THE

BORDER

READER

THE

GILBERTO ROSAS

BORDER

AND MIREYA LOZA, EDITORS

READER

Duke University Press Durham and London 2023

Project Editor: Jessica Ryan
Designed by Courtney Baker
Typeset in Portrait Text by Westchester Publishing Services

Library of Congress Cataloging-in-Publication Data
Names: Loza, Mireya, editor. | Rosas, Gilberto, [date] editor.
Title: The Border reader / Gilberto Rosas and Mireya Loza.
Description: Durham : Duke University Press, 2023. | Includes
bibliographical references and index.
Identifiers: LCCN 2022061124 (print)
LCCN 2022061125 (ebook)
ISBN 9781478024934 (paperback)
ISBN 9781478020257 (hardcover)
ISBN 9781478027195 (ebook)
Subjects: LCSH: Emigration and immigration law—Mexican-American
Border Region. | Mexican-American Border Region—Emigration and
immigration—Social aspects. | Mexican-American Border Region—History. |
BISAC: SOCIAL SCIENCE / Ethnic Studies / American / Hispanic
American Studies | HISTORY / United States / General
ClassificatLCion: C JV6475 .B68 2023 (print) | LCC JV6475 (ebook) |
DDC 325.72/1—dc23/eng/20230414
LC record available at https://lccn.loc.gov/2022061124
LC ebook record available at https://lccn.loc.gov/2022061125

Cover art: Mexico-US border, Tijuana 2014. © Ingrid Hernández.
Courtesy the artist.

Contents

Acknowledgments

Bringing *The Border Reader* to fruition has been a herculean task. It's been difficult to grapple with selecting these pieces as so much scholarship is worthy of being reproduced in this reader. And new scholarship is transforming this area every day.

The project has taken years and years, and years. And while such a project demands multiple volumes, our goal was to provide a preliminary cross-section of key works. Limitations in terms of space and breadth made this process much more challenging, as well as navigating the world of copyright and reproduction. While we would have liked to cover all the currents in Border Studies, the scope and scale of this project limited those possibilities.

The generous support of what was then called the Illinois Program in Research in the Humanities (now The Humanities Research Institute), under the robust guidance of Antoinette Burton, funded "Borders and Migrations in the Americas" (2015–2016) reading group, enabling conversations among the editors as well as a cohort of graduate students including Verónica Méndez, Brenda Garcia, Alana Ackermann, Raquel Escobar, and Carolina Ortega. The reading group culminated with a final talk given by our colleague, friend, and immigration attorney Virginia Raymond, JD, PhD, on immigrant detention. Soon thereafter, the University of Illinois Campus Research Board, specifically its Funding Initiative for a Multiracial Democracy, under the stewardship of our respected colleague Cynthia Oliver in the Office of Vice Chancellor for Research, generously awarded resources for the subventions of the selected works as well as support of Research Assistants in the production of this volume.

We are also extremely lucky that both Verónica Méndez and Steven McCutcheon Rubio joined the team and tracked down copyrights, navigated publishing limits, and helped us cross the finish line. We are very grateful to the attention, time, and care they dedicated to this project.

Ken Wissoker has been patient and thoughtful in his feedback with the multiple starts and stops of the project, as we pulled together the pieces, waded into the complexities of reproducing these works, and navigated publishing in the era of COVID, where everything slows. We also appreciate his careful selection of critical anonymous reviewers. We are also tremendously grateful to our colleagues in Latina/o Studies, Anthropology, History, and other departments at UIUC who supported the intellectual life of this project, as well those from the University of Texas' robust diaspora.

We are also fortunate to have the support of friends and family that have cheered us on every time we felt stuck and bound by the slow nature of producing an edited collection of previously published works. We are indebted to Korinta Maldonado, Teo and Maya, Gilbert Arthur Rosas and Cecilia Mora Rosas, Monica and Tommy. As well as Mike Amezcua, Pedro Loza, Marcelina Loza, Patricia Peña, Eric Peña, Juan Loza, Rosalba Loza, and Daniel Loza.

THE

BORDER

READER

Introduction:
On Theories from the Ends

GILBERTO ROSAS AND MIREYA LOZA

As Mercedes, BMWs, and other luxury vehicles zoom over the Rio Grande through special lanes, Pintos, Chevys, and pick-ups sit on the bridge. They wait their turn to cross, spewing brown toxins into the air. Dogs press their snouts into wheel wells, onto tires, into trunks. They seek people, drugs, or other contraband. Helicopters buzz the desert landscape from above. Infrared sensors document defiant life below.[1] Border guards move on foot, bikes, horses, and all-terrain vehicles; and the walls, fences, and infrared sensors testify to the effectiveness of crossings of all sorts. Be they from Mexico, Central America, Haiti, Cuba, China, or elsewhere across the globe, would-be border crossers abandon their ways of life and confront border guards, police, the National Guard, and their complex mirroring in vigilantes, *polleros* or human smugglers.[2] The border increasingly has become a site of militarized surveillance and border enforcement with deadly repercussions, as policy makers turned their attention toward racialized anxieties about irregular border crossers.[3] Now the border stages the latest wave of migrants: Central Americans, Africans, and Middle Easterners, sometimes with their families, and their efforts to be heard. They seek asylum.

Anti-border or post-citizenship formations animate the US-Mexico border region. They inspire alternative representations in art and popular music. They infuse alternative kin relations, geographies, desires, and economies. These dynamics render the US-Mexico border as material and imaginary. It is both utopic and dystopic. It is militarized and peaceful; organized and chaotic; masculine and feminine; it is straightening and queering; it is sometimes white, sometimes brown, and always Other; it is where untold wealth and regimes of impoverishment brutally collide. As with all borders, the international boundary between the United States and Mexico troubles distinctions between strangers and enemies, between the criminal and the law-abiding, between immigrant and citizen.

The US-Mexico border specifically, and borders generally, have grown in importance as border controls and undocumented border crossings have intensified across the globe. Be it the boundaries between the United States and Mexico, Israel and Palestine, or Guatemala and Mexico; the channels between Europe and Africa; or the genocidal partitioning of India, territorial divisions incite regimes of differentiation, typically as racialization. Such divisions also incite dreams of post- or non-bordered worlds. Indigenous communities whose sovereign assertions point to a different order, the alien-nated and their transborder kin networks, and other critical communities in border regions bear memories of different borders, moments when the boundaries between countries were largely immaterial or experienced on radically different terms.

The Border Reader curates some of the foundational scholarship on the region, its daily life, and its tensions. From linguistic studies of the criminal argot of smugglers, to insistences on the region's normalcy, to smug confirmations of US superiority, to romanticized folklores of resistance in *corridos* and related forms, to studies on health and immigration policy, questions about who, what, and which language—English, Spanish, Yoeme, or even Q'anjob'al—represent the border remain pertinent. Perhaps, what has sparked the most scholarship is the foundational intervention of Chicana scribe Gloria Anzaldúa's 1987 text *Borderlands: La New Mestiza* and its literary interpretation of the border as a larger metaphor. As Anzaldúa's conception of the border gained popularity, the North American Free Trade Agreement and the growing militarization of the border acted as catalysts for material interpretations and stringent debates.[4] The 1990s also gave rise to a contemporary generation of families caught in a moment of securitized borders and migrations, with fewer options toward documentation or related kinds of legal footing in the United States.

The empirical bent of earlier border studies should be contrasted with the theoretical interventions of those who take the border as a site of epistemic rupture, interventions, and departures.[5] Scholars like María Josefina Saldaña-Portillo,

Sonia Saldívar-Hull, Emma Perez, Patricia Zavella, and Alicia Schmidt Camacho show how feminist, queer, and critical race scholars, including Chicano and
Latino scholars, indigenous scholars, and scholars of indigeneity, as well as those
vested in questions of decoloniality have mobilized the border to press against
dominant theories of societies, cultures, the state, and related questions.

The Border Reader offers a vibrant alternative canon for scholars and students
in a range of fields including Anthropology, History, English, Spanish, Postcolonial, and Ethnic Studies. Although some consider the US-Mexico border
a spectacle,[6] this international boundary instigates a range of new questions
about empire, subjectivity, and violence, as well as a return to older questions.
It draws attention to the places where these quandaries play out and to its complex legacies, reverberations, and attenuations. The border, then, is not only an
enforced division that transverses particular terrains but an imagined site that
moves through the nation. The barbed wire cuts well after its crossing.

The Border Reader places selected works in conversation to highlight the
longue durée of intellectual production and critical reverberations instigated
by the US-Mexico divide. It is for this reason that The Border Reader moves
thematically, rather than chronologically, placing certain interventions at the
forefront. Clearly, there are significant omissions. The literature on this region
is rich, deserving, and underappreciated. We didn't include literature on populations of the region, for example, worthy of a reader of their own.

The first section, "Locating the Border," suggests that the US-Mexico border region can serve as a fertile site for understanding borders, migrations, and
other movements across the globe. In the border region, people and nation-states
negotiate power, citizenship, cultural citizenship, and related processes as well
as questions of empire. In this respect, "American empire," as Gilbert González
and Raúl Fernández argue, fueled twentieth-century Mexican immigration to
the United States. Moving toward understanding how immigration and criminal law constitute legal violence, Cecilia Menjívar and Leisy J. Abrego show how
Central Americans experience border crossing and life thereafter. Gilberto Rosas
captures the lessons from the border as a space of death, life, and subjection, as
they relate to asylum and related legal proceedings. Alejandro Lugo provides a
critical exemplification of locating the border as a site of theory-making. Transfeminist Sayak Valencia Triana insists on the geopolitical coordinates of the
other side of the border, Tijuana, Baja California, in this case, to underline the
"spectacular violence" of criminal syndicates in Mexico and their complexity
with dominant regimes of masculinity, globalization, and the Mexican government. In sum, these contributions underline how imperial projects rework relationships of power in the US-Mexico border region for some, and erode the
hegemonies of the US and Mexico evident the region for others.

The following section of *The Border Reader*, "Documenting Identities," takes stock of the undocumented identities in the actual border region and the borderlands of academic discourses. The selections speak to some of the shifting analytical paradigms that have reframed our understanding of the US-Mexico border by underscoring the complexity, dynamisms, and diversity of peoples inhabiting and moving through this contested space. In a look at quotidian expression, Américo Paredes provides a study of Mexican machismo and challenges the extent to which machismo is unique to Mexico and Mexican culture. Drawing on notions of racialization, as well as government documents and policies, Martha Menchaca's contribution underscores the often-repressed and overlooked racial histories of contemporary Mexican Americans in the Southwest. Offering a critical understanding of the intersectionality of race and sexuality for Mexican migrants, Lionel Cantú reconfigures understandings of queer communities across borders. Patricia Zavella's chapter "Migrations," excerpted from her influential *I'm Neither Here nor There,* documents how gender inflects the undocumented migrant self, mobilizing a concept that she refers to as "peripheral vision" that is inspired by Gloria Anzaldúa.

Although themes of gender and sexuality infuse this reader, "En/Gendering Borders" elaborates on the gendered contours of life at the border and in border thinking. Renato Rosaldo's pioneering "Changing Chicano Narratives" underlines a shift to Chicana foundational figures in border thinking. Sonia Saldívar-Hull's "Feminism on the Border" conjures an expansive vision of feminism that renders visible the intersections of gender, class, and race that shape the lived experiences of women of color. Martha Balaguera draws on border theory, participant observation and interviews conducted with *chicas trans* at migrant shelters in Mexico, this study sheds light on how gender and geographical transitions shape each other, blurring distinctions of shelter and homelessness, motion and boundedness, and freedom and unfreedom. José Limón contrasts a Chicano carnivalesque barbeque scene with certain dominant Mexican discourses about masculinity and in spite of its deep gendered contradictions.

The following section, "Othering Spaces, Othering Bodies," engages with scholarship on the body and space at the intersection of race, immigration, and deviance. The selected readings explore the multiple ways through which the US-Mexico border has become imagined as a site of "illegality," how immigrant bodies themselves become racialized and excluded from the body politic, and how dead immigrant bodies serve as sites for Mexican and US governments to assert authority. The physical border is reinforced not only through militarization but through cultural imaginings and the desire for an orderly social world juxtaposed by disorder, chaos, and feelings of lawlessness projected onto sister cities such as El Paso and Juárez or Tijuana and San Diego. The fantasy and the reality transform the people, products, and wildlife that pass through these spaces. White middle-class Americans in San Diego, as Ramón Gutiérrez shows, demarcate the dividing line that spatially separates an orderly and pure America from a deviant Tijuana. Bodies are categorized, examined, and placed within or outside discourses of belonging. Advancing a historical analysis of race, immigration, and disability, Natalia Molina offers and examination of how public health and immigration discourses defined Mexican immigrants as culturally or physically unfit for citizenship. Eithne Luibhéid's "'Looking Like a Lesbian'" exemplifies how the policing of identities at the US-Mexico ports of entry consolidate heteronormative identities. Alicia Schmidt Camacho calls on us to consider migrant melancholia as a framework to understand not only the material consequences of immigration but also its psychological toll, as expressed through narratives that constitute a political act against the substantive erosion of citizenship.

The works in "Border Crossings" render these experiences visible and chart the material consequences of migration. Roberto Gonzales and Leo Chavez capture the nightmares of illegality, how certain youth are situated in regimes of despair, marginality, and hopelessness. Carlos Vélez-Ibáñez's "Regions of Refuge in the United States" which crosses the border in its own right and draws on the work of Gonzalo Aguirre Beltrán (1979), maps the lived contours of Mexican immigrant and Mexican American communities who make up impoverished and socially stratified urban and rural ecologies of the United States, and how people both thrive and suffer in these restrictive/spaces. Recasting the debates on undocumented migration, Néstor Rodríguez asserts that undocumented crossings by laborers should be considered a political act in defiance of state regulation. In an effort to reveal the relational racial construction of indigeneity across borders, Mireya Loza places indigenous Mexican communities at the center and recasts the history of the Bracero Program.

Emergent border, post-border, and anti-border panoramas are explored in the final section, "New Cultural Imaginaries." Néstor García Canclini explains hybridity as he sees it developing in Tijuana in a conversation with Fiamma Montezemolo. In unpacking border epistemes, scholars have highlighted new narratives about experiences along the borderlands. Rosa-Linda Fregoso delves into border femicides, in an essay charting the politics of witnessing. In an effort to contextualize the relationship between mass incarceration and immigration, Kelly Lytle Hernández calls for a reexamination of the origins of immigration control. As both a personal exploration, an archaeological rumination of border history, and a piece of border poetics, Gloria Anzaldúa vindicates the in-betweenness of Chicana/o identities that stems from their positionality in the geographical and metaphysical space of the borderlands. The power of a hybrid language and fluid identities are inherently subversive to the very systems of oppression that produced them. Closing this reader, María Josephina Saldaña Portillo, in "Wavering on the Horizon of Social Being," underlines the racial governmentalities unleashed by the Treaty of Guadalupe Hidalgo and its insistence on stripping away Mexican character and holding in abeyance savage Indianness in order to receive the benefits of United States citizenship.

The Border Reader demands an examination of border subjectivities as produced by and in between multiple nations and uneven relationships of power and privilege. Historically and culturally, communities grapple with the meaning and the consequences of this relationship as it is experienced politically, spatially, and corporeally in their daily lives, their complex relations, their feelings, and their rich and creative cultural expressions.[7]

NOTES

1   See Gilberto Rosas, *Barrio Libre: Criminalizing States and Delinquent Refusals of the New Frontier* (Durham: Duke University Press, 2012).

2   Some of the earliest vigilantes of the border, the Texas Rangers, worked to bring about a new racial order on the state level, while later groups were organized on the federal level to enforce laws that restricted entry. By 1904 men hired to patrol the border by the US Immigration Service assigned a keen group of officers to enforce the Chinese Exclusion Act. They also looked to exclude immigrants infected with contagious diseases, illiterates, and those too poor to pay the head tax. Later, these men would turn their eye toward what they deemed were dangerous rabble-rousers of the Mexican Revolution. For more on the Texas Rangers and Texas border violence see Monica Muñoz Martinez, *The Injustice Never Leaves You: Anti-Mexican Violence in Texas* (Cambridge, MA: Harvard University Press, 2018); Elliot Young, *Catarino Garza's Revolution on the Texas-Mexico Border* (Durham: Duke University Press, 2004). For more on the history of the Border Patrol see Kelly Lytle Hernández, *Migra!: A History of the US Border Patrol* (Berkeley: University of California Press, 2010).

3   For some of the expansive literature on the militarization of the border, border securitization, and related frameworks see Miguel Antonio Levario, *Militarizing the Border: When Mexicans Became the Enemy* (College Station: Texas A&M Press, 2012). Also see Rosas, *Barrio Libre*. It draws on Timothy J. Dunn, *The Militarization of the U.S.-Mexico Border, 1978–1992: Low-Intensity Conflict Doctrine Comes Home* (Austin: Center for Mexican American Studies, 1996); Jonathan Xavier Inda, *Targeting Immigrants: Government, Technology, Ethics* (Malden, MA: Blackwell Publishing, 2006); Joseph Nevins, *Operation Gatekeeper: The Rise of the "Illegal Alien" and the Making of the U.S.-Mexico Boundary* (New York: Routledge, 2002); and Miguel Diaz-Barriga and Margaret E. Dorsey, *Fencing In Democracy: Borders Walls, Necrocitizenship, and the Security State* (Durham: Duke University Press, 2020).

4   See, for example, Josiah Heyman, "The Mexico-United States Border in Anthropology: A Critique and Reformulation," *Journal of Political Ecology* 1, no. 1 (1994): 43–66.

5   See Robert R. Alvarez, "The Mexican-US Border: The Making of an Anthropology of Borderlands," *Annual Review of Anthropology* 24 (1995): 447–70.

6   On the border as spectacle, see Nicholas P. De Genova, "Migrant 'Illegality' and Deportability in Everyday Life," *Annual Review of Anthropology* 31, no. 1 (October 1, 2002): 419–47.

7   See Alex E. Chavez, *Sounds of Crossing: Music, Migration, and the Aural Poetics of Huapango Arribeño* (Durham: Duke University Press, 2017) for some of the latest literature on transborder expressive culture and politics.

PART I

LOCATING

THE

BORDER

Empire and the Origins of Twentieth-Century Migration from Mexico to the United States

GILBERT G. GONZÁLEZ AND RAÚL FERNÁNDEZ

The [migrant] is forced to seek better conditions north of the border by the
slow but relentless pressure of United States' agricultural, financial, and oil corporate
interests on the entire economic and social evolution of the Mexican nation.
—ERNESTO GALARZA, 1949

Preamble

In this essay we show how the twentieth-century appearance of a Chicano minority population in the United States originated from the subordination of
the nation of Mexico to U.S. economic and political interests.[1] We argue that,
far from being marginal to the course of modern U.S. history, the Chicano
minority, an immigrant people, stands at the center both of that history and of
a process of imperial expansionism that originated in the last three decades of
the nineteenth century and that continues today.

Several challenges to conventional interpretations of Mexican migration and
the Chicano experience derive from this approach. This century-long exodus
of Mexicans to the United States has often been perceived as an "American"

problem, affecting welfare, education, culture, crime, drug abuse, and public budgets, to be solved by get-tough measures, such as California's Proposition 187, and softer policies, such as those of immigrant rights agencies. In contrast, we take the position that migration signifies a Mexican national crisis, reflecting Mexico's economic subordination to the United States and the limitations placed upon its national sovereignty by that domination. A century of mass border crossings displays the breaking apart of the social fabric of the Mexican nation and its resettlement in enclaves across the United States as a national minority.

The social and political repercussions of this subordination have been enormous. More than a century of domination by the United States increasingly undermined the social and political cohesion of Mexico, causing dislocation to its domestic agriculture and industry as well as migration to the United States–Mexico border and into the United States itself. In his 1911 classic exposé, *Barbarous Mexico*, John Kenneth Turner addressed the dismantling of the Mexican nation. "The partnership of Díaz and American capital," he argued, "has wrecked Mexico as a national entity. The United States government, as long as it represents American capital . . . will have a deciding voice in Mexican affairs."[2] Washington preferred economic domination by U.S. corporations to the direct annexation of Mexico. As John Mason Hart has persuasively demonstrated, U.S. capital realized that policy objective and established its supremacy in Mexico by the late nineteenth century.[3] Mexico became the first foreign country to fall under the imperial umbrella of the United States.

The practice of territorial conquest and expansion in pursuit of, or as a consequence of, commercial developments is very old; from the Romans to the Aztecs to nineteenth-century Great Britain, this characteristic has been shared by most imperial powers. Over the last century, however, the United States, along with other global powers, developed an empire of a new type, a transnational mode of economic domination similar to but in important respects different from previous imperial regimes.

While the United States throughout its history has engaged in numerous acts of territorial aggression and conquest—like other historical centers of power—its particular mode of empire building and maintenance emerged when the growth of large corporations and financial institutions became directly involved in alliance with local elites, in the formally independent economies and politics of other countries. Simultaneously, these large conglomerates of finance and production came to dominate the government of United States, using the power of the state to jockey for position with other world powers. This practice of empire construction and management was aptly captured by U.S. Secretary of State John Foster Dulles in the 1950s: "[T]here [are] two ways of dominating a foreign nation," he remarked, "invading it militarily or controlling it financially."[4] In the case of Mexico, U.S. policy preferred financial over military control.

Mexico and the U.S. Model of Empire Building

A transnational mode of imperial hegemony has defined U.S. relations with the rest of the world throughout the twentieth century. Mexico provided the first testing ground. The United States initiated new mechanisms of empire in the late 1870s when it became the senior partner in an alliance with the local Mexican elite personified in the figure of dictator Porfirio Díaz. Using threats of military intervention, U.S. capital interests invested heavily in the construction of railroads in Mexico. These initial intrusions were quickly followed by massive investments in mining, cattle farming, and cotton production. After Mexico, the United States moved swiftly to establish economic control and political influence southward. The United States launched the War of 1898 for a variety of motives: to insure that no sovereign and independent nation appeared in Cuba upon the defeat of the Spanish empire; to establish a military presence guaranteeing the security of its investments; and to establish strategic outposts to secure and control commerce and investments in the Caribbean and East Asia. U.S. political leaders defended the war with rhetoric of supporting the underdog, a rationale to allay public unease over war and manipulate public opinion. The War of 1898 was followed quickly by the U.S.-supported secession of the province of Panama from Colombia, ensuring U.S. control of interoceanic trade. At the same time, large U.S. investments in Mexico and Cuba took place via the company town model in agriculture, railroad construction, and mining.[5]

Beginning at the turn of the century, investment by U.S.-based corporations in Latin America, in cooperation with archaic land-based elites and bolstered by the U.S. military and the threat of annexation, transformed the hemisphere into a series of neocolonial republics. Mexico became something of a laboratory for the imperial experiments; few events of significance in the history of twentieth-century Mexico were not decisively influenced by the power of U.S. economic, political, and, as a last recourse, military power.[6] A few examples will suffice: The United States played a determining role in the outcome of the 1910 Mexican Revolution; after World War II the United States provided the money, propaganda, and logistics to control the labor and social movements in which the ideas of socialism were taking root, not only in Mexico but throughout Latin America;[7] in the 1990s the United States established NAFTA to secure further its investments in Mexico and to restrict access for investment there by competitors. The freedom and security of U.S. capital thus remained a constant in U.S. policy toward Mexico in the twentieth century.

This establishment of U.S. imperial hegemony over Mexico and other Latin America nations has long been acknowledged in Latin America as central to local histories and identity. From the 1880s to the 1930s, major Mexican and Latin American thinkers, including Jose Vasconcelos, Jose Martí, Jose Enrique Rodó, and Eugenio María de Hostos, placed U.S. presence in Latin America as central to their essays on Latin America's future. The profound awareness of the United States that pervades the lives, history, politics, and economics of Latin American countries is not matched by a parallel knowledge in the United States of its southern neighbors. In the academy, official U.S. historiography dates national emergence onto the global scene to World War I, privileging U.S. activity in Europe over decades of investment, interference, and invasions into Mexico and other southern neighbors. As a subset of official U.S. history, the study of the Chicano national minority has largely been constructed in an atmosphere in which "race matters," and culture, too, but empire does not. Insofar as the U.S. transnational mode of hegemony is acknowledged, it is not seen as essential or even related to understanding the origins and development of the Chicano national minority.[8]

The Push-Pull Thesis: The "Official" Line on Mexican Migration

Since the first decade of the twentieth century, academic studies of Mexican migration to the United States established one basic theoretical construct—the push-pull thesis, modeled upon conventional supply and demand economics. The thesis reduces the causes of migration to sets of conditions within the sending country and the host country, conditions that *function independently* of each other. In one country, a push (supply), usually attributed to poverty, unemployment, or political unrest, motivates people to consider a significant move; in the other country, a pull (demand), usually a shortage of labor, operates to attract the disaffected. In tandem, they synergistically lead to transnational migration.

Following the political militancy and cultural nationalism of the late 1960s, numerous studies focused on the origins of the Mexican population in the United States. These stemmed from the interest not only of Chicano activists but also of academics attracted to the issues raised by the regional political rebellion. As the Chicano Studies research agenda matured, immigration, particularly in the 1900–1930 period, gained a central place in many studies. The original push-pull thesis, as enunciated by the U.S. Industrial Commission on Immigration in 1901 and repeated by Victor S. Clark in 1908 and by Manuel Gamio and Paul S. Taylor in the early 1930s, became an article of faith among a new generation of academics destined to dominate the field to the end of the century.[9]

Many academics simply made the 1910 Revolution the principal push factor operating in the 1900-1930 era.[10] Consequently, when the UCLA Mexican American Study Project turned its attention to immigration in the late 1960s, the theoretical scenario had been set: "The Mexican revolutionary period beginning in 1909-1910 spurred the first substantial and permanent migration to the United States," the report's authors wrote. "By liberating masses of people from social as well as geographic immobility, [the Revolution] served to activate a latent migration potential of vast dimensions."[11]

To be sure, different research projects often emphasized particular conditions that modified the form in which push-pull ostensibly manifested. There *were* variations on the theme. A number of authors viewed the policies of Díaz as similar to European elites' expropriation of peasants' lands and the simultaneous de-peasanting of the countryside. Some saw the extension of railroads throughout Mexico as the key element that made migration possible. For others, the devastation of the Mexican Revolution and its aftermath precipitated the early twentieth-century migrations. A survey of the more significant studies of the last twenty years reveals a collage of factors that propel migration; seldom is the "push" viewed as the result of one factor alone. Currently, most students of Mexican migration and border studies agree that a complex of "push" factors, such as low wages, unemployment, poverty, and political oppression have operated at various times to create the conditions leading to Mexican migration over the course of the twentieth century.[12] The "pull" factors—high wages and labor demand in the United States—are taken as a given.

Around 1970 the push-pull thesis came under critical scrutiny, resulting in refinement but not substantial overhaul. Condemned as a neoclassical artifact, the thesis was ostensibly supplanted by a set of theoretical approaches to explain Mexican migration. The new paradigms—social capital theory, segmented market theory, new economics theory, and world systems theory—challenged push-pull. The first three of these contended that the old economic categories— wages, poverty, surplus population, and unemployment—inadequately explain the "push" of Mexican migration, particularly the long-term trends appearing since roughly 1970. World systems theory, on the other hand, contended that global capitalism reaching into the remotest corners of Mexico uprooted peasants from the land and caused unemployment; both conditions drive migration. In spite of the claim that these approaches go beyond the limitations of the push-pull paradigm, we shall argue below that the basic premises of push-pull have not been completely uprooted by these modifications.

Most analysts of migration seem to view the "push" factors, such as Porfirian policies, the 1910 revolution, low wages, and surplus population, as operating independently of the economic power of the United States. Implicit in the argument is the contention that an autonomous modernization process, not unlike what occurred in Europe, led to Mexican migration to the United States. In short, older versions and modern variations of push-pull inherently assume that Mexican migration—from 1900 to the present—followed from independently stimulated economic progress in Mexico. Largely absent in discussions of migration are two questions: Is it appropriate to conflate all migrations into a single "one size fits all" paradigm? And, if the forces of supply and demand work to eliminate economic *disequilibria*, why has there been an apparent permanent *disequilibrium* that no amount of migration from Mexico (or modernization therein) has been able to root out and that remains in effect more than a century after it began?[13]

Recent "Refinements" to Push-Pull

Recent research by sociologists has pointed out that migration continued unabated since the 1960s when economic conditions in Mexico were relatively good. Studies analyzed noneconomic factors and questioned whether these factors affected the decision to migrate. Framed in such a perspective, emphasis swung to the role of "agency," or the independent decision making of the migrants as they "negotiated" their migratory treks. Social capital theory configured transnational migrant networks linking communities divided by national borders. Migrants summoned motivations, constructed pathways, and provided the resources that propelled migrations over the long term. Theoretically, a culture of migration establishes a social network across borders that feeds migrations. Migration, in other words, exists autonomously above the economic and political life of Mexico. As migrants cross the border, they allegedly define the border on their own terms, reconfiguring sociopolitical spaces. Ultimately, recent sociological models have celebrated migration as "transnational resistance" to internationalized economic and political imperatives.[14]

According to this perspective, migration evolved into an institutionalized "self-feeding process" with a life of its own. Tautological in essence, migration is explained by migration; migrants migrate because, as "historical actors," they have voluntarily chosen to create a culture of migration. Nevertheless, the question of origins, of the factors that send the first migration and lead to subsequent migrations, is left, by default, to push-pull. The original sin, push-pull, prompts the first migrations, but, once the sin is committed, the migration assumes a *self-generating* state. The only true national and/or transnational factor of significance in this theory is the migration itself. Rational choices made by migrants, to acquire commodities or reestablish community, cultural lifestyle, and family ties, motivate migrations. Such analyses relegate international economic relations to the margins and ignore the economic domination that we address here; instead, they home in on the "independent" decision making of migrants.[15]

A second theoretical design arising from the critique of push-pull, the segmented labor market model, emphasizes an economic aspect of the receiving country, precisely the structured dependence of modernized, "post-industrial" forms of production upon the continued flow of cheap immigrant labor. An insatiable thirst for cheap labor drives migration. Adherents to this position contend that the old push conditions—wage differentials, surplus population, and so forth—are secondary if not irrelevant. However, while the push side of the equation evaporates, the pull side—that is, the demand for labor in the receiving country—functions as before. Note that both the social capital theory and the segmented labor market theory view the two economically interconnected countries as *economically independent of each other* and ignore transnational financial *domination* with respect to the process of migration. Like the original push-pull theory, these revisions separate the process of migration into two interacting but independent operations.[16]

A third model, new economics theory, contends that migration is explained "by measures of risk and the need for access to capital" rather than by the workings of the labor market.[17] According to Douglas Massey, "Considerable work suggests that the acquisition of housing, the purchase of land, and the establishment of small businesses constitute the primary motivations for international labor migration."[18] Here the push argument seems to have been supplanted by factors other than wages; however, this theoretical model, like social capital theory, stands well within the old model. New economics theorists argue that the sending country fails to supply needed capital, land, and business opportunities. These contentions fit into the push-pull model as it was first articulated nearly a century ago: The host country has something that the sending country lacks; hence, people migrate to satisfy a felt need, and a neoclassical equilibrium is established (or should be established).

In these critiques of push-pull theory, basic assumptions replicate the old model. For one, migrants have a felt need that Mexico cannot meet—thus, a push. Secondly, the United States has the conditions and wherewithal to satisfy migrants' yearnings—therefore, a pull. Lastly, the national economies of Mexico and the United States are interactive (often described as "interdependent") but without domination exerted by either party.[19]

Finally, the world systems model causally links global capitalism with migrations. In this view, direct foreign investments generate economic development in sending countries, which removes natives from farming lands or causes unemployment in traditional occupations, creating a body of migrants within the country. Saskia Sassen, perhaps the best-known world systems theoretician of migration, rightly points out how foreign investment in export agriculture modernizes production, which simultaneously upsets traditional farming practices, removes small farmers from the Mexican countryside, and resettles them in cities. Some migrate to the northern states where foreign-owned assembly plants advertise employment. Ultimately, that same surplus labor migrates to the United States where immigrant labor is in constant demand.[20]

While a thorough discussion of world systems theory is beyond the purview of this essay, our basic differences with world systems theory as applied to Mexican migration to the United States stem from 1) the emphasis on direct investments, 2) the implicit argument that modernization via foreign financing equals the development experienced by Europe in the nineteenth century, and 3) the exclusive attention to the post-1960 period. First, direct investments are only one type of foreign capital that has affected the national economy of Mexico. Other types of capital have had serious consequences for the economy and society as well. For example, U.S. government lending programs, private philanthropic organizations like the Rockefeller Foundation and others, as well as economic development programs (loans) run by the International Monetary Fund (IMF), the World Bank, and the trade policies of the World Trade Organization, have had a decided impact on the economy and society of Mexico. Second, world systems theory implicitly parallels notions of the great nineteenth-century European migrations, which occurred via an indigenous capitalist modernization and consequent de-peasanting of the land. In the case of Mexico, we contend that foreign economic incursions led to a colonial status, resulting in neither indigenous, capitalist-driven modernization nor dependent modernization, but rather one under foreign control that removes peasants from the land to other parts of Mexico and to the United States. Third, regarding the proposition that the post-1960s migrations are distinct from those of earlier decades, we argue that U.S. economic domination over Mexico has remained more or less constant over the course of the twentieth century. While world systems theory does point to the significance of foreign investments in the removal of people from the countryside and their migration to cities and northern assembly plants, the model holds that the roots of migration derive from global capital, or direct foreign investment, which "modernizes" the Mexican economy. Accordingly, Mexico and the United States are sovereign nations as in the first versions of the push-pull thesis, each in its own way subject to the nuances of global capital and interdependent in the process. The theory ignores government-to-government lending programs, bank capital, massive foreign debt, and empire; the "world system" is all one massive capitalist system covering the entire globe, in which issues of inequality and domination become obscured.

In social capital theory, the segmented labor model, new economic theory, and world systems theory, the core premise of push-pull—the imbalance of independent conditions in sending and host countries—still obtains in spite of critiques. A real alternative requires a reconceptualization of migration within the context of empire.

Economic Conquest: Porfirian Mexico, 1876–1910

A critical examination of the push side of the thesis requires that we analyze the economic policies carried out by the Mexican government in the 1880–1910 period and their social consequences. It is necessary to take another look at four processes: first, the building of Mexico's railroads by U.S. companies; second, the investment of U.S. capital in mining and smelting; third, the effects of the above modernization projects on Mexico's agriculture; and fourth, the displacement of large segments of Mexico's peasant population as a consequence of the foreign-induced modernization.

We will show that foreign monopolistic economic interests—not the much vaunted *cientificos*—were the principal architects of the policies implemented by the Porfirio Díaz administrations and that these policies resulted in the subjection of Mexico to domination of a new type: a transnational mode of economic colonialism. While Porfirian policies forcibly removed peasants from ancestral village lands, it is wrong to assume that these were policies wholly designed in Mexico City. Like the construction of railroads, oil exploration and exploitation, mining, and agricultural investments by foreign capital, the removal of peasants from village lands emanated from the integration and exploitation of Mexican natural resources into foreign, primarily U.S., industrial production.

Not only Mexico but all of Latin America fell under the gaze of U.S. foreign policy at the end of the nineteenth century. The United States saw Mexico as the doorway to Latin America's riches, but only if it remained under U.S. economic tutelage. U.S. policy essentially followed the dictum of no less a patron of imperialism than Cecil Rhodes, who envisioned Mexico as the material fountain of empire. "Mexico," he once observed, "is the treasure house from which will come the gold, silver, copper, and precious stones that will build the empires of tomorrow, and will make the future cities of the world veritable Jerusalems."[21] The United States changed the plural "empires" to the singular "empire."

The 1865 victory of the Northern armies in the U.S. Civil War failed to deter the cry for "all of Mexico" that lingered in the minds of adventurous entrepreneurs and their supporters in the United States. In 1868 a spate of articles in the *New York Herald* and other metropolitan newspapers called upon the United States to establish "a protectorate over Mexico." Voices of opposition to such a policy were heard; not all were enthralled by the easy victories of 1848 and the imagined expansion to the isthmus. Anti-annexationists responded with an economic alternative free of any humanitarian impulses. William S. Rosecrans, speculator and promoter of Mexican railroads, while serving as minister to Mexico, anticipated future U.S. policy toward Mexico in his response to the newspaper articles. Rosecrans urged that Americans abandon the notion of "all of Mexico." "Pushing American enterprise up to, and within Mexico wherever it can profitably go," he claimed, "will give us advantages which force and money alone would hardly procure. It would give us a peaceful conquest of the country."[22]

A number of Rosecrans's contemporaries engaged the discussion as to whether U.S economic interests required annexation. One prominent American investor, Edward Lee Plumb, wrote, "If we have their trade and development meanwhile we need not hasten the greater event [annexation]." Former President U. S. Grant, himself an investor in Mexico's railroads, leaned toward the Rosecrans position. According to David M. Pletcher, "Grant's fragmentary writings about Mexico . . . suggest that in the last years of his life he developed toward that country an ideology of economic imperialism closely similar to that of other promoters."[23] Former U.S. commercial attaché Chester Lloyd Jones reiterated this approach decades later in *Mexico and Its Reconstruction* (1921):

> The economic advantage that would result to the United States from annexation as contrasted to that which may follow independence and friendship is doubtful. Mexican trade, both import and export, is already almost inevitably American and investments will be increasingly so. . . . A friendly, strong, and independent Mexico will bring greater economic advantages than annexation that certain classes of Mexicans fear and some citizens of the United States desire.[24]

However, when Jones set down his policy recommendations, Mexico was well on the way to being "an economic satellite of the United States."[25]

U.S. capital first conquered the Mexican railroad system (which, for all practical purposes, was an extension of the American system), then the mining and petroleum industries, and, concurrently, trade between the two countries. The social consequences reverberated throughout Mexico in the form of mass removal of people from village lands, the ruin of artisans and craftsmen, the creation of a modern working-class subject to the business cycle, and the appearance of a migratory surplus population. That migratory population first appeared within Mexico in both a rural-to-urban movement and a south-to-north movement; as the tide of U.S. investments grew, the migratory distances increased and crossed over to the United States.

Mexico began to build its railroads during the administration of Benito Juárez (1867–1872), who granted a concession to a British company to build between Mexico City and Veracruz. His successor, Sebastián Lerdo de Tejada, continued the Juárez policies but refused to allow railroad lines to be built toward the north for fear that they might become a military advantage to the United States. Following a period of political instability, military strongman Porfirio Díaz took over Mexico's government in 1876. Díaz inaugurated the period of economic liberalism—forerunner of the current NAFTA-style neoliberalism—by selling railroad concessions to large U.S. railroad companies in the northern states. Within three years, concessions and $32 million in subsidies to U.S. corporations provided for the construction of five railroads in Mexico. Extending 2,500 miles from south to north, these lines provided a route to the interior of Mexico from which mineral ores and agricultural products were transported to the United States.[26]

These developments occurred simultaneously with the development of railroads in the southwestern United States by the same corporate interests. By 1902 U.S. investments in Mexican railroads amounted to $281 million with the northern states of Sonora, Coahuila, and Chihuahua the main recipients. Fully 80 percent of all investments in railroads in Mexico emanated from the United States.[27] By 1910 U.S. corporate capital had largely financed the building of 15,000 miles of track, providing a basic infrastructure that would insure the transport of raw materials northward and technology south.

By the dawn of the twentieth century the United States controlled the Mexican economy. According to U.S. Consul-General Andrew D. Barlow, 1,117 U.S.-based companies and individuals had invested $500 million in Mexico. Railroads were the cornerstone of the modernization process, initiated, designed, and constructed by foreign capital. Railroads enabled myriad economic activities, principally those under foreign control, including mining, export of agricultural products, and oil production. In 1902 Walter E. Weyl observed that railroads "permitted the opening up of mines" and stimulated "agriculture, and manufacturing by establishing foreign markets."[28] While foreign investments entered Mexico "at an astonishing rate," Mexican national markets for raw materials like copper were practically nonexistent or, in the case of coffee, sugar, and henequen, severely limited. Consequently, both U.S. enterprises and those owned by Mexicans marketed their commodities primarily in foreign outlets. Railroads were indispensable for the increased export of raw materials and agricultural products and the import of tools, machinery, and other products supporting the modernized sectors of the economy.

Before 1880, for example, copper was processed through the centuries-old patio method for deriving precious metals from ore. "Railroads," commented

Marvin Bernstein, "aided mining from their very inception."[29] This aid, however, worked to the detriment of established miners using archaic techniques. According to mining engineer H. A. C. Jenison, writing in the *Engineering and Mining Journal-Press* in 1921, railroads "made the more remote regions accessible, made the transportation of heavy machinery possible, and the shipment of low-grade ores to smelters profitable." Consequently, about one-sixth of rail mileage was "mineral railroad," but conversely "most railroads counted upon mineral shipments."[30]

Under the stimulus of terms largely favorable to corporate investors rather than smaller individual stakeholders, U.S. capital thus assumed nearly complete control of railroads, oil, agriculture, and mining, as well as substantial control of Mexico's finances, communication (telegraphs, telephones), and urban transport. Mexico had passed into the hands of foreign economic interests. As historian Robert G. Cleland wrote in 1927:

> large numbers of foreign companies, most of them which were American, entered Mexico. As the foreigner became interested in the industry, the Mexican gradually withdrew; little by little the important properties passed out of his control, until by 1912, of a total investment in the mining business estimated at $323,600,000, he could lay claim to less than $15,000,000.[31]

American investors held $223 million, and of the total invested in Mexico, nearly 68 percent originated from foreign sources. Foreign capital's power multiplied through its control of key areas of the economy. Every review of the evidence came to the same general conclusion: "Foreign investment [almost entirely of U.S. origin] was on the order of two-thirds of the total for the decade of 1900–1910; foreign ownership by 1910 has been estimated at half the national wealth."[32] For all practical purposes, the regional elites—the *comprador caciques*—and their representatives serving as the Mexican government provided the midlevel managing agency for foreign capital.

Internal Migration: The First Step toward Emigration

Even as the railroads made the export of agricultural products to the United States and Europe a lucrative possibility, Mexican wealth remained concentrated in the semi-feudal hacienda. Enrichment without social change encouraged *hacendados* to transfer production from subsistence to cash crops for export. Coffee, fruits, henequen, hides, cattle, sugar, cotton, and other goods entered the international marketplace. For good measure, the large exporters received favorable transit rates that discriminated against domestic traders and forced the latter to produce for local consumption or not at all.[33] Hacienda export production, developed by and dependent upon railroads, was equally significant for the effects upon the peasantry. The economic spur of the railroad promoted land expropriation laws, under the aegis of liberal land reform, and effected the legalized transfer of free peasant village holdings to nearby haciendas. Based on the locations of recorded violent peasant rebellions contesting land seizures between 1880 to 1910, the majority of land expropriations during the Díaz era occurred along or near planned or operating railway routes. These activities, however, were entirely dependent upon the effects of rail transport and production geared to foreign markets. Evidence points to similar patterns in other parts of Mexico. For example, in the northern state of Sonora, sales of empty public land to speculators "faithfully mirror the history of the Sonora railroad."[34]

Interestingly, the railroads, which had little effect upon industrial development, strengthened the precapitalist economic form, the hacienda. However, the hacienda, originally organized for self-sufficiency, engaged in cash crop production on an extended scale to the detriment of staple crops, causing shortages of basic foodstuffs. Corn production fell by 50 percent between 1877 and 1910, and bean production declined by 75 percent, forcing the nation to rely on costly imported staples. At the same time, exports of raw materials, like henequen, coffee, sugar, hides, oil, and ores, grew at an annual rate of 6.5 percent.[35] In 1910 Mexico was exporting a quarter of a million pounds of henequen a year, supplying Midwestern farmers with twine for binding hay. While Mexico's foreign trade grew "tenfold between the mid-1870s and 1910," the average Mexican's diet fell below the levels of the pre-Díaz period as prices for staples rose much faster than wages.[36] The state-sponsored expropriations—the mass removal of hundreds of thousands of peasants from former village subsistence holdings— was the first phase toward the transnational migration that would occur a few years later.

The first victims of Mexico's modernization—that is, economic conquest— were the peasants. By 1910, 90 percent of the central plateau's villages owned no communal land; meanwhile, the haciendas "owned over half of the nation's territory."[37] The army of dispossessed moved from village to town and city and, as the northern mining districts opened up, from south to north. No wonder that over the course of the Porfiriato the village-to-city migration would lead to a dramatic population growth in the provincial capitals, 89 percent, which outstripped the national increase of 61 percent.[38] The most dramatic increase occurred in the nation's capital, where migrating peasants began to settle in substantial numbers. According to Michael Johns, "Railroads and expanding haciendas threw so many off their lands in the 1880s and 1890s that nearly half of the city's five hundred thousand residents . . . were peasants."[39] Daily, the new arrivals searched for quarters as best they could, cramming into over-crowded lodgings. An estimated 25,000 homeless moved into *mesones*, a form of nightly shelter for transients. Men, women, and children could be found sleeping on mats in single rooms, huddled against the cold. Others lived in more permanent quarters, tenements or *vecindades*, which, while not as inhospitable as the *mesones*, were nonetheless overflowing. John Kenneth Turner estimated that at least 100,000 "residents" were without stable shelter.[40]

From this pool, the city's aristocracy and foreign (mainly American) businesspeople selected their domestic servants: drivers, cooks, babysitters, housecleaners, and laundresses. Some 65,000 in 1910 accounted for 30 percent of the capital's workforce.[41] This growing labor pool eventually supplied other regions as well. Labor recruiters working for textile manufacturers, henequen plantations, railroads, mines, and oil operations also targeted displaced peasants. Many ended up in Yucatan henequen estates as virtual slaves, working alongside thousands of Yaqui Indians forcibly removed from their Sonoran homelands to make room for land speculators and railroad builders.[42] As railroads expanded their radius of operations and as ownership of mines shifted from small prospectors to Americans, the search for labor became a key element in the modernization process. The northern trade routes from the central region, which normally occupied 60,000 pack mules, underwent a profound change with the advent of railroads. Early Latin Americanists noted this change. Frank Tannenbaum wrote that in the past the "surplus crop was . . . loaded upon the backs of pack mules or in some instances on the backs of men and carried to the nearest trading center, often days of travel away. More recently it has been delivered to the nearest railroad station."[43] Walter E. Weyl confirmed the gradual displacement in his study:

> the muleteer is now relegated to a lesser sphere of activity and a lower position in the national economy. The driver of the mule car is slowly giving way to the trained motorman, and before long the vast army of *cargadores*, or porters, will go the way which in other cities has been trod by the *lenadores* and *aguadores*—"the hewers of wood and drawers of water."[44]

Others besides mule packers were cast aside as wagon drivers, weavers, shoe-makers, tanners, soapmakers, and others found that they could not compete against the new enterprises and imported goods; they too joined the army of dispossessed and unemployed, the burgeoning migrant labor pool.[45]

In a 1908 study for the U.S. Bureau of Labor, Victor Clark noted that underemployment and unemployment interacted with the internal demand for labor to cause a northward migration from the central plateau of Mexico along the railroad routes:

The railroads that enter Mexico from the United States run for several hundred miles from the border through a desert and very sparsely settled country, but all of them ultimately tap more populous and fertile regions. Along the northern portion of their routes resident labor is so scarce that workers are brought from the south as section hands and for new construction. This has carried the central Mexican villager a thousand miles from his home and to within a few miles of the border, and American employers, with a gold wage, have had little difficulty in attracting him across that not very formidable dividing line.

Clark later noted that, "Like the railways, the mines have had to import labor from the south; and they have steadily lost labor to the United States." Clark interviewed one mining operator who in one year brought 8,000 miners from the south to work in Chihuahua. On the whole, continued Clark, "there is a constant movement of labor northward inside of Mexico itself to supply the growing demands of the less developed states, and this supply is ultimately absorbed by the still more exigent demand . . . of the border States and Territories of the United States."[46]

In his review of the Porfiriato, Mexican historian Moisés González Navarro wrote that this "human displacement from the countryside" was a "phenomenon seen for the first time."[47] Approximately 300,000 persons left the south to settle in the north primarily during the last decade of the Porfiriato, a massive and permanent shift in the nation's population generated by foreign-controlled modernization.[48] One mining engineer lamented that "The call for labor is greater than can be supplied by the native population."[49] Another remarked that "The increase in number of mining operations in recent years has been so great as to make the securing of an adequate supply of labor a difficult problem."[50] At mid-century, scattered mines operated by small contingents of laborers had toiled intermittently, often in a "hand to mouth affair," but by the century's end some 140,000 worked the mines and smelters, and most of these were internal migrants.[51] Another 30,000 to 40,000 were employed annually on the railroads in the 1880s and 1890s. It is no wonder the population growth in the north surpassed that of any other area of Mexico.[52]

Along the rail routes, cities like Torreón and Gomez Palacio expanded enormously, as did ports like Guaymas and Tampico, due to the transport of people and/or export of goods. In 1883 Torreón was classified as a *rancheria*, a collection of ranches. By 1910 it had earned the title "city" with a population of over 43,000. Nuevo Laredo grew from 1,283 in 1877 to 9,000 in 1910; Nogales, which could not claim anything more than desert and some tents, blossomed into a thriving border port of 4,000 within two years after the train passed through.

Ciudad Lerdo offers a reverse example of the power of the railroads to determine population placement. In 1900 the city had contained 24,000 inhabitants, but, when the railroad bypassed it, the population declined to fewer than 12,000.[53]

The growth of the city was the other side of the demographic shift from the central plateau to the north. In the case of the north, population growth was most pronounced in the mining areas. Company towns like Cananea, El Boleo, Nacozari, Navojoa, Copola, Concordia, Santa Eulalia, Santa Rosalia, Batopilas, and Esperanzas sprang from virtual wilderness into thriving mining camps within a few years. American employers believed that company housing—albeit segregated, with Americans living apart from the Mexican labor force—was necessary to attract and control labor.[54] Cananea offers a representative example of localized change. A mining engineer reviewing the Greene Consolidated mining operations in 1906 wrote, "La Cananea presents a wonderful contrast to its earlier appearance. . . . [W]here eight years ago there were no persons other than a few warring prospectors . . . is now a camp of 25,000 persons with all the necessities and most of the comforts of civilization."[55] The Cananea operations required the labor of 5,500 regular men, with 8,000 to 9,000 listed as employees.

The Esperanza mining region in Coahuila experienced a similar profound change. In five years the area had grown from several villages to a population of 10,000, the mines employing 2,000. Batopilas, in Chihuahua, grew from 300 to 4,000, employing 900 miners. Mulegé, a port near the copper boomtown of El Boleo in Baja California, demonstrates the secondary effects that mining had on the region. The small port grew from 1,500 in 1880 to 14,000 in 1910. Similarly, Nogales, Hermosillo, El Paso, and other cities that depended on mine-driven commerce paralleled the growth in the mining enterprises themselves.

The reconfiguration of the centuries-old demographic pattern in Mexico comprised the first step in migrations to the United States. Crucially, the economic forces that propelled the population shifts were not indigenous to Mexico. Rather, they emanated from large-scale foreign corporate enterprises operating under the protection of the U.S. government's foreign policy.

Migration and Emigration

"In the southern section of the Western division, immigration from Mexico has become an important factor," stated the 1911 *Report* of the U.S. Immigration Commission. Indeed, even before the launching of the full-scale battles of the 1910 revolution (which were not to occur until 1913 to 1915), emigration had become a part of Mexican life. According to available statistics, Mexican labor began to enter the United States in sizable numbers after 1905, partly as a result of the south-to-north internal migrations in Mexico. Later migrations occurred in response to the economic depression in the United States that caused a slowdown of mining, motivating a northward migration. Data on Mexican migration shows that the numbers declined between 1905 and 1907 from 2,600 to 1,400. However, the numbers rose steeply in 1908 to 10,638, reaching 16,251 in 1909 and 18,691 in 1910. But these figures tell only part of the story. In 1911 the Immigration Bureau noted that at least 50,000 Mexicans without documentation crossed the border annually. The cyclic pattern of migration of superfluous labor from Mexico had begun to take root.

The argument made for the push of the Mexican Revolution does not answer why the migrations, documented and undocumented, appeared before the onset of the revolution or why the migrations slowed during the revolution but increased in the 1920s, well after the fighting had terminated.[56] It is entirely probable, even without the 1910 civil war, that emigration would have moved in the same upward direction. This is precisely what happened from the 1940s forward without the violence of war. The war probably exacerbated a preexisting condition rather than created it.

Moreover, the argument that the railroads as a transportation system inspired migration cannot withstand scrutiny. If railroads *per se* fostered the mass movement, then why did the migrations begin a quarter of a century *after* trains began running from Mexico City to the U.S. border? Furthermore, if wages were the stimulant, then emigration should have occurred earlier rather than in the middle of the first decade of the twentieth century, since wages were always lower in Mexico than in the United States. (This was particularly true during the depression of the 1930s.)

Abundant evidence suggests that the hacendado class provided a major impetus to emigrate since the hacendados perceived the dispossessed peasants as a potential political hazard and therefore financed migration journeys. In El Paso, Victor Clark interviewed several young migrants and was surprised to find evidence of lending by "patrons" in support of emigration, "sometimes a political officer—in one case a judge—and sometimes a merchant, possibly also a landowner."[57] Years later, Paul S. Taylor also found evidence of lending to the unemployed. In Jalisco, Taylor noted, "Anyone with money engaged in the business of assisting persons to migrate," and "hacendados prefer to let the workers get away so they won't congregate in pueblos and ask for land."[58] Clearly, there are serious problems with the conventional mode of analysis. The usual push arguments and the recent modifications simply cannot hold up to the evidence.

The Ebb and Flow of Migration, 1950–1970

Data on migration indicate that the flows are cyclical as well as long-term in nature. The original push-pull thesis and its newer versions cannot explain what accounts for this pattern. A constant (i.e., a steady disparity in the level of income and wages, or migrant networks, or the like) cannot logically account for variations in the pace of migration. Rather, one must turn again to concrete historical developments to explain those changes.

Despite the upheaval of the 1910 revolution, U.S. investment in the 1920s either retained its position garnered during the Díaz years or increased in significance.[59] With the coming of the global depression that began in the early 1930s, economic activity by U.S. companies at home and abroad diminished. The evidence shows that migration from Mexico declined after 1930 following the 1910–1930 upward trend. The slowdown in migration lasted until the early 1950s when it picked up again. Seeking the causes of this rebound, we once again turn to the pattern of U.S. economic activity in Mexico.

Beginning in the early 1940s, U.S. investments in Mexico began to rise once again in new forms. In Mexico, the depression of the 1930s brought to power what would become the future Partido Revolucionario Institucional (PRI) under its paternalistic leading figure, Lázaro Cárdenas. Like Franklin D. Roosevelt's New Deal, the Cárdenas government used the economic power of the state as never before in Mexico to maintain and protect the free market/private property social contract.

Under the Partido Revolucionario Mexicano (forerunner of the PRI), foreign investment flowed once again: It tripled from 1940 to 1950, and doubled again by 1958.[60] But the profile of the investment was different. Guided by the governing party, the national government instituted in 1934 a major public finance and development institution, the Nacional Financiera, which became the pillar of the economy. Nacional Financiera invested heavily in works of irrigation, highways, and electric power. Of the decades from 1940 to 1970, a period of rapid economic growth in Mexico, it has been said that "[n]o financial institution in Mexico has contributed more to the economic growth of that country than Nacional Financiera."[61]

Beginning in the early 1940s, U.S.-based banks and financial institutions began to invest in Mexico through loans to the Nacional Financiera. Some of the lending institutions included the U.S. Export-Import Bank, the Bank of America, the Chase Manhattan Bank, and eventually the International Bank for Reconstruction and Development (World Bank). Between 1942 and 1959 more than $900 million (mostly of U.S. origin) had been invested in major works of infrastructure in Mexico by way of the Nacional Financiera.[62] By 1953 foreign loans accounted for the single largest—about one-third—source of equity funds available to the institution.[63] This allowed U.S. capital to maximize its leverage over decision making while minimizing risks: U.S. financial institutions were in the driver's seat of the economic policies of the Nacional Financiera.

The investments financed by the Nacional Financiera had a tremendous impact both on Mexico's economy and on migration to the United States. A significant proportion of the investment went into major irrigation projects, the most important of which were located in the northern border states. The irrigation projects began in the early 1940s and included the Falcón Dam on the Rio Grande and the Rio Fuerte Irrigation Project in the state of Sonora. A tremendous increase in agricultural production followed. For example, cotton production in areas like the Mexicali Valley made Mexico the largest cotton exporter in the world.[64] Cotton production itself developed under the close control, through credit and marketing channels, of a U.S. agribusiness giant, Anderson Clayton (AC).

Mexican growers did not sell their product in the international market but through Anderson Clayton (and other U.S. companies), which monopolized the harvest and provided credit, seed, and fertilizers to the producers (much as AC had done in California's San Joaquin Valley in the 1930s). This company also managed cotton production in the countries with which Mexico competed in the world market: Brazil and the United States. In the late 1960s such control enabled AC to engage in cotton "dumping," reminding the Mexican government who was boss.[65] The opening up of irrigated lands in Sinaloa and Sonora allowed also for the production of "winter vegetables" beginning in the late 1940s, creating additional pockets of U.S. agribusiness control. The Pan-American Highway—another Nacional Financiera project—facilitated the marketing of Mexican vegetables in the United States. Thus, the export of tomatoes from Mexico's northeast increased from less than a million pounds in 1942 to 14 million in 1944.[66] The denationalized character of this production was evident as other U.S. corporations joined AC in effectively taking over Mexico's agribusiness, from production and the sale of machinery and fertilizers to the processing and merchandising of agricultural goods. The method of political control that John Foster Dulles described was complete: Mexico was borrowing money from U.S. banks to develop irrigation projects and transportation, thereby making possible the growth of U.S.-controlled agriculture in the northern tier of Mexican states.

With the growth of agriculture came population shifts, continuing the pattern begun in the late nineteenth century. Outside of the tourist-driven economies of Acapulco and Quintana Roo, only three Mexican states, all border states, showed an astonishing rate of growth of 45 percent or above in the

1950–1960 period (Baja California 232 percent, Tamaulipas 61 percent, and Sonora 45 percent).[67] Between 1950 and 1960 the total population of the eight major *municipios* of the Mexican border (Tijuana, Mexicali, Nogales, Ciudad Juárez, Piedras Negras, Nuevo Laredo, Reynosa, and Matamoros) increased by 83 percent, from less than 900,000 to 1.5 million. By 1970 the population had reached a total of 2.3 million. Between 1960 and 1969 the population rose by 45 percent in the northern border states (Baja California, Sonora, Chihuahua, Coahuila, Nuevo León, and Tamaulipas) in contrast with a figure of 31 percent for the nation as a whole. In 1970 fully 29 percent of the border population came from other parts of the country.[68]

Between 1950 and 1970 further ties developed across the Mexico–United States border. Subordination to U.S. corporations and the U.S. government provided the opportunity to construct a giant agribusiness economy on both sides of the border that relied on the ready supply of cheap labor from the interior of Mexico. An evident consequence of this relationship was one of the most spectacular mass movements of people in the history of humanity. The northward migration of people from all corners of Mexico to its north and, for many, eventually to the United States was motivated by the same general force, *the economic dislocation caused by U.S. capital—not an amorphous "global" capital—in Mexico*, the pace of the movement modulated in a cyclical manner by the relative intensity of U.S. economic intrusion. This movement turned the border area into a highly urbanized region. Simultaneously, migration constantly propelled the growth of the Chicano minority in the United States in a variety of forms: regulated and unregulated, legal and illegal, cyclical and long-term.

The Current Cycle, 1970–2000

As in the post–World War II period, U.S. investments in Mexico between 1970 and 2000 shifted away from mining and railroads toward industrial manufacturing. U.S. corporations made their way through direct purchase into the most dynamic sectors of local industry, especially in the 1960s. This trend occurred most notably in consumer durables, chemicals, electronics, department stores, hotels and restaurants, and the food industry, whereby United Fruit (later known as Dole), Heinz, Del Monte, and General Foods became very visible; 225 subsidiaries of U.S.-based corporations operated in the manufacturing sector.[69] U.S. investment in manufacturing concentrated around Mexico City, which accounted for 50 percent of the total manufacturing production of the country in 1975. Although this geographical concentration shifted, in the meantime Mexico's dependence on foreign loans increased. Between 1950 and 1972 the foreign debt grew at an average annual rate of 23 percent, reaching $11 billion by the latter year.

A chronic balance-of-payments problem, resulting from Mexico's reliance on the export of primary commodities and on foreign loans, made the situation worse. Beginning in the late 1960s, Mexico's hardly independent government had no choice but to accept lenders' terms. At the behest of international creditors, economic policies once again resulted in massive economic and demographic dislocation, contributing to a further increase of migration into Mexico's northern region, which became not only highly urbanized but acquired a new role as a major staging area for further migration to the United States.

In 1967 Mexico took a giant step in the complete abdication of its economic sovereignty when it established the Border Industrial Program along its northern border, beginning the transformation of the entire area into a gigantic assembly operation. The sad story of the maquiladora program in all its sordid details has been told elsewhere.[70] Suffice it to say that the maquilas, like a narcotic drug, made Mexico even more dependent while failing to solve its unemployment problems or help the country to become self-sufficient, developed, and modern.

For the purposes of our argument, the maquiladora program made the border states of Mexico, and specifically its border cities, into magnets for poverty-stricken, unemployed masses seeking work in the growing assembly plant industry. The maquiladoras have turned Mexico's northern border into an enclave with few links to the rest of the economy. Into the border area flowed duty-free manufacturing inputs to be assembled into final products for entry into the United States or export to other countries. The northern tier of Mexico has become a direct appendage of U.S. manufacturing, replicating the examples of railroads and mining in the Mexican economy during the early 1900s.

Simultaneous with the development of the maquiladora program, other significant changes affected Mexican agriculture. Between 1940 and the late 1960s, Mexico's countryside provided the basic food staples to its growing urban population. However, pressure from international lenders and agribusiness multinationals caused Mexico's central government to eliminate subsidies to small agricultural producers, who then began to abandon their farm plots to join the migration streams. Into the breach moved the United States, which turned the same agricultural lands into mechanized farms, producing commodities for export to the United States. In the 1970s the rate of growth of basic staples like corn, beans, and wheat began to fall behind population growth. To cover the precipitous decline in staple food production, a problem not seen since the Porfiriato, the country was forced to import basic food supplies.[71] However, imports have not fed Mexico's people satisfactorily. Infectious diseases and other illnesses linked to malnutrition and economic underdevelopment became rampant by the late 1980s.[72]

The 1990s witnessed the signing of the North American Free Trade Agreement (NAFTA), the most recent and devastating example of how U.S. domination over Mexico continues to misdevelop and tear apart the socioeconomic integrity of that society. The U.S. government and major corporate interests promoted NAFTA as a weapon in their trade competition with Europe and Japan. Under the "free trade" slogan, the proposed treaty would ostensibly serve two purposes. First, it would enable U.S. enterprises willing and able to invest in Mexico to take advantage of that country's cheaper wages. Mexico was to become a platform for the export of manufactured commodities to the United States and world markets. Major U.S. corporations, in particular automobile manufacturers, stood to benefit greatly from this scheme. Second, the treaty would, in effect, simultaneously deny to other economic powers the advantage of operating in and exporting from Mexico. Briefly put, the United States sought to create with Mexico (and Canada) an economic bloc to compete against Europe and Japan.

In its quest, the United States could count upon the leadership of Mexico's governing party, the PRI, and President Carlos Salinas. Under his leadership, Mexico undertook a set of wide-ranging measures to make NAFTA a reality. First, to demonstrate resolute support for market-oriented policies and attract foreign capital, the Mexican government broke up numerous government enterprises and laid off thousands of employees. Hundreds of state companies and institutions were sold or "privatized." The government enacted laws to "flexibilize" the labor market, restricting wage increases, curtailing vacation and sick-leave time, extending the work-week, and increasing management powers over the firing and hiring of temporary workers (known in the United States as downsizing). The elimination of trade protection meant that by 1993 nearly 50 percent of Mexico's textile firms and 30 percent of leather manufacturing firms had gone bankrupt. By the time of the signing of the treaty, Mexico's population had become severely polarized in terms of wealth and income.[73]

The actual signing of NAFTA revealed that Mexico was only as strong a bargainer as the weakest of the 535 U.S. parliamentarians. U.S. President Bill Clinton succeeded in obtaining a majority vote in Congress only by guaranteeing a multitude of senators and representatives protection for their districts against any competition that might result from NAFTA. For example, a Texas congressman agreed to vote in favor of NAFTA only after Clinton promised that the Pentagon would add two more cargo planes to a production order previously awarded to his district. A Florida representative voted for the treaty only after the State Department agreed to seek the extradition of an individual residing in Mexico who was accused of a crime in the United States. A lawmaker from Georgia opted for the treaty in exchange for promises by the Agriculture

Department that limits would be imposed upon increasing imports of peanut butter from Canada. Even small U.S. producers of brooms were protected from Mexican competition. Throughout the entire humiliating process, not a peep was heard from the Salinas government. In the end, "free trade" meant that Mexico would be completely open to U.S. goods, but U.S. producers were safely guarded against Mexico's products.

Rather than a free trade agreement, NAFTA could be better described as a "free investment" agreement. During the 1980s, tariffs levied by Mexico against the United States had steadily declined. NAFTA codified these changes, and, more importantly, it opened up investment opportunities in Mexico, protected against nationalizations, and eliminated all restrictions against U.S. ventures in Mexico. Of course, the "free investment" part would be limited under a section of the treaty entitled "rules of origin." These rules defined as domestic any inputs originating in Canada, the United States, and Mexico. Other imputs (for example, those from Japan) were classified as "foreign," and any products assembled with them became liable to export limits. In other words, after NAFTA it became more difficult for Japanese or European investors to ship products into Mexico for assembly and export to the United States.

NAFTA was never envisioned as a development policy for Mexico. All announced plans, forecasts, and decisions by U.S. multinationals relied on the low wages prevalent in Mexico as the key variable involved. Further displacement of peasants, massive migration, and the destruction of what remains of domestic Mexican agriculture will follow on the heels of NAFTA's complete opening to competition with the large U.S. agribusiness consortiums. Under NAFTA, Mexico has agreed to subject all land to privatization—that is, sale and speculation. For example, it returned Indian lands to the same juridical status that gave rise to Mexico's famed agrarian revolt over ninety years ago.[74]

Almost to the day of the first anniversary of the signing of NAFTA, the newly installed administration of Ernesto Zedillo faced a catastrophic devaluation of the national currency. Mexico's image changed from an investor's paradise to a disheveled financial hulk, a virtual economic protectorate of the United States. The United States set up conditions for a bailout that were, according to newspaper reports, too sensitive even to be published in Mexico. Eventually it became known that the U.S. plan required Mexico to hand over all revenues from its oil sales and gave to U.S. banks the right to supervise and enforce further privatizations and measures of austerity. Everything was now up for sale: bridges, airports, toll roads, ports, telephones, and so on. In the meantime, thousands of farmers, business people, and consumers went broke because they could not pay bills, meet debts, or finance mortgages. Contemporary estimates indicate that in the first two months of 1995 nearly 600,000 jobs were lost. A whopping 30 percent of Mexico's labor force, 11 million people, were reported unemployed in mid-1995.[75]

The U.S. embassy in Mexico, demonstrating U.S. resolve to remain committed to its plans for Mexico, referred positively to rising unemployment and bankruptcies as the "Darwinian effects" of NAFTA. Embassy officials praised its "stabilizing" effects upon the economy and called it the "bright spot" in the Mexican catastrophe. Taking advantage of the plummeting wage levels in Mexico relative to the dollar, the United States benefited enormously as 250 companies set up shop in the border area in the first three months of 1995. Apparently, Mexico should have been grateful that, in exchange for millions of unemployed and thousands ruined, a handful of Mexicans—a new generation of migrants—obtained jobs toiling in border cities for a miserable wage assembling products for reshipment to the United States. In the long run, the devastating effects of NAFTA upon Mexico's remaining agricultural production and urban manufacturing will throw onto the migration highways an even larger number of people desperately looking to make a living, thereby enlarging at a faster pace the mass of Mexican migrants in the United States. NAFTA is a particularly telling example of the unity of push and pull, as well as the role of U.S. domination in dismembering Mexico and creating a Chicano national minority in the United States.

Conclusion: A Network of Domination

Under NAFTA, steadily dropping manufacturing employment (outside of the maquila sector) points to the deindustrialization of Mexico. While manufacturing employment stood at 2,557,000 in 1981, it fell to 2,325,000 in 1993 and to 2,208,750 by 1997, a 13 percent drop from 1981. This brought with it lower living standards, as many workers moved from permanent to lower wage contingency work that lacked benefits and union protection. The destruction of Mexico's industrial base is particularly pronounced in the area of capital goods. Between 1995 and 1997 alone, following the peso debacle, 36 percent of the nation's 1,100 capital goods plants closed down. In all, 17,000 enterprises of all kinds went bankrupt shortly after the crisis exploded. Meanwhile, employment opportunities in the lowest-paying categories ballooned by 60 percent, dragging 5 million people to the official category of "extreme poverty." Manufacturing production has been reduced to the maquiladora sector, situated largely in the northern confines of the country, and to an increasingly concentrated manufacturing system dominated by a few U.S. industrial giants involved in production for export.[76]

The debacle in national industry has also materialized in agriculture with catastrophic consequences. According to a Mexican analyst, the opening of agricultural markets by the NAFTA treaty has led to the rapid ruin of what remained of Mexico's production of basic staples and to the dumping of cheap U.S. corn, wheat, and beans into Mexico. One hundred years of U.S. empire building has produced what 300 years of Spanish rule could not accomplish: the complete inability of the Mexican nation to produce enough to feed its own people. The migratory consequences are staggering: Millions will be forced to leave Mexico's countryside in the next decade.[77]

The demographic impact of this transformation of Mexico's economy has already caused a dramatic shift in the nation's population distribution. Since the 1960s the northern *municipios* feature one of the fastest-growing populations in the world. There appears no end in sight. The population there, which topped 4 million in 1995, is expected to double by 2010 and more than triple by 2020. Ciudad Juárez, for example, has grown fivefold since 1970, reaching one million. According to the Associated Press, each day "an estimated 600 new people arrive from Mexico's poor provinces hoping for work" in Ciudad Juárez—or nearly 220,000 new arrivals a year. Internal migrants in desperate straits will later surface as international migrants confronting the dangers of the militarized border.[78]

Today, this process intensifies the Mexicanization in the many barrios across the United States, forging a distinct demographic form in which immigrants either outnumber the second generation or reach a level of parity not seen since the 1930s. Migrants are the fastest-growing sector of the Chicano population; approximately 40 percent were born in Mexico, up from 17 percent four decades ago.[79] Had it not been for the Great Depression and World War II, the migratory movement of the 1900 to 1930 period would have proceeded without respite. That interruption made possible a distinctive Mexican American generation and later the Chicano generation. However, once migration resumed its previous pace, a cultural pattern that first surfaced in the 1920s reappeared in the 1960s. We foresee this Mexicanization overwhelming the older enclaves, remaking older barrios into immigrant centers, and thus reshaping the Chicano version of ethnic politics forged in the 1960s.

If there were any doubts about the false dichotomy between push and pull factors in the case of Mexico, the maquila program, NAFTA, and the agricultural collapse have erased them. For the most part, historians and social scientists have chosen not to scrutinize push-pull in this manner. Rather, social science perspectives have, in head-in-sand fashion, chosen to focus away from these "macro" factors toward the agency of migrants who, having constructed networks of migration, are regarded as the self-generators of migration. To be sure, Mexican immigrants have taken active roles and made significant choices in the construction of their lives, families, and communities. But it defies the evidence to insist that the explanation for Mexican migration to the United States lies within the immigrants' subjectivity. A simpler and more powerful explanation for Mexican migration northward to the United States, and the consequent development of the Chicano national minority, focuses on the 100 years of economic domination by centers of transnational economic power in the United States. Bit by bit, this tighter and tighter network of domination has succeeded in disarticulating the Mexican economy, destroying its domestic industry and local agricultural production, creating demographic dislocation, and, in the process, turning an increasing portion of its population into a nomadic mass of migrant workers who eventually emerge as the Chicano national minority. The rise of the Chicano national minority is not an event marginal to U.S. history. Quite the opposite, it has been central to the construction of the U.S. neocolonial empire.

Epilogue

In an earlier essay we challenged the widespread view that contemporary Chicano history originated in the aftermath of the 1848 conquest.[80] By focusing on economic transformations, we questioned the conventional periodization of Chicano history and argued that the nineteenth- and twentieth-century Spanish-speaking populations of the southwestern United States were largely two different populations. A focus on the War of 1848—the presumed starting point of Chicano history—obscures the relationship between the establishment of U.S. hegemony over Mexico, which came decades later, and the development of the Chicano national minority in the United States in the twentieth century.

We must distinguish the annexation of 1848 and the ensuing institutional integration of Mexican territory into the United States from the economic conquest of the late nineteenth and early twentieth centuries. Rather than the commonly held belief that the Mexican-American War of 1848 led to the construction of the Chicano minority, this study proposes that the origins of the Chicano population evolved from the economic empire established by corporate capitalist interests with the backing of the U.S. State Department. The political and economic repercussions of 1848 had virtually ended by the last decade of the nineteenth century. Furthermore, at no time did the 1848 annexation cause continuous internal migration, the mass population concentration along the border, the bracero program, low-wage maquila plants, Mexico's agricultural crisis, and, more importantly, a century of migrations to the United States. Those historical chapters, derived from the economic subordination of Mexico, forged the modern Chicano national minority.

NOTES

Reprinted with permission from the University of California Press. This essay originally in the *Pacific Historical Review* 71, no. 1 (February 2002): 19–57.

1 Chapter epigraph taken from Ernesto Galarza, "Program for Action," *Common Ground*, 10 (1949).

2 John Kenneth Turner, *Barbarous Mexico* (Chicago, 1911), 256–257.

3 John Mason Hart, *Revolutionary Mexico: The Coming Process of the Mexican Revolution* (Berkeley, 1997), chapters 5–7.

4 As quoted in the *Ottawa (Canada) Monitor*, Sept. 1995.

5 See, for example, Jonathan C. Brown, *Oil and Revolution in Mexico* (Berkeley, 1993); William E. French, *A Peaceful and Working People: Manners, Morals, and Class Formation in Northern Mexico* (Albuquerque, 1996); G. M. Joseph, *Revolution from Without: Yucatan, Mexico, and the United States, 1880–1924* (Durham, N.C., 1988); Ramon Eduardo Ruiz, *The People of Sonora and Yankee Capitalists* (Tucson, 1988); Mark Wasserman, *Capitalists, Caciques, and Revolution: The Native Elite and Foreign Enterprise in Chihuahua, Mexico, 1854–1911* (Chapel Hill, N.C., 1984).

6 There are a number of studies that look at the characteristics of the cooperation between Mexico's elites and powerful U.S. monopolies that descended upon Mexico at the end of the nineteenth century. In addition to those listed in note 5, see Robert Freeman Smith, *The United States and Revolutionary Nationalism in Mexico, 1916–1922* (Chicago, 1972), and Hart, *Revolutionary Mexico*, chapters 5 and 6.

7 See, for example, Clarence Clendenen, *The United States and Pancho Villa: A Study in Unconventional Diplomacy* (Ithaca, N.Y., 1961); Friedrich Katz, *The Secret War in Mexico: Europe, the United States and the Mexican Revolution* (Chicago, 1981); Gregg Andrews, *Shoulder to Shoulder? The American Federation of Labor, the United States, and the Mexican Revolution* (Berkeley, 1991); and Hart, *Revolutionary Mexico*.

8 Gilbert G. González, *Mexican Consulates and Labor Organizing: Imperial Politics in the American Southwest* (Austin, Tex., 1999).

9 See Mario Barrera, *Race and Class in the American Southwest: A Theory of Racial Inequality* (Notre Dame, Ind., 1979), 68–69; U.S. Industrial Commission, *Reports of the Industrial Commission on Immigration*, 15 (Washington, D.C., 1901), lxxxix. The report's conclusions about the cause of migration were based on the testimony of a former commissioner of immigration of the port of New York. As a witness before the U.S. Industrial Commission, he stated that "Those people who come for settlement in this country have a desire and feel the ability in themselves to expand, to look out for larger and better fields for their activity than they can find at home." *Reports of the Industrial Commission on Immigration*, 15, 183. See also Victor S. Clark, *Mexican Labor in the United States*, Department of Commerce and Labor, Bureau of Labor Bulletin No. 78 (Washington, D. C., 1908), 505; Manuel Gamio, *Migration and Immigration to the United States: A Study of Adjustment* (Chicago, 1930), 171; and Paul S. Taylor, *A Spanish-Mexican Peasant Community, Arandas in Jalisco, Mexico* (Berkeley, 1933), 40.

10 For a summary of sociological critiques of push-pull theories, see Alejandro Portes and Robert L. Bach, *Latin Journey: Cuban and Mexican Immigrants in the United States* (Berkeley, 1985); Stephen Castles and Mark J. Miller, *The Age of Migration: International Population Movements in the Modern World* (New York, 1993); Ewa Morawska,

"The Sociology and Historiography of Immigration," in Virginia Yans-McLaughlin, ed., *Immigration Reconsidered: History, Sociology, and Politics* (New York, 1990), 192.

11 Leo Grebler, Joan W. Moore, Ralph C. Guzman, and Jeffrey Lionel Berlant, *The Mexican American People: The Nation's Second Largest Minority* (New York, 1970), 63.

12 The examples of push-pull are many; the following are but a few: Leo R. Chavez, "Defining and Demographically Characterizing the Southern Border of the U.S.," in John R. Weeks and Roberto Ham-Chande, eds., *Demographic Dynamics of the U.S.-Mexico Border* (El Paso, Tex., 1992); Douglas S. Massey, Rafael Alarcón, Jorge Durand, and Humberto González, *Return to Aztlan: The Social Process of International Migrations From Western Mexico* (Berkeley, 1987), 108; Mark Reisler, *By the Sweat of Their Brows: Mexican Immigrant Labor in the United States, 1900–1940* (Westport, Conn., 1976), 14; Arthur F. Corwin and Lawrence A. Cardoso, "Vamos al Norte: Causes of Mass Migration to the United States," in Arthur F. Corwin, ed., *Immigrants and Immigrants: Perspectives on Mexican Labor Migration to the United States* (Westport, Conn., 1978), 39; David Maciel and Maria Herrera Sobek, "Introduction," in David Maciel and Maria Herrera Sobek, eds., *Culture Across Borders: Mexican Immigration and Popular Culture* (Tucson, 1998), 4; Camille Guerin-Gonzales, *Mexican Workers and the American Dreams: Immigration, Repatriation, and California Farm Labor, 1900–1939* (New Brunswick, NJ, 1994), 27–30; George J. Sánchez, *Becoming Mexican American: Ethnicity, Culture, and Identity in Chicano Los Angeles, 1900–1945* (New York, 1993), 20, 39; Richard Griswold del Castillo and Arnoldo de León, *North to Aztlan: A History of Mexican Americans in the United States* (New York, 1996), 60–61; Antonio Rios-Bustamante, ed., *Mexican Immigrant Workers in the United States* (Los Angeles, 1981); Frank D. Bean, Rodolfo de la Garza, Bryan Roberts, and Sidney Weintraub, eds., *At the Crossroads: Mexico and U.S. Immigration Policy* (New York, 1997).

13 There are a few exceptions. Barrera's *Race and Class in the Southwest* briefly pointed out that the push-pull notions were difficult to separate. Alejandro Portes also points to weaknesses in "From South of the Border: Hispanic Minorities in the United States," in Yans-Mclaughlin, ed., *Immigration Reconsidered*. Portes generally identifies the role of U.S. expansion and intervention in Mexico, which he lumps with "postcolonial" societies. Upon closer examination, he appears to be referring to the territorial acquisition following the Mexican-American War of 1846. He specifically places the origin of the northward migration on the activities of labor recruiters, not on the social dislocations caused by U.S. investments. Interestingly, Saskia Sassen also emphasizes the "emergence of a multinational labor market" consequent to the "internationalization of capital." She writes that investments by U.S. railroad and agricultural corporations and the Border Industrial Program "are all processes which created a labor market." The U.S.-Mexican border artificially divides this "labor market"; hence, migration responds to the international labor marketplace. Saskia Sassen, "U.S. Immigration Policy Toward Mexico in a Global Economy," in David Gutiérrez, *Between Two Worlds: Mexican Immigrants in the United States* (Wilmington, Del., 1996).

14 See the special issue of the *Journal of American History* 86 (1999), edited by David Thelen, titled "Rethinking History and the Nation-State," 427–697.

15 See, for example, Nestor Rodriguez, "The Battle for the Border: Notes on Autonomous Migration, Transnational Communities, and the State" in Susanne Jonas and

Suzie Dod Thomas, eds., *Immigration: A Civil Rights Issue for the Americas* (Wilmington, Del., 1999); for a variation on this theme, see David M. Reimers, *Still the Golden Door: The Third World Comes to America* (New York, 1985), 128–29; Vicki Ruiz, *From Out of the Shadows: Mexican Women in Twentieth-Century America* (New York, 1998), 163; Pierrette Hondagneu-Sotelo, *Gendered Transitions: Mexican Experiences of Migration* (Berkeley, 1994); Douglas Massey, "The Social Organization of Mexican Migration to the United States," in David Jacobson, ed., *The Immigration Reader: American in Multidisciplinary Perspective* (New York, 1998), 213–14; and David Jacobson, "Introduction" in *The Immigration Reader*, 11. Jacobson writes that "Mexican migration reflects the earlier development of social networks that sustain it."

16   See, for example, Wayne Cornelius, "The Structural Embeddedness of Demand for Mexican Immigrant Labor: New Evidence from California," in Marcelo M. Suarez-Orozco, ed., *Crossings: Mexican Immigration in Interdisciplinary Perspective* (Cambridge, Mass., 1998), 141–42, and Robert Smith, "Commentary," in Orozco, *Crossings*.

17   Douglas S. Massey and Kristin E. Espinosa, "What's Driving Mexico-U.S. Migration? A Theoretical, Empirical, and Policy Analysis," *American Journal of Sociology* 102 (1997), 953.

18   Massey and Espinosa, "What's Driving Mexico-U.S. Migration?," 954.

19   See Reimers, *Still the Golden Door*; Frank D. Bean, W. Parker Frisbie, Edward Telles, and B. Lindsay Lowell, "The Economic Impact of Undocumented Workers in the Southwest of the United States," in Weeks and Ham-Chande, eds., *Demographic Dynamics*.

20   Saskia Sassen, "Foreign Investment: A Neglected Variable," in Jacobsen, ed., *The Immigration Reader*; Saskia Sassen, *Globalization and Its Discontents: Essays on the New Mobility of People and Money* (New York, 1998), chapter 6.

21   Quoted in P. Harvey Middleton, *Industrial Mexico: Facts and Figures* (New York, 1919), frontispiece; for a slightly different version, see Alfred Tischendorf, *Great Britain in Mexico in the Era of Porfirio Díaz* (Durham, N.C., 1961), 75.

22   David M. Pletcher, *Rails, Mines, and Progress: Seven American Promoters in Mexico, 1867–1911* (Ithaca, N.Y., 1958), 38.

23   Pletcher, *Rails, Mines, and Progress*, 38, 79–80.

24   Chester Lloyd Jones, *Mexico and Its Reconstruction* (New York, 1921), 299, 310. Mexican elites anticipated the policy design. Onetime Mexican representative in Washington, Matias Romero, proposed an economic conquest in an 1864 speech before a gathering of New York City's prominent citizens. Guests included the largest capitalists; names like Aspinwall, Astor, Fish, and Clews filled the list. Romero advised: "The United States are the best situated to avail themselves of the immense wealth of Mexico. . . . We are willing to grant to the United States every commercial facility. . . . This will give to the United States all possible advantages that could be derived from annexation, without any of its inconveniences." Matias Romero, *Mexico and the United States* (New York, 1898), 385.

25   Pletcher, *Rails, Mines, and Progress*, 3.

26   Ruiz, *The People of Sonora*, 14–15; Wasserman, *Capitalists, Caciques, and Revolution*, 108–9.

27   In his authoritative 1921 review of Mexican railroads, Fred Wilbur Powell stated that "Mexican railroad development was *the result of foreign capital and enterprise,*

attracted by national franchises or 'concessions' and encouraged by subsidies" (emphasis added). Fred Wilbur Powell, *The Railroads of Mexico* (Boston, 1921), 1.

28 Walter E. Weyl, *Labor Conditions in Mexico*, Bulletin of the U.S. Department of Labor, No. 38 (Jan. 1902), 52.

29 Marvin D. Bernstein, *The Mining Industry in Mexico, 1890-1950* (New York, 1964), 35.

30 Bernstein, *The Mining Industry in Mexico, 1890-1950*, 33. Booster advertising that offered sure bets on Mexican investments cajoled American investors. Railroads, it was said, guaranteed lucrative profits and vast wealth; they awaited only the enlightened administration of the American investor. David M. Pletcher, "The Development of the Railroads in Sonora," *Inter-American Economic Affairs* 1 (1948), 1-2. One pamphlet published by the U.S. government announced that "the opening up of new mining districts is largely due to Americans, both through the improved mining methods and through the development of railroads built by our capital." International Bureau of the American Republics, *Mexico: Geographical Sketch, Natural Resources, Laws, Economic Conditions, Actual Development, Prospects of Future Growth* (Washington, DC, 1904), 233.

31 Robert G. Cleland, "The Mining Industry of Mexico: A Historical Sketch," *Mining and Scientific Press* (July 2, Nov. 5, 1921), [part 1] 13; Wasserman, *Capitalists, Caciques, and Revolution*, 76.

32 John Sheahan, *Patterns of Development in Latin America* (Princeton, N.J., 1987), 297; Joseph, *Revolution from Without*, 30, 51, 62; Wasserman, *Capitalists, Caciques, and Revolution*, 46.

33 John Coatsworth, *Growth Against Development: The Economic Impact of Railroads in Porfirian Mexico* (DeKalb, Ill., 1981), 123-124.

34 Coatsworth, *Growth Against Development*, 158, 170. John Mason Hart makes this same point: "In the midst of land seizures associated with the planning of the new railroad system, peasant uprisings ranged from Chihuahua in the north to Oaxaca in the south." Hart, *Revolutionary Mexico*, 41, 170. See also French, *A Peaceful and Working People*, 37-47; Ruiz, *The People of Sonora*, 16-17; Wasserman, *Capitalists, Caciques, and Revolution*, 109.

35 Coatsworth, *Growth Against Development*, 145.

36 Michael Johns, *The City of Mexico in the Age of Díaz* (Austin, Tex., 1997), 14.

37 Roger D. Hansen, *The Politics of Mexican Development* (Baltimore, 1971), 27; Nathan L. Whetten, *Rural Mexico* (Chicago, 1948), 89.

38 Moisés González Navarro, *El Porfiriato: La Vida Social* (Mexico City, 1957), 20.

39 Johns, *The City of Mexico*, 64.

40 Turner, *Barbarous Mexico*, 116.

41 Johns, *The City of Mexico*, 30.

42 Evelyn Hu-Dehart, "Pacification of the Yaquis in the Late Porfiriato: Development and Implications," *Hispanic American Historical Review* 54 (1974), 77.

43 Frank Tannenbaum, *The Mexican Agrarian Revolution* (Washington, DC, 1929), 126.

44 Weyl, *Labor Conditions in Mexico*, 91.

45 See Rodney D. Anderson, *Outcasts in Their Own Land: Mexican Industrial Workers, 1906-1911* (De Kalb, Ill., 1976), 48-50. Anderson writes that "the artisans added to the growing numbers of rural people forced off their lands by enclosure."

46 Clark, *Mexican Labor in the United States*, 470–71. See also French, *A Peaceful and Working People*, 42–43.

47 González Navarro, *El Porfiriato*, xvii, 25.

48 Friedrich Katz, "The Liberal Republic and the Porfiriato, 1867–1910," in Leslie Bethell, ed., *Mexico Since Independence* (New York, 1991), 89.

49 E. A. H. Tays, "Present Labor Conditions in Mexico," *Engineering and Mining Journal* 84 (1907), 622.

50 Allen H. Rogers, "Character and Habits of Mexican Miners," *Engineering and Mining Journal* 85 (1908), 700.

51 See Cleland, "The Mining Industry of Mexico," [part 2] 640.

52 J. Fred Rippy, *Latin America and the Industrial Age* (New York, 1947). Jonathan Brown, "Foreign and Native-Born Workers in Porfirian Mexico," *American Historical Review* 98 (1993), 798.

53 González Navarro, *El Porfiriato*, 23.

54 Rogers, "Character and Habits of Mexican Miners," 701. See also Brown, *Oil and Revolution in Mexico*, 80–81. Brown writes that the Veracruz state population increased by 280,000 between 1890 and 1910, the oil boom years cited by personages like Edward Doheny, who developed the Veracruz area oil explorations.

55 Dwight E. Woodbridge, "La Cananea Mining Camp," *Engineering and Mining Journal* 82 (1906), 623. This citation also applies to the following paragraph.

56 See French, *A Peaceful and Working People*; Brown, *Oil and Revolution in Mexico*; Wasserman, *Capitalists, Caciques, and Revolution*; Ruiz, *The People of Sonora*; Smith, *The United States and Revolutionary Nationalism in Mexico*.

57 Clark, *Mexican Labor in the United States*, 472.

58 Taylor, *A Spanish-Mexican Peasant Community*, 44.

59 Smith, *The United States and Revolutionary Nationalism*, 34.

60 Howard F. Cline, *Mexico: Revolution to Evolution, 1940–1960* (New York, 1963), 244.

61 Benjamin Higgins, *Economic Development: Problems, Principles, and Policies* (New York, 1968), 643.

62 Cline, *Mexico*, 245.

63 Higgins, *Economic Development*, 645.

64 W. Whitney Hicks, "Agricultural Development in Northern Mexico, 1940–1960," *Land Economics* 53 (Nov. 1967), 396.

65 Raúl A. Fernandez, *The United States-Mexico Border: A Politico-Economic Profile* (Notre Dame, Ind., 1977), 108.

66 Fernandez, *The United States-Mexico Border*, 123.

67 Raúl A. Fernandez, *The Mexican American Border Region: Issues and Trends* (Notre Dame, Ind., 1989), 61. It is interesting to note that during the cotton boom years (1940–1960), the border *municipios* where cotton was the main agricultural product (Mexicali, Juárez, Reynosa, and Matamoros) registered the highest rates of population growth. On the other hand, during the years of the cotton crisis (1960–1970), the same municipalities suffered a sharp drop in their populations.

68 Fernandez, *The Mexican American Border Region*, 108.

69 See Fernandez, *The Mexican American Border Region;* Fernandez, *The United States-Mexico Border*.

70 Fernandez, *The United States-Mexico Border*.

71 David Barkin and Blanca Suarez, *El Fin de la Autosuficiencia Alimentaria* (Mexico City, 1982); Ruth Rama, "Some Effects of the Internationalization of Agriculture on the Mexican Agricultural Crisis," in Steven E. Sanderson, *The Americas in the New International Division of Labor* (New York, 1985).

72 Hart writes: "Mexico in 1987 constitutes an economic and social disaster . . . 70 percent of the children suffer from malnutrition. . . . The World Health Organization estimates that 107,000 Mexican children died in 1983 from three diseases for which immunization is available." Hart, *Revolutionary Mexico*, 378.

73 Carlos Heredia and Mary E. Purcell, "The Polarization of Mexican Society," paper prepared for the NGO Working Group on the World Bank, Development Group for the Alternative Policies, Dec. 1994.

74 González, *Mexican Consuls and Labor Organizing*, 12, 14–15; James D. Cockcroft, *Mexico: Class Formation, Capital Accumulation, and the State* (New York, 1983), 91.

75 González, *Mexican Consuls and Labor Organizing*, chapter 6.

76 *International Report* 12 (March–June 1994); 13, (Feb.–July 1995). Raúl Fernández, "Perspectivas del Tratado de Libre Comercio de Norteamerica," *Deslinde* [Bogotá, Colombia], 13 (March–April 1993). James M. Cypher, "Developing Disarticulation within the Mexican Economy," *Latin American Perspectives* 28, no. 3 (2001): 11–37.

77 Victor S. Quintana, "La Catastrofe Maicera," *La Opinion*, April 17, 1999; Chris Kraul, "Growing Troubles in Mexico," *Los Angeles Times*, Jan. 17, 2000. Kraul writes that, due to corn imports from the United States, "one fifth of the 250,000 families who were working the land in Guanajuato in 1990 have since left their farms . . . a population shift that has been repeated across Mexico." The Free Trade Agreement "mandated the end of the costly subsidy program"; John Coatsworth, "Commentary" in Suarez-Orozco, ed., *Crossings*, 75–78; Philip Martin, "Do Mexican Agricultural Policies Stimulate Emigration?" in Bean, de la Garza, Roberts, and Weintraub, eds., *At the Crossroads*.

78 "A Call to Action is Needed at U.S. Border," *Los Angeles Times*, May 9, 1999; Mark Stevenson, "Border Factories Target of Fury over Mass Killings of Women," *Orange County (Calif.) Register*, April 4, 1999; Ham-Chande and Weeks, "A Demographic Perspective of the U.S.-Mexico Border," in Weeks and Ham-Chande, eds., *Demographic Dynamics*.

79 Frank D. Bean and Marta Tienda, *The Hispanic Population in the United States* (New York, 1987), 110; Marcelo M. Suarez-Orozco, "Introduction: Crossings: Mexican Immigration in Interdisciplinary Perspectives," in Suarez-Orozco, ed., *Crossings*, 7; Gilda Laura Ochoa, "Mexican Americans' Attitudes and Interactions Towards Mexican Immigrants: A Qualitative Analysis of Conflict and Cooperation," *Social Science Quarterly* 81 (March 2000), 84–105.

80 Gilbert G. González and Raúl Fernández, "Chicano History: Transcending Cultural Models," *Pacific Historical Review* 63 (1994), 469.

Legal Violence: Immigration Law and
the Lives of Central American Immigrants

CECILIA MENJÍVAR AND LEISY J. ABREGO

Concha is in Honduras, the native country of one of the fastest-growing im-migrant populations in the United States.[1] The country's stagnant economy resulting from the Central American Free Trade Agreement with the United States and the devastation of Hurricane Mitch in 1998, along with recent po-litical turbulence in the country, have led to massive outmigration in the past decade and a half. Comparing the migration of two family members at differ-ent points in time, Concha describes the effects of U.S. immigration and bor-der policy changes on peoples' perceptions of a successful migration:

> When my brother went [to the United States, 15 years ago] the idea was
> to send money. One considered that a successful migration, when people
> who went sent money here. Now, no. Now it's another thing with all the
> dangers on the way there, the crossing of the border. Now it's successful
> if they make it there alive. One is left here with so much anguish. It's just
> so worrisome to see a loved one go [to the United States].

As Concha relates, the definition of a successful migration today, compared to
15 years ago, has been reduced to simply surviving the trip. Having accepted

the dangerous terms of migration, immigrants and their families understand them as a "new normal," perhaps even expected, aspect of migration and settlement. In this essay, we analyze how Central American immigrants in tenuous legal statuses experience current immigration laws in qualitatively different and more negative ways than in the recent past.[2] We argue that this change is rooted in the effects of an increasingly fragmented and arbitrary field of immigration law gradually intertwined with criminal law, and we label the current practices *legal violence*.

The Central American case provides a fruitful starting point to analyze how the legal context of reception produces vulnerabilities among contemporary immigrants. Guatemalan, Honduran, and Salvadoran immigrants have multiple legal statuses resulting from an array of U.S. foreign and immigration policy decisions, bringing into sharp relief the consequences of specific laws on groups and individuals (see Menjívar, n.d.). Grounding our analysis on immigrants' experiences, we use a theoretical lens that makes visible different forms of violence inherent in the implementation of the law, particularly when these become normalized and accepted (Menjívar 2011, n.d.). Like Central Americans, many immigrants in the United States and in other major receiving countries around the world are facing similar predicaments. Thus, our objective is twofold: (1) to inspire comparative work by offering an analytical lens that can capture the experiences of other immigrants in unresolved legal statuses today and (2) to theorize about the place of the law in shaping everyday life more generally.

The legal violence lens is particularly useful in the study of immigrants and immigration as it grasps the complex and often overlooked effects of the law on immigrants' paths of incorporation and assimilation. A central theme in sociological studies of immigration, past and present, has been the incorporation or assimilation of immigrants into the receiving society. This question preoccupied the early scholars whose work set the foundations of American sociology (e.g., Park 1950; Thomas and Znaniecki 1996), and it has sustained considerable attention. Over the decades, debates have revolved around whether immigrants follow a purported straight-line path, as in Milton Gordon's (1964) classic conceptualization in which, over time, they become similar to the majority group in terms of norms, values, and behaviors, or perhaps a "bumpy line," as in Herbert J. Gans's (1992) view. Contemporary debates have centered on whether the paths of incorporation of contemporary immigrants differ from those of immigrants from the turn of the past century (Waldinger and Perlmann 1998; Portes and Rumbaut 2001; Rumbaut and Portes 2001; Kasinitz et al. 2008). Scholars have identified various factors, including immigrant groups' human capital levels and the occupational opportunities that receive them, as catalysts for successful incorporation. New formulations, building on earlier foundational questions and focusing on the second generation, have refined the theoretical tools for the understanding of immigrant incorporation. For instance, in what has been called the "new assimilation theory," Alba and Nee (2003) highlight the crucial role of civil society organizations, past and present, in facilitating assimilation. And exponents of the segmented assimilation framework propose variegated paths of incorporation in which structural factors in the context of reception can lead to stagnant or downward mobility, straight-line assimilation, or an alternative path in which immigrants become successful by staying close to their ethnic group (Portes and Zhou 1993).

The segmented assimilation framework has been especially useful in identifying structural forces that block or facilitate mobility: poor urban schools, inequalities in job market opportunities, racialization (Portes and Zhou 1993; Portes, Fernández-Kelly, and Haller 2005), and immigration laws, for example, shape immigrant "modes of incorporation" (Portes and Böröcz 1989, 620). Along with economic, social, and human capital factors, and the contexts of exit and reception, the segmented assimilation model incorporates immigration laws of the receiving country as a key analytical feature to understand the various paths of immigrant incorporation. Theoretically, we build on this tradition to further examine the potential effects of immigration laws on immigrants' incorporation, and, in doing so, we focus on the law's underside—the sometimes hidden and violent effects. This is particularly relevant today, as many immigrants are spending longer periods of time as undocumented or in uncertain legal statuses with significant long-term consequences (Menjívar 2006a, 2006b). And although we do not directly examine the long-term effects of current laws, in highlighting this aspect of the context of reception, we contribute to broader discussions of the place of immigration law (not of legal status per se) on immigrant incorporation.

Much of the current discourse implicitly assumes that legal status is intrinsic to individuals; however, migrant illegality (and legality) is legally constructed (De Genova 2005; Ngai 2007; Donato and Armenta 2011). Immigration laws restrict the movement of some individuals but allow the admission of others (Hao 2007), thereby making and unmaking documented, undocumented (Calavita 1998; Ngai 2004), and quasi-documented immigrants. These practices establish a social hierarchy anchored in legality as a social position (Menjívar 2006b), as legal categories grant immigrants access to goods, benefits, and rights in society (Massey and Bartley 2005). As such, immigration laws today create a new axis of stratification that, like other forms of stratification, significantly shapes life chances and future prospects (Menjívar 2006a, 2006b).

To bring to the fore the complex manner in which the law exerts its influence and control, we examine the harmful effects of the law that can potentially obstruct and derail immigrants' paths of incorporation. We use the term *legal violence* to refer to these effects, as they are often manifested in harmful ways for the livelihood of immigrants. Importantly, although we note cases of interpersonal aggression, or physical violence, we concentrate on those instances that are not directly physically harmful and that are not usually counted and tabulated; indeed, our analysis draws attention to the accumulation of those damaging instances that are immediately painful but also potentially harmful for the long-term prospects of immigrants in U.S. society. We trace immigrants' experiences to the laws, their implementation, and the discourses and practices the law makes possible.

Forms of Violence: Structural, Symbolic, and Legal

According to sociologist Mary Jackman (2002), two dominant assumptions have guided most examinations of violence: (1) that violence is motivated by the willful intent to cause harm presumably resulting from hostility and (2) that violence is socially or morally "deviant" from mainstream human activity. Thus, "when violence is motivated by positive intentions, or is the incidental by-product of other goals, or is socially accepted or lauded, it escapes our attention" (Jackman 2002, 388). This approach, therefore, leaves out sources of material injuries, "such as loss of earnings, destruction, and confiscation; the psychological outcomes of fear, shame, anxiety, or diminished self-esteem; and the social consequences of public humiliation, stigmatization, exclusion, banishment, and imprisonment, all of which can have deeply devastating consequences for human beings" (393). Ignoring these less dramatic, often less visible, forms of causing injuries results in a "patchy, ad hoc conception of violence" (395). Through our analysis of immigrants' experiences with immigration law, we heed Jackman's call to open up the sociological optic to the examination of violence and focus on those instances that might, otherwise, elude attention.

To theorize about legal violence, we link specific laws and their implementation to particular outcomes in three central facets of study participants' lives: family, work, and school. These are vital spheres of life through which immigrants come into contact with institutions in the wider society and thus are key areas to examine when assessing long-term incorporation and paths of assimilation. As such, they also represent the most salient spheres of life through which immigrants experience the effects of the law.

Drawing from the scholarship on structural and symbolic violence, we utilize a lens that identifies harmful outcomes of the law in the lives of individuals (see Menjívar 2011, n.d.).[3] The concept of legal violence incorporates the various, mutually reinforcing forms of violence that the law makes possible and amplifies. This lens allows us to capture the aggravation of otherwise "normal" or "regular" effects of the law, such as the immigrants' predicament that results from indefinite family separations due to increased deportations; the intensification in the exploitation of immigrant workers and new violations of their rights; and the exclusion and further barring of immigrants from education and other forms of socioeconomic resources necessary for mobility and incorporation. All of these instances constitute forms of structural and symbolic violence that are codified in the law and produce immediate *social suffering* but also potentially long-term harm with direct repercussions for key aspects of immigrant incorporation.[4]

Moreover, the legal violence lens exposes the contradictions on which the formulation and implementation of immigration law rests: the various laws at federal, state, and local levels today seek to punish the behaviors of undocumented immigrants but at the same time push them to spaces outside the law. This dual contradictory goal makes immigrants simultaneously accountable to the law but also excludes them from legal protections or rights, or in Chavez's (2008) conceptualization, it forces them to live in the nation but not be perceived as part of the nation. Finally, the concept of legal violence also allows us to bring into focus the far-reaching consequences of laws enacted in a regional center of power as these have a spillover effect that engulfs as well the lives of the nonmigrant relatives and communities in countries from which immigrants originate (see also Coleman 2007; Massey 2007).

The different forms of violence we examine are linked and mutually constitutive. At the macro level, patterned forms of structural violence are "rooted in the uncertainty of everyday life caused by the insecurity of wages or income, a chronic deficit in food, dress, housing, and health care, and uncertainty about the future which is translated into hunger" (Torres-Rivas 1998, 49). This type of violence is considered structural because it is borne through and concealed in exploitative labor markets and discriminatory educational systems that impose inequality on society (49). As the anthropologist Paul Farmer (2003) observes, suffering that results from structural violence is "'structured' by historically given (and often economically driven) processes and forces that conspire . . . to constrain agency" (Farmer 2003, 40). Structural violence is particularly evident in the living conditions and limitations of the poor. For example, although malnutrition and lack of access to goods and services do not result in immediate killings, over many years, for the most vulnerable members of society, they do effectuate a slow death (Galtung 1990). In Galtung's (1990) classic conceptualization, exploitation (in its various forms) lies at the core of the archetypal violent structure. Thus, attention to forms of inequality and abuses of immigrants' labor that are made possible by specific laws under the current immigration regime highlights not only immediate social suffering but also how the law can block access to society's goods and services that promote integration and success. These violations of rights are, in turn, linked to and mutually constitutive of symbolic violence.

An important aspect of the violence we address is its normalization, for which we turn to the work of Pierre Bourdieu. Following Bourdieu (1998), symbolic violence refers to a range of actions that have injurious consequences, to the internalization of social asymmetries, and to the legitimation of inequality and hierarchy, ranging from racism and sexism to expressions of class power. It is about the imposition of categories of thought on dominated social groups who then accept these categories and evaluate their conditions through these frames and think of their predicament as normal, thus perpetuating unequal social structures.[5] In this conceptualization, "The dominated apply categories constructed from the point of view of the dominant to the relations of domination, thus making them appear as natural. This can lead to a systematic self-depreciation, even self-denigration" (Bourdieu 1998, 35). Since the lens through which social actors see the social world is derived from the same social world, they (mis)recognize the social order, including, for instance, the power of the law in their everyday lives, as natural. In this way, inequalities and rights violations in the social order can go unquestioned because "it is the law." Individuals who endure these power inequalities, however, are fully aware of the effects, but the conditions are so overwhelming and structures so omnipotent that there is little room for questioning this natural order of things (Kleinman 2000).[6] Symbolic violence, moreover, "is exercised upon a social agent with his or her complicity" (Bourdieu and Wacquant 2004, 273) and manifested through individuals' feelings of inadequacy, mutual recrimination, and exploitation of fellow victims. These processes, in turn, divert attention away from the forces that created the conditions of violence in the first place (Bourgois 2004a, 2004b). Thus, individuals come to understand their marginalized positions as natural and can then become contributors to their own plight but also actors in trying to change those conditions.[7]

Drawing on these conceptualizations of structural and symbolic violence (see Menjívar 2011, n.d.), we argue that legal violence best explains the living conditions and experiences of contemporary immigrants in tenuous legal statuses in the United States as well as in other major immigrant-receiving countries.[8] Legal violence captures the suffering that results from and is made possible through the implementation of the body of laws that delimit and shape individuals' lives on a routine basis. Under certain circumstances, policy makers and political leaders enact laws that are violent in their effects and broader consequences. Although their effect may be considered a form of both structural and symbolic violence, we refer to it as legal violence because it is embedded in legal practices, sanctioned, actively implemented through formal procedures, and legitimated—and consequently seen as "normal" and natural because it "is the law."[9]

Legal violence, in the interpretation that we advance here, is embedded in the body of law that, while it purports to have the positive objective of protecting rights or controlling behavior for the general good, simultaneously gives rise to practices that harm a particular social group. In these cases, the law enables various forms of violence against the targeted group. For contemporary immigrants, legal violence is rooted in the multipronged system of laws at the federal, state, and local levels that promotes a climate of insecurity and suffering among individual immigrants and their families. To be sure, legal violence against immigrants is not a new phenomenon (see, e.g., Takaki 1989; Espiritu 1997; De Genova 2004). The lens we employ based on today's practices, therefore, may shed new light on the violent effects of immigration law in the past, such as the Chinese Exclusion Act of 1882 and Operation Wetback in the 1950s. However, in today's regime, which increasingly links civil immigration with criminal laws (Miller 2005; Inda 2006), the threat of deportation has been used with unprecedented vigor to make even permanent legal residents vulnerable to deportation (Kanstroom 2007).[10] A key point is that beginning in the early 1990s and progressively after the attacks of September 11, 2001 (Donato and Armenta 2011), lawmakers have converged civil immigration law with criminal law, relying on a vast state technology that enables the merging of the two for border but also interior social control (Kanstroom 2007). Indeed, the reorganization of the Immigration and Naturalization Service (INS) under the Department of Homeland Security (DHS) created in the aftermath of 9/11 to safeguard the country against terrorism (Borja 2008) has increasingly linked immigrants with terrorists and criminals, helping to move immigration matters from the civil to the realm of criminal law. This process has fashioned a violent context for immigrants already in the country, where social suffering becomes commonplace, normalized, and familiar. This new approach to immigration, undocumented and documented alike (Kanstroom 2007; Donato and Armenta 2011), has created a new context that requires a fresh lens to unearth its violent effects.[11]

Unlike most punitive laws that target the behavior of individuals, current immigration laws and their implementation target an entire class of people mostly with noncriminal social characteristics, such as language spoken or physical appearance, that associate them with a particular immigration status. Although the focus of these laws is immigrants in uncertain legal statuses they also target their U.S.-born family members as well as documented immigrants (and other noncitizens). And importantly, whereas immigration law has moved toward a convergence with criminal law, there are now fewer (and more restrictive) avenues for immigrant legalization. These parallel tracks have created a population caught in uncertain legal statuses with very limited legal options but living with the omnipresent threat of deportation. We bring together a variety of situations that when taken individually may be interpreted (or perhaps dismissed) as aberrations or exceptions but when examined collectively across different contexts reveal group vulnerabilities specifically linked to the law and its administration. Moreover, each of the situations we analyze relates to areas long examined in assessments of immigrant assimilation. In this way we link the immediacy of the violent effects of the law with cumulative, long-term consequences for immigrants' futures.

Immigration Law as Legal Violence

Immigrants receive a combination of rewards and penalties depending on whether they are naturalized U.S. citizens, legal permanent residents, temporarily protected, or undocumented (Massey and Bartley 2005). Immigrants with a greater degree of legal protections are much more likely than those in tenuous statuses to fare better; in general, documented immigrants earn more, work in safer jobs, and can apply for and obtain various forms of educational and housing aid. Legal status determines access to health care (Menjívar 2002; Holmes 2007), housing (Painter, Gabriel, and Myers 2001; McConnell and Marcelli 2007), higher education (Abrego 2006, 2008b), and employment (Simon and DeLey 1984; Uriarte et al. 2003; Walter et al. 2004; Gonzalez 2005; Fortuny, Capps, and Passel 2007; Takei, Saenz, and Li 2009). Legal status also has been found to affect immigrants' health risks (Guttmacher 1984), vulnerability in the streets (Hirsch 2003), domestic violence (Salcido and Adelman 2004), wages in the labor market (Massey, Durand, and Malone 2002), and family dynamics (Rodriguez and Hagan 2004; Menjívar 2006a; Menjívar and Abrego 2009). In every case, immigrants who are undocumented or in tenuous statuses are more vulnerable, and many of them incorrectly believe they have no legal protections; thus, to evade detention and deportation, they avoid denouncing physical abuse and crime (Menjívar and Bejarano 2004) and refrain from seeking formal health care (Okie 2007). Today's immigration regime exacerbates these situations and creates a wider gap between immigrants and various social institutions (see Capps et al. 2007).

Immigrants in tenuous legal statuses, however, are not the only class of immigrants harmed by the current immigration regime. Despite the very real differences between the paths of documented and undocumented immigrants in various spheres of life, documented immigrants (e.g., legal permanent residents) also have been progressively losing rights as they are also targets of new laws and increasingly at risk of deportation (Kanstroom 2007). This is a new development resulting from today's immigration regime.

Legal categories are also tied to negative perceptions of undocumented immigrants, which are produced and maintained through their representations in mass media (Chavez 2008). For example, immigration raids are often covered in the media in a manner that associates immigrant workers with criminality—even when these are still matters of civil law.[12] These practices solidify perceptions of immigrants in tenuous legal statuses as criminals and portray them as less than human in the minds of viewers and listeners, contributing to normalizing and then justifying maltreatment against immigrants who are perceived as lawbreakers. In effect, sociologist Douglas Massey, relying on work on cognitive science from social psychology, notes that in the minds of U.S. citizens, undocumented immigrants (alongside sex offenders, drug dealers, and those perceived to be lazy welfare recipients) are considered "despised, out-group members" (Massey 2007, 14). Massey warns that this is dangerous terrain: undocumented immigrants "are not perceived as fully human at the most fundamental neural level of cognition, thus opening the door to the harshest, most exploitative, and cruelest treatment that human beings are capable of inflicting on one another" (150). This is how symbolic violence permeates perceptions, interactions, and ultimately shapes the treatment accorded to immigrants, with short- and long-term consequences for their lives.

The growing nexus between immigration and criminal law is evident in the 1996 Illegal Immigration Reform and Immigrant Responsibility Act (IIRIRA) and its implementation. This act makes even documented immigrants deportable and includes language that criminalizes a wide range of behaviors. For example, immigrant workers in tenuous legal statuses are being charged with aggravated felony for using borrowed Social Security numbers in order to work. Indeed, the term *aggravated felony* has been expanded to include a broadening array of what were previously considered to be relatively minor crimes (even misdemeanors). In Phoenix, Arizona, for instance, the Maricopa County Sheriff's Office (MCSO) refers to the crime suppression sweeps conducted in predominantly Latino neighborhoods as efforts to combat identity theft (Creno 2009).[13] This is how the language of the media mingled with public officials' narratives contributes to normalize images of immigrants as criminals, setting conditions for mistreatment.

The legal context also includes federal programs run by Immigration and Customs Enforcement (ICE) that are meant to round up criminals and terrorists, further fusing images of immigrants with criminals and terrorists. The National Fugitive Operations Program, an ICE program that seeks to integrate immigration and border control, is meant to focus resources on immigrants with criminal records, but it also includes "fugitives without criminal conviction." Thus, in practice, these enforcement tactics—broadcast in the media and garnering public attention—persuade the public that federal and state governments are moving to solve the immigration problem, even when government statistics show that the arrests capture mostly immigrant workers without criminal records.[14] Importantly, broadcasting reports of these raids, which have become a common strategy to detain and deport immigrants in recent years, sustains immigrants' fear of deportability (De Genova 2002). As De Genova observes, the mere threat of deportation, even when not coupled with the practice of deportation, is key to the power of the law and what makes undocumented immigrants potential targets of abuse. And although there is insufficient funding and inadequate means to actually deport all undocumented immigrants, the perennial threat of deportation is encoded in the law.

Immigration categories into which contemporary immigrants are classified have created the possibility for the dramatic expansion of the "illegality" we see today (De Genova 2002, 2004; Massey et al. 2002), categories that determine immigrants' rights, their position in society, and also their treatment. Moreover, targeted by (mis)representations, immigrants often internalize their status, accept these conditions as normal, and may even feel deserving of mistreatment (Abrego 2011). Our argument, then, is not simply that immigrants are an especially vulnerable group or that current laws disenfranchise contemporary immigrants. This point has already been examined and effectively argued before (Piore 1979; Hagan 1994; Cornelius 2001). Instead, we argue that immigrants in tenuous legal statuses today experience the multipronged system of immigration laws and their implementation, aided by a vast technological infrastructure and state bureaucracy, as a form of violence due to the blurring of immigration and criminal law that leads to a progressive exclusion of immigrants from "normal" spaces and societal institutions. This transformation has immediate and long-term consequences that, cumulatively, can contribute to thwarting their incorporation into the host society.

Legal Context

Structural and political violence have shaped in interrelated ways Central American immigrants' lives in their countries of origin as well as in the United States.[15] The political conflicts that lasted approximately three decades in Guatemala and 12 years in El Salvador, along with related political and economic dislocations in Honduras, have shaped U.S.-bound migration flows from those countries, as well as U.S. immigration policies toward these immigrants. On the receiving end, the U.S. government has responded with legal actions in a span of more than two decades that have failed to recognize Central Americans as refugees of geopolitics in their homelands; thus, many Guatemalans,

Hondurans, and Salvadorans have entered, and many remain in the United States, as undocumented immigrants or only temporarily protected.

In the United States, the legal status of the majority of Central American immigrants has been marked by prolonged uncertainty embedded in laws with few avenues for legalization (Menjívar 2006b). From the initial years of Salvadorans' and Guatemalans' massive migration to the United States in the early 1980s, they have been granted temporary permits, a barrage of applications, reapplications, long processing periods for their applications, and the threat of imminent deportation, while remaining ineligible for important forms of legal protection or social services. Although Hondurans are increasingly leaving contexts of heightened political violence, they, too, have been received in the United States with the same temporary treatment and legal uncertainty that characterizes the reception of Guatemalans and Salvadorans.

Despite commonalities with other national-origin groups that have been granted refugee status, throughout the 1980s fewer than 3% of Salvadoran and Guatemalan applicants were given political asylum. Immigrants' rights groups lobbied on their behalf, and eventually in 1991 Congress granted temporary protected status (TPS) from deportation to Salvadorans, which allowed them to live and work in the United States for a period of 18 months; it was extended multiple times and ended in September 1995. In 1990, as a result of the settlement of a class-action suit (*American Baptist Churches v. Thornburgh* [ABC] legislation) against the INS, Salvadorans and Guatemalans were allowed to resubmit asylum applications, thereby improving the success rate of these applications. Another pathway to legal status—legalization under the Immigration Reform and Control Act (IRCA) of 1986—was available to a relatively small percentage of Central Americans who arrived in the United States prior to the January 1, 1982, deadline. The thousands who arrived during and after the height of the political conflicts in their countries were ineligible for IRCA provisions. To add complexity to the Central Americans' legal story, benefits of the 1997 Nicaraguan Adjustment and Central American Relief Act (NACARA) were extended only to some Guatemalans and Salvadorans (and not to any Hondurans).

Although elite and middle-class Hondurans have been migrating in small numbers to the United States since the late 1800s, large-scale Honduran migration started in the 1980s. Recently, the working poor have fled en masse from the economic destabilization, growing instability, and the natural and economic devastation resulting from Hurricane Mitch in 1998 (Portillo 2008). They are joined by Guatemalans and Salvadorans who continue to migrate despite the official end of civil conflicts in those countries in 1997 and 1992, respectively. The structures of inequality at the root of the civil conflicts—and of emigration—are still in place and are now exacerbated by high rates of unemployment and underemployment and high levels of violence associated with "common crime" in the three Central American countries.[16] And the social channels for Central American migration have expanded as more individuals have relatives and friends in the United States (PNUD 2005; Menjívar 2006a).

El Salvador suffered two earthquakes in early 2001 that worsened the social, political, and economic problems left by years of civil war. Salvadorans who arrived after the earthquakes were granted TPS for a period of nine months, a dispensation that has already been extended several times and at the time of this writing will expire on March 9, 2012. Similarly, Hondurans arriving after Hurricane Mitch in 1998 were granted TPS, which has been renewed multiple times; it is currently set to expire July 5, 2013. And while Guatemala also endured the destruction of Hurricane Stan in late 2005, Guatemalans have never been granted TPS.[17] For the Hondurans and Salvadorans on TPS, its inherent temporariness is made clear by multiple deadlines for application and reregistration and, importantly, by announcing extensions just a month or two prior to the current TPS expiration. Each group has different deadlines and registration procedures, including different applications for TPS and for employment authorization, and various application and renewal fees.

The legal context for Central American immigrants is further shaped by IIRIRA.[18] Among other things, IIRIRA reduced the threshold for crimes and offenses that may be considered grounds for deportation (Stumpf 2006).[19] In effect, IIRIRA has facilitated the removal of hundreds of thousands of immigrants for a wider range of criminal offenses (Rodriguez and Hagan 2004). The year before IIRIRA passed there were 69,680 deportations; this figure has increased every year, reaching a record of 392,000 in 2010 (U.S. DHS/ICE 2010) and surpassing it in fiscal year 2011 with 396,906 deportations (U.S. DHS/ICE 2011). Between 2000 and 2009, 149,833 Guatemalans, 159,265 Hondurans, and 105,397 Salvadorans were deported.[20] And whereas in 1998 these three Central American groups accounted for approximately 9% of total deportations, they made up 17% in 2005 and 21% in 2008, remaining in the top four groups (with Mexico) of deportees in the past few years.[21] This was done through the creation of two mechanisms of IIRIRA that (*a*) made it possible to deport legal immigrants who have been convicted of a felony at any time in the United States, even when they have already completed their sentences, and (*b*) created the 287(g) program, which allows local police to enter into agreements with ICE to target and detain "criminal illegal aliens." With an emphasis on deporting even documented immigrants who have ever committed a felonious crime, thus expanding the categories of noncitizens subject to deportation and augmenting the list of offenses for which they can be deported (Hagan et al. 2011), IIRIRA has legitimated and normalized the perception of immigrants as criminals (and potential terrorists).

Although the 287(g) agreement was created in 1996, it was promoted and used after the attacks of September 11, 2001—a move that further ties terrorist activities with civil immigration matters and invokes concerns about national security in immigration matters. And though all law enforcement involves discretion, the implementation of 287(g) has been linked to racial profiling practices that criminalize immigrants. Indeed, concerns and complaints about the use and implementation of 287(g) have led the federal government to adopt other enforcement strategies. Thus, in 2008 it introduced "Secure Communities," which along with 287(g), is part of ICE's Agreements of Cooperation in Communities to Enhance Safety and Security (ACCESS). Secure Communities uses biometric information to "modernize and transform the criminal alien enforcement model through technology, integration, and information sharing . . . to improve public safety."[22] This program is based on electronic data sharing (Kohli, Markowitz, and Chavez 2011), through which the fingerprints of anyone arrested or booked by local police are checked against the Department of Homeland Security databases and the FBI. This program operated in 14 jurisdictions in 2008, had expanded to 660 jurisdictions by 2010 (U.S. Department of Homeland Security 2010), and, at the time of this writing, it is expected that it will be in place in every jurisdiction in the nation by 2013 (Kohli et al. 2011). And whereas the 287(g) program is voluntary (it is up to the municipalities), the Secure Communities program is a national mandatory program for all municipalities. Thus, increasingly, strategies that associate immigrants with dangerous criminals (and terrorists) expand and make immigrants—documented and undocumented alike—vulnerable to the legal system.[23]

Although the legal context that Guatemalans, Hondurans, and Salvadorans face is primarily dictated at the federal level, through ordinances, laws, and agreements such as Secure Communities and 287(g), the state and local levels have acted in conjunction to create a multilayered context that makes violent consequences possible.[24] Thus, in recent years, immigrants' legal uncertainty and risk have been aggravated by a barrage of local-level ordinances targeting the activities of undocumented immigrants. These ordinances range from penalties to city contractors and private businesses for hiring undocumented immigrants, to revoking licenses when businesses are found to hire them, to attempts to bar landlords from renting to them.[25] Significantly, the language used in local measures parallels the federal trend toward criminalizing immigrants. For instance, in Arizona, a law created to penalize human smuggling was reinterpreted to charge individual immigrants as coconspirators in their own smuggling, thereby making unauthorized entry a criminal rather than a civil offense. And with a new tactic denominated "attrition through enforcement," these laws do not seek to apprehend everyone but to implement routine practices that tie immigrants to criminality and debates about national security. Thus, while this multilevel, multipronged approach to restrict immigration may not necessarily decrease levels of immigration, it does make the lives of immigrants particularly difficult by legitimizing more restrictions and normalizing and facilitating violence in immigrants' lives. Even as these laws, or specific policies, seem to change continually, the associated practices and the messages they send have short- and long-term consequences for immigrants' incorporation.

Data and Methods

We did not start out searching for indications of violence in immigrants' lives; rather, in an inductive fashion, their stories and words led us to reflect on the violent effects that current immigration law has on their lives. Our study participants described their legally rooted circumstances in words that evoke the suffering we might associate with more obvious and direct forms of violence, such as those who lived in situations of political violence or war (e.g., torture, pain, anguish, etc.).

The data on which this essay is based come from several studies, which permit us to elucidate the broad reach and ramifications of the legal context. Menjívar draws on a series of studies of Latin American–origin immigrants in the Phoenix metropolitan area that she conducted between 1998 and 2010. This time span has allowed her to capture how immigrants have perceived and reacted to changes to federal and local laws (for further details, see Menjívar [2001, 2003, n.d.]; Menjívar and Bejarano [2004]). In addition, data for this essay come from in-depth, semistructured interviews that Menjívar and McKenzie conducted with women in Honduras in December 2007 and January 2008 (for further details, see McKenzie and Menjívar [2011]). Abrego draws on two separate studies. Between June 2004 and September 2006, she conducted 130 in-depth interviews with Salvadoran families in the midst of long-term separation (for more details, see Abrego [2009]). And from 2001–6, she carried out a longitudinal study that focused on access to higher education for Guatemalan, Mexican, and Salvadoran undocumented high school and college students in Los Angeles (for a detailed description, see Abrego [2008b]).

Given the quick pace of change and ongoing developments in immigration law, we also draw on newspaper articles from around the country to supplement some of the empirical points we make. These articles detail similar incidents as those our study participants shared and provide further evidence of the generalized nature of contemporary legal violence. Although our main empirical focus is on three aspects of immigrants' lives—family, work, and school—in line with our argument that the laws of the powerful country have a "spillover" effect (see Coleman 2007), we begin by briefly contextualizing the immigrants' journey into the country and the consequences of the current immigration regime that reaches beyond the confines of U.S. national borders.

Legal Violence and the Journey North

Perhaps reflecting the interconnectedness of immigrant origins and destinations, the effects of current U.S. immigration policies are not neatly contained within the U.S. territory or confined only to immigrant communities in the United States. This is especially visible among the growing numbers of immigrants traveling without a visa (and by land). Under new border enforcement policies in place since the early 1990s, smugglers have significantly changed strategies; rather than being individuals who assist in border crossing, they are now members of smuggling rings with state-of-the-art equipment akin to (and often being confused with) drug cartels (see Spener 2009).[26] Through new operations, they move people in ways that are indistinguishable from human trafficking, often exposing immigrants to shootings and kidnappings, as well as extortion at drop houses in the United States (Tobar 2009) and Mexico. In this process, the smugglers, who are themselves immigrants, injure their coethnics in ways that resemble terror techniques used by authoritarian regimes in Latin America (see Menjívar and Rodríguez 2005). The smugglers' actions incite physical violence that spills over to nonimmigrants who live in the migration corridor where the smuggling rings operate (Tobar 2009). These organized rings have emerged in tandem with border policies that seek to protect the border in the context of national security. And though the building of fences and increased militarization of the southern U.S. border does not necessarily reduce the number of immigrants crossing, it fuels a thriving business in smuggling that benefits both law enforcers and law evaders (Andreas 2001), while creating conditions for multiple forms of violence for immigrants and for nonmigrants along the migration corridor in Central America and Mexico.

Although the passage through Mexico has always been risky for Central Americans (Menjívar 2000), new U.S. border policies in place since the mid-1990s have made this journey increasingly dangerous, a situation that has multiplicative effects on the lives of migrants and their families left behind. In fact, almost all respondents in our studies who traveled by land shared stories of perilous journeys north. Mauricio, a Salvadoran man who was deported from Mexico twice before making it to the United States on his third attempt in 2003, recounted some of the experiences he endured and witnessed:

There were 87 of us and they packed us up into a trailer truck for 16 hours. And for all of us to fit, we had to be so close to each other, and I couldn't take it anymore, I needed to move.... And then we started to walk across the desert. All you desire is water and food. We used our shirts to drain some muddy rain water that remained in a plastic bag that was stuck to a tree. That's how thirsty we were! ... And at one point, we all had to run in different directions, and once the [border patrolmen] were gone, we went back to look for the Guatemalan man who was with us. He was already really tired and we didn't find him. The smuggler wanted to keep going, and who knows what happened to that poor man because we still had to walk many hours and it was so cold that night. I don't know if he survived. He probably didn't.

Tales like these are not uncommon among Central American migrants crossing several international borders to arrive in the United States (see also Coutin 2007; Behrens 2009).

Notably, for unauthorized travelers the journey is not confined to physical injuries, and such harm does not end with their arrival in the United States. The increasingly difficult border crossing has promoted a significant increase in smugglers' fees (Spener 2009). The trip today requires that immigrants invest amounts of money and incur large debts; thus, often their first task upon arrival is to pay off the money they owe. As Gardner (2010) observed among Indian immigrants in Bahrain, this debt becomes a fulcrum for various forms of violence for the immigrants and their families back home. Many participants in our studies struggle to repay their debt, and most owe so much that it takes them years to repay. Suyapa, a mother of five in Honduras, described how payment of the debt has lengthened her husband's intended stay in the United States: "Manuel tells me he expects to be in the United States for six years ... because right now it's been three years and he still owes half of the money he borrowed." Thus, during this extended time, much of the money immigrants earn goes to reduce their debt rather than to help their relatives, as they originally intended.

Although immigrants are responsible for earning the money to repay their loans, the nonmigrant relatives directly manage the everyday dealings with debt collectors and the looming threat of having their family's houses or land seized as collateral for failure to pay on time (McKenzie and Menjívar 2011). Examining this link to the relatives back home highlights how the threat of deportation in the United States effectively constrains the immigrants' options to provide for their families in their countries of origin. Also in Honduras, Rosa described an interaction in which a debt collector intimidated her: "The lady [who loaned us the money] always sends her husband to the house to ask, 'What's happening with the money?' Last year he came and asked me, 'What do you think about your husband? Are you going to pressure him to pay the money, or are we going to have to take away your land?'" Several other study participants in the home countries described similar experiences—sometimes outright extortion—in dealing with debt collectors after their relatives attempted the trip north. These instances can be traced to the policies that have made border crossing increasingly dangerous and as such exacerbate various forms of violence among the immigrants' and the non-migrants' relatives alike.

Families back home are also affected by other aspects of their relatives' journeys (Hammock et al. 2005). Family members described taxing periods when their loved ones are in transit to the United States, when information about them is scant. Norma, in Honduras and with two sons working in the United States, recounted her experiences during her sons' travels, "I even got sick. My nerves were terrible, so that it was impossible to be calm. I just passed the time crying, crying. Because I listened to the news—of the murders, people falling from the train, the gang holdups . . . all of that." Thus, this knowledge of the dangers of traveling to and entering the United States affects nonmigrant family members in multiple ways.

These examples demonstrate how U.S. immigration laws, along with the militarization of the Mexico-U.S. border, set up conditions conducive to an increase in the immigrants' (and their families') suffering beyond the territorial jurisdiction of U.S. immigration law. This is due to the powerful position of the United States as a "strong state" in this migration region. The higher costs and the consequent debts contribute to exacerbate immigrants' vulnerability and facilitate exploitation among coethnics, here and there, highlighting how physical, structural, and symbolic forms of violence coalesce in the context of immigration legislation to affect lives beyond U.S. territorial boundaries.

FAMILY

Once they arrive in the United States, the effects of the current immigration regime are manifested in several ways in the lives of Central American immigrants, from lengthy and uncertain family separations as a result of raids and deportations, to children being cut off from basic services such as access to higher education and health care, to the insecurity of wages and worries about not having enough money to buy food or pay rent. Some of these situations may be more recognizable as "violent" because they evoke strong immediate emotions, such as the case of a Honduran mother who was taken into custody during an immigration raid at her home in Ohio. The mother is pictured in newspapers, distraught and in tears, as she was separated from her

9-month-old daughter (Preston 2007). Other cases are more subtle but equally damaging (in the short and long term). We turn our attention to these cases, as they embody the various forms of violence to which we point here and are also instances with the potential to have consequential effects for long-term immigrant incorporation.

Study participants in Los Angeles and Phoenix shared experiences that, while not physically violent, are legally violent because immigration laws create the conditions in which they occur. They are members of a class of individuals whose experiences demonstrate the law's harmful and potentially long-lasting damaging effects. At a recent gathering in Los Angeles, Marta, a Salvadoran college student, shared with her peers:

> I was in the waiting room at the clinic last week, sitting next to this girl who was like my age. We were talking about where our parents are from and how we haven't been back, when she gets a call on her cell phone. Somebody was calling to tell her that her mother had just been deported! . . . Now, every day, I leave the house and I don't know if me or my parents will be back. It could be any of us, any of these days, and it's so scary. . . . We started to talk about what will happen with my little sister because she's a U.S. citizen, but who is she going to stay with here if we get deported?

Much like stories of living in a directly violent context such as war, Marta describes the fear that pervades her daily life anytime she leaves her home. Her family members' experiences exemplify how deportability is lived: because several of them are in tenuous legal statuses, they may be detained and later deported at any moment. This vulnerability, made possible by immigration laws and their implementation practices, instills fear in immigrants (and their families) who live with the very real possibility of forced family separation (see Capps et al. 2007; Hagan, Eschbach, and Rodríguez 2008). Such feelings affect how immigrants perceive their current place in U.S. society and can affect long-term paths of incorporation.

With the exponential surge in ICE raids and deportations since the mid-2000s, there is increasing fear and insecurity among immigrants—those who are undocumented but also among the documented, particularly among those who have a relative with uncertain status. Clara, a Salvadoran woman in Phoenix, shared the strategies she and her husband have adopted in their daily lives to plan for "the worst," as she put it. The couple works together cleaning model homes at night in a suburb of Phoenix; he is undocumented, and she has a temporary work permit but both feel equally insecure because TPS is technically not fully documented status. Deeply cognizant of the frailty of their legal situation, they never ride together in the same car.

Look, Cecilia, this situation is scary; it gives us fear. Yes, everyday, I don't lie to you, it's constant. So no, we don't drive together. What if we are stopped and we get deported? We'll be taken to jail, and the kids, what? Who's going to take care of them? Who's going to stay with them? We worry; we live anguished. So he goes in one car, with our neighbor, and I go in another one, with my cousin. The same when we go to the market. He goes in one car and I go in another. So no, we try to never, no, we're never in the same car. Never. Who knows what can happen. . . . We must take precautions.

As Clara's words highlight, deportability is palpable in daily life, as even commuting between home and work or shopping for groceries involves "anguish" and careful deliberation to avoid the possibility of being separated from loved ones. Her words denote the "terror" that individuals living in Latino communities experience (Caspa 2008) or the "reign of terror," as former Phoenix mayor Phil Gordon called the daily intimidations that undocumented immigrants endure in Arizona's Maricopa County today (Finnegan 2009).

In another part of the interview, Clara (and her husband) identified the threat of raids as the source of their anxiety. In their experience, there is no comparison between how the "situation was before" and how "the situation is now." Since the mid-2000s, Clara has felt gradually more vulnerable and threatened, particularly by the actions of the MCSO, a vigorous advocate (and user) of the 287(g) agreement and the Secure Communities programs. Indeed, Clara has telephoned Menjívar on a few occasions to ask if she knows where a raid might take place next. Their deportability and the ever-present threat of raids—that are unannounced and can happen anytime, anywhere—keep the immigrants on alert at all times, much like a constant state of emergency (see Taussig 1992). But for the general public these raids are normalized as a response to a perceived problem that law enforcement needs to address.

For families who are separated due to migration, legal status plays a central role in determining parents' labor market experiences and therefore the amount of money they can send to their children back home (Abrego 2008a). This is another instance in which U.S. law spills over beyond the nation's borders. Many immigrants' families in the home countries do not receive sufficient remittances and cannot make ends meet because the remitting relative is in detention or local-level laws have reduced their employment opportunities and they are still repaying debts acquired to cover the costs of the trip. Without funds, children are unable to eat properly or attend school regularly, and their health and academic achievements are compromised (Abrego 2008a). For example, Ana, in El Salvador, is thin and likely malnourished even though she receives money from her father. His uncertain legal status in the United States kept him from applying for worker's compensation when he hurt himself at work. Since then, he has moved from job to job, being unemployed months at a time and deported a couple of times. He sends between $50 and $100 per month, but this sum has to be divided among six siblings.[27] To survive, Ana spreads throughout the day food that would typically constitute one meal. She makes this sacrifice because, at the age of 24, she is still in high school and wants to graduate. Her schooling situation is the result of years of insufficient remittances to cover education-related expenses and of the general conditions of structural violence and unequal access to education in El Salvador. Ana's predicament highlights the intertwined nature of legal and structural violence that affects those here and their families there. The injuries of structural violence—poverty, malnutrition, unequal access to education—that the father sought to rectify with migrant remittances have not abated, and the legal violence he now experiences as an immigrant in the United States has contributed to exacerbate those conditions for his family back home.

Legal violence shapes the experiences of families living in the United States in multiple ways but, in particular, by hampering their links to institutions and thus affecting patterns of incorporation (Menjívar 2006a). Families report going to great lengths to avoid contact with social service providers, even when children in those families are eligible to receive social services by virtue of being U.S. citizens by birth (Capps et al. 2007). A Guatemalan mother in Phoenix said that although she needed aid for her two U.S.-born toddlers, she would not apply for food stamps. Due to the economic recession and to employers' fears of being sanctioned for hiring unauthorized immigrants, her family's income sources were very limited. Like this mother, parents with uncertain legality who are expected to ensure the welfare of children refrain from doing so when deportation and family separation are real possibilities. It is in this manner that contemporary laws negatively impact immigrants' immediate well being and future prospects.

Many study participants described feeling as if they were under siege. Within the family realm, legal violence frames everyday lives, from parents having to leave children behind in the home country for uncertain periods of time to leaving the house in fear every day for work or for grocery shopping—basic family functions for economic and physical survival. The accumulated pressure of persistent vulnerability and deportability makes basic family needs difficult to meet, with the potential to thwart these immigrants' paths to successful integration into U.S. society. Increasingly lengthy and uncertain family separations, normalized in the context of enforcement today, bring to light the underlying contradictions of legal violence in immigrant communities: while the law seeks to remove them from society, by pushing them outside the boundaries of juris-diction, it simultaneously includes them by criminalizing their presence.

WORK

Aside from the laws' widespread effects on families, legal violence also shapes immigrants' work experiences. It is widely known that many immigrants earn low wages in jobs with no benefits (Milkman, González, and Narro 2010). How-ever, the recent activities of the National Fugitive Operations Program, by tar-geting undocumented workers, facilitates various forms of immediate abuse in the workplace as well as long-term consequences for immigrant workers and their perceptions of their rights and civic participation. Workplace raids (or, as they are called in Arizona, employer sanctions investigations), made possible by the 287(g) agreement, Secure Communities, and IIRIRA in general, have increased scrutiny and suspicion of immigrant workers, especially Latinos.[28]

For instance, Josefina, an immigrant with legal permanent resident status in Phoenix, reflected on the "nervousness" she experiences. Although she is not undocumented, she feels vulnerable in public places, particularly on her way to work and while she is at work at the plastics factory where she is employed. She thinks these days it is "more secure" to be a U.S. citizen:

> You have no idea how much I want to be a citizen, so that I don't have to carry my *mica* (green card) everywhere I go, so I don't have to think all the time that I will be stopped and deported because now they're de-porting even people who are here legally, just because of how you look! So yes, I'm really desperate to be a citizen. I am already taking English classes and as soon as I become eligible, I'll apply.

Even though Josefina has been living in the United States since 1993, in 2010 she was one year short of becoming eligible to apply for citizenship because her permanent legal resident application (through marriage) took more than a decade to be finalized. Her case demonstrates that legal violence and its as-sociated stress can affect all immigrants—documented or undocumented.[29] Furthermore, by fueling immigrants' fear, their deportability, or the threat of being removed, the law creates situations ripe for mistreatment, as often em-ployers either cooperate with law enforcement or refuse overtime pay to their immigrant workers, deny them breaks, or fire them right before payday. These situations, in turn, shed light on how structural and symbolic violence coales-cence in immigrants' lives through legal violence.

Contrary to common assumptions, immigrant workers are not underval-ued (and underpaid) because of the work they do; rather, they are limited to labor sectors rampant with abuse precisely because they are undervalued. This is accomplished through the legal regime in place, media portrayals, and the public discourse that depict them as outside the law, as undeserving, and as law breakers, which together erase their contributions to society. This type of treatment, sanctioned by the law, sets the stage for further mistreatment. For instance, like his compatriots arrested with him, a Guatemalan worker in the 2008 Postville, Iowa, raid, where 400 mostly (Maya) Guatemalans were taken to detention centers, could not understand all the charges filed against him. However, his words provide a glimpse into how this act, where the workers were separated from family and community (many of whom had been living with tenuous statuses for a decade or longer),[30] reverberates to the individuals and contributes to their self-condemnation in a matter that evokes the symbolic violence embedded in these actions. According to the interpreter, "No matter how many times his attorney explained it, he kept saying, 'I'm illegal, I have no rights. I'm nobody in this country. Just do whatever you want with me'" (Preston 2008). Apparently, this man had internalized the devaluation that comes from the implementation of the law by accepting and confirming his own self-depreciation. Identifying himself entirely by his "illegal" status, he conformed to the notion that he had "no rights."

For the first time in his long career, the interpreter in the Iowa case felt compelled to share details of the Guatemalan workers' court hearing and public display of violence (Camayd-Freixas 2009). Prior to the implementation of current policies, these workers would have been apprehended and swiftly deported. But immigration policies today require that undocumented workers also be charged with aggravated identity theft when they use false documents to secure employment.[31]

Our study participants described similar incidents at their work sites. In Phoenix, some local law enforcement agencies have taken a particularly strong stance and have collaborated with ICE on raids, regular traffic stops, and checkpoints, and volunteer posses have been deputized to patrol streets, perform sweeps, and conduct armed workplace raids. Marcos is a study participant who works as a day laborer in a small community of Latinos and Yaqui Native Americans that has a contract with the MCSO for police protection. MCSO deputies perform random patrols there, often demanding IDs from pedestrians. These crime-suppression operations, as they are officially called, occur in predominantly Latino neighborhoods throughout the Phoenix Metropolitan area over which the MCSO has jurisdiction. Marcos describes how members of his community deal with the threat of raids there:

For instance, someone sees the sheriff [MCSO officers], let's say there, on Baseline [Avenue], coming this way . . . with a huge trailer and sometimes horses and armed . . . yes, about 50 or 60 officers. That person then calls a friend and tells him, "look the sheriff is here, don't go out of the house" and this person calls a cousin or a friend and then these people call others and that's how everyone finds out and no one leaves the house, not even to go to the market. We look through the window, open the curtain a little, to see if they're still there, to see if it's safe to go out.

Marcos's description is reminiscent of scenes of direct political violence that some of these immigrants lived in Central America during the decades of civil war. And aside from the immediate fear, raids affect immigrants' ability to work. Marcos, like Clara and her husband above, commented that when they hear that MCSO officers will be in a particular area of the valley, they do not go to work there, and, in the case of Marcos, he does not even go to the corner to seek day work. Menjívar drove through the small town mentioned above on a day that a traffic suppression sweep was expected to take place and, except for sheriff patrol cars everywhere and two large commando units parked two blocks apart, found desolate streets and empty street corners where day laborers typically congregate to wait for potential employers.[32] The highly visible presence of law enforcement (or potential presence, as they can show up any time) affects the day laborers' experiences by facilitating a decrease in wages, creating safe spaces for dishonest employers, and generally making workers more vulnerable (Arriero 2009). Clara added that car washes have become "dangerous" places of work because they have been the target of raids. Consequently, even before the economic recession began, employment options for immigrants with tenuous legal statuses had started to decrease.

In addition, in 2007 Arizona passed the Legal Arizona Workers Act, a law that went into effect on January 1, 2008, and allowed the state to suspend or revoke the licenses of businesses that intentionally or knowingly hire undocumented immigrants.[33] This law was the first in the country in which a state sought to gain control of a federal function, and it represents a national trend in local-level attempts to regulate immigrant workers. Although its purported objective was to reduce the number of undocumented immigrants in the state, the law mainly has exacerbated their already vulnerable living situations. Fearful employers began to fire workers who could not produce proof of work eligibility even before the law officially went into effect. Thus, many lost their jobs, and their economic insecurity increased, with repercussions in different spheres of their lives—both in the United States and in their origin countries. Those who have stayed in their jobs have been made more susceptible to unpaid hours, increased workloads, and dismissal without cause. This is the case of Floridalma, a Guatemalan who arrived in Phoenix in 2004 and initially worked at a furniture factory. She was fired soon after the 2008 law went into effect and since then has been earning a living mainly by cleaning houses. She had to start working as an assistant to a woman who "owns" the route of houses they clean, and even though the woman charges $70 per house, Floridalma said she only gets $15 per house. Although she said this is the direct result of the 2008 law, she also blamed her "boss" for not paying her enough. This is how legal violence works: it creates conditions for the dominated to harm others in their same position, and it also contributes to the obstruction of traditional paths of incorporation by keeping immigrants in dead-end jobs with precarious working conditions for longer, uncertain periods of time.

Legal violence also affects workers in more subtle but equally harmful ways. Manuel, a Salvadoran who has had temporary protected status on and off for 17 years, is meticulous about renewing his work permit even before the deadline. He always has been outspoken and "tells it like it is." However, lately he has changed his views and now prefers not to complain at work. He was the victim of abuses by a foreman and asked Menjívar for help in writing a letter of complaint to the owner of the company but never sent the letter. A bit surprised, Menjívar asked him why. "Because these days you can't say anything. [A] couple of years ago, in another time, I would have sent it in. But now I'm afraid, you know, with the times now, we all live afraid." Even though Manuel realizes that it is "not OK" for his employer not to pay him overtime, to give him only one 15-minute break a day, to refer to him using ethnic slurs, and to regularly threaten to call the feared *migra*, Manuel is now afraid to speak up. Symbolic violence, through legal violence, exerts its influence on workers who live in fear and begin to think that they have no rights and accept "normal abuses," as Manuel explained.

Similarly, Nelson, a Salvadoran immigrant in Los Angeles who earns less than the minimum wage as a warehouse worker, describes his predicament:

> You see that without papers it is very difficult to be hired just anywhere. So my brother-in-law found me a job [in] a company where the trailer trucks come and you pack them and unpack them. That is hard work because they don't care if one is tired, if one needs to rest, or if [the weather is] too hot or too cold. And so, since they didn't even let us rest, I messed up my back and when I told them, they pretended not to hear me, they didn't do anything. I kept complaining and in the end they told me that if I couldn't do the work anymore, I should look for another job because they needed someone who could stay on schedule. And after that I still had to fight with them to get my last paycheck because they were saying that I worked too slowly. Up until now I still can't carry anything too heavy, so I haven't been able to find a steady job.

Due to his undocumented status, Nelson was afraid to apply for worker's compensation or to denounce the employer who fired him when he complained of back pain. Since losing his steady job, he spends most of his time at a day labor site, trying to get temporary, short-term jobs. Unfortunately, as he said, "in this kind of work, you don't earn enough." The current legal regime makes it possible for employers to pay low wages and to withhold health benefits and other basic legally mandated provisions, such as bathroom breaks and protective gear, when these are necessary for the job (Holmes 2007); thus, the law creates conditions under which workers' rights have diminished (see Walter et al. 2004).

The current legal system has direct, long-term effects as well, as it shapes how immigrants assess their futures. Nelson goes on to explain how the current system thwarts his American Dream:

> One comes here thinking that life will be better . . . but without papers, one's life is not worth much. Look at me; I have always been a hard worker . . . but I messed up my back working, carrying heavy things without any protection . . . and I can't do anything about it. What doctor is going to help me if I can't pay? And the worst part is, who's going to hire me now? How will I support my family?

Reminding himself that he came to the United States in search of economic opportunities, Nelson describes the sense of defeat that accompanies his legal status and now pervades him. Despite what he perceived to be his positive qualities—a hard worker who sought to improve his life—being "without papers" means being "without any protection" and being perceived as worthless. The violence that the current regime makes possible exacerbates the effects of structural violence when immigrants cannot support themselves and their families. Furthermore, it becomes entwined with symbolic violence when immigrants become participants in their own devaluation and accept this social order as normal and the consequences in their lives as expected. Unlike previous generations of immigrants, current immigrants in tenuous legal statuses are less likely to be upwardly mobile in their paths of incorporation in this country.

SCHOOL

Manifestations of legal violence are also evident among younger immigrants, particularly in school-related matters. Education is another key dimension in the path of immigrant assimilation and an area where the legal regime today leaves an indelible and long-lasting mark (Menjívar 2008). Schools are the main social institutions with which young immigrants interact, and education is especially influential in determining their day-to-day realities and their long-term incorporation experiences. The 1982 U.S. Supreme Court case, *Plyler v. Doe*, grants undocumented youths access to public schools in grades K–12, yet students speak of feeling unwelcome when their legal protections end after high school. Even students who have "played by the rules" and excelled in school are effectively blocked from college legally or financially, depending on the state in which they reside. In schools, legal violence manifests itself through blocked paths to mobility and intense stigmatization of the youth who otherwise feel a strong sense of belonging in U.S. society (Abrego and Gonzales 2010; Abrego 2011; Gonzales 2011).

Many undocumented and quasi-documented youth learn of their unauthorized status in high school when they have to fill out applications for internships, summer jobs, or college admission. Unable to provide a Social Security number for the applications, their parents are forced to explain the situation to them, often for the first time. By the time they learn that they are undocumented or that they are "waiting for the papers," many have been mostly socialized in the United States where, having had legal access to schools, they have developed a strong sense of belonging (Abrego 2008b). From that moment on, however, their legal status becomes an effective obstacle in their incorporation in U.S. society. As Alex, a Salvadoran junior in high school described it, before he learned of his status: "I used to leave my house to go to school every day and I didn't know anything. I didn't know I was undocumented. . . . I just went to class, hung out with my friends, you know, whatever normal things." Since learning of his status, Alex tries to keep pursuing his goals, but he lives with constant reminders of his vulnerability. In his worldview, as well as that of other youth in a similar situation, an undocumented status is an anomaly because many have lived in the United States all their lives. As a result, they feel stigmatized in the very society that they previously considered home.

Once these youth learn about their legal statuses, many develop an awareness of the negative connotations associated with their illegality. Astrid, a Salvadoran undocumented high school student recalled feeling uncomfortable at school when the classroom topic turned to immigration: "I hate how they call us 'illegal aliens.' I feel like telling them that I don't have antennae, I'm not a weirdo like they think." Concerned with the potential repercussions, however, she never shared these feelings with her peers. Similarly, Brenda, an undocumented Guatemalan high school student says, "they call us 'illegals' and they think we're committing crimes all the time and we're not." The undocumented label, created through immigration laws, weighs heavily on these youth who, like any other U.S. teenager, often want nothing more than to fit in. Importantly, during formative years in adolescence, even awareness of restrictive laws impacts the youngsters' identity development, with potential long-term repercussions. A survey conducted among middle school students in Phoenix found that awareness of SB 1070, the Arizona restrictive law passed in 2010 that is still on hold in federal court, was positively linked to perceptions of discrimination and negatively impacted the students' perceptions of being American: the more they were aware of this law, the more discrimination they perceived and the less American they felt (Santos, Menjívar, and Godfrey, in press). It would not be surprising to find a similar situation in states like Georgia and Alabama where equally or more severe immigration laws quickly followed the passing of the Arizona law.

The stigma these youth experience affects them in various ways. Youth in tenuous legal statuses must interact and share information about their status with gatekeepers and school officials to transition to higher education. Among other things, they have to request letters of recommendation and proof of school attendance to apply to college. Many students expressed the mental (and sometimes physical) distress they experienced whenever they disclosed their status to a new school official: unsure about teachers' and counselors' stances on immigration, they worried about being publicly ridiculed and targeted. Alisa, a Guatemalan high school student in Los Angeles, fidgeted with her fingers and looked away as she described this process: "I would get really nervous, but I had to tell them [teachers] because I just thought that they could help me. . . . It's stressful, you don't know if they will treat you different." Moreover, even when they overcome the stigma of the legal label, those who excel academically are often unable to attend college or to claim scholarships awarded to them, effectively being barred from traditional means to upward mobility.

Some youths with uncertain legal statuses, particularly those whose parents are undocumented, learn early on that their status makes them different, vulnerable, and even suspect. This is especially driven home by nervous parents who, when fearful of deportation, may not take their children, including U.S.-born children, to school. Afraid of being apprehended and separated, these families avoid interacting with officials in social service agencies, even when this means denying children the social, medical, and educational services they need. In the process, children learn to be fearful of authorities who may, at any moment during a regular activity such as attending school, separate them from their families or send them to a country they do not remember or simply do not know. For example, Jorge, a Salvadoran college student in Los Angeles, recalls being scared in school: "There would be fights and the cops would come and I would stay away, but I would think, 'what if immigration [how immigrants often refer to immigration authorities] comes and tries to find those of us who don't have a Social Security [card]?' . . . You try to go through your day like nothing, but in the back of your head, you're always scared."

The cumulative stress paired with the knowledge that life will change radically after high school leads to trumped aspirations and little motivation for many youth. Formerly high-achieving students explain their poor academic performance as a result of a lack of desirable opportunities (Abrego 2006). For instance, the daughter of a Guatemalan couple in Phoenix managed to keep a high grade point average for all four years of high school in spite of working alongside her parents cleaning houses and offices on weekends, but as graduation from high school approached, she confided in her mother: "I don't want to leave school. I want to flunk. I want to stay in school. I know that after this [finishing school], I will have nothing; I feel like my life will be over. I want to stay back a grade so at least I'll continue going to school." With few or no opportunities to regularize their status, and knowing that there is "no future" for them in U.S. society, these students' situations exacerbate the effects of symbolic and structural violence in their lives. David, a Guatemalan high school student in Los Angeles, had this to share during an interview with Abrego:

LA: Do you find that it's common at your school that there are people who talk about this, about not having their papers?

D: Yeah. . . . A lot of people want to go to college.

LA: And they know that they can't?

D: Yeah.

LA: What do you think that does to people?

D: It makes them give up. Like, why try? . . . when they find out they can't go to college because they don't have papers.

LA: Do you know a lot of people who have gone through that?

D: Some of my friends . . . Yeah, they give up. . . . They say, "why bother if I can't continue?"

David is quick to make the connection between his legal status and his desire "to go to college." In schools with large populations of students with various uncertain statuses, the knowledge that such statuses will keep them from attending college lowers their aspirations. This is the case of a Salvadoran family in Phoenix, in which all five members have different legal statuses and four of them have been waiting to receive their "papers" "any time" for approximately nine years (as of this writing). The mother, who attended two years of law school in her country, explained that in each of her children's cases they had to quit their educational objectives due to their legal statuses, and in her case, "I was a very good student. I have taken 38 credits at the community college, but when will I finish? When will I transfer and get my degree? We're not even talking about law school anymore . . . that's gone. I don't aspire to that anymore." In this way, the legal violence that keeps individuals in these situations is bound up with structural violence when it blocks their paths to upward mobility and keeps them on the margins of society, usually waiting for many years, often decades, to regularize their statuses.

An estimated 65,000 undocumented or legally uncertain students graduate from high schools throughout the United States every year (Passel and Cohn 2009). Although college students in tenuous legal statuses are eligible to pay in-state tuition in 12 states throughout the country (as of this writing), they are barred from federal and state financial aid—including grants, loans, and work-study programs.[34] With little or no financial resources (because most rely on their undocumented or partially documented parents' low wages), these students are often priced out of higher education, and their efforts toward upward mobility are trumped (Abrego 2006; Gonzales 2011). Camilo, a high-achieving Guatemalan student in Los Angeles, shares his frustrations: "Teachers always tell you not to worry about where the school is or how much it costs. They tell us we have so many options. But we [undocumented students] don't have those decisions. Our decision is whether or not we can pay for college." And students who have TPS or who are in the process of obtaining legal permanent residence are also barred from receiving financial aid. Alex, a Salvadoran high school student in Los Angeles whose father qualified for legalization through NACARA, was in his senior year when he received his work permit—one of the first steps in the process of obtaining legal residency. As he explains, "I'm so happy, I cried, I cried when I saw the letter. . . . And most likely I'm not going to get my papers by the time I graduate next year. . . . But it means I can apply to college. I can't apply for financial aid until I have the green card, but now at least I can work."

Legal violence also manifests itself in these youths' lives in ways similar to adults. Although *Plyler v. Doe* bars public schools from excluding undocumented children in grades K–12, these students are not protected from deportation outside of school grounds. Like their adult counterparts, undocumented youth may be targeted, detained, and deported for minor infractions, such as driving without a license (Jordan 2008). As more police departments nationwide work in conjunction with ICE through the 287(g) agreement or the Secure Communities program, students in tenuous legal statuses increasingly fear the possibility of being deported for minor offenses. Although they are protected in school, the fear of deportation extends into other extracurricular educational activities. Legal violence thus emerges outside school for these youth, as their legality exposes then to discriminatory treatment and stigmatization and leads them to fewer, if any, opportunities for advancement. This is evident when they try to get a job. Jovani, a Guatemalan high school student, describes his experiences as he becomes aware of his limitations to help his low-income family pay bills: "When I want to get a job, I can't. I want to drive, but I can't. . . . So yeah, it's kind of hard for me. . . . I get mad because my parents brought me. I didn't tell them to bring me, but I get punished for it, for not having the papers." The legal violence that his parents experience on the margins of society limits their wages, stands in Jovani's way of higher education, and blocks him from contributing through employment to improve his family's living conditions. In his frustration, he overlooks the legitimated power of immigration laws and incorrectly identifies the source of his vulnerability in his parents' decision to bring him to the United States. This is how structural violence and symbolic violence coalesce in legal violence to shape immediate experiences and long-term trajectories of incorporation.

Discussion/Conclusion

The question of immigrant incorporation has been an enduring concern for sociologists of U.S. immigration (Park 1950; Gordon 1964; Gans 1992; Thomas and Znaniecki 1996). Scholars have debated whether the process is akin to a smooth, linear progression, a single bumpy line, or even multiple lines aimed in different directions. In recent years, individual- and community-level factors have been identified as shaping immigrant integration (Portes and Zhou 1993; Portes and Rumbaut 2001; Alba and Nee 2003). In this essay, we build on theories that underscore the role of structural factors in immigrant assimilation and highlight especially the role of immigration laws in delimiting immigrants' short- and long-term integration experiences. We focus on Central American immigrants whose various legal statuses offer fruitful terrain to examine the potential effects of the law in the lives of immigrants.

The unprompted references to the immigration laws that govern the lives of our study participants in Los Angeles and Phoenix demonstrate the power of these laws. Designed to modify migratory practices and behaviors, these laws potentially violate individuals' human rights, make them suspect in the eyes of others, lead them to accept their self-depreciation as normal, and create conditions for immigrants to impose categories of domination on one another. Significantly, such consequences are not contained solely within U.S. borders—the presumed jurisdiction of U.S. immigration laws—but spill over to the countries of origin in various, complex ways. This results not just from immigrants' own ties to their relatives and communities of origin but also, and just as importantly, through the U.S. ties with and position of power relative to the immigrants' countries of origin.

Drawing on various conceptualizations of violence in a single framework, we have examined the harmful consequences of implementing a restrictive body of law that criminalizes individuals, and we refer to this phenomenon as *legal violence*. Following Jackman's (2002) call for refocusing the sociological optic to examine violence away from the willful intention to inflict pain between individuals, we shed light on legally sanctioned social suffering. Legal violence is at once structural in that it is exerted without identifiable perpetrators, and it is symbolic in that it is so thoroughly imposed by the social order that it becomes normalized as part of the cognitive repertoire of those exposed. Importantly, this type of violence is legal, sanctioned, and legitimated through formal structures of power that are publicly accepted and respected. The legal violence lens, with its ability to capture physical, structural, and symbolic violence as these are made possible through the law, exposes the intertwined nature of these forms of violence, as one form begets another, and allows the recognition of violent consequences of the law when they are present, particularly when these are perpetuated and embedded in structures of domination.

In the United States, as in other major receiving countries around the world, the symbolic violence embedded in constructions of immigrant legality has tightened the association between immigration and crime. Starting in the mid-1990s and intensifying after the attacks of September 11, 2001, there has been a convergence of immigration law with criminal law. Using this convergence as a starting point, the legal violence lens allows us to unearth the social suffering that the implementation of a multipronged legal system has for immigrants (and their families) today.

In the case of immigrants in tenuous legal statuses, legal violence is rooted in the legal system that purports to protect the nation but, instead, produces spaces and the possibility for material, emotional, and psychological injurious actions that target an entire group of people with a particular set of shared social characteristics. For analytical purposes, we demonstrated Central American immigrants' deportability and vulnerability in three distinct areas—family, work, and school—that are often examined in the context of assimilation frameworks because they represent key spheres of life through which immigrant incorporation is gauged. Importantly, although we analyzed each sphere separately, immigrants experience legal violence simultaneously and cumulatively in these three areas. Legal violence magnifies immigrants' vulnerability in these key areas and in other facets of life.

The concept of legal violence, therefore, advances immigration scholarship by revealing immigration law's harmful consequences in immigrants' quotidian practices. Some may argue that our findings are unsurprising. Intuitively, it makes sense that immigrants would feel vulnerable living without authorization or that they will modify their behaviors in response to changes in the law. However, the legal violence lens allows us to recognize how the legal regime harms both documented and undocumented immigrants through the convergence of criminal and civil immigration laws, as well as through the repeated use of discourses that portray immigrants as criminals. The contemporary immigration regime makes mistreatment not only possible but uneventful, familiar, and legal as individuals come to understand it as "the law." Such legally sanctioned violence is likely to have far-reaching and persistent effects because immigrants spend increasingly lengthy periods of time in these legal locations. In this way, immigration laws that seek to criminalize immigrants and their behaviors thwart the immigrants' integration and can hinder upward mobility in multiple ways. As Jiménez and López-Sanders (2011) argue, current immigration policies are detrimental for immigrants' long-term social and economic incorporation across multiple generations and risk creating an "illegal class" (see also Menjívar 2006b; Massey 2007). Thus, our study suggests a need for a more systematic interrogation of the role of immigration law in the process of immigrant integration. Shifting the focus to legal processes and their effects also allows for critical examinations of immigration and integration from the perspective of exclusion and human rights. And as people throughout the world continue to migrate to a handful of receiving countries, sociological analysis can help explain key processes at the root of questions about who belongs and why (Willen 2010).

NOTES

Reprinted with permission from the University of California Press. This essay originally in the *American Journal of Sociology* 117, no. 5 (March 2012): 1380–421.

1   All individuals' names in this essay are pseudonyms.

2   We do not discuss what factors led to the creation of these laws, the dynamics that preceded their implementation, or why they have been implemented now; such debates have been adequately covered elsewhere (see De Genova 2005; Wong 2005).

3   Other researchers have conceptualized the consequences of contemporary immigration laws in the lives of immigrants as forms of structural or symbolic violence. In a study of immigrant laborers in California, Holmes (2007) calls attention to the internalization of structural violence to explain how inequalities are maintained among farmworkers. From a medical anthropology perspective, Walter, Bourgois, and Loinaz (2004) examine the embodiment of structural violence that results in patterns of social suffering among undocumented Latino men. Examining the effects of deportation among undocumented immigrants in Israel, Willen (2007) notes that such campaigns represent forms of structural and symbolic violence that exacerbate the effects of the ever-present threat of deportation. Spener (2008) uses the concepts of personal, structural, and cultural violence to analyze the tragedies involved in crossing the Mexico-U.S. border. And in a study of Indian migrant laborers in Bahrain, Gardner (2010) uses the concept of structural violence to capture the consequences of labor recruitment practices.

4   We use the anthropologically informed term *social suffering* to analyze collective experiences of suffering among a large group of individuals (see Willen 2007).

5   Unlike scholars who capture state-induced violence on communities and individuals using a Foucauldian analysis that emphasizes surveillance and discipline to control individual bodies (Hekman 1996; Roberts 1997; Simon 2007), the legal violence concept is based on Bourdieu's work because this perspective provides a better understanding of the process through which laws with harmful consequences become part of the social order.

6   In the interest of space, we are not including a discussion of resistance and protest, which are critical aspects of how individuals and groups have responded to the effects of the law today (see Abrego 2011).

7   Auyero (in press) proposes a useful distinction when examining habituation to conditions of multisided violence between familiarization, as in "we are used to it," and desensitization, meaning that individuals are less likely to pay attention or notice. Following Auyero, we mean familiarization.

8   Legal violence is also related to, but distinct from, the violence revealed in the work of the legal scholar Robert Cover (1975). Unlike the legal violence framework, which includes symbolic and nonphysical forms of violence, one of Cover's central arguments is that to maintain order, the state must use its laws in direct and violent ways. These include practices such as returning people to slavery prior to the Civil War, capital punishment, and force by police officers. Cover also asserts that judges' legal interpretations are a form of direct violence when they result in subjects' loss of freedom, property, children, or even life (Minow, Ryan, and Sarat 1993). Certainly, these are convincing examples of law's violent effects, but the analytical lens we use here looks beyond these more explicit and direct violent consequences of the law.

9   Walter Benjamin (2001, 69), in his classical writings on violence, observed that "all violence as a means is either law-making or law-preserving."

10   As Kanstroom (2007) observes, there have been immigrants deemed excludable as criminals or as posing a political threat since the foundation of the nation. But today's regime differs in significant ways.

11   Hagan, Rodriguez, and Castro (2011) identify three periods of mass deportations in U.S. history, noting that the third, starting in the mid 1990s, is quantitatively and qualitatively different than the previous two.

12   Socially constructed phenomena can be closely linked to public fear (Glassner 1999; Best 2001), often with important political gains for particular groups (Glassner 1999).

13   Employer sanctions, on the other hand, even though codified into law for much longer, have not had nearly as damaging effects on employers (Calavita 1990; Medina 1997).

14   The outcome is that 287(g)—the program that allows local police departments to act as immigration agents—has had its largest impact on noncriminal immigrants, such as day laborers, street vendors, and drivers with broken taillights (Shahani and Greene 2009).

15   Notably, popular accounts of the current "immigration debate" fail to note that most Central Americans being targeted for immigration infractions in the United States

today had already experienced the devastation of civil wars and their aftermath in their own countries—conflicts substantially funded by the U.S. government.

16 The United Nations Human Development report for El Salvador (2008) shows that only 20% of the population has "dignified" employment in that country; see http://www.pnud.org.sv/2007/idh/content/view/28/100/ (accessed July 22, 2008).

17 Although hundreds of rural villages were annihilated, almost a quarter of a million Guatemalans disappeared or were killed during the civil conflict, and natural disasters compounded the human-made destruction, the U.S. Department of State has never recognized Guatemalans as deserving of temporary protection.

18 The IIRIRA expanded the range of crimes that make immigrants ineligible for permanent legal residence and permanent legal residents deportable, increased border control efforts, eliminated waivers through which undocumented immigrants in deportation procedures could petition to remain in the United States, and made it more difficult for them to obtain permanent legal residence.

19 Since IIRIRA became law, among the deported were permanent residents and refugees who left behind at least 1.6 million spouses and children, many of whom are U.S. citizens (Human Rights Watch 2007; Menjívar and Rumbaut 2008). Although we do not have figures for deportation-induced family separations among Guatemalans, Hondurans, and Salvadorans, given their deportation rates and their temporary statuses, we expect that many have been affected.

20 DHS Statistical Yearbook 2009, table 38, "Aliens Removed by Criminal Status and Region and Country of Nationality: Fiscal Years 2000 to 2009"; and DHS Statistical Yearbook 2000, table 66, "Aliens Removed by Criminal Status and Region and Country of Nationality, Fiscal Years 1993–2000."

21 Office of Immigration Statistics (U.S. Department of Homeland Security 2009).

22 For information from Immigration and Customs Enforcement about Secure Communities, see http://www.ice.gov/doclib/foia/secure_communities /securecommunitiespresentations.pdf.

23 Even though they constitute a relatively small percentage of the immigrant population, Guatemalans, Hondurans, and Salvadorans seem to feel the effects of stiffer laws more directly than other groups. This is evident in their proportionally large numbers among deportees. Also, one study in New Jersey found that among Latin American–origin immigrants, Guatemalans ranked at the bottom in a system of stratification based on legal status because ICE raids disproportionately target them (since Guatemalan Mayas are physically more easily identifiable), and, therefore, other Latinos sometimes avoid being associated with them (Adler 2006).

24 Some scholars (see Varsanyi 2008) argue that there has been a devolution of select immigration powers to local and state governments. While states are now active enforcers, we see these actions as adding a layer to the federal government's laws, in additive fashion.

25 Some of these ordinances are largely symbolic since they seek to bar undocumented immigrants from accessing services that were already unavailable to them.

26 Border enforcement policies include Operation Gatekeeper in California, Operation Safeguard in Arizona, and Operation Hold-the-Line in Texas, among others.

27 For context, in 2004 the estimated monthly expenses for most households in urban areas in El Salvador was $129.50 (PNUD 2005, 481).

28   As of this writing, the Obama administration has suspended workplace raids but
      has expanded the Secure Communities program and implemented workplace
      audits, or "silent raids," which facilitate deportations.

29   A recent report (Kohli et al. 2011) found that through Secure Communities the
      ICE has deported hundreds of U.S. citizens, which shows the effects of these
      strategies beyond their intended target—undocumented immigrants with criminal
      records.

30   According to recent estimates (Passel and Cohn 2011), two-thirds of the undocu-
      mented immigrants in the United States today have been in the country for more
      than 10 years, with a full one-third having resided in the country for 15 years or
      longer.

31   As of this writing, the U.S. Supreme Court ruled that using another person's docu-
      ments to work does not constitute identity theft (http://feetin2worlds.wordpress
      .com/2009/05/05/supreme-court-ruling-in-identity-theft-case-too-late-for-some
      -immigrants/). However, some local law enforcement agencies, like Arizona's
      MCSO, through a state law, have continued to raid workplaces and mingle civil and
      criminal law, in spite of the Supreme Court's ruling.

32   Due to concerns and complaints of abuse, the federal government terminated its
      agreement with the MCSO in 2009; thus, they can no longer conduct traffic sup-
      pression sweeps under the federal program, but the MCSO continues to conduct
      workplace raids under a 2008 state law to target businesses suspected of hiring
      undocumented workers described below.

33   Under the Legal Arizona Workers Act, employers who hire unauthorized work-
      ers can have their business licenses suspended for up to 10 days and be put on
      probation. A second offense can lead to a revocation of the license. It also requires
      Arizona employers to use E-verify, the federal electronic system to validate Social
      Security numbers and employees' immigration status.

34   For more information about in-state tuition laws throughout the country, visit
      http:// www.nilc.org/basic-facts-instate.html.

REFERENCES

Abrego, Leisy J. 2006. "'I Can't Go to College Because I Don't Have Papers': Incorpora-
    tion Patterns of Latino Undocumented Youth." *Latino Studies* 4 (3): 212–31.
Abrego, Leisy J. 2008a. "Barely Subsisting, Surviving, or Thriving: How Parents' Legal
    Status and Gender Shape the Economic and Emotional Well-Being of Salvadoran
    Transnational Families." PhD dissertation. University of California, Los Angeles,
    Department of Sociology.
Abrego, Leisy J. 2008b. "Legitimacy, Social Identity, and the Mobilization of Law: The
    Effects of Assembly Bill 540 on Undocumented Students in California." *Law and
    Social Inquiry* 33 (3): 709–34.
Abrego, Leisy J. 2009. "Economic Well-Being in Salvadoran Transnational Families:
    How Gender Affects Remittance Practices." *Journal of Marriage and Family* 71:1070–85.
Abrego, Leisy J. 2011. "Legal Consciousness of Undocumented Latinos: Fear and Stigma
    as Barriers to Claims Making for First and 1.5 Generation Immigrants." *Law and
    Society Review* 45 (2): 337–70.

Abrego, Leisy, and Roberto Gonzales. 2010. "Blocked Paths, Uncertain Futures: The Postsecondary Education and Labor Market Prospects of Undocumented Latino Youth." *Journal of Education of Students Placed at Risk* (JESPAR) 15 (1): 144–57.

Adler, Rachel H. 2006. "'But They Claimed to Be Police, Not *La Migra*!': The Interaction of Residency Status, Class, and Ethnicity in a (Post-PATRIOT Act) New Jersey Neighborhood." *American Behavioral Scientist* 50 (1): 48–69.

Alba, Richard D., and Victor Nee. 2003. *Remaking the American Mainstream: Assimilation and Contemporary Immigration*. Cambridge, Mass.: Harvard University Press.

Andreas, Peter. 2001. "The Transformation of Migrant Smuggling across the U.S.-Mexican Border." Pp. 107–25 in *Global Human Smuggling: Comparative Perspectives*, edited by David Kyle and Rey Koslowski. Baltimore: Johns Hopkins University Press.

Arriero, Elisabeth. 2009. "Slow Economy Spells Little Work for Day Laborers." *Arizona Republic*, July 27. http://www.azcentral.com/news/articles/2009/07/27/20090727dayl aborers0727.html.

Auyero, Javier, and Agustin Burbano de Lara. In press. "In Harm's Way at the Urban Margins." *Ethnography*.

Behrens, Susan Fitzpatrick. 2009. "Plan Mexico and Central American Migration." North American Congress on Latin America, New York City. http://nacla.org/node/5406.

Benjamin, Walter. 2001. "Critique of Violence." Pp. 62–70 in *Deconstruction: A Reader*, edited by Martin McQuillan. New York: Routledge.

Best, Joel. 2001. *Damned Lies and Statistics: Untangling Numbers from the Media, Politicians, and Activists*. Berkeley and Los Angeles: University of California Press.

Borja, Elizabeth C. 2008. "Brief Documentary History of the Department of Homeland Security: 2001–2008." Report. Department of Homeland Security History Office, Washington, D.C. http://www.dhs.gov/xlibrary/assets/brief_documentary_history_of _dhs_200l_2008.pdf.

Bourdieu, Pierre. 1998. *Masculine Domination*. Stanford, Calif.: Stanford University Press.

Bourdieu, Pierre, and Loïc Wacquant. 2004. "Symbolic Violence." Pp. 272–74 in *Violence in War and Peace*, edited by Nancy Scheper-Hughes and Philippe Bourgois. Malden, Mass.: Blackwell.

Bourgois, Philippe. 2004a. "The Continuum of Violence in War and Peace: Post-Cold War Lessons from El Salvador." Pp. 425–34 in *Violence in War and Peace*, edited by Nancy Scheper-Hughes and Philippe Bourgois. Malden, Mass.: Blackwell.

Bourgois, Philippe. 2004b. "U.S. Inner-City Apartheid: The Contours of Structural and Interpersonal Violence." Pp. 301–8 in *Violence in War and Peace*, edited by Nancy Scheper-Hughes and Philippe Bourgois. Malden, Mass.: Blackwell.

Calavita, Kitty. 1990. "Employer Sanctions Violations: Toward a Dialectical Model of White-Collar Crime." *Law and Society Review* 24 (4): 1041–70.

Calavita, Kitty. 1998. "Immigration, Law, and Marginalization in a Global Economy: Notes from Spain." *Law and Society Review* 32 (3): 529–66.

Camayd-Freixas, Erik. 2009. *Postville: La criminalización de los migrantes*. Guatemala City: F&G Editores.

Capps, Randy, Rosa María Castañeda, Ajay Chaudry, and Robert Santos. 2007. "Paying the Price: The Impact of Immigration Raids on America's Children." Report. Urban Institute, Washington, D.C. http://www.urban.org/UploadedPDF/411566_immigra-tion_raids.pdf.

Caspa, Humberto. 2008. *Terror in the Latino Barrio: The Rise of the New Right in Local Government*. Santa Ana, Calif.: Seven Locks Press.

Chavez, Leo R. 2008. *The Latino Threat: Constructing Immigrants, Citizens, and the Nation*. Palo Alto, Calif.: Stanford University Press.

Coleman, Matthew. 2007. "Immigration Geopolitics beyond the Mexico-U.S. Border." *Antipode* 39 (1): 54–76.

Cornelius, Wayne A. 2001. "Death at the Border: Efficacy and Unintended Consequences of U.S. Immigration Control Policy." *Population and Development Review* 27 (4): 661–88.

Coutin, Susan B. 2007. *Nations of Emigrants: Shifting Boundaries of Citizenship in El Salvador and the United States*. Ithaca, N.Y.: Cornell University Press.

Cover, Robert. 1975. *Justice Accused: Antislavery and the Judicial Process*. New Haven, Conn.: Yale University Press.

Creno, Glen. 2009. "44 Held in Sheriff's Office Raid on Phoenix Company: 35 Suspects Are Booked on Suspicion of ID Theft." *Arizona Republic*, August 14. http://www.azcentral.com/arizonarepublic/local/articles/2009/08/14/20090814raid0814.html?&wired. Accessed December 19, 2011.

De Genova, Nicholas P. 2002. "Migrant 'Illegality' and Deportability in Everyday Life." *Annual Review of Anthropology* 31:419–47.

De Genova, Nicholas P. 2004. "The Legal Production of Mexican/Migrant 'Illegality.'" *Latino Studies* 2 (2): 160–85.

De Genova, Nicholas P. 2005. *Working the Boundaries: Race, Space, and "Illegality" in Mexican Chicago*. Durham, N.C.: Duke University Press.

Donato, Katharine M., and Amada Armenta. 2011. "What We Know about Unauthorized Migration." *Annual Review of Sociology* 37 (1): 529–43.

Espiritu, Yen Le. 1997. *Asian American Women and Men: Labor, Laws, and Love*. Thousand Oaks, Calif.: Sage.

Farmer, Paul E. 2003. *Pathologies of Power: Health, Human Rights, and the New War on the Poor*. Berkeley and Los Angeles: University of California Press.

Finnegan, William. 2009. "Sheriff Joe." *New Yorker*, July 20, pp. 42–53.

Fortuny, Karina, Randy Capps, and Jeffrey Passel. 2007. "The Characteristics of Unauthorized Immigrants in California, Los Angeles County, and the United States." Report. Urban Institute, Washington, D.C. http://www.urban.org/uploadedpdf/411425_characteristics_immigrants.pdf.

Galtung, Johan. 1990. "Cultural Violence." *Journal of Peace Research* 27 (3): 291–305.

Gans, Herbert J. 1992. "Second Generation Decline: Scenarios for the Economic and Ethnic Futures of the Post-1965 America Immigrants." *Ethnic and Racial Studies* 15 (April): 173–92.

Gardner, Andrew M. 2010. *City of Strangers: Gulf Migration and the Indian Community in Bahrain*. Ithaca, N.Y.: Cornell University Press.

Glassner, Barry. 1999. *The Culture of Fear: Why Americans Are Afraid of the Wrong Things*. New York: Basic.

Gonzales, Roberto. 2011. "Learning to Be Illegal: Undocumented Youth and Shifting Legal Contexts in the Transition to Adulthood." *American Sociological Review* 76 (4): 602–19.

Gonzalez, Daniel. 2005. "Guatemalans Tops at Filling Area Roof Jobs." *Arizona Republic*, May 31, A1. http://www.azcentral.com/arizonarepublic/news/articles/0531roofers31.html.

Gordon, Milton. 1964. *Assimilation in American Life: The Role of Race, Religion, and National Origins*. New York: Oxford University Press.

Guttmacher, Sally. 1984. "Immigrant Workers: Health, Law, and Public Policy." *Journal of Health Politics, Policy and the Law* 9 (3): 503–14.

Hagan, Jacqueline Maria. 1994. *Deciding to Be Legal: A Maya Community in Houston*. Philadelphia: Temple University Press.

Hagan, Jacqueline, Karl Eschbach, and Nestor Rodríguez. 2008. "U.S. Deportation Policy, Family Separation, and Circular Migration." *International Migration Review* 42 (1): 64–88.

Hagan, Jacqueline, Nestor Rodriguez, and Brianna Castro. 2011. "Social Effects of Mass Deportations by the United States Government, 2000–2010." *Ethnic and Racial Studies* 34 (8): 1374–91.

Hammock, John, María Elena Letona, Gilma Pérez, and Ana Micaela Isen. 2005. "Testimonios de familias migrantes Salvadoreñas: Pobreza y trabajo." Report. Centro Presente, Boston. http://fletcher.tufts.edu/faculty/hammock/pdf/Testimonios%20 de%20familias%20migrantes%20salvadore%F1as-1.pdf. Accessed April 22, 2008.

Hao, Lingxin. 2007. *Color Lines, Country Lines: Race, Immigration, and Wealth Stratification in America*. New York: Russell Sage.

Hekman, Susan, ed. 1996. *Feminist Interpretations of Michel Foucault*. University Park: Pennsylvania State University Press.

Hirsch, Jennifer S. 2003. *A Courtship after Marriage: Sexuality and Love in Mexican Transnational Families*. Berkeley and Los Angeles: University of California Press.

Holmes, Seth M. 2007. "'Oaxacans Like to Work Bent Over': The Naturalization of Social Suffering among Berry Farm Workers." *International Migration* 45 (3): 39–68.

Human Rights Watch. 2007. "Forced Apart: Families Separated and Immigrants Harmed by United States Deportation Policy." *Human Rights Watch* 19, no. 3(G). http://www.unhcr.org/refworld/publisher,HRW,,USA,46a764862.0.html. Report. Human Rights Watch, New York City.

Inda, Jonathan Xavier. 2006. "Border Prophylaxis: Technology, Illegality, and the Government of Immigration." *Cultural Dynamics* 18 (2): 115–38.

Jackman, Mary R. 2002. "Violence in Social Life." *Annual Review of Sociology* 28: 387–415.

Jiménez, Tomás R., and Laura López-Sanders. 2011. "Unanticipated, Unintended, and Unadvised: The Effects of Public Policy on Unauthorized Immigration." *Pathways* (Winter): 3–7.

Jordan, Jessica. 2008. "Latino College Students Fear Deportation." *Gainesville Times*, October 9. http://www.gainesvilletimes.com/news/article/9556/.

Kanstroom, Daniel. 2007. *Deportation Nation: Outsiders in American History*. Cambridge, Mass.: Harvard University Press.

Kasinitz, Philip, John H. Mollenkopf, Mary C. Waters, and Jennifer Holdaway. 2008. *Inheriting the City: The Children of Immigrants Come of Age*. New York and Cambridge, Mass: Russell Sage Foundation and Harvard University Press.

Kleinman, Arthur. 2000. "The Violences of Everyday Life: The Multiple Forms and Dynamics of Social Violence." Pp. 226–41 in *In Violence and Subjectivity*, edited by Veena Das, Arthur Kleinman, Mamphela Ramphele, and Pamela Reynolds. Berkeley and Los Angeles: University of California Press.

Kohli, Aarti, Peter L. Markowitz, and Lisa Chavez. 2011. "Secure Communities by the Numbers: An Analysis of Demographics and Due Process." Report. University of California, Chief Justice Earl Warren Institute on Law and Social Polity, Berkeley. http://www.law.berkeley.edu/files/Secure_Communities_by_the_Numbers.pdf.

Massey, Douglas. 2007. *Categorically Unequal: The American Stratification System.* New York: Russell Sage.

Massey, Douglas, and Katherine Bartley. 2005. "The Changing Legal Status Distribution of Immigrants: A Caution." *International Migration Review* 39 (2): 469–84.

Massey, Douglas, Jorge Durand, and Nolan Malone. 2002. *Beyond Smoke and Mirrors: Mexican Immigration in an Era of Economic Integration.* New York: Russell Sage Foundation.

McConnell, Eileen Diaz, and Enrico Marcelli. 2007. "Buying into the American Dream? Mexican Immigrants, Legal Status, and Homeownership in Los Angeles County." *Social Science Quarterly* 88 (1): 199–221.

McKenzie, Sean, and Cecilia Menjívar. 2011. "The Meanings of Migration, Remittances, and Gifts: The Views of Honduran Women Who Stay." *Global Networks: A Journal of Transnational Affairs* 11 (1): 63–81.

Medina, Maria Isabel. 1997. "The Criminalization of Immigration Law: Employer Sanctions and Marriage Fraud." *George Mason Law Review* 643:669–731.

Menjívar, Cecilia. 2000. *Fragmented Ties: Salvadoran Immigrant Networks in America.* Berkeley and Los Angeles: University of California Press.

Menjívar, Cecilia. 2001. "Latino Immigrants and Their Perceptions of Religious Institutions: Cubans, Salvadorans, and Guatemalans in Phoenix, AZ." *Migraciones Internacionales* 1 (1): 65–88.

Menjívar, Cecilia. 2002. "The Ties That Heal: Guatemalan Immigrant Women's Networks and Medical Treatment." *International Migration Review* 36 (2): 437–67.

Menjívar, Cecilia. 2003. "Religion and Immigration in Comparative Perspective: Salvadorans in Catholic and Evangelical Communities in San Francisco, Phoenix, and Washington D.C." *Sociology of Religion* 64 (1): 21–45.

Menjívar, Cecilia. 2006a. "Family Reorganization in a Context of Legal Uncertainty: Guatemalan and Salvadoran Immigrants in the United States." *International Journal of Sociology of the Family* 32 (2): 223–45.

Menjívar, Cecilia. 2006b. "Liminal Legality: Salvadoran and Guatemalan Immigrants' Lives in the United States." *American Journal of Sociology* 111 (4): 999–1037.

Menjívar, Cecilia. 2008. "Educational Hopes, Documented Dreams: Guatemalan and Salvadoran Immigrants' Legality and Educational Prospects." *ANNALS of the American Academy of Political and Social Science* 620 (1): 177–93.

Menjívar, Cecilia. 2011. *Enduring Violence: Ladina Women's Lives in Guatemala.* Berkeley and Los Angeles: University of California Press.

Menjívar, Cecilia. N.d. "Central American Immigrant Workers and Legal Violence in Phoenix, Arizona." Manuscript. Arizona State University, School of Social and Family Dynamics, Tempe.

Menjívar, Cecilia, and Leisy Abrego. 2009. "Parents and Children across Borders: Legal Instability and Intergenerational Relations in Guatemalan and Salvadoran Families." Pp. 160–89 in *Across Generations: Immigrant Families in America,* edited by Nancy Foner. New York: New York University Press.

Menjívar, Cecilia, and Cynthia L. Bejarano. 2004. "Latino Immigrants' Perceptions of Crime and Police Authorities in the United States: A Case Study from the Phoenix Metropolitan Area." *Ethnic and Racial Studies* 27:120–48.

Menjívar, Cecilia, and Néstor Rodríguez, eds. 2005. *When States Kill: Latin America, the U.S., and Technologies of Terror.* Austin: University of Texas Press.

Menjívar, Cecilia, and Rubén G. Rumbaut. 2008. "Rights of Migrants." Pp. 60–74 in *The Leading Rogue State: The United States and Human Rights*, edited by Judith Blau, David Brunsma, Alberto Moncada, and Catherine Zimmer. Boulder, Colo.: Paradigm.

Milkman, Ruth, Ana Luz González, and Victor Narro. 2010. "Wage Theft and Workplace Violations in Los Angeles: The Failure of Employment and Labor Law for Low-Wage Workers." Report. UCLA Institute for Research on Labor and Employment, Los Angeles. http://www.irle.ucla.edu/events/2010/pdf/LAwagetheft.pdf.

Miller, Teresa. 2005. "Blurring the Boundaries between Immigration and Crime Control after September 11th." *Boston College Third World Law Journal* 25 (2005): 81–124.

Minow, Martha, Michael Ryan, and Austin Sarat, eds. 1993. *Narrative, Violence, and the Law: The Essays of Robert Cover*. Ann Arbor: University of Michigan Press.

Ngai, Mae M. 2004. *Impossible Subjects: Illegal Aliens and the Making of Modern America*. Princeton, NJ: Princeton University Press.

Ngai, Mae M. 2007. "Book Review: Working the Boundaries; Race, Space, and 'Illegality' in Mexican Chicago." *Latino Studies* 5 (4): 503–6.

Okie, Susan. 2007. "Immigrants and Health Care—at the Intersection of Two Broken Systems." *New England Journal of Medicine* 357 (6): 525–29.

Painter, Gary, Stuart Gabriel, and Dowell Myers. 2001. "Race, Immigrant Status, and Housing Tenure Choice." *Journal of Urban Economics* 49:150–67.

Park, Robert. 1950. *Race and Culture*. Glencoe, Ill.: Free Press.

Passel, Jeffrey, and D'Vera Cohn. 2009. "A Portrait of Unauthorized Immigrants in the United States." Report. Pew Hispanic Center, Washington, DC. http://www.pewhispanic.org/files/reports/107.pdf.

Passel, Jeffrey, and D'Vera Cohn. 2011. "Unauthorized Immigration Population: National and State Trends, 2010." Report. Pew Hispanic Center, Washington, DC. http://www.pewhispanic.org/files/2011/12/Unauthorized-Characteristics.pdf.

Piore, Michael. 1979. *Birds of Passage: Migrant Labor in Industrial Societies*. New York: Cambridge University Press.

PNUD (Programa de las Naciones Unidas para el Desarrollo). 2005. *Informe sobre desarrollo humano de El Salvador 2005: Una mirada al nuevo nosotros, impacto de las migraciones*. San Salvador: United Nations Development Program. http://www.pnud.org.sv/migraciones/content/view/9/105/.

Portes, Alejandro, and József Böröcz. 1989. "Contemporary Immigration: Theoretical Perspectives on Its Determinants and Modes of Incorporation." *International Migration Review* 23 (3): 606–30.

Portes, Alejandro, Patricia Fernández-Kelly, and William Haller. 2005. "Segmented Assimilation on the Ground: The New Second Generation in Early Adulthood." *Ethnic and Racial Studies* 20 (6): 1000–1040.

Portes, Alejandro, and Rubén G. Rumbaut. 2001. *Legacies: The Story of the Immigrant Second Generation*. Berkeley and New York: University of California Press and Russell Sage Foundation.

Portes, Alejandro, and Min Zhou. 1993. "The New Second Generation: Segmented Assimilation and Its Variants." *Annals of the American Academy of Political and Social Sciences* 530:74–96.

Portillo, Suyapa. 2008. "'Los Hondureños Somos Invisibles en Los Angeles': The Growing Honduran Immigrant Community in Los Angeles." Paper presented at the XXVII International Congress of the Latin American Studies Association, Montreal, 2007.

Preston, Julia. 2007. "Immigration Quandary: A Mother Torn from Her Baby." *New York Times*, November 17. http://www.nytimes.com/2007/11/17/us/17citizen. html?ex=1352955600&en=995bf8e6cb90c8de&ei=5088&partner=rssnyt&emc=rss.

Preston, Julia. 2008. "An Interpreter Speaking Up for Migrants." *New York Times*, July 11. http://www.nytimes.com/2008/07/11/us/11immig.html.

Roberts, Dorothy. 1997. *Killing the Black Body: Race Reproduction and the Meaning of Liberty*. New York: Pantheon.

Rodriguez, Nestor, and Jacqueline Maria Hagan. 2004. "Fractured Families and Communities: Effects of Immigration Reform in Texas, Mexico, and El Salvador." *Latino Studies* 2 (3): 328–51.

Rumbaut, Rubén G., and Alejandro Portes, eds. 2001. *Ethnicities: Children of Immigrants in America*. Berkeley and Los Angeles: University of California Press.

Salcido, Olivia, and Madelaine Adelman. 2004. "'He Has Me Tied with the Blessed and Damned Papers': Undocumented-Immigrant Battered Women in Phoenix, Arizona." *Human Organization* 63 (2): 162–72.

Santos, Carlos, Cecilia Menjívar, and Erin Godfrey. In press. "Effects of SB 1070 on Children." In *The Case of Arizona's Immigration Law* SB 1070, edited by Lisa Magaña and Erik Lee. New York: Springer.

Shahani, Aarti, and Judith Greene. 2009. "Local Democracy on ICE: Why State and Local Governments Have No Business in Federal Immigration Law Enforcement." Report. Justice Strategies, Brooklyn, N.Y. http://www.justicestrategies.org/sites/default/files/JS-Democracy-On-Ice.pdf.

Simon, Jonathan. 2007. *Governing through Crime: How the War on Crime Transformed American Democracy and Created a Culture of Fear*. Oxford: Oxford University Press.

Simon, Rita J., and Margo DeLey. 1984. "The Work Experience of Undocumented Mexican Women Migrants in Los Angeles." *International Migration Review* 18 (4): 1212–29.

Spener, David. 2008. "Global Apartheid, Coyotaje and the Discourse of Clandestine Migration: Distinctions between Personal, Structural, and Symbolic Violence." *Migración y Desarrollo* 10:115–40.

Spener, David. 2009. *Clandestine Crossings: Migrants and Coyotes on the Texas-Mexico Border*. Ithaca, N.Y.: Cornell University Press.

Stumpf, Juliet. 2006. "The Crimmigration Crisis: Immigrants, Crime, and Sovereign Power." *American University Law Review* 56:367–419.

Takaki, Ronald. 1989. *Strangers from a Different Shore: A History of Asian Americans*. Boston: Little, Brown.

Takei, Isao, Rogelio Saenz, and Jing Li. 2009. "Cost of Being a Mexican Immigrant and Being a Mexican Non-citizen in California and Texas." *Hispanic Journal of Behavioral Sciences* 31 (1): 73–95.

Taussig, Michael. 1992. *The Nervous System*. New York: Routledge.

Thomas, William I., and Florian Znaniecki. 1996. *The Polish Peasant in Europe and America*. Urbana: University of Illinois Press.

Tobar, Hector. 2009. "Hostage House in Compton an Example of Increasing Dangers for Illegal Immigrants." *Los Angeles Times*, August 4. http://latimesblogs.latimes.com/laplaza/2009/08/hostage-house-in-compton-an-example-of-the-increasing-dangers-for-illegal-immigrants.html.

Torres-Rivas, Edelberto. 1998. "Sobre el terror y la violencia política en América Latina." Pp. 46–59 in *Violencia en una sociedad en transición*. San Salvador: Programa de las Naciones Unidas para el Desarrollo. http://www.enlaceacademico.org/fileadmin/usuarios/El_Salvador/Natali/Documentos/ensayos.pdf.

Uriarte, Miren, Phil Granberry, Megan Halloran, Susan Kelly, Rob Kramer, Sandra Winkler, Jennifer Murillo, Udaya Wagle, and Randall Wilson. 2003. "Salvadorans, Guatemalans, Hondurans and Colombians: A Scan of Needs of Recent Latin American Immigrants to the Boston Area." Report. University of Massachusetts, Gastón Institute for Latino Community Development and Public Policy, Boston. http://scholarworks.umb.edu/gaston_pubs/134.

U.S. Department of Homeland Security. 2009. "Immigration Enforcement Actions, 2008: Annual Report." Office of Immigration Statistics, Washington, D.C. http://www.dhs.gov/xlibrary/assets/statistics/publications/enforcement_ar_08.pdf.

U.S. DHS/ICE (Department of Homeland Security/Immigration and Customs Enforcement). 2010. "Secretary Napolitano Announces Record-Breaking Immigration Enforcement Statistics Achieved under the Obama Administration." Press release, October 6. U.S. Department of Homeland Security, Washington, D.C. http://www.ice.gov/news/releases/1010/101006washtingtondc2.htm.

U.S. DHS/ICE (Department of Homeland Security/Immigration and Customs Enforcement 2011. "FY 2011: ICE Announces Year-End Removal Numbers, Highlights Focus on Key Priorities including Threats to Public Safety and National Security." Press release. U.S. Department of Homeland Security, Washington, D.C. http://www.ice.gov/new/releases/1110/111018washtingtondc.htm.

Varsanyi, Monica. 2008. "Rescaling the 'Alien,' Rescaling Personhood: Neoliberalism, Immigration and the State." *Annals of the Association of American Geographers* 98 (4): 877–96.

Waldinger, Roger, and Joel Perlmann. 1998. "Second Generations: Past, Present, Future." *Journal of Ethnic and Migration Studies* 24 (1): 5–25.

Walter, Nicholas, Philippe Bourgois, and H. Margarita Loinaz. 2004. "Masculinity and Undocumented Labor Migration: Injured Latino Day Laborers in San Francisco." *Social Science and Medicine* 59:1159–68.

Willen, Sarah S. 2007. "Toward a Critical Phenomenology of 'Illegality': State Power, Criminalization, and Abjectivity among Undocumented Migrant Workers in Tel Aviv, Israel." *International Migration* 45 (3): 8–38.

Willen, Sarah S. 2010. "Citizens, 'Real' Others, and 'Other' Others: The Biopolitics of Otherness and the Deportation of Unauthorized Migrant Workers from Tel Aviv, Israel." Pp. 262–94 in *The Deportation Regime: Sovereignty, Space, and the Freedom of Movement*, edited by Nicholas P. De Genova and Nathalie Peutz. Durham, N.C.: Duke University Press.

Wong, Carolyn. 2005. *Lobbying for Inclusion: Rights Politics and the Making of Immigration Policy*. Palo Alto, Calif.: Stanford University Press.

Necro-Subjection: On Borders, Asylum,
and Making Dead to Let Live

GILBERTO ROSAS

From *Barrio Libre*:

The grainy footage captures a cement ditch rife with undocumented, illegal, irregular movement. The scene is being filmed by a police officer,
a modality of "high intensity policing" that noncitizens are experiencing integral to "low intensity warfare" other border scholars have documented. The footage shows a group of mostly Hispanic police officers and
Border Patrol agents with their hands on their holsters on an overpass
about a half mile from the U.S.-Mexico border. The officers ask a group of
youth in the drainage ditch what they are doing—telling them to go back
to Mexico. The footage then shifts to the flash of a light cutting through
the darkness of the sewer tunnel behind the youth. A group of the undocumented materializes on the screen. They make their way northward
toward the bright sunlight of Nogales, Arizona. "El Enano," or the Dwarf,
suddenly wields a pipe. He strikes one of the denizens. He does it again
and again. A child in the group of migrants screams. "Stop." Another of
the young men of Barrio Libre seizes a migrant by his lapel of his western

shirt. With his other hand, he rips a chain off the neck of the unlucky man, who wears a cowboy hat. The officers above order the youth to stop.[1]

These *chúntaros*, uninitiated border-crossing hicks in cowboy drag, make themselves subject to death.[2] They would escape into the United States.

What of other noncitizens? What of the families, men, women, children who also breach the U.S.-Mexico border by attempting through crossing the desert? Although beautiful as documented by Amy Sara Carroll,[3] this terrain has been rendered treacherous. It is where thousands of irregular crossers of this international boundary have died, killed by an effective weaponization of the environs through deliberate policies of the United States government. Such border-crossers lack the cultural acumen of longstanding "Border People."[4] They end up in the "killing deserts."[5] Or, they may suffer other kinds of violence. It is normalized as natural in what Jason De Leon would later build on in his deep ethnography *The Land of Open Graves*.[6]

Neither random accidents nor natural disasters produce the death of noncitizen border-crossers in this terrain. They happen because states and governments designate certain groups to the racialized category of illegal.

People disappear forever. Animals, heat and cold, people smugglers, "delinquents," border control and migrants themselves, conspire. Death and the degradation of immigrant bodies, at the hands of wild animals, vigilantes, Border Patrol campaigns, are the result. They produce "deterrence," acknowledged in an admission by the U.S. authorities that "social violence would increase," if the Border Patrol was to adopt certain aggressive tactics that it did in the 1990s.[7] The rain and sun cause their corpses to slowly wear away, slowly deteriorating into nothingness.

The U.S.-Mexico border has become a zone of sacrifice. It pervades contemporary relations well beyond the actual international boundary.[8] Yet, the vast majority of immigrants who cross the U.S.-Mexico border irregularly live. These processes deepen relations of illegality and deportability, which some aptly term "deportation terror."[9]

What does it mean to almost die? What does it mean to expose oneself and possibly one's loved ones as subject to death and other cruel fates? What does it mean to be the subject of death and its politics? What does it mean to be disappeared, erased, to be made dead, socially if not politically? Or, more poignantly, what does it mean to *make dead to let live*?

Whole swaths of humanity are now condemned. They become surplus, rendered excess, an attribute of the inner solidarity of Western liberalism and the enduring presence of colonialist relations. They are disposed of and disappeared.

Drawing on the experiences of those that lack the privilege of citizenship in this anti-immigrant age, I advance the concept necro-subjection in this essay. The concept animates the history of the subject subordinated to the politics of death. Necro-subjection as a concept animates this neglected order of subjection, the entanglements of power, how it generates, penetrates, and produces psychic and somatic effects, how it may organize resistance, or more likely usher in refusals at the level of life itself.

Necro-subjection, conceptually, wrestles with living and the dead. It involves representing those who are made—and who make themselves—dead—in order to live. It is part of a larger project documenting and expressing contemporary brutalities without exacerbating indifference to obscene suffering and the demands to re-victimize immigrants, refugees, and asylum-seekers both in legal proceedings and in engaged traditions of scholarship, so that violence, spectacular and mundane are analyzed, recognized, and ultimately struggled against. The project, an ethnographic analysis of providing expert testimony on behalf of people fleeing Mexico's drug war in immigration proceedings and its methodological and theoretical implications and dilemmas, thus recognizes the complexity of working with groups struggling against systemic oppressions and how it infiltrates them and activist-scholarship alike.[10]

Necro-subjection is inextricably linked to racial liberalism. To garner asylum or other relief from deportation increasingly demands accounts of deep victimization on behalf of individuals and collectivities, playing to a deeply ingrained paternalism found in liberalisms of today. It coincides with the surveillance, policing, and detention of immigrants, echoing the birth of the prison industrial complex and the hyperincarceration of African Americans.[11] This order of subjection occurs among those attempting to irregularly cross the U.S.-Mexico border region, in politically related legal immigration proceedings, and many other hotspots across the globe, where surplus humanity threatens or appears to threaten the established polarity between them, us, and Other, between friends and enemies, where the whiteness of the social contract must be reaffirmed.[12]

This paper moves through multiple scenes where making dead to let live occurs, be it where I began this essay with the ethnography from my first book on the birth of a population of criminalized youth at the U.S.-Mexico border, their complex relation to the neoliberal reconfiguration of Mexico, and militarized policing practices implemented by both U.S. and Mexico in the border region, and the subjugation of undocumented border-crossing life, or my contemporary critically engaged ethnographic research project as an expert witness on behalf of others also seeking asylum and related legal remedies in immigration courts. Necro-subjection speaks to the emergence of the living dead, those who can never rest, evident in representations of zombies in popular culture, as the never-ending drug wars which I argue late in this essay reiterate the structures of settler colonialism.

Such figures link to a gradual zombification of rural life in certain parts of Mexico refusing dominant theorizations of the subject. They resonate with contemporary dystopic popular culture imaginaries, the brown figures of zombies. Neither wholly living or wholly dead, they abandon the everyday, the snuffing out of residual ways of life and the spectacular terror of privatized and public sovereigns. These walking dead complexly relate to the lived experience of race, class, gender, sexuality and related power differentials. Although many who flee Mexico, Central America, or other parts of the globe may not be indigenous, they flee its genocidal logics of dispossession. In the process, they may become new kinds of settlers.[13] These refugee-like zombies-in-the-making are often misrecognized as traditional immigrant laborers, given the longstanding imperial relationship of the U.S. and Mexico.[14] This emergent current of forced immigration to the United States refuses the merciless crossings through the killing deserts. They present themselves to the authorities at the U.S.-Mexico border. They request political asylum.

Brute force and social facts of violence no longer constitute an anomaly to late liberal rule, if they ever did, for those constituting or inhabiting the colonial "dark" side. Violence is unexceptional. Liberal consensus is now forged through the domination, subjugation, and the manipulation of the life and death, or better the death and life of the "new Poor." They are, as Sylvia Wynter puts it, "a category defined at the global level by refugee/economic migrants stranded outside the gates of the rich countries."[15] These postcolonial variants of Fanon's category of *les damnes* reaffirm how, as Quijano notes, the idea of race becomes the "most efficient instrument of social domination in the last 500 years."[16] No longer content to stay cordoned off in the hinterlands, the new refugees face a global xenophobia in their struggle to circumvent an increasingly globalized nativism. It demands contortions of life and death.

These new refugees flee. They escape. They desert. They refuse the tyrannies of the new normal as well as a return to the contemporary temporality. They refuse their residual life ways. Their mass movements constitute an abandonment of "slow death"[17] too much of the globe confronts.

Necro-subjective Demands in Asylum

Asylum is a protection granted to foreign nationals already in the United States or at its borders who meet the international standards of the "refugee."[18] The United Nations 1951 Convention and 1967 Protocols define a refugee as a person who is unable or unwilling to return to his or her home country, and cannot obtain protection in that country. Said person must have suffered persecution or hold a well-founded fear of persecution "on account of race, religion, nationality, membership in a particular social group, or political opinion." Congress incorporated this definition into U.S. immigration law in the Refugee Act of 1980. As a signatory to the 1967 Protocol, and through U.S. immigration law, the United States has legal obligations to provide protection and certain rights to those who qualify as refugees. To be awarded asylum involves accounting for membership in one of the protected categories, often taken as innate, such as sex, what the law designates as "color," or kinship ties. Asylum may also be awarded through what is referred to as a "particular social group," based on shared past experiences. It can range in meaning to include land ownership, or even small business ownership.

A similar legal remedy is the United Nations Convention against Torture and Other Cruel, Inhuman or Degrading Treatment or Punishment. It includes a provision that prevents expulsion to another state where there are substantial grounds for believing that the expellee would be in danger of torture or the infliction of pain or suffering, whether physical or mental, including punishment or coercion.

Moving forms of sociality crack open such legal categories. The law chases new subjectivities, as does social theory. Typically, and all too problematically cast as liberal entrepreneurial subjects extraordinaire, bent on the American dream of wealth and consumption, an emergent current of immigrant is fleeing the spectacular terror of the drug war in certain areas of Mexico. They also flee a less-recognized wearing away of residual ways of life, the kinds of life contemporary settler societies, to adapt Patrick Wolfe, snuff out, grind away, or abandon in far more banal ways.[19]

I sit in the witness stand and adjust the mic.[20] In this courtroom somewhere in the United States are a judge, two attorneys representing the Department of Homeland Security, "the respondents"—a couple and their three children—facing imminent deportation, their attorney, and a small audience, including some of their family members. A middle-aged husband and wife are trying to avoid deportation back to their onetime home, now dominated by a ruthless cartel.

Many thousands of others like this family are being held in detention centers in small towns in the United States. They refused to circumvent border enforcement, presenting themselves to the authorities at ports of entry into Texas, and requesting political asylum. An administratively appointed judge in the proceedings wields sovereign power. He decides who can move and who can settle, a core political struggle of the moment,[21] playing out in this case as whether to detain the couple, "remove" or deport them, or award them asylum.

The couple from Mexico fled a massacre. It was the horrendous culmination of what echoes certain private and indirect governance occurring elsewhere in the globe.[22] Short, quiet, humble, and middle-aged, the male head of household picked melons for living in a small agricultural village for a transnational agricultural company based in the United States. He and his coworkers began receiving threats to get off the fields, where they worked, a couple of years back. This man reported that if [they] "continued to work there they were going to be disappeared."

Then one day when he did not make it to work, a group of men armed with assault files killed nine of his co-workers in the fields. He explained in the court that "delinquents" had committed the crime—a gloss for those working in organized crime. One of his close friends was killed in this event. He feared what happened to his co-workers would happen to him. He also feared that his children would be kidnapped and suffer violence. Later, when a relative of this man was murdered, only his head was found.

Strange men began menacing his partner, looking for the man at his home. The couple fled to the United States. The couple sought relief from deportation by being granted asylum.

I must testify as to whether the "removal" of this couple, specifically their deportation to Mexico, places them in imminent danger. Immigration attorneys increasingly ask social science experts like me to corroborate testimony. This scenario underlines their incredibility; their existence demands validation. They have been officially rendered voiceless, effectively rightless in these proceedings.[23]

I consciously summon the demons—"the rapists . . . the murderers . . . the drug lords." I testify: "Mexico is experiencing the devastating effects of its drug war. Most experts agree it began near the end of 2006. The cartels rape and deploy sexual violence. They sever limbs and heads to intimidate law enforcement and civilians alike." I tell of the *fosos clandestinos*, mass graves that appear occasionally in Mexican media, of bodies consumed in acid. Of how human rights organizations describe Mexico as rife with human rights abuses. I explain that I am convinced that the levels of violence in the country are underreported.

I tell how NAFTA and its asymmetric terms of trade ravaged Mexico's rural economies, transforming areas into zones of undocumented immigration. Some of those who stayed behind soon cultivated marijuana and other drugs—primarily for consumption in the United States. I then rehearse the facts: the 160,000 deaths in Mexico tied to the drug war over the past decade; the 40,000 more who have "disappeared." I explain that Central American women, who are crossing the thickening border that Mexico has become, *know* to take birth control pills.

I feel blood pooling on my tongue. I spew it onto all-too-ready ears. I am seeking that ripe, imperially charged sensibility. I want to elaborate. I want to tell how U.S. addictions animate the carnage, how it feeds the dead. I want to tell of racisms in this age of human sacrifice, premature death,[24] vile misogyny and related exclusions of both sides of the U.S.-Mexico divide. I feed the hunger—neither the *carne* nor the carnality of power that cannot be lost[25]—for the social hegemonies about Mexico generally and Mexicans specifically as well as other parts of the globe. I want to suggest that they are tied to U.S. empire. I want to chart for the court the genealogies of military training and local machinations of empire. But there is little space for complexity. I hear myself explain, "There is blurring in daily life in large swaths of Mexico among elements of the local, national, and regional government and the cartels." I explain that Ciudad Juárez, a city on the U.S.-Mexico border opposite my hometown of El Paso, Texas, was more lethal than Afghanistan in 2010. Asylum cases often hinge on the government's unwillingness or inability to protect those at risk.

I paint a picture of this ordinary couple struggling in daily life. I describe how they toil, how the stained jeans that the man wears as he testifies are likely his only clothes; how he works, plays, and—yes—testifies in them. I speculate about the paltry government services, such as the underperforming public education—he finished sixth grade and she did not attend—eviscerated by the promises of a new liberalism that never came. I paint a picture of their home, with one light bulb that glows at night, cinderblock walls and dirt floors, homes similar to what I have seen in Nogales, Sonora, and across Mexico. The land itself and their will become subject to further dispossessions of privatized sovereigns.

I make dead to let live. I affirm imperial as late liberal common sense. Liberalism demands that my testimony is rife with the monstrous, the racist and gendered imperialist projections about Mexicans. Violent masculinities and victimized femininities are the heart of the case. They must be. I must render Mexicans and their situation back in their home country, so hopeless, so bleak, so full of imminent danger and so full of despair that the judge finds in favor of their application. I return to the mass disappearances, decapitations, and dismemberments, the clandestine graves, the tearing asunder of bodies, the menace.

I mobilize the specter of rape, again and again. Liberalism demands that the cartels, officialdom, the courts, and I, mobilize what Sayek Valencia terms "weaponized machismo"[26] and its corollary victimized femininity.

Necropolitical States

Appreciating "states" as both rich psychic interiorities and sovereignties that hold powers over life, death, racisms, capital, and multiple other power relations allows me to further unpack necro-subjection. These individuated or collective experiences speak to making dead to let live. When it comes to border enforcement, detention, and related questions such as asylum, deep and newly revealed histories of anti-Black racism generally and anti-Haitian xenophobia specifically animate U.S. immigrant detention, border enforcement, and deportation practices.[27]

A growing body of scholars and policy makers declare that the crisis in Mexico represents the failure of the Mexican state. Other scholars hold that the drug war cloaks more sinister forces, be it a clamping-down on social mobilization, the latest, intensified violent regime of dispossession, or related, longstanding collaborations between Mexico and the United States in the unruly governance of illicit commodities and their Baudrillardian confabulations.[28] Are these simply monstrous fables?

The established social hegemonies about Mexican immigration to the United States—their widespread rendering as "cheap," "disposable," "deportable," and increasingly "detainable," such awkward neologisms aside, labor—obscure those whose are forced to immigrate as an effect of politically organized state and state-like terror in Mexico. Nevertheless, hunger, starvation, regimes of impoverishment, and related forms of deprivation are normalized. They are the unremarkable, the inert violence of late racial liberalism,[29] rooted in histories of colonialisms, enslavement, and other dispossessions. The polarity between politically versus economically motivated alienage found in United States immigration law cuts too neatly. It lends itself to unfolding liberal rationalities.

This witnessing does not document "the criminal capture of the Mexican state," a certain technocratic discourse circulating among governing elites about Mexico, other parts of the globe, and increasingly about the contemporary United States. It is not that narco-traffickers or gangster Russians in other parts of the globe, secure in their mammoth wealth, their ill-gotten gains, have undertaken or are in the process of completing a criminal coup d'état, albeit from the side or above.[30] Imperial states, long about slavery and increasingly eviscerated of their better logics, increasingly exercise terror and torture as legitimation.

Spectacular terror is instrumental in a kind of capitalist accumulation has reconstituted itself since the 1970s, akin to what Karl Marx termed "primitive accumulation" in chapter 26 of *Capital*. It is based in dispossession, fraud, and violence. It involves the privatizing or cordoning-off of the commons, including indigenous lands and related strategic resources. Rosa Luxemburg, David Harvey, and others hold that such forms of accumulation must constantly be revitalized,[31] and consequently so are the long durées of "slavery, colonization, apartheid, capitalist alienation, immigration and asylum politics, postcolonial liberal multiculturalism, gender and sexual normativity, securitarian governmentality, and humanitarian reason" and related modes of anti-human-making and modes of dispossession.[32] They demand an analysis of "life itself" at the level of power and the subject, which normative accountings of the subject misrecognize, misapprehend.

Foucault's influential *Society Must Be Defended* underlines the inextricable ties among racism, state formation, life, and death. In this never-finished genealogy, modern racism is first articulated as a discourse of social war in the eighteenth century. It developed during the second half of the nineteenth century, absorbing important impulses from psychiatry as a means to protect society against the abnormal. Racism, in this formulation, "constitutes the necessary precondition that makes killing permissible." It essentially introduces "a break between what must live and what must die."[33] Racism articulates a *caesura* between worthy and unworthy life and resonates with the aforementioned formulations of contemporary racism as inextricably lethal—placing bodies closer and closer to death[34]—rather than the constructivist emphasis of racism strangling the contemporary liberal academy. Although Foucault's lectures lack any substantial discussion of European colonialism or the history of the idea of race, they deserve appreciation and invite an analysis of modes of making life and death as modes of biopolitical government. It impinges on individuals in their most basic relationship to themselves and others, as it does on collectivities. The integration of sovereign power (the "right of the sword") was complemented by a new right which does not erase the old right but which penetrates it, permeates it. "This is the right, or rather precisely the opposite right. It is the *power to 'make' live and 'let' die*. The right of sovereignty was the right to take life or let live. And then this new right is established: the right to make live and to let die." A certain death power animates this government of Others—allowing certain populations to die. Racism "constitutes the necessary precondition that makes killing permissible. It essentially introduces "a break between what must live and what must die" (2003: 254). It articulates a *caesura* between worthy and unworthy life and resonates with the aforementioned formulations of contemporary thinkers insisting on the lethality rather than constructivist emphasis of racism predominating in the liberal academy.

Contemporary projects of existence exert pressure on those competing analytics of the subject and subjection. They demand an epistemic rupture, a reversal of the modes of subjection articulated by Foucault and his army of followers in his profound and influential "Subject and Power" (1982), which seem well-suited to more harmonious political moments, but not to moments rife with crisis, where hierarchies and inequalities break through normativities and the reckoning with the question challenges instrumentalist reckonings with violence. Just as the Black slave and white supremacist foundations of capitalism scandalize the all-too-orthodox projects of working-class unity found in certain readings of Antonio Gramsci,[35] Achille Mbembe's fierce engagement with Foucault's concept of biopower from the contemporary postcolony and his demand for an analytics of necropolitics provokes its own scandal. Mbembe is concerned with figures of sovereignty. Yet, the central project to his conceptualization is "the generalized instrumentalization of human existence and the material destruction of human bodies and populations." He presents a reading of politics as the work of death. Starting from Hegel's account of death, "the human being truly becomes a subject—that is, separated from the animal—in the struggle and the work through which he or she confronts death."[36] Necropolitics captures certain lives in dark realms of jeopardy that increasingly have become normalized in parts of Mexico, Latin America, Europe and its one-time colonies, and in the *dark* arenas of the United States and other parts of the globe. The ultimate expression of sovereignty is to have the power and capacity to dictate who may live and who may die; and biopower is the domain of life over which power has taken control. Mbembe's essay draws on the concept of biopower and explores its relation to notions of sovereignty and the "state of exception" in order to answer many questions about the politics of death. Mbembe is concerned with figures of sovereignty whose central project is "the generalized instrumentalization of human existence and the material destruction of human bodies and populations." The notion of necropolitics and necropower help account for the various ways in which, in our contemporary world, war machines and states of exception are deployed in the interest of maximum destruction of persons and the creation of death-worlds, new and unique forms of social existence in which vast populations are subjected to conditions of life conferring upon them the status of living dead.

Mbembe argues that biopolitics fails to explain how the threat of violence, bodily destruction, and death prevail as a technique of governance in many contemporary settings, challenging Foucault's reliance on Western European examples. The Cameroonian philosopher instead draws on examples from the more politically volatile states of the postcolonial Africa and the Near East. They provide insights through which we can understand politics as a form of war in which the sovereign emerges through the determination of who dies or who does not and, therefore, lives. The meaning of death in necropolitics emerges in interpretations of corpses, killers, and those subject to them.

My concept of necro-subjection extends this project. It refuses its analytical closures of it and related schools of thought, thus following calls to "theorize with horror."[37] To wrestle with the actual existing multiple orders of oppression infiltrating this different kind of subjection demands decentering the center. The demand, foisted upon me by those seeking asylum, is to center the margins and peripheries, as illustrated on those who live on the jagged, illegal margins of societies. While Foucault's insight into biopolitical power's management and production of life remains crucial, the right to decide life and death is never completely excised from certain kinds of sovereign power, be it authoritarian or liberal democratic, and its deep ties to empire. A politics of life must commit "the subjugation of life to the power of death" or it lends itself to a politics and an analysis of the privileged.[38]

Necro-subjection moves to the center of analysis the subject forged in discourses and related micro-political processes of a once-robust liberalism to one that is increasingly dystopic. It emerges when "the right to punish" shifts "from the vengeance of the sovereign to the defense of society."[39] It captures those subjects who regularly face the horror of death, of being made—or even more complexly, making themselves—dead in order to let live. From a hail of bullets raining down from drones high in the sky in the Mideast to the almost banal slaughter of youth in public schools in the United States, what were one time promises of liberal statehood now seem increasingly intertwined with its constitution as securing against terror but also generating it, amplifying contemporary government's deep linkages to slavery, racism, misogyny, and capital. These complexities demand a theoretical and political commitment, a refusal to treat such oppressions as ancillary or superstructural.[40]

Necropolitics bring the politics of life and death to an analysis of never-ending warfare, the uneven distribution of disease, and other forms of social and discursive exclusions in modernity. They frame certain lives in dark realms of jeopardy that have become increasingly normalized in parts of Mexico, in Latin America, in Europe and its onetime colonies, in the dark arenas of the United States and other parts of the globe. Private armies, so-called "war machines," states of exceptions and related phenomena perversely birth death-worlds in their carnage as is accounted for in notion of necropolitics and necropower. These are new and unique forms of social existence in which vast populations are subjected to conditions of life conferring upon them the status of living dead. Under terms of necropower, the lines between resistance and suicide, sacrifice and redemption, martyrdom and freedom are blurred.[41] The suicide bomber becomes recognized as a subject through her death, echoing "revolutionary suicide" in African American thought, and suggestive of the influence of the Black Panthers on Foucault's oeuvre.[42] Perhaps the multiple corpses both discovered and not in the killing deserts should be considered so.

Imperial sovereignty-making violence or necropolitics ricochets. It devastates. It multiplies. It proliferates.

Nevertheless, necropolitics understates concurrent everyday dispossessions or structural violence prefiguring these killer relations. Necro-subjection privileges these histories. Necro-subjection emphasizes at the level of the subject, those who are birthed in and experience killer politics, as well as their kin, such as in drug-war-governed frontier zones of Mexico and Central America, the afore-mentioned "killing deserts," Occupied Palestine, the Dakota pipeline and else-where in the occupied Americas, and related settler societies. Necro-subjection accounts for those subjectivities which societies must be defended against.

The concept also privileges the birth of subjectivities that push beyond these ends of life. The concept captures the restlessness of those who are dying to live, of those contending with brutal dispossession, of those challenging official and privatized hetero-masculine sovereigns, who dictate, subjugate, and exercise ty-rannical rule. Making dead to let live registers how the contemporary demands articulating a theory of the subject engulfed in an extraordinarily Other politics of death and life. It is not exceptions that become the rule, nor the naturaliza-tion of camp-like spaces of liberal democracies, but in the daily workings of state and the law as it recoils, reconstitutes, and readdresses itself across much of the globe in new seemingly always violent rule. The concept chases subjectivities along axes of Otherness, or more precisely racism and its intersecting exclusions but more pertinently in also the material, physical subjections—the subject ef-fects—of threats over life, including the horrendous regime of violence against women termed *femicidio* or femicide, mass graves, and mass disappearances. The concept demands a reckoning with the life at the margins, life subjected as illegal, criminal, queer, or life cast as too Black, too brown, too Native, too Muslim. Necro-subjection is not a liberal analytics of resilience, nor survival. It is the contemporary subjection of the Other, often individuated through vio-lence, ensnared in the death struggle of contemporary capital and the terrify-ing, often perverse, private and indirect government of difference. Making dead to let live, moreover, grapples with the rich interiorities of necropolitics. The concept crystallizes a thick dimension to questions of the Subject and Power,[43] the birth of subjectivities and affects wracked in actual and structural relations of violence, its psychic effects and the proliferation of involved affects.

The concept invites certain politically useful caveats regarding these opera-tions. Race and intersections still bear potential; they may remain affirmative social identities, a position that subaltern genealogies have long recognized, and point to its limitations of certain traditions that see race and racism only as negative trajectories. In this respect, necro-subjection in the case of immi-gration courts or undocumented border-crossings demands recognizing long-standing or contemporary practices of escape,[44] as disruptive or potentially constituent of new potentialities. It thus follows notions of refusal, refusing of life itself. Necro-subjection thus pushes at potentialities beyond longstanding binaries of resistance and accommodation, and which may or may not ulti-mately infiltrate larger assemblages of culture and politics,[45] those oppositional forces, affects, and practices found outside traditional notions of politics.

Necro-subjectivities haunt. They flag the anomic zones of death and life struggles. They materialize in popular culture if one looks awry. In the television series *Breaking Bad*, mindless, ruthless young men, almost always phenotypically brown, wander through Albuquerque, bent on revenge against Walter *White*. There are the zombies on dystopic TV shows, always mindless, inevitably brown. These "walkers" in the parlance of television and a term that appears increasingly in Latina/o studies flit across our screens to co-emerge with the anti-citizens of nowhere yet everywhere, immigrant others.[46] They are Joaquin Dead: grotesque, dismembering, savage embodiments of radical non-humanness, epochal floating signifiers that devour majoritarian flesh, perhaps the most fundamental of "our" resources. They flit across our screens to co-emerge with the anti-citizens of nowhere yet everywhere, the immigrant others, the homeless denizens, damned to near-death existence. These ravenous subhumans devour white majoritarian flesh, ripping it from bodies with their teeth. Yet, as with most zombie nightmares, they quickly become fodder for the larger-than-life struggles, grist for the all-too-human struggles among the non-zombie; the protagonists practice killing for a semblance of the way things once were. Zombie fantasies mark a return of sorts. They are mere background noise in the semi-privatized warfare, and feeding on other flesh in once-settled regions of the world.

A reckoning with the Joaquin Dead demands a return to those wretched borders of death and life evident in asylum or related immigration proceedings, or when Others must cross the international boundary irregularly. Those who embody the limits and pressures of expulsion all too often bring only the clothes on their back soiled from the toil. They who have cultivated the land, now are losing everything to the private and indirect narco-governors, only to face detention, deportation, and other punishment upon entering the United States. They speak nonstandard or better indigenously marked Spanish, if they speak the dominant language at all, as I sometimes must explain to the courts. They speak in short sentences. They evoke impoverishment, their need for work, unaware that everything they say can be used against them. They live a carceral regime of sovereignty beyond the walls of detention centers and prisons that bleed into daily life,[47] as well as borders. Such differences become instrumental both in their caging and in their lines of flight. What necro-subjection and its derivatives crystallize is the continuities between liberalism and totalitarianism. It is felt first among the marginals, the Black and brown, the queer, the gender-nonconforming and always Others. The promises of liberal citizenship and of modernities, already, always illusory for those on the margins, shatter into fragmented, jagged, piercing hierarchies. Resurgent totalitarianism in the Western democracies, evident in Brexit and among Trump and other rulers, so intimate to liberal democracies despite the insistence otherwise, manifests first in dealings with difference.

Necro-subjection and the Drug War as Settler Colonialism

Drug wars are Indian wars. They are *not wars against drugs*. They are struggles *for* massive profits, trade routes, political power, and ultimately territory.[48] United States' addiction to illicit drugs shoots capital southward. "The state," as the official crystallization of power relations and which remains central to lived experience that the analytic of governmentality apprehends, is inextricably linked to the cartels. States both express hegemony and crystallized power relations. Drug trafficking is lucrative. Profits from the industry are estimated to be between $30 billion and $60 billion per year, which means that drug money is competitive with oil as the greatest source of revenue for Mexico. The Mexican government, particularly its army and police, has facilitated the drug trade for decades and has participated in it extensively. Given the enormous profits that the Mexican state stands to make in the drug business, its counternarcotic efforts may not represent a sincere effort to quash the drug industry. Drug wars effectively revitalize colonialist, neocolonialist, or perhaps settlerist dispossession of Other land, Other labor power, and Other resources. Deep infrastructures of racial capitalism are reconstituted in drug wars.

Drug war refugees, those who abandon these regimes of dispossession, must make themselves dead in order to live. These and related contestations birth brutal private and indirect reprisals, and a simultaneous affirmation of liberal presuppositions about abominable, monstrous, foreign difference, which victims must be saved from, in the Global North. Such ideologies render the United States a beacon of multicultural acceptance, a haven, although one that is rapidly collapsing.

Private and indirect governance must, again, be situated in deeper processes, the slow-killing off of particular ways of life in Mexico and other parts of the globe, such as contemporary Puerto Rico. Mexico's necropolitical turn, for example, emerged from the nineteenth-century civil strife that engulfed the country after independence which resulted in decades of economic stagnation. It produced a state that was particularly vulnerable to corruption. Lomnitz argues that the results of these phenomena are historically vast amounts of petty corruption, a large informal economy, and a tax base that is extremely small (the Mexican state relies very heavily on revenues from Pemex to fund itself—this accounts for up to 30 percent of the federal budget). Lomnitz also holds U.S. drug and gun control policies accountable for much of the current chaos, which preys on Mexico's weak and corrupt system of law enforcement.[49]

These inheritances of socially and historically produced oppressions meld onto populations and bodies. They are all too often taken as natural, given, *the order* versus *an order of things*. According to a 2014 report by the Consejo Nacional de Evaluation de la Política de Desarrollo Social (COEVAL), some 53.3 million Mexicans live in poverty and 20 million cannot meet their basic needs. This number represents more than 50 percent of Mexicans. Those in the top 10 percent earn 27 times as much as those in the bottom 10 percent. In OCED countries the difference tends to be ten times as much. A 2013 study by the Hay Group found that the base salary of executives in Mexico City averaged $10,000 a month, $417 less than a comparable executive in New York City, whereas the minimum wage in New York was $7.25 per hour, compared to $5.05 per day in Mexico City. The typical Mexican CEO earns 121 times the minimum wage, which is the largest gap in Latin America. More troubling, these figures do not even capture the 29 million Mexicans (out of an economically active population of 52 million) who work in the informal sector. Productivity in Mexico has soared since the 1980s. Wages have stagnated. Wages and salaries as a portion of GDP has fallen from 40 percent to 18.9 percent since the 1980s, and the value of the minimum wage has fallen by 80 percent. Mean income in Mexico in 2010 in constant dollars was lower than it was in 1990. Furthermore, a recent report by the Centro de Estudios Espinosa Yglesias in Mexico City found that while there was considerable social mobility within the middle class, the poorest Mexicans experience remarkably little social mobility. Another 2013 World Bank report found that Mexico had one of the worst rates of upward social mobility in Latin America.

Phenotypically rich but resource-deprived people compose the vast army of underpaid workers in terms of income, education, and social standing, with domestic workers, manual laborers, drivers, security guards, in Mexico. They keep the bleached middle and upper classes afloat in Mexico. Those residing in indigenous communities live in the most abject poverty, followed by rural migrants to the cities, especially the poorest among them. The latter are indigenous in drag, impoverished in their spoken Spanish and dress. They suffer discrimination in the cities, and are unable to climb the social ladder. They hold jobs in the service sector, as street performers, sellers of chiclets and cigarettes, or beggars; their persistent poverty serves as an explanation for their poverty. They are poor because they are Indian or they are Indian because they are poor. They appear as simple people and speak different kinds of Spanish. They deserve their life.[50] Or there are those who embrace criminalized life, newfangled cholos, and their pursuit of their Others, onetime *chúntaros* or the indigenous in mestizo drag, a bleak iteration of Central American life flowing through Mexico.[51]

These histories of oppression are long in Mexico. They date back to a colonial period in which the caste system (the precursor to nineteenth-century scientific racism) determined that indigenous peoples would provide colonized laborers for the newly discovered regions of the globe. Though posited as a system intended to protect a Republic of Indians from voracious Spaniards, the caste system effectively functioned as a guarantor of agricultural and public labor during the colonial epoch. Impoverished, phenotypically rich bodies built the roads, the airports, the metro. Generations later, rural, richly colored Mexicans now constitute a central part of both the Mexican and the U.S. quasi-chattel labor force in agriculture, and in urban settings. They constitute the labor that maintains the homes of the middle class and the rich. They feed the urban populations. And they work in the fields, where some become subject to the machinations of privatized sovereignties.

Notably, in the asylum proceedings, necro-subjection underlines how contemporary subjection of the Other often occurs on an already slowly dying figure, one on its way to becoming skeletal, which experiences the spectacular terror of contemporary private and indirect—or public and direct—government. Attorneys and experts, perversely, must interrupt the commonsense of Mexicans as a labor migration. Paternal, racial liberalism demands violent, macabre, grossly civilizationist narratives, in the practice of immigration proceedings, which drug war settler colonialism reinstantiates and from which they flee, to interrupt it. Those seeking asylum must be made dead in order to live. They become necro-subjects.

Conclusion

To be a pessimist of the intellect, but perhaps not the will, is to recognize that those who make themselves dead in asylum proceedings or risk their lives in irregular border-crossings (or other deadly ways) experience the violent instantiation as the Other subject in order that they can live. Necro-subjection, that is, is not the imposition of false consciousness, or mystification of social relations. It is the material subjugation of certain lives, which are situated socially, materially, discursively, and ideologically closer and closer to death.

To become a subject in difference today all too often demands a reckoning with orders of violence that are intractable, normative, normalized. These regimes are inextricably tied to race, or more precisely racism(s), and intersecting exclusions, recognitions, and related dynamics. Necro-subjection conceptually traces these dynamics. The concept becomes evident in this essay in the near-death experiences of those vying to cross the southern border of the United States through the deserts. The concept further brings flesh to theory in immigration proceedings where practices of expert testimony, affidavit-writing, or other kinds of expert analysis on current questions of asylum from

Mexico and elsewhere in the globe must underscore the horrendous. Other life must be characterized as full of pain, despair, brutality, and violence—making people dead—so that they might be freed from detention, deportation, or banishment to crime ridden homelands—so that they might live—reaffirming paternal liberal social hegemonies.

This discordance reverberates in how Black lives can only be made to matter in the wake of police violence, and related banalities of evil that indigenous peoples, Black people, Muslims, immigrants and those frequently racialized as immigrants, among other exclusion that Others experience, are birthed into relations of normative liberal politics. It crystallizes how certain life must be represented as exposed, vulnerable, precarious, a characterization evident in much contemporary ethnography, which some have characterized as "dark."[52] Necrosubjection crystallizes how discourses about Mexican rapists and other bad hombres infiltrate immigration court, setting the stage for critical, strategic redeployments, subversions, betrayals, following a long line of *vendidas*, capturing instantiations that feed my insurgent optimism of the will.

Those who experience making dead to let live become life that moves through sewers, under borders, beyond the law. It is the subjection from war-torn homelands for hyper-ghettoes. Necro-subjects may utter and enact refusals that infiltrate larger assemblages of culture and politics, or as life that waits in the shadows and refuses the contemporary. Or, those that are dying to live may march in the streets of Chicago, Los Angeles, New York, or demand a new order of asylum in U.S. immigration courts.

The killer impulse of "imperial sovereignty" (to return to the words of Mbembe) rifles through the concept necro-subjection. To become a subject in difference today all too often demands a reckoning with orders of violence that are untraceable, normative, normalized. These regimes are inextricably tied to race, or more precisely racism(s), and its intersecting exclusions. Predatory capitalism and its intersecting exclusions haunt practices of expert testimony, affidavit-writing, or offering other kinds of expert analysis, on current questions of removal to Mexico and the Northern Triangle, and accompanying questions of asylum. To characterize Other life as full of pain, despair, brutality, and violence—making people dead—so that they might be freed from detention, deportation, or banishment to crime-ridden homelands—so that they might live—reaffirms social hegemonies. It also captures a new current of immigration to the United States from Mexico: refugees, those typically thought of as coming from other countries, who confront a deeply held commonsense in the law and civil society that Mexicans constitute a labor immigration.

Their lives and homelands must be represented as so full of despair, pain, and hopelessness, so mired in relations of precarity and dispossession, their governments so full of graft and corruption. Their representations affirm imperial racisms and liberal presumptions of the racial, cultural, and civilizational exceptionalism of the United States. They must make themselves—or they must be made—dead, as do many other immigrants who cross the U.S.-Mexico border without documentation, as well as many others across the globe.

NOTES

Reprinted with permission from Johns Hopkins University Press. This essay originally appeared in *Theory and Event* 22, no. 2 (2019): 303–24.

The intellectual imprint of my collaborators and accomplices cannot be lost in the development of these ideas and this essay. I appreciate the feedback of Marisol de la Cadena, following my plenary "Life against the Edge" that I gave at the *Society for Cultural Anthropology* meetings in 2014, from where these ideas first stirred. Versions of this paper were later given at the Center for the Study of North America at the Universidad Nacional Autónoma de México (UNAM) at the invitation of Ariadna Estéves, and as a keynote at the annual Latino Studies conference at Indiana University at the invitation of Sylvia Martinez. My frequent conversations with Korinta Maldonado, Ellen Moodie, Brenda Garcia, Emily Metzner, and others are also of note.

1 See Gilberto Rosas, *Barrio Libre: Criminalizing States and Delinquent Refusals of the New Frontier* (Durham: Duke University Press, 2012). It draws on Timothy J. Dunn, *The Militarization of the U.S.-Mexico Border, 1978–1992: Low-Intensity Conflict Doctrine Comes Home* (Austin, TX: Center for Mexican American Studies, 1996); Jonathan Xavier Inda, *Targeting Immigrants: Government, Technology, Ethics* (Malden, MA: Blackwell Publishing, 2006); Joseph Nevins, *Operation Gatekeeper: The Rise of the "Illegal Alien" and the Making of the U.S.-Mexico Boundary* (New York: Routledge, 2002).

2 Gilberto Rosas, "Cholos, Chúntaros, and the 'Criminal' Abandonments of the New Frontier," *Identities* 17, no. 6 (December 15, 2010): 695–713.

3 Amy Sara Carroll, *The Desert Survival Series* (University of Michigan Digital Environments Cluster Series, 2014).

4 See Américo Paredes, *With His Pistol in His Hand: A Border Ballad & Its Hero* (Austin: University of Texas Press, 1971); Alejandro Lugo, *Fragmented Lives, Assembled Parts: Culture, Capitalism, and Conquest at the US-Mexico Border* (Austin: University of Texas Press, 2008).

5 Rosas, *Barrio Libre*.

6 Jason De León, *The Land of Open Graves: Living and Dying on the Migrant Trail* (Berkeley: University of California Press, 2015).

7 Rosas, *Barrio Libre*.

8 Gilberto Rosas, "The Thickening Borderlands: Bastard Mestiz@s, 'Illegal' Possibilities, and Globalizing Migrant Life," in *Critical Ethnic Studies: A Reader*, ed. Nada Elia et al. (Durham: Duke University Press, 2016), 344–59; Gilberto Rosas, "The Thickening Borderlands: Diffused Exceptionality and 'Immigrant' Social Struggles during the 'War on Terror,'" *Cultural Dynamics* 18, no. 3 (2006): 335–49; J. Inda, "Borderzones of Enforcement: Criminalization, Workplace Raids, and Migrant Counterconducts," in V. Squire, ed., *The Contested Politics of Mobility: Borderzones and Irregularity* (New York: Routledge Taylor & Francis Group, 2011), 74–91.

9   See Nicholas De Genova, "The Legal Production of Mexican/Migrant 'Illegality,'" *Latino Studies* 2, no. 2 (January 1, 2004): 160–85; Rachel Ida Buff, *Against the Deportation Terror, Organizing for Immigrant Rights in the Twentieth Century* (Philadelphia: Temple University Press, 2017).

10   Charles Hale, "What Is Activist Research?" *Items and Issues: Social Science Research Council* 2, no. 1–2 (January 1, 2001): 13–15.

11   Naomi Murakawa, *The First Civil Right: How Liberals Built Prison America* (Oxford: Oxford University Press, 2014).

12   Charles W. Mills, "Racial Liberalism," *PMLA*, 2008, http://www.mlajournals.org /doi/abs/10.1632/pmla.2008.123.5.1380.

13   See Lourdes Gutiérrez Nájera and Korinta Maldonado, "Transnational Settler Colonial Formations and Global Capital: A Consideration of Indigenous Mexican Migrants," *American Quarterly* 69, no. 4 (2017): 809–21; Jodi A. Byrd, *The Transit of Empire: Indigenous Critiques of Colonialism* (Minneapolis: University of Minnesota Press, 2011); S. L. Morgensen, "The Biopolitics of Settler Colonialism: Right Here, Right Now," *Settler Colonial Studies*, 2011, https://www.tandfonline.com/doi/abs/10 .1080/2201473X.2011.10648801.

14   See Gilbert G. Gonzalez and Raul A. Fernandez, *A Century of Chicano History: Empire, Nations, and Migration* (New York: Routledge, 2003).

15   Zygmunt Bauman, *Globalization: The Human Consequences* (New York: Columbia University Press, 1998); Sylvia Wynter, "Unsettling the Coloniality of Being/ Power/Truth/Freedom: Towards the Human, After Man, Its Overrepresentation—An Argument," *CR: The New Centennial Review* 3, no. 3 (2003): 257–337.

16   Franz Fanon, *The Wretched of the Earth* (New York: Grove Press, 2004); Aníbal Quijano, "¡Qué Tal Raza!," 1999, http://repositorio.flacsoandes.edu.ec/handle/10469/5724.

17   Lauren Berlant, "Slow Death (Obesity, Sovereignty, Lateral Agency)," in *Cruel Optimism* (Durham, NC: Duke University Press, 2011), 95–119.

18   I made a conscious political choice in my witnessing to break with protocol. As an expert witness, we are not supposed to discuss the specifics of cases. I've made a point of negotiating with immigration attorneys and their clients. I explain that I want to document what is occurring in my capacity serving as an expert witness, when I am asked to serve. To write about these occurrences and to draw on the respondent's stories is to commit a kind of betrayal. Ethnography, if one follows certain feminist directions in the discipline, must betray. See, for example, Patricia Zavella, "Feminist Insider Dilemmas: Constructing Ethnic Identity with Chicana Informants," in *Feminist Dilemmas in Fieldwork* (New York: Routledge, 2018), 138–59; and Kamala Visweswaran, *Fictions of Feminist Ethnography* (Minneapolis: University of Minnesota Press, 1994).

19   Patrick Wolfe, "Settler Colonialism and the Elimination of the Native," *Journal of Genocide Research* 8, no. 4 (January 1, 2006): 387–409.

20   I discussed the practices of testimony in immigration proceedings as one example of fugitive work in "Fugitive Work: On the Criminal Possibilities of Anthropology," https://culanth.org/fieldsights/1529-fugitive-work-on-the-criminal -possibilities-of-anthropology. Indeed, Berry, Chavez Arguelles, Cordis, Ihmoud, and Velasquez Estrada hold that a decolonizing and what they call "fugitive

anthropology" likely demands breaking with their "intellectual home." See Berry, Maya J., Claudia Chávez Argüelles, Shanya Cordis, Sarah Ihmoud, and Elizabeth Velásquez Estrada, "Toward a Fugitive Anthropology: Gender, Race, and Violence in the Field." Accessed August 15, 2018. https://www.academia.edu/35197382 /TOWARD_A_FUGITIVE_ANTHROPOLOGY_Gender_Race_and_Violence_in _the_Field.

21 See Achille Mbembe, "The Idea of a Borderless World," *Africasacountry.com*. Accessed November 21, 2018. https://africasacountry.com/2018/11/the-idea-of-a -borderless-world?fbclid=IwARocyScyyMMPqSMSSqMLdoyaVJmV17UiBhTQUP MGdoBGYt9X-ocmFKNMLGQ.

22 See Achille Mbembe, *On the Postcolony (Studies on the History of Society and Culture)*, 1st edition (Berkeley: University of California Press, 2003).

23 A. Naomi Paik, *Rightlessness: Testimony and Redress in U.S. Prison Camps Since World War II* (Chapel Hill: University of North Carolina Press, 2016).

24 In "Fatal Couplings of Power and Difference: Notes on Racism and Geography," *The Professional Geographer: Journal of the Association of American Geographers* 54, no. 1 (January 1, 2002): 15–24, Ruth Wilson Gilmore holds that racism constitutes politically organized premature death.

25 See José E. Limón, "Carne, Carnales, and the Carnivalesque," in *Dancing with the Devil: Society and Cultural Poetics in Mexican-American South Texas* (Madison: University of Wisconsin Press, 1994); Achille Mbembe, "The Banality of Power and the Aesthetics of Vulgarity in the Postcolony," *Public Culture* 4, no. 2 (January 1, 1992): 1–30.

26 Sayak Valencia Triana, "Capitalismo Gore: Narcomáquina Y Performance de Género," *Revista E-Misférica. Instituto de Performance Y Política* 8, no. 2 (January 1, 2011).

27 Jenna M. Loyd and Alison Mountz, *Boats, Borders, and Bases: Race, the Cold War, and the Rise of Immigration Detention in the United States* (Berkeley: University of California Press, 2018).

28 Oswaldo Zavala, *Los cárteles no existen: Narcotráfico y cultura en México* (Malpaso Ediciones SL, 2018); Melissa W. Wright, "Epistemological Ignorances and Fighting for the Disappeared: Lessons from Mexico," *Antipode* 49, no. 1 (May 16, 2016): 249–69.

29 Paul Farmer, "An Anthropology of Structural Violence," *By The Wenner-Gren Foundation for Anthropological Research* (2004): 3204.

30 See John K. Simon, "Michel Foucault on Attica: An Interview," *Telos* 19, no. 154–61 (January 1, 1974), in which Foucault holds that crime is "a coup d'état from below."

31 Paige West, *Dispossession and the Environment: Rhetoric and Inequality in Papua New Guinea* (New York: Columbia University Press, 2016); Rosa Luxemburg, *The Accumulation of Capital* (New York: Routledge, 2003).

32 Karl Marx, *Capital: A Critique of Political Economy, 3 Vols.* (Penguin Classics, n.d.); Carlos Fazio, *Estado de Emergencia, De La Guerra de Calderón a La Guerra de Peña Nieto* (Mexico City: Grijalbo, 2016).

33 Michel Foucault, *Society Must Be Defended: Lectures at the Collège de France, 1975–76*, ed. M. Bertani et al., vol. 1 (New York: Picador USA, 2003).

34 See Gilmore, "Fatal Couplings of Power and Difference."

35 Frank Wilderson, "Gramsci's Black Marx: Whither the Slave in Society?" *Social Identities* 9 (January 1, 2003): 1–17.

36 Achille Mbembe, "Necropolitics," *Public Culture* 15, no. 1 (January 1, 2003): 11–40.

37 François Debrix, *Global Powers of Horror: Security, Politics, and the Body in Pieces* (New York: Routledge, 2016), 6.

38 Mbembe, "Necropolitics," 39.

39 Michel Foucault, *Discipline and Punish: The Birth of the Prison* (New York: Vintage Books, 1979), 90.

40 See Cedric Robinson, "Racial Capitalism" in *Black Marxism: The Making of the Black Radical Tradition* (Chapel Hill: University of North Carolina Press, 1983), 9–28.

41 Mbembe, "Necropolitics," 40.

42 See Huey P. Newton, Eldridge Cleaver, and Black Panthers, "The Genius of Huey P. Newton" (San Francisco: Black Panther Party, Ministry of Information, January 1, 1970), https://www.freedomarchives.org/Documents/Finder/Black%20 Liberation%20Disk/Black%20Power!/SugahData/Books/Newton.S.pdf; Brady Thomas Heiner, "Foucault and the Black Panthers."

43 See Michel Foucault, "The Subject and Power," in *Michel Foucault, beyond Structuralism and Hermeneutics.*, ed. H. Dreyfus and Paul Rabinow, vol. 2 (Chicago: University of Chicago Press, 1982), 208–26.

44 See Kamala Visweswaran, *Un/common Cultures: Racism and the Rearticulation of Cultural Difference* (Durham, NC: Duke University Press, 2010); Silvia Federici, *Caliban and the Witch* (New York: Autonomedia, 2004).

45 For literature on refusal and related concepts, see Audra Simpson, *Mohawk Interruptus: Political Life across the Borders of Settler States* (Durham, NC: Duke University Press, 2014); Cathy Cohen, "Deviance as Resistance: A New Research Agenda for the Study of Black Politics," *Du Bois Review: Social Science Research on Race* 1, no. 1 (January 1, 2004): 27–45.

46 See Sujey Vega, *Latino Heartland: Of Borders and Belonging in the Midwest* (New York: New York University Press, 2015).

47 See Martha Balaguera, "Trans-Migrations: Agency and Confinement at the Limits of Sovereignty," *Signs: Journal of Women in Culture and Society* 43, no. 3 (2018): 641–64.

48 Curtis Marez, *Drug Wars: The Political Economy of Narcotics* (Minneapolis: University of Minnesota Press, 2004).

49 Claudio Lomnitz-Adler, *Deep Mexico, Silent Mexico: An Anthropology of Nationalism*, Public Worlds, vol. 9 (Minneapolis: University of Minnesota Press, 2001).

50 Alexander Dawson, "Politicians, Narcos, Missing Students, and Mexico's Crisis (SWP 47)," 2015.

51 See Rosas, *Barrio Libre*.

52 Sherry B. Ortner, "Dark Anthropology and Its Others: Theory since the Eighties," *HAU: Journal of Ethnographic Theory* 6, no. 1 (July 16, 2016): 47–73.

Reimagining Culture and Power against Late Industrial Capitalism and Other Forms of Conquest through Border Theory and Analysis

ALEJANDRO LUGO

border n. 1: an outer part or edge 2: BOUNDARY, FRONTIER . . .
4: an ornamental design at the edge of a fabric or rug
syn BORDER, MARGIN, VERGE, EDGE, RIM, BRIM, BRINK
borderland n. 1 a: territory at or near a border: FRONTIER
b: an outlying region
borderline n.: line of demarcation
bordure n.: border surrounding a heraldic shield
—WEBSTER'S NEW COLLEGIATE DICTIONARY

Ania Loomba: Now some people have offered a critique of Subaltern Studies saying that if you try and combine Foucault and Gramsci, it's like trying to ride two horses at the same time. And Gyan Prakash answers by saying then we all need to become stunt riders! . . . I wanted to ask you to comment in a little more detail on what you think is the potential of such combinations. Is this a productive tension at all between Foucault and Gramsci?

Edward Said: Extremely productive . . . the attempt to bring the two together involves in a certain sense breaking up the Foucauldian narrative into a series of smaller situations where Gramsci's terminology can become useful and illuminating for analytical purposes.—EDWARD SAID, "IN CONVERSATION WITH NEELADRI BHATTACHARYA, SUVIR KAUL, AND ANIA LOOMBA"

Introduction: The Borders of Border Theory

If we wanted to carry out an archaeology of border theory, how would we identify its sources and its targets?[1] Where would we locate its multiple sites of production and consumption, formation and transformation? What are the multiple discourses producing images of borders almost everywhere, at least in the minds of academics? In trying to answer these questions, though more with an exploratory spirit than with a definitive one, let us say that the sites, the sources, the targets, and the discourses can be variably characterized by the following: previously marginalized intellectuals within the academy (i.e., women and other minorities); the outer limits of the nation-state (i.e., the U.S.-Mexico border region); the frontiers of culture theory (i.e., cultural borderlands compared with cultural patterns); the multiple fronts of struggle in Cultural Studies (i.e., the war of position); the cutting edge of theories of difference (i.e., race, class, gender, and sexual orientation); and, finally, the crossroads of history, literature, anthropology, and sociology (i.e., Cultural Studies).

In this essay, I argue that to understand its political and practical importance, we must reimagine border theorizing (one that articulates to culture, capitalism, and conquest) in the realm of the inescapable, mountainous terrains of power (Derrida 1978; Foucault 1978) as the latter has operated through the expansion of Western empires since 1492, and as it has overlapped in the academy, in culture theory, in the global contexts of late industrial capitalism, and, in the last analysis (and perhaps most important), in the realms of the changing "nation" (Anderson 1991) and "state" (Hall 1986)[2]—under which current transnational academic practices continue to be enacted.

This privileging of the "nation-state" on my part relates to a current theoretical and political concern that has practical implications for the opening of more inclusive spaces under globalization, especially for the twenty-first century; for *the deterritorialization (and reterritorialization)* of the nation, politics, culture, and border theory; and, finally, for human agency (Martín-Rodríguez 1996; Morales 1996; Ong 1995). For Alejandro Morales, "Michel Foucault's concept of heterotopia explains border culture," and "life in the chaos of heterotopia is a perpetual act of self-definition gradually deterritorializing the individual" (1996, 23, 24). Regarding feminist practice in the global setting, Aihwa Ong argues that "diasporic feminists (and we should all be somewhat mobile to be vigilant) should develop a denationalized and deterritorialized set of cultural practices. These would have to deal with the tough questions of gender oppression not only in that 'other place' . . . but also in one's own family, community, culture, religion, race, and nation" (1995, 367). Finally, just as Manuel Martín-Rodríguez, following Deleuze and Guattari, argues that a "minor language" can erode a "major language from within," I argue that the border region, as well as border theory and analysis, can erode the hegemony of the privileged center by denationalizing and deterritorializing the nation-state and culture theory, respectively: "In other words, minor languages erode, as it were, a major language from within, deterritorializing it, breaking up its system's supposed homogeneity" (Martín-Rodríguez 1996, 86)—without uncritically reterritorializing it.[3]

Much more specifically, my analytical framework in this chapter is the following: I draw the contours of two theoretical parallelisms, both constituted by seemingly disconnected conceptual preoccupations. On the one hand, there is the critical articulation between Gramsci's notion of the *state and its dispersal* and Foucault's notion of *power and its deployment*;[4] on the other, we have Anderson's critique of the nation and R. Rosaldo's critique of culture in anthropology. I am particularly interested in Gramsci's uses of the terms "state," "force relations," and "war of position" and how they might relate to Foucault's "relations of force" and his faith in "the strategical model rather than the model based on law," as well as his strategic belief that "politics is *war* pursued by other means" (Foucault 1978, 93; emphasis added). I argue here that these connections of resistance against folk notions of the "head of the king [and] the spell of monarchy" (Foucault 1978, 88–89), that is, "the state/the law,"[5] are quite telling in themselves about the ways in which we have come to think about social life and culture inside and outside anthropology, which is my interest here. These critiques call for multiple discourses, wars of position, situated knowledges, positioned subjects, and different arenas of contestation in everyday life. Thus, the analysis presented here should help explain not only the recent production of theories of borders in resistance to our Westernized imagination but also how the latter system of domination is traced back to the sixteenth and seventeenth centuries. I strategically examine this complex sociohistorical articulation between border theory and the West, within anthropology, by juxtaposing Anderson's critique of the nation as an imagined community with Rosaldo's critique of culture as shared patterns of behavior.

By reflecting on these parallelisms—that between Gramsci's notion of the state and Foucault's notion of power (both being *dispersed* entities) and between Anderson's notion of the imagined community and R. Rosaldo's cultural patterns (both being *homogeneous* entities)—I hope to show how border theory at the turn of the twenty-first century in anthropology (i.e., R. Rosaldo's "cultural borderlands") cannot be properly understood without situating it in relation to changing discourses about the state (both colonial and modern), the nation, and culture in the nineteenth and twentieth centuries, at least as these imagined categories and periodizations are examined in the works of R. Rosaldo (*Culture and Truth*, 1993), Anderson (*Imagined Communities*, 1991), Foucault (*The History of Sexuality*, Vol. 1, 1978), and Hall ("Gramsci's Relevance for the Study of Race and Ethnicity," 1986), as well as throughout this book.[6]

By locating border theory at the crossroads of culture theory in anthropology, and at the crossroads of ideologies of the state and the nation, which in turn produced "anthropologies" that represented national hegemonic traditions (American, British, and French), I hope to show the political and epistemological limits under which we teach, write, do research, and theorize. One of my main arguments here is that border theory itself can contribute effectively to the exploration of these limits, as long as it is recognized to be (as theories of social life tend to be) a product of the codification of a "multiplicity of force relations . . . which by virtue of their inequalities, constantly engender states of power" (Foucault 1978, 93).[7]

The Current State of Culture: Cultural Borderlands vis-à-vis Cultural Patterns

Cultural borderlands should be understood, first of all, in relation to the previous dominant discourse about culture: cultural patterns. Renato Rosaldo has been very precise about the limitations of what he calls the "classic vision of unique cultural patterns":

> It emphasizes shared patterns at the expense of processes of change and internal inconsistencies, conflicts, and contradictions. By defining culture as a set of shared meanings, classic norms of analysis make it difficult to study zones of difference within and between cultures. From the classic perspective, cultural borderlands appear to be annoying exceptions rather than central areas of inquiry. (1993, 28)

Although I agree with R. Rosaldo's critical assessment of the social and political implications of the ideology of "cultural patterns," my vision of the way those cultural patterns have been created in the theoretical imagination of classic anthropologists is a bit different. In fact, the historical process through which we have come to theorize and think about culture, society, cultural patterns, and borderlands should be reconsidered if we want, as Foucault argued, "to cut off the head of the king" (1978, 88).

I propose here that the attempt to decipher the complex relation between structure and practice was and has been a dominant thinking channel or tool through which the concept of culture has been imagined, though more implicitly than explicitly. Let us see how the latter contention is manifested in the writings of some of anthropology's major and recent practitioners. By considering the sociopolitical and historical context in which anthropologists wrote, I hope to shed some light on why, after all, a discourse on culture and society emerged, especially in the context of capitalism and imperialism. The following discussion will eventually bring us back to an analysis of the role of the state, the law, and the nation in shaping our formulations of the concept of culture and of social life in general.

Marshall Sahlins has explicitly associated the concept of culture with a double existence: "In the dialectic of culture-as-constituted and culture-as-lived we . . . discover some possibility of reconciling the most profound antimony of social science theory, that between structure and practice: reconciling them, that is, in the only way presently justifiable—as a symbolic process" (1982, 48). Regarding "society," however, Sherry Ortner has also identified a dialectical polarity in what she calls "practice theory," which constitutes the attempt to understand "how society and culture themselves are produced and reproduced through *human intention and action*" (1984, 158; emphasis added). In 1984, Ortner argued that "the modern versions of practice theory . . . appear unique in . . . that society is a system, that the system is powerfully constraining, and yet that the system can be made and unmade through human action and interaction" (1984, 159). Ortner's similar treatment of both "society" and "culture" is less conspicuous, for our purpose here, than the way she imagines these theoretical constructs through pervasive critical dualisms: system and action, human intention and action. Sahlins's imaginings about culture, as lived and as constituted, also reproduce the pattern I am exposing here: the double existence of culture.[8]

Sahlins subjects this dialectic in culture to his "structure and history" approach (1981, 1982, 1985; see also R. Rosaldo 1980), whereas Ortner associates the dialectic in society with a general theory of "practice" (1984). Ortner in fact argues that this focus on "practice" emerged in the early 1970s as a result of such historical conjunctures as the New Left movement; she also suggests that "practice theory" became articulated in American anthropology when Bourdieu's *Outline of a Theory of Practice* was translated into English in 1977 (Ortner 1984).[9]

In what follows, I suggest that the dominant anthropological notion of culture is one that is constituted by the articulation of beliefs and action, structure and practice, culture as constituted and culture as lived, and/or system and action, and that it is the historical product of a specific "academic" response to the political relation between the state/the nation and its citizens—a relationship that can be traced to the nineteenth century. In fact, these larger sociohistorical forces became crystallized in Western academia through Durkheim's ([1893] 1933, [1912] 1965) own peculiar invention of "society" and through the German/American production of "culture" in Boasian anthropology.

Culture and the State

Before the late 1960s, certain socioeconomic and political events of the Victorian era contributed to the continued suppression of the explicit treatment of the structure/practice relation embedded in the concepts of "culture" and "society": to talk about human practice or praxis was to talk about history, conflict, change, and social transformation—theoretical concepts that could easily expose the colonial and capitalist encounters/enterprises of the nineteenth century and the first half of the twentieth century. Thus, until the early 1970s, the discourse on culture and society in the social sciences, and especially in anthropology, was dominated by the systematic analysis of the coordination of such dualisms as the individual and society, the individual and culture—ignoring the realities of "practice" (for examples of this pattern, see Barth 1966; Benedict 1934; Durkheim [1893] 1933, [1912] 1965; Malinowski 1944; Radcliffe-Brown 1952).

Consequently, due to the political suppression of conceptual binaries that included "practice" (praxis), the notions of "society" and "culture" were to be discussed in terms of "order," "harmony," "rules" (Durkheim [1893] 1933, [1912] 1965), "shared patterns of beliefs" (Benedict 1934; Boas 1963), and an antichaotic condition (Weber 1977). Political scientist Perry Anderson has appropriately noted that the work of Emile Durkheim, like that of Max Weber and Vilfredo Pareto, was haunted by "a profound fear of the masses and premonition of social disintegration" (1968, 4). He claims quite explicitly that sociology at the turn of the twentieth century "emerged as a bourgeois counter-reaction to Marxism," which, of course, was arguing at the time that class conflict was inevitable. It must be noted, however, that Durkheim was as much against the greedy capitalist on the loose at the time as against the "immorality" of the masses. Both of these threats confirmed for him, as an employee of the French state, the need for rules to monitor and control both the working classes and the utilitarian entrepreneur.

The intensification of class conflict had emerged as a product of industrial capitalism within the "West"; additionally, broader sociopolitical tensions were generated as a result of the retraction of some European colonialisms due to the nineteenth-century nationalist movements in Spanish America and Central

Europe. The expansion of U.S. colonialism at the turn of the twentieth century into the Philippines and Puerto Rico, for instance, also contributed to a generalized problem of the body politic within and outside the West (see B. Anderson 1991; Flores 1993; Foucault 1978; Hall 1986). Foucault[10] and Stuart Hall treat 1870 as a key historical moment regarding, respectively, the production of new sexualities and the expansion of the new imperialist colonialisms. According to Gramsci and Hall, this period in the latter part of the nineteenth century constitutes a historical transition in the nature of the "State" from a monarchical, dynastic body politic and its subjects to a "State" (read: nation/nation-state) in which the subjects become citizens, and thus, become loosely tied to the direct control of a centralized, lawlike apparatus; in this new political regime, individuals are indirectly monitored through the state's *dispersal of power* (Foucault 1978; Hall 1986). This process must be properly explained in the historical and geographic contexts of each newly emerging nation around the world.[11]

Stuart Hall describes Gramsci's vision of this critical transformation in Western history in this way:

> Gramsci bases this "transition from one form of politics to another" historically. It takes place in "the West" after 1870, and is identified with "the colonial expansion of Europe," the emergence of modern mass democracy, a complexification in the role and organization of the state and an unprecedented elaboration in the structures and processes of "civil hegemony." What Gramsci is pointing to, here, is partly the diversification of social antagonisms, the "dispersal" of power, which occurs in societies where hegemony is sustained, not exclusively through the enforced instrumentality of the state, but rather, it is grounded in the relations and institutions of civil society [schooling, the family, the factory, churches and religious life, and so on]. (1986, 18)

In addition to these institutions of civil society, Foucault adds "a multiplicity of discourses produced by a whole series of mechanisms operating in different institutions . . . demography, biology, medicine, psychiatry, psychology, ethics, pedagogy, and political criticism" (1978, 33). Regarding their dispersal, Foucault explicitly and forcefully noted, "So it is not simply in terms of a continual extension that we must speak of this discursive growth; it should be seen rather as a dispersion of centers from which discourses emanated, a diversification of their forms, and the complex deployment of the network connecting them" (1978, 34).

Weber (1958) documented the bureaucratization of modern institutions around the same time, after 1870 and into World War I. The "war of position" necessary for effective political resistance against the dispersal of power, and characterizing the new state of the "state," is powerfully stated in military terms:

> The "war of position" . . . has to be conducted in a protracted way, across many different and varying fronts of struggle. . . . What really counts in a war of position is not the enemy's "forward trenches" (to continue the military metaphor) but "the whole organizational and industrial system of the territory which lies to the rear of the army in the field"—that is, the whole structure of society, including the structures and institutions of civil society. (Hall 1986, 17, paraphrasing Gramsci)

Today's realization of the transformation of the nature of the cultural (from homogeneity to heterogeneity) as manifested by both "Cultural Studies" and the postmodern preoccupation with "dispersal," has clearly influenced Renato Rosaldo's redefinition of "culture" in terms of "borderlands," fragmentation, and contestation (as opposed to the exclusivity of shareability, coherence, and uniformity). It is necessary to quote Rosaldo at length from his book *Culture and Truth* (1993):

> The fiction of the uniformly shared culture increasingly seems more ten-uous than useful. Although most metropolitan typifications continue to suppress border zones, human cultures are neither necessarily coherent nor always homogeneous. More often than we usually care to think, our everyday lives are crisscrossed by border zones, pockets and erup-tions of all kinds. Social borders frequently become salient around such lines as sexual orientation, gender, class, race, ethnicity, nationality, age, politics, dress, food, or taste. Along with "our" supposedly transparent cultural selves, such borderlands should be regarded not as analytically empty transitional zones but as sites of creative cultural production that require investigation. (207–8)

In the past, from the moment Marxism became a threat to the late nineteenth-century European order, Marx and his followers were not only negatively sanc-tioned (suppressed) in major sociological and anthropological circles, but "met-ropolitan typifications" of culture and society (i.e., Durkheimian and Weberian traditions) quite willingly continued "to suppress" any alternative means of studying and analyzing social life in its entirety, that is, in a manner that such phenomena as disorder, chaos, fragmentation, contestation, resistance, and "the border zones" could be rigorously scrutinized. The notion of "cultural border-lands" is also closely associated with social identities or cultural diversity—that is, age, gender, class, ethnicity. However, for purposes of explaining what Ortner calls "human intention and action" or what Sahlins denotes as "structure and practice," Renato Rosaldo still depends on the dual aspect of social life (structure and agency) that, I have argued, has characterized our imaginings about both culture and society.

For example, in his examination of recent ethnographic experiments and in the new social analysis that he proposed, Rosaldo noted:

> Modes of composition have changed because the discipline's research agenda has shifted from the search for structures to theories of practice that explore the interplay of both structure *and* agency. In such endeavors, knowledge and power are intertwined because the observer's point of view always influences the observation she makes. Rather than stressing timeless universals and the sameness of human nature, this perspective emphasizes human diversity, historical change, and political struggle. (1993, xvii–xviii; italics in original)[12]

Thus, if the initial understanding of the "state" was complicit with rules, laws, and order, which must be followed or obeyed by its citizens or subjects, Victorian anthropologists (British, American, and French) quite willingly, with the same juridical attitude and "morality," traveled to other "non-Western" societies uncritically searching for the rules, traditions, orders, and coherent social systems to which human subjects (or informants, in the anthropologists' case) must accommodate and adhere. By "uncritical," I mean that these early twentieth-century scholars did not necessarily articulate in their writings the politics of the state over the production of social science itself. It is also true, however, that the dominant discourse on "law and society" had a key humanitarian angle that was used against an earlier vision of "natives" as lacking law and therefore having no rights to life and property.

Nonetheless, the Victorian focus on morality, order, and the state, with its many angles, dominated the anthropology practiced until the early 1970s, when the civil rights, New Left, and feminist movements and the decolonization of previously colonized "nations" disinterred Marxism (or Gramscian Marxism in England) from the academic cemetery deliberately constructed by "metropolitan scholars" (see R. Rosaldo 1993, chap. 1). Now that we recognize that "modern societies" constitute "arenas" of different social contestations, are we looking for similar contestations, fragmentations, dispersals, disorders, and chaos in "other"[13] societies, just as our ancestors looked for order, shared patterns, and coherent systems here and elsewhere?

Perhaps what is of major importance here is that our metaphors of social life have also been transformed along with our notions of culture, society, and the state. There has been a very persuasive replacement, not only displacement, of a metaphoric trope: the biological organism, which was supposed to maintain itself in equilibrium through systemic (political) order and (social) harmony, has been decidedly supplanted by the "war" metaphor, which sheds light on how "society" and "culture" constitute hegemonic battlefields where contestation itself (instead of reciprocity) is inescapably pervasive. As Foucault suggestively questions, "Should . . . we say politics is *war* pursued by other means?" (1978, 93; my emphasis).[14]

Although Gramsci's work on the state and culture was "rediscovered" in England as late as the 1950s and 1960s as a result of the sociopolitical movements of Birmingham, England (see Raymond Williams's *Politics and Letters*, 1979), through Gramscian "Cultural Studies" in American academia, the state has come to be imagined vis-à-vis its dispersal of power within "civil society" by being deployed on a battlefield of multiple social relations. Since the mid-1980s, through the critiques of such scholars as Renato Rosaldo, Donna Haraway (1986), and James Clifford (1986), American anthropologists began rigorous (re)search on the deployment, dispersal, and, ergo, fragmentation of society and culture, where identities and experiences are constantly being contested in specific sites or localized centers of power, such as the factory, the cafeteria, the city streets, and the buses.[15]

Nonetheless, despite the influence of cultural Marxism, the notion of culture being used in Cultural Studies has a strong connection to the culture concept constituted by "structure and practice," and that has characterized the academic imagination about the social and the cultural. Paul Willis, in his classic *Learning to Labor*, stated the following with regard to his use of the "cultural": "I view the cultural, not simply as a set of transferred internal *structures* (as in the notion of socialisation) nor as the passive result of the action of dominant ideology downwards (as in certain kinds of marxism) but at least in part as the product of collective human *praxis*" (1977, 3; my emphasis; note the inevitable duality structure/praxis). Following Gramsci, Hall presents the following definition of culture:

> [One might note the centrality which Gramsci's analysis always gives to the cultural factor in social development.] *By culture, here, I mean the actual, grounded terrain of practices, representations, languages and customs of any specific historical society. . . . I would also include that whole distinctive range of questions which Gramsci lumped together under the title,* the "*national popular*." . . . They are a key stake as objects of political and *ideological* struggle and *practice*. (1986, 26; my emphasis, but original italics on "national popular")

The dual aspect (ideology/practices, structure/praxis) associated with a general definition of culture, although not central, is self-evident. Along with this implicit double existence, in the last two decades, we have simultaneously treated, much more explicitly, culture as an arena of different social contestations. James Clifford notes, "Culture, and our views of it, are [sic] produced historically, and are actively contested" (1986, 18). He adds, "Culture is contested, temporal and emergent" (1986, 19). Its temporality, its instability, its contingency, and thus its fragmentation all give form to the theory of borderlands that R. Rosaldo (1993) and Anzaldúa (1987) call for in and outside social analysis.

Yet to limit the concept of culture to "contestations" while not recognizing its double life (as we tend to do regarding new theories of borders, culture, and social life) is to confuse culture with Gramsci's notion of the "State" in "modern societies." As Stuart Hall correctly argues about Gramsci:

> Gramsci elaborates his new conception of the state . . . it becomes, not a thing to be seized, overthrown or *smashed* with a single blow, but a complex formation in modern societies *which must become the focus of a number of different strategies and struggles because it is an arena of different social contestations.* (1986, 19; my emphasis, but original italics on "smashed")

In fact, I must emphasize that Gramsci associated culture not only with practices and representations but also with the "national popular." Why are culture and the idea of nation or nationalism so closely interrelated by Gramsci?

Culture and the Nation: Imagined Communities

At the turn of the twenty-first century, both culture and the state are perceived to be dispersed as well as consolidated or centralized. Yet some of us have privileged, in the last two decades of the twentieth century and even today, the dispersed and the fragmented. How were nationalism, the state, the nation, and culture perceived in the nineteenth century? In its classic mode (as Renato Rosaldo so eloquently reminded us and Chagnon's *Yanomamo* confirmed), culture was imagined, almost exclusively, to be shared, patterned, and homogenous. So, in a similar way, throughout the nineteenth century and the first half of the twentieth century, the nation, according to Benedict Anderson, came to be imagined in homogenous time, and as an imagined community: "The nation is always conceived as a deep, horizontal comradeship. Ultimately it is this fraternity that makes it possible, over the past two centuries, for so many millions of people, not so much to kill, as willingly to die for such limited imaginings" (1991, 7).[16]

These imaginings—whether from the first decade of the 1800s (Creole nationalism, i.e., Mexico); or from the 1820s or the 1850s of Central Europe (so-called vernacular/linguistic nationalisms, which were opposed to the hegemony of Latin); or from the "official nationalism" prior to the end of World War I (a nation/dynasty combination)—all culminated in the now-threatened "nation-state" that became the international norm after 1922 and at least until the 1970s. By the 1970s, the nation-state was politically and economically transcended, or at least challenged, by the strategic fragmentation of the manufacturing production process around the globe under late capitalism. In the specific case that has concerned this book, the Mexican state has been challenged by the deployment of mostly American maquiladoras not only throughout Mexico (thereby intensifying Mexico's dependency on foreign capital) but throughout the border metropolis of Ciudad Juárez; they are located in more than seventeen industrial parks strategically established in different sections of the city.[17]

Thus, the imagined community Anderson identifies in the idea of the nation is the imagined (shared) community R. Rosaldo identifies in the classic anthropological concept of culture, which was conceptualized in the period of "official nationalism" and discursively deployed throughout the consolidation of the "nation-state" (between 1922 and 1970).[18]

Two major historical forces (or, in Gramsci's terms, "*force relations*") that led to the nation as an imagined community were the emergence of print capitalism (the novel and the newspaper) and the gradual collapse of the hegemony of Latin (a collapse that gave rise to vernacular nationalisms within Europe).[19] Before these major historical and complicated political processes led to the initial versions of the nation (before the nineteenth century, more specifically before 1776), the political imagination regarding such taken-for-granted conceptualizations as "society" or "social groups" was characterized by fragmentation, intermarriage, and cultural and social heterogeneity—all predating a homogeneous imagined community.

For instance, Benedict Anderson has written in relation to this prenation, premodern stage, "The fundamental conceptions about 'social groups' were centripetal and hierarchical, rather than boundary-oriented and horizontal" (1991, 15). With regard to the dynastic, monarchic realm, Anderson notes that "in the older imagining, where [kingship] states were defined by centres, borders were porous and indistinct, and sovereignties faded imperceptibly into one another. Hence, paradoxically enough, the ease with which pre-modern empires and kingdoms were able to sustain their rule over immensely heterogeneous, and often not even contiguous, populations for long periods of time" (1991, 19). Regarding sexual politics, Anderson states that "in fact, royal lineages often derived their prestige, aside from any aura of divinity, from, shall we say, miscegenation? For such mixtures were signs of superordinate status [thus] . . . what 'nationality' are we to assign to the Bourbons?" (1991, 20–21). Consequently, assigning an essentialized identity about nationalism or culturalism to any subjectivity, before the nation, was not only difficult, but probably impossible.[20]

It is evident that heterogeneity preceded the "imagined community"—the nation, the nation-state, nationalism—all of which, I argue, influenced our academic notions of culture and society during the late nineteenth and most of the twentieth centuries. Thus, the heterogeneity discovered in the late twentieth century in theories of borderlands and fragmentation should not be limited exclusively to the collapse of classic norms from the mid-1960s to the mid-1980s; rather, our theories of culture, society, and identity should be analyzed in the contexts of much longer historical processes, such as (1) the monarchic kin relations in sixteenth-century New Spain and Spain; (2) the first attempts "to cut off the head of the king" in the early nineteenth century; and (3) the political transformation and/or reproduction of the nation-state throughout the twentieth century. This book has attempted to provide a comparative analysis of the heterogeneity of the late twentieth century and the heterogeneity associated with prenation contexts and politics in the sixteenth and seventeenth centuries; it is not that heterogeneity cannot coexist with homogeneity, but this strategy might serve as a point of departure from a possible prison of border thought.[21] At the same time, however, we must recognize that such identities as class, gender, sexuality, and ethnicity, as they were (and still are) articulated in the late twentieth century, are, in large part, products of the 1900s; in particular, they are products of a long history of resistance—the working-class, feminist, gay and lesbian, and civil rights movements of the 1960s as well the decolonization movements of Africa and Asia since the late 1950s (R. Rosaldo 1993).

We can now claim, then, that at the turn of the twenty-first century, the "state" has been strategically dispersed, both by current Gramscian thinking and by multinational corporations in this historic moment characterized by the dispersal of manufacturing production processes (as well as commodity consumption) throughout the world. Unfortunately, Benedict Anderson not only ignored the role of late capitalism in the redefinition of the nation-state after 1965 (when the maquiladora industry arrived in Mexico); he also did not perceive that the fascism of Mussolini had been produced through and by the ideology of the nation, which Anderson himself limits to an amorous feeling of patriotism. Anderson also ignores the major threat to the formation of the nation-state in the first decades of the twentieth century: the attempt to internationalize (read: denationalize, deterritorialize) the working classes.

It is perhaps at this analytic juncture that we must systematically articulate R. Rosaldo's theory of multiple subjectivities (so much needed for our understanding of the politics of difference under state citizenry) with pervasive late capitalism—which can be characterized not only by the fragmentation of the production process but also by the fragmentation of the working classes as a labor force (women, men, younger, older, educated, migrants, married, single, and so forth). Is it possible to reconcile the following seemingly irreconcilable statements about the politics and economics of difference? First, Rosaldo argues, "Social borders frequently become salient around such lines as sexual orientation, gender, class, race, ethnicity, nationality, age, politics, dress, food, or taste. . . . [S]uch borderlands should be regarded not as analytically empty transitional zones but as sites of creative cultural production that require investigation" (1993, 207–8). And second, Marxist feminist June Nash notes regarding the current global accumulation of capital that "sectors of the labor force based on gender, ethnicity, age, and education within both industrial core and peripheral nations are differentially rewarded and these differences, along with wage differences, between nations, determine the long-run movement of capital" (1983, 3).

Adding the wage differential to the "borderlands" equation does not allow us to separate "border zones" as "sites of creative cultural production" from "border zones" as "sites of lucrative manufacturing production" in the globalization of capital. Thus, is the theory of borderlands a critique or handmaid of capitalist discipline in this historical moment? Historically and theoretically, it can be both. Just as we must extend cultural borderlands into a critique of late-capitalist production, so we must transform the political economy of June Nash into a critical, global theory of multiple cultural subjectivities, which in fact R. Rosaldo offers. After all, one alternative lies in situating our theoretical concepts about social life not only in the larger contexts of history, colonialism, nationalism, and power, but also in micro-contexts of cultural specificity as well as in the Foucauldian recognition that academic research

> is a question of orienting ourselves to a conception of power which replaces . . . the privilege of sovereignty with the analysis of a multiple and mobile *field of force relations*, wherein far-reaching, but never completely stable, effects of domination are produced. . . . And this, not out of a speculative choice or theoretical preference, but because in fact *it is one of the essential traits for Western societies that the force relationships which for a long time had found expression in war, in every form of warfare, gradually became invested in the order of political power.* (Foucault 1978, 102, my emphasis)

In a post-9/11 world, and with the American invasion of Iraq as well as today's assault on Mexican immigrants, we are, at least in part, returning once again, at the beginning of the twenty-first century, to a situation in which "it is one of the essential traits for Western societies that the force relationships find expression in war, in every form of warfare."

In this broader context, it is worthwhile to note that through the ethnographic descriptions of class and cultural struggles throughout this book, we have turned R. Rosaldo's ideas of cultural borderlands into a simultaneous theory of class borderlands. Besides the need to identify in the world concrete situations concerning specific political mobilizations where people do in fact get together in street protests or in strikes at the workplace, for example, the fiction of a "shared class" seems, as Rosaldo argues about a "shared culture," "increasingly more tenuous than useful." I argue here that "social classes" are also characterized by border zones and that they are "neither necessarily coherent nor always homogeneous." Consequently, the working-class lives of the factory workers under study are always "crisscrossed by border zones, pockets and eruptions of all kinds," including, I will add, cultural ruptures. I have demonstrated, then, that "class borderlands" should also be regarded as creative sites of culture and class making and unmaking, both of which demand additional investigation within and beyond officially recognized borderlands.

From the Nature of the State to the State of Nature

The emphasis in this book on war, contestation, and power relations in society and culture along class, gender, and color lines, more than on a faithful commitment to Communist utopias, constitutes a strategy of resistance and opposition to the extreme conservatism permeating Durkheimian thinking, which dominated academic social thought throughout most of the twentieth century. The latter influential paradigm, however, was tied more to Thomas Hobbes, who wrote for an earlier British monarchy, than to Durkheim himself, who was reacting against late nineteenth-century labor unrest (Anderson 1968). In assigning the generalized transformations of societies to specific historical periods—for example, to 1870s historical events or, for that matter, to 1970s political occurrences and outcomes—one runs the danger of reducing the complexity of human relations to socially situated experiences (practice), which are in turn transformed into generalized visions of the world (structure). The problematic trick presents itself when the latter (structure) are confused with the former (practice), not in the recognition that one can lead to the other. The impermanence of either "structure" or "practice" allows for the analysis of the unintended consequences of "culture" and its politics, past and present.

"Situated knowledges" (Haraway 1986) in themselves are not necessarily, and have not always been, part of the "war of position" that Gramsci promoted. Durkheim's position about the state, morality, and society was situated as well, but relative to the state's need of the times, to restore so-called social order—both from capitalist rapacity (the greedy capitalist) and from worker unrest. Under late capitalism, Durkheim's vision of the sovereign state is in fact being politically challenged by multinational corporations, particularly in Mexico, but more specifically at the U.S.-Mexico border, and by a much-needed border theory that is produced by border subjects who claim citizenships that transcend boundaries (see Anzaldúa 1987; Lugo 1997, 2000b; Morales 1996; R. Rosaldo 1993).

Throughout most of the history of social science thinking, and even as early as 1642, Hobbes argued in his *Leviathan* ([1642] 1958), and in Latin (that is, before "the nation"), that the state of nature is inherently about chaos, disorder, and war, and that the only remedy is to impose a sovereign—the king—so that order and harmony will exist. Thus, we must realize that actual social life does not tend to obey "official mandates" or the most recent "theoretical paradigms." Human relations did not necessarily transform themselves from "chaos" to "order" under Hobbes, nor from "order" to "chaos" under Marx, nor (back again) from "chaos" to "order" under Durkheim, nor will they change from pure "order" to pure "disorder" under Gramscian, postmodernist, and borderland thinking.[22] Thus, just as culture changes, so does the state; needless to say, our concepts about them are also transformed according to distinct historical specificities.

Social life changes and reproduces itself both through cultural-historical contingencies and through the arbitrary, though still symbolically constituted, imposition of a politically legitimated force. It is our business to study the former and a matter of human integrity not only to scrutinize the latter but, more importantly, to prevent it. It is necessary that we continue our analytic flow from "Culture" to "culture," from the "State" to the "state," from "Order" to "order," from "Patterns" to "patterns," from "Chaos" to "chaos," and from "Border Crossings" to their "border inspections," as well as from "gender studies of women and gender studies of men" to "studies of gender" that comprehensively include both women and men. As Geertz persuasively noted in 1973, the anthropologist still "confronts the same grand realities that others . . . confront in more fateful settings: Power, Change, Faith, Oppression . . . but he [*sic*] confronts them in obscure enough [I'd say clear enough] places . . . to take the capital letters off them" (1973a, 21). It seems, after all, that one of postmodernism's major contributions to sociocultural analysis is, as Antonio Benítez-Rojo argues in *The Repeating Island: The Caribbean and the Postmodern Perspective*, its "lens," which "has the virtue of being the only one to direct itself toward the play of paradoxes and eccentricities, of fluxes and displacements" (1992, 271), that is, toward the simultaneous play of order and disorder, coherence and incoherence, chaos and antichaos, contestation and shareability, practice and structure, culture and history, culture and capitalism, and finally, patterns and borderlands (R. Rosaldo 1993). We should not privilege a priori one or the other; instead, we must continuously suspend each category in order to analyze the eccentricities of each. It seems to me that only by following these suggestions was I able to juxtapose the analysis of "assembled parts" in maquiladoras with the analysis of the fragmented lives of the maquila workers who assembled them, and I was able as well to examine the everydayness of late industrial capitalism as compared with the encounters of conquest and colonialism in the sixteenth century—all in the larger contexts of history and the present, the global economy and the local strategies of survival, and, finally, in the more intricate micro-contexts of culture and power. Ultimately, and without leaving the question of *meaning* behind, I suggest that we, as social analysts, must face the challenge to truly balance the interpretation of human culture and its borderlands with their respective inspections.

Conclusion

By examining Gramsci's notion of the state and its dispersal, Foucault's notion of power and its deployment, Anderson's critique of the nation, and R. Rosaldo's critique of culture, I have tried to spell out my critique of cultural analysis, Cultural Studies, and culture and border theory as these overlap one another in nationalist, capitalist, late-capitalist, colonialist, and related projects of politically legitimated force. My specific argument throughout this final chapter, however, has been fourfold. First, I have argued that our own folk conceptions of culture and society have been historically constituted by such dialectic dualities as beliefs and practices (Boas 1940), "symbolic structures and collective behavior" (Geertz 1973a, 251), structure and agency (Bourdieu 1977; R. Rosaldo 1980, 1993), human action and intention (Ortner 1984), and culture as constituted and culture as lived (Sahlins 1981, 1982, 1985).[23] Second, I have asserted that our received academic conceptions of culture and border, and of social life for that matter, have been heavily (but, for the most part, unconsciously) influenced by our capacity and incapacity to acknowledge the distinct transformations that the nature of the Westernized "state" has gone through in the past two hundred years (the academic recognition of everyday experiences along the U.S.-Mexico border region is a manifestation of this transformation, especially with the creation of Free Trade [Border] Zones around the world). Third, I have contended that these academic conceptions of culture and border have been the historical products of either political suppressions or political persuasions and other types of resistance (i.e., the emergence of minority scholars who have experienced life at the borderlands) to the center's domination. Finally, I have argued in this chapter that culture, constituted by both beliefs and practices, is not necessarily always shared or always contested, and that the crossroads and the limits or frontiers of these beliefs and practices (border theory) create, in turn, the erosion *from within* of the monopoly of culture theory as "cultural patterns" (to follow Martín-Rodríguez 1996, 86).

Regarding anthropology as a discipline, we must ask: What is the role of anthropologists in the production of a cultural theory of borderlands in the interdisciplinary arena? Anthropologists today can certainly redefine themselves vis-à-vis the emergent and newly formed academic communities that now confront us. At the turn of the twenty-first century, as Renato Rosaldo has argued, anthropologists must strategically (re)locate/(re)position themselves in the current scholarly battlefield of power relations.

To be effective in this conceptual/political relocation, however, both anthropologists and nonanthropologists who think seriously about the cultural must ask themselves the following question (which Roland Barthes would pose to anybody regarding the nature of interdisciplinarity): Is the concept of culture an object of study that belongs to no particular discipline? Only an antidisciplinary mood would allow us to answer in the affirmative. A cultural theory of borderlands challenges and invites academics to recognize the crossroads of interdisciplinarity, where "ambassadors" are no longer needed. Once the challenge and the invitation are accepted, border theorizing in itself can simultaneously transcend and effectively situate culture, capitalism, conquest, and colonialism, as well as the academy, at the *crossroads* (including the inspections), but only if it is imagined historically and in the larger and dispersed contexts of the nation, the state, the nation-state, and power (Foucault 1978).

Finally, at certain times we must question the tropes we tend to privilege the most—"culture," "nature," "humanity," "class," "race," "*mestizaje*," "border," "gender," "power." In this case, I prefer the "nonimagined community" as opposed to the "imagined one," for as Anderson told us, imagined communities kill people and people die for them. More importantly, we need to understand and explain the symbolic process—the structure of the conjuncture, that is, the complex articulation of culture, capitalism, and conquest both in the sixteenth and seventeenth centuries as well as in the late twentieth century and into the present—that has made it possible, over the past five hundred years, for so many millions of people, in this case in the Americas, not so much to die as to die slowly (and at times abruptly) *so that others may live well-off.*

NOTES

Reprinted with permission from the University of Texas Press. This essay originally appeared in *Fragmented Lives, Assembled Parts: Culture, Capitalism, and Conquest at the U.S.-Mexico Border*, 213–30 (Austin: University of Texas Press, 2008).

1   A different version of this chapter appeared as "Reflections on Border Theory, Culture, and the Nation" in *Border Theory* (1997), edited by Scott Michaelsen and David E. Johnson. Both my article in *Border Theory* and this particular version of it are dedicated with *mucho cariño*, admiration, and gratitude to one of my most important teachers, Renato Rosaldo.

2   In this chapter, "the nation" and "the state," though usually imbricated with each other, will be used as categorically distinct entities, respectively, as a changing imagined community (Anderson 1991) and as a changing governance apparatus (Hall 1986). These specific uses, and their implications for culture and border theories, will be examined throughout the chapter. Although this chapter reflects on the state of culture and the nation during the past two hundred years, it does not constitute in itself an exhaustive historical project. I wish mainly to point out some limitations and some new readings of these topics as they connect to issues raised throughout my book *Fragmented Lives*. Nonetheless, the analysis of the nation, culture, and the state will be presented here as a point of reference rooted in my discussion of both monarchy and empire in the U.S.-Mexico borderlands in chapters 2 and 3 of *Fragmented Lives*.

3   "Deterritorializing" from "within" is a multilinear process and a complicated political project. It is multilinear because there are several fronts of struggle: late capitalism, the nation-state, contested communities, colonizer/colonized relations, theory itself, and the individual subject, among many others. It is a complicated political project because agents inhabit multiple locations, creating immediate reterritorializing. For instance, I write from diverse but interconnected positions: as a cultural anthropologist who did fieldwork among maquila (factory) workers and who was trained in American institutions; as a Mexican who spent his childhood and was born in Ciudad Juárez, Mexico, but who became Chicano *en el otro lado* (on the other side) while continuing his secondary and university schooling in Las Cruces, New Mexico. While living in Las Cruces, I visited Ciudad Juárez (my grandparents) every weekend until I was twenty-two years of age; thus, I am also a borderer (*fronterizo*) whose everyday experiences could be unpredictably located at the Mexico (Ciudad Juárez)/Texas (El Paso)/New Mexico (Las Cruces) borders. In spite of my multiple locations and possibilities, however, in this chapter I would like to reflect on why, as academics, we have come to think seriously about "culture" and "borders" to begin with and how these two concepts can help us better critique the many forms of conquest that have impacted the working-class Mexican and indigenous communities considered in this book.

4   Foucault wrote that "the purpose of the present study [*The History of Sexuality*] is in fact to show how deployments of power are directly connected to the body" (1978, 151). These "deployments of power" overlap with the deployments of sexuality in the modern West. In Part Four, "Deployment of Sexuality," Foucault examines in detail the objectives, methods, domains, and periodizations through which power operated and dispersed itself from the late eighteenth century to the late nineteenth century in Europe (see 1978, 75–131). He also argues, as is well known nowadays, that power is omnipresent: "The omnipresence of power: not because it has the privilege of consolidating everything under its invisible unity, but because it is produced from one moment to the next, at every point, or rather in every relation from one point to another" (1978, 93).

5   Foucault wrote: "Law was not simply a weapon skillfully wielded by monarchs; it was the monarchic system's mode of manifestation and the form of its acceptability. In Western societies since the Middle Ages [and here we must include New Spain], the exercise of power has always been formulated in terms of law" (1978, 87). He adds, "One is attached to a certain image of power-law, of power-sovereignty, which was

traced out by the theoreticians of right and the monarchic institution. *It is this image that we must break free of, that is, of the theoretical privilege of the law and sovereignty, if we wish to analyze power within the concrete and historical framework of its operation. We must construct an analytics of power that no longer takes law as a model and code*" (1978, 90; my emphasis).

6   Interestingly, in his analysis of the nation, Benedict Anderson uses the same periodization that Foucault used to examine the deployment of sexuality and E. P. Thompson used to examine class and industrial capitalism: the late 1700s and the nineteenth century. For the most part, Rosaldo limited himself to the twentieth century.

7   Edward Said's more elaborate response to Ania Loomba's question about how to combine Gramsci and Foucault is worth stating much more fully here, especially since it is analytically relevant to my own historico-theoretical argument in this book: "Once you've begun to circulate a bit in Gramsci, you realize that he is talking about very different situations at very different times, and that there is a danger of abstracting from the situation to a general theoretical term—which is almost impossible, I mean the danger is almost too great. Nevertheless, Gramsci, unlike Foucault, is working with an evolving political situation in which certain extremely important and radical experiments were taking place in the Turin factories in which he was involved, and from them he generalized periodically, I mean in a periodical form. You don't get that sense in Foucault; what you get instead is a sense of teleology where everything is tending toward the same end . . . The introduction of historical, what I would call a historical context, to Foucault is extremely important and worth doing" (Said 2002, 10).

8   In fact, Sherry Ortner organizes her highly influential essay on "practice theory" (1984) along such dialectics as system/action, structure/practice.

9   In chapter 5 of *Fragmented Lives*, I showed how this double life of culture is manifested in the electronics maquiladora through an analysis of how specific notions of laziness at the workplace reproduce ideologies of masculinity and machismo as well as the working-class experience.

10 Foucault associates this periodization—"1870"—with the production of the homosexual as "a personage, a past, a case history, and a childhood, in addition to being a type of life" (1978, 43). He adds, "We must not forget that the psychological, psychiatric, medical category of homosexuality was constituted from the moment it was characterized—Westphal's famous article of 1870 ['Archiv fur Neurologie'] on 'contrary sexual relations' can stand as its date of birth. . . . The sodomite had been a temporary aberration; the homosexual was now a species" (Foucault 1978, 43).

11 As we have seen in the case of Mexico, the question of *mestizaje* as a national project emerged at the same time that the nation-state was trying to consolidate itself immediately after the Mexican Revolution of 1910–1920. Before the Mexican Revolution, especially immediately after independence, Mexico struggled with its monarchic legacy (with the exception of Benito Juárez's presidency, which coincided with and against the French invasion of the 1860s). In the context of world politics of the late nineteenth century, the Porfiriato (1877–1911) carried the seeds of exploitation that led to the Revolution, which in turn led to the production of the "state" identified by Gramsci in the 1930s (Gramsci himself was a contemporary of President Lázaro Cárdenas).

12   Also, while analyzing the work of literary theorist Kenneth Burke, Rosaldo wrote:

> Recent social thinkers [Giddens 1979; Ortner 1984] have updated Burke's style of analysis by identifying the interplay of "structure" and "agency" as a central issue in social theory. Most central for them, in other words, is the question of *how received structures shape human conduct, and how, in turn, human conduct alters received structures.* (1993, 104; my emphasis)

13   Of course, the self/"other" distinction has been both contested and problematized in most recent writings of culture and power.

14   In his experimental ethnography, *Dancing with the Devil,* José Limón applies the metaphor of war in ways I am suggesting here, but following Gramsci's "war of maneuver" and "war of position." In the following quotation, Limón uses the metaphor of war quite appropriately to depict the racial struggle between Mexicans and Anglos in South Texas: "For it is a basic premise and organizing metaphor for this essay that since the 1830's, the Mexicans of south Texas have been in a state of social war with the 'Anglo' dominant Other and their class allies. This has been at times a war of overt, massive proportions; at others, covert and sporadic; at still other moments, repressed and internalized as a war within the psyche, but always conditioned by an ongoing social struggle fought out of different battlefields" (1994, 16).

15   Also, feminist anthropologists were, and have been, at the forefront of this exciting anthropology produced in the late twentieth century (see especially the provocative and theoretically sophisticated volumes *Uncertain Terms* [1990], edited by Faye Ginsburg and Anna Tsing, and *Women Writing Culture* [1995], edited by Ruth Behar and Deborah Gordon—two among many others).

16   For some very useful critiques of Benedict Anderson's *Imagined Communities,* the works of the following authors stand out: in Subaltern Studies, Chatterjee (1993) and Chakrabarty (2000); in Latin Americanist anthropology, Thurner (1997) and Lomnitz (2001). My own border reading of this text vis-à-vis *Culture and Truth* attempts to contribute to the necessary dialogue on two of the most important essays of late twentieth-century U.S.-based scholarship (R. Rosaldo's and Anderson's).

17   The presence of hundreds of maquiladoras in Ciudad Juárez, as well as the fragmented life that they create, makes the working-class men and women part of the articulation of domination of both industrial and state capital; after all, the Mexican state, particularly in northern Chihuahua, has been mostly controlled by elite families, themselves industrial entrepreneurs.

18   Of course, this notion of culture as shared patterns of behavior still reigns in some quarters.

19   In *The Making of the English Working Class* (1966), E. P. Thompson examined the role of print "capitalism" in the radicalization of the working and middle classes in England during the early nineteenth century. This kind of radicalization, through print, has not occurred in Ciudad Juárez, although in his *Terror of the Machine* (1997), Devon Peña briefly documented a few such historical moments in the early 1980s.

20   This imagined and practiced kingship led to the domination and conquest of Nueva España, Nueva Galicia, Nueva Vizcaya, and Nueva Mexico.

21 See chapter 2 of *Fragmented Lives* for the encounters of conquest both Hernán Cortés and Juan de Oñate had with uncertain, unidentified groups of people, not yet "labeled" by the Europeans, on the coast of Mexico and in what came to be New Mexico.

22 One of the most important contributions of Renato Rosaldo's thinking is precisely his sensitivity to analysis of power as it is found in patterns and borderlands, chaos and order, subjectivity and objectivity, and culture and politics. None of these entities holds a monopoly on truth. This is Rosaldo's most important message regarding culture, identity, and power/knowledge.

23 I have also argued that if within anthropology such dialectics as "practice and structure" and "beliefs and action" do not explicitly appear in early anthropological debates about culture and the individual, the individual and society, the individual and social structure, or culture and the environment, it is because "practice," as a category of analysis, was suppressed due to its implication for political mobilizations on the part of colonized subjects, the working poor, and other subaltern subjects—the usual targets of anthropologists throughout most of the twentieth century.

Also, anthropologists have historically privileged such analytical domains as cognition, symbols, the environment, decision making, the superorganic, and personality, among many others, in trying to get to the cultural or the social in human beings. Yet, all these categories acquire meaning for academics only to the extent that they can explain or interpret people's beliefs and actions. Thus, we inevitably return to the "structure/practice" duality that, I argue, has constituted our dominant discourse on culture and power—so far.

REFERENCES

Alonso, Ana María. 1995. *Thread of Blood: Colonialism, Revolution, and Gender on Mexico's Northern Frontier*. Tuscon: University of Arizona Press.

Alonso, Ana María, and María Teresa Koreck. 1988. "Silences: Hispanics, AIDS, and Sexual Practices." *difference* 1: 101–24.

Alvarez, Robert R., Jr. 1995. "The Mexican-U.S. Border: The Making of an Anthropology of Borderlands." *Annual Review of Anthropology* 24:447–470.

Anderson, Benedict. 1991. *Imagined Communities: Reflections on the Origin and Spread of Nationalism*. Rev. ed. London: Verso.

Anzaldúa, Gloria. 1987. *Borderlands/La Frontera: The New Mestiza*. San Francisco: Spinsters/ Aunt Lute.

Anzaldúa, Gloria. 1989. "The Homeland, Aztlán/El Otro México." In *Aztlán: Essays on the Chicano Homeland*, ed. Rudolfo A. Anaya and Francisco A. Lomelí, 191–204. Albuquerque: University of New Mexico Press.

Behar, Ruth. 1993. *Translated Woman: Crossing the Border with Esperanza's Story*. Boston: Beacon Press.

Behar, Ruth. 1995. "Writing in My Father's Name: A Diary of Translated Woman's First Year." In *Women Writing Culture*, ed. Ruth Behar and Deborah A. Gordon, 65–82. Berkeley: University of California Press.

Behar, Ruth, and Deborah A. Gordon, eds. 1995. *Women Writing Culture*. Berkeley: University of California Press.

Bejarano, Cynthia L. 2002. "Las Super Madres de Latino América: Transforming Motherhood and Houseskirts by Challenging Violence in Juárez, Mexico; Argentina; and El Salvador." *Frontiers* 23 (1): 126–50.

Bejarano, Cynthia L. 2005. *"¿Qué Onda?": Urban Youth Cultures and Border Identity.* Tucson: University of Arizona Press.

Berdahl, Daphne. 1999. *Where the World Ended: Re-Unification and Identity and the German Borderland.* Berkeley: University of California Press.

Bonilla, Frank, et al. 1998. *Borderless Borders: U.S. Latinos, Latin Americans, and the Paradox of Interdependence.* Philadelphia: Temple University Press.

Borofsky, Robert, ed. 1994. *Assessing Cultural Anthropology.* New York: McGraw-Hill.

Burden, Philip D. 1996. *The Mapping of North America: A List of Printed Maps 1511–1670.* London: Raleigh Publications.

Carrillo, Héctor. 2002. *The Night Is Young: Sexuality in Mexico in the Time of AIDS.* Chicago: University of Chicago Press.

Castellanos, Alicia G. 1981. *Ciudad Juárez: La vida fronteriza.* Mexico City: Editorial Nuestro Tiempo.

Castillo, Debra A., and María Socorro Tabuenca Córdoba. 2002. *Border Women: Writing from La Frontera.* Minneapolis: University of Minnesota Press.

Chagnon, Napoleon. 1992. *Yanomamo.* 4th ed. Fort Worth, TX: Harcourt Brace College Publishers.

Chakrabarty, Dipesh. 2000. *Provincializing Europe: Postcolonial Thought and Historical Difference.* Princeton: Princeton University Press.

Chatterjee, Partha. 1993. *The Nation and Its Fragments: Colonial and Postcolonial Histories.* Princeton: Princeton University Press.

"Ciudad Juárez, Chihuahua, 1999." 1999. *Document.* Ciudad Juárez, Mexico: Desarrollo Económico de Ciudad Juárez, A.C.

"Ciudad Juárez en cifras—1991: Estadísticas socioeconómicas básicas." 1991. *Document.* Ciudad Juárez, Mexico: Desarrollo Económico de Ciudad Juárez, A.C.

Cline, Howard. 1972. "Ethnohistorical Regions of Middle America." In *Guide to Ethnohistorical Sources,* Part One, ed. Howard Cline, 166–83. Handbook of Middle American Indians Series. Austin: University of Texas Press.

Conway, George Robert Graham (G. R. G.). 1940. *Postrera voluntad y testament de Hernando Cortés, Marqués del Valle. Introducción y notas por G. R. G. Conway.* Mexico City: P. Robredo. (Orig. pub. 1939.)

Cortés, Hernán. 1986. *Hernán Cortés: Letters from Mexico.* Trans. and ed. Anthony Pagden. New Haven: Yale University Press.

De Genova, Nicholas, and Ana Y. Ramos-Zayas. 2003. *Latino Crossings: Mexicans, Puerto Ricans, and the Politics of Race and Citizenship.* New York: Routledge.

Dubois, Laurent. 1995. "'Man's Darkest Hours': Maleness, Travel, and Anthropology." In *Women Writing Culture,* ed. Ruth Behar and Deborah A. Gordon, 306–21.

Ehrenreich, Barbara. 1983. *The Hearts of Men: American Dreams and the Flight from Commitment.* New York: Anchor Press.

Elliot, J. H. 1986. "Introduction: Cortés, Velázquez, and Charles V." In *Hernán Cortés: Letters from Mexico,* trans. and ed. Anthony Pagden, xi–xxxvii. New Haven: Yale University Press.

Encinias, Miguel, Alfred Rodríquez, and Joseph P. Sánchez, trans. and eds. 1992. *Historia de la Nueva México, 1610*. By Gaspar Pérez de Villagrá. Albuquerque: University of New Mexico Press.

Fernandez, James W. 1986. *Persuasions and Performances: The Play of Tropes in Culture*. Bloomington: Indiana University Press.

Fernández-Kelly, María Patricia. 1983. *For We Are Sold, I and My People: Women and Industry in Mexico's Frontier*. Albany: State University of New York Press.

Flores, Juan. 1993. *Divided Borders: Essays on Puerto Rican Identity*. Houston: Arte Público Press.

Foucault, Michel. 1978. *The History of Sexuality*, Vol. 1. New York: Pantheon.

Fregoso, Rosa Linda. 2003. *meXicana Encounters: The Making of Social Identities on the Borderlands*. Durham: Duke University Press.

Fusco, Coco. 1995. *English Is Broken Here: Notes of Cultural Fusion in the Americas*. New York: New Press.

García Sáiz, Maria Concepción. 1989. *The Castes: A Genre of Mexican Painting* [Las castas mexicanas: Un género pictórico americano]. Milan, Italy: Olivetti.

Ginsburg, Faye, and Anna Lowenhaut Tsing, eds. 1990. *Uncertain Terms: Nogotiating Gender in American Culture*. Boston: Beacon Press.

González Obregón, Luis. 1959. *México viejo: 1521–1821*. Mexico City: Editorial Patria.

Gordon, Deborah A. 1995. "Border Work: Feminist Ethnography and the Dissemination of Literacy." In *Women Writing Culture*, ed. Ruth Behar and Deborah A. Gordon, 373–89. Berkeley: University of California Press.

Griswold del Castillo, Richard. 1990. *The Treaty of Guadalupe Hidalgo: A Legacy of Conflict*. Normal: University of Oklahoma Press.

Gutiérrez, Ramón A. 1991. *When Jesus Came, the Corn Mothers Went Away: Marriage, Sexuality, and Power in New Mexico, 1500–1846*. Stanford: Stanford University Press.

Gutmann, Matthew C. 1996. *The Meanings of Macho: Being a Man in Mexico City*. Berkeley: University of California Press.

Gutmann, Matthew C. 2000. "A (Short) Cultural History of Mexican Machos and Hombres." In *Gender Matters: Rereading Michelle Z. Rosaldo*, ed. Alejandro Lugo and Bill Maurer, 160–84. Ann Arbor: University of Michigan Press.

Guzmán Betancourt, Ignacio, ed. 1998. *Los nombres de México*. Mexico City: Miguel Angel Porrúa.

Hall, Stuart. 1986. "Gramsci's Relevance for the Study of Race and Ethnicity." *Journal of Communication Inquiry* 10 (2): 5–27.

Heyman, Josiah McC. 1991. *Life and Labor on the Border: Working People of Northeastern Sonora, Mexico, 1886–1986*. Tucson: University of Arizona Press.

Heyman, Josiah McC. 1998. *Finding a Moral Heart for U.S. Immigration Policy: An Anthropological Perspective*. American Ethnological Society Monograph Series, No. 7. Arlington, VA: American Anthropological Association.

Hill, Sarah. 2003. "Metaphoric Enrichment and Material Poverty: The Making of 'Colonias.'" In *Ethnography at the Border*, ed. Pablo Vila, 141–65. Minneapolis: University of Minnesota Press.

Humboldt, Alejandro. [1882] 1998. "Ensayo politico sobre el reino de la Nueva España, 1808–1822." In *Los nombres de México*, ed. Ignacio Guzmán Betancourt, 199–201. Mexico City: Miguel Angel Porrúa.

Jackson, Robert H., ed. 1998. *New Views of Borderlands History*. Albuquerque: University of New Mexico Press.

Julyan, Robert. 1998. *The Place Names of New Mexico*, Rev. ed. Albuquerque: University of New Mexico Press.

Kearney, Michael. 1991. "Borders and Boundaries of State and Self at the End of Empire." *Journal of Historical Sociology* 4 (1): 52–74.

Kelleher, William F., Jr. 2003. *Troubles in Ballybogoin: Memory and Identity in Northern Ireland*. Ann Arbor: University of Michigan Press.

Kuhn, Josh. 1997. "Against Easy Listening: Audiotopic Readings and Transnational Soundings." In *Every-night Life: Culture and Dance in Latin/o America*, ed. Celeste Fraser Delgado and José Esteban Muñoz, 288–309. Durham: Duke University Press.

Lavie, Smadar, and Ted Swdenburg. 1996. *Displacement, Diaspora, and Geographies of Identity*. Durham: Duke University Press.

Lewin, Ellen. 1995. "Writing Lesbian Ethnography." In *Women Writing Culture*, ed. Ruth Behar and Deborah A. Gordon, 322–35. Berkeley: University of California Press.

Lewis, Laura A. 2000. "Black, Black Indian, Afromexicans: The Dynamics of Race, Nation, and Identity in a Moreno Mexican Community (Guerrero)." *American Ethnologist* 27 (4): 898–926.

Lewis, Laura A. 2004. "Modesty and Modernity: Photography, Race, and Representation on Mexico's Costa Chica (Guerrero)." *Identities: Global Studies in Culture and Power* 11 (4): 471–99.

Limón, Jose. 1994. *Dancing with the Devil: Society and Cultural Poetics in Mexican-American South Texas*. Madison: University of Wisconsin Press.

Lipschutz, Alejandro. 1944. *El indoamericanismo y el problema racial en las Américas*. Santiago, Chile: Editorial Nascimiento.

Lomnitz, Claudio. 2001. *Deep Mexico, Silent Mexico: An Anthropology of Nationalism*. Minneapolis: University of Minnesota Press.

Lugo, Alejandro. 1990. "Cultural Production and Reproduction in Ciudad Juárez, Mexico: Tropes at Play among Maquiladora Workers." *Cultural Anthropology* 5 (3): 173–96.

Lugo, Alejandro. 1997. "Reflections on Border Theory, Culture, and the Nation." In *Border Theory: The Limits of Cultural Politics*, ed. Scott Michaelsen and David E. Johnson, 43–67. Minneapolis: University of Minnesota Press.

Lugo, Alejandro. 2000a. "Destabilizing the Masculine, Refocusing 'Gender': Men and the Aura of Authority in Michelle Z. Rosaldo's Work." In *Gender Matters: Rereading Michelle Z. Rosaldo*, ed. Alejandro Lugo and Bill Maurer, 54–89. Ann Arbor: University of Michigan Press.

Lugo, Alejandro. 2000b. "Theorizing Border Inspections." *Cultural Dynamics* 12 (3): 353–73.

Lugo, Alejandro. 2003. "Gender Matter: Women, Men, and the Production of Feminist Knowledge." In *Disciplines on the Line: Feminist Research on Spanish, Latin American, and U.S. Latina Women*, ed. Anne J. Cruz, Rosilie Hernández-Pecoraro, and Joyce Tolliver, 79–100. Newark, DE: Juan de la Cuesta Press.

Lugo, Alejandro, and Bill Maurer. 2000. "The Legacy of Michelle Rosaldo: Politics and Gender in Modern Societies." In *Gender Matters: Rereading Michelle Z. Rosaldo*, ed. Alejandro Lugo and Bill Maurer, 16–34. Ann Arbor: University of Michigan Press.

Lutz, Catherine. 1995. "The Gender of Theory." In *Women Writing Culture*, ed. Ruth Behar and Deborah A. Gordon, 249–66. Berkeley: University of California Press.

MacKinnon, Catharine A. 1982. "Feminism, Marxism, Method, and the State: An Agenda for Theory." In *Feminist Critique: A Critique of Ideology*, ed. Nannerl O. Keohane, Michelle Z. Rosaldo, and Barbara C. Gelpi, 1–30. Chicago: University of Chicago Press.

Maciel, David R., and María Herrera-Sobek, eds. 1998. *Culture across Borders: Mexican Immigration and Popular Culture*. Tucson: University of Arizona Press.

Martínez, José Luis, ed. 1990. *Documentos cortesianos*. Vol. 1–4. Mexico City: Fondo de Cultura Económica.

Michaelsen, Scott, and David E. Johnson, eds. 1997. *Border Theory: The Limits of Cultural Politics*. Minneapolis: University of Minnesota Press.

Morales, Alejandro. 1996. "Dynamic Identities in Heterotopia." In *Alejandro Morales: Fiction Past, Present, Future Perfect*, ed. José Antonia Gurpegui, 14–27. Tempe, AZ: Bilingual Review Press.

Morner, Magnus. 1967. *Race Mixture in the History of Latin America*. Boston: Little Brown.

Newton, Judith, and Judith Stacey. 1995. "Reflections on Studying Academic Men." In *Women Writing Culture*, ed. Ruth Behar and Deborah A. Gordon, 287–305. Berkeley: University of California Press.

Oboler, Suzanne. 1995. *Ethnic Labels, Latino Lives: Identity and the Politics of (Re)Presentation in the United States*. Minneapolis: University of Minnesota Press.

O'Laughlin, Bridget. 1974. "Mediation of Contradiction: Why Mbum Women Do Not Eat Chicken." In *Woman, Culture, and Society*, ed. Michelle Zimbalist Rosaldo and Louise Lamphere, 301–18. Stanford: Stanford University Press.

Olwig, Karen Fog, and Kirsten Hastrup, eds. 1997. *Siting Culture: The Shifting Anthropological Object*. New York: Routledge.

Opler, Morris E. 1983. "The Apachean Culture Pattern and Its Origins." In *Handbook of North American Indians*, Vol. 10: Southwest, ed. Alfonso Ortiz, 368–92. Washington, DC: Smithsonian Institution.

Ortiz, Victor. 2003. "El Paso as an Eternal Yet Not Last Frontier." In *Ethnography at the Border*, ed. Pablo Vila, 236–50. Minneapolis: University of Minnesota Press.

Ortner, Sherry. 1984. "Theory in Anthropology since the Sixties." *Comparative Studies in Society and History* 26 (1): 126–66.

Pagden, Anthony. 1986. "Translator's Introduction." In *Hernan Cortes: Letters from Mexico*, trans. and ed. Anthony Pagden, xxxix–lxvii. New Haven: Yale University Press.

Paredes, Américo. 1968. "Folk Medicine and the Intercultural Jest." In *Spanish-Speaking People in the United States, American Ethnological Society Proceedings of the 1968 Annual Spring Meeting*, ed. June Helm, 104–19. Seattle: University of Washington Press.

Pena, Devon G. 1997. *The Terror of the Machine: Technology, Work, Gender, and Ecology on the U.S.-Mexico Border*. Austin: University of Texas Press.

Perez-Firmat, Gustavo. 1994. *Life on the Hyphen: The Cuban-American Way*. Austin: University of Texas Press.

Robertson, Donald. 1959. *Mexican Manuscript Painting of the Early Colonial Period: The Metropolitan Schools*. New Haven: Yale University Press.

Romero, Mary. 2003. "Nanny Diaries and Other Stories: Imagining Women's Labor in the Social Reproduction of American Families." *DePaul Law Review* 52 (3): 809–47.

Romero, Mary. 2005. "Violation of Latino Civil Rights Resulting from INS and Local Police's Use of Race, Culture, and Class Profiling: The Case of the Chandler Roundup in Arizona." *Cleveland State Law Review* 52 (1&2): 75–96.

Rosaldo, Renato. 1993. *Culture and Truth: The Remaking of Social Analysis*. Boston: Beacon Press. (Orig. pub. 1989.)

Rosaldo, Renato, and William Flores. 1997. "Identity, Conflict, and Evolving Latino Communities: Cultural Citizenship in San Jose, California." In *Latino Cultural Citizenship: Claiming Identity, Space, and Rights*, ed. William v. Flores and Rina Benmayor, 57–96. Boston: Beacon Press.

Ruiz, Vicki L., and Susan Tiano, eds. 1987. *Women on the U.S.-Mexico Border: Responses to Change*. Boston: Allen and Unwin.

Sahlins, Marshall. 1985. *Islands of History*. Chicago: University of Chicago Press.

Said, Edward. 2002. "In Conversation with Neeladri Bhattacharya, Suvir Kaul, and Ania Loomba." In *Relocating Postcolonialism*, ed. David Theo Goldberg and Ato Quayson, 1–14. Malden, MA: Blackwell Publishing.

Saldívar, José David. 1997. *Border Matters: Remapping American Cultural Studies*. Berkeley: University of California Press.

Salzinger, Leslie. 2003. *Genders in Production*. Berkeley: University of California Press.

Schirmer, Jennifer. 1994. "The Claiming of Space and the Body Politic within National-Security States: The Plaza de Mayo Madres and the Greenham Common Women." In *Remapping Memory: The Politics of TimeSpace*, ed. Jonathan Boyarin, 185–220. Minneapolis: University of Minnesota Press.

Spyer, Patricia. 1998. "Introduction." In *Border Fetishisms: Material Objects in Unstable Spaces*, ed. Patricia Spyer, 1–11. New York: Routledge.

Staudt, Kathleen, and Irasema Coronado. 2002. *Fronteras No Más: Toward Social Justice at the U.S.-Mexico Border*. New York: Palgrave Macmillan.

Taussig, Michael. 1987. *Shamanism, Colonialism, and the Wild Man: A Study in Terror and Healing*. Chicago: University of Chicago Press.

Taussig, Michael. 1998. "Crossing the Face." In *Border Fetishisms: Material Objects in Unstable Spaces*, ed. Patricia Spyer, 224–44. New York: Routledge.

Tedlock, Barbara. 1995. "Works and Wives: On the Sexual Division of Textual Labor." In *Women Writing Culture*, ed. Ruth Behar and Deborah A. Gordon, 267–86. Berkeley: University of California Press.

Thompson, Edward P. 1966. *The Making of the English Working Class*. New York: Vintage Books.

Thurner, Mark. 1997. *From Two Republics to One Divided: Contradictions of Postcolonial Nation-making in Andean Peru*. Durham: Duke University Press.

Tiano, Susan. *Patriarchy on the Line: Labor, Gender, and Ideology in the Mexican Maquiladora Industry*. Philadelphia: Temple University Press.

Timmons, W. H. 1990. *El Paso: A Borderlands History*. El Paso: Texas Western Press.

Torres-Saillant, Silvio. 2002. "Problematic Paradigms: Racial Diversity and Corporate Identity in the Latino Community." In *Latinos Remaking America*, ed. Marcelo M. Suárez-Orozco and Mariela M. Páez, 435–55. Berkeley: University of California Press.

Valdivia, Angharad. 2005. "Geographies of Latinidad: Deployments of Radical Hybridity in the Mainstream." In *Race, Identity, and Representation in Education*, 2nd ed., ed. Cameron McCarthy et al., 307–17. New York: Routledge.

Valeri, Valerio. 1990. "Both Nature and Culture: Reflections on Menstrual and Parturitional Taboos in Huaulu (Seram)." In *Power and Difference: Gender in Island Southeast Asia*, ed. Jane M. Atkinson and Shelly Errington, 253–72. Stanford: Stanford University Press.

Vélez-Ibáñez, Carlos G. 1996. *Border Visions: Mexican Culture of the Southwest United States*. Tucson: University of Arizona Press.

Vélez-Ibáñez, Carlos G. 2004. "Regions of Refuge in the United States: Issues, Problems, and Concerns for the Future of Mexican-Origin Populations in the United States." [Malinowski Award Lecture, 2003]. *Human Organization* 63 (1): 1–20 (Ernesto Galarza Applied Research Center Monograph Series No. 2, University of California, Riverside).

Vila, Pablo. 2000. *Crossing Borders, Reinforcing Borders: Social Categories, Metaphors, and Narrative Identities on the U.S.-Mexico Frontier*. Austin: University of Texas Press.

Washington-Valdez, Diana. 2005. *Cosecha de Mujeres: Safari en el desierto mexicano*. Mexico City: Océano.

White, Hayden. 1973. *Metahistory: The Historical Imagination in Nineteenth-Century Europe*. Baltimore: Johns Hopkins University Press.

Wilson, Thomas W., and Hastings Donnan, eds. 1998. *Border Identities: Nation and State at International Frontiers*. Cambridge: Cambridge University Press.

Wright, Melissa. 1998. "'Maquiladora Mestizas' and a Feminist Border Politics: Revisiting Anzaldúa." *Hypatia* 13 (3): 114–31.

Young, Gay. 1986. *The Social Ecology and Economic Development of Ciudad Juárez*. Boulder: Westview Press.

Tijuana Cuir

SAYAK VALENCIA TRIANA

The foundation for the future politics of social transformation and rupture lies in the very processes of subjectivization and singularization in opposition to the dominant modes; these processes should allow for the permanent reinvention of the word and of ways of being.—VIRGINIA VILLAPLANA, *zonas de intensidades* [Zones of intensities]

First, I see it as essential to begin this essay by analyzing a number of elements of the regional, geopolitical, and social context within which Tijuana is circumscribed. According to Wikipedia:

> Tijuana is a Mexican city, belonging to the state of Baja California. It is the most populous city in the state and is located 105 miles to the west of the state capital, Mexicali, and approximately 30 minutes north of Ensenada. The city is the seat of the municipality of the same name and is known by other nicknames, including "the corner of Mexico" or "the door to Mexico." Its slogan is *"Aquí empieza la patria"* [The homeland begins here]. It is the westernmost city in Latin America; Tijuana is located in Mexico's sixth-largest metropolitan zone, but, combined with

Rosario, Tecate, and San Diego (California), it comprises the largest "transnational" metropolitan zone in Mexico, with more than 5 million inhabitants.[1]

I've attempted to show the geopolitical coordinates of the city because it is regularly referenced in a decontextualized way, following a style of postmodern overrepresentation that glorifies the reinterpretive dystopias of the economy and subjectivity as "new and radically open horizons: the insurrections of the peripheral areas show us that the inhabitants of these areas are the living material, the flesh of the masses of which the globalized world is made."[2] This creates a tautology in the representations of this border in international academic works.

Nevertheless, most of these interpretations ignore or disregard the regional context of Tijuana. The city is part of the state of Baja California and has been governed for more than twenty years by the Partido Acción Nacional (PAN; National Action Party), with its clear conservative and reactionary inclinations; for example, in 2008, the PAN amended the constitution to make abortion illegal in Baja California (in the seventh article of the first paragraph). During September 2011, the PAN successfully convinced the Mexican Supreme Court to back said reform, which criminalized the right of women to make decisions about their own bodies, penalizing any kind of abortion from the point of conception on, regardless of whether or not the pregnancy was caused by rape. It's ridiculous and unacceptable to call abortion the murder of a fetus, since the fetus is actually cell tissue which may or may not continue growing; this discourse is silent when it comes to the real obscenities of hunger, the fierce, repressive violence against women and queer subjects, the derealization of the living in favor of the economy, slavery and child prostitution, immigration and its dead in the state.

In my opinion, the prohibition of abortion in the state is a distraction tactic of patriarchal institutions, represented by doctors, fathers, priests, lovers, rapists, etc., so as not to have to speak of themselves or about the ultraviolent context in which Baja California lives on a daily basis. Talking constantly about women, their bodies, their sexuality, and their choices is the best way to continue controlling us; it's a clear way to avoid the enunciation of an autonomous discourse about their own issues. As Virginie Despentes states: "Men like to talk about women. That way, they don't have to talk about themselves. How can it be explained that in the last thirty years no (traditional) man has produced an innovative text on masculinity? When will there be a masculine emancipation?"[3]

As a transfeminist,[4] I consider this question of antiabortionism to be essential for a more located analysis of the everyday context in Tijuana, an analysis that must take into account the weight of conservatism in the state itself, as well as the conservatism of San Diego County. Within this context, the question arises: can queerness develop in a conservative context?

Accordingly, we should remember that the emergence of the queer movement in the United States is composed of distinct movements in opposition to Reaganism (from the 1980s to the early 1990s) and to its neoliberal, conservative project, which sought to disassemble the welfare system, endangering sexual and racial minorities both economically and existentially. In this way, the rise of the queer movement is due to a combination of economic, political, and social factors. Of this multiplicity of factors, we can highlight two: (1) the emergence of AIDS as an illness, stigmatizing people designated as "risk groups," i.e., homosexuals and drug users; (2) the mobilization in Southern California of black and Chicana lesbians, who rebel against the standard of the white, heterosexual, middle-class woman used as a political category by the feminist movement. This complex popular movement set forth a new model of identity politics, which, as a reaction against the normalizing tendency of supposedly oppositional political movements, resists their definition as women, lesbians, or homosexuals in order to vindicate themselves as queer subjects (that is, as *different* or *strange, minority*). This new conceptualization doesn't just include sexual options that are different from the heterosexual norm; rather, any person who suffers some type of discrimination because of social class, race, culture, or sexual identity is identified as *queer*: in Deleuze and Guattari's terms, the *becoming-minorities*.

Thus, it's clear that if the emergence of the queer in Tijuana as a movement of dissidence and radical criticism hadn't occurred, it would have had to be invented. This is because the current regional and national contexts demand social mobilization and criticism of the apparatuses of power and of the technologies of gender, which have created a fertile field for the increasing use of spectacular violence and have led to its economic profitability, as well as an iconization of violent masculinity and the emergence of *endriago* subjectivity.

In order to be able to discuss the possibility of queerness in TJ, I think it is necessary to make visible the complexity of the criminal networks in the Mexican context, and its connections with rampant neoliberalism, globalization, the narcomachine, the binary construction of gender as political performance, and the creation of capitalistic subjectivities, recolonized by the economy and represented by Mexican criminals and drug traffickers, who within the taxonomy of gore capitalism[5] receive the name of *endriago* subjects.

We will begin by talking about what we understand as masculine gender performance, that is: the acritical obedience of men to a performance of the gender norms dictated by hegemonic masculinity, which holds as one of its most deeply entrenched values economic respectability like *"indifference to danger, contempt for feminine virtues and the affirmation of authority on any level."*[6] That is to say, in order to be a legitimate male in the Mexican context, who (re)produces and reaffirms his gender identity, he must assume and uphold the choreographies (movements, relational behaviors) constructed by sociocultural hegemony for masculinity. This fulfillment of hegemonic, masculinist demands is repeated until they become artificially naturalized and understood as the *essence* of masculinity.

However, what is the relationship between this acritical representation (performance) of the choreographies of masculinity and the Mexican state and the narcomachine? The nexus emerges in the following way: the term *macho* is highly implicated in the state construction of Mexican identity; after the revolutionary struggles, the use of this term expands in Mexico as a sign of national identity. During that period the term *machismo* was associated with the working and peasant classes, since in the incipient configuration of the Mexican nation, the *macho* became a superlativization of the concept of man that later would become naturalized artificially as a *national social heritage* and would no longer be restricted to the subaltern classes. The constructions of gender in the Mexican context are intimately related to the construction of the state.

Thus, in light of the contextual situation of contemporary Mexico (the unraveling of the social fabric, the breakdown of the state and the rise of conservatism), we need to make the connections between the state, and the criminal class visible, since both of them uphold the maintenance of a violent masculinity, related to the construction of the national. In the present day, this nexus has social, economic, and political implications, leading to a high number of human casualties. This is because of the masculinist logic of the challenge and the struggle for power; if maintained, this logic will legitimate the criminal class as subjects with full rights to carry out violence: this being one of the main orders to follow, according to the demands of hegemonic masculinity, national machismo, gore capitalism, and heteropatriarchy.

In addition to the connection between gender performance and the construction of the Mexican state as a *machista* state, we must also add the economic demands of contemporary capitalism, which demands all individuals be hyperconsumers in order to be considered legitimate members of the g-local capitalist structure. In addition, we must also consider the colonialism that underlies Mexican idiosyncrasy, in which there is a desire to whiten oneself through economic empowerment, as well as homophobia: a ghost that accompanies hegemonic masculinity. All these elements add up to a Molotov cocktail for the construction of capitalistic subjectivities, which in this essay we call endriago subjects, in whom we see crystallized all the previously mentioned factors.

We take the endriago from medieval literature, specifically the book *Amadís de Gaula.*[7] This follows Mary Louise Pratt's thesis, which affirms that the contemporary world is governed by *the return of the monsters.*[8]

The endriago is a literary character, a monster, a cross between a man, a hydra, and a dragon. It is characterized by its large stature, agility, and beastliness. It is one of the enemies that Amadís de Gaula must confront.[9] In the book, it is described as a being endowed with defensive and offensive elements sufficient to provoke fear in any adversary. Its fierceness is so great that the island where it lives is described as an uninhabited locale, a kind of earthly hell where the only people who can enter are knights whose heroism borders on madness; the descriptions of these locales resemble those of contemporary border zones.[10]

We make this analogy with the literary figure of the endriago, who is one of the Others, unacceptable and the enemy, since its construction was based on a colonialist optic that is still present in many parts of the planet that are considered ex-colonies, places which are being economically recolonized by the demands of global production and hyperconsumption, creating new ultraviolent, destructive subjects who make up the rank and file of gore capitalism and the narcomachine.

However, apart from the characteristics attributed to this literary figure, and shared by the endriago subjects, these have another set of characteristics and contexts that we will detail now. The endriago subjects arise out of a specific context: post-Fordism. This makes clear and traces a basic genealogy to explain the connection between poverty and violence, between the birth of endriago subjects and gore capitalism.

In the contemporary global context, we find that "petty crime, robbery, and scams tend to be justified as easy ways to acquire money and to participate in the dominant lifestyles with which the media bombards us."[11] With this epistemological alteration in the conception of violence, it comes to be perceived as a tool for personal self-affirmation, and at the same time as a means of subsistence; this turn is especially evident in border zones, Tijuana being a key example.

In terms of the identity characteristics of the endriago subject, we can mention the fact that said subject is anomalous and transgressive, combining a logic of lack (poverty, failure, dissatisfaction) and a logic of excess, a logic of frustration with a logic of heroification, a hate drive and a utilitarian strategy. We understand endriago subjects as a set of individuals who circumscribe a capitalistic subjectivity, filtered through globally precarious economic conditions, along with a subjective agency from ultraviolent practices that incorporate, in a self-referential, delimiting way, "the systems of direct connection between the great productive machines, the great machines of social control and the psychic instances that define perception of the world,"[12] as well as the fulfillment of demands of gender prescribed by hegemonic masculinity. The everyday context of Tijuana is formed within the previously mentioned structure in a paradoxical way: on the one hand, the endriago subjectivities, the economic transactions and the double standards of the political class; on the other hand, Tijuana as a young city that disobeys and makes pertinent a critique of this retrograde system, which is conservative because it seeks to preserve certain values of oppression, discrimination, and fear of difference and of becoming-minorities, but Tijuana is made up of these becomings and of contradictory multitudes.

From my point of view, it is also crucial to analyze what we understand by *queer*. In another article in this same book ("Technicolor? Or Just Rainbow Tinted Lenses . . ."), Jennifer Donovan and I asked ourselves if it was appropriate to label Tijuana as a queer geography. This (self-)questioning was founded in two motives: (1) We refused to impose a hegemonic and ethnocentrist vision on semiotics, choreographies, and processes specific to the city in order to make them "easily" identifiable; (2) We were opposed to treating the term queer as another label in the capitalist market, exportable to diverse contexts and phenomena, without considering the geopolitical context of the city. Both of these concerns can be found in this essay as well. Nevertheless, once the context of Tijuana has been presented briefly, we will move to situate what we understand as queer and in what way this term can be used to describe certain recreational and micropolitical practices in the city.

The term *queer* is complicated since it cannot be applied universally, nor in a totalizing way, although I am conscious that said concept was reappropriated and resignified during the struggles of becoming-minorities in the United States during the 1980s and taken up again during the 1990s by certain feminist theoreticians, like Teresa de Lauretis, Judith Butler, and Eve Kosofsky Sedgwick, who built a discursive corpus about those oppositional movements that later would be called Queer Theory.

Nevertheless, the richness of the term exceeds that genealogy; in this sense, if we confront the problem of the translation of the term into Spanish, the dictionary throws us a list of words like the following: "strange, weird, unwell, dejected, mad, eccentric, outlandish, bizarre, suspicious, mysterious, false"; whereas *queerness* means something like "strangeness, weirdness, ridiculousness."[13] If we dig a little deeper, it is said that the term *queer* is derived from the Latin *torquere*, which means twisted; this meaning at the root of the term would create another genealogy, no longer attributing the copyright solely to the Anglo-Saxon context, which has been the cause of multiple debates and rejections of the queer and its applicability in the Latin American context.

Beyond the etymological debates (which for me seem to be fundamental and justified) and the complexity of the translation/transfer of the term to other geopolitics, for this essay it is important to say that *queer* refers above all to those who are able to evade interpretative unidirectionality, who are able to be unintelligible at first sight, those people outside of the simple models and frames of hegemonic representation, which is not very difficult to achieve in a g-local world that is presumed to be "white" even though the majority of its inhabitants are not "white." Thus, the queer would be a massive thing, more specifically, of the masses opposed both to the traditional political institutions that present themselves as sovereign and universally representative, and to the heterocentric, sexopolitical epistemologies that still dominate the production of politics, economics, science, discourse, gender, and somatopolitics.

So then, we understand the queer as a type of choreographic flow of becoming-minorities; now we still need to investigate how this concept can be applied or refer to the social, political, cultural, and geographic space of Tijuana. With this in mind, we endorse said concept as possible in the context of Tijuana in its phonetic, improper/deviant/Hispanicized form: *cuir*. We are inspired by the "The International Cuir," which argues: "The variation *queer/ cuir* [. . .] registers the geopolitical inflection towards the south and from the peripheries, in counterpoint to colonial epistemology and Anglo-American historiography."[14]

Once these points have been made clear/explicit, we can then have a dialogue about the term *cuir* and the way in which this phenomenon, in existence, coexists with the three most insidious clichés about the city: *Tijuana, laboratory of postmodernity, Tijuana, city of passage,* and *Tijuana, city of vice.* Subsequently, we will analyze whether the city can be considered as representative of cuir geography.

Tijuana, Laboratory of Postmodernity

From the mid-1990s through the present decade, much has been written about Tijuana; in fact, Tijuana has suffered a kind of overrepresentation and glorification by cultural studies and other disciplines, beginning with the famous quote by the Argentinian anthropologist Néstor García Canclini who said about the city: "[Tijuana is] a modern, contradictory cosmopolitan city with a strong definition of itself [. . .] this city is, along with New York, one of the major laboratories of postmodernity."[15]

Even prior to the popularization and exoticization of Tijuana as the epitome of postmodernism, the city already had attained, in the Mexican social imaginary, a *leyenda negra* (black legend) because of its location on the border.

It is said that illegality is characteristic of borders, that these territories have been created to this end, that that is the function they serve within the state. In any case, these affirmations do not apport anything at a discursive level, since "naturalizing" the conditions of a territory with a word like *postmodern*, to the level of exalting it, places us in an acritical and resigned position in regard to the potentiality of our actions to redirect that "nature."

Tijuana, City of Passage

Tijuana is also interpreted as a *ciudad de paso* (city of passage). Nevertheless, we consider it more appropriate to read Tijuana as a *trans-city* since this prefix implies a displacement, not just physically but also between languages and economic perspectives "opposite the cities of California that consider themselves post-peripheral, wealthy metropolises."[16] Tijuana appears as a postapocalyptic landscape, an indisputable product of neoliberalism, while simultaneously becoming a key city in the New World Order, demonstrating that this *New Order* is far from fulfilling other, noneconomic pacts.

This *state of passing through* that converts Tijuana into a trans-city can be identified in its lack of urban planning, in its architecture dotted with emergency constructions, in which golf courses coexist with shantytowns; we find the widest possible array of constructions, from houses made of refuse materials to enormous mansions built in a style we could classify as *narcoarchitecture*.

We must not forget that space affects bodies through biopolitics and somatopolitics; in this sense, the emergency architecture of Tijuana could be read as falling outside the paradigms of traditional beauty and livability. This positions the city and the bodies that live in it within social exchanges closer to *cuir* politics than the discursive hegemony; however, these bodies and the city itself play a fundamental role in the world order, because of their flexibility and their capacity to adapt to the changes required by the conditions of competitiveness and economic and existential precarization, brought about by economic globalization.

Tijuana, City of Vice

Tijuana's proximity to the globalized world's most influential economic and political power means that the city, since it is located at a strategic geographic point, becomes an ideal zone for the transit of illegal products and services that attempt to enter the U.S. market, as it is one of the most prosperous consumer markets in history. The reading of Tijuana as a *city of vice* must be inscribed and codified in relation to the First World's demands for leisure and consumption.

In the case of Tijuana, this relationship necessitates an analysis of the U.S. market, since said market is considered to be the principal consumer of services offered by gore capitalism to satisfy its practical and recreational necessities.

In this regard, we can reflect on the fact that the supply of gore services and the management of violence as the principal source of income for Tijuana's economy are founded on the fulfillment and also the reappropriation of the logics of the U.S. market.

Looking at the three interpretative clichés of the city, Tijuana could be considered a capital subjected to the New World Order, which shows us a countergeography produced by gore capitalism, understanding as countergeography what Saskia Sassen affirms in this regard:

> I call these circuits countergeographies of globalization because they are: (1) directly or indirectly associated with some of the key programs and conditions that are at the heart of the global economy, but (2) are circuits not typically represented or seen as connected to globalization, and often actually operate outside and in violation of laws and treaties, yet are not exclusively embedded [though neither can they be completely separated from these circuits] in criminal operations as is the case with the illegal drug trade.[17]

The concept of countergeography of globalization in some way refers, like an interpretation of space-city, to the way in which becoming-minorities are treated, discriminated against and exploited by hegemony. For that reason, we can say that *Tijuana is cuir* insofar as it has a problematic relationship with its context and insofar as it is a zone that can be considered, like the majority of borders, as a *national sacrifice zone*. We use this term to refer to the boundaries between poor countries and powerful countries; within these boundary zones, double dynamics are established that make these territories a space where *anything goes*, that is to say, they are considered the garage of the two countries.

Similarly, these are portal-territories in which undesirable and desirable merge, and simultaneously, hybridize these characteristics and make the application of a traditional axiology hard to conceptualize, creating a kind of eschatological rupture because of which they are conceived of as self-cannibalizing and sinister. Tijuana is one of these *backdoor cities*, cities that challenge intelligibility, that exceed the interpretive frames. Thus, the city is directly related with the agencies of the queer masses and with the necessity to begin to establish a movement of radical, transfeminist critique, as well as the need to posit other masculinities that reorient the capitalist, homophobic, *machista*, and gore structure, which is crystallized in the dynamics of the city through extreme violence executed by endriago subjects.

NOTES

Reprinted with permission from the author. This essay originally appeared in *Queer Geographies* (Beirut, Tijuana, Copenhagen, Dinamarca, Museet for Samtidskunst, 2014), 90–95.

1   Wikipedia Tijuana: http://es.wikipedia.org/wiki/Tijuana.

2   Antonio Negri and Giuseppe Cocco, "La insurrección de las periferias," in: *Revista Caosmosis*, July 10, 2007. http://caosmosis.acracia.net/?p=509.

3   Virginie Despentes, *Teoría King Kong* (Barcelona: Melusina, 2007): 118–20.

4   The transfeminist movement can be understood as an articulation both of thought and of social resistance; this movement is able to retain certain suppositions of the feminist struggle as necessary for acquiring rights in certain geopolitically diverse spaces, and at the same time includes the element of mobility between genders, corporealities, and sexualities leading to the creation of strategies applicable in situ. These strategies are identified with the Deleuzean idea of minorities, multiplicities, and singularities that make up a reticular organization capable of a reappropriation and intervention irreducible to the slogans of defense of women, identity, liberty, or equality, that is, it brings together a variety of living revolutions.

5   We propose the term *gore capitalism* to refer to the reinterpretation of the global, hegemonic economy in (geographically) borderland spaces; in our case we posit as an example of this phenomenon the city of Tijuana, the border located between Mexico and the United States, known as *the last corner of Latin America*. We take the term *gore* from a cinematographic genre that refers to extreme and categorical violence. Thus, with gore capitalism we refer to the explicit and unjustified spilling of blood (as a price the Third World pays, as it embraces adherence to the logics of an increasingly demanding capitalism), to the extraordinarily high percentage of viscera and dismemberings, frequently mixed with organized crime, gendered and the predatory uses of bodies, all this by means of the most explicit violence as a tool of *necroempowerment*. Cf. Sayak Valencia, *Capitalismo Gore* (Barcelona: Melusina, 2010).

6   Carlos Monsiváis, "¿Pero hubo alguna vez once mil machos?" *FEM*, no. 18 (April–May 1981): 9.

7   It is a masterpiece of fantastic medieval literature in Spanish and the most famous of the so-called *libros de caballería* (books of chivalry), which were extremely popular during the sixteenth century on the Iberian Peninsula.

8   Mary Louis Pratt, "Globalización, Desmodernización y el Retorno de los Monstruos," Third Gathering on Performance and Politics, Universidad Católica. Lima, Peru, 2002.

9   Amadís de Gaula would represent the knight and the inherited values of all Western culture. Amadís would be the Western subject par excellence, the nonmonster, the non-Other; that is, the universal subject without fissures that later would be defended by the logics of the Enlightenment and humanism.

10 By *border* territories, we mean borders in general, but we emphasize the borders in Northern Mexico that are next to the United States and especially Tijuana, Ciudad Juárez, and Tamaulipas, which fit perfectly as they are territories that have been overrun for decades by the drug cartels, human traffickers, prostitution, and the different repressive forces of the State, thus made into a battlefield, a territory

in a state of emergency that clearly shows the connections between the state and organized crime in Mexico.

11 Gilles Lipovetsky, *La felicidad paradójica. Ensayo sobre la sociedad hiperconsumista* (Barcelona: Anagrama, 2007), 184.

12 Félix Guattari and Suely Rolnik, *Micropolítica: Cartografías del deseo* (Madrid: Traficantes de Sueños, 2006), 41.

13 *Debate Feminista* 16 "Raras rarezas" (October 1997): 9.

14 "La internacional cuir. Transfeminismo, micropolíticas sexuales y video-guerrilla." http://www.museoreinasofia.es/programas-publicos/audiovisuales/internacional-cuir.html.

15 Néstor García Canclini, *Culturas híbridas. Estrategias para entrar y salir de la modernidad* (Barcelona: Grijalbo, 1989), 293–94.

16 Mike Davis, *Ciudades Muertas. Ecología, catástrofe y revuelta* (Madrid: Traficantes de Sueños, 2007), 113.

17 Saskia Sassen, *Contrageografías de la Globalización. Género y ciudadanía en los circuitos transfronterizos* (Madrid: Traficantes de Sueños, 2003), 66.

PART II

DOCUMENTING

IDENTITIES

The United States, Mexico, and *Machismo*

AMÉRICO PAREDES

One of the most widely discussed Mexican national types is the *macho,* the superman of the multitude. He has preoccupied psychologists, sociologists, philosophers, historians, poets, and even folklorists. Some, like folklorist Vicente T. Mendoza, have explained him as a phenomenon caused by the climate, or as a result of tendencies inherited by the Mexicans from the people of Andalusia.[1] On the other hand, many others have explained *machismo* in terms of Freudian theories. *Machismo*—so they tell us—has its origins in the Conquest, when Hernán Cortés and his conquistadors arrived in Mexico and raped the women of the Aztecs. From this act of violence is born the *mestizo,* who hates and envies his Spanish father and despises his Indian mother—in both cases as a result of his Oedipal complexes. Various Mexican writers have taken this line, but Samuel Ramos may be singled out as the initiator and Octavio Paz as one of the most eloquent defenders of this theory. In Argentina, too, Ezequiel Martínez Estrada applied a similar point of view to the *gaucho.*[2] The characteristic traits of *machismo* are quite well known: the outrageous boast, a distinct phallic symbolism, the identification of the man with the male animal, and the ambivalence toward women—varying from an abject and tearful posture to brutal disdain. The Mexican *macho,* Santiago Ramírez tells us, "is terribly fond of all articles of clothing symbolizing masculinity: the hat (either the fancy sombrero or the wide-brimmed Borsalino), the pistol, the horse or automobile are his pleasure and his pride."[3] *Machismo* finds expression in Mexican folklore, especially in the folksong. As Felipe Montemayor states, "The folksongs of Mexico are openly tearful and addressed to the woman who has gone away with another man 'who is no doubt more of a man than I am,' . . . in which he openly admits his frustration and failure; as for the rest, they are strings of phrases typical of one rejected, who tries to conceal his humiliation or the scorn directed at him by resorting to aggressive or compensatory forms."[4]

If all this has resulted from the rape of some Indian women by the soldiers of Cortés, then Mexican *machismo* is very ancient indeed. It has existed some four centuries at least, if one is to suppose that effects follow soon after causes. It should be possible, then, to make an interesting study of the folkloric expressions of Mexican *machismo,* from the time of the first *mestizo* up to the present. Such a work cannot be expected from either psychologists or poets, to whom we owe but superficial references to Mexican folksong and other folkloric genres. We would expect it from a folklorist, a Vicente Mendoza for example. And in truth, there is at least one study by Vicente T. Mendoza on this subject, "El machismo en México al través de las canciones, corridos y cantares," published in Buenos Aires in 1962.[5] In this essay, one of the last left us by the late Mexican folklorist, we are told that "there are two kinds of *machismo:* one that we could call authentic, characterized by true courage, presence of mind, generosity, stoicism, heroism, bravery," and so forth and "the other, nothing but a front, false at bottom, hiding cowardice and fear covered up by exclamations, shouts, presumptuous boasts, bravado, double talk, bombast. . . . Supermanliness that conceals an inferiority complex."[6] Mendoza goes on to cite more than thirty Mexican folksongs as examples of what he calls "authentic" and "false" *machismo.*

There are at least three points of interest in this study of Mendoza's. The first is his definition of the two kinds of *machismo.* Mendoza's "false" *machismo*— with its "presumptuous boasts, bravado, and double talk"—is what all other writers on the subject would call the "real" *machismo,* that configuration of attitudes which has so preoccupied writers as divergent as Samuel Ramos and Octavio Paz. What Mendoza calls "authentic" *machismo* is no such thing. It is simply courage, and it is celebrated in the folksongs of all countries. Admiration for the brave man who dies for the fatherland, for an ideal, or simply because he does not want to live without honor or without fame is found among all peoples. It is the heroic ideal in any time and in any country. Furthermore, the examples of boastful songs that Mendoza gives us date from the last third of the nineteenth and the first third of the twentieth centuries. That is to say, they belong to the period of the Revolution or to the times of Porfirio Díaz, immediately preceding the revolutionary period. Finally—and this is the most surprising thing of all—in all the examples Mendoza gives us of folksongs illustrative of Mexican *machismo*, not once does there occur the word *macho* or any of its derivatives. The heroes of the folksongs cited by Mendoza "die like men"; they are said to be "real men," and they are "valiant" or "brave." But they are never *machos*. The words *macho* and *machismo* occur repeatedly in the essay, but only in Mendoza's discussion of this supposedly Mexican phenomenon.

If the reader believes that the examples given by Mendoza are not representative, he can consult the major collections—those of Vázquez Santa Ana, Rubén Campos, and others including Mendoza himself.[7] The reader will find no traces of *machismo* in the songs of the colonial period, the war of independence, or even the Reformation. He will encounter many brave men in those songs, but rarely will he find the bully. The Mexican bully as a folkloric type begins to appear in the *décimas* printed in the last two decades of the nineteenth century, in leaflets from presses like that of Antonio Vanegas Arroyo and with titles like "El Guanajuateño," "El Valiente de Guadalajara." Let us emphasize that these boastful *décimas* of the last part of the nineteenth century are of a decidedly comic character. They abound in humorous sayings and proverbial phrases. A *décima* from "El Guanajuateño" (The Man from Guanajuato) may serve as an example for the whole genre:

No se arruguen, valentones,
traigan dispuestos sus fierros
que aquí está "El Guanajuateño"
para darles sus lecciones.
Acérquense los matones
que yo no les tengo miedo,
firme y parado me quedo
esperando cuchilladas;
me parecen enchiladas
que me trago las que puedo.[8]

Don't back down on me, you bravos, and carry your blades at ready; here's a man from Guanajuato, to teach you a thing or two. Come a bit closer, you bullies; I am not afraid of you. Here I stand, firm and erect, awaiting your thrusts to parry; to me they're like enchiladas, and I'll guzzle all I can.

One must be extremely ingenuous to think that we have here a faithful picture of the Mexican bravo in real life. The man who is convinced that life is not worth living does not waste time on well-turned phrases and colorful words. Artistic boasting is found among Mexican males, but almost always it is the buffoon of the group who cultivates this genre. Usually he is the drunkest and least courageous member of the group, whose lack of valor and manliness gives him a certain minstrel-like license. It is this type, and not the bravo, who is described in the *décimas de valientes*. And let us also keep in mind: the boastful protagonist of these *décimas* says he is "a real man," "valiant," and "brave." He may compare himself with the tiger and the panther, or he will say that he is "a fever on stilts." But he never calls himself a *macho*.

The Mexican boast turns serious once the Revolution begins, and then it passes from the *décima* to the *corrido*. The idea of manliness existed in the Mexican *corrido* before the Revolution, as Mendoza shows in his study, for example in the *corrido* of "Demetrio Jáuregui":

> *Le contestó Don Demetrio:*
> *—Yo no me vine a rajar,*
> *yo vine como los hombres*
> *aquí a perder o ganar.*[9]

Don Demetrio replied, "I didn't come to back out of a fight; I came here like a man, either to win or to lose."

Now the *corrido* picks up the kind of boast seen earlier in the *décima*, no longer in jest, however, but with all the seriousness of spirits inflamed by the Revolution. For example, in the corrido "De la persecución de Villa," the singer pokes fun at the efforts made by Pershing's forces to capture Pancho Villa:

> *Qué pensarán los "bolillos" tan patones*
> *que con cañones nos iban a asustar;*
> *si ellos tienen aviones de a montones*
> *aquí tenemos lo mero principal.*[10]

What did these Gringo Bigfoots think, that they scare us with cannon. They may have piles of airplanes, but we have the thing that really counts.

"The thing that really counts" is, of course, courage—concentrated in the testicles of the Mexicans—what will give them the advantage over all the cannon and airplanes of the United States. Here we come much closer to what is usually meant by *machismo*. Another *corrido* of the same era presents the same attitudes even more explicitly, this one being "Los ambiciosos patones":

> *Se va a mirar muy bonito de gringos el tenderete,*
> *después no quedrán la gorda; les sudará hasta el copete.*

La verdad, yo les suplico que traigan a sus gringuitas,
porque estamos enfadados de querer a las inditas,
sé que las tienen bonitas, gordas y bien coloradas,
ahora es tiempo, camaradas, de pelear con muchas ganas,
que les vamos a "avanzar" hasta las americanas.[11]

It will be a pretty sight, to see all those Gringo corpses; they will flinch from the tortilla, and they will sweat up to here. In truth, I hope they will bring their Gringo women along, because we are getting tired of loving our Indian girls. I know that they have some nice ones, plump and with red faces. Now is the time, my comrades, to fight with a will; there will be lots of plunder, even American women.

This last song has the melody of a *corrido*, but the text is composed in *décimas*. Moreover, the influence of the braggart type of *décima* may be seen in the number of proverbial phrases it contains, such as "they want to scare us with the dead man's pallet," "they are going to stake out their hides," and "go slow in reaching in there, or you'll get your hand full of thorns." It must be noted it is in the *corridos* about United States intervention in the affairs of Mexico where we find these examples of what could be called the "boast taken seriously." Nevertheless, the word *macho* does not occur in these *corridos* either. Not until the 1940s, during World War II, do we begin to run across it. Mendoza published a *corrido* entitled "De pistoleros y moronistas" ("About gunmen and partisans of Morones"), collected in 1949 but dating from the period between 1940 and 1946, the administration of President Manuel Ávila Camacho. The last stanza goes like this:

¡Viva el pueblo siempre macho! ¡Agustín el general!
y ¡Viva Ávila Camacho y la vida sindical![12]

Long live the people, who are always *machos*! Long live Agustín, the general! Long live Ávila Camacho and the labor unions!

In another *corrido*, very popular in the 1940s, the protagonist brags about Mexican courage, and how the Mexicans are going to wreak havoc on the Axis once Mexico decides to join in the war, adding that their president is "Ca . . . macho!" In still another song of the same period, threats are hurled at the Axis nations, as the singer says:

Yo soy puro mexicano
y me he echado el compromiso con la tierra en que nací
de ser macho entre los machos,
y por eso muy ufano yo le canto a mi país.

I am a true-blue Mexican, and I have an obligation to the land where I was born, to be a *macho* among *machos*; and that is why I proudly sing to my country.

In these *corridos* of the 1940s, where we do find the word *macho*, we almost always see it in association with other well-defined factors. One of these is the grim figure of the *pistolero*, one of the most dismal products of the post-revolutionary period. This is the man of the Revolution projected into peace-time, and therefore out of his element: the pistol-toting bully who sates his brutal impulses by trampling on the common citizen, and who can do it with impunity because he has money or political influence or simply because he is the bodyguard of some congressman or governor. Another factor is World War II, in which Mexicans took almost no part, in which they were not threatened by danger, desolation, or death—as they were during the Revolution. This is why the boasts ring so false in the *corridos* of the 1940s as compared to those of the Revolution. The revolutionary boasts directed against the United States arose from a situation both dangerous and real, and they expressed the sentiments of a majority of Mexicans. The boasts against the Axis during the 1940s sound like those of a little man who hurls threats while hiding behind a protector much larger than he. And let us remember that in this case, the "protector" was the tra-ditional enemy, the United States. A third factor is the accident that in this pe-riod the last name of the Mexican president included the sound *macho*. I am not suggesting that the word *macho* was not used in Mexico prior to the 1940s, or that *machismo* would not have appeared in Mexico if Ávila Camacho had not been president. But we must remember that names lend reality to things. The name of Camacho—because it rhymes with *macho* and because it was well-known when other factors favored *machismo*—gave to both word and concept a popularity they did not have before. Before that time *macho* had been almost an obscen-ity, and consequently a word less used than *hombre* or *valiente*. Now it became correct, acceptable. After all, wasn't it in the name of the president himself?

Then appear the *corridos* for which Mexico is known abroad, the same ones cited repeatedly by those who deplore *machismo*. The following stanzas exem-plify the style:

> ¡Traigo mi cuarenta y cinco
> con sus cuatro cargadores!
> ¡Y traigo cincuenta balas,
> las traigo pa' los traidores!

I'm wearing my forty-five with its four cartridge clips! And I carry fifty bullets; they are for renegades!

And another one, even more foolish:

¡Caramba, yo soy su rey
y mi caballo el segundo!
¡Ora se hacen a mi ley
o los aparto del mundo!

Caramba, I am your king; and my horse is second only to me! Now you will bow to my law, or I'll send you from this world!

Such *corridos* were disseminated in Mexico and abroad by the voices of popular singers like Pedro Infante and Jorge Negrete. That is to say, these were moving-picture *corridos*. And when one says moving pictures, one says middle class. These have been the songs of the man from an emergent middle class, a man who goes to the movies, has enough money to buy a car, and enough political influence to go around carrying a gun. During World War II, it was this middle class that became emotional hearing Pedro Infante sing:

¡Viva México! ¡Viva América!
¡Oh pueblos benditos de Dios!

Long live Mexico! Long live America! Oh, nations blessed by God!

The feelings of the common man are revealed in a well-known anecdote. The news that Mexico has just declared war against the Axis reaches a little Mexican village. The authorities lead the people in the execution of various "vivas" to Mexico. In a pause a voice is heard yelling, "¡Viva México, and death to the Gringos!"

"Shut up, stupid!" they tell him. "The Gringos are our allies." "But how?" he says. "If it isn't the Gringos, then who are we fighting?"

It seems, then, that Mexican *machismo* is not exactly as it has been painted for us by people who like to let their imaginations dwell on the rape of Indian women. *Machismo* does not appear in Mexican folklore until very recent times. In a more-or-less comic form, it was characteristic of the lower classes in pre-Revolutionary times. In a more sentimental and meretricious style, it is identified today with the Mexican middle class. We note, furthermore, a certain influence of the United States. All this makes us ask: How Mexican is *machismo* and to what degree is it a Hispanic, a New World, or a universal manifestation?

We know that courage and virility have always been identified as the ideal traits of the male, and that both primitive and modern man often have equated the coward with the homosexual. Among some groups it has been the custom to dress in woman's clothes any man who did not show sufficient courage in battle. There is no lack of examples making direct identification between courage and manliness. In an Eskimoan song published by C. M. Bowra, an old man remembers his youth, when he was a great hunter. And he sings:

> I remember the white bear,
> With its back-body raised high;
> It thought it was the only male here,
> And came towards me at full speed.
> Again and again it threw me down,
> But it did not lie over me,
> But quickly went from me again.
> It had not thought
> Of meeting other males here,
> And by the edge of an ice-floe
> It lay down calmly.[13]

Let us take a second example from the Nordic peoples, of times past but not very remote, from the *Volsunga Saga*. Two heroes, Sinfjotli and Granmar, prepare to duel to the death; and as a preamble Sinfjotli says to his opponent:

> Dim belike is grown thy memory now of how thou wert a witch wife on Varinsey, and wouldst fain have a man to thee, and chose me to that same office of all the world; and how thereafter thou wert a Valkyrie in Asgarth, and it wellnigh came to this, that for thy sweet sake should all men fight; and nine wolf-whelps I begat on thy body in Lowness, and was the father to them all.[14]

Except for the archaic English, this might be a *pelado* doing the Mexican equivalent of the "dozens" with another of his type. But let us move to the eighteenth century, to the classical English poet John Dryden and his famous ode on Alexander the Great, which includes a kind of refrain that has become proverbial, "None but the brave, None but the brave, None but the brave deserve the fair." That is to say, the most valiant and vigorous *macho* wins the coveted female, a poetizing of the natural selection of the species before Darwin was even born. Yet, this is also the theme of many *Märchen*, and of numberless plots in our popular literature, movies, and television.

The ingredients of *machismo*, then, are found in many cultures; however, what has been observed in Mexico is a whole pattern of behavior, a popular philosophy, so to speak. Is Mexico unique in this respect? Martínez Estrada would have said no, since he thought he had found the same thing in the Argentine *gaucho*. But let us look in the opposite direction, and we will find a country— the United States—where something very similar to Mexican *machismo* took place, with lasting influences on folklore, literature, and even politics.

The North American *macho* first appears in the 1820s and 1830s. This was for the United States a time of revolution, the age of Andrew Jackson. Earlier the country had been dominated by the aristocrats of the Atlantic coast, the big landholders of Virginia and the rich merchants of New England. They talked, dressed, and lived in the English manner; their poets and fiction writers were mediocre imitators of the Europeans. The age of Jackson brings radical changes; the country openly enters its nationalistic period. The man of the forest—the frontiersman dressed in animal skins—becomes a political force, and the aristocrats of the coast look with horror at the vulgarity of the new leaders. In letters we have the dawning of a truly North American literature, which goes from the humorists of the 1820s to the novelist Mark Twain, and from him to the modern North American writers.[15] In folklore, the North American nationalistic movement is expressed in the tradition of the man from the backwoods, dressed in animal skins and armed with knife and long rifle. This figure—at the same time hero and buffoon—is expressed folkloristically in the tall tale, the humorous anecdote in which the stranger or Anglicized aristocrat from the coast is ridiculed, and the boast. Above all in the boast. The North American bully boasts of his vulgarity—the one thing the European and the Easterner held most against him. He thinks of himself as the bravest and most ferocious man in the world; he can fight more men, love more women, and drink more whiskey than any other man alive. He compares himself to the bear and the tiger, to the alligator and the hurricane. He challenges the whole world with rowdy yelling; he leaps in the air and then struts around. In short, he is the spitting image of the Mexican *pelado* making out as the bravo from Guadalajara or the panther from Guanajuato.

We need not stress that the North American *macho* expressed feelings of inferiority in respect to European culture. The North American was trying to attain a true independence within his own country, to fashion a culture of his own. In order to reach his goal, he would boast even of his weaknesses. On the other hand, he could not completely ignore the technological superiority of Europe and his own East. He could laugh at English literature, at Italian music, and at French dancing masters; but he knew that the English navy ruled the seas, and that his rifle had been made by Eastern craftsmen. Technology enabled him to conquer the West, although he always tried to deny it, giving the credit to his own manliness. Then came the Civil War, after which the United States began its march toward industrial and military world power. On the national level, Anglophobia gave way to Anglo-Saxonism, the glorification of a supposed Anglo-Saxon type.[16] During the period from 1870 to 1914, North American *machismo* undergoes some interesting changes. The *macho* becomes civilized, at least part of him. In folklore the frontiersman remains a comic character. The tall tales and the jokes in which the frontiersman appears as a boor continue to be told. That is to say, as a historical figure the *macho* persists in his role of buffoon. But the hero takes on new types (or stereotypes). In movies and dime novels, the *macho* becomes the cowboy. In serious literature he reappears as protagonist in the novels of Frank Norris, Jack London, and other writers of the naturalist school.[17]

In passing from folklore to the naturalistic novel, the North American *macho* loses not only his comic character but also his sexuality; that is to say, he becomes a Puritan *macho*, adjusting to the novelistic tradition of the times. He is all muscle and virility, but he releases his energy in orgies of violence against his enemies. The female still is the reward of his exploits, but all he does is show off in front of her—seriously now, and not in jest as the frontiersman had done. When he is not committing acts of barbarism against other men, he is a model of sobriety, filial love, and courtesy. In sum, he bears a surprising resemblance to the *charro* of recent Mexican movies, who—after shooting down half a dozen men—goes into church all loaded down with his guns, to sing a pious song to the Virgin of Guadalupe.

Aside from his asexual character, the *macho* of the naturalistic novel differs from the frontier *macho* in another respect: his nationalism turns into racism. The protagonist is always Anglo-Saxon, of course, and the cowardly, bad types are men darker than he—Italians, Portuguese, Spaniards, Mexicans, or Indians. The plot shows us that the blond *macho* is more of a *macho* than the dark ones; and therefore, he is Nature's chosen, according to the law of the jungle and the struggle for existence. This is nothing less than the superman as "blond beast," some forty years before Hitler. Furthermore, only the Anglo-Saxon blond is superior; the German, the Scandinavian, and the Irishman appear in the role of comedians or well-intentioned simpletons. This is a result, on the one hand, of Darwin's theories and, on the other, of the North American impulse toward empire and world power during this time. The pattern has its parallels in politics, and it is here that we find a historical figure, one single man, who symbolizes this second stage of North American *machismo*. This is Theodore Roosevelt—politician, cowboy, cavalry colonel, undersecretary of the navy, president, and a devotee par excellence of novelistic *machismo*. Not only in politics but in his personal life, Roosevelt made a determined effort to present before the public the figure of the *macho*, with all its strengths and weaknesses. Sickly as a child, myopic as to be almost blind, Roosevelt made it his business to show the world that, in spite of his physical deficiencies, he was just as good as any other man. It was this preoccupation that led him to try the most dangerous tasks of the hunter, the cowboy, and the soldier.

After World War I, a decided shift from *machismo* to feminism occurs in the United States, but it is not immediately apparent in literature. On the contrary, it is at this time that a figure analogous to Roosevelt appears in North American literature, this being the novelist Ernest Hemingway—the most hallowed interpreter of the *macho*. The popularity of Hemingway's works in the period between the two world wars—as much among the critics as with the general public—shows us the attraction the *macho* still had for the North American, although in real life the man of the United States made less and less of a show over his masculinity. Hemingway himself understood this, and almost all his novels and short stories develop the theme of *machismo* in Spain, Mexico, or Cuba. Today Hemingway is scorned by the critics. This is not surprising, since the protagonist of the novels now acclaimed by the critics no longer is the *macho* but the homosexual—the other extreme, or perhaps the same thing seen from another point of view. And although Hemingway has not been rejected by the general public, his works no longer are as popular as are novels of the type begun by Mickey Spillane. These are an exaggeration of the Hemingwayesque theme: the *macho* heroes are fierce, sexual, and brutally sadistic with the female. They do not stop with a simple beating, as might the "primitive" man. They riddle their women with bullets, a favorite target being the woman's belly. In North American folklore also, *machismo* is not completely a thing of the past. The boast and the tale still are cultivated among white folk groups. In the cities, meanwhile, the North American Negro has developed a genuinely *macho* folklore, with heroes that are bad men of insatiable sexual appetites. Their feats are narrated in folk poems and stories of an exaggerated obscenity. In the poetry are many boasts such as the following, taken from Roger Abrahams's book about the Philadelphia Negro:

I live on Shotgun Avenue, Tommygun Drive,
Pistol Apartment, and Room 45.[18]

This brings to mind what Santiago Ramírez has to say about the Mexican's fondness for pistols, big hats, and automobiles—above all for the pistol, symbol par excellence of *machismo*. A sexual symbol, the disciples of Freud would tell us; and in truth, *pistola* is one of the many terms that the Mexican uses for "penis." But the pistol has other meanings for the Mexican, historical meanings related to the clash of cultures in the West, especially in the region of the Great Plains. The Spaniards arrived at the borders of the Great Plains centuries before the North Americans appeared, but they never occupied these areas. One of the obstacles they encountered were mounted Indians like the Comanches, who gave a lot of trouble to the Spanish garrisons on the edge of the plains. Then come the North Americans; and in less than fifty years they totally subdue the Indians, occupy the Great Plains, and civilize the whole area. To what did the North American owe the ability to do in half a century what the Spaniard did not even begin in three? In a work on the subject, entitled precisely *The Great Plains*, the well-known Texas historian Walter Prescott Webb has explained it very simply: the North Americans were racially superior to the Spaniards. The Spaniards, being Europeans, were able to conquer inferior races like the Mexican Indians, in whose veins—Webb tells us—flowed ditch water instead of blood. But the Comanche was too fierce to be overcome by Spaniard or Mexican. Only the Anglo-Saxon could be a manlier man than the Comanche; and in subduing the Comanche the Anglo-Saxon proved his superiority over other Europeans like the German, the Scandinavian, and the Italian. As Webb tells it, the men who conquered the Great Plains all had English or Scottish names.[19]

No better examples exist of the influence of *machismo* in the academic world than the books of Walter Prescott Webb, in which we find an almost infantile admiration for the man who totes a gun and wears boots and a big hat. The explanation by this distinguished historian of the conquest of the Great Plains in terms of manliness—and exclusively of Anglo-Saxon manliness—ignores well-known facts: all classes of men participated in the conquest of the West, including Negroes, and the technology of eastern United States was a decisive factor in the superiority the North American of the West gained over Indians and Mexicans.[20] The surprising thing is that these facts were well known to Webb himself, since he discusses them with erudition and insight in other chapters of *The Great Plains*.[21] It seems to have been necessary for Webb, the man of the West, to reveal his personal feelings, boasting of the manliness of his region and its independence with respect to the East. Then Webb the historian gives us a careful study of the role played by the technology of the East in the conquering of the Great Plains: the importance of the repeating rifle, barbed wire, windmills, the revolver, and machines for large-scale agriculture. What he says about the revolver is of special interest for us.

The old long rifle was the North American's ideal weapon while he conquered the forests east of the Mississippi, where he fought in the woods on foot. But when he emerged on the plains, the North American found himself at a great disadvantage. His rifle, which he had to load through the muzzle with a ramrod, was an ineffective weapon against Indians and Mexicans, who were men on horseback. Once he fired his rifle, the North American had only his knife to defend himself with, and in the use of this weapon he found the Mexican a dangerous adversary.[22] The Indian was even more formidable, since he could discharge twenty arrows in the time necessary to load a rifle.[23] Furthermore, both Mexicans and Indians used the lance as well. Confronted with this problem, the North Americans in the West seriously considered two solutions that were not at all heroic. One was to build a series of forts on the borders of the Great Plains to contain the Indians—that is to say, precisely what the Spaniards had done. The other was the settling of French colonists in these same areas, to serve as a buffer between the Indians and the North Americans.[24] But it did not become necessary to carry out these projects, and the reason was the technology of the East. In New Jersey an artisan from Connecticut, Samuel Colt, began to produce the first revolvers in 1838. The North American army showed little interest in them, but the Texans and other men of the West received them with enthusiasm.[25] In 1844 the revolver was put to the test for the first time in a battle between Texans and Comanches; each Texan was armed with two revolvers and a rifle. The Indians fled in disorder; the revolver had changed the balance of power on the Great Plains in favor of the man with the two pistols.[26] A quarter of a century later, the Winchester rifle replaced the revolver as the preferred weapon in the Great West, but the revolver—as a result of its initial impact—remained the symbolic weapon as much in folklore as in popular literature, and later in the movies and on television.

The revolver not only changed the character of conflict with the nomadic Indian, but it also revolutionized the North American concept of manliness. Let us not forget that, before the arrival of the North American in the Great West, the Mexican had faced the Indian armed only with lance and knife, as did the Argentine *gaucho* against the Indian of the pampas. The North American, Webb tells us, recognized the Mexican as an "artist with a knife."[27] Webb says it not in admiration but in a contemptuous tone, since it is part of the tradition of *machismo* in the United States to scorn the man with the knife, who is always given the role of coward and traitor.[28] It was not always this way, for there was a time when the North American boasted of his skill with the knife and held it in such high esteem that he gave personal names to his favorite blades, as did the medieval knights to their swords. This was, naturally, before the revolver, in the days of the backwoodsman, typified by Davy Crockett, who died in the defense of the Alamo against the troops of Santa Anna. Another of the defenders of the Alamo was James Bowie, whose name became a synonym for knife, because Bowie was a virtuoso in what Martínez Estrada calls "the art of cutting throats."[29] Considering the derogatory associations later given the knife in the folklore of the United States, it is truly ironic that legend should picture Bowie at the Alamo, knife in hand against the Mexican muskets. And in truth, if we imagine a confrontation between two men—one armed with a rifle or revolver and the other with a knife—which of the two would we say is taking the greater risk? Let the Knight of the Sad Countenance give us the answer, in the celebrated disquisition on arms and letters that Don Quixote makes in the chapters dealing with the Captive of Algiers.

Happy the blest ages that knew not the dread fury of those devilish engines of artillery, whose inventor I am persuaded is in hell receiving the reward of his diabolical invention, by which he made it easy for a base and cowardly arm to take the life of a gallant gentleman; and that, when he knows not how or whence, in the height of the ardour and enthusiasm that fire and animate brave hearts, there should come some random bullet, discharged perhaps by one who fled in terror at the flash when he fired off his accursed machine, which in an instant puts an end to the projects and cuts off the life of one who deserved to live for ages to come.[30]

Cervantes reveals his own sentiments, no doubt, since he was maimed as a result of one of those "accursed machines." But he also expresses the feelings of most soldiers of his time. This is also the point of view in *Martín Fierro*, where we see the valiant *gaucho*, with "the one that never misfires" in his hand, facing cowards and scoundrels armed with revolvers and muskets.[31] But if we are gun-toters ourselves, we cannot accept such a judgment. We must change the situation, and thus it was in the North American tradition. The knife was made the weapon of the renegade, of the coward; the pistol became the weapon of the *macho*, the brave man. A paradox? It is, in truth, but it agrees with the tendency to change an unpleasant reality by inverting it, the very thing that is at the base of *machismo*.

Understandably, the Mexican did not immediately accept the North American's point of view. In much of Mexican folklore the steel blade retained its character as a suitable instrument for admirable deeds, and it was considered a very "Mexican" weapon as well. In a *corrido* from central Mexico of the 1930s, "Conversation between Two Rancheros," we hear of a migrant worker who returns to Mexico from the United States, full of Gringo ways and saying insulting things about Mexico. His *compadre*, who had stayed home on the farm, takes out his huge knife to punish him. Seeing the knife, the Americanized migrant falls on his knees and begs forgiveness for having offended the fatherland.[32] By this time, however, the Mexican had learned to use the revolver. The *norteño*, the Mexican from the border, recognized its worth at an early date by having been on the receiving end of more than one revolver. It is through the border *corrido*—in *norteño* folklore—that the revolver enters the folklore of Mexico, as the Mexican folk hero first abandons the knife for the gun. This corresponds with actual fact, for the border Mexican was a man with a pistol in this hand by the end of the 1850s. In 1859, when Juan Nepomuceno Cortina rebelled against North American authority in Texas, he did so after a shootout with a North American city marshal who had beaten one of his mother's farmhands. From Cortina on, the protagonists of the border *corrido* are men "pistol in hand." That is to say, they fight "American style," as we are told in a *corrido* from Sonora, "De Cananea":

Me agarraron los cherifes
al estilo americano—
como al hombre de delito—
todos con pistola en mano.

The deputies arrested me, in the American style—as they would arrest a criminal—all with pistols in their hands.

"With a pistol in his hand" or "with his pistol in his hand" becomes a conventional phrase in the *corrido* of the border between Mexico and the United States, distinguishing it from the *corrido* of southern Mexico, where this formula rarely appears before the 1930s. The man with pistol in hand is rarely a bully in the *corridos*. He pursues other goals, as did Cortina, defending himself against the abuses of an oppressive authority.

In a *corrido* from Coahuila, as late as the 1930s, a young man named Arnulfo and a state policeman gun each other down after the policeman slaps Arnulfo, simply because Arnulfo did not lower his eyes when the policeman looked at him. After the two are dead, the singer tells us in a fit of enthusiasm:

¡Qué bonitos son los hombres
que se matan pecho a pecho,
cada uno con su pistola,
defendiendo su derecho!

How beautiful it is to see two men gun each other down, standing face to face! Each with his pistol, each defending his right!

Something remains of the *corridos* on the clash-of-cultures theme, but this also sounds like *machismo*—presented in a situation like that of a Wild West movie. And there is good reason for the resemblance, since there is a very close relationship between Hollywood and the gun-toting *macho*, the *pistolero*. Let us return to the North American *macho* with his pistol in hand, and we will find him converted into the cowboy. Why the cowboy became the type chosen to synthesize the *macho* is another question, but let us look at these two figures—the *macho* and the cowboy—in relation to that great North American *macho*, Theodore Roosevelt. Roosevelt's admiration for cowboys was excessive, almost childish. He lived with them, working at their tasks, in order to prove his manliness. Later, during the Cuban war, he formed a regiment of cowboys, putting into practice his conviction that the cowboy was the best soldier possible because he was the epitome of all the austere, manly virtues. Nothing speaks more emphatically—Mody C. Boatright tells us in a study entitled "Theodore Roosevelt, Social Darwinism, and the Cowboy"—of Roosevelt's delight in the life of the cowboy than the fancy and expensive clothes he wore. Boatright quotes from a letter written by Roosevelt to his sister:

> I wear a sombrero, silk neckerchief, fringed buckskin shirt, sealskin chaparajos, or riding trousers, alligator hide boots, and with my pearl-hilted revolver and my beautifully finished Winchester rifle, I shall be able to face anything.[33]

The cowboy was taken almost totally from the Mexican tradition, but the North American made some important contributions, among them the pistol, the Stetson hat (an adaptation of the Mexican sombrero), and in our days the substitution of the horse with the Cadillac of the rancher-turned-millionaire. The pistol, above all—first the revolver and then the forty-five automatic with its four cartridge clips. A phallic symbol perhaps, but in a much more direct sense a symbol of power—and of the abuse of power as well. A symbol of the manliness of the bully, the *macho* of the movies, who guns his rival down in the middle of the street, lifts the girl to his saddle, and rides into the sunset on his faithful horse. Or on his Cadillac, heading for Houston, or Austin, or Washington. The pistol above all—symbol of the overbearing bully. The Mexican knew this well enough, from the day the first Colts arrived on the border. Harassed, dispossessed by the man with the gun, the Mexican lost no time in wishing to be a man with a gun also. And so it was that the Mexican took back from the North American something he had lent him, the figure of the *vaquero*; but he received his loan with interest, since the *vaquero* returned as cowboy—a *pistolero* and a *macho* among *machos*.

It would be an overstatement to say that the Mexican *macho* is merely a mirror image of the North American cowboy (although it is not much more extravagant to claim that he originates in Oedipal complexes caused by the Conquest). But any evaluation of Mexican *machismo* will not be complete if the following point is ignored: the fundamental attitudes on which *machismo* is based (and which have caused so much distress to those wishing to psycho-analyze the Mexican) are almost universal. What might distinguish Mexican *machismo* is not the presence of those attitudes but their undeniable exaggeration; yet, this is not peculiar to the Mexican, since something very similar has occurred in a modern and neighboring country, the United States. There is no evidence that *machismo* (in the exaggerated forms that have been studied and condemned in Mexicans) even existed in Mexico before the Revolution. Available evidence suggests that it is a phenomenon dating from the 1930s to the present, that is to say, from the period after the Revolution. There is an intriguing parallel between North American and Mexican *machismo*. In the United States the sense of manliness is exaggerated during the 1820s and 1830s, because of a growing sense of nationalism, resulting in greater participation by the common man in the democratic process of the country, as well as in a marked feeling of hostility and inferiority toward Europe, especially toward England. During this period the idea of North American manliness is mainly unconscious and expresses itself generally in folkloric forms, especially in the boast and the tall tale. Nor is this supermanliness completely divorced from reality, since it occurs at a time when the North American male becomes an explorer and conqueror, extending the borders of his country farther and farther to the west.

An analogous period in Mexico is the Revolution and the years immediately preceding it. The boundaries extended by the Mexican during this time are not geographic but of the spirit. Nevertheless, the attitudes are more or less the same: a growing feeling of nationalism accompanied by sentiments of distrust and inferiority toward outsiders, particularly toward the United States; and a movement toward democracy and equality. As with the North American during the 1820s and 1830s, such sentiments in the Mexican were for the most part unconscious; and they were expressed in folkloric forms—in the artistic boast during the final years of the Díaz regime and in the *corrido* during the Revolution. Again, it may be said that the Mexican sense of manliness had a firm basis in reality during the Revolution, when struggle and death were accepted as daily occurrences.

North American *machismo* becomes artificial and grotesque when the frontier ends, when the Wild West disappears and men no longer live in the midst of conflict and danger. Then comes on scene the cowboy, fabricated by the cheap popular writers, the *macho* of Theodore Roosevelt's type, with the fancy cowboy suit, the pearl-handled revolver, and the enormous spectacles of the myopic scholar. Close after him comes the cowboy of the cities, the "Professional Texan" with his white Stetson, his embroidered boots, and his Cadillac. The sense of manliness passes from folklore to the movies and popular literature, where we have the scorned woman abused by the man, at times physically tortured by the *macho* in forms of undoubtedly sexual symbolism. North American *machismo* in this late and exaggerated form goes even farther than does Mexican *machismo*, since the North American type is dignified in serious literature, in the novels of Frank Norris, Jack London, Ernest Hemingway, and many other lesser writers. In Mexico, too, the sense of manliness typical of the Revolution is converted into exaggerated *machismo* once the period of armed conflict has ended, more or less by 1930. This is also the date, by the way, that Vicente Mendoza singles out as marking the end of the truly folk *corrido*.[34] The *corrido* after 1930, according to Mendoza, passes from folklore to the movies and other mass media.

Both in Mexico and in the United States, *machismo* betrays a certain element of nostalgia; it is cultivated by those who feel they have been born too late. The North American *macho* acts as if the Wild West had never come to an end; the

Mexican *macho* behaves as if he is still living in the times of Pancho Villa. But we must make an important distinction. The United States began with feelings of inferiority toward England; today it is perhaps England that may feel inferior in respect to its former colony. Such is not the case with Mexico, since despite its undeniable progress it still lives under the shadow of the old Colossus of the North, today more colossal than ever. And here, at least, Samuel Ramos may have been right. But he also remarked that to feel inferior is not the same as being so.[35] We might add that to feel poor and to be poor are not exactly the same thing; and even more, that often the first is a necessary condition in doing away with the second. Upward-moving groups and peoples on the go are among those most disposed to feelings of inferiority. Both in the United States and in Mexico, *machismo*, despite all its faults, has been part of a whole complex of impulses leading toward a more perfect realization of the potentialities of man.

NOTES

Reprinted with permission from Indiana University Press. This essay was translated from Américo Paredes, "Estados Unidos, Mexico y el Machismo," *Journal of Inter-American Studies* 9 (January 19670): 65–84, by Marcy Steen. The essay originally appeared in English in the *Journal of the Folklore Institute* 8, no. 1 (June 1971): 17–37.

1   Vicente T. Mendoza, *Lírica narrativa de México: El corrido* (*Estudios de Folklore*, no. 2) (Mexico, Instituto de Investigaciones Estéticas, 1964), 34; "El machismo en México al través de las canciones, corridos y cantares," *Cuadernos del Instituto Nacional de Antropología* 3 (Buenos Aires: Ministerio de Educación y Justicia, 1962), 75.

2   Ezequiel Martínez Estrada, *Radiografía de la pampa*, 2 volumes (Buenos Aires: Editorial Losada, 1942; first ed. 1933).

3   Santiago Ramírez, *El mexicano: Psicología de sus motivaciones* (Mexico: Editorial Pax-México, 1959), 63.

4   Felipe Montemayor, "Postemio antropológico," *Picardía mexicana* (Mexico: Libro Mex, 1960), 229–30.

5   Mendoza, "El machismo en México," 75–86.

6   Mendoza, "El machismo en México," 75–76.

7   It is necessary to include the collections of *décimas* as well as those of *corridos, canciones*, and *cantares*.

8   Vicente T. Mendoza, *La décima en México* (Buenos Aires: Instituto Nacional de la Tradición, 1947), 611.

9   Mendoza, "El machismo en México," 9.

10   Mendoza, *Lírica narrativa*, 95.

11   Mendoza, *Lírica narrativa*, 82.

12   Mendoza, *Lírica narrativa*, 146.

13   C. M. Bowra, *Primitive Song* (*Mentor Books* MT 499) (New York: New American Library, 1962), 122.

14 William Morris, trans., *Volsunga Saga: The Story of the Volsungs and Niblungs*; with a new introduction by Robert W. Gutman (*Collier Books* BS 66) (New York: Crowell-Collier Publishing, 1962), 113.

15 We must remember that there is another literary tradition oriented toward Europe, that of Henry James.

16 Locally, especially in the center of the country, where there are many people of Germanic and Scandinavian ancestry, Anglophobia persists even today.

17 See Maxwel Geismar's *Rebels and Ancestors: The American Novel 1890–1915* (New York: Hill and Wang, 1963) concerning *machismo* in these authors.

18 Roger D. Abrahams, *Deep Down in the Jungle: Negro Narrative Folklore from the Streets of Philadelphia* (Hatboro, Pa., Folklore Associates, 1964), 147.

19 Walter Prescott Webb, *The Great Plains* (Boston: Ginn and Company, 1931), 144–38, 509.

20 See page vi of the preface of *The Great Plains*, where Webb considers the conquest of the Great Plains as "a new phase of Aryan civilization."

21 Especially chapters V, VII, and VIII.

22 Webb, *The Great Plains*, 168.

23 Webb, *The Great Plains*, 169.

24 Webb, *The Great Plains*, 180–84.

25 Webb, *The Great Plains*, 167–79.

26 Webb, *The Great Plains*, 173–75.

27 Webb, *The Great Plains*, 168.

28 Note, for example, this passage from a so-called history book. The famous bandit Billy the Kid has captured several Mexicans and taken their weapons: "The Kid examined the knives, lying on the ground beside the fire. They were of the finest steel and workmanship. He admired the knives and had an impulse to keep them, but he gave another order. 'Throw these on the coals. Only renegades use knives.'" William Lee Hamlin, *The True Story of Billy the Kid* (Caldwell, ID: Caxton Printers, 1959), 209–10.

29 Martínez Estrada, vol. I, 64.

30 John Ormsby, trans., *Don Quixote of the Mancha* I (Barcelona, Spain: Limited Editions Club, 1933), 374.

31 José Hernández, *Martín Fierro* (*Colección Austral*, No. 8) (Buenos Aires: Espasa-Calpe Argentina, 1938), 51, 54, 89.

32 Paul S. Taylor, "Songs of the Mexican Migration," *Puro Mexicano* (*Publications of the Texas Folklore Society*, No. 12) (Austin: Texas Folklore Society, 1935), 241–45.

33 Mody C. Boatright, "Theodore Roosevelt, Social Darwinism, and the Cowboy," *Texas Quarterly* 7 (1964): 17.

34 Mendoza, *Lírica narrativa*, 14.

35 Samuel Ramos, *El perfil del hombre y la cultura en México* (*Colección Austral*, No. 1080) (Mexico: Espasa-Calpe Mexicana, 1951), 52.

The Spanish Settlement of Texas and Arizona

MARTHA MENCHACA

During the late seventeenth century, Spain initiated its next colonization phase, identifying Texas and Arizona as the preferred sites (Polzer 1976:36–37; Weber 1992:154). The *entradas* were launched by the military and the church. Franciscan fathers were in charge of the missions in Texas, while the Jesuits founded the missions in Arizona (Engelhardt 1929:14; Polzer 1976:34; Weber 1992:95).[1] Before colonies could be established, however, Indian alliances had to be forged and places for future colonies identified.

Texas Colonial Settlements

The colonization of Texas began in 1690 when two missions were established in the northeast (Chipman 1992:88; Morfí 1935). Approximately twenty-nine missions were erected throughout the Spanish period (Chipman 1992:108–9, 148–49; cf. Weber 1992:150). Some lasted a few months, while others continue to serve a congregation today, such as Mission San José and Mission San Juan de Capistrano. The settlement of Texas was prompted by the threat of a French invasion (Bannon 1970:94). France's monarch, Louis XIV, disregarded Spain's claim to North America and failed to honor the 1493 papal bull giving Spain legal right over most of the New World (Hoffman 1973). By the seventeenth century most European countries disagreed with the papal bull and proposed that land in the New World belonged to the country that had military possession of it. To establish an official claim to East Texas and Louisiana, Louis XIV commissioned René Robert Cavelier de La Salle to establish colonies. In 1685 La Salle founded Fort Saint-Louis near Matagorda Bay, in East Texas (Chipman 1992:87). Although the colony failed after most settlers met their deaths at the hands of Indians, France continued its crusade, concentrating its energies in northeastern Texas.

To avert a French invasion, the Spanish crown commissioned Captain Alonso de León to take a party of soldiers and missionaries into the northeast border area of Louisiana and Texas (Pertulla 1992). They were to establish two mission settlements among the Hasini Indians, a subdivision of the Caddo. Franciscan father Damién Mazanet was in charge of the colonies and was assisted by four friars (Newcomb 1986). On 20 March 1690 León departed from Monclavo, Coahuila, and led his party toward the northeast (Bannon 1970:102). His troops were ordered to remain there until the fathers were safely situated but to leave as soon as possible, to assure the Indians that the fathers came in peace. The fathers set camp in a Hasini village called Nabedaches and soon established two missions nearby. After a year the crown sent a troop of soldiers to replenish supplies, because giving gifts to the Indians was an effective way of befriending them (Weber 1992). Apparently the first two years were successful, and a large number of Indians came to visit the fathers. Relations began to deteriorate, however, when the military stopped coming to replenish supplies. As supplies dwindled, so did the interest of the Hasini converts. Compounding the fathers' problems was their inability to grow crops in arid soil (Newcomb 1986). They gradually became more dependent on the Indians and were unable to prove the worth of their farming technology. In New Mexico the *entradas* had been partially successful because the Spaniards had demonstrated to the Pueblo Indians the advantages of having allies with advanced agricultural technology (Engelhardt 1930). This process was not replicated in the northeast, and in 1694 the Hasini forced the missionaries to leave (Newcomb 1986:287).

Although the first *entrada* failed, neither the crown nor the Catholic Church abandoned the efforts to colonize Texas. New plans were drafted after the royal government learned that France had ceased its attempts to colonize the northeast. Now the colonization of Texas could proceed in an area closer to the northern colonies already founded in the present states of Coahuila and San Luis Potosí (Alessio Robles 1934; Frye 1996). Establishing colonies in close proximity to one another was better strategically. If a colony was under attack, troops could quickly be mobilized and a large counterattack could be mounted. In 1700 and

1703 three missions were established along the current Texas-Mexico border, near present-day Monclova (Newcomb 1986:36). Although these missions were part of the Texas-Coahuila mission program, the buildings were erected on what is today the Mexican side of the border. Fortunately for the fathers, the missions flourished and attracted a large neophyte population (Campbell 1977). Alliances were also established with a large number of Tejas and Coahuiltecan Indians living in *rancherías* located near the missions (Chipman 1992; Weber 1982).[2]

Throughout Texas and other parts of the Southwest many Indians lived in villages politically led by a chief or headman, in contrast to the theocratic government commonly practiced among the Pueblo Indians of New Mexico. These communities were called *rancherías*. In most cases *ranchería* Indians refused to move when they were invited to live in the missions, so their chiefs were asked to relocate their villages near the missions. Fathers expected the *ranchería* Indians to become Christians and to adopt Spanish customs in terms of dress style, to register their villages as ally settlements in a garrison or presidio, and to send members of the *rancherías* to the missions (Ezzell 1974; Polzer 1976). Because *ranchería* Indians were not economically dependent upon the Spanish and were not under daily surveillance as were the mission Indians, the fathers knew that their interethnic relations were fragile and that the Indians' way of life had to be respected. During periods of war, *ranchería* allies were also expected to form military auxiliaries and to assist the Spanish in fighting mutual enemies (Kessell 1989).

In turn the Christianized *ranchería* Indians expected a reciprocal relationship, with the soldiers protecting them from common enemies and the fathers giving them supplies (Engelhardt 1930). Through this relationship many *rancherías* officially became part of Spanish municipalities and legal subjects of the crown (see *Byrne v. Alas et al.*, 1888:525, 526; Weber 1982).

Civilian Colonies

In 1716 the first civilian colony was established in Texas (Castañeda 1936:47–49). Once again plans were prompted by renewed French threats in the northeast (Weber 1992).[3] A successful French colony had been established in Natchitoches, along the present northeast Texas-Louisiana border. Making matters worse for Spain, France granted entrepreneurs willing to fund colonies permission to establish camps in the northern region of Texas (Castañeda 1936:22–24). This gave investors title to the land they controlled.

Spain determined that Texas must be settled to avert any further French *entradas*. It became necessary to start populating several regions with soldiers, civilians, Indians, and mission fathers. In preparation for the arrival of the colonists, Spanish soldiers and missionaries were commissioned to explore Texas and to select sites for settlement. At this time most of these soldiers came from Coahuila, and a large number of them were from the Tlaxcalan towns of Saltillo and San Esteban (Hernández Xochitiotzin 1991; Meade de Angulo n.d.).

In mid-February 1716 Captain Domingo Ramón took approximately seventy-eight colonists into the northeast (Bannon 1970:112; Castañeda 1936:47). These settlers included nine priests, three lay brothers, dozens of colonists, and twenty-five soldiers. Many of the soldiers also brought their families. Among the colonists were *criollos, mestizos,* and *peninsulares.* Only seven of the colonists were Indian, and one was Black (Castañeda 1936:45–47). As the colonists migrated north, they stopped many times along their route to rest and to greet friendly Tejas Indians. The settlers finally arrived in the northeast on 26 June 1716 (Bannon 1970:114). They established a presidio five miles west of the Neches River and erected five missions nearby among various ethnic subdivisions of the Caddo Indians.[4] Although their initial journey succeeded, they soon experienced severe hardships when their gifts dwindled and they were no longer welcomed. Within two years the Caddo Indians became increasingly hostile and repeatedly attacked the settlers.

When the royal government in Mexico City received news of the problems, it became necessary to reassess the colonization project; if military assistance was not made available, it was only a matter of time before the Indians destroyed the settlements. Clearly, if the colonists needed help it was unrealistic to expect the military from Coahuila to dispatch a cavalry unit in a timely manner. It therefore became necessary to establish a second colony midway between the northeast and Coahuila. A temporary militia could be assembled there and dispatched while a larger cavalry group came from Coahuila (Bannon 1970). Upon hearing the news that a second colony was to be established, Father Antonio de San Buenaventura de Olivares, the head missionary of the Coahuila missions, took immediate action and petitioned the crown for the colony to be established in San Antonio and for all religious matters to be in his charge. In 1690 Father Olivares had sent Agustín de la Cruz, a Tlaxcalan neophyte, to explore present San Antonio and the current Texas-Coahuila border (Baga 1690:96). Upon his return, De la Cruz reported that the region was inhabited by peaceful village-dwelling Indians. Nearly two decades later Father Olivares visited the area and reported to the royal government that the Indians of San Marcos and San Antonio were well suited for mission life.

In 1718 Father Olivares's petition was approved by the royal crown. His plans were to erect a mission and a civilian settlement populated by Indians and governed by *peninsulares* (Weber 1992:163). These plans came to a temporary halt when Martín de Alarcón, the governor of Coahuila and Tejas, was appointed to recruit the settlers and establish a civilian colony. Although Father Olivares was commissioned to found the first mission in San Antonio, it was Alarcón who was appointed to control all secular matters in the colony. Their views on who should settle San Antonio clashed.

Alarcón, like Olivares, preferred to select Spaniards to settle San Antonio. This became an unrealistic goal, however, because Alarcón was only able to recruit a handful of Spaniards. Most of the people willing to take the journey into the frontier were people of color (Castañeda 1936:87). According to Alarcón, only *mulattos, lobos, coyotes,* and *mestizos* from Coahuila were prepared to risk their lives in exchange for land. Nonetheless, Olivares distrusted these colonists because he considered them half-breed savages and feared that if war broke out they would betray the Spanish. He believed that the colonists of color were not the best agents of Spanish acculturation since they still practiced Indian dances and traditions and could easily revert to their parents' lifestyle. Father Olivares several times attempted to delay the departure of the colony until a larger number of *peninsulares* could be recruited. Alarcón, unable and unwilling to fulfill the father's request, began the trek toward San Antonio after agreeing to return and recruit more *peninsulares.*

The colonists were divided into two companies. The first company departed from Mission San José, located along the current Texas-Coahuila border. It was composed of Father Olivares, two missionaries, twenty-five soldiers, and about five Indians raised by Olivares since childhood (Castañeda 1936:35). The second company, stationed in Saltillo, Coahuila, was composed of Alarcón and seventy-two settlers (Chipman 1992:117).[5] The settlers included many of the soldiers' families as well as a large number of artisans (de la Teja 1991). The two companies departed in early April and arrived in San Antonio several days apart. Father Olivares took a direct route to San Antonio and arrived on 1 May 1718 (Bannon 1970:117). On that day Father Olivares founded Mission San Antonio de Valero—the chapel that later became the Alamo. Alarcón arrived five days later, as he took a scouting route to explore the coast before proceeding to San Antonio.[6] Presidio de Béjar was formally founded upon his arrival, and the settlers clustered inside it. They were the first members of what later was destined to become the largest civilian settlement in Texas—Villa of San Fernando de Béjar,[7] later renamed San Antonio. At this time the settlers remained under military governance and could not establish a town council because people of color did not have the right to govern themselves (de la Teja 1991). The crown did not give them this privilege until a decade later, after a large colony of *peninsulares* arrived in San Antonio. Furthermore, these settlers were not awarded land grants and were only issued occupancy land rights (de la Teja 1991).

After the colonists settled in San Antonio, Father Olivares charged that the colonists of color were unacculturated and untrustworthy and therefore asked

Alarcón to return immediately to recruit *peninsulares*. Alarcón ridiculed the father's request, responding that unlike Olivares, who had access to Spanish missionaries from the apostolic colleges, he could recruit no such Spaniards. In a letter dated 22 June 1718, Olivares derogatorily characterized the colonists of color as savage half-breeds who were less civilized than the Indians and asked the viceroy, the marqués de Valero, to force Alarcón to recruit other people:

> Such people are bad people, unfit to settle among gentiles, because their customs are depraved, and worse than those of the gentiles themselves. It is they who sow discontent and unrest among them and come to control the Indians to such an extent, that by means of insignificant gifts they make them do what they please. When it is to their interest, they help the Indians in their thefts and evil doings, and they attend their dances and *mitotes* just to get deer and buffalo skins from them.... It is with this sort of people, Your Excellency, that he wishes to settle the new site on the San Antonio and the Province of Tejas. (Father San Buenaventura de Olivares, in Castañeda 1936:87)

Although Father Olivares's request went unheeded, the crown did give him permission to send for additional Christian Indians from Tlaxcala and from the northern missions. They were to be used as models and beneficiaries of a Christian lifestyle (Bolton 1960:15; Castañeda 1936:73). Father Olivares also requested that Tlaxcalan masons and sculptors be transferred to San Antonio, as they were specialists in constructing mission buildings and designing iconographic religious art. Sculptors and masons from the Tlaxcalan town of San Esteban, Coahuila, were brought for the specific purpose of sculpting religious images on the mission buildings (Castañeda 1936:80). By 1720 San Antonio had a colonial population of 300 and several hundred mission Indians (Weber 1992:193).

The Northeast

While Olivares and Alarcón disputed over San Antonio, news arrived that the colonists of the northeast could no longer survive among the Indians and were prepared to abandon their post. Alarcón immediately departed for Presidio Nuestra Señora de los Dolores and later visited the missions, where he observed a pattern of disorder and despair. Most colonists were sick, their supplies depleted, their houses in disrepair, their fields destroyed by the Indians, and most of the missions empty, as the neophytes were better off on their own. Apparently, the local Indians and the French from Natchitoches had conspired to drive the colonists out. Alarcón assessed the damage and determined that it was necessary to retreat temporarily. He had to receive permission to do so, however. Matters got worse, and the colonists could no longer wait. While the viceroy assessed the petition, French soldiers attacked Mission San Miguel de los Adaes and forced everyone to flee. News of the attack reached the other northeast settlements. The settlers were warned that unless they abandoned their homes a French battalion of 100 soldiers was prepared to kill them. Father Antonio Margil, the head missionary of the northeastern missions, attempted to calm the settlers and temporarily convinced them to stay. He suggested that they congregate in Mission Concepción until the Spanish cavalry arrived. When the settlers arrived at Concepción, a sense of despair and panic prevailed. Many of the settlers, unwilling to wait for military aid, opted to withdraw immediately to San Antonio. Unable to assure the colonists of their safety, the fathers allowed them to leave. After accompanying the refugees to San Antonio, Fathers Margil and Espinosa returned to the northeast.

Although the crown allowed the settlers to leave, the recolonization of the northeast resumed in 1721 (Chipman 1992:121). The crown appointed José Azlor de Vera to launch a counterattack. Don José was officially known as the marqués de Aguayo. Two years earlier he had been appointed governor and captain-general of Texas and Coahuila. To fulfill his commission, Aguayo raised a force of 85 soldiers and 500 recruits to repopulate northeastern Texas (Castañeda 1936:122; Chipman 1992:120). It is uncertain what percentage of the colonists were people of color; Aguayo's reports did not provide a demographic description, indicating only that a large number of them were Indian, *mestizo*, and Black (Castañeda 1936:130). Although a census was not taken by Aguayo, Spanish census enumerators in 1777 reported that over 50 percent of the 130 families living in the northeast were people of color: 62 were classified as Spanish, 49 as partially Black, 13 as Indian, 5 as Black, and 1 as *mestizo* (Tjarks 1974:324–25).

Aguayo's forces departed from Monclavo, Coahuila, and arrived on the Neches River around mid-July 1721 (Bannon 1970:121). They were greeted by Father Espinosa and by the former mission Indians of the dismantled missions. Aguayo left a number of soldiers to reconstitute the Presidio of San Francisco (Weber 1992). After resting, he proceeded to the site where Mission San Miguel had previously stood, approximately twelve miles from Natchitoches. There he received a delegation of French soldiers who diplomatically asked him to place his colony somewhere else. Aguayo ignored the request and proceeded to establish Presidio de Nuestra Señora del Pilar de Los Adaes. He also assisted Father Margil to reconstitute Mission San Miguel, which was located near the presidio and renamed San Miguel de Los Adaes. To protect the settlements and to ward off further French attacks, Aguayo reinforced the presidio with a hundred soldiers and left artillery and six cannons behind. Twenty-eight of the soldiers were joined by their families, helping to populate and set claim to the northeast (Castañeda 1936:144). This region came to be known as Los Adaes. Before leaving the northeast, Aguayo reestablished six of the mission settlements and left two well-fortified presidios (Chipman 1992:123, 126).

Aguayo then moved south to fight further French intrusion and to solidify Spain's claim along the coast of Texas. After resting for the winter in San Antonio, he reassembled his troops and marched toward Matagorda Bay, where the French had built a fort. In 1722 his troops seized the fort and in its place founded Presidio Nuestra Señora de Loreto (Bannon 1970:121). Mission del Espíritu Santo de Zúñiga was also established nearby. Approximately ninety soldiers were left to protect these two settlements. After four years the settlements were moved inland near the Guadalupe River (Chipman 1992:127). The new location proved to be beneficial because it was accessible to a larger number of Christian *ranchería* Indians. The presidio was renamed Presidio Nuestra Señora de la Bahía del Espíritu Santo. The settlements remained small yet stable, and two decades later Mission Rosario was founded nearby. This region came to be known as La Bahía.[8]

The friars were able to develop a successful tutelage relation with hundreds of *ranchería* allies and establish a thriving cattle economy. In 1758 Mission Espíritu Santo alone owned 3,200 head of cattle, 1,600 hundred sheep, and 20 saddle horses (Castañeda 1939:23). Moreover, many Indians came to visit their relatives in the missions and were allowed to live there temporarily. In 1763 the missions had a total neophyte population of 312 and a colonial population of fifty families (Castañeda 1939:23, 25).[9] The colonists consisted of fifty soldiers, their nuclear families, and extended kin. Fourteen of the soldiers guarded the missions and lived on the grounds, while the rest of the colonial population lived in the presidio. Furthermore, 1777 census records indicate that the settlement in La Bahía was multiracial (Tjarks 1974:324). Approximately 53 percent of the settlers were registered as Spanish ($N=370$), 27 percent as Indian ($N=185$), 3 percent as *mestizo* ($N=24$), and 17 percent as of partially Black descent ($N=117$) (Castañeda 1939). As time passed, La Bahía's strategic location became increasingly important, and a third mission was built at present Refugio.[10] The Christian Indian population, however, continued to prefer to live in their villages rather than in the missions.

Success and Failures: Laredo and West Texas

Between 1747 and 1773 Spain expanded its colonization of its northeastern frontier (Beers 1979:97). Many missions and presidios were built in Texas and in a newly established territory called Nuevo Santander (Castañeda 1938). In

1749 Nuevo Santander was founded along the current border between south-eastern Texas and the Mexican state of Tamaulipas.[11] Six thousand people were recruited to move there (Weber 1992:194), including seven hundred Tlaxcalan families (Bolton 1960:15; Simmons 1964:105). Although most of the colonists established their ranches in Tamaulipas, the purpose of the Nuevo Santander colony was to populate the far northern frontier and to create an infrastructure to help protect colonial settlements in Texas.

Over twenty-three towns were established in Nuevo Santander. Laredo was founded in 1755 on what is today Texas soil and soon became a stable community (Alonzo 1998:34; Castañeda 1938). The Indians near Laredo were friendly and allowed missionaries to visit them. One of the *rancherías* became a mission *visita* called Visita San Agustín de Laredo, with about 500 Christian Indians (Castañeda 1938:161). A settlement called Dolores was established near Laredo by twenty-three families. Dolores remained a ranching community throughout its existence and did not grow into a town (Alonzo 1998:80). By the turn of the nineteenth century Laredo had over 718 residents, according to the census, including 321 Spaniards, 155 *mulattos*, 121 *mestizos*, and 111 Indians (Hinojosa 1983:124). The Visita of San Agustín had over 1,500 Indians (Alonzo 1998:54). Altogether, by that time Nuevo Santander had grown to over 20,000 settlers, with a sizable population residing on what is today the Texas side of the border (Weber 1992:195).

Unlike the flourishing communities in Nuevo Santander, the newly established settlements in West Texas failed. Spain began its colonization project in 1747 (Castañeda 1938:226). Spanish soldiers tried to enact treaties with the Lipan Apache, who controlled the region. The Lipan Apache first appeared in West Texas during the late 1600s, and by the mid-1700s hundreds more had arrived (Alonso 1995; Swanton 1984:323). If Spanish colonies were to be established in West Texas, it was necessary to befriend the Apache. Thus, the first Spanish *entrada* began with the founding of Mission Cíbola on the border between Texas and Chihuahua, at the conjunction of the Rio Grande and the Concho River near present-day Presidio, Texas (Castañeda 1938:226).[12] The mission was specifically founded for the Lipan Apache. The *entrada* failed; within a year the settlement was destroyed and the mission fathers and neophytes were killed.[13] The Spaniards once again attempted to colonize West Texas by establishing Presidio San Luis de Las Amarillas in 1757 and Mission Santa Cruz de San Sabá a year later, both located near the San Sabá River and present Menard (Beers 1979:96). The furnishings and supplies used for the San Sabá settlements came from the failed missions of San Marcos and Georgetown.[14] Both Texas missions had been built for the Apache.

Learning from the experience at Mission Cíbola, the Spanish had a new strategy: to populate West Texas solely with Indians. The plan was to place

Indians in Apache territory on the theory that the Apache would not kill other Indians. In the northern states of Coahuila and San Luis Potosí, where similar *entradas* had been launched into hostile territory, sending Indian pioneers had apparently deflected the anger of the local Indians. Nine Tlaxcalan families and several fathers were sent to populate the mission at San Sabá (Castañeda 1938:394, 407). Although at first the settlements in San Sabá attracted many Lipan Apache families, and the presidio became a popular trading post, the life span of the mission was short. The Comanche and Lipan Apache did not want the colonial settlements and were angered that some Apache groups had befriended their enemies. The Comanche, like the Apache, saw the Spanish as intruders. Although most Comanches lived in North Texas, a few *rancherías* had moved to West Texas and more were advancing west (Chalfant 1991:5). Thus, when the San Sabá settlements were established, hostile Indians raided the mission's livestock and in general made life miserable for the colonial residents (Chipman 1992; Corbin 1989). Within a year the mission was burned, and the survivors were forced to flee to San Antonio. Only the presidio was left standing.

The destruction of the mission led the royal governmnt to reconsider its plans and temporarily cease the missionization of the Lipan Apache. In 1762, however, several Lipan Apache groups agreed to resume alliances and to be missionized (Castañeda 1939:42, 169). Two missions were established north of the Nueces River and forty leagues from present San Sabá in an area called El Cañón. The missions immediately attracted a neophyte population of over 700 Indians. In addition Chief Tacú and Chief El Chico, who controlled over 3,000 *ranchería* Indians, became allies of the Spanish (Castañeda 1938:398, 1939:108). Although these chiefs did not move their villages into the mission compounds, they actively became engaged in mission life. Once again, however, hard times befell the fathers as enemy Indian groups attacked El Cañón settlements and the presidio at San Sabá (Swanton 1984). This time the presidio was also destroyed. In 1767 all settlements in West Texas were destroyed (Bannon 1970:139).

In spite of the ongoing defeats the royal government ordered the colonization of West Texas to resume. It was painfully clear, however, that no settlements could be established near San Sabá and that another site had to be selected. In 1773 a new site south of San Sabá near the location of the failed mission of Cíbola was selected (Castañeda 1938:223–32). This region was called La Junta. Presidio del Norte at La Junta was built approximately three miles south of the city of Presidio and north of the Rio Grande (Beers 1979:97).[15] Finally, a permanent settlement had been established in Apache territory. Throughout its duration it remained a small and popular trading post.

The Canary Islanders and a Flexible Casta System

In 1731 fifty-five *peninsular* families came to San Antonio from the Canary Islands, enlarging the size of the White population. A few of these people later dispersed throughout Texas (Poyo 1991a:41). They were brought for the explicit purpose of governing the non-White population, as Spanish law prohibited non-Whites from holding positions on the town council. In Texas the royal government appointed the town council, called a *cabildo* (Haring 1963; Menchaca 1993; Poyo 1991b).

Canary Islanders were given special privileges because they were *peninsulares*. Besides being eligible for the *cabildo*, they qualified for the most prestigious occupations within the military and were accorded the title *hidalgo* (see Poyo 1991b; *Recopilación de leyes de los reynos de las Indias* 1774: Book 3, Title 10, Law 12). For example, ten Canary Islanders were given life appointments as councilmen, sheriff, notary, land commissioner, city attorney, and two magistrates who ruled on the legalities of community life (Poyo 1991a:42). Likewise, the Texas census of 1793 indicates that in San Antonio nearly 100 percent of the Canary Islanders were employed as professionals and farmers, while nearly 40 percent of the nonmission Indians and racially mixed peoples were employed as laborers and servants (Poyo 1991b:88, 93).

As *hidalgos*, the Canary Islanders were also eligible to receive land grants twice the size of those of other subjects and temporarily be exempt from paying taxes (see Castañeda 1936:296–301, 1938:90; Graham 1994). This land distribution policy adversely affected many *mestizos* who arrived to San Antonio after the Canary Islanders. Since the best land in San Antonio was owned by the missions, and the Canary Islanders were given most of the remaining irrigable land, the new immigrants received land without water and therefore were unable to become farmers (Poyo 1991b:89). Many worked as servants or field hands as a means of supporting themselves. The non-White settlers who arrived before the Canary Islanders were much better off, however, because they had obtained fertile land. They were not issued patents, but they did receive occupancy rights.

Although the racial caste system was transported to Texas, it was less rigid than in the interior. In Texas commoners of color could move out of their legal racial categories if they performed heroic acts for the state (Forbes 1966:245; *Recopilación de leyes de los reynos de las Indias* 1774: Book 7, Title 5, Laws 10 and 11). In the interior of Mexico such permission was uncommon and generally only accorded to wealthy individuals (see McAlister 1963; Seed 1988). The best-known case of racial mobility in Texas is that of Antonio Gil Y'Barbo, a well-respected *mulatto* (Tjarks 1974:326). He was one of the settlers of Los Adaes and had established a successful ranch called El Lobanillo. In 1772, after a series of

Indian attacks, the colonists from northeastern Texas were forced to flee to San Antonio (Poyo 1991b:97). While in San Antonio, Los Adaesanos elected Y'Barbo as their spokesperson (Castañeda 1939). After a year, Los Adaesanos became restless and asked to leave because they had been given farmland that was impossible to cultivate. Without land they were limited to selling their labor. After repeated petitions to leave San Antonio, Y'Barbo was given permission to establish a new colony and immediately began traveling throughout the northeast and the Gulf Coast. In 1774 he found several suitable places along the northeast coast near the villages of Caddo and Orcoquisac Indians (Poyo 1991b:97). The settlers spread along the coast and inland and founded the town of Bucareli (Block 1976, 1979; Castañeda 1936). The royal government rewarded Y'Barbo by appointing him captain and chief justice of the colonists. In spite of his racial lineage, Y'Barbo was later promoted to lieutenant governor and captain of the northeast (Tjarks 1974).

Historian Gerald Poyo (1991a) found in a study of the *casta* system in San Antonio that Y'Barbo's case was not unique: non-Whites could change their racial status and obtain the classification of *criollos* if they held a special skill. For example, census enumerators allowed individuals to change their racial classification. Poyo found it was common for *mestizo* and *afromestizo* craftsmen who were cobblers, blacksmiths, tanners, carpenters, or sculptors to move up in social standing. Many craftsmen who were identified in the 1770 census as *mestizos* or *afromestizos* (i.e., *coyotes, mulattos,* and *lobos*) were classified as *criollos* by the 1790s (Poyo 1991b:94, 95).

Poyo contends that the flexibility of Texas's racial order benefited the White population, since a large number of the people of color were financially secure ranchers. After the arrival of the Canary Islanders, the royal government was prepared to bring in more *peninsular* families. Plans were aborted, however, because local authorities reported that the Canary Islanders were dependent upon the other settlers (de la Teja 1991). Instead local authorities recommended that frontierspeople from towns in Coahuila, Zacatecas, Querétaro, Guanajuato, San Luis Potosí, Tula, and Jalpa be recruited (Tjarks 1974) because they were better suited to frontier life. This context led to improved interracial relations in San Antonio, because the Canary Islanders found life difficult and had to rely on their neighbors. Scholars attribute the prosperity of a larger number of the non-White settlers to the type of subsistence activities they engaged in (see Poyo and Hinojosa 1991). Many non-White settlers in San Antonio who established ranches which emphasized stock raising rather than farming were able to make handsome profits by selling hides and meat.

The Canary Islanders' inability to exploit the mission Indians also contributed to the racial leveling of the inhabitants of San Antonio. The fathers held tight control over the mission Indians and prohibited colonists from employing them. Without a free labor force the large land grants the *peninsulares* received were useless because they had insufficient numbers of employees to work their fields. Furthermore, since enslaving Blacks in Texas was also uncommon, most Canary Islanders did not have access to slave labor. The Spanish censuses in Texas indicate that between 1782 to 1821 the number of slaves never exceeded 37, the majority of them women (*Residents of Texas 1782–1836*). These labor conditions placed the Canary Islanders and other *peninsulares* at a disadvantage and generated the social ambiance for a flexible racial order, where non-White neighbors had to be treated diplomatically. Such flexible race relations were manifested in interracial marriages. In 1793 church records indicate that approximately 18 percent of the White population married non-Whites in San Antonio ($N = 47$ out of 257) and 28 percent ($N = 26$ out of 92) in the northeast (Tjarks 1974:331).

The Christian Indians

In San Antonio, La Bahía, and northeastern Texas there were thirteen active missions in 1763 with a neophyte population of over 2,354; each mission was also associated with one to three Christian *ranchería* villages (Castañeda 1939:14, 23, 40). The missions in San Antonio were the most successful. By 1768 there were over twenty-three Indian tribes affiliated with the five San Antonio missions (Castañeda 1939:6, 8). The Coahuiltecans were the most numerous, followed by the Jumanos and the Lipan Apaches (Castañeda 1939: 6–14). Over 5,115 Christian *ranchería* Indians had been baptized in the San Antonio missions, and 1,246 were resident neophytes (Castañeda 1939: 6, 8, 9, 14). Many of the *ranchería* Indians were second-generation Christians and had adopted some of the Spaniards' ways. They lived a sedentary life and had established farms and ranches (Castañeda 1936; John 1991; Morfí 1780; Weber 1982). Moreover, in the missions the Indians had adopted the town council form of government (Castañeda 1938:17).

The missions at La Bahía were also able to attract local Indians. Several Karankawa ethnic subdivisions were represented at the missions, including Cocos, Tamiques, and Xarananes (Castañeda 1938:187, 1939:40–44). Unlike the San Antonio missions, however, the missions at La Bahía never exceeded a membership of over 300 per mission and in the 1800s dwindled to a few families. La Bahía missions were poorly stocked, and when supplies dwindled people left. Many Indians would return only to visit the fathers or when goods were restocked. The fathers attributed the high attrition rate to the local terrain, which made agriculture difficult. They claimed that the main problem, however, was the royal government's failure to invest in this region because the Indians were peaceful and did not pose a threat.

A similar situation occurred in Laredo. The church petitioned the royal government for assistance to missionize the local *ranchería* Indians and asked for funds to establish a mission in Laredo, as several chiefs had agreed to relocate their villages there (Castañeda 1938:150, 172). The petition was rejected on the basis that there was plenty of room for neophytes at La Bahía and it was not necessary to give supplies to Indians who were peaceful. Although missions were not established, the Indians continued to attend church services at Laredo and to trade with the colonists (Castañeda 1938; Hinojosa 1983). Tejones and various ethnic subdivisions of the Coahuiltecan Indians, including the Nazos, Comecrudos, Pintos, and Narices visited Laredo.

The missions in the northeast were only able to attract a few families and basically failed. In 1765 King Charles III of Spain directly commissioned the marqués de Rubí, a royal inspector, to write a status report on the northern frontier colonies, including Texas (Hendricks and Timmons 1998:3). Rubí recommended that the northeast be abandoned because the Indians were unwilling to be missionized.

Rubí's Policy Recommendations

In 1768 Cayetano María Pignatelli Rubí Corbera y San Climent, commonly known as the marqués de Rubí, submitted a report entitled *Dictamen* on the status of the northern frontier and recommended that the northeast settlements in Texas be abandoned because the French no longer posed a military threat in that region (Hendricks and Timmons 1998:3). It was also wise to retreat temporarily from the northeast, which had become a battle zone. By the time of Rubí's visit thousands of Apaches and Comanches lived in Texas, competing for land inhabited by local Caddo groups and colonial settlers. Warfare between the colonists and the Apaches and Comanches often erupted in the west and north. Although the colonists had some Indian allies, they were outnumbered. Rubí recommended that the northeast missions be abandoned and the territory be left to the Comanches. The settlers and Indian allies would be relocated to San Antonio or La Bahía, where they could assist in the fortification of these stable communities. Through nuclear fortification a gradual expansion from the center into the periphery would be possible. A similar plan had succeeded two centuries earlier in the Gran Chichimeca when the colonists concentrated their energies on the fortification of Zacatecas and then gradually moved outward.

Rubí further recommended that, instead of colonizing the north, funds be spent in southwestern Texas near Presidio del Norte at La Junta to create another heavily fortified zone such as San Antonio. This area would serve as a resting place for settlers traveling from San Antonio to El Paso or Santa Fe. The idea was to create a line of missions from La Bahía to other parts of the Southwest (Castañeda 1939:253). A single cordon of presidios situated forty leagues (a hundred miles) apart could halt any invasion (Hendricks and Timmons 1998). Rubí proposed as part of the presidial plan that Laredo be further developed and converted into a military center. If the crown invested in this large peaceful Indian population, it could be converted to a powerful military force to use against hostile Indians.

Rubí also offered a very unpopular opinion that was heatedly rejected by the missionaries. He recommended that Spain terminate all Lipan Apache alliances (Castañeda 1939:256–58). Rubí charged that the Lipan Apache allies were treacherous and unreliable, a liability rather than an asset. He also proposed ending all alliances for strategic reasons; he envisioned that the Comanche would massacre the Apache if the Spanish did not intervene. If this occurred the number of troublesome Indians would decline, and the colonists could concentrate their energies on subduing the Comanche. The Catholic Church disagreed, as many Apaches had joined the San Antonio missions and lived in peace. Likewise, Presidio del Norte at La Junta had a large Lipan Apache ally population (Castañeda 1938:223–32). To the Catholic Church Rubí's plan to abandon the Lipan Apaches was a disgrace and an insult to the advances the fathers had made.

The royal government chose to implement only part of Rubí's recommendations regarding Texas. It continued its alliance with Apache groups, but agreed to evacuate the northeast. In 1772, after several Indian raids, the southward exodus began (Poyo 1991b:97).[16] Rubí's recommendations were only temporarily implemented, however. As previously mentioned, within a year of moving to San Antonio, Los Adaesanos found life unbearable and returned to the northeast. Antonio Gil Y'Barbo led 347 Los Adaesanos to the northeast and left nineteen *afromestizo* families behind (Castañeda 1939:317; Tjarks 1974:320, 323). Within a few years Los Adaesanos were attacked by Comanches and forced to move once again. Though this was a tragic event, their new homeland was much safer, because the local Indians left them alone. In 1779 they finally established a permanent colony and called it Nacogdoches (Chipman 1992:206).[17] It became Mexico's northeasternmost frontier settlement.

The Racially Diverse People of Texas

By the late eighteenth century the settlers of Texas were concentrated in four regions: Nacogdoches, San Antonio, La Bahía, and Nuevo Santander. Censuses taken between 1780 and 1798 indicate that the nonmission settlements in these regions were multiracial (Poyo 1991b; Tjarks 1974). The majority of the settlers were classified as Spaniards and *afromestizos*, while Indians and *mestizos* constituted the smallest percentages. For example, in San Antonio (excluding the mission communities) 61 percent of the residents in 1780 were registered as Spaniards ($N=885$), 25 percent as *afromestizos* (*mulattos, lobos,* or *coyotes*) ($N=361$), 6 percent as Indians ($N=85$), and 3.5 percent as *mestizos* ($N=51$) (Tjarks 1974:324–25).[18] Furthermore, though the largest number of residents were registered as Spaniards, the majority of the heads of household were *afromestizo*. About eighty-six of the families reported that the male head of household was an *afromestizo* (Tjarks 1974:328). That same year in La Bahía the census reported a similar demographic composition. In the nonmission settlements 63 percent ($N=340$) reported that they were Spaniards, 34 percent *afromestizos* (*mulattos, lobos,* or *coyotes*) ($N=183$), and 4 percent *mestizo* ($N=21$) (Tjarks 1974:324–25). Furthermore, the census identified 52 percent of the heads of households as *afromestizos* (Tjarks 1974:328). A similar pattern emerged in Laredo. The 1789 census reported that 45 percent were Spanish ($N=321$), 22 percent *afromestizo* ($N=155$), 17 percent *mestizo* ($N=121$), and 16 percent Indian ($N=111$) (Hinojosa 1983:124). In 1793 in Nacogdoches 24 percent were Spaniards ($N=109$), 28 percent *afromestizo* (*mulatto, lobo,* or *coyote*) ($N=130$) 2 percent Black ($N=10$), 26 percent *mestizo* ($N=117$), and 6 percent Indian ($N=29$) (Tjarks 1974:324–25).[19]

The interior of Texas failed to attract a large number of settlers and only grew to a colonial population of 4,000 by 1803 (Weber 1992:299). Most people who moved to the far northern frontier chose to settle in Nuevo Santander, which later became the Mexican side of the border. Historians David Weber (1992:195) and Donald Chipman (1992:163) attribute Texas's failure to attract a large colonial population to two main factors. First, the ongoing Apache and Comanche raids in the west and northeast made Texas an undesirable place to live. Second, when new settlers arrived in San Antonio and La Bahía the best land was reserved for the Christian Indians and what was left over was parceled out to *peninsulares* (Jackson 1986). Exacerbating this land tenure practice was the refusal of the royal crown to issue titles to newcomers and to allocate land to the children of the settlers. Most newcomers had to enter the labor market because they could not become farmers or ranchers.

Though most people did not want to settle in what today is the interior of Texas, other parts of the area continued to grow. El Paso Valley, which was part of the territory of New Mexico during the Spanish period, attracted a large colonial and mission Indian population and by 1790 had over 3,140 colonists (Weber 1992:195) and 2,000 Christian Indians (Metz 1994:17). By 1819 Laredo had grown to 1,418 (Hinojosa 1983:123). The interior of Texas was part of the colonial and cultural infrastructure of the northern frontier and was closely linked to Nuevo Santander, which had grown to 56,937 by 1810 (Alonzo 1998:40). In these areas the royal crown continued to grant people title to land and to accommodate the growth of the native population. In addition to the colonists, there was a sizable Christian Indian population that was part of colonial society.

The Founding of Arizona

Arizona's colonization is radically different from the pattern in the rest of the southwestern territories settled by Spain. Arizona's desert regions, its extremely hot climate, and the danger posed by the Apache were deterrents to building large colonial settlements. In other territories the first colonists were brought by a person commissioned by the viceroy, but in Arizona the migratory movements were composed of extended family units who generally followed kinsmen stationed as soldiers or officers in the frontier (Engstrand 1992). Arizona was the least populated of the Spanish territories in the Southwest. Its colonial population primarily grew through the conversion of local people into Christian Indians. During the Spanish period, the Indians living in the missions or presidios became acculturated, and their children followed a similar cultural path. Many of the colonists were second-generation acculturated Indians, rather than Spanish or *mestizo* immigrants.

Arizona's colonization history is intertwined with the founding of northern Sonora, Mexico, which was colonized under the same seventeenth-century program (Spicer 1981). This entire region was known as Pimería Alta. In 1692 the first mission buildings were erected in northern Sonora, rather than in Arizona (Spicer 1981:123). Overall, approximately twenty-four missions were founded by the Jesuits in Arizona and northern Sonora (Kessell 1976:7, 10; Polzer 1976:36–37). Most of the missions only lasted a few years.

During the first years of the conquest of northern Sonora, missions were built near Indian *rancherías* that did not pose a threat to the missionaries. Meanwhile, in Arizona friars visited Indian villages near present Tucson, but did not erect any buildings (Polzer 1976:37).[20] Though the visits were infrequent, these early *entradas* into Arizona were planned and supervised by the Sonoran Rectorate of Nuestra Señora de Los Dolores. At this time Spanish-Indian relations were peaceful in both regions (Bolton 1960; Spicer 1981).

In the early 1720s, however, when colonists arrived in large numbers and settled near the missions of northern Sonora, relations turned hostile. Conflicts arose over land disputes, as the Christian *ranchería* Indians inhabited the best land along the rivers and the Sonoran settlers were unwilling to abide by preestablished territorial boundaries. Upon seeing the mission fathers' inability to convince the settlers to respect their land, the Indians turned on them and refused to be their allies. The Christian Indians burned several missions, ousted the colonists, and for over a decade suspended most communication with the church.

Relations resumed in Pimería Alta when missionaries regained the trust of some Opata and Upper Pima groups in 1732 (Kessell 1976:2). These initial alliances were prompted by the fear that many Indians had of the Apache (Smith 1962b). At that time hundreds of Apaches descended into Arizona and Sonora and began to occupy territory already claimed by other Indians. The Opata and Pima, to protect their land, resumed their alliances in return for military assistance. Spaniards took advantage of the intertribal conflict and used this as an opportunity to recolonize Pimería Alta. This time, however, the church and royal government shifted the colonization project to southern Arizona.

The mission system in Arizona finally gained a foothold in 1732 (Kessell 1976:2; Spicer 1981:122), when the missions of San Xavier del Bac and San Miguel de Guevavi and the mission *visita* of Tumacácori were established. Parish buildings were erected in San Xavier and Guevavi.[21] Although a parish was not built in Tumacácori at this time, it received regular visits from the fathers, masses were offered, and new converts were baptized. From these mission settlements the fathers were able to reach more Indians living in nearby communities. Eventually about ten mission *visitas* were founded in the Santa Cruz and San Pedro valleys of southern Arizona (Kessell 1976:7).[22] The Upper Pima became the largest Indian group to be missionized.[23]

While the first missions were being erected in Arizona, a series of Indian revolts once again erupted in northern Sonora. Hundreds of Christian Indians rebelled against the illegal kidnapping of their kinfolk. The mission fathers tried to intervene, but were unable to stop the kidnappings. The revolts led to the temporary collapse of the northern Sonora missions, leaving only the missions in Arizona standing. Unlike the Indian conflicts of northern Sonora, relations between the Christian Indians and the Spanish in Arizona remained peaceful and generated the ambiance to permit a modest expansion of the mission system.

The Arrival of the Colonial Settlers in Arizona

The first colonists to settle in Arizona arrived in groups of extended families following kinsmen stationed as soldiers or officers on the frontier. The northward move began in the 1720s, when the Indian rebellions in northern Sonora forced people to find new homes (Mattison 1946:276). They settled on the current Sonora-Arizona border and established farms above Guevavi, where a large Christian *ranchería* was located. Some years later silver mines were discovered in southern Arizona, prompting more Sonoran settlers to move north. Several mining camps were established near the newly built missions at Guevavi and San Xavier del Bac. To protect the families from Apache attacks, a presidio was established southeast of Mission Guevavi, on the Mexican side of the present

Arizona border in 1741 (Engstrand 1992:121). Eight families moved to the presidio that year, and later a number of them moved further north. They dispersed themselves throughout Arizona's Santa Cruz and San Pedro valleys and began establishing mining camps and ranches. A few years later more settlers moved to Arizona and settled in Mission Guevavi and in the Santa Cruz Valley, where the *visitas* of Aribaca and Sópori had been established (Mattison 1946:277). In 1753 Presidio Tubac was founded to protect the growing population (Engstrand 1992:134; Kessell 1976:2). Its superior fortification attracted many frontier families as well as several Christian Indian families.[24] Within a few years Presidio Tubac became a lively community with over 500 colonists in residence and the social focal point of the ranching families (Mattison 1946:283). Captain Juan Bautista de Anza was the commander of the presidio and was put in charge of 120 soldiers and their families (Dobyns 1962:10).

By 1762 Tubac had become the main colonial center, and its inhabitants constituted one-third of the 1,500 colonists in Arizona (Mattison 1946:277). When the royal crown sent the marqués de Rubí to inspect the status of the Spanish settlements, however, he observed that Tubac could easily be destroyed by a large-scale Apache raid and advised that its population be moved near Tjkshon, the largest allied *ranchería*. Tjkshon was inhabited by over 400 Upper Pima Indians and was surrounded by numerous Christian *rancherías* (Dobyns 1962:11). It was impossible for hostile Indians to penetrate this zone. Tjkshon was well fortified and had a massive wall surrounding its church and adobe buildings (Dobyns 1962).[25]

Rubí's recommendations were implemented a few years later after Captain Hugo O'Conor arrived to supervise the move and determine the future of Tubac. In 1775 he resettled the colonists across the river from Tjkshon and founded Presidio Tucson (Dobyns 1976:58). Tjkshon and the presidio became the foundation of present-day Tucson and the center of the colonial population. By 1797 Presidio Tucson had over 297 colonists in residence (Dobyns 1962:28). Although a new presidio was established, Tubac was not abandoned. Several Indian soldiers and their families remained behind, forming a small community of acculturated Indians.

Residential Patterns

In the presidios most colonists were given small plots of land to build houses and grow gardens. Those colonists who moved to the missions were also given small plots of land adjacent to the Indians' fields (see Engstrand 1992). Although settlers were given land to subsist on, only elites such as officers, their families, or affluent subjects were issued property deeds. To obtain a deed people had to prove that they had funds to make structural improvements (construct a house, cultivate the land, or build stables or other types of buildings) and that the land grant would be permanently inhabited. A petitioner had to present a claim outlining how the grant would be subdivided into several parcels and submit a map indicating where houses, ranches, farms, or mining camps would be constructed.

During the Spanish period, only four land grants were issued (see Mattison 1946).[26] Three of the grants were awarded to colonists and one allocated to a community of acculturated Indians from Tumacácori. The land grants were enormous and were inhabited by the extended kin of the petitioners. The first land grant was awarded to the Otero family in 1789 (Mattison 1946):282). The Otero land grant was subdivided into four farming lots (*suertes*), each consisting of approximately three leagues (total 13,314 acres); in addition approximately one-eighth of a league (800 acres) was reserved to build the main family ranch and house (Mattison 1946); Engstrand 1992:243).[27] The second land grant was issued in 1807 to a community of Tumacácori Indians. They were awarded over 52,000 acres (Mattison 1946:291–94; see Mattison 1967). The third land grant, called La Canoa, was issued to the Ortiz brothers in 1821 (Mattison 1946:294–97). This land grant was situated five leagues from Tubac and was subdivided into four cattle ranching lots (*sitios*), totaling 46,696 acres. The fourth land grant, called San José de Sonoita, was issued to the Herrera brothers that same year (Mattison 1946: 298–99). This land grant was the original site of the abandoned mission *visita* of Sonoita. It consisted of nearly two square leagues totaling approximately 8,874 acres, subdivided into two lots (*sitios*) to establish cattle ranches. Although only four land grants were issued, many families were permitted to establish permanent ranches in southern Arizona, in Aribaca, Santa Cruz, Sonoita, San Rafael de la Sanja, San Bernardino, and several other places in the San Pedro Valley (Mattison 1946: 286).[28]

Blurred Racial Categories among the Colonists

In Arizona the officers' families formed the upper class, while the soldiers' families were the commoners (Dobyns 1976; Engstrand 1992). The officers and their families claimed to be White, while the commoners were clearly people of color. Although the officers most likely were White, there were few *peninsulares* among them. Iris Engstrand's study *Arizona hispánica* (1992) illustrates this point. According to Engstrand, presidial records indicate that most officers were *criollos* and were part of second- or third-generation military families from Sonora, Sinaloa, or Coahuila. Engstrand also found that most of the *peninsulares* in Arizona were missionaries. Although she identified documents indicating that the officers were *criollo*, she found few records to verify the race of their relatives. This vagueness is partly due to the scarcity of racial data in Arizona's colonial censuses and marriage records.[29] Racial terms were usually used only in military and mission roll documents. Missionaries and military officers, who were often responsible for preparing the census reports on the civilian population, preferred to use cultural rather than racial terms. The label "gente de razón" was often used in reference to non-Indians (Collins 1970; Dobyns 1976:65, 137–39).

Moreover, Engstrand found that baptismal records frequently did not include the entire family racial history in an effort to hide the true racial identity of a child. For example, when a child's father was a Spaniard, the race of the mother was omitted and the child was classified as *criollo* (Engstrand 1992:160). In most census records, except for the mission Indians, missionaries preferred to classify their parishioners as *vecinos* or *peones* in order to avoid indicating their actual racial identity (Engstrand 1992:254–55). *Vecino* was a social class and not a racial category, referring to the landed elite, whereas *peón* denoted a foot soldier and his family (see Gutiérrez 1991:82). Ramon Gutiérrez also concludes that missionaries preferred to emphasize common cultural attributes rather than distinguishing people by race, since the categories of *mestizo* and Indian carried a social stigma. The only racial categories that are certain are those used to classify the military personnel and the mission Indians. Officers were classified as Spaniard, while soldiers were counted as Indian, *mestizo*, and *afromestizo* (Dobyns 1962:23–27, 1976:153, 171–73).

The families of the officers claimed that they were of pure Spanish descent and primarily intermarried among themselves (Dobyns 1976). For example, elite marriage networks included the de Anza, Elías González, Vildosola, Díaz del Carpio, Otero, Robles, Carrillo, and Aro y Aguirre families (Engstrand 1992:160, 274–76). Moreover, these families lived in relative luxury. Their homes were well furnished, their children were schooled by tutors, and they imported clothes from Europe or from the interior of Mexico. Unlike the elites, soldiers and Christian Indian families lived in modest adobe homes, with beds, stools, and tables serving as their sole furniture. They also dressed modestly (Engstrand 1992:159–61). Although social class differences distinguished the colonists, they remained a closely knit community and socialized during weddings, birthdays, funerals, and most everyday life events.

Among the commoners, intermarriage between soldiers and Indian women was an accepted practice and was encouraged by the royal crown. The Royal Order of 1790 gave soldiers incentives to marry local indigenous women (Mattison 1946:281–82). A soldier who married an Indian woman was given four square leagues of land, which was a tremendous amount of land for a commoner.[30] The order was designed to attract males to Arizona and encourage them to become permanent residents. In this way, Arizona's population would increase and the culture of the soldiers would be diffused to their wives and kin.

Throughout Arizona's Spanish period eleven colonial villas were founded (Kessell 1976:138, 311). Because of Apache attacks, however, most villas were abandoned after a few months and the colonists forced to move to the presidios, missions, or *visitas* (Smith 1962a). By the end of the Spanish period the colonial population was concentrated in Tucson, Tubac, and the missions of Tumacácori and San Xavier del Bac, as well as dispersed on the ranches. During the early nineteenth century, the colonial population ranged from 1,800 to 2,291 (Dobyns 1962:29; Kessell 1976:246). This estimate included the colonists who were not mission neophytes or residents of Christian *rancherías*.

Christian Indians

In the late eighteenth century the size of the Christian Indian population grew, and so did the demand for missions (Kessell 1976: chapter 3). Although many *ranchería* Indians were willing to become neophytes, the royal government was reluctant to establish new missions because of the threat that the Apaches posed outside the fortified zones.[31] Establishing new missions would be a financial disaster if they came under attack. As the size of the Christian Indian population expanded, some *visitas* were structurally improved to accommodate new converts and took on the character of mission pueblos: adobe homes were built, and some pueblos even had modest parishes. A priest was not in residence but visited the Indians regularly. The fathers selected a spokesperson to govern the mission pueblos. If the pueblo was composed of one *ranchería*, the chief became the spokesperson; if it was composed of more than one *ranchería*, one of the chiefs was selected. The spokesperson was officially granted the title of *gobernador* and acted in the capacity of a mayor. The fathers also encouraged the *gobernadores* to reorganize their tribal governments into town councils (Ezzell 1974:121–27). The *gobernadores* were encouraged to select two assistants, called *alcaldes*.

Five of the *visitas* became mission pueblos, including Tjkshon, Sonoita, Calabazas, La Purísima, and Tumacácori (Engstrand 1992:177; Kessell 1976:311).[32] Most were located within a short distance of the missions or presidios. It was common for secularized Indians or *ranchería* allies to reside in the mission pueblos, while space in the missions was reserved for recent converts (Kessell 1976:788–89). The missions and mission pueblos were inhabited throughout the Spanish period and only temporarily abandoned during Apache attacks, except for the mission at Guevavi, which was dismantled after a series of sustained Apache attacks during the late 1760s (Engstrand 1992:122; Kessell 1976:57). Soon Tumacácori was elevated to a mission and took its place.

Mission settlements were usually inhabited only by Indians. The church preferred to separate the neophytes as a means of avoiding the problems that had arisen in Sonora, where the colonists enslaved Indians and generated the conditions for revolts. Only when colonial settlements were under attack were colonists allowed to seek temporary refuge in the mission settlements. By 1774 the mission communities contained 168 colonists and 2,018 Christian Indians (Kessell 1976:88).

The largest number of missionized Indians were Opatas, Upper Pimas, and Papagos (Dobyns 1962; Ezzell 1974; Spicer 1981). Many of these Indians assimilated into Spanish society by moving into the mission pueblos and adopting some of the ways of the colonists. In one case several Indian groups chose to replicate the Spanish township pattern. After having lived in the missions, several secularized Opata and Upper Pima families established a town that was independent of the colonists and the church. In 1807 they received a land grant from the royal crown and called their community Tumacácori (Mattison 1967:72). They established ranches and farms on 52,000 acres (Mattison 1946:291–94), while reserving 6,770 acres to establish civic buildings (see Kessell 1976:207–12; Mattison 1967:72).[33]

Indians also chose to become part of Spanish society by relocating their *rancherías* near the missions or presidios (Collins 1970; Doyle 1989; Kessell 1976; Polzer 1976). Often they did so because of their fear of the Apache, as in the case of hundreds of *ranchería* Indians who moved near Presidio Tucson (Dobyns 1962). A census taken in 1825 by Lieutenant Mariano de Urrea indicates that approximately 9,200 Indian allies were dispersed in ten *rancherías* near Tucson and scattered nearby in the Santa Cruz Valley (Kessell 1976:264). Other Indians chose not to move, yet became allies of the Spanish. Many Pima, Papago, and Yuma Indians who lived west of the Santa Cruz Valley and along the present border of Sonora and Arizona formed military alliances of convenience (Ezzell 1974). They were farmers and sought the aid of their colonial neighbors during harvest season. Likewise, throughout the Spanish period the colonists sought the military assistance of their Indian allies. For example, the early 1760s, the mid-1770s, and 1781 were periods of intense Spanish-Apache conflict (Dobyns 1962:20, 40, 82; Engstrand 1992:197–98, 228). Because the Apaches were so successful in their raiding, the colonial settlements were confined to the San Pedro and Santa Cruz valleys.

Although the fathers were able to Christianize many Indians, the Navajo and most Apaches resisted.[34] The Navajo distanced themselves in the far north, while most Apaches remained feared enemies.

Reprinted with the permission of the University of Texas Press. This essay originally appeared in *Recovering History, Constructing Race: The Indian, Black, and White Roots of Mexican Americans* (Austin: University of Texas Press, 2001), 97–126.

1   In Arizona Franciscans replaced the Jesuits in 1767 (Engelhardt 1929: 306), when the Jesuit order was expelled from Mexico.

2   "Tejas Indians" is a general term applied to Indians native to Texas. The Coahuiltecans were the largest subdivision of the Tejas (Salinas 1990).

3   See Beers (1979) for a review of the political reorganization of Texas between 1689 and 1836. Over time, Texas was under the direct command of either the viceroy or the king. Furthermore, its political jurisdiction was reconfigured six times, making Texas a separate province or part of the internal or eastern provinces.

4   Bannon (1970:114) states that only four missions were founded among the Caddo Indians of the northeast.

5   Castañeda (1936:35) proposes that only thirty-eight of the seventy-two settlers in Alarcón's colony were not Indians.

6   Chipman (1992:117) claims that Alarcón's party arrived in San Antonio on 25 April 1718.

7   A villa was a settlement larger than a town and smaller than a city (see Graham 1994; Hendricks and Timmons 1998).

8   After Don Pedro de Rivera's military inspection of 1727, the soldiers stationed at La Bahía were reduced to twenty (Bannon 1970:123). Rivera reported that La Bahía was excessively militarized for a zone surrounded by peaceful Indians.

9   Chipman (1992:180) estimates that only 200 neophytes were regular residents at the missions of La Bahía.

10 After their initial founding, the settlements at La Bahía were moved to different locations. The presidio and Mission Espíritu Santo were moved from the Guadalupe River to the San Antonio River (Beers 1979:96; Chipman 1992:147–50, 201). After three moves, Mission Refugio was established in present Refugio.

11 See Beers (1979) for a history of the political shifts in the governance of the Province of Texas and Nuevo Santander.

12 In 1684 six missions were established on the Mexican side of the border between Texas and Chihuahua, at the conjunction of the Rio Grande and the Concho River (Castañeda 1936:328). This region was known as La Junta. Mission Cíbola was established over half a century later on the U.S. side of the border. It was also part of the La Junta colonization project.

13 The exact date when Mission Cíbola was destroyed is unknown since Captain José Idoyaga arrived at the mission after the inhabitants had been dead for what appeared to be a long time (Castañeda 1938:224). Very little is known about Mission Cíbola because most of the documents concerning the mission were burned.

14 In 1748 several missions were established in present Milam County along the San Gabriel River (Bannon 1970:136; Castañeda 1938:362–87). The missions were later relocated to San Marcos and New Braunfels. Ten years later the mission neophytes and church belongings were transferred to the newly established mission at San Sabá.

15 In 1759 Presidio del Norte was initially founded on the south side of the Rio Grande (Beers 1979:97; Castañeda 1938:223–32). After Apaches destroyed the presidio, it was moved across the river to what is today U.S. soil.

16 Over sixty soldiers and their families lived in Presidio de Los Adaes and thirty-one soldiers and their families in Presidio de San Agustín de Ahumada (Castañeda 1939:34, 39). The missions were also abandoned, and the few neophytes living there were taken to San Antonio (Castañeda 1936:231).

17 The Spanish plaza in Nacogdoches originally stood in the center of town. In the 1930s it was moved near the cemetery. This information was provided by Carolyn Spears, curator of the Stone Fort Museum, Nacogdoches, Texas.

18 No racial or ethnic data were included for eighty-one persons (Tjarks 1974:324–25).

19 Data were not offered for sixty-two inhabitants. Percentages are based on a total of 457 inhabitants (Tjarks 1974:325).

20 Spicer (1981:123) states that in the late 1600s *visitas* were also established among the Pima of Arizona in Quiburí, Gaybanipitea, and Gubo.

22 Swanton (1984:363) argues that the first mission buildings in Arizona were erected in 1731.

21 There is disagreement over how many *visitas* were established in Arizona. Engstrand (1992:179) claims there were ten, Kessell (1976:7) fourteen, and Dobyns (1962:23–25) nine.

23 Scholars distinguish between the Upper Pima, who lived in Arizona, and the Lower Pima, who lived in Sonora (see Spicer 1981).

24 In 1776 temporary presidios were established in the Santa Cruz and San Pedro valleys. After a series of sustained attacks, the presidio at Sópori was moved to Sonora and the presidio along the border near San Bernardino was abandoned and later transformed into a ranch (Beers 1979:311; Kessell 1976:98–99, 109, 169, 245).

25 Navajos sometimes also attacked the colonial settlements, but for the most part they remained at a distance and only on occasion migrated south (Officer 1987). Their history is more closely intertwined with the colonial settlements of New Mexico.

26 Often titles were not issued because people abandoned their ranches after Apache attacks and new claimants moved when an area was recolonized (Beers 1979). Allegedly many ranches were not inhabited long enough to merit issuing property deeds.

27 One league amounted to approximately 1,100 varas or 4,438 acres (see Margadant S. 1991:91).

28 Rancho San Bernardino was located on the border between Arizona and Sonora (cf. Beers 1979:310; Engstrand 1992:179; Kessell 1976:10).

29 Dobyns (1976:171–73) claims that census records from Presidio Tucson indicate that the officers' families were Spanish.

30 There is no evidence indicating that the soldiers who married Indian women were issued property deeds.

31 Two missions located on the border between Arizona and California, La Concepción and San Pedro y San Pablo de Bicreñer, lasted a short period (Kessell 1976:7; Weber 1992:259).

32 On the Mexican side of the border between Arizona and Sonora several other *visitas* were converted into mission pueblos (see Kessell 1976).

33 The Tumacácori land grant covered part of the mission land of the abandoned *visita* of Calabasas and part of the nearly dismantled mission at Guevavi.

34 Weber (1992:233) found that in 1793 several Apache *rancherías* settled near Tucson and formed colonial alliances. The number of inhabitants is estimated to have reached 2,000.

REFERENCES

Aguirre, Beltrán, Gonzalo. 1946. *La población negra de México, 1519-1810*. Mexico City: Ediciones Fuente Cultural.

Alessio Robles, Vito. 1934. *Saltillo en la historia y en la leyenda*. Mexico City: A. del Bosque Impresor Pensador Mexicano.

Alonzo, Armando C. 1998. *Tejano Legacy: Rancheros and Settlers in South Texas, 1734-1900*. Albuquerque: University of New Mexico Press.

Altamira, Rafael. 1988. *Historia de la civilización española*. Barcelona: Instituto de Estudios "Juan Gil-Albert," Fundación Altamira.

Appiah, Anthony Kwame, and Henry Louis Gates. 1999. *Africana: The Encyclopedia of the African and African American Experience*. New York: Basic Civitas Books.

Ayers, James J. 1886. *Spanish and Mexican Grants in California, Complete to February 25, 1886*. Sacramento, Calif.: State Printing.

Bancroft, Hubert Howe. 1964. *Register of Pioneer Inhabitants of California 1542-1848*. Los Angeles: Dawson's Book Shop.

Bandelier, Adolph F. 1990. *The Discovery of New Mexico by the Franciscan Monk Friar Marcos de Niza in 1539*. Trans. and ed. Madeline Turrell Rodack. Tucson: University of Arizona Press. (1st ed. 1886.)

Bannon, John Francis. 1970. *The Spanish Borderlands Frontier 1513-1821*. New York: Holt, Rinehart and Winston.

Bautista Pino, Pedro. 1812. Exposición sucinta and sencilla de la Provincia del Nuevo México. Reprinted in *Three New Mexico Chronicles*, ed. H. Bailey Carroll and J. Villasana Haggard, 211-61. Albuquerque, NM: Quivira Society, 1942.

Bayle, Constantino. 1931. España y el clero indígena de América. *Razón y Fe: Revista Quinceñal Hispano Americana* 94 (405): 213-25.

Beers, Henry Putney. 1979. *Spanish and Mexican Records of the American Southwest*. Tucson: University of Arizona Press.

Beers, Henry Putney. 1976. *A History of Jefferson County, Texas: From Wilderness to Reconstruction*. (Master of arts thesis, Lamar University.) Nederland, TX: Nederland Publishing.

Bolton, Herbert E. 1966. *Anza's California Expeditions: An Outpost of Empire, Volume 1*. New York: Russell and Russell.

Bolton, Herbert E. 1921. *The Spanish Borderlands*. New Haven, Conn.: Yale University Press.

Borah, Woodrow. 1983. *Justice by Insurance: The General Indian Court of Colonial Mexico and the Legal Aides of the Half-Real*. Berkeley: University of California Press.

Bowden, Jocelyn J. 1971. *Spanish and Mexican Land Grants in the Chihuahua Acquisition*. El Paso: Texas Western Press.

Bowman, J. N. 1958. The Resident Neophytes of the California Missions 1769-1834. *Historical Society of Southern California Quarterly* 40 (2): 138-48.

Bravo Lira, Bernardino. 1970. *Formación del derecho occidental: Con especial referencia a la Península Ibérica.* Santiago, Chile: Editorial Jurídica de Chile.

Brayer, Herbert O. 1949. *William Blackmore: The Spanish-Mexican Land Grants of New Mexico and Colorado, 1863-1878.* Denver, Colo.: Bradford-Robinson.

Carroll, H. Bailey, and J. Villasana Haggard. 1942. *Three New Mexico Chronicles.* Albuquerque, N.M.: Quivira Society.

Carroll, H. Bailey, and J. Villasana Haggard. 1939. *Our Catholic Heritage in Texas 1519-1936, the Mission Era: The Passing of the Missions 1762-1782, Vol. 4.* Austin, Tex.: Von Boeckmann-Jones Company.

Carroll, H. Bailey, and J. Villasana Haggard. 1938. *Our Catholic Heritage in Texas 1519-1936, the Mission Era: The Missions at Work 1731-1761, Vol. 3.* Austin, Tex.: Von Boeckmann-Jones Company.

Carroll, H. Bailey, and J. Villasana Haggard. 1936. *Our Catholic Heritage in Texas 1519-1936, the Mission Era: The Winning of Texas 1693-1731, Vol. 2.* Austin, Tex.: Von Boeckmann-Jones Company.

Chapman, Charles E. 1930. *A History of California: The Spanish Period.* New York: Macmillan Company.

Chipman, Donald. E. 1992. *Spanish Texas 1519-1821.* Austin: University of Texas Press.

Coupe, Douglas R. 1994. *The Limits of Racial Domination: Plebeian Society in Colonial Mexico.* Madison: University of Wisconsin Press.

Cowan, Robert G. 1977. *Ranchos of California.* Los Angeles: Society of Southern California, American Offset Printers.

Creamer, Winifred, and Jonathan Haas. 1991. Pueblo: Search for the Ancient Ones. *National Geographic* 180 (4): 84-99.

Creamer, Winifred, and Jonathan Haas. 1986. *The Protector de Indios in Colonial New Mexico, 1659-1821.* Albuquerque: University of New Mexico Press.

Dale, Edward E. 1951. *The Indians of the Southwest: A Century of Development and the United States.* Norman: University of Oklahoma Press.

Deloria, Vine, Jr., and Clifford M. Lytle. 1988. *American Indians, American Justice.* Austin: University of Texas Press.

Dobyns, Henry F. 1976. *Spanish Colonial Tucson: A Demographic History.* Tucson: University of Arizona Press.

Doyle, David E. 1989. The Transition to History in Northern Pimería Alta. In *Columbian Consequences, Vol. 1, Archaeological and Historical Perspectives on the Spanish Borderlands West,* ed. David Hurst Thomas, 139-158. Washington, D.C.: Smithsonian Institution Press.

Doyle, David E. 1930. *Missions and Missionaries of California: Upper California, Vol. 2.* 2nd ed. Santa Barbara, Calif.: Mission Santa Barbara.

Doyle, David E. 1929. *Missions and Missionaries of California: Lower California, Vol. 1.* 2nd ed. Santa Barbara, Calif.: Mission Santa Barbara.

Doyle, David E. 1913. *Missions and Missionaries of California: Lower California, Vol. 3, Part 2.* San Francisco, Calif.: James H. Barry Company.

Engstrand, Iris H. W. 1992. *Arizona hispánica.* Madrid, Spain: Editorial Mapre.

Engstrand, Iris H. W. 1991. An Enduring Legacy: California *Ranchos* in Historical Perspective. In *Spanish and Mexican Land Grants and the Law,* ed. Malcolm Ebright, 36-47. Manhattan, Kans.: Sunflower University Press.

Ezzell, Paul H. 1974. The Hispanic Acculturation of the Gila River Pimas. *American Anthropologist Memoir 90*. Milwood, NY: Kraus Reprint.

Frye, David. 1996. *Indians into Mexicans: History and Identity in a Mexican Town*. Austin: University of Texas Press.

Galarza, Ernesto. 1964. *Merchants of Labor: The Mexican Bracero Story*. Santa Barbara, Calif.: McNally and Loftin Publishers.

Garrison, Myrtle. 1935. *Romance and History of California Ranchos*. San Francisco: Harr Wagner Publishing Company.

Garza, Leonel, comp. 1980. Agencia mexicana ante la Comisión General de Reclama- ciones entre México y los Estados Unidos—Reclamaciones mexicanas. Reprint of the original 1852 manuscript. In *Indece [sic] de propetarios [sic] originales con la pagina y numero de reclamacion*, 1–13, 102–57. N.p.: Asociacion de Reclamantes of Texas Land Grant Heirs.

Garza, Leonel, comp. 1964. *Aztecs under Spanish Rule: A History of the Indians of the Valley of Mexico*. Stanford, Calif.: Stanford University Press.

Gillespie, Susan. 1989. *The Aztec Kings: The Construction of Rulership in Mexican History*. Tucson: University of Arizona Press.

Graham, Joe S. 1994. *El Rancho in South Texas: Continuity and Change from 1750*. Kingsville: University of North Texas Press.

Gutiérrez, Ramón A. 1991. *When Jesus Came, the Corn Mothers Went Away: Marriage, Sexual- ity, and Power in New Mexico, 1500–1846*. Stanford, Calif.: Stanford University Press.

Haas, Lisbeth. 1995. *Conquests and Historical Identities in California 1769–1936*. Berkeley: University of California Press.

Hanke, Lewis. 1949. *The Spanish Struggle for Justice in the Conquest of America*. Philadelphia: University of Pennsylvania Press.

Hanke, Lewis. 1992. Thoughts after Sixty Years as a Southwestern Archaeologist. In *Emil W. Haury's Prehistory of the American Southwest*, ed. J. Jefferson Reid and David E. Doyle, 435–64. Tucson: University of Arizona Press.

Heizer, Robert F., and Alan F. Almquist. 1977. *The Other Californians: Prejudice and Dis- crimination under Spain, Mexico, and the United States*. Berkeley: University of California Press.

Hendricks, Rick, and W. H. Timmons. 1998. *San Elizario: The Spanish Presidio to Texas County Seat*. El Paso: University of Texas at El Paso.

Hernández Xochitiotzin, Desiderio. 1991. *Crónica de 400 de las familias tlaxcaltecas, 1591–1991*. Tlaxcala, Mexico: H. Ayuntamiento de Tlaxcala, General Archives of the State of Tlaxcala, File Diaspora Tlaxcalteca.

Hoover, Mildred Brooke, Hero Eugene Rensch, and Ethel Grace Rensch. 1966. *Historic Spots in California*. 3rd ed. Revised by William N. Abeloe. Stanford, Calif.: Stanford University Press.

Hull, Elizabeth. 1985. *Without Justice for All: The Constitutional Rights of Aliens*. Westport, Conn.: Greenwood Press.

Hurtado, Albert. 1988. *Indian Survival on the California Frontier*. New Haven, Conn.: Yale University Press.

Hutchinson, Cecil Alan. 1969. *Frontier Settlement in Mexican California: The Hijar-Padres Colony and Its Origins, 1769–1835*. New Haven, Conn.: Yale University Press.

Hutchinson, Cecil Alan. 1975. *Storms Brewed in Other Men's Worlds: The Confrontation of Indians, Spanish, and French in the Southwest, 1540–1795.* College Station: Texas A & M University Press.

Johnson, John. 1989. The Chumash and the Missions. In *Columbian Consequences, Vol. 1, Archaeological and Historical Perspectives on the Spanish Borderlands West,* ed. David Hurst Thomas, 365–75. Washington, D.C.: Smithsonian Institution Press.

Johnson, John. 1976. *Friars, Soldiers, and Reformers: Arizona and the Sonora Mission Frontier 1767–1856.* Tucson: University of Arizona Press.

Konvitz, Milton R. 1946. *The Alien and the Asiatic in American Law.* Ithaca, NY: Cornell University Press.

Larroyo, Francisco. 1946. La educación. In *México y la cultura,* ed. Arturo Barocio et al., 584–625. Mexico City: Secretaría de Educación Pública.

Leonard, Olen E. 1943. The Role of the Land Grant in the Social Organization and Social Processes of a Spanish-American Village in New Mexico. Doctoral dissertation, Louisiana State University.

León-Portilla, Miguel. 1975. *Pre-Columbian Literatures of Mexico.* Norman: University of Oklahoma Press.

Levtzion, Nehemia. 1973. *Ancient Ghana and Mali.* Bungay, Suffolk, UK: Richard Clay.

Lipe, William. 1978. The Southwest. In *Ancient Native Americans,* ed. Jesse Jennings, 327–401. San Francisco, Calif.: W. H. Freeman.

Lynch, John. 1964. *Spain under the Habsburgs: Empire and Absolutism, 1516–1598, Vol. 1.* New York: Oxford University Press.

Margadant S., Guillermo. 1991. Mexican Colonial Land Law. In *Spanish and Mexican Land Grants and the Law,* ed. Malcolm Ebright, 85–99. Manhattan, Kans.: Sunflower University Press.

Mason, William M. 1986. Alta California during the Mission Period, 1769–1835. *Masterkey* 60 (2/3): 4–14.

Mason, William M. 1946. Early Spanish and Mexican Settlements in Arizona. *New Mexico Historical Review* 21 (4): 273–327.

Mason, William M. 1957. The Privileges of the Pardos. In *The Fuero Militar in New Spain, 1764–1800,* 43–54. Gainesville: University of Florida Press.

Menchaca, Martha. 1999. The Treaty of Guadalupe Hidalgo and the Racialization of the Mexican Population. In *The Elusive Quest For Equality: 150 Years of Chicano/Chicana Education,* ed. José F. Moreno, 3–29. Cambridge, Mass.: Harvard Educational Review.

Menchaca, Martha. 1997. Early Racist Discourses: The Roots of Deficit Thinking. In *The Evolution of Deficit Thinking: Educational Thought and Practice,* ed. Richard R. Valencia, 13–40. Stanford Series on Education and Public Policy. London: Falmer Press.

Menchaca, Martha. 1995. *Mexican Outsiders: A History of Marginalization and Discrimination in California.* Austin: University of Texas Press.

Menchaca, Martha. 1993. Chicano Indianism: A Historical Account of Racial Repression in the United States. *American Ethnologist* 20 (3): 583–603.

Merriam, Clinton Hart. 1955. *Studies of California Indians.* Berkeley: University of California Press.

Metz, Leon C. 1994. *El Paso Chronicles: A Record of Historical Events in El Paso, Texas.* El Paso, Tex.: Mangan Books.

Meyer, Michael, and William L. Sherman. 1995. *The Course of Mexican History.* New York: Oxford University Press.

Minter, Alan H. 1993. Indian Land Claims in Texas during the Twentieth Century. Paper archived at the Texas General Land Office, Austin.

Mörner, Magnus. 1967. *Race Mixture in the History of Latin America.* Boston: Little, Brown and Company.

Morrow, William W. 1923. *Spanish and Mexican Private Land Grants.* San Francisco: Bancroft-Whitney Company.

Morrow, William W. 1986. *The Indians of Texas: From Prehistoric to Modern Times.* Austin: University of Texas Press.

Officer, James E. 1987. *Hispanic Arizona, 1536–1856.* Tucson: University of Arizona Press.

Omi, Michael, and Howard Winant. 1994. *Racial Formation in the United States: From the 1960s to the 1990s.* New York: Routledge. (1st ed. 1986.)

Ortiz, Alfonso. 1991. Through Tewa Eyes: Origins. *National Geographic* 180 (4): 5–13.

Palacios Preciado, Jorge. 1988. *La esclavitud de los africanos y la trata de negros: Entre la teoría y la práctica.* Tunja, Boyacá, Colombia: Magister en Historia, Escuela de Posgrado de la Facultad Educación, Universidad Pedagógica y Tecnológica de Colombia.

Palmer, Colin. 1981. *Human Cargoes: The British Slave Trade to Spanish America, 1700–1739.* Urbana: University of Illinois Press.

Perry, Richard J. 1991. *Western Apache Heritage.* Austin: University of Texas Press.

Perry, Richard, and Rosalind Perry. 1988. *Maya Missions: Exploring the Spanish Colonial Churches of Yucatan.* Santa Barbara, Calif.: España Press.

Polzer, Charles W. 1976. *Rules and Precepts of the Jesuit Missions of Northwestern New Spain.* Tucson: University of Arizona Press.

Powell, Philip Wayne. 1952. *Soldiers, Indians and Silver: The Northward Advance of New Spain, 1550–1600.* Berkeley: University of California Press.

Reader, John. 1997. *Africa: A Biography of the Continent.* London: Hamish Hamilton.

Robinson, William W. 1948. *Land in California.* Berkeley: University of California Press.

Rodríguez Flores, Emilio. 1976. *Compendio histórico de Zacatecas.* Zacatecas, Mexico: Academia Comercial Heroes del 64.

Ross Browne, J., comp. 1850. *Report of the Debates in the Convention of California, on the Formation of the State Constitution, in September and October, 1849.* Washington, DC: John J. Towkes Printers.

Rush, Philip S. 1965. *Some Old Ranchos and Adobes.* San Diego, Calif.: Neyenesch Printers.

Salinas, Martín. 1990. *Indians of the Rio Grande Delta: Their Role in the History of Southern Texas and Northwestern Mexico.* Austin: University of Texas Press.

Sánchez, Federico A. 1986. Rancho Life in Alta California. *Masterkey* 60 (2/3): 15–25.

Santa Paula Water Works et al. v. Julio Peralta, 1893–1898. Reel no. 38, case no. 001458. Superior Court, Ventura County, California.

Sauer, Carl. 1934. The Distribution of Aboriginal Tribes and Languages in Northwestern Mexico. *Ibero-Americana* 5: 65–74.

Scholes, France V., and Harry P. Mera. 1940. Some Aspects of the Jumano Problem. *Carnegie Institution Contributions to American Anthropology and History* 6: 265–99.

Seed, Patricia. 1988. *To Love, Honor, and Obey in Colonial Mexico: Conflicts over Marriage Choice, 1574-1821*. Stanford, Calif.: Stanford University Press.

Seed, Patricia. 1994. Hispanic Homesteading in Arizona 1870 to 1908, under the Homestead Act of May 20, 1862, and Other Public Land Laws. Arizona General Land Commission Publication. Archives and Correspondence. Altadena, California.

Spicer, Edward. 1981. *Cycles of Conquest: The Impact of Spain, Mexico, and the United States on the Indians of the Southwest 1533-1960*. 7th rpt. Tucson: University of Arizona Press.

Steward, Julian. 1933. Ethnography of Owens Valley Paiute. *University of California Publications in American Anthropology and Ethnology* 33 (3): 233-350.

Swanton, John R. 1984. *The Indian Tribes of North America*. 4th rpt. Bureau of American Ethnology, No. 45. Washington, DC: Smithsonian Institution Press. (First printed 1952.)

Swanton, John R. 1990. *Iron Cages: Race and Culture in Nineteenth-Century America*. 2nd ed. New York: Alfred A. Knopf.

Texas General Land Office. n.d. Espada Mission Land Records. File 121: 45. Austin: Texas General Land Office.

Texas General Land Office. 1983. *El jade de México: El mundo esotérico del "Chalchihuite."* Mexico City: Panorama Editorial, S.A.

Tjarks, Alicia. 1974. Comparative Demographic Analysis of Texas, 1777-1793. *Southwestern Historical Quarterly* 77 (Jan.): 291-338.

Tyler, Ron, ed. 1996. New Handbook of Texas History, Vol. 3. Austin: Texas State Historical Association. @

Vigil, James Diego. 1984. *From Indians to Chicanos: The Dynamics of Mexican American Culture*. Prospect Heights, Ill.: Waveland Press. (1st ed. 1980.)

Villagrá, Gaspar Pérez de. 1933. *History of New Mexico*. Trans. Gilberto Espinosa. Los Angeles: Quivira Society. (1st printing 1610.)

Vinces Vives, Jaime. 1972. *Approaches to the History of Spain*. Berkeley: University of California Press.

Wagner, Henry R., and Helen R. Parish. 1967. *The Life and Writings of Bartolomé de las Casas*. Albuquerque: University of New Mexico Press.

Weber, David J. 1992. *The Spanish Frontier in North America*. New Haven, Conn.: Yale University Press.

Weber, David J. 1982. *The Mexican Frontier, 1821 to 1846: The American Southwest under Mexico*. Albuquerque: University of New Mexico Press.

Williams, David A. 1998. *Bricks without Straw: A Comprehensive History of African Americans in Texas*. Austin, Tex.: Eakin Press.

Byrne v. Alas et al., 16 Pacific Reporter 523-529 (Supreme Court of California 1888).

United States v. Wong Kim Ark, 169 U.S. 649-732 (1898).

Laws of Texas, Vol. 1 (1898).

A Place Called Home: A Queer Political Economy
of Mexican Immigrant Men's Family Experiences
LIONEL CANTÚ

Driving the Interstate 5 Freeway, near San Diego and the San Onofre border
checkpoint, there are large yellow signs graphically depicting a fleeing family
(father leading, mother, and child—legs flailing behind). The almost surreal
signs are meant to warn motorists of the danger of "illegal" immigrant families
trying to cross the busy lanes. This image reveals not only the extreme risks
that many immigrants are willing to take to get to the United States but also
the way in which we imagine these immigrants. While most motorists probably do not think of a sexual message when they see the warning sign, it's there
for us to see; if we only really look. The sign is symbolic at multiple levels: a
nuclear family unit, heteronormative in definition, a threat to the racial social
order by virtue of its reproductive potential. The sign is also symbolic of the
current state of international migration studies: sexuality is an implicit part of
migration that has been overlooked—ignored.

In this essay I examine some of the ways in which sexuality, understood as
a dimension of power, has shaped the lives, intimate relationships, and migratory processes of Mexican men who immigrate to the United States.[1] More specifically, I utilize ethnographic data to examine how traditional family relations and

alternative support systems such as "chosen families" (Weston 1991) influence migration among Mexican immigrant men who have sex with men (MSMs). The men whom I interviewed and introduce in this essay had a variety of sexual identities both prior to and after migration. An important part of my research, therefore, is to examine from a queer materialist perspective dimensions that shape the social relations of families of origin and families of choice and thus, the intimate context by which identity itself is shaped. I argue for a theoretical move toward a *queer political economy* in order to understand the dynamics that shape "the sexuality of migration" and the fluidity of identities in a global context. In the first section of this essay I briefly discuss how I conceptualize this theoretical framework (specific to the issues discussed here). I then discuss the ways in which these theoretical concepts are grounded in the everyday experiences of Mexican immigrant men.

Queering the Political Economy of Family and Migration

Queer theory, a conceptual framework that by its very logic resists definition and stability (Jagose 1996), has become both an area of growing influence and an entrenched resistance in the social sciences. These tensions and contradictions are due in part to an increased focus on issues of identity (including that of nation, race/ethnicity, gender, and sexuality) among scholars from a variety of disciplines with different theoretical perspectives and empirical concerns. Yet these tensions are rooted in queer theory itself, descended from the more modernist concerns of early gay- and lesbian-studies scholars and the postmodern influence of semiotics and the work of Foucault.

Queer theorists more closely aligned with the semiotic tradition have built upon Foucault's assertion that sexualities and identities can only be understood through discursive strategies and an "analytics of power" that examines the multiple sites where normalization occurs through discourse and knowledge production (Cousins and Hussain 1984; Foucault 1990 [1978]; Martin 1988). However, an analytics of power restricted purely to an examination of textual discourse, void of a material context, is obviously limited. There are, of course, numerous normalizing sites, including the body (which has received particular attention as an inscribed "text"), but my concern here lies with that of the family. As I demonstrate in the following discussion, the family and the home (or household) is a site where normalizing rules of gender and sexual conduct and performance are taught on a daily basis.

More recently there has been a move toward a queer materialist paradigm that asserts that "all meanings have a material base" from which cultural symbols and identities are constructed (Morton 1996; see also Gluckman and Reed

1997; Seidman 1996). Furthermore, it is "the examination of the complex social conditions (division of labor, production, distribution, consumption, class) through which sexual preference/orientation, hierarchy, domination, and protest develop dialectically at a particular time and place" (Bennett 1996). Thus, in this section I briefly outline a queer materialist paradigm for analyzing the social relations between family, migration, and sexual identity.

The link between "gay" identity and socioeconomic forces[2] has been asserted by gay- and lesbian-studies scholars since at least the late 1960s with the work of Mary McIntosh (1968) and Jeffrey Weeks (1977). In his seminal article "Capitalism and Gay Identity," John D'Emilio (1993) asserts that the modern construction of a gay identity is the result of capitalist development and the migration of homosexuals to urban gay communities in San Francisco, Los Angeles, Chicago, and New York after World War II. In a similar vein, Gayle Rubin argues that gay identity is a result of the rural to urban migration of "homosexually inclined" men and women where communities and economic niches (which Rubin calls a "gay economy") were formed based on a shared identity as an "erotic minority" (1993 [1984]).

Key to these arguments is an understanding of how capitalist development has shaped and transformed *family* relations and structure. D'Emilio argues, "Only when *individuals* began to make their living through wage labor, instead of parts of an interdependent family unit, was it possible for homosexual desire to coalesce into a personal identity—an identity based on the ability to remain outside the heterosexual family and to construct a personal life based on one's attraction to one's own sex" (1993:470).

D'Emilio's argument thus expanded the historical materialist understanding of the patriarchal heterosexual-family structure long argued by feminists (cf. Donovan 1992; Hennessy and Ingraham 1997) and even Engels (1993 [1942]) and made more evident the relationship between the political economy of the modern family and sexual identity. This argument asserted that the economic interdependence of family members constrained gay identity formation and that these bonds were loosened by capitalist development.

Yet, the "capitalism/gay identity" argument is limited in several important ways. First, it fails to capture the complexity of stratified-power relations beyond a simple class argument even if held to the Western-industrial experience. Racial/ethnic dimensions are notably absent and must also be considered especially when family-economic interdependence plays so central a role in the paradigm. In the case of international migration, family-economic interdependence may continue to play an important role in relations and identity even while reconfigured through migratory processes and when new systems of support are created. Second, while most social constructionists agree that gay identity is linked with capitalist development, this body of literature fails to capture the multiplicity and fluidity of sexual identity and fails to conceptualize capitalist development as a global phenomenon with implications for sexuality and migratory patterns on a global scale. Unfortunately, migration-studies scholars have in turn ignored this literature marked as "gay studies" and have not examined how sexuality may shape migratory processes.

There are a number of theoretical-migration models that postulate the reasons why migration begins or the conditions that perpetuate it.[3] Traditionally, microlevel theories focus either on the rational choice of the individual or on the household;[4] while macrolevel theories examine the structural forces of capitalist societies such as the labor market, trade relations, or economic intervention by nations.[5]

In the 1980s other "social" factors also began to receive analytical attention, but not until Sylvia Pedraza's 1991 article, "Women and Migration: The Social Consequences of Gender," were feminist concerns taken seriously by migration scholars. Part of the reason for the delay (and continued resistance) in recognizing gender as an important dimension of analysis within migration studies has been the limited scope through which migration scholars have viewed the "economic" realm. For many, gender was perceived as a social factor subsumed by the economic or considered to be a variable of analysis, like age or education, that simply needed to be added to migration studies.

Feminist scholars, however, assert that gender is a much more complex dimension. For instance, while migration scholars argue that social networks and modes of incorporation such as ethnic communities and economies are an important aspect of personal transition linking migrants to social, cultural, familial, and economic resources, most studies have conceptualized social networks either in terms of familial relationships or in terms of men's labor networks, without theorizing how gender itself might shape these relations. As Pierrette Hondagneu-Sotelo demonstrates in her book *Gendered Transitions* (1994), gender is more than a variable of migration; rather, it is a dimension of power relations that shapes and organizes migration. Similarly, sexuality is a dimension of power that I contend also shapes and organizes processes of migration and modes of incorporation.

In this essay I examine the relations between materialist forces, family, migration, and sexual identity. A queer materialist or political economy paradigm is central to my analysis, for such a paradigm allows identity to be understood not only as a social construction but also as being fluid—that is, constructed and reconstructed depending upon social location and political economic context. Furthermore, my analysis is informed by what Anzaldúa (1987) refers to as "mestiza consciousness" (also sometimes referred to as border theory), in which the incongruities of binary systems are made visible as are the intersections of multiple marginal positions and relations of power. My analysis is thus centered on "the borders" in its conscious effort to incorporate structural dimensions of "the borderlands" into an identity that is constructed and draws meaning from marginality.

Border Crossers: Family, Migration, Identity

The immigrant men I interviewed for my research ranged in age from their early twenties to early forties and lived in the greater Los Angeles area. I met these men during my dissertation research fieldwork from 1997 through December 1999 by making initial contacts through organizations, fliers, and friends and then using a snowball sampling technique to meet others. While each of these men's stories was in its own way unique, there were also similarities that became more evident as my research progressed.

Most of the men came from the Pacific states of Mexico, and approximately two-thirds came from the state of Jalisco. About half described their communities of origin as small cities or towns, with only a couple describing their origins as rural; migration to larger cities (such as Guadalajara or border cities such as Tijuana) prior to migrating to the United States was also a common experience.[6] All the men included here were sixteen years old or older when they immigrated. Most came from lower middle-class Mexican backgrounds[7] and had at least a high-school education. Like many of their straight counterparts, many were undocumented. Only two of the men I met were not working at the time of their interview; one man was unable to work due to health reasons related to AIDS/HIV, and the other was looking for work. Several of the men were actually holding down more than one job, one full-time and one part-time. The average annual income of the men was between twenty and twenty-five thousand dollars. Their fluency in English was relative to their time in the United States, but none of the men were completely fluent.[8] Due in part to this, the men interviewed reported daily lives that were for the most part Spanish speaking. In addition, nearly all estimated that more than 75 percent of their social circles were Latino.

In the following paragraphs I introduce seven of the twenty men I interviewed formally.[9] I selected these particular interviews as representative of the range of experiences related to me. However, the interview excerpts I have included should not be considered representative of all Mexican-immigrant men to the United States who have sex with men—the diversity of experiences is far greater than can be captured here. The men I have included identified as either bisexual or homosexual (gay) at the time of the interviews. In addition, I do not include the voice of transgendered Mexican immigrants, although some of the men do have experience with crossdressing.[10] Yet the voices represented here do reveal the complexity of the sexuality of migration and the importance of including sexuality in our analysis. I will first provide a general description of these men and then discuss their experiences as they relate to family, migration, and sexual identity.

> *Lalo* is a thirty-three-year-old immigrant from Guadalajara, Jalisco. The fifth of nine children, Lalo comes from what he describes as a "very poor" class background. He migrated to the United States in 1983 and is a legal resident who currently lives in Fountain Valley.
>
> *Armando* is a thirty-two-year-old Mexican national born in the state of Jalisco where he spent eight years in a seminary studying to be a priest. He is the oldest of eight children (four boys and four girls). He moved to the United States in 1995 and is an undocumented immigrant. He currently lives in Santa Ana but was living in Los Angeles with his brother when we met.
>
> *Gabriel* is a twenty-three-year-old undocumented immigrant who has lived in the Orange County area for the past five years. He works as a medical assistant. The fourth of six children, Gabriel moved to the United States from Nayarit, Mexico, in 1993 when he was eighteen. Gabriel is now living in Fullerton.
>
> *Paco* is the youngest of six children, four sisters and a brother. His father died three months after he was born and Paco was raised by his mother and older siblings. Paco is a legal resident of the United States although he immigrated illegally in 1990.
>
> *Roberto* is in his early forties and has lived in the United States since migrating from Mexico in 1994. The fourth of five children, he comes from a prestigious and well-to-do family in Nayarit, Mexico. Although never married, Roberto has a teenaged son who lives in Mexico with the son's mother. Roberto now lives in the San Fernando Valley and works as an AIDS educator for a Latino community organization.
>
> *Manuel* is thirty years old, identifies as bisexual, and currently is un-employed although he worked as a registered nurse in Guadalajara, Mexico. He is the third of eight children (seven boys and one girl) and grew up in Tlaquepaque, a town famous for its artisans and now considered part of the Guadalajara metro area. A Jehovah's Witness, he considers himself to be very religious. Due to his HIV status, he moved to the United States in 1996 to be with his family and is an un-documented immigrant. He lives with his family in Santa Ana, who know of his condition but are not aware of his sexual identity.

Carlos migrated from Guadalajara in 1990 and is currently seeking political asylum in the United States based on his sexual orientation. Because Carlos was an active member of the Democratic Revolutionary Party (PRD), an opposition party to Mexico's ruling Institutional Revolutionary Party (PRI), Carlos fears that he may be imprisoned or murdered if he returns to Mexico. He now lives in Los Angeles.

Family Life in Mexico

Social scientists have historically given great attention to the role of *la familia* in Latino culture. Scholarship often points to Latino "familism"—defined as the value and preservation of the family over individual concerns (Moore and Pachon 1985; Williams 1990)—as the contentious source of both material and emotional support and patriarchal oppression. The stereotype is problematic for a number of reasons, not the least of which is the fact that the same argument could be made of most families regardless of their cultural context.[11] Thus, in this section, while I discuss how the early family lives of Mexican immigrant MSMs influenced migratory processes, my aim is not to reproduce a cultural pathology of *la familia* but, rather, to examine the family as a site where normative constructions of gender and sexuality are reproduced and in which the dynamics of migration are materially embedded.

During my interviews, most of the men remembered their lives as children in Mexico fondly.[12] Yet, even when memories of early family life were positive, the daily lessons of normative masculinity learned by these men often resulted in emotional conflicts. I asked them to share with me their memories of family life and educational experiences in order to understand more fully the processes by which normative gender roles and sexuality are learned. Most early childhood memories were shared with smiles and consisted of generally carefree days: playing typical games and going to school. Most of the men also reported that they were good students who received awards for their scholarship and genuinely seemed to have enjoyed school. However, even men such as Paco, who reported that his childhood was "a great time . . . a very beautiful stage of my life," expressed a sense of inner conflict rooted in normative definitions of masculinity.

These conflicts were even more pronounced for men such as Lalo, whose memories of early life in Mexico were not good ones. Recounting his childhood Lalo told me,

> As I child I was very mischievous. I was sexually abused when I was seven by the neighbor, a man of forty. It was a childhood experience that affected me greatly. This person continued to abuse me, he would give me money,

later I would go looking for him myself and I was like his "boyfriend" until I was nine. I knew what he was doing was wrong so I never told anyone.

Paternostro (1998) reports that child sexual abuse by a family member is a common phenomenon in Latin America (whether it is more prevalent than other countries is debatable). In fact, Lalo was not the only man I interviewed who was sexually abused as a child, but he was the most forthcoming about the experience.[13] Later in the interview he explained that he had also been abused by two older male cousins and that when he told his father about the abuse, his father's response was to rape him for being a "*maricón*."

None of the sexually abused men, including Lalo, remember connecting these experiences to homosexuality at the time of their occurrence; in part because they didn't really know what homosexuality was. Lalo explained that although he had never heard the word "homosexual," words such as "*maricón*" and "*joto*" were commonly heard in his home. However, Lalo related these terms to effeminate men or *vestidas* like the man in his neighborhood who dressed like a woman. Many informants related similar experiences. Carlos explained, for example, "Across from us lived the town *maricón*. In every town there is the drunk and the *maricón*, and the *maricón* lived across the street." As children the question of what a *maricón* was remained somewhat of a mystery; although they knew it wasn't anything "good." For instance, it wasn't until later that Lalo started to understand what "homosexual" meant. He explained,

> After about the age of twelve or thirteen there was a lot of sexual play among the boys of the *colonia*. We would masturbate one another. There were about twelve of us in the group and we would form a circle and masturbate one another. Later, couples would form and we would penetrate one another. Now they are all grown up and married but there was a lot of sexual play when we were kids. . . . There were some boys who would refuse to join us, saying, "that's for *maricones*" or "you're going to be a *joto* or a woman." It was then that I started to understand but I never thought that I was going to be like a woman.

Masculine discourse that devalues the feminine and equates homosexuality to the feminine, is of course, not particular to Mexican culture (cf. Fellows 1996; Murray and Roscoe 1998). However, as Lalo explained, homosexuality and femininity are not popularly understood as synonymous.[14] "Being a *joto* is to not be man. Neither a man nor a woman, it is to be an abomination, a curse." Prieur's (1998) recent work on male-to-female transgendered residents of Mexico City supports Lalo's analysis and suggests that class perspectives are an important dimension of its construction. Thus the relationship of homosexuality to the feminine is more complex than a synonymous equation implies. Homosexuality is not only the opposite of masculinity, it is a corruption of it, an unnatural form that by virtue of its transgression of the binary male/female order poses a threat that must be contained or controlled.

The liminal/marginal location of homosexuality, perhaps best understood as shaped by what Almaguer (1993) refers to as a sex/gender/power axis, is reproduced through messages in everyday life. Discussing his daily chores at home, Paco explained,

> My duties at home in particular, well, they were almost never designated to us. I liked very much to sweep, mop, wash the dishes, and when [my mother and sisters] would make cake I always liked to be there when they were preparing it. But, only when my mom and my sisters were there, because my brother would often be in the United States. I always liked to help my mom and my sisters, but when my brother would get there, I always had to hide or not do it because he would tell me "You are not a woman to be doing that, that's for the *maricones*." Then, since I was scared of him, I wouldn't do it anymore. But it was what I liked to do, up till now; I like cleaning very much and chores like that. I like to cook very much, I like to have everything clean—I've always liked that.

When I asked Paco to discuss the issue of "women's work" in more detail, he explained,

> In Mexico they say "Oh, a homosexual person or a *maricón* or a *joto* are those persons that are dressed like women." They always have a little of that mentality. For example, there were times that a guy named Luis would pass by and he always left his nails long and his hair long like a woman. He had a bag, and he would put on women's pants or a woman's blouse, and he might have put on make-up but not a lot, but obviously he would go around like a woman. Then all the people, well, they said things, but in my family one time I heard my mother call him, she would call them *frescos* (fresh), there goes this *fresco*, there goes that *fresco*, I would hear my mom say that. Then, I would get angry when I would hear that, because I would say "Well, I am not like that, but I am attracted to young men."

Armando expressed learning the same type of sex/gender message through child's play. Armando explained that he liked to play with paper dolls and more than anything liked to cut out the clothes, yet he hid when he did so. When I asked him why, Armando replied, "It's the only game I remember playing secretly. I knew my parents wouldn't like it. I thought it was perfectly normal, it was only bad because it was something that little girls do."

The struggle that Paco and Armando relate in attempting to negotiate the perceived contradictions of sex, gender, and sexual identities was a common theme of many of my interviews. Participants expressed a certain sense of isolation or "not belonging" and not wanting to disappoint their families. Even learning to emulate normative gender and sexual performances was not, in itself, sufficient to resolve these conflicts. For some men, these tensions were a catalyst for migration itself.

Leaving Home

One of the questions that I asked immigrant interviewees was what their top three reasons for immigrating were. After analyzing the answers given, it became clear that sexuality was indeed an influencing reason for migration and that "family" dynamics were often linked to these reasons. However, understanding how sexuality actually influenced these decisions was not always as clear-cut as having people respond, "it was my sexuality"—although that sometimes happened. For example, Lalo told me, "Ninety percent of the reason I migrated was because of my sexuality." Such reasons obviously resonate with D'Emilio's (1993) and Rubin's (1993 [1984]) models of rural to urban migration by gay men and women seeking greater anonymity and gay life in the cities. Yet, in order to understand more fully how sexuality is linked to other socioeconomic dimensions, one must attempt to connect the micro with the meta and macro dimensions of life. That is to say, one cannot separate individual reasons for migration from the larger processes that shape people's everyday lives and perceived choices. Several themes did arise from the interviews, sometimes from the same source, and these themes are implicated in a queer political economy in different ways.

For example, all of the men I interviewed, in one form or another, gave financial reasons for migrating to the United States. And indeed, immigration scholars have traditionally placed a great deal of emphasis on economic reasons for migration, yet to a great degree their vision of the economic realm is extremely limited. The social inequalities of sexuality, like race and gender, are integrally linked to the economic structures of society. Groups that are marginalized as sexual minorities are constrained by the limits of discrimination and prejudice that may limit their socioeconomic opportunities. Thus, when immigrants, who are a sexual minority, say that they immigrated for financial reasons, part of the analysis must include sexuality. For instance, even the person I interviewed in Mexico who owned his own pesticide and fertilizer business felt the constraints of heterosexism. Business networks, he explained, depend upon having the right image, which means a wife, children, and social events tied to church and school. Clearly, as a gay man he was outside this world. His class privilege and the fact the he is his own boss, however, permit him to remain in Mexico relatively free from some of the pressures that drive others to migrate.[15]

Thus, while men such as Lalo clearly migrate to escape a sense of sexual oppression, for others the decision to migrate to the United States is influenced by a combination of sexual liberation and economic opportunities. For example, Gabriel moved to the United States from Nayarit, Mexico, when he was eighteen but explained that he had begun to prepare himself for immigrating at sixteen. When I asked him why, he explained that he had two major reasons for coming to the United States:

> First, I wanted to get a better level of education. And the second reason was sexuality. I wanted to be able to define myself and have more freedom with respect to that. I wanted to come here to live, not to distance myself from my family but to hide what I already knew I had. I knew I was gay but I thought I might be able to change it. I needed to come here and speak to people, to learn more about it, because in Mexico it's still very taboo. There isn't so much liberation.

Gabriel's experience reveals how the tension of sexual desire versus "not wanting to distance" oneself from family may serve as a migratory "push." Yet while he clearly moved to the United States seeking a more liberal sexual environment, it was not just a personal matter, it was also because he felt he had limited economic opportunities as a gay man in Mexico. Staying in Mexico might very well have meant either attempting to create a heteronormative family or dealing with social and economic discrimination as a gay man.

Sometimes homosexual relationships might have subtle influences such as serving to establish or expand social networks or they might have a more direct influence driving migration itself. For instance, Roberto explained to me that he was quite happy with his life in Mexico as a civil servant but that people had begun to gossip about his sexual orientation and he feared for his job security, especially since he had recently learned that he was HIV positive. Roberto had met a man from the United States who was vacationing in Mexico and had maintained a friendly relationship with the man. When the American suggested to Roberto that he move to the United States to live with him, Roberto took advantage of the opportunity and moved to Los Angeles. Although he is no longer in a relationship with the American, they continue to be friends. In such a case, new (transnational) social bonds are created similar to the kinship networks that migration scholars argue facilitate migration, yet these are not blood-based but, rather, based on affiliation-transnational gay networks.

Finding Their Way Home

Adapting to life in the United States is difficult for any migrant, but for immigrants like Lalo, who migrate to the United States expecting a gay utopia, the reality of life in the United States can be quite a blow. Indeed Lalo had returned to Mexico for two years after first migrating to the United States because of his disillusionment, returning only when he realized that his prospects as a gay man were limited in Mexico. Thus, for Lalo, home was no longer Jalisco. While there are a number of important aspects of an immigrant's experiences adapting to their new home, in this section I focus on how sexuality might be related to a migrant's adaptation and incorporation. Specifically, I am concerned here with both kin networks and the home as mechanisms for adaptation.

In her discussion of gay and lesbian kin relations, Weston (1991) demonstrates how gays and lesbians construct "chosen" families based on shared affinities and relationships of both material and emotional support. Kinship (biological) plays a central role in migration as a means through which immigrants receive support and acquire important knowledge for survival and adaptation (cf. Chavez 1992). While the Mexican men I interviewed often utilized kinship networks to these ends, they also depended upon networks that were similar to those described by Weston. About half of the immigrants I spoke with utilized preexisting gay networks to migrate to the United States. They were like Lalo, who migrated with the help of a gay compatriot already living in Los Angeles, and like Roberto, who came with the help of a gay American. But even some of those who utilized kin networks for initial migration also used gay networks for meeting other gay Latino men, finding gay roommates, making job contacts, and acquiring other types of information. The existence and use of these alternative networks depended to a large extent on how the men identified sexually, to what extent they were "out of the closet," and, to some extent, on their ability to speak English (and thus expand their networks into the mainstream gay world).

For instance, although Paco migrated and found his first job using kinship networks, he was soon able to develop a gay network as well.

> My second job was in a company where they made pools. I obtained that job through a [gay] friend, an American, who is the person, the third person that I have to thank about my legal status here in this country. He helped me get the job because it was the company of a friend of his. In the morning I would clean the offices and then I would go to the warehouse and take inventory or I would clean the warehouse or cut fiberglass, or things like that. And they paid me well at that time but I worked only a few

hours. So after that, since they said "Oh, you clean so well," and they had some very beautiful houses, over in Laguna Beach. Sometimes I would stay over because I could not finish in the weekend. The owners of the company were gay. They would go to San Francisco, or wherever they were going, they always traveled on the weekend, they left me the key, "Here is the stereo and here is the television," and everything like that because I had to sleep over. Then I would go home when they returned on Sundays.

Ironically, Paco is one of the people who assured me that sexuality had not influenced his migratory experiences in the least. This excerpt, however, reveals that gay-social networks were an aid in his finding work. In addition, Paco shares a home with a lesbian niece and has allowed other gay immigrants to stay with him temporarily until they are able to move on.

Carlos also made use of gay networks in a similar manner. When he migrated to the United States, he first lived for two months in Watsonville, California, with a brother and then went to live in Milwaukee for two years with his two sisters, who are lesbians. He then moved to Los Angeles after meeting and starting a relationship with a gay man. Like Paco, Carlos revealed that his gay friends had helped him find work and even helped him out financially. "Because of my gay friends, I have never gone without," he said.

Both Paco's and Carlos's experiences also point to the fact that sexuality is an important dimension of immigrant-household arrangements. While recent immigration literature has discussed the importance of household arrangements as "landing pads" for migrant adaptation (cf. Chavez 1992, 1994), the sexual dimensions of these arrangements are missing from the analyses. For an individual who has migrated to the United States seeking a more liberal sexual environment, it makes little sense to live in a home constrained by heteronormative relations. While about half of the Mexican men I interviewed originally lived with family members when they migrated, most had formed alternative living arrangements as soon as they were able to. Lalo's home exemplifies this alternative type of arrangement.

When I first met Lalo he was living in Santa Ana in an apartment he shared with three other immigrant men, all gay. Since our first meeting, Lalo has moved twice and has had a number of different roommates, always gay Latino immigrant men. Sometimes the men, especially if they were recent immigrants, would stay only a short time until they found another place to live. It was clear that Lalo's home was a landing pad, but it was one where Latino men could be openly gay, support one another, and share information that was essential for adaptation. Although the men did not explicitly define these relations as "family," they did sometimes refer to each other affectionately as siblings (sometimes as "sisters" and sometimes as "brothers"). Regardless of how these relationships were labeled, it was clear that an alternative support system had been created. It is precisely in this type of living arrangement that many men discover the space that transforms the way they think about themselves and their sexual identities.

Migrating Identities

One of the contributions of postmodern (including queer theory) and postcolonial literature is that identity is no longer understood as something inherently fixed and stable. Rather, identity is understood as mutable and plural—that is, the subject is the intersection of multiple identities (race/ethnicity, gender, sexuality, and so forth) that change and have salience at different moments in time and place. Given the dramatic sociospatial changes that immigrants experience, their sexual identities cannot therefore be assumed stable. As Iain Chambers puts it, "identity is formed on the move" (1994:25). The effects of migration upon the sexual identities of Mexican immigrant MSMs are ultimately linked to their emotional and material relationships to their biological families and the degree to which they have been able to resolve the normative sexuality and gender conflicts that fed their desire to migrate.

I asked the men I interviewed if they felt that they had changed at all since migrating to the United States. Nearly all of the men responded with a resounding yes. The changes they described generally centered around racial, gender, sexual, and class identities. Most of the men inevitably referred to a more liberal sexual environment as a reason for their transformation. Migrating to the United States was for many men one step in a series toward what might be called "a journey to the self."[16] For Gabriel, the desire to live in a place where he could develop his human potential as a gay man was a driving force in his decision to immigrate. He added,

> I have two names, Gabriel Luis, and my family calls me Luis. I've always said that Luis is the person who stayed in Mexico. Once I came here, Gabriel was born. Because, like I've told you, once I was here I defined myself sexually and I've changed a lot emotionally, more than anything emotionally, because I found myself.

This journey of self-discovery is intimately linked to resistance to the normative gender and sex regimes I have described earlier. While earlier scholarship asserted that Mexican male sexual identities were based on the active or passive (*activo/pasivo*) role of the participant (where only the passive was deemed homosexual) more recent research, including my own, finds that Mexican sexual identities are more complex.

Most interviewees remembered first being aware of their attraction to boys or men in early childhood. Some remembered being attracted to the same sex as young as age four, but the majority of recollections were a bit later. Carlos remembered, "I was around eight years old. I could recognize the beauty of men. But from then on it was an issue of denial." The pressure to conform, or as Lalo described, *"la lucha de no querer ser gay"* (the struggle of not wanting to be gay) took a toll on most of the men I interviewed but perhaps was most eloquently described by Armando. He explained that he had been tormented by schoolmates after around the fourth grade who would call him *joto* and *maricón*. He stated,

> But I learned how to hide it better, so it wasn't noticeable. I no longer isolated myself, instead I would mix with the troublemakers at school so that their reputation would rub off on me and so no one would tell me anything anymore. A new student arrived who was even more obvious than me and to a certain extent he was my salvation. Everyone focused their attention on him and it was a load off of me. It gave me the opportunity to get closer to the other students and do everything that they did, to act like them, have girlfriends, and not be the "good boy" anymore—to take on the heterosexual role.

Armando would later join a seminary in an attempt to escape his sexual feelings and began to lift weights so that his appearance was more masculine. Eventually, however, he realized he needed to face who he "really" was.

> I feel that I lost a lot of my essence as a homosexual during that time. I see it like that now. At that time I only wanted to be part of a group, to be accepted. It's horrible to feel marginalized, in a corner, abnormal. In my attempts to be like everyone else wanted me to be I lost much of myself.

Two months after migrating to the United States, seeking the freedom to be a gay man, he confessed to a cousin, with whom he was staying, that he was gay. She told him that she accepted and loved him as he was but that he needed to talk to his brothers. Armando told his brothers one by one and they all accepted his homosexuality (although it was by no means easy). He then decided to tell his widowed mother. At the time of our interview it had been five months since he had written his mother a five-page letter explaining his struggle to accept himself. A month later Armando's mother wrote him back asking forgiveness and assuring him that he would have her support and unconditional love. Armando has been able successfully to integrate his calling to service with his desire to be true to himself. He now works as an AIDS educator and program coordinator for an organization that serves gay Latino men.

Like Armando, other men who migrated to the United States also came out to their families and some found acceptance as well. In some of these men's cases it seems that the acceptance is in part tied to a reversal in family roles. Where once they were dependent upon their families for support, now their families are dependent upon them. Thus, while Almaguer (1993) has argued that economic interdependence stifles a gay identity from forming among Latino MSMs, my research reveals that it may actually facilitate familial acceptance. For instance, since migrating to the United States Lalo has also gained acceptance from the family who threw him out of the house. He explained to me that he has sent money to Mexico to have his mother's house repaired and to pay for his brother's tuition and that his family now respects him. Lalo related, "I'm much more secure now. I'm not afraid to say I'm a homosexual. I'm content being gay and I can help others. I'm stronger and have achieved a lot of things."

Thus the transformation in economic roles and physical separation has allowed Lalo the opportunity to be both gay and accepted by his family.

There were, however, a couple of men I interviewed who were openly gay prior to migrating to the United States. In both cases these men had upper-class backgrounds. The difference that class makes in mitigating the effects of homophobia is significant and needs to be studied more closely. For example, when I asked Roberto about his son he laughed out loud and said,

> Oh my son! My son was the product of an agreement. His mother knew that I was gay. My partner of ten years and I lived together [in Tepic, Nayarit] and she lived in front of us. She knew of my relationship with Alejo and the three of us would go out to dance. In a small town, well, it was known that she was the friend of "the boys." We would go out to dance, she would come to our home to watch television, listen to music, or have a drink. Then one day she told me flat out that she wanted to have my baby. Then between the jokes I began to understand and between the jokes we ended up in bed. We had sex for two or three months and one day she called me and told me she was pregnant. I was twenty-three or twenty-four and was completely out of the closet with my family and I didn't care about anything.

Without a doubt, Roberto's class privilege allowed him to not "care about anything" as an openly gay man. In all probability it also shaped his gay-social networks that allowed him to migrate to the United States.

To be clear, for those men who do not have such privileges in Mexico, migrating to the United States does not necessarily afford them these privileges either. While there may be more space to be gay in the United States, migrating has its costs. For example, as Carlos lamented,

Being away from Mexico creates a strong nationalistic feeling with a lot of nostalgia. You begin to notice how different the system is here than in Mexico, an economic system that changes your life completely—a system where one forgets about other things that in Mexico were a priority. Here one lives life from the perspective of money. Working and making enough money to pay your bills is more important than having friends and doing what you like. In Mexico it's very different. It's more important to have friends. One lives less a slave to the clock. One forgets these things and becoming aware of that has made me very sad.

Discovering the virulence of racism in the United States seems to counterbalance any feelings of sexual liberation. I asked the men, in an open-ended manner, if they had ever experienced discrimination (without defining the type). Nearly all of the men responded in ways similar to Carlos: "For being Latino, for not speaking English perfectly, for the color of my skin." The irony, of course, is that in their attempts to escape one form of bigotry, most of the Mexican men I interviewed discovered that not only had they not entirely escaped it but they now faced another. As Lalo said, "It wasn't true that homosexuals are free, that they can hold hands or that Americans like Mexicans." Under these circumstances the role of a support system becomes all the more important and for queer Latino-immigrant men this often means that new families must be created.

Building Family

I was naively surprised by the responses I received when I asked immigrant men about their future plans. I suppose that I had allowed myself to become so immersed in the migration literature that I was expecting to hear something more along the lines of "return to Mexico and start my own business." More common, however, were responses such as Paco's:

I want to be anywhere close to the person I love, to support me. If it's in Mexico, a lot better because I would have my family and that person near me. But, more than anything, right now I worry a lot for my own person and for the partner who I think will be what I wait for in my life. And I see myself in a relationship with a lot of affection, and maybe by then, living with that person, together. And maybe even to get married.

In response to my next question, "So your plans for the future are to have a partner?" Paco answered:

A stable partner, be happy, and give them all my support, and I would help that person shine, succeed in anything I could help. I will try to do it all the time. If he accomplishes more than I have it will make me very happy because in that aspect I am not egotistical. And still more things that are positive; get more involved in helping people that need me, in every aspect. Be happy, make my partner happy, above all make myself happy, and my family, my friends, all the people that like me, and I like.

This type of response does not exclude dreams of material wealth and entrepreneurship, but it centers and gives priority to affective dimensions—to building new families. The desires for stable relationships reflect not only the difficulty for maintaining such relationships in Mexico but also the isolation that these men feel in the United States. This isolation that gay Mexican immigrant men feel is due in some measure to language difficulties, but racial and class issues also play into it. For instance, Carlos explained to me that although he was in a relationship at the time of our interview he didn't see much of a future in it:

I don't have many expectations for my relationship because my partner is not Latino. I think that, ideally, for a stable relationship I need to be with a Latino . . . someone who identifies as Latino. Someone intelligent and a little more cultured. Someone who has the capacity to go to an art or photography exhibit and enjoy it. Someone open-minded, open to learning from other cultures and who is financially independent.

The problem, of course, is that the social location of Mexican immigrant MSMs in the United States is a marginal one. Stability is not easily established and financial independence may take years to accomplish, if at all. The problem is exacerbated by the fact that there are few public spaces where Latino gay men can openly meet one another. Thus, creating family or even a sense of community depends in no small part upon the ability of queer Latinos to build a new home with limited resources and external support.

"Who do you turn to for support?" I asked the men I interviewed. The standard response was: "family and friends." Yet it is clear from my discussions with these men, and the data presented here, that these relationships (whether biological or chosen) were sometimes strained, always evolving, and ultimately negotiated. A queer materialist analysis of the experiences of Mexican-immigrant men who have sex with men reveals the ways in which dimensions of family, migration, and sexual identity intersect and are embedded within a political economy. Many of the men interviewed felt marginalized by hetero-normative definitions of masculinity reproduced through and embodied in the traditional family. These norms, reproduced in daily activities since childhood, marginalize not only men with "feminine" characteristics but also those able to pass, who were instilled with a fear of discovery. Associations of femininity with homosexuality created a sense of confusion in some men who, although attracted to men, did not identify as feminine. The economic liability that derived from not creating a heteronormative family unit as an adult also influenced the immigration process. These strict gender/sex regimes were powerful enough to drive many men to migrate to the United States in search of a more liberal environment.

A queer political-economy perspective of migration also aids in unveiling how sexuality has shaped processes and strategies for adaptation such as social networks and household arrangements. Alternative relations to biological families, which serve as systems of support, are created based on sexual orientation. The members of these "chosen families" assist one another through the trials and tribulations of being a queer Mexican-immigrant man. Such assistance takes a variety of forms, including helping with migration itself, sharing knowledge and resources such as job information, and even sharing households.

New economic arrangements mean that some men find that they are empowered to come out to their biological families as gay men and maintain a level of acceptance and respect from their loved ones. Shared space is also an important dimension linked to the futures of these gay men. Faced with a sense of isolation and a deep desire to form stable relationships—which they were prevented from having in Mexico—space becomes the base for adaptation, community, and shared futures. Thus, for many men who have come to identify as gay, new family structures become a means by which dreams may be realized.

Although my focus has been on Mexican-immigrant men, there are larger implications that need to be explored. When we understand sexuality as a dimension of power (that intersects with other dimensions such as race, gender, and class) in which certain groups are privileged over others, then these implications become more visible. For instance, Argüelles and Rivero (1993) argue that some immigrant women have migrated in order to flee violent and/ or oppressive sexual relationships or marriage arrangements, which they contest. Little research has been conducted on Latinas in general; far less exists on the intersections of migration and sexuality (regardless of sexual orientation). While it is clear that biological families reproduce normative constructions of gender and sexuality, the ways in which these norms and power relations influence different groups of people in terms of migration and identity is not understood. I hope the research presented here will be a step toward the development of a queer materialist paradigm by which the sexual dimensions of migration can be understood and by which further research may be conducted.

NOTES

Reprinted with permission from John Wiley and Sons. This essay originally appeared in *Perspectives on Las Américas* (New York: John Wiley, 2008), 259–73.

1   This essay represents part of a larger dissertation research project entitled *Border Crossings: Mexican Men and the Sexuality of Migration*. The author gratefully acknowledges the comments and suggestions of the editors and Nancy Naples, as well as the funding support of the Social Science Research Council's Sexuality Fellowship Program and the Ford Foundation, which made this research possible. In addition, the author wishes to express his gratitude to the men who participated in this project.

2   While recent debates between social constructionists and what are sometimes belittlingly called essentialists have heated up with genetic research, I assume that sexuality is more complex than the either/or debates allow for. I therefore focus on the social aspects of sexuality, i.e., the social constructionist perspective. The constructionist argument has also been made from a cultural perspective. In his classic study of the Sambia of New Guinea, anthropologist Gilbert Herdt (1994 [1981]) examined the cultural meanings of homosexuality and masculinity in a nonindustrial society and demonstrated, through his examination of "boy-inseminating rituals," that meanings of homosexuality and norms of gender are not universal but, rather, are culturally constructed.

3   This section of my discussion is meant to highlight and illustrate only part of the theoretical framework of my research and my ideas for "queering" it.

4   C. M. Wood (1982) attempts to reconcile these differences by focusing on the household as a unit of analysis that bridges micro- and macro-economic concerns, but the household analysis also has its limitations, including a bias toward the individual actor that obscures some of the macrolevel dimensions of migration such as the role of the state and sociocultural influences. In addition, a focus on the household *exclusively* tends to conceal dimensions of the transnational or binational household and other adaptive strategies by assuming (in at least some of the literature) a nuclear household configuration with one head and fully shared resources— that a household has a choice is a problem of reification as well.

5   Douglas Massey and his coauthors (Massey, Arango, Hugo, Kouaouci, Pellegrino, and Taylor 1993; Massey and Espinosa 1995) categorize various theories of international migration into five conceptual frames, which I highlight: neoclassical economics, the new economics of labor migration, segmented labor market theory, social capital theory, and world systems theory.

6   This urban migration generally occurred during the participants' childhood and was not a common experience of their adult life.

7   Distinguishing social class was a difficult task in large part because the Mexican middle class is quickly disappearing from the country's socioeconomic landscape and also because of the international relativity of social class definitions. My measure of class is, therefore, informant defined and takes into account the men's educational and career backgrounds as well as that of their parents.

8   Interviews were conducted in Spanish and translated by the author.

9   The names of research participants are pseudonyms.

10 I do not mean to suggest that cross-dressing and transgender are the same.

11 For further elaboration of the ways in which stereotypical cultural arguments pathologize Latino culture, see Cantú (2000).

12 All the men came from households with more than one child.

13 For ethical reasons, I did not pressure any of my interviewees to discuss traumatic experiences in more detail than they were comfortable with. I had informed all of them prior to the interview that if there were questions with which they felt uncomfortable, they could choose not to answer them and/or end the interview at any time they so wished.

14 While earlier research on Mexican homosexuality found that the homosexual label was applied to only passive (anally receptive) men—*pasivos*—this view seems to be changing (see Carrier 1995).

15 See Cantú (1999) for more on the queer life in Mexico as it relates to migration.

16 I do not mean to imply that there is some essential or "true" sexual nature that awaits "discovery"; rather, I utilize the term as a means to convey informants' expressed understanding of their sexual journeys.

REFERENCES

Almaguer, Tomás. 1993. "Chicano Men: A Cartography of Homosexual Identity and Behavior." In Henry Abelove, Michèle Aina Barale, and David M. Halperin, eds., *The Lesbian and Gay Studies Reader*. New York: Routledge.

Anzaldúa, Gloria. 1987. *Borderlands/La Frontera: The New Mestiza*. San Francisco: Spinsters/Aunt Lute.

Argüelles, Lourdes, and Anne M. Rivero. 1993. "Gender/Sexual Orientation Violence and Transnational Migration: Conversations with Some Latinas We Think We Know." *Urban Anthropology* 22 (3/4): 259–76.

Bennett, James R. 1996. Introduction to "Materialist Queer Theory: A Working Bibliography." In Donald Morton, ed., *The Material Queer: A LesBiGay Cultural Studies Reader*. Boulder, Col.: Westview Press.

Cantú, Lionel. 1999. "Border Crossings: Mexican Men and the Sexuality of Migration." PhD diss., University of California, Irvine, 1999.

Cantú, Lionel. 2000. "Entre Hombres/Between Men: Latino Masculinities and Homosexualities." In Peter Nardi, ed., *Gay Masculinities*, 224–46. Thousand Oaks, Cal.: Sage.

Carrier, Joseph. 1995. *De Los Otros: Intimacy and Homosexuality Among Mexican Men*. New York: Columbia University Press.

Chambers, Iain. 1994. *Migrancy, Culture, Identity*. London: Routledge.

Chavez, Leo. 1992. *Shadowed Lives: Undocumented Immigrants in American Society*. San Diego, Cal.: Harcourt Brace Jovanovich.

Chavez, Leo. 1994. "The Power of the Imagined Community: The Settlement of Undocumented Mexicans and Central Americans in the United States." *American Anthropologist* 96 (1): 52–73.

Cousins, Mark, and Athar Hussain. 1984. *Michel Foucault*. New York: Macmillan.

D'Emilio, John. 1993. "Capitalism and Gay Identity." In William B. Rubenstein, ed., *Lesbians, Gay Men, and the Law*. New York: New Press.

Donovan, Josephine. 1992. *Feminist Theory*. New York: Continuum.

Engels, Frederick. 1993 [1942]. *The Origin of the Family, Private Property and the State, in the Light of the Researches of Lewis H. Morgan*. New York: International.

Fellows, Will, ed. 1996. *Farm Boys: Lives of Gay Men from the Rural Midwest*. Madison: University of Wisconsin Press.

Foucault, Michel. 1990 [1978]. *The History of Sexuality*. Trans. Robert Hurley. New York: Pantheon.

Gluckman, Amy, and Betsy Reed, eds. 1997. *HomoEconomics: Capitalism, Community, and Lesbian and Gay Life*. New York: Routledge.

Gutmann, Matthew C. 1996. *The Meanings of Macho: Being a Man in Mexico City*. Berkeley: University of California Press.

Hennessy, Rosemary, and Chrys Ingraham, eds. 1997. *Materialist Feminism: A Reader in Class, Difference, and Women's Lives*. New York: Routledge.

Herdt, Gilbert H. 1994 [1981]. *Guardians of the Flutes: Idioms of Masculinity*. New York: McGraw-Hill.

Hondagneu-Sotelo, Pierrette. 1994. *Gendered Transitions: Mexican Experiences of Immigration*. Los Angeles: University of California Press.

Hondagneu-Sotelo, Pierrette, and Michael Messner. 1994. "Gender Displays and Men's Power: 'The New Man' and the Mexican Immigrant Man." In Harry Brod and Michael Kaufman, eds., *Theorizing Masculinities*. Thousand Oaks, Cal.: Sage.

Ingram, Gordon Brent, Anne-Marie Bouthillette, and Yolanda Retter. 1997. *Queers in Space: Communities, Public Places, Sites of Resistance*. Seattle, Wash.: Bay Press.

Jagose, Annamarie. 1996. *Queer Theory: An Introduction*. New York: New York University Press.

Martin, Biddy. 1988. "Feminism, Criticism, and Foucault." In Irene Diamond and Lee Quinby, eds., *Feminism and Foucault: Reflections on Resistance*. Boston: Northeastern University Press.

Massey, Douglas S., Joaquin Arango, Graeme Hugo, Ali Kouaouci, Adela Pellegrino, and J. Edward Taylor. 1993. "Theories of International Migration: Review and Appraisal." *Population and Development Review* 19(3): 431–67.

Massey, Douglas S., and Kristin Espinosa. 1995. "What's Driving Mexico–U.S. Migration? A Theoretical, Empirical, and Policy Analysis." Unpublished paper.

Mclntosh, Mary. 1968. "The Homosexual Role." *Social Problems* 16(69): 182–92.

Moore, Joan, and Harry Pachon. 1985. *Hispanics in the United States*. Englewood Cliffs, NJ: Prentice-Hall.

Morton, Donald, ed. 1996. *The Material Queer*. Boulder, Col.: Westview Press.

Murray, Stephen O. 1995. *Latin American Male Homosexualities*. Albuquerque: University of New Mexico Press.

Murray, Stephen O., and Will Roscoe, ed. 1998. *Boy-Wives and Female Husbands: Studies in African Homosexualities*. New York: St. Martin's Press.

Paternostro, Silvana. 1998. *In the Land of God and Man: Confronting Our Sexual Culture*. New York: Dutton.

Pedraza, Silvia. 1991. "Women and Migration: The Social Consequences of Gender." *Annual Review of Sociology* 17: 303–25.

Prieur, Annick. 1998. *Mema's House, Mexico City: On Transvestites, Queens, and Machos*. Chicago: University of Chicago Press.

Rubin, Gayle. 1993 [1984]. "Thinking Sex: Notes for a Radical Theory of the Politics of Sexuality." In Henry Abelove, Michèle Aina Barale, and David M. Halperin, eds., *The Lesbian and Gay Studies Reader*, 3–44. New York: Routledge.

Seidman, Steven, ed. 1996. *Queer Theory/Sociology*. Cambridge, Mass.: Blackwell.

Weeks, Jeffrey. 1977. *Coming Out: Homosexual Politics in Britain from the Nineteenth Century to the Present*. London: Quarter.

Weston, Kath. 1991. *Families We Choose: Lesbians, Gays, Kinship*. New York: Columbia University Press.

Williams, Norma. 1990. *The Mexican American Family: Tradition and Change*. Dix Hills, N.Y.: General Hall.

Wood, Charles, H. 1982. "Equilibrium and Historical Structural Perspectives on Migration." *International Migration Review* 16(2): 298–319.

Migrations

PATRICIA ZAVELLA

Llegamos a la frontera a puros penas.

(We arrived at the border with nothing but grief.)
—"PACTO DE SANGRE," LOS TIGRES DEL NORTE

If crossing the border is hampered by surveillance and possible detention and the representation of migration is seen as an onslaught to the nation, the state and social boundaries that migrants traverse by crossing the border are equally fraught. In this essay I explore the process of border crossing by migrants in Santa Cruz County, both across the U.S.-Mexico border and within the United States. I also discuss how discourses about migration are gendered, evoking parallels between the experiences of men and women as well as those that are distinct.

Many assume migrants' main motivation for transnational migration is unemployment, especially for those with low educational attainment, which prevents them from finding work opportunities in Mexico. However, the vast majority of experienced migrants from Mexico, overwhelmingly men, were employed before they left for the United States.[1] Most of the male migrants I interviewed had some sort of work prior to migration and many of the women who migrated as adults worked for wages as well. Thus, failure to find work at home does not seem to be the primary reason that undocumented migrants from Mexico have come to the United States. Other important economic considerations are the wage differential between the United States and Mexico, extreme poverty or displacement in regions within Mexico, job quality, long-term employment prospects in the United States, or recruitment within Mexico by firms from the United States.[2]

There are also many social and personal reasons for embarking on the long journey north in what Lionel Cantú Jr. calls a "journey of the self."[3] The decision to migrate usually entails the ability to mobilize exchange through social networks, which begins long before migration actually occurs.[4] The decision regarding who will migrate often takes place as potential migrants secure resources for the journey itself, gather knowledge about migrant routes, and negotiate the approval or even blessings of loved ones. As Judith Adler Hellman writes, "Indeed, if we can find any predictor that would account for the decision to undertake the journey northward it is the presence of family, village, or neighborhood networks that facilitate and stimulate people to consider resolving their problems by joining friends and relations al otro lado, on the 'other side.'"[5] Much of the recent research on transnational migration notes the prominence of transnational *family* networks, the "underbelly of the global penetration of capitalism."[6] According to Carlos Vélez-Ibáñez and Anna Sampaio, "In Mexico, 61 percent of households have a relative currently residing in the United States and 73 percent of Mexican households have some social connection with someone in the United States."[7]

Social networks that include distant relatives, friends, neighbors, coworkers, or acquaintances are important sources for finding reliable coyotes (Mexican border specialists) to make the trip safer or contacts who can provide sustenance or temporary lodging during the journey. Between 1965 and 1985, the use of paid coyotes increased from 40 percent to about 75 percent.[8] In a survey in Mexico by Wayne Cornelius and his colleagues of 603 recently returned and potential first-time migrants in west-central Mexico, 90 percent of the respondents hired a coyote. Further, because increased border surveillance has pushed migrant crossing points east to more dangerous routes through the deserts, the average fee paid to coyotes has increased dramatically as migrants need the aid of experienced guides. According to a study, the median fee paid to coyotes rose from $924 in 1982–92 to $1,783 (in U.S. dollars) in 2002–4 and the fee has increased even more since.[9] Increasingly, migrants do not want to face the dangers of multiple crossings on their own.

Migrants' social connections are critical for successful migration yet are not uniformly available for all potential migrants. Cecelia Menjívar points out that the functions of social networks vary tremendously and in some cases networks weaken with immigration: "The shifting, processual nature of informal networks makes it difficult to define them unambiguously as enduring or frail."[10] In addition, the reproduction of migration is also social and more likely to occur in villages or regions where there is a history of migration. Some villages in west-central Mexico have a hundred-year history of sending migrants to the United States.[11] In some regions of Mexico, there is a rich tradition of hometown associations, social clubs, or festivals funded by migrants that make migration something to be expected.[12] The presence of a social infrastructure that supports migration is crucial as potential migrants reflect upon their lives and contemplate moving.

In *Ni aquí, ni allá* (neither here nor there), María Luisa de la Garza argues that migrants undergo a profound reconstruction of self as they anticipate and then experience the process of migration. According to de la Garza, migrants begin their journeys after evaluating their options in Mexico and, especially for the poor, coming to the conclusion, "I'm tired of not being anybody so I decided to improve my luck."[13] Migrants reflect on the possibilities of gaining a life (*ganarse la vida*) and feeling more self-respect. They anticipate valuing the decisions and taking actions in pursuing their dreams of creating new lives through migration. However, this decision making entails a process of reconstructing their selves that carries some costs, as she explains: "So as to realize this plan [to migrate], there has to be an unavoidable and cruel requirement: that to *improve* their lives, migrants must *worsen* them. In effect, to be able to become *someone* they have to detach themselves from all the resources they have, material and social."[14] De la Garza suggests that migration entails a social death, particularly if one crosses the border without documentation through dangerous routes. She states: "One who decides to emigrate leaves *what s/he has*, annuls *what s/he can* and almost stops *being*, if not actually *existing*."[15]

I agree with de la Garza that migrants reconstruct their selves through planning, reflection, and participation within the migration process. Further, being without any state documentation in a foreign country verifying one's existence in itself can be deeply disorienting, as any traveler who has lost a passport can attest. One feels vulnerable, unmoored, and anxious that there may be dire legal, economic, or social repercussions. Without legal papers, most of us long for evidence of belonging someplace. In addition, migrants' detachment is emotional as they anticipate the possibilities of never seeing their loved ones again, never returning to their homes, and fearing the unknown of the journey or of their new destinations. However, de la Garza's use of *emigrar* (emigrate) is telling for it assumes that migration is in one direction—toward the United States—and overstates the disappearance of the self, since feeling uprooted is a far cry from no longer being. Further, de la Garza ignores how gender may shape a person's decision to migrate and adapt in new locations with profound implications for a sense of self. I suggest that migrants work long and hard to overcome a sense of displacement and emotional turmoil by cultivating their social networks and social infrastructure of support prior to and while crossing the border and then again as they attempt to start their new lives and these processes are gendered.

Policies and representations construct gendered differences in migration where more men have migrated to the United States until the passage of the Immigration Reform and Control Act in 1986. In the post-IRCA era, Mexican men were more likely to be apprehended: Between 2005 and 2008, 97 percent of apprehensions by the Border Patrol were along the U.S.-Mexico border and 91 percent were Mexican nationals. Nearly 84 percent of those apprehended were men.[16]

Migration is shaped by the relative opportunity structures for men and women in places of origin and destination. Shawn Kanaiaupuni suggests that migration from Mexico has been predominantly male because of several social processes: men are considered to be the breadwinners due to patriarchal social norms. If employment structures do not provide adequate wages, men are more likely to migrate and where there are significant employment opportunities for women, male partners tend not to migrate. However, the presence of children influences men to migrate if they do not earn enough income to support their families in Mexico, whereas for women the effect is less direct. Generally the presence of children makes geographical mobility difficult and the cost of raising a family is lower in Mexico than in the United States: "Hence married women with children are more likely to remain in the sending communities while male family members migrate."[17] Other important predictors of women's migration include level of education, prior marital status, and the strength of their social networks in the United States. Even if they have children, women who are no longer in conjugal relationships are more likely to migrate, particularly if they have strong social networks in the United States. Women with higher levels of education also tend to migrate, given the low returns on their human capital investments in Mexico compared to those for men.[18] Some indigenous people expect women to be accompanied by men during the journey al norte.[19]

Increasingly women are migrating with the support of their own social networks and without authorization.[20] In the post-IRCA era, women make up about one-third of the unauthorized migrants.[21] By 1995, women were 57 percent of authorized migrants from Mexico.[22] Women are less likely to cross by themselves compared to men, and women are much more likely to use the services of a coyote vouched for in their communities.[23] Women often articulate economic rationales for migrating—*para superarse* or to get ahead, especially in relation to their children—or the desire to join up with female kin who have found work in the United States.[24] That women view these responsibilities as their primary impulse for migrating, traditionally expected of men, indicates that gender relations are shifting in Mexico.

In this essay, I examine gendered migration—the practices through which men and women move across space—and the effects of these types of migration on their subjectivities. I explore the following questions: How did transnational migrants decide to move great distances across an international boundary? For migrants within the United States, how did they move across social borders? For all migrants, how did their adaptation affect their sense of selves? I argue that as men and women contemplate transnational migration, they do not necessarily comply with traditional gendered expectations. Rather, gender has complex influences on the decision to migrate and in turn is shaped by migration as migrants find themselves in new circumstances. Once migrants arrive at their destinations and attempt to adapt, they construct peripheral vision, a perspective in which their comparisons between Mexico and the United States are based on a sense of marginality. Mexican American migrants within the United States also experience peripheral vision as they, too, experience marginality in relation to poverty, racialization, gender, and stereotypes about being from Mexico.

An Infrastructure of Support

Migrants from Mexico are aware of changes in immigration policies and practices as well as the numerous threats along the route, called the Devil's Highway, to the north.[25] Ninety percent of all households in Mexico have access to television, often through satellite dishes, and Spanish-language news programs regularly discuss the treatment of migrants and troubles with crossing the border in great detail.[26] In 1997, the INS began broadcasting a "Stay Out, Stay Alive" campaign, featuring television commercials and newspaper advertisements in Mexico and other countries, warning people about the dangers of evading immigration checkpoints and trying to cross the border illegally. There are gendered differences in awareness of television reports about the dangers of migration in one survey of migrant communities: 45 percent of men had heard about the dangers of border crossing on television while only 28 percent of the women had.[27] In 1999, the INS began using the radio to broadcast alerts warning potential migrants about the dangers of crossing the border. These were made graphic when the U.S. Department of Homeland Security issued a

Spanish-language radio and television campaign called "No Más Cruces en La Frontera (No More Crosses on the Border)" at a cost of $1.5 million.[28] Others have written popular or scholarly texts on the dangers that children and adults face when they ride trains that originate in southern Mexico or Central America in which they could be maimed or killed while jumping from one train to another or they may be beaten, robbed, or raped by fellow migrants or by members of gangs or state officials.[29] In light of these possible dangers, social networks are crucial for providing information on how to minimize the risks of migration.

The process of reconstructing the self is evident in the range of responses by my research participants to questions about how they contemplated migration. Virtually everyone who crossed without authorization came with relatives, spouses, or close friends. Only the taciturn Israel Mata migrated by himself at thirteen: "I came alone—not even with friends. My life has been a lone road. [Wasn't it dangerous?] No. Lots of stops [before arriving in south Santa Cruz County]." Yet he did not experience a social death and kept in close contact with kin in Mexico. The necessity of social networks led Roberto May to the following conclusion: "I would recommend to anyone thinking of coming, if you don't have anyone, neither family nor religion to help you, why are you thinking of migrating? Don't go."

Poverty was a powerful motivator, yet it was not the sole reason for planning such a huge undertaking as migration to the United States. Iliana Lomas, who migrated from a small village in the state of Michoacán in 1993 at nineteen, for example, had the following memory: "We were from the poorest of the poor. There one could work but it [wages] only covered food. I was the one that told my mother, we have to save up [for the trip] for one never knows." Eliana Zambrano also migrated at nineteen, arriving in Santa Cruz County in 1971. She recalled living in a compound (*rancho*) in the countryside in Michoacán where they were so broke, they harvested cactus to sell as food: "I'd work all day taking out the thorns and I'd come home all cut up. Sometimes people didn't have money so they would pay us in tortillas. . . . And because I suffered, I told my grandmother, 'I'm going to leave.'" Lucio Cabañas, who left rural Jalisco at fifteen with his male kin, also in 1971, said, "My father died and we were living in a very difficult situation. There was no vision of how we would make it; there was no future. So I stopped my schooling because there was no economic support and that was the motive for coming here. My brother had already made arrangements with the coyote and he said I could come along." Eliana had become a widow when she was nineteen and had little recourse but to migrate so she could support her child.

The wage differential between the United States and Mexico is a powerful reason for deciding to migrate; it has been estimated the difference between the minimum wage in the United States and in Mexico is often more than eleven to one.[30] Armando Amodor, who came in 1982 from a rural setting and had worked in the fields in Jalisco, voiced the importance of this factor: "Well, they are paying more here than the wages they can pay in Mexico and you do the same work." Iliana Lomas also made explicit comparisons in wages: "There in Mexico everything is very expensive. Here also, everything is very expensive but since we live here, we are like the middle class over there in Mexico. And there [in Mexico]? We are among the most poor. Because we know how much we earn. We work from 8 to 5 packing strawberries and we earn 20 pesos. . . . We barely earn enough to eat. And here, you work one day to buy a pair of pants and over there, no. It is very difficult over there." Gloria García, also from rural Michoacán, believed that "the difference is that here [in the United States] one can gain a better life. If one works hard one can succeed in what one wants and there in Mexico, no. Even though you work hard you cannot succeed there [in Mexico] because the wages are so low. And one just cannot make it. I think that is the greatest difference between Mexico and the United States." Yet potential migrants are well aware that consumption costs in the United States are large as well, where migrants must purchase housing and daily expenses in dollars, and sometimes they earn below minimum wages in the United States if they are undocumented. Economic motivations are only part of the reasoning for migration.

Some scholars suggest that the decision to migrate is not an individual one but made in relation to one's family, household, or even community to overcome failures in labor markets or a lack of credit, capital, or insurance to finance businesses. Often migrants come with particular goals in mind—to build a home or improve the parents' house, to prepare for marriage and a family, or to start a small business. Indeed, Douglas Massey and his colleagues argue that a stint of labor in the United States is the poor man's credit card, a source of generating a significant sum for funding economic or social projects.[31] Iliana Lomas recalled the powerful incentive of easy earnings inspired by the talk of those who had returned: "They [potential migrants] think that over there [in the United States] they are going to sweep up the money."

In order to raise enough funds to migrate, many work and save up the funds or they take out loans from relatives, friends, or moneylenders in Mexico or the United States. Yet borrowing from kin has gendered dimensions as well. In one survey in a migrant community, 94 percent of women migrants versus 50 percent of male migrants had received financial support from family in Mexico or the United States for their most recent crossing.[32] One woman in one of the focus groups I organized stated her mother saved $17,000 so the entire family could migrate. Eliana was able to finance her journey by moving to her cousins' home in Tijuana and helping them with their small business. Her husband, Jorge, chimed in: "At that time many people, who themselves were poor, told her, 'I'll take you [across the border], I'll help you get across. You start working and you can pay in small payments as best you can.' They [the cousins] sent her to their sons who knew a coyote.... It was a way of showing their affection for her." Loans imply that the recipient of the funds is trustworthy and will maintain contact after migration and repay the loan. If potential migrants sell off their belongings to raise cash for the journey, they indeed are preparing for a clean departure with only social and emotional relations to tie them to their places of origin.

In addition to economic factors, there were other reasons for migrating: some personal experiences related to gendered expectations. Women in rural villages sometimes chafe under patriarchal surveillance and control, which is often inflicted by their mothers-in-law if their partners have migrated. Besides having few work opportunities, rural women (single and married) are subject to gossip if they leave their homes without accompaniment: Attending church or visiting relatives is fine but walking the streets for no good reason raises questions about women's reputations and subjects them to the threat of sexual assault.[33] When Brenda Casas, for example, was fourteen she had problems with her mother while living in a small town in Jalisco: "She said that I was a rebel but I just wanted some liberty. Not liberty to walk around like a loose woman (*libertina*), to drink, or for ruin (*perdiciones*). I wanted the liberty to know things, to have friends, to go out and breathe fresh air; not to be closed up in the house."

Others migrate out of the need to reunite their families with expectations that traditional gender relations would continue. Isabella Morales, who left Oaxaca in 1989, discussed her motivation for migration: "Well, I came because he [her spouse] was working here and, well, we had nothing there." Flora Ramos wanted to unite with her parents and sisters, who had migrated previously, and fulfill her notions of being a good daughter: "Above all it was to be with them." Whether they came to follow their spouses or find more opportunities than provided in rural villages, women were aware that even in rural California, life is different. Bety Martínez, from rural Zacatecas, felt relief after leaving the gendered surveillance in her hometown: "I have lived more here. Here people don't snoop so much and don't criticize so much. And there [her village], where people are from the countryside, they notice everything. And if a woman starts to go out with a boyfriend, they begin to criticize her. Here you can see women go out." Ester Moreno, who returned to rural Jalisco with her adolescent daughter, recalled: "We [women] are controlled; that is the norm. But there [her village] it is *more* controlled." One member of a focus group seemed wistful as she explained: "When you come here [California], you expect more, but you live in poverty."

Others have more idiosyncratic reasons for migrating. Ana Acuña, for instance, decided to come (with authorization) in 1993 and help her sister who became ill while pregnant, and then Ana decided to overstay her visa because of the economic crisis in Mexico.[34] Some women came seeking refuge from abusive male kin, lovers, or partners, seeking distance from the pressures to remain in compromising relationships. One woman in a focus group commented determinedly: "I wanted to start a new life without him." Gloria García decided to migrate because of economic reasons and because her partner would not take responsibility for their unborn child. He didn't believe she would come accompanied by her sister: "Since I was going to be there [in Michoacán] alone without any help, how was I going to support my son? I didn't know if he was going to send money or not. So I came alone." Several came as adolescents, as did Rosario Cabañas from Guanajuato at fourteen, accompanying their families who started new lives together. María Pérez left Mexico City when she was twenty-eight after completing her master's degree. She was seeking a means to continue her education and some adventure after a breakup with her lesbian lover. After completing college, Frida hoped her trip to the United States was the beginning of her world travels. Most women and men had multiple reasons for migration.

These varied reasons are related to the multiplicity of communities of origin by my research participants as well as their diverse social locations. Migrants who responded to the survey were from nineteen states in Mexico. The largest number of the core participants were from the classic sending region of west-central Mexico, confirming local lore about chain migration. In particular, there are large numbers of migrants locally from Gómez Farias in Michoacán and San Pedro Tesitán in Jalisco—those from the latter village hold an annual celebration in Watsonville in South County.[35] The largest number of survey respondents were from Michoacán, but the next largest group was from Oaxaca, confirming local observations and information from the Mexican Consulate that in the late 1990s migrants from Oaxaca began arriving in Santa Cruz County in significant numbers.[36] And while the overwhelming majority of survey respondents listed Spanish as their first language, twenty-five individuals spoke Mixtec as their first language and another spoke Triqui: key markers of indigenous status in Mexico. Unlike other regions, where there are close ties between sending and receiving communities, these data indicate the diverse regional and ethnic backgrounds of Mexican migrants in Santa Cruz County.[37] These findings suggest the prominence of agriculture in this part of California, which attracts recent migrants and also provides possibilities for long-term work as well as the availability of jobs in the service sector.

Finally, there are other motivations for migration. In communities with a strong migrant tradition, remaining at home may seem distasteful and downright lonely. I have done field research in rural communities in the Mexican states of Jalisco, Guanajuato, Yucatán, and Oaxaca where mainly women, children, and elders reside because so many men have left for the United States. The expectation that one should leave forms what Kandel and Massey call a "culture of migration" transmitted across generations and through social networks.[38] In addition to worries about abandonment, women voice their sense that they are old-fashioned, outside modernity if they remain in Mexico to struggle there. In focus groups in Oaxaca in particular, women were animated in expressing their observations that "everyone is leaving; there are only women and elders left. . . . And when the husbands return, they get their wives pregnant and then they leave." When I visited San Pedro Tesitán, residents there claimed there are more migrants in south Santa Cruz County than in the village itself in Mexico.

Gendered notions of masculinity and femininity are also considerations when making the decision to migrate. Especially in those communities that have a long history of transnational migration to the United States, going *al norte* has become almost a rite of passage by members of young men's social networks as a means of asserting their masculinity by continuing their work histories.[39] Norma Ojeda de la Peña finds that young male migrants enter the labor force earlier and have more jobs than young female migrants.[40] Pablo, who migrated in 1994, was frank about his desire to remain in Mexico: "I didn't *want* to emigrate. They say, 'It's better to live poor but happy.' But my cousins were coming so I thought, why not?" The camaraderie, encouragement, and pressure by his cousins to leave Mexico and prove his manhood were compelling. Others felt a deep sense of tradition regarding the prospect of migrating. Gerónimo explained how migration reflected expectations about masculinity: "I think it comes from the heritage of your father. Your father is going to influence you to work, to move. You are going to do everything, look for the means to sustain your family." Making enough money to build one's own home was a powerful incentive for young men, in part because initially it seemed to entail a temporary investment in migration and the results were readily apparent, as Salvador recalled: "Well many of the young men come for the adventure, they say. All the young men come thinking, 'See that guy, he built his home and I can too. Up there [in the United States] I can work it' (*lo hago allá aventurar*)." Roberto decided to focus on soccer rather than his studies and when he informed his mother, she was upset: "She said, 'You leave. I don't want you in this house. I don't want lazy people here.' She told me this on Sunday and she bought my ticket [for the bus] and by Wednesday I was gone." For these men, the desire or pressure to migrate and find jobs so they could support their families or build their own homes were the material expressions of masculine responsibility.

Women also were attuned to the tradition of migration especially if relatives had migrated previously. Brenda recalled that her relatives encouraged her: "They talk about the positive aspects, 'If you go, you will be in seventh heaven with me. I am going to help you.' But when you get here it is very different." Eliana, who had migrated with the help of kin in Tijuana and with women relatives who provided housing and food when she arrived, had a similar experience: "Ever since I was a child I heard about Watsonville and I wanted to come here. I would tell my grandmother, 'I want to go to the north; I want to go there and I want to know,' and she'd say, 'You can't go; it's too far.' I always had it in my head as a girl that I wanted to come here to Watsonville."

The expectation that one would migrate also affected women's notions of femininity. In response to my question about how she crossed, Rosa Guzmán, who migrated at fifteen in 1964 from rural Michoacán, told the following story. Her mother accompanied her on the long bus ride to a border city. They met up with an aunt who crossed her with authorization and then she traveled alone to join her spouse. Rosa disclosed: "That story makes me cry. But I had the courage to stand up to this life and there has been tremendous change. I left my village, my family, and my parents." She marveled at her ability to take on the extraordinary travails normally taken on by men: "How could I come here so far away?"

Mónica Estrada was pushed into migrating: "My sister brought me over because my mother was very sick and I was the only single one at home. My sister worked at Green Giant and she got me a job there. She said, 'You are old enough and I'm not going to be supporting you; you have to work.' And I had never worked before." Carmela Zavala's mother encouraged her to leave since she was divorced with four children: "Someone invited me and my mother said, 'Well, you are alone, why don't you go? You could make more money and support your children.' More than anything, she pushed me: 'Go dummy; if someone invited me I'd go. See what you learn. Leave the kids with me. And if things go well you can take them too and it goes badly, well, you can come back.' And that's how I got animated." These women, uprooted from their homes in Mexico, found unexpected strength and new possibilities for womanhood.

The tangible rewards of migration are evident in many communities throughout Mexico. Often there are whole neighborhoods with "migrant homes," newly built houses—some quite ostentatious, painted in bright colors with elaborate wrought-iron fences—or homes undergoing construction with the homeowner (male or female) directly supervising the work. Further, families of migrants are eager to show off their wealth and give tours of their relatives' homes, which tend to be furnished with both locally constructed furniture and items brought back from the United States. They proudly enumerate on which trip they brought each small appliance. I call these *las casas tristes* (sad homes) since they are empty because their owners must work in the United States to continue earning dollars to finish their construction and furnishings while their relatives look after the empty homes.[41] To migrants in the United States and their families in Mexico, casas tristes are tangible representations of unfulfilled dreams about returning to live in Mexico and how a stint in *el otro lado* will allow one to fulfill gendered expectations. Isabella, for example, had a home in Oaxaca and her in-laws were supervising the construction, which was almost completed. She felt anxious because she was waiting for permanent U.S. residence before returning home, so she could come back if need be. She wrung her hands as she expressed her maternal desires for a better life for her children yet worried about how they would adapt to life in Mexico: "I think my kids will miss the school because everything is very different." She hoped to receive her green card within a year, "*si dios quiere* (God willing)."

Many women expressed their desires in relation to their children as the rationale for migration, particularly the wish that their children would receive more education than they had. Deferring any aspirations for themselves, these women emphasized, "I did it for my kids, so they would have a better life." Whether parents decide on stage migration, bringing only some children or leaving them all behind, is carefully considered. Important factors are the ages of their children or other close relatives, whether the children would be old enough to work once they arrive, whether there are reliable caregivers—typically close relatives—and whether they have enough resources. María Muñoz twisted her hands and seemed anxious as she recalled their process of family stage migration that eventually brought together a couple and two children left behind with their grandparents: "He [her husband, Pedro] crossed first; then later I came and then we brought the children. He had been here a year and a half when the children came. My daughter Mónica [second to the youngest] did not cross with me; when I came I wanted her with me but she stayed there [in Mexico] waiting." Pedro added: "A woman smuggler passed Mónica in her car. And then my son, Juan, was crossed by the woman smuggler who had brought Mónica." María finished the story: "And then my youngest daughter, Lisa, was born and with that citizen child one can petition [for authorization]. At that time [the mid-1970s] it was easy to become documented here." When parents leave children in the care of kin, they agonize over when and how to bring them over, filled with anxiety during their children's migration process.

At times women had to choose between seeking a better future for their children over close relatives who would remain behind, which was extremely painful. Aurora Bañales explained her thinking about migrating: "My mother didn't like the idea of me coming and even more of me bringing my son, who was little [two years old]. She was afraid; she would say that I was going to die on the road, that I would get dehydrated. She would say, 'What are you going to do alone? What if you get lost, or something happens? Or your son gets sick and you will be so far away? When will you return?' [Aurora's voice cracked and tears came to her eyes as she remembered her mother's words.] She warned me in a very direct way: 'These eyes that see you now will not see you return!'" As much as she hated the thought of leaving her mother, Aurora steeled herself emotionally and made the trip despite her mother's opposition. These women's experiences confirm other scholars' findings that children's futures are key factors in the decisions to migrate to the United States.[42]

Those women who migrated alone usually had some social support. Vicenta Fernández, for example, recalled crossing the border at twenty-six in 1963: "I crossed [the border] legally. No one brought me; I came by myself. I walked alone. I think in those days there was more respect than now. There is no way that I would walk alone now." She came to join her father who had worked as a bracero and lived in Los Angeles and her father's kin picked her up at the bus station when she arrived.

Other women found ways to play on gendered expectations and further their own agendas. For example, when she was pregnant but unmarried at thirty, Iliana threatened her fiancé that she would marry someone else unless he brought her to the United States as his wife. Her family amassed the equivalent of $5,000 for the crossing of five of them, which included her parents: "I warned him: I'll get married! [to someone else]." Apparently he believed her since he brought her over to live with him in Santa Cruz, where their child was born.

Whatever their particular rationale for migration, these migrants had reflected upon the opportunities available where they lived and for varied reasons decided to try their luck in the United States. They were well aware that their circumstances were unstable in comparison to others and were contingent upon the vagaries of the Mexican economy and the possibility for finding employment in the United States, as well as particular fluctuations in their personal lives. From the point of view of those with limited options, migration to the United States seemed the means to accomplish their goals of starting new lives. While many research participants articulated their decisions in traditional gendered terms— men wanted to fulfill breadwinner responsibilities or women wanted to help their children—often their circumstances required flexible accommodations.

Border Crossings

Not surprisingly, those who were authorized to migrate to the United States had a relatively easy time crossing the border; they simply caught a bus or plane, drove with others, or, in some cases, walked across the border. Yet as

I heard these stories they reminded me of the inevitable anxiety that comes even when Mexicans who are U.S. citizens try to cross back into the United States from Mexico. I recall the time a college friend and I were searched for no apparent reason other than his having long hair. Another time, when crossing in a car, one of my sisters had been asleep and was too groggy to respond to questions by the border official about her country of birth. Worried we would be detained, several of us yelled at her, "Dede, tell him where you were born!" To our great relief she muttered, "Maine," and we were allowed back in the country. Even if authorized to enter the United States, looking "illegal" can seem arbitrary, a judgment based on the whim of border officials.[43]

For those who made a clandestine entry, at times it was remarkably straight-forward to cross the border into the United States. Migrants often journey by buses or flights that have lines directly from sending regions to the border. Particularly prior to Operation Gatekeeper (implemented in 1994), the undoc-umented found many ways to cross the border although the risks were often very high. As Joel García, who crossed the first time in 1990, phrased it: "In those days if they got you it was because you were an idiot (un pendejo) or had fucked-up luck (una suerte de la chingada). It was really easy." Several examples illustrate how men were able to cross the U.S.-Mexico border sin papeles (with-out authorization). Regardless of whether the journey is made with the help of a coyote or not, often elaborate precautions are taken such as bringing water, canned food (sardines or tuna are favorites since they contain protein and salt), and plastic bags if crossing the river; wearing durable shoes and clothes; and discarding unnecessary items such as wallets or purses. Some migrants did not want to go into detail about the actual crossing since it brought up painful memories. Lucio was succinct: "As illegals, we had to suffer on one side [of the border] or the other and we had to suffer the crossing, not the coyote." Others were more expansive. Armando paid $250 in 1982 for a smuggler to get him across the mountains near Tijuana. He was nineteen and at the time was not too worried about the danger: "One comes to take the risk. Some say it's easy, others that it's difficult. There is much danger at the border." Salvador crossed in 1985 by walking through underground sewage tunnels between Tijuana and San Ysidro after he was chased by the Border Patrol: "At that moment I real-ized the desperation for living; it was so horrible. Before one does not imagine the consequences, the gravity of the danger that the smugglers put us through. They tell us, 'This is how you are going to cross' and 'This will be your route.' But you have to go where they take you." José, who crossed without authori-zation in 1987, long before cumbersome security measures were implemented in airports, recalled a relatively easy crossing the first time: "I was lucky and crossed over by airplane. A friend helped me buy a ticket and advised me how to do it. I got on the plane as if nothing was wrong and we arrived in Los Angeles; they did not check anything. My brother was there at the airport and he took me to his house. And luck was with me because the week before my other brother bought a ticket and they checked him and detained him. . . . I lasted for two years working in construction [as a day laborer]. Each day I went back to the same place and at the end they were paying me about $14 an hour. But I couldn't stand being alone, without my kids and my wife, and I returned to Mexico." His low wages as a taxi driver in Mexico City pushed him to return to California again. He saved money with the hope of bringing over his wife and children. These men had crossings filled with moments of worry, anxiety, and the loss of social moorings, yet they did not suffer social deaths since they maintained ties with those in Mexico.

Prior to 1994, it was relatively easy to bring children. Celia Tejeda, whose parents crossed in Texas, said, "At that time [1942] it was no big deal. People would swim over the river and cross it [the border]. Especially there where I was raised [in South Texas]." Melissa García, who crossed in 1983, was pregnant at the time: "The crossing was easy in those days. I crossed in a car with various people. The smuggler crossed us in a large car and there weren't many difficulties like there are now. And he brought us to Santa Cruz. My brother paid $300." Antonio, who was born in Tijuana and brought to the United States as a young child in 1980, also recalls a relatively easy crossing: "There was some people that we knew in San Diego that had papers and they have six or seven kids of their own. So they would leave a couple in San Diego and then bring a few other ones from Tijuana and mix them in there. So that family decided to bring us with them." Carmela, who crossed five times before staying in the United States in 1992, was once detained near Tijuana and deported in Mexicali, about sixty-eight miles to the east. She was separated from her minor son, yet she was not particularly worried since the friend she was crossing with was trustworthy: "I didn't worry that they left me off in Mexicali because I knew that person [her friend] would go where they left me off. She was a person who would help me. You live in the moment when you are crossing. I knew that if I told her, 'come for me,' that she would." One woman who was sent across with coyotes before her mother crossed through the mountains teared up as she recalled a traumatic experience as a child: "I was waiting for her out in the middle of nowhere with that woman [smuggler] and when I saw her [her mother] I started screaming, 'Hurry, the *migra* [Border Patrol] is going to get you!' I must have been about four." It wasn't until she was in high school that she was able to obtain documentation. Despite the anxiety and even long-term trauma these experiences generated, they illustrate that the border enforcement practices prior to 1994 were easier to circumvent.

A successful border crossing signals a man's masculinity, his ability to persevere despite life-threatening obstacles. And when the Border Patrol catches them, transnational migrants often make multiple attempts until they have a successful crossing. Returning home without having crossed successfully would leave them in dire straits with no way to repay any loans they had secured for the journey and a bruised sense of masculinity. One man said, "It's a high price one pays to earn dollars here [in the United States]."

As those who migrate increasingly include more women and youths, the strength confirmed by a successful crossing is no longer only a sign of masculinity. Women come to see themselves as *macha*—tough, independent, or a tomboy. Brenda, for example, recalled: "My boyfriend said he was going to come and get me [in Mexico] and I told him no. Because my mother had me working like a servant, working as a babysitter, cleaning the house, cooking, all the responsibilities. And I wasn't going to clean the whole house for a domineering old lady. So I crossed with my aunt, using her child's birth certificate." Women also found an inner strength they never knew they had: "*Aguanté la cruzada* (I endured the crossing)," said one woman in a focus group. Jesús Martínez-Saldaña argues that the border defines a migrant's relationship to the United States: "To Mexicans intent on crossing into this country, the border represents an artificial sociopolitical trench which divides human beings along national and racial lines; it must be defied, whether to seek work, unify the family, or carry out other activities."[44]

When Operation Gatekeeper started in 1994, there was increased militarization of the U.S.-Mexico border.[45] Border enforcement policies provided funds to build fences in high-traffic areas such as San Diego–Tijuana and El Paso–Ciudad Juárez and have pushed migrant border crossers into the mountainous Sonoran Desert between Yuma, Arizona, in the west and Nogales, Mexico, in the east, with deadly consequences. With daytime temperatures of up to 130 degrees, and nighttime lows below freezing, migrants and even Border Patrol officers can die of exposure or dehydration. In addition, border crossers suffer fatigue, blistered feet, sun and windburn, extreme hunger, or snake and spider bites. To many, this type of crossing was a gauntlet of death.

In the post–Operation Gatekeeper era, migrants have developed extensive networks of coyotes, whose knowledge of local conditions, authorities, and safer routes can make the difference between a difficult and life-threatening trip, particularly for those journeying from Central America. Even when migrants have coyotes to guide them through dangerous terrain, however, migrants expose themselves to an underground world of crime where border bandits may rob or assault them.[46] In contrast to those who had crossed in earlier periods, Alfredo seemed very sad as he recalled the dangers of crossing the border for the first time in 1996: "I tried to cross through Tijuana and couldn't do it. Later I went through Tecate [about forty miles east of Tijuana]. That was a bitch of a crossing. We walked for two days. All I remember was walking, walking, walking, seeing ranches and we wouldn't get there. Then I fell and couldn't walk anymore; my legs gave out. I was alone at the border. I didn't know anyone. I was fifteen years old." While socially unmoored, his recently acquired travel companions became critical sources of social and emotional support that helped him persevere despite the life-threatening circumstances as Alfredo explained: "Some of the guys told me, 'You can do it! Don't get left behind!'" Another man who crossed in 2003 had a difficult experience that was all too common: "Before I used to go [to Mexico] and come back each year. It used to cost me about $300. Now I can't. Each time it is more difficult and for that reason more expensive. The last time, after everything, it cost me $1,500 and worse, they left me in the desert." His voice broke as he said, "I can't tell the whole story" yet later indicated he found others to travel with. Several others described riding in vehicles with special compartments or of riding in the trunk of a car or a van piled on top of one another. Not surprisingly, many were disheartened by these experiences.[47] Alfredo recalled thinking: "Was this how my dream was starting out?" These men endured physical and emotional traumas of crossing that were still painful to describe years later. Yet I found very little evidence of social deaths. Indeed, the traumas created the social support migrants received occasionally from coyotes but mainly by their fellow crossers who helped them in various ways, including keeping up their morale so they could continue.

Women's experiences crossing the border varied but, compared with men, they had similar difficulties, which were mitigated by the presence of kin. Young women (between fifteen and twenty-four years old) are more likely to migrate only if they have family members in the United States and women are no more likely to bring their children with them than men.[48] Yet members of social networks may help them with the journey. Flora, for example, migrated without authorization with her spouse and four children for the first time in 1984 when she was twenty-nine by walking through the mountains near Tijuana. She recalled: "I carried the baby and my husband carried my [5-year-old] daughter and my older son and daughter walked on their own. We walked all night and through dawn." They arrived in a neighborhood in southern California where the dogs began barking. Flora laughed nervously as she recalled running and stooping behind fences so no one would see them but admitted to being scared at the time. Ángela Román, who crossed many times with her parents when she was a child, crossed in 1985 when she was twenty-four by swimming the Rio Grande with her partner: "I came here very scared. Many said that I should cross through the river and that scared me even more.

I said, 'I don't know how to swim' and they would ask me, 'So how are you going to cross?' For me it was very difficult passing there." She was caught and sent back twice. The second time, after questioning her in English when she did not understand a word, the Border Patrol detained her for three days: "It got worse. I cried and cried because we lived really far away and I saw lots of people [detained] and, well, it scared me." Josefa Ruíz came with her daughter and her friend to Watsonville in 1985 when she was thirty-one. An employer paid the smuggler's fee and had them repay it by working. Aurora tried to cross several times in 1991 when she was eighteen, including once with someone else's permanent residence card when she had to dye her hair black, but she was apprehended each time until finally she was successful. She returned to Mexico and tried to cross again in 1994. She had a fifteen-month-old son who she sent across the border with her sister-in-law and waited a week in Tijuana before she and her spouse were able to cross. The couple paid $2,000 to a coyote. Her story was chilling since she had to rely on a smuggler who was unknown:

I was worried because I was in Tijuana and I didn't have money for a hotel or to come home and my son was already here [in Santa Cruz]. . . . We finally found a coyote that would take us across by the river. . . . We waited in the bushes until it was dark. Then the coyotes made us take off our clothes and put them in a black garbage bag, which they would fill with air so it would float and help those of us who couldn't swim. The water was moving fast and two girls got swept away. My husband pulled me along and the coyote went after the girls. The migra was on the other side, waiting, so we couldn't move right away until they left. Afterwards some taxis arrived and they took us to a house where they gave us used clothes and something to eat. And we called my brother-in-law to come and pick us up.

At the time of her interview with me, Aurora's mother was very ill but she would not go to Mexico to see her since she would have to cross without authorization again. She seemed very upset by these circumstances—"I'm afraid of the return [to the United States]." Her inability to go home reinforced the emotional difficulty of leaving the country. Eliana grew weary of coming and going: "I stayed for a time there [in Mexico] and for a time here. And I didn't want to go home because I suffered during the crossing. So I sought out a job here, taking care of an old woman." Relatives also were quite helpful. Eliana recalls her crossing experience: "And we arrived at the house of my cousins. And I felt as if I was at home. They gave us food and a place to sleep; we stayed for a month and I never worried about food. Afterwards I sent them $50 and he appreciated that. He said, 'You were the only one who helped me.'" Aurora was also hesitant to go back to Mexico because of the cost of migrating: "He [her partner] says that now everything is more difficult. It took him three days walking through the mountains. And he had to sleep on the ground. It takes more money [than before] to be able to come and go."

In addition to the dangers discussed above, women faced the risk of sexual assault. Sylvanna Falcón argues that sexual violence by state representatives (e.g., Border Patrol agents or members of the National Guard) is integral to the maintenance of control at the border. Since the perpetrators are not screened beforehand and receive few sanctions if there are complaints, in essence the state allows violence against women in this militarized zone. She documents multiple instances of abuse by members of the Border Patrol, where women were intimidated, sexually harassed, or assaulted.[49] Women are also vulnerable to sexual assault from coyotes or by fellow migrants—at times an entire group of women can be violated one after the other. To avoid these abuses, women must find reliable coyotes that are integrated into migrant social networks and known for their integrity, or they may need their kin or partners to cross with them to provide protection.[50]

None of the women I interviewed disclosed any experience with sexual violence while traveling to the United States yet they were well aware of the dangers and some had close calls. Iliana said, "Thanks be to God, nothing happened to us. God helped us and we crossed well. Because many times they say that when one is crossing, your own people will rob you. And they violate the women; all of that. And I never saw anything like that and neither did my mother." Gloria told the story of her crossing in Tijuana in 1994 when she was twenty years old:

> They tell you beforehand, "Don't go with just anyone because there are always people who rob your money and leave you with nothing." Then this happened to us [nervous laughter]: We met up with some smugglers who said they were going to cross us. Well, we went with him and we trusted him and he said, "Give me the money that you brought for the crossing." So we gave it to him. And much later that night a woman [smuggler] came by and she said, "Well, it's a miracle that you girls are here," and that really scared us. I told my friend, "Why didn't you warn me that they might leave us?" And she said, "How would I know what they are going to do?" So I learned from experience. And thank God they didn't just dump us there.

Flora, when remembering her second crossing, said, "I was really tired. And the coyote proposed to my mother and father that we [three sisters] stay with them and cross someplace easier. And I said, 'No, I don't want to stay with someone I don't know.' I told my parents, 'I prefer to walk hours and hours.'

Obviously I was afraid. I didn't know those people." Josefa, who took a bus with two women relatives from Mexico City to Tijuana, recalled that when they arrived, three men followed them all over the city: "They really scared us. They seemed like low-lifes [mal vivientes]. So we called someone we knew." The women ended up staying for a month, working for pittances and living in really bad conditions. Their luck changed and they found a woman coyote that brought them directly to Watsonville with promises of jobs, yet before they arrived they were completely broke with no money for food or lodging. She said, "No one knew who they were. And they left us without anything, not even a nickel. I didn't have anything [money] to return or to move forward. That's how so many people are lost at the border, even their lives." Eliana made several attempts to cross without authorization—once through the mountains and once by the river near Tijuana. She chuckled as she remembered how her brother and cousin picked her up by the arms and carried her across the river, where the water was up to her neck, teasing her: "He said, 'I'm not going back to your north. It's a hassle up there.'" She tried crossing once by train before her final successful attempt: "On the train there are a lot of risks. I was afraid they were going to close the boxcar. . . . And then they detained us in Mexico where there's lots of corruption and they take away whatever few cents you have hidden or they hit you. That time I was afraid. We had run into some people that would turn you in. The fear came not from the Border Patrol—the Border Patrol doesn't do anything—but the people. Yeah, I suffered but our Heavenly Father took care of me." Hitching rides on trains is extremely dangerous, and migrants have been left in Mexico with severed limbs and other injuries.[51]

In addition, if women migrate on their own, the journey al norte is fraught with symbolic danger since migrant folklore suggests that women who cross by themselves must exchange sex with the smugglers for a safe journey. For this reason, some women start taking contraceptives to avoid impregnation while in transit.[52] A number of men were sympathetic to the risk that women face in crossing the border. Joel, for example, said, "I've heard that sometimes their own smugglers are the ones who rape women. They rape them on the journey across the border. And if the women don't give in, they'll leave them there. That is not good."

Those women and men who migrated after 1994 often were bitter about the anxiety, humiliation, and occasionally the trauma associated with crossing the border. Joel, who crossed five times between 1990 and 2004 and perhaps exaggerated when he claimed there had been "dozens of attempts," recalled the time he was extorted by the federal police in Nogales. He believed this harassment was because he was indigenous: "There were eight of us, all from Oxkutzcab [a city in Yucatán with a high proportion of Mayas] in a taxi and they pulled us over and made us strip, even our underwear. They told us we had to pay 200 pesos each for our 'crimes,' which of course were made up. We asked, 'Why?' And they said, 'Because we said so!' And if we didn't pay they would be sure to find drugs on us. That was fucked-up." Others hear about the experiences of those who have already migrated and had a difficult time adjusting. Mariana, for example, recalled her relatives telling her not to go: "They said, 'You should understand that it is not easy over there [in the United States]. It is worse over there than here. There, people don't have anywhere to live; sometimes they don't have anything to eat.' I thought about it a lot and fig-ured, but that cannot be, lots of people are comfortable over there. Sometimes one's pride gets in the way. How could I go and then return without anything?" Eliana took great satisfaction in her ability to finally pay off the smugglers who came to her work site (the fields) to collect their fees and played on gender ste-reotypes: "That day we didn't have anything [to pay them]. And he [the coyote] got angry but he told his friend, 'You don't have a reason to get angry because women are better at paying off than men; women pay more.' He told the men, 'You have more shame than they do [the women].' Well I worked really hard and eventually I finished paying them off!" Clearly the smugglers kept in close contact long after Eliana and her sisters had arrived.

It is difficult to estimate how many unauthorized migrants cross the bor-der each year, which in places can be quite porous. People can swim or boat around, climb over, swim across or dig under, undermining the fixity of the border. However, one indication is the increased number of people attempt-ing to cross the border. In the 261 miles of border that makes up the Tucson sector, there were 491,771 crossings in 2004, up 253 percent from ten years ago. During this ten-year period, the number of Border Patrol agents tripled.[53] Fur-ther, there has been a surge in the number of smugglers driving cars loaded with undocumented migrants after Border Patrol agents became more adept at spotting false documents. In 2003 the number of migrants concealed in ve-hicle trunks or compartments was nearly 50,000; by 2004 that number had nearly doubled.[54] Between 2001 and 2006, authorities discovered twenty-one tunnels designed to move people and drugs across the U.S.-Mexico border near Tijuana, including one with a cement floor, water pump, and electricity.[55]

In 2007, to prevent migrants or terrorists from walking across the border, Congress authorized a $3 billion fence to gain "operational control" over the southern border with funds for fortifications of border fences and vehicle bar-riers, camera and radar towers, and unmanned aerial vehicles.[56] Congress had approved the Secure Fence Act in 2006 and exempted the border project from state and federal environmental safety and labor laws. Legislation to authorize building a wall along the entire 1,952-mile border, which would cost billions of dollars, was proposed in the House of Representatives.[57]

Policies and practices designed to secure the border have led to more danger for those crossing. In an important study, "Death at the Border," Karl Eschbach and his colleagues found that between 1993 and 1996 approximately 1,185 undocumented migrants died from drowning, environmental factors (e.g., hypothermia, heat stroke, or dehydration), or auto-pedestrian accidents while crossing the border.[58] Scholars estimate that about 23 migrants died every year prior to the implementation of Operation Gatekeeper and 300 died per year after its implementation.[59] Migrant deaths from vehicles, which numbered 227 between 1987 (when California began keeping records) and 1991, forced the state to construct a special eight-mile fence and to post signs cautioning migrants near the border in San Clemente about the dangers of crossing freeways on foot.[60] In 2001, Eschbach and his colleagues provided an update: "Every year more than three hundred people die while attempting to enter the United States clandestinely from Mexico as a result of intensified border enforcement policies, mainly because entry attempts have been pushed away from densely populated areas to more dangerous areas of the border."[61] Drawing on data from Mexican consulates and the Mexican Ministry of Foreign Relations, Wayne Cornelius calculates that 3,182 migrants died between 1995 and 2004, and Gilberto Rosas documents over 3,600 corpses that have been found since the late 1990s in the "killing deserts."[62] Further, many thousands of migrants disappear during their journeys, never to be heard from again, causing anguish and search parties on both sides of the border.[63] Migrant deaths after arrival in the United States have increased as well. In 2006, Mexican consulates across the United States recorded 10,622 shipments of bodies for burial back home, 7 percent more than in 2005 and 11 percent more than in 2004. The consulates spent $4 million in 2006 to help repatriate bodies to Mexico, up from $3.4 million in 2005.[64]

For those with very large social networks, the dangers of crossing the border are not experienced in isolation. I can recall several instances when local activists had returned to Mexico on pressing family matters and entire communities—some unknown to them—worried about their journey back to the region. One elderly couple's story about crossing by being shut inside a car trunk circulated beyond their social networks while another couple who walked through the desert after visiting family in Oaxaca had many of us checking weather reports and hoping for their safe return. These stories circulate on both sides of the border. For those who have defied the trench between the United States and Mexico, their senses of selves shift as they feel anxiety yet a sense of relief and even pride at accomplishing their goals related to starting a new life.

Neither Here nor There

Upon arrival in the United States, migrants often feel exhausted, demoralized, or disoriented. Bety pointed out that one could spot the newly arrived: "They look timid, embarrassed, without confidence, with a desire to return back. But after a few days they don't want to return anymore." Once migrants cross the border, particularly if they crossed without authorization, it is important to reestablish contact with friends and loved ones left behind. In practice, migrants' communication with family members in Mexico varies tremendously. On one end of the continuum are those who keep frequent contact with family members in Mexico. One man had lived in the United States for twelve years to save money since his own health was deteriorating. His wife's health problems were his reason for migrating in the first place and he had been able to pay for her medical attention through the remittances he sent home. I visited her in Mexico in the course of another research project and she was open about her severe depression in part because of her husband's absence. So he called every day to try and make her feel better until he could return home, which he hoped would be in the near future. Others call regularly but communicate selectively, diminishing their own struggles with poverty wages in the United States, which affect their ability to send remittances for consumer goods in Mexico.[65]

Those who want to keep in close communication with those back home have a number of options. Long-distance phone calls are relatively easy and inexpensive. Phone cards can be purchased in many retail outlets in working-class barrios. One study found that 57 percent of female migrants and 37 percent of male migrants call home at least once a week.[66] Cell phones are often expensive for those with low incomes and most have poor or erratic service in rural areas in Mexico or the United States.[67] In the United States by 2005, 87 percent of all Latino households had telephone service in their homes, compared to 96 percent of whites and 86 percent of blacks.[68] More than any other ethno-racial group, Latinos are more likely to opt for cellular phones over ground lines, in part because prepaid plans do not require a credit check that may require a Social Security number, and, if one moves frequently, the cell phone is portable.[69] If migrants have Internet access, many small towns in Mexico have Internet cafés where, for modest fees, one can send and receive electronic mail with those outside the country.[70] Some entrepreneurs are establishing transnational Internet communication that includes real-time images of both parties.

At the other end of the continuum are migrants who have lost complete contact with their relatives at home for several reasons. In some rural villages in Mexico, there can be limited phone service with one telephone shared by an entire village—something I witnessed in rural Guanajuato, which has high emigration rates. In these cases, the caller has to call and ask someone to fetch someone else and then call back later, or an announcement is broadcast over loudspeakers and the intended recipient has to drop everything and come to the phone. Further, if breadwinners cannot afford to send money home or they get involved in new intimate relationships, they may not want to call home. Thus whatever social contact can be maintained by long-distance communication is highly dependent on migrants' resources and social investment in keeping in contact with partners or kin in Mexico.

Research on women left behind in Mexico shows that they often feel depressed, lonely, and powerless in the face of men's autonomy and ability to maintain or abandon family ties. Nelly Salgado de Snyder discusses the emotional and psychological toll on wives left behind when men migrate from Mexico to the United States. In her survey of 202 rural and semirural Mexican women whose spouses had migrated, 72 percent had spouses who visited them, 23 percent reported their spouses never returned but kept in contact, and 5 percent did not know the whereabouts of their spouses.[71] In addition, there may be significant shifts in gender relations and sexuality if women start running homes, businesses, or farms or establish new intimate relationships when their partners leave.[72]

My own encounters with men in Mexico who failed to migrate successfully indicate they also feel powerless and sad; they feel somehow less of a man for not being able to carry through on masculinist expectations. During a conversation in rural Guanajuato, an elderly woman berated her brother in front of me for being useless (*inútil*) since his journey to Tijuana and failure to cross the border meant he returned home empty-handed. She then could not migrate since she was expected to cook and clean for him. The man explained that he had been unable to make it despite several tries and, hanging his head in shame, agreed that he was useless. In the eyes of those women or men who are abandoned or left behind, migrants who do not keep in contact may experience social death or the emotional toll can continue for many years. Part of the stress of watching family members leave for el norte is the lack of information: how they fared during the crossing, whether they secured housing or a job, and whether they feel comfortable in the new locale. Yet despite the availability of technology that allows international communication, for financial reasons it may take weeks or even months for migrants to contact kin at home.[73] The Mexican folk saying, "Those who leave, leave sighing and those who remain, remain weeping," conveys well the anxiety and sadness associated with migration.

The facility of international communication becomes even more important when migrants decide to remain in the United States. Scholars find that increased border enforcement has led to migrants remaining in the United States for longer durations, something that many migrants I interviewed experienced.[74]

Cornelius found that 37 percent of his respondents stayed longer than expected on their most recent sojourn in the United States while 79 percent knew someone who remained in the United States because of stronger border enforcement. Further, those who have greater knowledge of border conditions and who know someone who has died while crossing the border are more likely to migrate. Fuentes, L'Esperance, Pérez, and White conclude that increased border enforcement either has no statistically significant effect on the propensity to migrate or their effects are in the opposite direction and they increase potential migrants' determination to cross the border: "We find that stronger border enforcement has not significantly reduced unauthorized migration to the United States."[75] Josefa's thinking confirmed this finding: "People say, 'When I get my papers [authorization] then I'll go back to Mexico two or three times.' Until then, you can't even think about going back." About 40 percent of core participants and 36 percent of the survey respondents had returned to Mexico. Those who had returned ranged from the undocumented men who returned annually to those who returned once for family emergencies.

A number of the migrants I interviewed disclosed that their initial plans had been to work for a few years and then return to Mexico. Particularly when they first arrived, migrants would compare their wages to Mexican wages with the latter coming up short, as Eliana explained: "I thought to myself, things go better for me here than over there." In addition to the difficulty of crossing the border, a number of factors kept migrants here: They could not save up enough money to return home, they were discouraged by corruption in Mexico that contributed to few economic opportunities, or they became accustomed to living in the United States. They went through a binational process of reflection, peripheral vision, to figure out what would be best. Ana, for example, explained: "What motivated me to stay here was when we began to see a lot of economic crisis in Mexico." Bety recalled: "The first time I came here it was a real struggle and after four years I returned home. But it was really hard there too [in rural Zacatecas] and I didn't *want* to come back [here]. [But] that's why people stay here; it seems better. And time passes without returning and you start forgetting your family and you get accustomed to being here and you get distanced [from home]."

Perhaps the most significant reason for remaining in the United States despite initial plans to stay temporarily was related to children: Parents wanted them to complete their educations in the United States or the children did not want to live in Mexico. Particularly for those children born in the United States, citizenship conferred rights and opportunities that were too good to pass up. Brenda, whose daughters are U.S. citizens, illustrated her rationale: "I see the difference in this aspect. Here my daughters can study and have a career. They can receive financial aid from the government and in Mexico they would not be able to. Because in Mexico they are not going to have resources for students; they don't even give student loans like they do here."

The higher standard of living was another reason for staying in the United States. Consuelo Gutiérrez has considered returning to rural Michoacán but then recalled what it would mean in daily life: "When my children protest too much I tell them: 'I'll save up and take you to Mexico so you can really see the difference between the United States and Mexico.' Because here the poorest do not live like they do in Mexico—there the poverty is dire. You have a little house but nothing [else]. Here the apartments are good, even if you have to sleep on a mat but there the homes are nothing but cement and earth with bone chilling cold."

Even if apprehended multiple times, unsuccessful migrants hesitate to return home and face the debts and gossip, which becomes yet another reason to remain in the United States. From recent and potential migrants' perspectives, the cost/benefit ratio still strongly favors migration. The majority of migrants from Mexico are able to send remittances on a regular basis although the percentage is declining, reflecting a rising sense of uncertainty about whether migrants would stay in the United States as well as difficulties finding work.[76]

Economic exchanges help keep migrant families in communication with those in Mexico. Migrants sent $3.7 billion to Mexico in 1995 and by 2007 the amount increased to $26.1 billion, an increase of 605 percent. However, remittances fluctuate in relation to the economy in the United States and by 2008, the recession led to a decline in remittances sent to Mexico at $25.1 billion.[77] Remittances are used overwhelmingly for everyday survival of family members: "An estimated 20 percent of Mexican families [in Mexico] are absolutely dependent on remittances to meet their needs for food, clothing, and shelter."[78] Of remittances sent, 67 percent are used for food and basic consumption, 9 percent for health needs, 3 percent for family home improvement, 2 percent for home construction, and 2 percent for education of family members.[79] Collective remittances sent by hometown associations became so prominent the Mexican government instituted programs to leverage and direct their use in Mexico.[80]

Those who were able to return to Mexico for visits often took great pains to display their relative wealth and to conceal the difficulties of their living conditions. Carmela, for example, chuckled as she disclosed her extraordinary impression management: "When you go back to Mexico that is the first impression that you give to people. That every day you look very sharp, with high heels, and only when you come here do you understand that you don't use any of those clothes. Why? Because you are always going to work. Here the only time you wear nice clothing is when you go to church. And that is the deceit, that people don't tell you how things really are in the United States." Many migrants, especially those who left behind family members, contemplated the possibility of returning to Mexico. However, a return would be possible if they had saved enough money or accomplished their initial goals. With increased border enforcement, the number of Mexicans who have returned to Mexico has declined. In 1992 about 20 percent of migrants returned home after six months. By 1997, that figure declined to 15 percent, and by 2000 only 7 percent returned after six months.[81]

There are gender patterns regarding return migration. Belinda Reyes and her colleagues conducted a survey with return migrants. They found that women are more likely to stay in the United States for long durations: 40 percent of the women stay longer than fifteen years, compared to 20 percent of the men, a finding that confirms those of other scholars showing women have a relatively easier time finding employment and adjusting to life in the United States than men.[82] Further, human capital and access to work are deciding factors about whether to stay or return to Mexico. Reyes found that "within two years, over 50 percent of those with less than an elementary school education, 70 percent of the people employed as agricultural workers, and 50 percent of the unauthorized migrants in the sample return to Mexico."[83] Further, nearly 70 percent of the unemployed return to Mexico within the first year after migration. She concluded that those who remain in the United States are quite different from those who return to their Mexican homeland: "Those who chose to stay in California have the best employment experiences, the highest wages, and the most education—just the kind of selection that has been the key feature of U.S. immigration for many generations."[84]

The return home can be emotionally difficult. Carmela, who had two children in Mexico and a son born in the United States, had a checkered work history as she moved from job to job, often being unemployed and pushed into the informal sector. She considered returning to Mexico, especially when she gets "totally demoralized." However, she admitted that her pride got in the way: "But with the situation I'm in now how could I do that and reunite with my two sons? My pride keeps me here. How can I return to Mexico after ten years without anything?" She considered returning to school, beginning with English as a Second Language classes. Yet that too was difficult: "How is it that I've been here ten years and I don't know how to speak English?" Feeling torn like this had gone on for some time and her resolution was to tough it out for a few more years: "I decided to stay here until my son finishes high school. Then I can return to Mexico and he will find a well-paid job. So I am here with my [other] kids in Mexico, waiting."

Upon arriving in the United States, transnational migrants feel in between Mexico and the United States. They weigh their options about possibly returning to Mexico or remaining in the United States, mindful of economic, political, or social considerations on both sides of the border.

Migration within the United States

While migrants who crossed the border certainly endured a number of travails, Mexican Americans born in the United States often also experience migration. The majority of the Mexican American interviewees and survey respondents had considerable experience moving from place to place. For the most part, these were children uprooted by their families' ongoing search for work and cheap places to live. Dominique Ponce, for example, whose parents were born in South Texas and migrated to Santa Cruz where she was born and raised, had lived in eight different homes in this city by the time she was twenty-two years old, when I interviewed her. The Mexican Americans I interviewed who had worked as farmworkers as children migrated from Texas to Michigan or Chicago and then to California or to agricultural valleys in Oregon and Washington.[85] Jennie Guerra, originally from Texas, migrated to Santa Cruz County as a teenager and then within this region in between stints of working at the cannery in the late 1960s. She recalled her migrant adolescence: "They would put me on call for Green Giant [cannery] so I would go and work sorting the tomatoes on the machine. We'd work from eight to ten hours a day in the summer. We'd go to Hollister [about twenty miles away], and we'd go to San Juan Bautista [about fifteen miles away] and we'd be working all the time. There was no way that you could stay home if you wanted to work. There was always a job. Either the fields, factories, anywhere you wanted to work there was always a job here." Dirana Lazer also had a migrant childhood, moving from Los Angeles where she was born to Mexico when her parents moved back temporarily, then to El Paso, Los Angeles, and Santa Barbara before she struck out on her own: "I came to San Francisco 'cause my father worked here for the Navy as a welder so I got to know the city and I just fell in love with it. When I got here I had $10 in my pocket." The combination of large families and low incomes made moving to better homes or labor markets, even if on a whim, strategies of the poor.

Mexican American migrants did not face life-threatening journeys but they did experience deep poverty; this was especially true for migrant farmworkers who lived in camps, sheds, or low-cost housing in various places that often had poor plumbing, heating, or cooking facilities. In addition, migrants often were unable to remain in one school for very long, leading to disruptions in their educations. As newcomer children, often they felt excluded from social groups for their inappropriate clothing, for their poverty, or, if moving to predominantly white locales, for being from Mexico. Monique Rodríguez recalled: "People think that I was illegal in the United States. They would make fun of me. That's okay. I knew it's not true anyway."

As Dominique narrated her troubles fitting in as the new kid in school, she reminded me of children who migrated from Mexico, as well as of my own migrant childhood. My siblings and I were "Air Force brats" and my family moved frequently every time my father was transferred to another Air Force base. We had to explain repeatedly to teachers and schoolmates that we were not from Mexico and always had to prove ourselves. When we finally settled in Southern California when I was ten, my explanations to Mexican migrants then centered on explaining why Spanish was not my first language. Like Dominique and other Mexican Americans, I could relate to migrants' experiences of displacement even if I had not crossed the border and Spanish was not my first language.

Mexican Americans also had narratives of crossing borders, this time state boundaries, where some regions (like Texas or Colorado) were known for their lack of hospitality or downright racism toward Mexicans. In their encounters with racism while traveling in the United States, Mexican Americans found common experiences with transnational migrants who moved from place to place as they searched for stable work, to join up with kin, or to find better living conditions. As undocumented workers who traveled the Southwest and Northwest, Los Tigres del Norte performed their music for largely Mexican migrant audiences. They also experienced discrimination firsthand. In Idaho in 1969, for example, they were refused service at a restaurant that had a sign stating "No Mexicans Allowed," commonplace throughout the Southwest. In addition, the musicians had to go hungry once because a gas station worker refused to make change so they could purchase food at vending machines. They were refused service in Del Rio, Texas, at a Piggly Wiggly store in 1970. When I told Jorge Hernández that I was also denied service in Texas at a barbecue café in the 1970s, he responded: "We felt it in our own flesh (*en carne propia*) what it's like to be humiliated." I could very much empathize with the Hernándezes' shock and pain at being treated so poorly.

Further, while moving frequently within the United States does not carry the same risks or emotional freight as crossing an international boundary, many Mexican Americans can relate to the feeling of displacement involved with migration. Often U.S. citizens hear firsthand the stories of crossing the border by neighbors, friends, coworkers, or their extended kin (like my brother-in-law). Mexican Americans are forced to reflect upon the dangers that transnational migrants face because of the arbitrary border policies that affect people they know. And since often they are racialized in a similar manner, Mexican Americans may come to feel a sense of identification and sympathy with the travails of daily life experienced by undocumented Mexicans.

Conclusion

Whether they migrated to the United States with or without authorization or within the United States, migrants were negotiating changes in their selves. For those who anticipate crossing *sin papeles*—without authorization—the process of displacement begins. Migrants say their goodbyes, dispose of their possessions, and brace themselves for the possible dangers to come. Gender expectations were prominent in their migration experiences. Many men called upon traditional gender expectations, placing themselves at great risk so they could find work and support their families in Mexico or the United States. Women also journeyed to fulfill these responsibilities so they could enter the labor market and provide economic support to their families in both sites. Finding themselves in Santa Cruz County, a beautiful area of the world where the cost of housing is very high yet there are jobs to be found, many struggled to make ends meet. Transnational migrants compared their circumstances in the United States with those in Mexico, constructing peripheral vision, a perspective in which their lives, while still filled with challenges, were mostly better in the United States than in Mexico.

The life histories and focus groups with migrants indicate migration without authorization prior to 1994 was difficult and at times incredibly distasteful but not necessarily life-threatening if migrants had planned well and had good guides or experience and some luck. After the implementation of Operation Gatekeeper and greatly increased border surveillance, however, unauthorized migrants found crossing the border to be much more difficult and dangerous, exposing them to desert terrain or the river, unscrupulous smugglers, and, for women, threats of sexual violence and sullied reputations. Those who return to Mexico were well aware of the displacement that their compatriots faced, as were those who crossed with authorization or who had not crossed at all but moved around within the United States.

In addition to the cold calculation that goes into planning to migrate, the emotional dimension was prominent in interviews with migrants. If they migrated without authorization, they were subject to a range of emotions: the demoralization about the dangers, desperation for living, terror when left alone, fear of being caught or sexually violated, intimidation from border officials and the police, humiliation when caught, and shame and distress when anticipating returning with nothing, leading some to neglect those left behind. The narratives about crossings illustrated how migrants grappled with these emotions and their changing sense of selves.

However, I found no evidence that migrants experience social death while crossing the border. Several had harrowing crossing experiences where they were detained or faced life-threatening circumstances, were robbed, shaken down, or almost raped and were traumatized by these threats. Yet all of the transnational migrants managed to find support from kin, fellow travelers on the road, or those left behind even though they started their lives anew by establishing social exchange with those in the United States. As migrants try to adapt, working to repay their loans, keeping in contact and sending remittances home, providing social and emotional sustenance, and surmounting as best they could the barriers caused by great distances, they are re-creating their lives in the United States. And while men's ability to survive the rigors of crossing the border seemed to fulfill traditional notions of masculinity, women also acted *muy machas*, strong and determined, "like men."

Mexican American migrants within the United States also experienced journeys of the self that were somewhat different since most of them migrated as children with their families. However, they also experience peripheral vision as they experience racialization, marginality in relation to poverty, and assumptions that they are migrants from Mexico. Yet despite some social distances from transnational migrants, often they sympathized with them, aware of the dangers and travails they experience daily.

Regardless of how they arrived in Santa Cruz County, most migrants experienced a sense of loss, grieving what was left behind and nostalgic for the possibilities of return, tempered by their invisibility in the public sphere except for anti-immigrant discourse (prior to the immigrant rights protests). Despite often long-delayed realization of their dreams, the incentives of finding work make the risks of crossing into or moving within the United States a necessity. Whether it is across an international boundary or state border, migration, even if under the most trying conditions, provides the possibilities for becoming somebody and gaining a life. In many ways, migrants embody the structure of feelings that they are neither fully from here nor from there.

NOTES

This essay originally appeared in *I'm Neither Here nor There* (Durham: Duke University Press, 2011).

1   Gaytan, Lucio, Shaiq, and Urdanivia, *Contemporary Migration Process*, 36.
2   Cantú, "The Peripheralization of Rural America"; Kochhar, "Occupational Status and Mobility"; Massey, Durand, and Malone, *Beyond Smoke and Mirrors*; Reyes, "Dynamics of Immigration."
3   Cantú, *Sexuality of Migration*.
4   Massey, Alarcon, Durand, and Gonzalez, *Return to Aztlán*; Menjivar, *Fragmented Ties*; Paris Pombo, *La historia de Marta*; Zabin, Kearney, Garcia, Runsten, and Nagengast, "Mixtec Migrants in California Agriculture." Castaneda, Manz, and Davenport (2002) discuss the migration process for Guatemalans, who, like other Central Americans, cross more than one border as they travel through Mexico to the United States.

5   Hellman, "Give or Take Ten Million," 218.
6   Basch, Glick Schiller, and Blanc-Szanton, *Nations Unbound*, 170.
7   Vélez-Ibáñez and Sampaio, *Transnational Latina/o Communities*, 42.
8   Massey, Durand, and Malone, *Beyond Smoke*, 59.
9   Cornelius, "Introduction," 78 percent of returned migrants believe it is "very dan-
     gerous" to cross the border without authorization; 64 percent of the respondents
     know of someone who died trying to cross through desert or mountains (Fuentes,
     L'Esperance, Perez, and White, *Impacts of US Immigration Policies*, 64, 73).
10   Menjivar, *Fragmented Ties*, 35.
11   Massey, Alarcon, Durand, and Gonzalez, *Return to Azlán*.
12   Stephen, *Transborder Lives*.
13   De la Garza, *Ni Aqui, Ni Alla*, 35. She is particularly interested in how subjectivity in
     relation to migration is expressed through corridos. For the fifth edition, this book
     was given the Social Science Award "Cortes de Cadiz" in Spain.
14   De la Garza, *Ni Aqui Ni Alla*, 36, her italics.
15   "El que decide emigrar deja *lo que tiene*, anula *lo que puede* y casi deja de *ser*, cuando
     no verdaderamente de *existir*" (de la Garza, *Ni Aqui Ni Alla*, 37, her italics). She is
     subscribing to the discourse in Mexico that migrants are lost to the nation, effec-
     tively abandoning their country and patrimony when they migrate to the United
     States (Durand, "From Traitors to Heros").
16   Rytina and Simanski, *Apprehensions by the U.S Border Patrol*, 2.
17   Kanaiaupuni, *Reframing the Migration Question*, 1318. Also see Hirsch, *Courtship After
     Marriage*; Hondagneu-Sotelo, *Gendered Transitions*.
18   Reyes, *Dynamics of Immigration*.
19   Chavira-Prado, *Work, Health, and the Family*.
20   Cerrutti and Massey, *On the Auspices of Female Migration*; Massey, Durand, and
     Malone, *Return to Aztlán*; Segura and Zavella, *Women and Migration*.
21   Massey, Durand, and Malone, *Beyond Smoke and Mirrors*, 134.
22   Cerrutti and Massey, *On the Auspices of Female Migration*, 187.
23   Cerrutti and Massey, *On the Auspices of Female Migration*, 187; Donato and Patterson,
     "Women and Men on the Move."
24   Malkin, *Reproduction of Gender Relations*; Stephen, *Transborder Lives*; Velasco Ortiz,
     Women, Migration and Household Survival Strategies.
25   Urrea, *The Devils Highway*.
26   J. Castañeda, *The Mexican Shock*.
27   Valdez-Suiter, Rosas-Lopez, and Pagaza, *Gender Differences*, 107.
28   Casillas, *Sounds of Belonging*, 153–56; Spagat, "Ads Target Illegal Crossings."
29   Arguelles and Rivero, *Gender Sexual Orientation*; Falcon, *Rape as a Weapon*; Nazario,
     Enrique's Journey; O. Ruiz, *Los Riesgos de Cruzar*. In a well-known tragedy, eighteen
     men (including two smugglers) were trapped inside a sealed boxcar and died of
     asphyxiation and heat stroke at Sierra Blanca, Texas, in 1987. The Mexican govern-
     ment paid for the return of the bodies because their families could not afford the
     expense and a funeral home in Ciudad Juarez donated the caskets. Adolfo Aguilar
     Zinser (*Why Mexican Migrants*, A21), the former Mexican ambassador to the United
     Nations, wrote, "Death is not uncommon among the thousands of immigrants
     who travel every day through the southwest, walking through deserts, hiding in

trunks [of cars] and boxcars. The extraordinary aspect of the incident at Sierra Blanca is that so many died at one time."

30 Gaytan, Lucio, Shaiq, and Urdanivia, *The Contemporary Migration Process*, 41. According to the World Bank, the estimated per capita income for Mexico is $7,310 and the estimated per capita income for the United States is $43,560. See http://web.worldbank.org, accessed on June 22, 2007.

31 Massey, Durand, and Malone, *Return to Aztlán*, 11.

32 Valdez-Suiter, Rosas-Lopez, and Pagaza, *Gender Differences*, 102.

33 While men are certainly vulnerable to being sexually assaulted while migrating or as a motivation for migration, the research thus far has focused on women's experiences (Argüelles and Rivero, *Gender/Sexual Orientations*; Gonzalez-Lopez, *Erotic Journeys*).

34 The Pew Hispanic Center (2006a, 4) estimates that 1.7 percent of nonimmigrant visa holders from Mexico eventually became unauthorized migrants, a low number reflecting the diffculty of obtaining visas.

35 A research team based at El Colegio de Michoacán and also local news stories documented the relationship between migrants and settlers between Watsonville and the village of Gomez Farias in Michoacán (Lopez Castro, *La Casa Dividida*; Biasotti, *A Tie That Binds, They Send Money, Going North*).

36 Personal communication, Bruno Figueroa, former Consul General for the San Jose office of the Mexican Consulate, July 9, 2005.

37 Smith, *Mexican New York*. Three respondents to the survey migrated from El Salvador, Guatemala, and Nicaragua.

38 Kandel and Massey, *The Culture of Mexican Migration*.

39 Chavez, *Shadow Lives*; Kearney, *Borders and Boundaries*; Massey, Alarcon, Durand, and Gonzalez, *Return to Aztlán*.

40 Ojeda de la Pena, *Transborder Families*.

41 Zavella, *Engendering Transnationalism*.

42 Cerrutti and Massey, "Auspices of Female Migration"; Hirsch, *A Courtship After Marriage*; Orellana, Thorne, Chee, and Lam, *Transnational Childhoods*; Abel Valenzuela, *Gender Roles and Settlement*.

43 Eithne Luibhéid (1998) discusses how women who "looked like lesbians" experienced harassment, detention, and deportation prior to 1990 when Congress repealed immigration provisions that excluded lesbians and gay men.

44 Martinez-Saldana, *La Frontera del Norte*, 376–77. He ran a successful campaign in 2004 to become the first migrant legislator in his home state of Michoacán, Mexico. See http://www.jesusmartinez.org, accessed on September 31, 2004; and Garcia, "Poll."

45 Nevins, *Operation Gatekeeper*.

46 See Pérez, "Tianguis" for an autobiography about these dangers.

47 According to Achotegui (2004), "the Ulysses Syndrome," the disorientation and trauma related to immigration, can endure for years.

48 In a survey with 347 respondents in migrant-sending communities, the majority of women were young (between fifteen and twenty-four) and all of the women migrants had family in the United States (Valdez-Suiter, Rosas-Lopez, and Pagaza, *Gender Differences*, 102, 108). This survey only interviewed women if male heads

of households were not present, and this may have undersampled women migrants.

49 Members of the National Guard, who began helping patrol the border in 2006, were charged with human smuggling (Blumenthal, *Three Guardsmen;* Falcón, *Rape as a Weapon of War*). Olivia Ruiz (2001) and Sonia Nazario (2006) discuss the rape of Central American women migrants who are subject to violence crossing through Mexico's southern and northern borders.

50 Valdez-Suiter, Rosas-Lopez, and Pagaza, *Women Migration and Household Survival Strategies*, 107. Nazario (98) cites research where one in six detained women migrants say they were sexually assaulted.

51 Nazario, *Enrique's Journey*.

52 Falcón, *Rape as a Weapon of War;* Farr, *Sex Trafficking;* Menjívar, *Fragmented Ties*, 69–71.

53 See Lipton, *Despite New Efforts*.

54 Marosi, *Smuggling*, B1. Smugglers recruit U.S. high school students to drive cars with concealed passengers, so Border Patrol agents have begun to give talks at high schools warning students of the risks.

55 Archibold Officials; McKinley, *At the Mexican Border*.

56 Gaouette, *Senators*.

57 Werner, *Bill*.

58 Eschbach, Hagan, Rodriguez, Hernandez-Leon, and Bailey, "Death at the Border," 1; also see Massey, Durand, and Malone, *Beyond Smoke and Mirrors*, 114. This research counted only those deaths of noncitizens or residents of the United States that occurred in counties that touched the U.S.-Mexico border in circumstances that indicated that those who died were probably crossing without authorization. The researchers did not count deaths in the interior of Mexico or the United States, which may well include those in transit across the border. They estimate that this is an undercount due to the disappearance of some bodies down the river or in the desert or mountains as well as occasional lack of clarity about jurisdiction over deaths in the river.

59 Inda, *Targeting Immigrants*, 43.

60 Mydans, *One Last Deadly Crossing*.

61 Eschbach, Hagan, and Rodriguez, *Migrant Deaths*, 1.

62 Cornelius, *Introduction;* Rosas, *The Managed Violences of the Borderlands*.

63 Stephen, *Transborder Lives*.

64 Porter, *In Return Home*.

65 Schmalzbaur (2008) suggests that when parents choose not to tell children about their own poverty yet send expensive consumer goods, familial inequalities may persist for some time.

66 Valdez-Suiter, Rosas-López, and Pagaza, "Gender Differences," 108.

67 From 2000 to 2004, there were fifty-four telephone lines and thirteen Internet users per every one hundred people in Mexico (UNICEF, "At a Glance: Mexico," http://www.unicef.org/infobycountry/mexicoestatistics.html#26, accessed on January 29, 2008).

68 National Telecommunications and Information Administration, "Falling through the Net II: New Data on the Digital Divide," cited in Casillas, *Sounds of Belonging*, 267.

69 Casillas, *Sounds of Belonging*, 250.

70 In 2005, less than half of the population had cell phones, and only 9 percent of households in Mexico had Internet access (Porter 2007).

71 Salgado de Snyder, *Family Life Across the Border*, 393.

72 Aysa and Massey (2004) find that the greater the amount of the remittances received the lower the likelihood that wives left behind will enter the labor force in rural areas. However, in urban areas, the absence of a husband has a modest effect on whether wives will participate in the labor force. Also see Goldring; A. López, *The Farmworkers' Journey*; McGuire and Martin, "Fractured Migrant Families"; Plaza, "Sexuality and Gender."

73 For poignant letters written by migrants to those left behind, see Siems (1992) and the film *Letters from the Other Side*, directed by Heather Courtney (2006).

74 Reyes, *Dynamics of Immigration*; Passel, *Unauthorized Migrants*. Seventy percent of migrant seasonal farmworkers surveyed in Idaho, a relatively new region of settlement, plan to remain in the United States permanently (Chavez, Wampler, and Burkhart, *Left Out*, 413).

75 Fuentes, L'Esperance, Perez, and White, *Impacts of U.S. Immigration Policies on Migration Behavior*, 73. Eighteen percent of women and 14 percent of men cited the diffculty of crossing the border as their top reason for *not* migrating (Valdez-Suiter, Rosas-Lopez, and Pagaza 2004, 105). Also see Massey, Durand, and Malone, *Beyond Smoke and Mirrors*.

76 The percentage of Mexicans who regularly make remittances fell to 64 percent in the first half of 2007, down from 71 percent in 2006 according to a survey by the Inter-American Development Bank's Multilateral Investment Fund. The drop was the steepest in states where Latin American immigration is most recent. http://www.iadb.org/news/articledetail.cfm?artid=3985&language=EN&arttype=PRm, accessed on August 13, 2007.

77 Banco de Mexico, "Estadisticas de Balanza de Pagos," cited in Alvarez Bejar 2009, 10. Remittances continue to be the second highest source of foreign income in Mexico (Cortina and de la Garza, *Immigrant Remitting Behavior and Its Developmental Consequences for Mexico and El Salvador*; Orozco, *The Remittance Market Place*).

78 Hellman, *Give or Take Ten Million*, 218.

79 Cortina and de la Garza, *Immigrant Remitting Behavior and Its Developmental Consequences for Mexico and El Salvador*, 14.

80 In 1993 the state government of Zacatecas and the federal government started a program, Dos por Uno, to double remittances and channel them into infrastructure development and business start-ups in Mexico, and this program evolved to Three for One in 1999 when local government began to participate. There are now Dos por Uno programs in other Mexican states (Bada 2004).

81 Cornelius, "Introduction," 11; Reyes, Johnson, and Van Swearingen, *Holding the Line?*, 32–33.

82 Reyes, *Dynamics of Immigration*, x; Hirsch, *Courtship of Marriage*; Hondagneu-Sotelo, *Gendered Transitions*.

83 Reyes, *Dynamics of Immigration*, ix.

84 Reyes, *Dynamics of Immigration*, iv.

85 For autobiographies by Mexican American migrant farmworkers, see Buss, *Forged under the Sun*; and Hart, *Barefoot Heart*.

REFERENCES

Achotegui, Joseba. "Immigrants Living in Extreme Situation: Immigrant Syndrome with Chronic and Multiple Stress (The Ulysses Syndrome)." *Norte: The Spanish Association of Neuropsychiatry* 7, no. 21 (2004): 39–53.

Álvarez Béjar, Alejandro. "Impacts and Sociopolitical Dimensions of the Financial Crisis amongst US and Mexican Workers." Paper presented at the conference "Work and Inequality in the Global Economy: China, Mexico and the U.S.," Institute for Research on Labor and Employment, UCLA, Los Angeles, October 7–9, 2009.

Archibold, Randal C. "Officials Find Drug Tunnel with Surprising Amenities." *New York Times*, January 27, 2006, A12.

Argüelles, Lourdes, and Anne M. Rivero. "Gender/Sexual Orientation Violence and Transnational Migration: Conversations with Some Latinas We Think We Know." *Urban Anthropology* 22, no. 3–4 (1993): 259–75.

Aysa, María, and Douglas S. Massey. "Wives Left Behind: The Labor Market Behavior of Women in Migrant Communities." In *Crossing the Border: Research from the Mexican Migration Project*, edited by Jorge Durand and Douglas S. Massey, 131–46. New York: Russell Sage Foundation, 2004.

Bada, Xóchitl. "Clubes de Michoacanos Oriundos: Desarrollo y Membresía Social Comunitarios." *Revista Migración y Desarrollo* 2 (2004): 82–103.

Basch, Linda, Nina Glick Schiller, and Cristina Blanc-Szanton. *Nations Unbound: Transnational Projects, Postcolonial Predicaments, and Deterritorialized Nation-States.* Langhorne, Pa.: Gordon and Breach Science, 1994.

Biasotti, Marianne. "A Tie That Binds: Watsonville's Sister Village." *Santa Cruz Sentinel*, January 14, 1996a, A14.

Biasotti, Marianne. "They Send Money from Watsonville, When Able." *Santa Cruz Sentinel*, January 14, 1996b, 14A.

Biasotti, Marianne. "Going North Means Survival to Gomez Farias Residents: Region Sends More Workers to U.S. Than Any Other in Mexico." *Santa Cruz Sentinel*, January 15, 1996c, A1.

Blumenthal, Ralph. "Three Guardsmen Charged with Human Smuggling: Texas Soldiers Were to Aid Border Patrol." *New York Times*, June 12, 2007, A12.

Buss, Fran Leeper. *Forged under the Sun/Forjado bajo el sol: The Life of María Elena Lucas.* Ann Arbor: University of Michigan Press, 1993.

Cantú, Jr., Lionel. "The Peripheralization of Rural America: A Case Study of Latino Migrants in America's Heartland." *Sociological Perspectives* 38, no. 3 (1995): 399–414.

Cantú, Jr., Lionel. *The Sexuality of Migration: Border Crossings and Mexican Immigrant Men.* New York: New York University Press, 2009.

Casillas, Dolores Inés. "Sounds of Belonging: A Cultural History of Spanish-Language Radio in the United States, 1922–2004." PhD diss., University of Michigan, 2006.

Castañeda, Jorge G. *The Mexican Shock: Its Meaning for the U.S.* New York: Free Press, 1995.

Castañeda, Xóchitl, Beatriz Manz, and Allison Davenport. "Mexicanization: A Survival Strategy for Guatemalan Mayans in the San Francisco Bay Area." *Migraciones Internacionales* 1, no. 3 (2002): 103–23.

Cerrutti, Marcela, and Douglas S. Massey. "On the Auspices of Female Migration from Mexico to the United States." *Demography* 38, no. 2 (2001): 187–200.

Chavez, Leo R. *Shadowed Lives: Undocumented Immigrants in American Society*. Fort Worth: Harcourt Brace, 1992.

Chávez, Maria, Brian Wampler, and Ross E. Burkhart. "Left Out: Trust and Social Capital among Migrant Seasonal Farmworkers." *Social Science Quarterly* 87, no. 5 (2006): 1012–29.

Chavira-Prado, Alicia. "Work, Health, and the Family: Gender Structure and Women's Status in a Mexican Undocumented Migrant Population." *Human Organization* 51, no. 1 (1992): 53–64.

Cornelius, Wayne A. "Controlling 'Unwanted' Immigration: Lessons from the United States, 1993–2004." *Journal of Ethnic and Migration Studies* 31, no. 4 (2005): 775–94.

Cornelius, Wayne A. "Introduction: Does Border Enforcement Deter Unauthorized Immigration?" In *Impacts of Border Enforcement on Mexican Migration*, edited by Wayne A. Cornelius and Jessa M. Lewis, 1–15. La Jolla: Center for Comparative Immigration Studies, UCSD, 2007.

Cortina, Jeronimo, and Rodolfo O. de la Garza. "Immigrant Remitting Behavior and Its Developmental Consequences for Mexico and El Salvador." Los Angeles: Tomás Rivera Policy Institute, 2004.

De la Garza, María Luisa. *Ni aquí, ni allá: El emigrante en los corridos y en otras canciones populares*. Sevilla, Spain: Fundación Municipal de Cultura, 2005.

Donato, Katerine M., and Evelyn Patterson. "Women and Men on the Move." In *Crossing the Border: Research from the Mexican Migration Project*, edited by Jorge Durand and Douglas S. Massey, 111–30. New York: Russell Sage Foundation, 2004.

Durand, Jorge. "From Traitors to Heroes: 100 Years of Mexican Migration Policies." *Washington: Migration Policy Institute*, March 2004.

Eschbach, Karl, Jacqueline Hagan, and Nestor Rodríguez. "Migrant Deaths at the U.S.-Mexico Border: Research Findings and Ethical and Human Rights Themes." LASA *Forum* 2001, 7–10.

Eschbach, Karl, Jacqueline Hagan, Nestor Rodríguez, Ruben Hernandez-Leon, and Stanley Bailey. "Death at the Border." Houston: University of Houston, Center for Immigration Research, 1997.

Falcón, Sylvanna M. "Rape as a Weapon of War: Militarized Rape at the U.S.-Mexico Border." In *Women and Migration in the U.S.-Mexico Borderlands: A Reader*, edited by Denise A. Segura and Patricia Zavella, 203–23. Durham: Duke University Press, 2007.

Farr, Kathryn. *Sex Trafficking: The Global Market in Women and Children*. New York: Worth, 2005.

Fuentes, Jezmin, Henry L'Esperance, Raúl Pérez, and Caitlin White. "Impacts of U.S. Immigration Policies on Migration Behavior." In *Impacts of Border Enforcement on Mexican Migration: The View from Sending Communities*, edited by Wayne Cornelius and Jessa M. Lewis, 54–73. La Jolla: Center for Comparative Immigration Studies, University of California, San Diego, 2007.

Gaouette, Nicole. "Senators Commit $3 Billion for Border." *San Jose Mercury News*, July 27, 2007b, 5A.

Garcia, Edwin. "Poll: 62% Disapprove of Driver's License Bill." *San Jose Mercury News*, March 4, 2005b, 1C, 2C.

Gaytán, Seidy, Evelyn Lucio, Fawad Shaiq, and Anjanette Urdanivia. "The Contemporary Migration Process." In *Impacts of Border Enforcement on Mexican Migration: The View from Sending Communities*, edited by Wayne Cornelius and Jessa M. Lewis,

33–51. La Jolla: Center for Comparative Immigration Studies, University of California, San Diego, 2007.

Goldring, Luin. "Gendered Memory: Constructions of Rurality among Mexican Transnational Migrants." In *Creating the Countryside: The Politics of Rural and Environmental Discourse*, edited by Melanie E. DuPuis and Peter Vandergeest, 303–29. Philadelphia: Temple University Press, 1996.

González-López, Gloria. *Erotic Journeys: Mexican Immigrants and Their Sex Lives*. Berkeley: University of California Press, 2005.

Hart, Elva Treviño. *Barefoot Heart: Stories of a Migrant Child*. Tempe: Bilingual Press, 1999.

Hellman, Judith Adler. "Give or Take Ten Million: The Paradoxes of Migration to the United States." In *Latin America after Neoliberalism: Turning the Tide in the 21st Century?*, edited by Eric Hershberg and Fred Rosen, 213–31. New York: New Press, 2006.

Hirsch, Jennifer S. *A Courtship after Marriage: Sexuality and Love in Mexican Transnational Families*. Berkeley: University of California Press, 2003.

Hondagneu-Sotelo, Pierrette. *Gendered Transitions: Mexican Experiences of Immigration*. Berkeley: University of California Press, 1994.

Inda, Jonathan Xavier. *Targeting Immigrants: Government, Technology, and Ethics*. Malden, Mass.: Blackwell, 2006.

Kanaiaupuni, Shawn Malia. "Reframing the Migration Questions: An Analysis of Men, Women, and Gender in Mexico." *Social Forces* 78, no. 4 (2000): 1311–47.

Kandel, William, and Douglas S. Massey. "The Culture of Mexican Migration: A Theoretical and Empirical Analysis." *Social Forces* 80, no. 3 (2002): 981–1004.

Kearney, Michael. "Borders and Boundaries of State and Self at the End of Empire." *Journal of Historical Sociology* 4, no. 1 (1991): 52–74.

Kochhar, Rakesh. "The Occupational Status and Mobility of Hispanics." Washington, DC: Pew Hispanic Center, 2005.

Lipton, Eric. "Despite New Efforts along Arizona Border, 'Serious Problems' Remain." *New York Times*, March 14, 2005, A16.

López, Ann Aurelia. *The Farmworkers' Journey*. Berkeley: University of California Press, 2007.

López Castro, Gustavo. *La casa dividida: Un estudio de caso sobre la migración a Estados Unidos en un pueblo michoacano*. Zamora, México: El Colegio de Michoacán, Asociación Mexicana de Población, 1986.

Luibhéid, Eithne. "'Looking Like a Lesbian': The Organization of Sexual Monitoring at the United States–Mexican Border." *Journal of the History of Sexuality* 8, no. 3 (1998): 477–506.

Malkin, Victoria. "Reproduction of Gender Relations in the Mexican Migrant Community of New Rochelle, New York." In *Women and Migration in the U.S.-Mexico Borderlands: A Reader*, edited by Denise A. Segura and Patricia Zavella, 415–37. Durham: Duke University Press, 2007.

Marosi, Richard. "Smuggling by Car Accelerates." *Los Angeles Times*, April 24, 2005, B1, B6.

Martínez-Saldaña, Jesús. "La Frontera del Norte." In *Over the Edge: Remapping the History of the American West*, edited by Valerie J. Matsumoto and Blake Allmendinger, 370–83. Berkeley: University of California Press, 1999.

Massey, Douglas S., Rafael Alarcón, Jorge Durand, and Humberto González. *Return to Aztlán: The Social Process of International Migration from Western Mexico*. Berkeley: University of California Press, 1987.

Massey, Douglas S., Jorge Durand, and Nolan J. Malone. *Beyond Smoke and Mirrors: Mexican Immigration in an Era of Economic Integration*. New York: Russell Sage Foundation, 2002.

McGuire, Sharon, and Kate Martin. "Fractured Migrant Families." *Family and Community Health* 30, no. 3 (2007): 178–88.

McKinley, James C. Jr. "At Mexican Border, Tunnels, Vile River, Rusty Fence." *New York Times*, March 23, 2005, A8.

Menjívar, Cecilia. *Fragmented Ties: Salvadoran Immigrant Networks in America*. Berkeley: University of California Press, 2000.

Mydans, Seth. "One Last Deadly Crossing for Illegal Aliens." *New York Times*, January 7, 1991, A1, B8.

Nazario, Sonia. *Enrique's Journey: The Story of a Boy's Dangerous Odyssey to Reunite with His Mother*. New York: Random House, 2006.

Neuhauser, Linda, Doris Disbrow, and Sheldon Margen. "Hunger and Food Insecurity in California." Berkeley: California Policy Seminar, 1995.

Nevins, Joseph. *Operation Gatekeeper: The Rise of the "Illegal Alien" and the Making of the U.S.-Mexico Boundary*. New York: Routledge, 2002.

Ojeda de la Peña, Norma. "Transborder Families and Gendered Trajectories of Migration and Work." In *Women and Migration in the U.S.-Mexico Borderlands*, edited by Denise A. Segura and Patricia Zavella, 327–40. Durham: Duke University Press, 2007.

Orellana, Marjorie Faulstich, Barrie Thorne, Anna Chee, and Wan Shun Eva Lam. "Transnational Childhoods: The Participation of Children in Transnational Migration." *Social Problems* 48, no. 4 (2001): 572–91.

Orozco, Manuel. "The Remittance Marketplace: Prices, Policy, and Financial Institutions." Washington: Institute for the Study of International Migration, 2004.

París Pombo, María Dolores. *La historia de Marta*. Mexico City: Universidad Autónoma Metropolitana, Unidad Xochimilco, 2006.

Passel, Jeffrey S. "Unauthorized Migrants: Numbers and Characteristics." Washington: Pew Hispanic Center, 2005.

Pérez, Ramón. "Tianguis." In *Diary of an Undocumented Immigrant*, translated by Dick J. Reavis. Houston: Arte Público Press, 1991.

Pew Hispanic Center. "Modes of Entry for the Unauthorized Migrant Population." Washington, DC: Pew Hispanic Center, 2006a.

Plaza, Rosío Córdova. "Sexuality and Gender in Transnational Spaces: Realignments in Rural Veracruz Families Due to International Migration." *Social Text* 92, no. 3 (2007): 37–55.

Porter, Eduardo. "In Return Home to Mexico Grave, an Industry Rises." *New York Times*, June 11, 2007.

Reyes, Belinda I. "Dynamics of Immigration: Return Migration to Western Mexico." San Francisco: Public Policy Institute of California, 1997.

Reyes, Belinda I. "U.S. Immigration Policy and the Duration of Undocumented Trips." In *Crossing the Border: Research from the Mexican Migration Project*, edited by Jorge Durand and Douglas S. Massey, 299–320. New York: Russell Sage Foundation, 2004.

Reyes, Belinda I., Hans P. Johnson, and Richard Van Swearingen. "Holding the Line? The Effect of the Recent Border Build-Up on Unauthorized Immigration." San Francisco: Public Policy Institute of California, 2002.

Rosas, Gilberto. "The Managed Violences of the Borderlands: Treacherous Geographies, Policeability, and the Politics of Race." *Latino Studies* 4, no. 4 (2006): 401–18.

Ruíz, Olivia. "Los Riesgos de Cruzar: La Migración Centroamericana en la Frontera México-Guatemala." *Frontera Norte*, January–June (2001): 7–42.

Rytina, Nancy, and John Simanski. "Apprehensions by the U.S. Border Patrol: 2005–2008." Washington, DC: Department of Homeland Security, Office of Immigration Statistics, 2009.

Salgado de Snyder, Nellie. "Family Life across the Border: Mexican Wives Left Behind." *Hispanic Journal of Behavioral Sciences* 15, no. 3 (1993): 391–401.

Schmalzbaur, Leah. "Family Divided: The Class Formation of Honduran Transnational Families." *Global Networks* 8, no. 3 (2008): 329–46.

Segura, Denise A., and Patricia Zavella, eds. *Women and Migration in the U.S.-Mexico Borderlands: A Reader*. Durham: Duke University Press, 2007.

Siems, Larry, ed. *Between the Lines: Letters between Undocumented Mexican and Central American Immigrants and Their Families and Friends*. Tucson: University of Arizona Press, 1992.

Smith, Robert Courtney. *Mexican New York: Transnational Lives of New Immigrants*. Berkeley: University of California Press, 2006.

Spagat, Elliot. "Ads Target Illegal Crossings: U.S. Aims to Prevent Mexicans from Risking Lives, Including Kids." *San Jose Mercury News*, August 19, 2005, 10A.

Stephen, Lynn. *Transborder Lives: Oaxacan Indigenous Migrants in the U.S. and Mexico*. Durham: Duke University Press, 2007.

Stephen, Lynn. "Nuevos Desaparecidos: Immigration, Militarization, Death, and Disappearance on Mexico's Borders." In *Security Disarmed: Gender, Race, and Militarization*, edited by Barbara Sutton, Sandra Morgen, and Julie Novkov, 79–101. New Brunswick, N.J.: Rutgers University Press, 2008.

Urrea, Luis Alberto. *The Devil's Highway: A True Story*. New York: Little, Brown, 2004.

Valdez-Suiter, Elisabeth, Nancy Rosas-López, and Nayeli Pagaza. "Gender Differences." In *Impacts of Border Enforcement on Mexican Migration: The View from Sending Communities*, edited by Wayne A. Cornelius and Jessa M. Lewis, 97–114. La Jolla: Center for Comparative Migration, University of California, San Diego, 2004.

Valenzuela Jr., Abel. "Gender Roles and Settlement Activities among Children and Their Immigrant Families." *American Behavioral Scientist* 42, no. 4 (1999): 720–42.

Velasco Ortiz, Laura. "Women, Migration, and Household Survival Strategies: Mixtec Women in Tijuana." In *Women and Migration in the U.S.-Mexico Borderlands: A Reader*, edited by Denise A. Segura and Patricia Zavella, 341–59. Durham: Duke University Press, 2007.

Vélez-Ibáñez, Carlos G., and Anna Sampaio, eds. *Transnational Latina/o Communities: Politics, Processes, and Cultures*. Lanham, Md.: Rowman and Littlefield, 2002.

Werner, Erica. "Bill to Propose Border Fence, 2,000-Mile Structure Could Cost Billions." *San Jose Mercury News*, November 3, 2005, 5B.

Zabin, Carol, Michael Kearney, Anna García, David Runsten, and Carole Nagengast. "Mixtec Migrants in California Agriculture." Davis: California Institute for Rural Studies, 1993.

Zavella, Patricia. "Engendering Transnationalism in Food Processing: Peripheral Vision on Both Sides of the U.S.-Mexico Border." In *Transnational Latina/o Communities: Politics, Processes, and Cultures*, edited by Carlos G. Vélez-Ibáñez and Anna Sampaio, 225–45. Lanham, Md.: Rowman and Littlefield, 2002.

Zinser, Adolfo Aguilar. "Why Mexican Migrants Suffocate in Boxcars." *Toronto Star*, July 10, 1987, A21.

PART III

EN/GENDERING

BORDERS

Changing Chicano Narratives

RENATO ROSALDO

Social thinkers must take other people's narrative analyses nearly as seriously as "we" take our own. This transformation of "our" objects of analysis into analyzing subjects most probably will produce impassioned, oblique challenges to the once-sovereign ethnographer. Both the content and the idioms of "their" moral and political assertions will be more subversive than supportive of business as usual. They will neither reinforce nor map onto the terrain of inquiry as "we" have known it. Narrative analyses told or written from divergent perspectives, as I have said, will not fit together into a unified master summation. A source at once of insight and discomfort, the dilemma of "in-commensurability," or lack of fit among diverse narratives, makes it imperative to attend with care to what other people are saying, especially if they use unfamiliar idioms and speak to us from socially subordinate positions. Taking account of subordinate forms of knowledge provides an opportunity to learn and productively change "our" forms of social analysis. It should broaden, complicate, and perhaps revise, but in no way inhibit, "our" own ethical, political, and analytical insights.

What follows works in the manner of a case history that explores three Chicano narratives with a view to assessing their value as analyses of the concept of culture. The first, *"With His Pistol in His Hand": A Border Ballad and Its Hero*, was published in 1958 by Américo Paredes.[1] It concerns a ballad about a south Texas Mexican man who shoots an Anglo-Texan sheriff and becomes the object of a manhunt. At once a study in folklore and a piece of social criticism, the work now addresses a wider social movement as well as a professional audience. The second, *Barrio Boy*, was published in 1971 by Ernesto Galarza.[2] Written toward the end of a career, the bilingually entitled autobiography tells of an early childhood spent in a village of Nayarit, Mexico, and then of a move north to Sacramento, California. This book appeared shortly after the mobilization of the Chicano movement in the late 1960s. The third, *The House on Mango Street*, was published in 1986 by Sandra Cisneros.[3] Written by a young woman, this short-story cycle speaks with a playful diction that often approaches the nursery rhyme. Rather than telling of the journey "north from Mexico," the protagonist remains stationary in a Chicago neighborhood that changes around her as she comes of age. This work envisions a politics of identity and community not yet realized either in social analysis or in the Chicano movement.

The three narratives tell of the Chicano warrior hero. The first portrays him in a positive light, the second mocks him, and the third displaces him. Despite their differences of tone, these tales of "how we got to be the way we are" follow an Edenic mythic pattern of an idealized initial condition, a fall, and subsequent struggles to survive, and perhaps thrive, into the present. These continuities and changes in Chicano narrative forms reveal shifting conceptions of culture. Once a figure of masculine heroics and resistance to white supremacy, the Chicano warrior hero now has faded away in a manner linked—at least in the texts under discussion—to the demise of self-enclosed, patriarchal, "authentic" Chicano culture. The trajectory of the three narrative analyses moves Chicano identity from bounded cultural purity through the mockery of patriarchs to encounters at the border zones of everyday life.

The Chicano narratives speak to changing conceptions of culture, not only as a concept in social analysis but also as a vital resource for a developing politics of identity and community. For Chicanos, "our" felt oppression derives as much from cultural domination as from the brute facts of poverty. During my junior high school days in Tucson, Arizona, for example, Chicano students could be obliged to bend over and grab their ankles so that teachers could give them "swats" with a board. This punishment somehow fit the "crime" of speaking Spanish in school. Or consider how Anglo-Americans who learn a second language in college become "cultured" and "broaden their horizons," but Chicanos who enter elementary schools already speaking another language suffer from a "deficit" and are labeled "at risk." In "our" everyday lives, cultural domination surfaces as myriad mundane sites of cultural repression and personal humiliation. For "us," questions of culture encompass social analysis, and much more.

The Chicano narratives studied in this chapter weave together laughter, politics, culture, and patriarchy. They prominently include borders as sites where identities and cultures intersect. Their distinctively Chicano forms of irony provoke knowing chuckles more often than belly laughs. When the protagonists speak in self-deprecating voices, their humor can be so understated that its wit, not to mention its barbed edges, often escapes straight-faced readers and listeners. Culturally distinctive jokes and banter play a significant role in constituting Chicano culture, both as a form of resistance and as a source of positive identity.[4] Rather than defusing grievances, the incongruities thus exposed offer analytical insight potentially useful for mobilizing popular resistance based on inequities of race and class.

Américo Paredes: The Chicano Warrior Hero

The author of *"With His Pistol in His Hand,"* Américo Paredes, was a pioneer in the field of Chicano studies. He entered the university after World War II, when he was in his 30s, after having been in succession a singer, a poet, and a journalist. His gift for language shows both in his poetry and in his multifaceted academic writings on folklore, literature, and anthropology. Now an eminent professor emeritus at the University of Texas at Austin, he began his academic career in the mid-1950s, when the Chicano movement had not yet emerged as a widely recognized social phenomenon.

When Paredes wrote *"With His Pistol in His Hand,"* during the 1950s, anti-Mexican prejudice throughout the Southwest and California was even more evident than today. In south Texas, where this prejudice was particularly virulent, it took courage to challenge the dominant ideology of Anglo-Texan racial superiority. José Limón has described the publication of Paredes's book as a struggle against Anglo-Texan white supremacy. Even after the manuscript's publication, Limón says, an ex–Texas Ranger asked the press for Paredes's address, so that he could "shoot the sonofabitch who wrote that book."[5] Paredes, it seems, had touched a nerve. Under the circumstances, one marvels that the book's narrator can speak with a fine blend of scholarly integrity, low-key chuckles, and devastating criticism.

Always reread from ever-changing "present" vantage points, past narratives rarely continue to be the "same" in their cultural meanings. In part, changing readings reflect changing audiences. At the time of its publication, for example, Paredes's work reached local and professional audiences; a decade later, it was inserted into the Chicano movement in a manner neither its author nor its early readers could have foreseen. Thus "relocated," the book took on new cultural significance. Yet again, from the perspective of feminist thought in the late 1980s, Paredes's work now appears dated in its idealization of a primordial patriarchy, and ahead of its time in so clearly seeing the interplay of culture and power. To project a heterogeneous, changing heritage into the future, "we" Chicanos must continually reread past narratives in order to recover courageous early works without reifying them as sacred relics more fit for veneration than dialogue and debate.

Writing in an understated manner, Paredes uses a nostalgic poetic mode to depict his Garden of Eden. He describes a pastoral patriarchy that governed the Rio Grande region from the arrival of Mexican settlers in 1749 to the Mexican-American War of 1848. In a culturally distinctive version of Frederick Jackson Turner's notion of frontier democracy, Paredes asserts that in primordial times benevolent patriarchs maintained a cohesive and egalitarian social order. "Social conduct," he says, "was regulated and formal, and men lived under a patriarchal system that made them conscious of degree. The original settlements had been made on a patriarchal basis, with the 'captain' of each community playing the part of father to his people" (11). If taken literally, Paredes's view of the frontier social order seems both pre-feminist and as implausible as a classic ethnography written and read in accord with classic norms. How could any human society, even one as egalitarian as that of the Ilongots, function without inconsistencies and contradictions?[6] Did patriarchal authority engender neither resentment nor dissent? Read as poetic vision, however, the account of primordial south Texas Mexican society establishes the terms for verbally constructing the warrior hero as a figure of resistance. It enables Paredes to develop a conception of manhood rhetorically endowed with the mythic capacity to combat Anglo-Texan anti-Mexican prejudice.

The treaty following the War of 1848 definitively shattered the Edenic epoch of primordial pastoral patriarchy. After nearly a century of relatively peaceful existence, the patriarchs were deposed, the united land was divided, and the border was drawn. In mythic terms, Rio Grande Mexicans fell from innocence when their earthly paradise was split asunder: "It was the Treaty of Guadalupe that added the final element to Rio Grande society, a border. The river, which had been a focal point, became a dividing line. Men were expected to consider their relatives and closest neighbors, the people just across the river, as foreigners in a foreign land. A restless and acquisitive people, exercising the rights of conquest, disturbed the old ways" (15). The intrusive border brought a definitive end to the old way of life. From this point onward, primordial pastoral patriarchy (whatever its historical status) definitively survives only as folklore and as an idealized vision of manhood.

Lest there be any confusion, Paredes's narrative about the invasive border tells the history of his own ancestral past. He is not an immigrant. Neither he nor his Mexican ancestors moved after about 1750; instead, military conquest transformed the Rio Grande from a fertile place of gathering together into a barbed line of demarcation. The imposition of the border compelled friends and relatives to become citizens of two distinct nations. Long before his birth, Paredes's ancestral homeland had thus become south Texas. He was born into a world dominated by an aggressive group that spoke a foreign language. But they were the immigrants, not he. Not unlike blacks and Native Americans, Chicanos cannot readily be absorbed to a standard history of immigration and assimilation.

After telling about how the border invaded south Texas, Paredes's tone becomes quietly ironic. "In the conflict along the Rio Grande," he says, "the English-speaking Texan (whom we shall call the Anglo-Texan for short) disappoints us in a folkloristic sense. He produces no border balladry. His contribution to the literature of border conflict is a set of attitudes and beliefs about the Mexican which form a legend of their own and are the complement to the *corrido*, the Border-Mexican ballad of border conflict" (15). Although Mexicans sing their resistance with fine *corridos*, Anglo-Texans impose their domination with prosaic attitudes and beliefs. Doomed to lose the shooting wars, Mexicans use *corridos* of enduring value to counter Anglo-Texan claims to cultural supremacy. In his social criticism, Paredes speaks obliquely, deftly, pointedly, bilingually.

When Paredes speaks in more detail about border conflict, he plays with ironic parallel constructions that move between the perspectives of Mexicans and Anglo-Texans. He begins with the Anglo-Texan legend about Mexicans. In this view, Mexicans are cruel, cowardly, treacherous, and thieving because their mixed blood (Spanish and Indian) has made them degenerate. Mexicans are said to recognize the superiority of Anglo-Texans, especially the finest of their breed, the Texas Rangers. The Anglo-Texan legend about Mexicans circulated in popular attitudes and beliefs, which were reflected in and reshaped by printed works extending from nineteenth-century war propaganda to twentieth-century scholarship: "The truth seems to be that the old war propaganda concerning the Alamo, Goliad, and Mier later provided a convenient justification for outrages committed on the Border by Texans of certain types, so convenient an excuse that it was artificially prolonged for almost a century. And had the Alamo, Goliad, and Mier not existed, they would have been invented, as indeed they seem to have been in part" (19). Gradually unrolling his punch line, Paredes suggests that the writings of Anglo-Texan scholars not only justified the abuse of Mexicans but were also, in part, invented.

Mexican perceptions of Anglo-Texans, on the other hand, appear in sayings, anecdotes, and ballads about the Texas Rangers rather than in authoritative print. Without American soldiers, the sayings go, Rangers would not dare enter the border region. In this view, the cowardly Rangers never fought face-to-face against armed Mexicans, but shot them in the back or in their sleep. Many a tale tells of how Rangers killed innocent (often unarmed) Mexicans and planted rusty old guns on their corpses to justify their claims to have shot them in self-defense while pursuing thieves. Paredes hastens to say that such perceptions are partisan: "I do not claim for these little tidbits the documented authenticity that Ranger historians claim for their stories. What we have here is frankly partisan and exaggerated without a doubt, but it does throw some light on Mexican attitudes toward the Ranger which many Texans may scarcely suspect. And it may be that these attitudes are not without some basis in fact" (25). His rhetorical tactic nicely parallels and opposes that used to summarize Anglo-Texan perceptions. Once again, he ends by reversing himself, but this time he accents how Mexican perceptions rest on a significant grain of truth, not a large dose of invention.

Throughout his discussion of border conflict, Paredes himself becomes a warrior hero who battles against Anglo-Texan academic opponents. His devastating critique of J. Frank Dobie's and Walter Prescott Webb's influential work on the folklore and history of Texas shows how their (often unreliable) writings celebrate Anglo-Texans and denigrate their fellow citizens of Mexican ancestry.[7] Paredes exposes their work as a version of popular Anglo-Texan white supremacy dressed in academic garb. In being prejudiced and quick on the inference, Dobie and Webb appear to be latter-day incarnations of the Texas Rangers.

In his own good time, Paredes settles down to tell the ballad of Gregorio Cortez. Like his rendition of pastoral patriarchy, Paredes uses a poetic voice to display an updated version of the ancient ideal of manhood: "That was good singing, and a good song; give the man a drink. Not like these pachucos nowadays, mumbling damn-foolishness into a microphone; it is not done that way. Men should sing with their heads thrown back, with their mouths wide open and their eyes shut. Fill your lungs, so they can hear you at the pasture's further end. And when you sing, sing songs like *El Corrido de Gregorio Cortez*. There's a song that makes the hackles rise. You can almost see him there—Gregorio Cortez, with his pistol in his hand" (34). Descendants of the primordial patriarchs, these country men live in the old style. Unaided by microphones, their voices carry across the pasture and make their listeners feel *muy gallo*, literally very rooster, very male like a fighting cock, with rising hackles. The descendants of the warrior hero singing across the pasture probably should be understood more poetically than literally. Like Gregorio Cortez and Américo Paredes himself, the singer of *corridos* becomes a latter-day warrior hero, a figure of masculine heroics and resistance to Anglo-Texan domination.[8]

When Gregorio Cortez himself enters, he does so as a horseman who shouts his name in battle and whose heroic deeds are remembered and sung in ballad form. As Paredes notes, "Cortez sounds not like a Border vaquero [cowboy, or buckaroo] but like an old, name-proud hidalgo [nobleman]. It is this medieval pride in name that is the basis of the challenge as it appears in the Border *corrido*, pride in a name that has been earned through deed and not through birth or wealth" (236). His deeds as a warrior horseman confer the aura of medieval nobility on his person. When he boldly shouts his name in battle ("Yo soy Gregorio Cortes"), he elevates the humble *corrido* until it assumes the grandeur of the medieval epic. The Chicano warrior hero has grown larger than life to combat Anglo-Texan assertions of cultural and racial supremacy. It was a grand moment. Yet, as shall be seen in a moment, changing Chicano narratives have dismantled these masculine heroics, and reworked, without destroying, "our" forms of cultural resistance.

Ernesto Galarza: The Mocking of the Warrior Hero

The author of *Barrio Boy*, the late Ernesto Galarza, was a scholar-activist. Like Paredes, he is revered by Chicano scholars and activists. Without holding an academic position, he distinguished himself as an organizer and a writer. Throughout his life he helped organize agricultural workers, and he conducted research on the political economy of agribusiness. He wrote works of scholarship, poetry, and children's stories.

In Galarza's autobiography, both the warrior hero and the Edenic myth occupy central places, but they are mocked rather than treated with poetic reverence. In this respect, Galarza's work at once parallels and subverts Paredes's narrative. The shift in attitudes that separates the works by Paredes and Galarza probably derives as much from changing sociohistorical conditions as from the fact that the former writes as a folklorist and the latter as a student of agricultural economics. The chasm between the virtually unchallenged assimilationism of 1958 and the mobilized Chicano community of 1971 informs the two narratives. Writing about south Texas during the 1950s, Paredes called for Mexican cultural resistance to domination by the numerical minority of Anglo-Texans. For him, the critique of ideology appeared most urgent. In contrast, Galarza urged confrontation with established political authorities that governed the residentially segregated urban barrios of northern California in the early 1970s. For him, the analysis of capitalism and its bureaucratic administrative apparatus seemed most crucial. Shaped by distinct disciplinary predilections and differing historical circumstances, the two writers set complementary yet divergent agendas for social analysis.

Galarza's work has often been read with solemnity, as if it were written in a flat earnest manner. Yet the work is marked by heteroglossia, a play of English and Spanish, and by an understated, often self-deprecating humor through which his political vision becomes apparent.

Barrio Boy opens soberly enough, with an Edenic scene of Mexican rural life. "The pine kindling," Galarza says, "was marvelously aromatic and sticky. The woodsmen of the pueblo talked of the white tree, the black tree, the red tree, the rock tree—*palo blanco, palo negro, palo colorado* and *palo de piedra*. Under the shady canopies of the giants there were the fruit bearers—*chirimoyas, guayabas, mangos, mameyes*, and *tunas*" (6). Life is peaceful. Nature is aromatic, colorful, and abundant. The praise song of Galarza's pastoral opening makes the primordial environment into a bountiful upland tropical paradise.

However, an extended meditation on the *zopilote*, the turkey buzzard, interrupts the pastoral opening.

> But of all the creatures that came flying out of the *monte*—bats, doves, hawks—the most familiar were the turkey vultures, the *zopilotes*. There were always two or three of them perched on the highest limb of a tree on the edge of the pueblo. They glided in gracefully on five feet of wing spread, flapping awkwardly as they came to rest. They were about the size of a turkey, of a blackish brown color and baldheaded, their wrinkled necks spotted with red in front. Hunched on their perch, they never opened their curved beaks to make a sound. They watched the street below them with beady eyes. Sometimes during the day, the *zopilotes* swooped down to scavange in the narrow ditch that ran the length of the street, where the housewives dropped the entrails of chickens among the garbage. They gobbled what waste the dogs and pigs did not get at first. (6)

As ugly in appearance as it is graceful in flight, this scavenger becomes a mock national bird for Galarza's natal village of Jalcocotán, Nayarit, Mexico.

Governed by male heads of family, or *jefes de familia,* Jalcocotán formally resembles Paredes's primordial Rio Grande society ruled by benevolent patriarchs. Yet Galarza introduces the term *jefe de familia* by talking not about the deceased patriarch, Grandfather Félix, but about his successor, a diminutive matriarch named Aunt Tel:

> Doña Esther, my Aunt Tel, as I called her, was a small person. Something over five-feet-five, she was fair-skinned and hazeleyed. She seldom laughed, for when we came to Jalco she had already had enough grief to last a person a lifetime, the least of which was the responsibility for two younger brothers and a sister after the death of Grandfather Félix. He,

too, had been a rigid *jefe de familia*. She had lived all her life under authority but it had not bent her will; standing up to it she was more than a
person—she was a presence. When she was alone in the cottage with us
she told jokes about animals and foolish, stuck-up persons. She smiled
mostly with her eyes. (17)

Endurance, resilience, and her twinkling eyes make the matriarch Aunt Tel an
inspiring presence in young Ernesto's life.

In his oblique criticism of patriarchal authority, Galarza moves from Aunt
Tel to Coronel, the dominant rooster of Jalcocotán. As Paredes suggested in
his depiction of the ballad singer, to be *muy gallo* is to be a real man. Fighting
cocks are widely celebrated as symbols of manhood in Mexican speech and
song, as indicated by Galarza's introduction of the rooster Coronel, challenging all within earshot: "Coronel always held himself like a ramrod, but he stood
straightest when he was on top of the corral wall. From up there he counted his
chickens, gave the forest a searching look, and blasted out a general challenge
to all the world. With his flaming red crest and powerful yellow spurs, Coronel
was the picture of a very *jefe de familia*" (23). If Jalcocotán's national bird is a
mock eagle, the turkey buzzard, its dominant *jefe de familia* is a mock patriarch,
the rooster Coronel.

By interrupting the Edenic scene and by displacing the *jefe de familia*, Galarza
sets the stage for a mock cockfight that pits the rooster Coronel against the
nameless turkey buzzard. The parodic cockfight occurs in the world of women,
children, and animals, without adult male witnesses. In any case, it is all over
in a moment, and the turkey buzzard flies off with the prize, a heap of chicken
guts, while the rooster Coronel stays behind to claim victory:

> Coronel, standing erect among the litter gave his wings a powerful stretch,
> flapped them and crowed like a winning champ. His foe, five times larger,
> had fled, and all the pueblo could see that he was indeed *muy gallo*.
>
> Seeing that Coronel was out of danger, Nerón and I dashed to tell
> the epic story. We reported how our rooster had dashed a hundred times
> against the vulture, how he had driven his spurs into the huge bird inflict-
> ing fatal wounds, Nerón, my dumb witness, wagged his tail and barked. (31)

The cockfight mocks the village's established authorities, the *jefes de familia*,
so obliquely that most readers miss its irony. Because it deals with seemingly
nostalgic childhood memories about rural village life, the narrative probably
appears innocent. Although their self-deprecating postures and their plain
speech can be deceptive, Galarza and Paredes freely use irony, satire, mockery,
and double meaning.

When Galarza describes a *corrido* songfest, his account must be taken tongue in cheek. It has none of the poetic solemnity of Paredes's depiction of a man who throws his head back as he belts out the *corrido* of Gregorio Cortez:

> When some of the *compadres* got drunk, usually on Sundays, there was singing in some corral or in the plaza. Women and children took no part in these affairs, which sometimes ended in fights with machetes. We couldn't help hearing the men's songs, which became louder with the drinking. They sang the *corrido* of Catalino, the bandit who stood off hundreds of *rurales*, the mounted police who chased him up and down the Sierra Madre year in and year out. In his last battle, Catalino was cornered in a canyon. From behind a boulder he picked off dozens of rurales with his Winchester, taking a nip of *aguardiente* between shots, and shouting to his persecutors: "Acérquense, desgraciados, aquí está su padre." The rurales, like anybody else, did not like to be called wretched punks especially by an outlaw who boasted he was their father. In Mexico for such an insult you paid with your life. They closed in until Catalino lay dead. They chopped off his head and showed it in all the pueblos of the Sierra Madre, which made Catalino hero enough to have a ballad composed about him. It was generally agreed that he was from Jalcocotán where the bravest men were to be found, especially on Sunday nights when they were drunk. (48–49)

Nobody's masculine reputation escapes Galarza's parodic gaze. The *rurales* are mortally insulted by Catalino, who in turn becomes a hero by having his head chopped off. And the village men become the region's best and bravest only during their drunken Sunday night songfests. Galarza's deft, ironic touch deflates an overblown masculine ethic, but leaves the men's humanity intact.

After Galarza's move north to Sacramento, his mockery of patriarchal authority continues, but in a new context and with new consequences. In California, young Ernesto used his English-language education to translate for his elders as they negotiated with established Anglo authorities: "When troubles made it necessary for the *barrio* people to deal with the Americans uptown, the *Autoridades* [authorities], I went with them to the police court, the industrial accident office, the county hospital, the draft board, the county clerk. We got lost together in the rigamarole of functionaries who sat, like *patrones* [bosses], behind desks and who demanded licenses, certificates, documents, affidavits, signatures, and witnesses" (252). Speaking from a bicultural border zone, Galarza juxtaposes the Mexican figures of the *Autoridad* and the *patrón* with North American bureaucratic offices and official documents. The idiom that once mocked *jefes de familia* in a Mexican village now undercuts the authority of state officials in Sacramento. The whimsical sense for incongruities that informs Galarza's vision of Jalcocotán shapes a bilingual text that, unbeknownst to them, verbally transforms Anglo-American authorities into Mexican bosses.

The autobiography's conclusion thus brings into focus Galarza's lifetime concern with Chicano and working-class struggles against Anglo-American capitalist domination. Paredes elevates primordial patriarchs in order to endow their successors with mythic potency for combatting Anglo-Texan prejudice; Galarza mocks Mexican patriarchs in order to gain a critical idiom for subverting Anglo-American political authorities. Although one inflates patriarchy and the other deflates it, both writers displace and transform the primoridal patriarchs so that they can play an emancipatory role in Chicano struggles of resistance.

Sandra Cisneros: The Fading of the Warrior Hero

The author of *The House on Mango Street*, Sandra Cisneros, is a young woman who grew up in the Mexican community of Chicago. A writer and a teacher, she graduated from the Iowa Writers Workshop, and she has taught creative writing at an alternative school for dropouts in Chicago. For her, writing is a craft and a form of empowerment. At once widely accessible and unobtrusively bilingual, her writing reflects concerns at once Chicana, feminist, and broadly political.

Cisneros's work grows out of a wider movement. During the 1980s, the most creative modes of imagining Chicano identity have emerged less often from social thinkers than from creative writers, particularly from short-story cycles authored by women. It is no accident that a marginal genre, such as the short story, should become a site for political innovation and cultural creativity. Literary theorist Mary Louise Pratt has argued, for example, that the short-story cycle's formal marginality (as compared with the novel) makes it a particularly likely arena for experimentation, for the development of alternative moral visions, and for the introduction of women and teenagers as central protagonists.[9] In the case at hand, young Chicana authors have written against earlier versions of cultural authenticity that idealized patriarchal cultural regimes that appeared autonomous, homogeneous, and unchanging.

Esperanza, the central protagonist of *The House on Mango Street*, tells a gender-specific coming-of-age story that develops a distinct strand of her cultural heritage. More matriarchal than patriarchal, her vision reaches back to her great-grandmother and forward to herself. Yet her constant play, her deceptively childlike patter, subverts oppressive patriarchal points of cultural coherence and fixity.

Esperanza does not orient to a remembered ancestral homeland in Mexico or anywhere else. Unlike the works of Paredes and Galarza, Cisneros's narrative invokes neither a primordial pastoral patriarchy nor a primeval tropical village. If Esperanza has a cultural anchor, an Edenic reference point, it is the house of her dreams, paradoxically tucked away in a future that never arrives. "I knew then," she says, "I had to have a house. A real house. One I could point to. But this isn't it. The house on Mango Street isn't it. For the time being, Mama said. Temporary, said Papa. But I know how those things go" (9). The bilingualism of this prose is subtle enough to be ignored by Anglo readers. In her own public readings, however, Cisneros pronounces mango with the 'a' of "all," not that of "hat," and she accents Mama and Papa on the second syllable, not the first. Even life in the *barrio* appears not as near-documentary portraits of grinding poverty but as Esperanza's oblique statement that the American Dream has eluded her; she has no home, not even a room, of her own, and in her child-hood she never will.[10]

In one of her short stories, she plays with themes of the warrior hero—the horseman, the name shouted in combat, and the *corrido* which sings of his deeds—destabilizing each as she goes. Let me illustrate by citing "My Name" in its entirety:

In English my name means hope. In Spanish it means too many letters. It means sadness, it means waiting. It is like the number nine. A muddy color. It is the Mexican records my father plays on Sunday mornings when he is shaving, songs like sobbing.

It was my great-grandmother's name and now it is mine. She was a horse woman too, born like me in the Chinese year of the horse—which is supposed to be bad luck if you're born female—but I think this is a Chinese lie because the Chinese, like the Mexicans, don't like their women strong.

My great-grandmother. I would've liked to have known her, a wild horse of a woman, so wild she wouldn't marry until my great-grandfather threw a sack over her head and carried her off just like that, as if she were a fancy chandelier. That's the way he did it.

And the story goes she never forgave him. She looked out the window all her life, the way so many women sit their sadness on an elbow. I won-der if she made the best with what she got or was she sorry because she couldn't be all the things she wanted to be. Esperanza. I have inherited her name, but I don't want to inherit her place by the window.

At school they say my name funny as if the syllables were made out of tin and hurt the roof of your mouth. But in Spanish my name is made out of a softer something like silver, not quite as thick as sister's name Magdalena which is uglier than mine. Magdalena who at least can come home and become Nenny. But I am always Esperanza.

I would like to baptize myself under a new name, a name more like the real me, the one nobody sees. Esperanza as Lisandra or Maritza or Zeze the X. Yes. Something like Zeze the X will do. (12–13)

Esperanza inhabits a border zone crisscrossed by a plurality of languages and cultures. Multiple subjectivities intersect in her own person, where they coexist, not in a zone of free play but each with its own gravity and density. Moving between English and Spanish, her name shifts in length (from four letters to nine), in meaning (from hope to sadness and waiting), and in sound (from being as cutting as tin to as soft as silver). In contrast to Gregorio Cortez, she does not stand in one place, looking straight ahead, and shout, "Yo soy Esperanza."

Like her grandmother, Esperanza is a horse woman, but not a female imitation of the *hidalgo*, the male warrior horseman. No, she was born, of all things, in the *Chinese* year of the horse; in her heterogeneous cultural world, the Chinese and the Chicano readily come into play together. Both Chinese and Mexicans agree, she says, because neither culture likes its women strong.[11] Her narrative moves, as if along links in a chain of free associations, and great-grandmother Esperanza undergoes a metamorphosis from a rider, the horse woman, to the beast itself, a wild horse of a woman.

Her patrimony, the *corrido*, has been reduced to Mexican records that sound like sobbing. Although she accepts her matronymy (that is, her name), Esperanza refuses to assume her great-grandmother's place by the window. As she concludes the tale, Esperanza yet again turns things topsy-turvy by baptizing her invisible, real self: Zeze the X. Nothing stands still, especially not her name.

Near poems, the short stories evoke twin threats to her person in the form of sexuality and physical danger. Yet the power of these threats deceptively appears in the patter of "childlike" diction that often imitates nursery rhymes:

Across the street in front of the tavern a bum man on the stoop.

Do you like these shoes?
Bum man says, Yes, little girl. Your little lemon shoes are so beautiful.
    But come closer. I can't see very well. Come closer. Please.
You are a pretty girl, bum man continues. What's your name, pretty girl?
And Rachel says Rachel, just like that.

Now you know to talk to drunks is crazy and to tell them your name is worse, but who can blame her. She is young and dizzy to hear so many sweet things in one day, even if it is a bum man's whiskey words saying them.
Rachel, you are prettier than a yellow taxi cab. You know that.
But we don't like it. We got to go, Lucy says.
If I give you a dollar will you kiss me? How about a dollar? (39)

That this is a Chicana version of "Little Red Riding Hood" becomes evident as the bum man asks her to draw nearer, virtually saying, "The better to see you, my dear." His threatening presence echoes the clichéd warning of parents who say to their children, "Don't take candy from strangers." Instead of candy, the bum man offers saccharine words, calls her a pretty girl, praises her shoes, compares her with a yellow cab, and, in the end, offers a dollar for her kiss.

Esperanza depicts her sexual awakening as a process at once sensuous and dangerous. The story entitled "Hips" plays back and forth, metaphorically, between her suddenly present hips and a brand new Buick: "One day you wake up and there they [your hips] are. Ready and waiting like a new Buick with the keys in the ignition. Ready to take you where?" (47). In a later story, she is bursting: "Everything is holding its breath inside me. Everything is waiting to explode like Christmas. I want to be all new and shiny. I want to sit out bad at night, a boy around my neck and the wind under my skirt" (70). Esperanza interweaves her sexuality, her rounding hips, and images of automobiles. Not unlike a car, she is polished and ready to go (where?). In being "bad," she moves toward the sensuous, pleasurable, threatening edges of her world.

In this play of desire and threat, Esperanza meets dangers by gracefully moving on. If her sexuality resembles a new car, her grace is danced. "And uncle," she says, "spins me and my skinny arms bend the way he taught me and my mother watches and my little cousins watch and the boy who is my cousin by first communion watches and everyone says, wow, who are those two who dance like in the movies, until I forget that I am wearing only ordinary shoes, brown and white, the kind my mother buys each year for school" (46). Her grace resides in her person, not in her ordinary shoes. Never standing in one place, she uses the dance to counter male violence and efforts to confine and subordinate her. She just moves on, in her dance of life.

Cisneros opens fresh vistas in what Américo Paredes saw as the inextricably intertwined realms of culture and politics. In her narrative analysis, the concept of culture undergoes a metamorphosis. The warrior hero has seen better days. No longer can he serve as the "unified subject" around which Chicano sagas of masculine heroics revolve. Yet what the concept of culture loses in purity and authenticity, it gains in range and engagement. As embodied in Cisnero's short-story cycle, Chicano culture moves toward the borderlands, the spaces that readily include blacks, Anglos, mundane happenings of every-day life, and heterogeneous changing neighborhoods. Certain border crossings involve literal immigration, in which a number of people move in and out of the neighborhood, or a "wetback" with no last name dies anonymously in an accident, or a fat woman who speaks no English sits by the window and plays homesick songs. Others appear as more figurative border dances through which Esperanza makes her way in a world of desire and threat, budding sexuality and dangerous male violence.

In trying new narrative forms, Cisneros has developed a fresh vision of self and society; she has opened an alternative cultural space, a heterogeneous world, within which her protagonists no longer act as "unified subjects," yet remain confident of their identities. Esperanza's name itself twists and twirls until it reaches the end of its alphabet, "Zeze the X." In moving through a world laced with poverty, violence, and danger, Esperanza acts at once assertive and playful. She thrives, not just survives, as she dances through her unpredictable world with grace and wit. For all her grace, however, Esperanza does not just take on personas and remove them, as if they were so many old shoes; unlike the less encumbered French literary theorist Roland Barthes, Esperanza feels the weight of the multiple identities that intersect through her person.

On a more reflexive note, I should like to conclude by underscoring the analytical import of the interplay between "their" (Anglo-American) narratives and "ours" (Chicano). In the case at hand, the implications of Sandra Cisneros's short-story cycle came to me quite gradually. It took time—from initially conceiving my article "Grief and a Head-hunter's Rage" onward—for the concept of a multiplex personal identity to move in alongside its predecessor, the "unified subject," and for the notion of culture as multiple border zones to find a place next to its predecessor, the "homogeneous community." Yet it would be difficult to exaggerate the major role played by the narrative analyses of Paredes, Galarza, and Cisneros in my charting a path for renewing the anthropologist's search for meaning.

Certain readers may also wish to know that my point of departure in the next chapter, a critique of Max Weber's masculine heroics, followed on the heels of reading Cisneros, but with a major difference. The human and analytical limitations of Weber's passionate detachment struck me all at once, not gradually. This realization left me feeling at once deeply disoriented and excited at new possibilities for the social analyst as a "positioned subject." On the one hand, disciplined work habits went by the wayside because I could do nothing but wander around while things sank in at their own pace. On the other hand, new topics opened up because my attention was somehow drawn to works not usually included in the canon of interdisciplinary works for cultural studies. My inquiry, it seemed, was on a meander. Once absorbed, however, the critique of Weber proved central in organizing my thoughts for much of this book [*Culture and Truth*].

Reprinted with permission of the author. This essay originally appeared in *Culture and Truth: The Remaking of Social Analysis*, 147–67 (Boston: Beacon Press, 1993).

1   Américo Paredes, *"With His Pistol in His Hand": A Border Ballad and Its Hero* (Austin: University of Texas Press, 1958). All further references to the book appear in the body of the paper, cited by page number.

2   Ernesto Galarza, *Barrio Boy* (New York: Ballantine Books, 1972). All further references to this book appear in the body of the paper cited by page number. For another reading of *Barrio Boy*, see Jose Saldivar, "Caliban and Resistance: A Study of Chicano-Chicana Autobiography," paper delivered at the Chicano Colloquium Series, Stanford Center for Chicano Research, March 22, 1986.

3   Sandra Cisneros, *The House on Mango Street* (Houston: Arte Publico Press, 1986). All further references to this book will appear in the body of the paper, cited by page number.

4   The political potential of juxtaposing multiple discourses has most recently been confirmed in the distinctively Filipino carnivalesque overthrow of the seemingly all-powerful Marcos dictatorship. In one moment, Filipinos wept in fear for their lives as they stood firm before tanks; in the next moment, they turned to buy ice cream or joke with friends. On the role of humor in the politics of Chicano culture, see Américo Paredes, "The Problem of Identity in a Changing Culture: Popular Expressions of Culture Conflict along the Lower Rio Grande Border," in *Views across the Border: The United States and Mexico*, ed. S. R. Ross (Albuquerque: University of New Mexico Press, 1978), 68–94; José E. Limón, "Agringado Joking in Texas-Mexican Society: Folklore and Differential Identity," *New Scholar* 6 (1977): 33–50. For a fuller list of their pertinent works, see Renato Rosaldo, "Chicano Studies, 1970–1984," *Annual Review of Anthropology* 14 (1985): 405–27.

5   See José Limón, "The Return of the Mexican Ballad: Americo Paredes and His Anthropological Text as Persuasive Political Performance," SCCR Working Paper no. 16 (Stanford Center for Chicano Research, 1986). See also José E. Limón, "Americo Paredes: A Man from the Border," *Revista Chicano-Riquefia* 8 (1980): 1–5. The intensity of anti-Mexican prejudice among Anglo-Texans in the late 1950s appeared to call for a male hero capable of agonistic combat. One should add that the reputation of south Texan Anglo-American prejudice against Mexicans remains legendary, at least among its recipients.

6   For a less idealized view of primordial south Texas Mexican society, see David Montejano, *Anglos and Mexicans in the Making of Texas, 1836–1986* (Austin: University of Texas Press, 1987).

7   This reflexive comparison of Paredes's scholarly production with the deeds of the warrior hero deepens when one considers the beginning scholar's successful resistance to the University of Texas Press editor who initially refused to publish his manuscript unless he removed the critique of Walter Prescott Webb. See Limón, "The Return of the Mexican Ballad," 29.

8   José Limón compares the form of Paredes's narrative with the ballad form itself. See Limón, "The Return of the Mexican Ballad."

9   Mary Louise Pratt, "The Short Story: The Long and the Short of It," *Poetics* 10 (1981): 175–94.

10 Along with the story entitled "A House of My Own" (100), this passage invites comparison with Jean Briggs's retreat to "a tent of her own." The allusion to Virginia Woolf probably speaks for itself.

11 For an earlier reworking of the warrior hero from a woman's point of view, see Maxine Hong Kingston, *Warrior Woman: Memoirs of a Girlhood among Ghosts* (New York: Vintage Books, 1977).

Feminism on the Border:
From Gender Politics to Geopolitics

SONIA SALDÍVAR-HULL

Is it possible for Chicanas to consider ourselves part of this "sisterhood" called feminism? Can we assume that our specific interests and problems will be taken care of by our Marxist *compañeros*? In her essay, "Feminism, Marxism, Method, and the State," Catharine MacKinnon decrees that "[s]exuality is to feminism what work is to marxism: that which is most one's own yet most taken away" (1982, 515). MacKinnon argues that while we can draw parallels between Marxist and feminist methodologies, we must remember not to conflate these two "theories of power and its distribution" (1982, 516), that one theory must not be subsumed into the other. She continues:

> What if the claims of each theory are taken equally seriously, each on its own terms? Can two social processes be basic at once? Can two groups be subordinated in conflicting ways, or do they merely cross-cut? Can two theories, each of which purports to account for the same thing—power as such—be reconciled? Or, is there a connection between the fact that the few have ruled the many and the fact that those few have been men? (517)

But to the Chicana, a woman with a specific history under racial and sexual and class exploitation, it is essential that we further problematize the feminist/ Marxist discussion by adding the complication of race and ethnicity. Our feminist sisters and Marxist compañeros/as urge us to take care of gender and class issues first and race will naturally take care of itself. Even MacKinnon, as thorough as she is, constantly watching that she herself does not recreate a monolithic "woman," uses footnotes to qualify the difference between the white woman's and the black woman's situations. She claims to have checked her statements "to see if women's condition is shared, even when contexts or magnitudes differ" (520, note 7). If her check system fails, then "the statement is simply wrong and will have to be qualified or the aspiration (or the theory) abandoned" (520, note 7).

My project does not suggest that we abandon the aspiration nor the theory. It does insist, however, that our white feminist "sisters" recognize their own blind spots. When MacKinnon uses the black woman as her sign for all dispossessed women, we see the extent to which Chicanas, Asian-American, Native American, or Puerto Rican women, for example, have been rendered invisible in a discourse whose explicit agenda is to expose ideological erasure. Chicana readings of color *blindness* instead of color consciousness in "politically correct" feminist essays indicate the extent to which the issues of race and ethnicity are ignored in feminist and Marxist theories. Theorists such as Rosaura Sánchez, Alma Gómez, Cherríe Moraga, Mariana Romo-Carmona, Gloria Anzaldúa, and Helena María Viramontes, working collectively as in *Cuentos* (Gómez, Moraga, and Romo-Carmona 1983) and individually as in *Borderlands* (Anzaldúa 1987), insist on illuminating the complications and intersections of the multiple systems of exploitation: capitalism, patriarchy, and white supremacy.

As Chicanas making our works public—publishing in marginalized journals and small, underfinanced presses and taking part in conferences and workshops—we realize that the "sisterhood" called feminism professes an ideology that at times comes dangerously close to the phallocentric ideologies of the white male power structure against which feminists struggle. In her essay, "Ethnicity, Ideology, and Academia," Rosaura Sánchez reminds us of the ideological strategies that the dominant culture manipulates in order to mystify "the relation between minority cultures and the dominant culture" (1987, 80). She points out that U.S. cultural imperialism extends beyond the geopolitical borders of the country, "but being affected, influenced, and exploited by a culture is one thing and sharing fully in that culture is another" (1987, 81). If we extend the analogy to feminism and the totalizing concept of sisterhood, we begin to understand how the specific interests of Anglo-American and other European feminists tend to erase the existence of Chicana, Puerto Rican, Native American, Asian-American, and other Third World feminisms. Indeed, feminism affects and influences Chicana writers and critics, but feminism as practiced by women of the hegemonic culture oppresses and exploits the Chicana in both subtle and obvious ways.

When white feminists begin to categorize the different types of feminisms, we in turn can begin to trace the muting of issues of race and ethnicity under other feminist priorities. Elaine Showalter in *A Literature of Their Own* charts the "stages" of writing by women into the categories of "feminine, feminist, and female" (1977, 13). She first establishes that *all* "literary subcultures, such as black, Jewish, Canadian, Anglo-Indian, or even American," go through phases of imitation, internalization, protest, and finally self-discovery (1977, 13). In addition to the misrepresentation of what "literary subcultures" write, Showalter creates an ethnocentric, Eurocentric, middle-class history of women's writing.

Her penchant for creating literary history, however, does not stop with British women. In "The Feminist Critical Revolution," she again maps out "phases," this time of feminist criticism (1985). Feminist criticism, in Showalter's program, progresses from critiques of sexist texts by men, to the rediscovery of the female literary tradition, then finally, and presumably most advanced, to the revision of literary theories to take into account women's own interpretations, a type of essentialism that assumes the universality of Woman's experience. When we look at a Chicana literary project like Helena María Viramontes's "The Cariboo Cafe" (1985), published at the same historical moment as Showalter's essay, however, we can see how her model does not contain Chicana writers or our agendas.

Liberal, Anglo-American feminists are not alone in the recreation and representation (colonization) of women's literary history. In "Women's Time" (1981) Julia Kristeva also defines the phases of feminism. Sounding alarmingly like a version of racist anthropologist Lewis Henry Morgan's (1877) categories of savagery, barbarism, and civilization, which structure the evolution of societies, Kristeva sets up her own hierarchies. The most "primitive" would be the position that women in the United States would call liberal feminism. While not denying the political importance of this phase, the struggle for universal suffrage, equal pay for equal work, abortion rights, and so on, Kristeva nonetheless sees the limits of this ahistorical, universalist, globalizing stage. Next on the evolutionary scale is the radical feminist phase, a reductive, essentialist feminism where women "demand recognition of an irreducible identity, without equal in opposite sex and, as such, exploded, plural, fluid" (1981, 19). A mixture of these two feminisms, Kristeva explains, constitutes the dominant European feminism. For Kristeva it is the final "signifying space" that she privileges. Sounding extremely premature in her optimism that there has been a real change in sexist institutions of power, she is ready to abandon "the very dichotomy man/woman as an opposition between two rival entities" (1981, 33).

This dichotomy, she claims, belongs to the metaphysical. "What can 'identity,' even 'sexual identity,' mean in a new theoretical and scientific space where the very notion of identity is challenged?" (1981, 33–35).

While the first three categories Kristeva outlines are defined politically, the category she advocates for herself is dangerously apolitical as well as ahistorical. Even if we accept that Kristeva specifies European feminisms, her own category assumes a universalist privilege. Nowhere in Kristeva's essay do we get a sense that she even considers women of color in her theories.

Toril Moi, in a text that unfortunately is beginning to be used as the textbook for introductory feminist theory courses, polarizes Anglo-American feminism against European feminism. She goes to great lengths to critique various Anglo-American feminists, often citing that they have not gone far enough in their politics: "The central paradox of Anglo-American feminist criticism is thus that despite its often strong, explicit political engagement, it is *in the end* not quite political enough; not in the sense that it fails to go *far* enough along the political spectrum, but in the sense that its radical analysis of sexual politics still remains entangled with depoliticizing theoretical paradigms" (1985, 87–88). Only one paragraph earlier, however, Moi has just issued an apologia for omitting "black or lesbian (or black-lesbian) feminist criticism in America" (1985, 87). Not only does she assume that she can conflate the concerns of all women of color in the United States as "black" or "lesbian" or a reductionist combination of the two, but she continues to show her bias against non-European feminist theory by stating that "*in so far as textual theory is concerned* there is no discernible difference between these three fields [Anglo-American, black, and lesbian criticism]" (1985, 86). After homogenizing all women of color as black and/or lesbian, and doing it all in a single paragraph, Moi takes this opportunity to further chastise Anglo-American, heterosexual, middle-class women who have made their own concerns universal. Moi's own neglect of race or ethnic specificity in the United States mirrors the way that white supremacy institutes its racist ideology. Clearly, Chicana feminists cannot look to their Eurocentric "sister" for discussions of our specific positions.

In our search for a feminist critical discourse that adequately takes into account our position as women under multiple oppressions we must turn to our own "organic intellectuals." But because our work has been ignored by the men and women in charge of the modes of cultural production, we must be innovative in our search. Hegemony has so constructed the idea of method and theory that often we cannot recognize anything that is different from what the dominant discourse constructs. We have to look in nontraditional places for our theories: in the prefaces to anthologies, in the interstices of autobiographies, in our cultural artifacts, our *cuentos*, and if we are fortunate to have access to a good library, in the essays published in marginalized journals not widely distributed by the dominant institutions. While Chicana academics do publish feminist essays in journals such as *Crítica*, *The Americas Review* (formerly *Revista Chicano-Riqueña*), and *Third Woman*, I will focus on one specific type of Chicana feminism that deconstructs the borders erected by Eurocentric feminism.

The prefatory *testimonio* to *Cuentos: Stories by Latinas* (1983)—collectively written by the editors Alma Gómez, Cherríe Moraga, and Mariana Romo-Carmona—offers such a site of radical Chicana and Latina theory. The editors identify themselves as "U.S. Third World women," writers who want to break the tradition of silence imposed upon them by the pressures of the dominant culture which works against the viability of an oral tradition. The realities of women of color under capitalism in the United States urge the Latina woman to write. The material realities of life in the urban barrio or ghetto cannot sustain, in the authors' words, "a tradition which relies so heavily on close family networks and [is] dependent upon generations of people living in the same town or barrio" (1983, vii).

The Gómez, Moraga, and Romo-Carmona project explodes all of Showalter's assumptions about women's writing. As women whose daily existence confronts institutionalized racism, class exploitation, sexism, and homophobia, the U.S. Third World woman does not enjoy the luxury to privilege one oppression over another. While recognizing that Latinos are not a homogeneous group, the editors acknowledge that "as Latinas in the U.S., our experience is different [from that of white people]. Because living here means throwing in our lot with other people of color" (1983, x). Unlike Anglo-American and European feminists, Gómez, Moraga, and Romo-Carmona reject Eurocentrism and "claim 'la mezcla,' la mestiza, regardless of each author's degree of indio, africano, or european blood" (1983, x).

While Showalter's model insists that the first stage of feminist criticism looks back to find a literary tradition, the collaborators of *Cuentos* believe that in order to forge a new affiliation among working-class people of color in the United States who share a kinship of exploitation, looking to a romanticized past is a luxury in which we cannot indulge. Instead, the stories they present are tied to the specific historical imperatives of the woman of color.

By the time Cherríe Moraga and Gloria Anzaldúa each writes her own foreword to the second edition of their breakthrough anthology, *This Bridge Called My Back* (1983), their feminism on the border, or bridge feminism, can issue a full-fledged manifesto for their brand of radical feminism. Moraga also begins to bridge the chasm between radical women and oppressed men, acknowledging that if the volume were written in 1983 rather than in the original 1979, "it would speak much more directly now to the relations between women and men of color, both gay and heterosexual" (Moraga, foreword to the second edi-

tion, n.p.). In the four years between editions she envisions a more internationalist *Bridge* that would affirm the connections between U.S. people of color and
other "refugees of a world on fire."

As Moraga elaborates her feminist agenda, the many ways in which this
feminism differs from the Showalter, Moi, and Kristeva versions of feminism
become clear. The Chicana feminist does not present "signifying spaces," but
material geopolitical issues that redirect feminist discourse. No longer limiting
the feminist agenda to issues of race, class, ethnicity, and sexual orientation,
Moraga expresses solidarity with the Third World people struggling against the
hegemony of the United States. The issues that Moraga presents in 1983 remain
urgent in 1988:

> The U.S. is training troops in Honduras to overthrow the Nicaraguan
> people's government.
> Human rights violations . . . on a massive scale in Guatemala and El Sal-
> vador (and as in this country those most hard-hit are often the indig-
> enous peoples of those lands).
> Pinochet escalates political repression in Chile.
> The U.S. invades Grenada.
> Apartheid continues to bleed South Africa.
> Thousands of unarmed people are slaughtered in Beirut by Christian mi-
> litia men and Israeli soldiers.
> Aquino is assassinated by the Philippine government.
> And the U.S.? The Reagan administration daily drains us of nearly every
> political gain made by the feminist, Third World, and anti-war work
> of the late 60's and early 70's. (Moraga, foreword to the second edi-
> tion, n.p.)

In the same way that we must break with traditional (hegemonic) concepts of genre to read Chicana feminist theory, working-class women of color
in other Third World countries articulate their feminisms in nontraditional
ways and forms. The Chicana feminist acknowledges the often vast historical,
class, racial, and ethnic differences among women living on the border, but the
nature of hegemony practiced by the united powers of patriarchy, capitalism,
imperialism, and white supremacy promotes an illusion of an irreconcilable
split between feminists confined within national borders. We must examine
and question the First versus Third World dichotomy before we accept the opposition as an inevitable fissure that separates women politically committed in
different ways from any common cause.

In her testimony, *Let Me Speak* (1978), Bolivian activist Domitila Barrios de
Chungara acknowledges the separation between "First" and "Third World

feminists: "Our position is not like the feminists' position. We think our liberation consists primarily in our country being freed forever from the yoke of imperialism and we want a worker like us to be in power and that the laws, education, everything, be controlled by this person. Then, yes, we'll have better conditions for reaching a complete liberation, including a liberation as women" (Barrios 1978, 41). Her statement, however, is problematized by her occasion for speaking. As a participant at the UN-sponsored International Year of the Woman Conference held in Mexico City in 1975, Barrios witnessed co-optation of "feminism" by governments which use women and women's issues to promote their own political agendas. Barrios observed Imelda Marcos, Princess Ashraf Pahlevi, and Jihan Sadat as some of the conference's "official" Third World representatives. We begin to reformulate the dichotomy when we no longer choose to see these representatives as "Third World feminists," but as agents of their respective governments: agents of patriarchy, capitalism, and imperialism. Suddenly the First World/Third World dichotomy emerges as the arena where the split between the ruling class and the working class, between those in power and the disenfranchised, is exposed.

When Barrios disassociates herself from "feminism," she means feminism as defined by women and men of the dominant class. In the paragraph immediately following the one cited above, Barrios speaks as a working-class, socialist-feminist, affiliating herself with border feminists like Moraga and Anzaldúa. Unlike feminists whose political considerations must take into account their positions in an academic institution, Moraga, Anzaldúa, and Barrios consider themselves community activists first and, in the case of Moraga and Anzaldúa, academics second. Indeed, the tension between academic and community pressures erupts in Anzaldúa's own text, *Borderlands/La Frontera* (1987), in a mixture of autobiography, poetry, identity politics, and academic footnotes.

Barrios, for her part, speaks as the union organizer of the Bolivian tin miner's wives, the Housewife Committee of Siglo XX. "For us," she asserts:

> The important thing is the participation of the compañero and the compañera together . . . if women continue only to worry about the house and remain ignorant of the other parts of our reality, we'll never have citizens who'll be able to lead our country. . . . And if we think of the central role played by women as the mothers who have to forge future citizens, then, if they aren't prepared they'll only forge mediocre citizens who are easily manipulated by the capitalist, by the boss. (1978, 41)

While she echoes the rhetorical strategy of the nineteenth-century U.S. feminist Margaret Fuller (1845), who also argued that women be given equal education in order to teach the children, what to Fuller may have been a conscious rhetorical strategy is to Barrios a cultural imperative as a working-class woman in Bolivia.

If Barrios's point of reference is that of a heterosexual woman who does not question woman's role as mother, we must remember her historical context as a working-class woman in Bolivia, the poorest country in South America. History forces her to accept her position as primary nurturer, as the one who will teach the children about the struggle. History, however, also forces her to act in untraditional ways that ultimately place her in the middle of social and political involvement and in the hands of the Bolivian torturers. Considering the historical and economic realities of Barrios's position as a Bolivian woman, her own discourse echoes Moraga's internationalist agenda:

> We know there's a long struggle ahead, but that's what we're all about. And we aren't alone. How many peoples are in the same struggle! And, why not say it? Every people needs the solidarity of others, like us, because our fight is big. So we have to practice proletarian internationalism that many people have sung about, and many countries have followed. Many other countries suffer persecutions, outrages, murders, massacres, like Bolivia. (1978, 42)

While the publication date of Showalter's *A Literature of Their Own* (1977) coincides with Barrios's experiences at the Woman's Year Conference in 1975, the two women's concerns and contexts allow for little else in common. Likewise, Kristeva's deconstruction of the metaphysical constitution of masculine and feminine offer few solutions to the issues that concern women like Barrios and the other border feminists. Moi's admitted ignorance of the existence of any other marginalized women in the United States speaks for itself. MacKinnon's pledge to accept her premises as "simply wrong" if they do not apply to racial complications at least places her feminism closer to that of Barrios, Anzaldúa, Moraga, Gómez, and Romo-Carmona.

But what is "border feminism," which I have begun to use to specify as a type of Chicana feminism? Is it a new discursive practice or methodology that would legitimize the specificity of Chicana/black/lesbian . . . feminisms in Moi's eyes? Or is it simply a rearticulation of Anglo-American feminism with the added twist of color consciousness?

In *Borderlands/La Frontera* (1987) Gloria Anzaldúa examines the dynamics of race, class, gender, and sexual orientation. Whereas Barrios's historical context does not permit her to recognize lesbian issues as valid political concerns, women like Anzaldúa insist on complicating what at first appear as simple, clear-cut issues. For Anzaldúa feminism emerges as the force that gives voice to her origins as "the new *mestiza*." This "new *mestiza*" is a woman alienated from her own, often homophobic culture, as well as from the hegemonic culture. She envisions the new *mestiza* "caught between *los intersticios*, the spaces between the different worlds she inhabits" (1987, 20). If compañeras like Barrios cannot allow themselves the luxury of bourgeois feminism, a possible alternative is this "bridge feminism" that deconstructs geopolitical boundaries. Anzaldúa's "feminism on the border" begins to do just that. It is a feminism that exists in a borderland not limited to geographic space, a feminism that resides in a space not acknowledged by hegemonic culture. Its inhabitants are what Anzaldúa calls "*Los atravesados* . . . : squint-eyed, the perverse, the queer, the troublesome, the mongrel, the mulato, the half-breed, the half-dead; in short, those who cross over, pass over, or go through the confines of the 'normal'" (1987, 3). By invoking racist, homophobic epithets, Anzaldúa explodes the power that the dominant culture holds over what is "normal" or acceptable.

Whereas the earlier works of women like Angela de Hoyos articulate Tejana feminist issues, Anzaldúa makes the leap from the history of colonization by the United States to the history of colonization as a *mestiza*, a Native American woman. And although some Chicana critics reject the internal colony model because, as María Linda Apodaca states, "when the land was conquered the Mexican population in the Southwest was small given the total land mass" (1986, 110), the specific history of the Tejano/Tejana urges us to remember that there is not one single Chicano/Chicana experience in the United States. Apodaca's assumptions neglect to acknowledge historical specificity of the Tejanas/Tejanos who were forced to live under a reign of terror in post–1845 Texas.

In the poem "Hermano," Angela de Hoyos taunts the Anglo usurper by reminding him of his own immigrant status. He is told to "scare up your little 'Flor de Mayo'—/ so *we* can all sail back / to where we came from" (1975, 13, emphasis added). While De Hoyos identifies with her European heritage, the Pinta, the Niña, and the Santa María of the Spanish conquerors, Anzaldúa, in opposition, insists on identifying with the indigenous Indian tribes as well as with the African slaves who mixed with the conquerors resulting in the *mestizo*. She bases her political, feminist position on the Chicana's history within multiple cultures: indigenous Mexican, African, and always "grounded on the Indian woman's history of resistance" (1987, 21).

Anzaldúa's text is itself a *mestizaje*: a postmodernist mixture of autobiography, historical document, and poetry collection. Like the people whose lives it chronicles, *Borderlands* resists genre boundaries as well as geopolitical borders. The text's opening epigraph is an excerpt from a song by the *norteño* conjunto band Los Tigres del Norte. But if Anzaldúa's historical ties are closer to the *corrido* tradition than to the historical imperatives of postmodern theory, hers is the new *corrido* of the *mestiza* with a political analysis of what it means to live as a woman in a literal and figurative Borderland. She tells us that "The U.S.-Mexican border *es una herida abierta* (is an open wound) where the Third World grates against the first and bleeds. And before a scab forms it hemorrhages again, the lifeblood of two worlds merging to form a third country—a border culture" (3). Through issues of gender politics Anzaldúa locates personal history within a history of the border people. Legitimacy belongs to the Anglo hegemony, the indigenous population is nothing more than an aberrant species. To the white power structure the *mojado* (wetback) is the same as the *mexicano de este lado* (Mexican from the U.S. side). As she chronicles the history of the new *mestiza*, Anzaldúa explores issues of gender and sexual orientation that Chicano historians like David Montejano, Arnoldo De León, and Rodolfo Acuña have not adequately addressed. Presenting this other history of Texas that Anglo-Texans like J. Frank Dobie (1936) and Walter Prescott Webb (1935) never mention, Anzaldúa further merges autobiography with historical document. Her family history becomes the history of the Chicana/o experience in south Texas after colonization and occupation by U.S. forces. Those who dared resist were lynched by the Texas Rangers. "My grandmother," Anzaldúa informs us, "lost all her cattle / they stole her land" (8). The history of dispossession is transmitted orally from one generation to the next; Anzaldúa's mother tells the story of *her* widowed mother who was cheated by the Anglo usurper: "A smart *gabacho* lawyer took the land away *mamá* hadn't paid taxes. No *hablaba inglés*, she didn't know how to ask for time to raise the money" (8).

Autobiography for the new *mestiza is* the history of the colonization of indigenous Southwestern peoples by Anglo-American imperialists intent on their manifest destiny. Texas history, in Anzaldúa's revision, is incomplete without the presentation of the Mexican woman who dares to cross the border. She is the one who is the most easily exploited, physically as well as sexually. The *coyote* can enslave her after raping her. If she is lucky enough to make it to the U.S. side, she can look forward to laboring as a maid "for as little as $15 dollars a week" (12).

Once she establishes a working definition of the *mestizo* border culture with which she identifies, Anzaldúa begins her internal critique of that world. Because she is so much a part of this world, she can penetrate its inner dynamics and understand the oppressions that it in turn uses to control women within the culture. When Anzaldúa tells us how she rebelled, we can see the intense power that the Chicano culture holds over women: "*Repele, Hable pa' 'tras. Fuí muy hocicona. Era indiferente a muchos valores de mi cultura. No me deje de los hombres. No fuí buena ni obediente*" (I argued. I talked back. I was quite a bigmouth. I was indifferent to many of my culture's values. I did not let the men push me around. I was not good nor obedient) (15, my translation). The ideal woman for the people of the borderland is one who stands behind her man in silence and passivity. If she refuses her female role as housekeeper, she is considered "lazy." To study, read, paint, write are not legitimate choices for the *mestiza*. Her testimony rings true for many Chicanas who struggle against their gender indoctrination. That her history exists for us to study is a testament to her resistance: "Every bit of self-faith I'd painstakingly gathered took a beating daily. Nothing in my culture approved of me. Había agarrado malos pasos [I had taken the wrong path]. Something was 'wrong' with me. *Estaba más allá de la tradición* [I was beyond the tradition]" (16, my translation).

"Cultural tyranny" for the Chicana feminist imposes an additional hegemonic power against which she must struggle. She must not only contend with the racism of the dominant Anglo-American restraints, she must also resist the oppressive yoke of the sexist Chicano culture:

> Culture is made by those in power—men. Males make the rules and laws; women transmit them. How many times have I heard mothers and mothers-in-law tell their sons to beat their wives for not obeying them, for being *hociconas* (big mouths), for being *callejeras* (going to visit and gossip with neighbors), for expecting their husbands to help with the rearing of children and the housework, for wanting to be something other than housewives? (16)

Anzaldúa's gender politics are always aware of the women who are agents of the patriarchy.

In addition, Anzaldúa understands that for the new *mestiza* an education is imperative for liberation. But the realities of living in a borderland, a muted culture in the midst of the hegemonic power of the United States, the chances are slim that a Chicana will survive the battle against the combined forces of a sexist Chicano culture and the racist power of the dominant culture. Furthermore, economic exploitation ensures that Chicanas stay in their place because "as working class people our chief activity is to put food in our mouths, a roof over our heads and clothes on our backs" (17).

Anzaldúa's project problematizes further still the traditions of Chicanismo, when, as a lesbian Chicana, she forces the homophobes of the Chicano community to see their prejudice. If the heterosexual Chicana is ostracized from her culture for transgressing its rules of behavior, for the Chicana lesbian "the ultimate rebellion she can make against her native culture is through her sexual behavior" (19). She makes the "choice to be queer" and as a result feels the ultimate exile from her homeland, cultural as well as geographic. She transforms the bourgeois concept of "safety" and "home" to concepts she can carry with her along with her political commitments. As a Chicana "totally immersed" in her culture, she can choose to reject the crippling aspects of traditions that oppress women and silence homosexual men and women. Her refusal to "glorify those aspects of my culture which have injured me and which have injured me in the name of protecting me" signals the agenda for the new *mestiza*, the border feminist (22). The border feminist that Anzaldúa presents is a woman comfortable with new affiliations that subvert old ways of being, rejecting the homophobic, sexist, racist, imperialist, and nationalist.

In addition to gender transgressions that Anzaldúa's new *mestiza* introduces, new subject matter for poetry is another "aberration" that the Chicana feminist presents. African Americanists from Ida B. Wells (1969) to Hazel Carby (1985) and Wahneema Lubiano (1987) have explored the terroristic method by which the dominant culture kept the black people under control: the law of the rope. Likewise, Chicanos, particularly in Texas, have lived under the threat of lynching. But while historian Arnoldo De León investigates lynching as an institutionalized threat against Tejanos, it takes Anzaldúa's poem, "We Call Them Greasers," to flesh out the ramifications of the lynch law to Chicanas. In the poem whose title pays tribute to De León's history, *They Called Them Greasers* (1983), the connection between the history of oppression of nineteenth-century African slaves and ex-slaves and nineteenth-century *mestizos*/Chicanos emerges. Narrated by the Anglo-American usurper, this example of what Barbara Harlow (1987) has called resistance poetry speaks of how Tejanos lost their lands and often their lives. The Anglo narrator assumes the role of deity as he forces the Tejanos to place their hats "over their hearts" and lower their eyes in his presence. He rejects their collective farming techniques, cultural remnants of indigenous tribal traditions of the *mestizo*. He sneers, "they didn't even own the land but shared it." The Tejano "troublemakers" who actually have "land grants and appeal to the courts" are called laughingstocks, "them not even knowing English" (134). For the Anglo-American imperialist literacy in Spanish or any other nonstatus language is by their definition illiteracy. The women, in particular, suffer an additional violence before they are murdered by the gringo.

While Chicano (male) historians have done much to expose the realities of violent acts against the Tejanos, they have, to a great extent, been reluctant to voice the perhaps unspeakable violence against Tejanas. Even Américo Paredes in his breakthrough text, *"With His Pistol in His Hand"* (1958), cannot articulate the violence that Gregorio Cortez's wife, Leonor Díaz Cortez, must have suffered in the four months that she spent in a Texas jail, incarcerated for her husband's alleged crime (87). During the Ranger's manhunt for Cortez, a Mexican woman is alleged to have given information to the sheriff leading to Cortez's capture. Paredes states: "The woman, whoever she was, at first refused to talk, but 'under pressure' told Glover where Cortez was going. . . . What sort of pressure Glover used, whether it was physical or psychological, there is no way of telling" (1958, 68). Precisely because "there is no way" for a male historian to tell the history of the Chicana, it takes Anzaldúa's voice to articulate the violence against nineteenth-century Tejanas. In "We Call Them Greasers" she finds the words that acknowledge the history of violence against the Tejana. This history includes rape as institutionalized strategy in the war to disempower Chicano men. While the Tejano is tied to a mesquite tree, the Chicano version of the African American hanging tree, the gringo rapes the Tejana.

> She lay under me whimpering.
> I plowed into her hard
> kept thrusting and thrusting
> felt him watching from the mesquite tree
> heard him keening like a wild animal
> in that instant I felt such contempt for her
> round face and beady black eyes like an Indian's.
> Afterwards I sat on her face until
> her arms stopped flailing,
> didn't want to waste a bullet on her.
> The boys wouldn't look me in the eyes.
> I walked up to where I had tied her man to the
> tree and spat in his face. Lynch him, I told the
> boys. (134–35)

Once the rapist gains total control over the Tejano through the violation of his woman, the rapist can feel only contempt for her. Within the hierarchy of powerlessness the woman occupies a position below the already inferior brown man. While De León chronicles how Anglo-American occupiers made their conquests and massacres more bearable by comparing their victims to animals, similarly, by emphasizing the *mestiza's* "Indian" features, the Anglo-American imperialist further relegates the Chicana to the savagery of the Indian (1983, 14–23). Anzaldúa's reluctance to condemn the passive observers, "the boys," in the poem is not because of a misguided loyalty to the gringo, but an implicit recognition of the power of the class structure even in nineteenth-century Texas where the rich land barons controlled all their workers, regardless of race or ethnicity.

In poems like "sus plumas el viento," "Cultures," and "sobre piedras con lagartijos," Anzaldúa reasserts her solidarity with the exploited men and women along the border. "El sonavabitche" protests the exploitation of undocumented farm workers in places like Muncie, Indiana. Her poetry exposes the methods by which unscrupulous farmers create a modern-day slave system. Hiring undocumented Mexican laborers to work their fields, they tip off the Immigration and Naturalization Service (INS) for a raid before payday.

The Chicano narrator expresses solidarity with his undocumented compañeros when he refuses to work for the *sonavabitche* who has used the INS tactic "three times since we've been coming here / *Sepa dios* [God knows] how many times in between. / Wets, free labor, *esclavos* [slaves]. / *Pobres jijos de la chingada* [Poor sons of whores]. / This is the last time we work for him / no matter how *fregados* [desperate] we are" (126–27, my translation).

Finally, it is in the poem "To live in the Borderlands Means You" that Anzaldúa sums up her definition of the new *mestiza*, the feminist on the border. She is one who "carries five races" on her back, not Hispanic, Indian, black, Spanish, or Anglo, but the mixture of the five which results in the *mestiza, mulata*. She's also "a new gender," "both woman and man, neither" (194). While not rejecting any part of herself, Anzaldúa's new *mestiza* becomes a survivor because of her ability to "live *sin fronteras* [without borders] / be a crossroads" (195).

While Anzaldúa transgresses aesthetic boundaries in her text, transgresses gender boundaries in her "choice" to be a lesbian, transgresses ethnicity and race in her formulation of the new *mestiza* combining Native American, Spanish, African, and even Anglo "blood" to form a *mestizaje*, her project is nonetheless articulated within the vital history of the Texas Chicana. If history is what forces Anzaldúa's escape into what Jenny Bourne (1987) has called "identity politics" in her essay, "Homelands of the Mind," it is because the only history for the Chicana is the history of the *mestiza*'s colonization by both the Spanish conquerors and the Anglo-American imperialists in their conquest of south Texas. Once Anzaldúa establishes a history of the border people who "were jerked out by the roots, truncated, disemboweled, dispossessed, and separated from [their] identity and [their] history" (8), the Chicana feminist can turn to other concerns. Patricia Fernández-Kelly's *For We Are Sold, I and My People* (1983) presents a history of the *mestiza* laboring in the exploitative *maquiladora* (factory) system that Anzaldúa alludes to in her own work. In addition, Anzaldúa calls attention to the unwritten history of the *mestizas* in the *colonias* of south Texas and the border cities like El Paso and Ciudad Juárez, homelands of contemporary victims of U.S. multinational corporations. These people are being poisoned by the water they are forced to store in chemical drums that once held carcinogens (*Austin American Statesman*, 27 March 1988).

The Chicana feminist's theory and methodology are ideological analysis, materialist, historical research, as well as race, class, and gender analysis. It is never an ahistorical "politics of equal oppressions" (Bourne 1987, 16) because Chicana feminism develops from an awareness of specific material experience of the historical moment. Unlike the feminism of sisterhood, "feminism which is separatist, individualistic and inward-looking" (Bourne 1987, 2), Chicana feminists look "inward" in moments of self-exploration and see themselves as daughters of non-Western, indigenous tribes. Anzaldúa's feminist discourse leads her to look inward only for a deeper understanding of a larger erased history.

Anzaldúa's text can be seen as a bridge that forms a continuum between her collaboration with Moraga in *This Bridge Called My Back* (1983) and Helena María Viramontes's "The Cariboo Cafe" in her collection, *The Moths and Other Stories* (1985). One of the Chicana contributors to the *Cuentos* anthology (Gómez, Moraga, and Romo-Carmona 1983), Viramontes continues the internationalist connection with women in Latin America and other Third World countries. If Anzaldúa's antihegemonic strategy is to recreate border history for the *mestiza*, in "The Cariboo Cafe" Viramontes's strategy is to expose the extent of the political power of the United States. Viramontes presents the oppression of the reserve army of laborers that the United States creates and then designates as "other," the "illegal" immigrants. In this story Viramontes shows us that we *can* combine feminism with race and class consciousness, even if we recognize the fallacies of an all-encompassing "sisterhood." In this Chicana political discourse Viramontes commits herself to a transnational solidarity with other working-class people who like all nonindigenous tribes are immigrants to the United States. In *The Political Unconscious* Fredric Jameson has said that "history is what hurts" (1981, 102). For the most recent wave of brown immigrants who come to the United States in search of political freedom, the pain intensifies when they realize that for the brown, black, and Asian races, the suppressed history of the United States is the history of exploitation as well as racism.

"They arrived in the secrecy of night, as displaced people often do, stopping over for a week, a month, eventually staying a lifetime" (Viramontes 1985, 61). So Viramontes begins her history of the displaced immigrants of the eighties. They are the "illegal aliens," the racist label by which the U.S. government designates an exploited subculture it has created. As James Cockcroft asks: "if so many employers and all consumers depend so heavily on these people, then why is it that they are viewed as a "problem" or as "illegals"? Human beings can *do* illegal things, but can a human being actually *be* illegal? Moreover, since when under capitalism is it an illegal act to sell one's labor power for a low wage to an employer engaged in a socially approved business?" (Cockcroft 1986, 64).

In "The Cariboo Cafe" Viramontes interweaves narrative voices to give the history of the undocumented worker in the United States. Viramontes gives the story of the killing of an undocumented female worker wider political significance in the heteroglossic versions (see Bakhtin 1981, 263) of life at the borders, at the periphery of North American society.

The Cariboo Cafe is the center around which Viramontes constructs her revision of history. The cafe, a sleazy diner on the wrong side of the tracks, attracts the outcasts of late capitalism. Burned-out drug addicts, prostitutes, and undocumented workers frequent the place run by a petty bourgeois man who becomes the mouthpiece of the dominant society. While his speech places him in the working class, he spouts the ideology of the dominant class. What to him are unexamined platitudes, "family gotta be together" (73), are for outsiders like the undocumented workers ideologically charged, an ideology that Viramontes resists and unmasks in her tale. Viramontes transforms this cynical short-order cook with a grease-stained apron into a grotesque Uncle Sam, a living contradiction of core and periphery. The great irony here is that this man is almost as much a victim of the capitalist system as are the undocumented workers. If the new immigrants are exploited by capital as they labor in the sweatshops of the garment warehouses, this Anglo-American has been similarly victimized by the imperialistic urges of a U.S. government that led the country into a war in Southeast Asia. We learn that the man's only son is dead; it still haunts him that he will never know "what part of Vietnam JoJo is all crumbled up in" (73).

The owner of what the workers call the "zero zero place" is able to voice the dominant ideology not because of a class privilege, but because of his privilege as a white man. It is here that Viramontes exposes how the hegemonic forces of race, class, and gender intersect and collide. When she gives equal weight to the voices of the young daughter of undocumented workers and to a Salvadoran political refugee, Viramontes gives voice to the counterhegemonic.

The first voice we hear in the story is that of Sonya; we see the urban landscape through her eyes. Both her parents work so that the family may one day have a "toilet [of] one's own." For the feminist reader this turn of phrase resonates of Virginia Woolf's desire for financial independence for the woman writer, but it also reminds us of the vast difference between the concerns of bourgeois feminists and border feminists. Sonya is a latchkey child whose duties as a female include caring for her younger brother, Macky. The children lose the key to their apartment and get lost trying to find their way to safety. A premise for survival in hostile territory for these children is never to trust the police; the "polie" is "La Migra in disguise and thus should always be avoided" (61). Lost, the children see "a room with a yellow glow, like a beacon light at the end of a dark sea" which Sonya thinks will be a sanctuary from the alleys and the dead ends of the urban barrio. Ironically, the beacon is the "zero, zero place" (64).

In the "double zero cafe" we hear the story of the children's fate in flashback. The cafe owner tells his version as if he were on trial. Indeed, Viramontes *is* putting U.S. immigration policies and ideology on trial. The man constantly presents himself as honest, yet in the same breath he admits to lacing his hamburgers with something that is "not pure beef." He thinks that he redeems himself when he proclaims, at least "it ain't dog-meat" (64). Then he remembers the basic contradiction of the "American" ideal: "It never pays to be honest." He continues his version of how it came to be that a Salvadoran refugee was killed in his cafe. When he first saw "that woman," he immediately labeled her as Other: "Already I know that she's bad news because she looks street to me. Round face, burnt toast color, black hair. . . . Weirdo" (65). Through his voice we hear the articulation of the dominant race's rationale for excluding brown races from integration into the U.S. society. Because immigrants of different skin color belie the melting-pot myth, it is harder for them to be accepted in the same way that European emigrants have been accepted in the history of U.S. colonization. When the woman speaks Spanish to the children with her, he states: "Right off I know she's illegal, which explains why she looks like a weirdo" (66). Here Viramontes unmasks how the dominant marginalize on the basis of color and language.

Only when we get the third voice does Viramontes allow us to realize what has happened to the lost children of the first section. They have been taken by a Salvadoreña who mistakes Macky for her missing son. This woman is a modern day *llorona* (the wailing woman of *mestizo* folklore) who has fled her country after her own child was murdered by the right-wing, U.S.-backed government. The child is one of the countless *desaparecidos* in those countries whose dictators the U.S. government keeps in power.

The Salvadoreña tells her story and, indeed, becomes the modern-day wailing woman; in this version she represents all women who are victimized by conquering races and classes. The Salvadoreña represents all women "who come up from the depths of sorrow to search for their children; . . . [she] hear[s] the wailing of the women and know[s] it to be [her] own" (68–69). In his essay "On Language as Such and on the Language of Man," Walter Benjamin argued that the lament "is the most undifferentiated, impotent expression of language; it contains scarcely more than the sensuous breath" (1978, 329). Viramontes uses the lament motif in this story not only to expose the socially sanctioned, passive roles for women within the patriarchy, but to show the powerlessness of the victims of repressive governments, and thus, the lament contains much more than Benjamin would have it contain.

In her abjection the Salvadoreña believes Macky is her son. She cares for him and cannot understand why the cafe owner would call her act a kidnapping. For her, as for the children, the police here are no different from the police in the country she has fled. They will take her son away from her. She resists arrest and throws boiling coffee at the man pointing a gun at her forehead. With the Salvadoreña's final act of resistance Viramontes explodes the boundaries of family, of safety, and of home.

From Anzaldúa's important revision of Texas history to the theoretical proclamations by the collective voices of Moraga, Gómez, and Romo-Carmona to Viramontes's questioning the constitution of family, Chicana feminism challenges boundaries defined by the hegemony. When Eurocentric, liberal feminists define "theory" and "methodology," they become part of the hegemonic power that constructs the idea of "method" and "theory"; they cannot recognize racial or ethnic difference. Chicana feminism, both in its theory and method, is tied to the material world. When feminist anthologizers like Toril Moi cannot recognize Chicana theory, it is because Chicanas ask different questions which in turn ask for a reconstruction of the very premises of "theory." Because the history of the Chicana experience in the United States defines our particular *mestizaje* of feminism, our theory cannot be a replicate of white feminism nor can it be only an academic abstraction. The Chicana feminist looks to her history (to paraphrase Bourne's plea for feminist praxis) to learn how to transform the present. For the Chicana feminist it is through our affiliation with the struggles of other Third World people that we find our theories and our methods.

NOTE

This essay originally appeared in José David Saldívar and Hector Calderon, eds., *Criticism in the Borderlands*, 203-20 (Durham: Duke University Press, 1991).

REFERENCES

Anzaldúa, Gloria. 1987. *Borderlands/La Frontera: The New Mestiza*. San Francisco: Spinsters/Aunt Lute.

Apodaca, María Linda. 1986. "A Double Edge Sword: Hispanas and Liberal Feminism." *Crítica* 1, no. 3:96-114.

Bakhtin, M. M. 1981. *The Dialogic Imagination: Four Essays*. Edited by Michael Holquist. Translated by Caryl Emerson and Michael Holquist. Austin: University of Texas Press.

Barrios de Chungara, Domintila. 1978. *Let Me Speak! Testimony of Domitila, a Woman of the Bolivian Mines*. With Moema Viezzer. New York: Monthly Review Press.

Benjamin, Walter. 1978. "On Language as Such and on the Language of Man." In *Reflections: Essays, Aphorisms, Autobiographical Writings*, ed. Peter Demetz, 314-32. New York: Harcourt Brace Jovanovich.

Bourne, Jenny. 1987. "Homelands of the Mind: Jewish Feminism and Identity Politics." *Race and Class* 29, no. 1:1-24.

Carby, Hazel V. 1985. "'On the Threshold of Woman's Era': Lynching, Empire and Sexuality in Black Feminist Theory." *Critical Inquiry* 12:262-77.

Cockcroft, James D. 1986. *Outlaws in the Promised Land: Mexican Immigrant Workers and America's Future*. New York: Grove Press.

De León, Arnoldo. 1983. *They Called Them Greasers: Anglo Attitudes toward Mexicans in Texas, 1821-1900*. Austin: University of Texas Press.

Dobie, J. Frank. 1936. *The Flavor of Texas*. Dallas: Dealy and Lowe.

Fernández-Kelly, María Patricia. 1983. *For We Are Sold, I and My People: Women and Industry in Mexico's Frontier*. Albany: State University of New York Press.

Fuller, [Sarah] Margaret [marchesa d'Ossoli]. [1845] 1971. *Woman in the Nineteenth Century*. New York: Greely & McElrath; New York: W. W. Norton.

Gómez, Alma, Cherríe Moraga, and Mariana Romo-Carmona, eds. 1983. *Cuentos: Stories by Latinas*. New York: Kitchen Table: Women of Color Press.

Harlow, Barbara. 1987. *Resistance Literature*. New York: Methuen.

Jameson, Fredric. 1981. *The Political Unconscious: Narrative as a Socially Symbolic Act*. Ithaca: Cornell University Press.

Kristeva, Julia. 1981. "Women's Time." *Signs* 7, no. 1:13–35.

Lubiano, Wahneema. 1987. "The Harlem Renaissance and the Roots of Afro-American Literary Modernism." In *Messing with the Machine: Four Afro-American Novels and the Nexus of Vernacular, Historical Constraint, and Narrative Strategy*, 44–87. PhD diss., Stanford University, Stanford, Calif.

MacKinnon, Catherine. 1982. "Feminism, Marxism, Method and the State: An Agenda for Theory." *Signs* 7, no. 3:515–44.

Moi, Toril. 1985. *Sexual/Textual Politics: Feminist Literary Theory*. London: Methuen.

Moraga, Cherríe, and Gloria Anzaldúa. 1983. *This Bridge Called My Back: Writings by Radical Women of Color*. New York: Kitchen Table: Women of Color Press.

Morgan, Lewis Henry. [1877] 1963. *Ancient Society or, Researches in the Line of Human Progress from Savagery through Barbarism to Civilization*. New York: H. Holt; ed. Eleanor Burke Leacock. Rev. ed. Cleveland: World Publishing.

Paredes, Américo. 1958. *"With His Pistol in His Hand": A Border Ballad and Its Hero*. Austin: University of Texas Press.

Sánchez, Rosaura. 1977. "The Chicana Labor Force." In *Essays on La Mujer*, ed. Rosaura Sánchez and Rosa Marínez Cruz, 3–15. Los Angeles: Chicano Studies Center, UCLA.

Sánchez, Rosaura. 1987. "Ethnicity, Ideology and Academia." *Americas Review* 15, no. 1:80–88.

Showalter, Elaine. 1977. *A Literature of Their Own: British Women Novelists from Bronte to Lessing*. Princeton: Princeton University Press.

Showalter, Elaine. 1985. "The Feminist Critical Revolution." In *The New Feminist Criticism: Essays on Women, Literature and Theory*, ed. Elaine Showalter, 3–17. New York: Pantheon Books.

Viramontes, Helena María. 1985. *The Moths and Other Stories*. Houston: Arte Público Press.

Webb, Walter Prescott. 1935. *The Texas Rangers: A Century of Frontier Defense*. Boston: Houghton Mifflin.

Wells, Ida B. 1969. *On Lynching*. New York: Arno Press and New York Times.

Trans-migrations: Agency and Confinement at the Limits of Sovereignty

MARTHA BALAGUERA

Since the late twentieth century, Central Americans have headed north to Mexico and the United States, first as refugees of Cold War armed conflicts and then to escape gang violence, extreme poverty, extractive economies, and environmental degradation (García 2006; O'Neil 2016). Nowadays, a refugee crisis comparable to the Syrian context ignites the Americas, even as the militarized responses of both the US and Mexican governments have solidified a genuine detention-deportation regime (UNHCR 2014b; Suárez, Knippen, and Meyer 2016). As reports from the UN High Commissioner for Refugees (UNHCR) have noted, rising numbers of women and unaccompanied minors have crossed international borders in the region, fleeing for their lives (2014b, 2015). Increasingly, the presence of *chicas trans* on the run is apparent in the upsurge of asylum requests in both countries, and trans bodies tend to fill detention facilities, shelters, and the migrant trails across Mexico (UNHCR 2015; Cidón Kiernan, Hernández Flores, and Lucero 2017).[1]

While policy makers and journalists have been gradually compelled to attend to the specific needs of trans migrants and refugees, their reports are inherently descriptive and centered on the perspectives of nation-states and the international system of refugee rights. With a broader focus, feminist and queer scholars have made important contributions to the intersectional understanding of global migrations. Prominent research topics include sex work (Cheng 2010, 2012/2013; Shah 2014), transnational reproductive politics (Briggs 2012), and global care chains (Yeates 2009). In these areas of research, authors complicate the meaning of agency and oppression, and relate their analyses to questions of labor and economic exploitation. Scholars have also critically addressed the question of how migration policy has historically shaped national citizenship, whether through the exclusion of deviant sexualities and queer identities (Luibhéid 2002, 2013; Shah 2011) or by granting rights in ways that curtail the radical democratic potential of queer politics (Reddy 2011). Together, these works underscore how the disparities of the capitalist global political economy shape intersections of gender, sexuality, and migration, increasingly marked by the militarized policing of borders (Rosas 2012). In turn, these works interrogate "notions of Western superiority" and representations of third-world migrants and asylum-seekers as inherently victimized, backward, homophobic, or violent (Luibhéid 2002, 113–14). For even when states remove admission exclusions based on gender and sexuality, the trope of saving marginal others from oppressive societies through immigration policy and the recognition of the refugee condition becomes a form of "discursive" colonization that effaces the implication of Western imperial powers in processes of mass displacement around the world (Mohanty 1986, 333).

However, the embodied experiences of *chicas trans* in the context of mass migrations in the Americas, that is, the ways in which their displacement and confinement in motion unfold—and what that tells us about the changing nature of state sovereignty and contemporary regimes of government at the border and beyond—remain undertheorized. Although the field of transgender studies has sought to critically trans migration scholarship—that is, extending "queer studies' turn to the global" (Cotten 2012, 1)—there are few empirical analyses to date about the meaning of large-scale political phenomena grounded in *chicas trans*'s stories of migration. The US-Mexico border, to be precise, has long captured the imagination of feminist scholars across disciplinary fields.[2] Within transgender studies, Vek Lewis has written about the ways in which trans mobility is policed and foreclosed at the US-Mexico border, offering a reexamination of "the liberatory presumptions of border zones" that undermines the image of the borderlands as a geography relatively exempt from the closures of nation-states (Lewis 2012, 52–53). My approach resembles this line of inquiry, interrogating how trans mobility becomes an object of control at different sites. Yet rather than focusing on a border zone, I emphasize the process of transit across the Central America–Mexico–United States migration circuit.

In this essay, I reflect on the lived experiences of transit of three *chicas trans* I met during my fieldwork in Mexico within the shelter network that assists migrants and refugees from south to north. Here, transit denotes both the experiential state of finding oneself crossing Mexico en route to the United States and a space-time where questions about the nature of state power are productively explored through the intersectional analysis of gender, migration, and confinement. Thus, while feminist and queer analyses of migrations and the state have tended to privilege permanence over transience by focusing on places of settlement, I focus on the space-time of transit through an intersectional lens, shedding light on how trans migrant *chicas* undergo gender and geographical transitions that shape each other, revealing unanticipated meanings of home, refuge, mobility, freedom, and unfreedom.

While in transit, *chicas trans* are disproportionately targeted by the state and are often locked up in detention centers, jails, and prisons. However, as my ensuing analysis shows, what I call "confinement in motion" transcends the material conditions of these institutions and multiplies beyond state coercion. Uniquely intersectional, yet not singular, *chicas trans*'s experiences of confinement expose the workings of a carceral regime of sovereignty beyond the walls of the prison. Insofar as the requirements of global accumulation continuously set people in motion, mass migrations have become a paramount "defining issue . . . of the twentieth-first century" (Betts, quoted in Conlon and Hiemstra 2016, 1). Yet migratory flows have not remained untamed, undisciplined, but have been incorporated into contemporary global governance through confining practices and devices. As Eithne Luibhéid, citing Michel Foucault, has argued, the policing of borders becomes an opportunity to discipline and surveil women by tying them into the "'carceral archipelago' of modern society" (2002, xv). For *chicas trans* in transit, this tie transcends any contact with the state.

Natalia: Trans/transit/transition

Natalia agreed to give me an interview during the inauguration of the recently opened migrant shelter for unaccompanied minors in Mexico City after I heard her tell an audience of about fifty people that she was not in Mexico out of a desire to improve her life but because her own friends had banished her from the barrio back in Honduras.[3] Having left her home in the countryside at the age of eight after being violently shamed for her nonbinary gender by her own relatives, Natalia grew up on the streets of Tegucigalpa, first as a homeless child and later as a sex worker. Her friends were other urban dwellers of the red-light district where she lived. Many of them were young men, members of Mara Salvatrucha (MS13), one of the powerful gangs that were "exported" from

Los Angeles to Central America through large-scale deportations of "offending non-citizens" since the mid-1990s (Wolf 2014, 127). Because Natalia refused to sell drugs on their behalf at the brothel where she worked, MS13 gang members hounded and attempted to kill her.

When I interviewed Natalia the next day, she was lying on the floor of the still-unfurnished female bedroom. Although the shelter was not initially conceived as a closed facility, the day of the inauguration staff and volunteers saw the need for stricter rules about smoking, loitering, and begging on the street. Aggressions from neighbors who opposed the opening of the shelter had created tensions, and the most reasonable decision seemed to be to limit migrants' mobility and conduct to appease a hostile surrounding community. However, the new rules upset Natalia, as she felt confined in a place that was supposed to protect her.

As she recounted the details of her first migration from the countryside to the city and the extreme poverty she endured while living in the streets as a child, her face nevertheless lit up when she told me about her first engagement in sex work at the age of eleven. Sex work had allowed her to buy food and pay rent; it had been a successful way out from a life of painful precarity. And, while it is common to hear from trans migrants that one of the biggest challenges of gender transitioning is the economic cost of having one's options largely reduced to sex work, Natalia's early transit in gender and forced migration meant that she could only compare her situation as a refugee to the perils of home and homelessness. However, Natalia was also aware of the dangers of sex work for a trans girl like her, working in public space. In fact, she felt much freer from precarity and violence when she started working at a brothel in lieu of the streets at the age of fifteen.

It was this sense of safety that the threat of forced recruitment by the MS13 promised to end. Natalia had managed to make ends meet and build community in the brothel, while also sustaining her gender transition. For once, she had felt sovereign in her body and life; selling drugs for the gang would have been a setback for her. As Svati Shah argues, a "range of services, and modes of remuneration and exchange . . . occur under the auspices of sexual commerce" (2014, 113). In this sense, trans sex workers become coveted recruits for the drug-selling business. They are also recruited to traffic drugs into the prisons where gang members are locked in. However, as the stories of *chicas trans* illustrate, nonbinary individuals are especially exposed to gang violence. They often become coerced lovers of gang members, as is common for cis women as well. For *chicas trans* it entails the additional risk of being punished by the gang, whose collective performance of hypermasculinity entails homophobic and transphobic violence.[4]

Reflecting about her self-presentation reminded Natalia that she no longer felt sovereign in her own body after being displaced by the MS13, that her second forced migration out of Honduras jeopardized her gender as it did her home:

> Had this situation not happened to me, I would still be in Honduras. I wouldn't be here. . . . You know? I used to do fine at work. I used to earn good money. But now, look at me. . . . Every night, I used to pray to God to cover me, to come in my aid. . . . And I did fine. I'd fancy up. . . . Not like nowadays. I look at myself and I start crying. I suffer. I never thought I'd live like this. . . . I always had my money. . . . If I work, I know that I'll have money. And if I don't, it won't fall from the sky. That's what happens. And I feel that I'm now living the same as what I lived when I was a child.

For Natalia, being homeless and a refugee were similar predicaments, ones that hampered her gender transition through enforced poverty. Natalia faced the dangers of sex work by entrusting her life to God because, as many *chicas trans* I have met in Mexico acknowledge, "you never know if you will come back or what will happen to you with a client."[5] Yet a relative sense of safety at the brothel made her work easier, and her gender performance possible: she "fancied up." In contrast, Natalia resented depending on the protection of the shelter: while the politics of respectability that the shelter endorsed confined her in the building, the loss of economic autonomy infantilized her. Ironically, Natalia felt equally constrained by the precarity of living in the streets of Tegucigalpa as a child and the precarity of receiving humanitarian assistance in Mexico City. Homelessness and life at the shelter felt quite alike.

Among *chicas trans*, oral histories of displacement can reveal unanticipated meanings of home, work, (un)freedom, and (un)safety in the globalized periphery of transnational migration circuits. Being on the street, on one's own, can be as constraining as staying at a migrant shelter, despite—or precisely due to—the benign character of the latter, where a young woman fleeing violence might in principle find herself "saved."[6] These counterintuitive experiences are not singular to trans individuals set in motion throughout the Americas. Yet the stark intersections between geographical and gender transitions are particularly telling for considering large-scale political change, like the transformations of state power in late capitalism, in a new light. Importantly, behind the apparent movement of often forcibly displaced *chicas trans*, their stories elucidate the ways in which confinement multiplies in everyday life, beyond explicitly carceral facilities. In Natalia's case, being forced into motion was a form of confinement, while at different parts of her spatial journey carceral techniques of power proliferated.

Feminist and queer scholarship on the subject highlights the parallels between the "impossible" subject positions of trans individuals and (im)migrants, allowing for comparative analyses of legal categories and enforcing practices (Spade 2009, 368). Beyond comparing, by "transing" migration studies, it is possible to deepen our understanding of place, movement, borders, the body, political subjectivity, and, I would argue, state sovereignty (Cotten 2012, 1–3). For one, there are key intersections between gender transition and mass incarceration: historically, trans bodies have been disproportionately targeted by punitive and coercive institutions and have also fiercely challenged discretionary enforcement and the excessive use of state force (Stanley and Smith 2011).[7] Although trans people are only a minority of international migrants and incarcerated populations, their particular standing, often at the limits of state sovereignty and other power structures, makes their experiences crucial for understanding human mobility and confinement in the present.

In turn, the emerging field of detention studies has grown out of cross-fertilizations between critical prison and migration studies. This literature has focused on, first, aggregate patterns pertaining to migrant detention; and, second, embodied experiences of immigrants and asylum seekers in confinement. Among the former, critical analyses have illuminated macro patterns of detention and deportation while also accounting for otherwise less explored dimensions like race and gender. Ethnic studies scholar David Hernández analyzes the parallels between, and intertwining of, the figure of the "global detainee"—criminalized within the framework of the war on terror, "[allowing] the United States to push its borders outward and expand its detention project globally"—and that of the "immigrant detainee"—in principle constrained to domestic policy both at the border and within the US nation (2016, 303–4). As Hernández argues, a major force behind the creation of a global regime of exception and legal obscurity that racially targets noncitizens for incarceration is the reliance on private "surrogates and subcontractors," which combines with "racist fears" that are nowadays directed mainly toward Latino men in the United States (321).

Similarly, sociologist Tanya Golash-Boza uses a world-systems framework to explain the racial and gender composition of US migrant detentions and deportations across time. She identifies a temporal correlation between cyclical capitalist crises and the appearance of a "politics of fear" aimed at men of color (2016, 492–94). As she argues, in the United States, economic recessions have made possible the mass incarceration of black men, on the one hand, and mass deportations of Latino men, on the other. These two patterns took place in the aftermath of the 1970s and 2008 crises of global capitalism, respectively, leading to major transformations of production structures that affected certain occupations and social groups more strongly than others (Golash-Boza 2016).

If we now look at the literature on detained migrants' embodied experiences, two major themes are worth noting. First, scholars have examined the human face of national-level immigration policies when seen from the perspective of everyday life in detention, paying especial attention to the interactions between caregivers and bureaucrats, on the one hand, and detained migrants on the other. In this vein, geographer Nick Gill (2016) and criminologist Mary Bosworth (2014) offer a window into the hidden yet expansive world of migrant detention. While Gill emphasizes how functionary-noncitizen relationships are shot through with an ethics of "distance" despite being established in the context of daily practices of care (2016, 16), Bosworth points to the "relational nature of power in the face of mass mobility" with a slightly more hopeful, even if "uncertain," prospect regarding the effects of recognition and identification stemming from face-to-face interactions (2014, location 243).

A second theme appears in the edited volume *Intimate Economies of Immigrant Detention* (Conlon and Hiemstra 2016). In it, contributors employ microlevel analyses of the global profit generated by immigrant detention, not only for transnational corporations but also a range of actors (2016, location 213). The essays grapple with the everyday workings of immigrant detention, bringing to light activities and sites that would not otherwise count as economic (2016, location 241). The volume makes a strong case for a transnational feminist approach— which it shares with Hernández and Golash-Boza—showing the global scope of "intimate" intersections between confinement, mobility, and dispossession.

In sum, this scholarship addresses the overlapping structures of gender and race in how states have responded to international migrations. Yet if gender studies have fruitfully met with both carceral and migration scholarship, contributing to the burgeoning literature on detention, there is much room for research that foregrounds the stark intersecting transitions undergone by trans bodies in motion/confinement. Moreover, while detention studies often conjure the broad notion of confinement, analyses are almost always concerned exclusively with strictly carceral facilities administered by the state (or its subcontractors, such as jails, prisons, and detention centers).[8] However, the lived experiences of *chicas trans* in transit and confinement have multiplied at myriad sites. Based on participant observation and interview data collected at migrant shelters in Mexico, I trace the proliferation of experiences of confinement throughout this extended borderland—an extension that has been the result of both an outward transfer of US immigration enforcement from domestic to foreign policy and an inward expansion of border policing in Mexico from the geographical frontier to the inner territory. As the following discussion of cases illustrates, by looking at intersecting transitions of gender, migration, and confinement, we gain a better grasp of the workings of sovereignty beyond state prerogative.[9] That is, an emphasis on the context of transit as a heuristic for intersectional analysis makes it possible to analyze a broader carceral regime of sovereignty central to our fluctuating geography of power.

Rosario: Being Forced into Motion as Confinement

Migrants in transit who find themselves in shelters in Mexico exemplify the interwoven threads of displacement and confinement.[10] In the summer of 2016, I met Rosario, a *chica trans* who was making her fifth journey from Guatemala to the United States. At that point, she had been deported four times—three times from the United States and once from Mexico. She had also been in migrant detention and prison in the United States for different lengths of time.

Rosario first left Guatemala with the help of her mother in 2005. She had decided to start a new life in the United States, where she assumed she could begin her gender transition and live a life free from transphobia. She crossed Mexico in about two weeks, but upon entering the United States, she was detained and deported. A year later, Rosario embarked on a second journey. Her mother had perished during Hurricane Stan in October 2005, and Rosario lacked support from the rest of the family to live as a trans person. In her second journey, her brother accompanied her to the border city of Tecún Umán, where numbers of Central Americans cross daily on rafts to Mexico through "Paso del Coyote," a strait of Río Suchiate about a mile away from the official border checkpoint. Crossing Mexico has always been full of dangers, including assaults, kidnappings, rapes, and detentions, with risks growing ever more quickly in the past decade. In her initial trips, poverty led Rosario to exchange sex for rides along the way. In her narrative, these exchanges were often represented as the expected cost of her journey as a *chica trans*. After a few days, Rosario crossed successfully to the United States, where she lived in Texas for eight years. There, Rosario could work and start her transition: she had breast surgery, had hormone replacement therapy, and let her hair grow. However, that change also limited her work opportunities to sex work in public space. As she met new people and started to know her rights, she filed an application for asylum, but her "transgender status" did not necessarily constitute a strong case to seek refuge (Luibhéid 2002, 153–54; Cidón Kiernan, Hernández Flores, and Lucero 2017).

As a *chica trans* and sex worker, Rosario quickly faced the reality of being persecuted by the police state (Castillo, Rangel Gómez, and Delgado 1999, 401; Stanley and Smith 2011, 5, 8). In the context of the war on drugs and the war on terror, she became a clear target during raids in search of "criminals." In

2009, Rosario was apprehended on charges of prostitution and drug posses-sion. Later, she was arrested one more time while driving without a license, which is a common way for undocumented immigrants to enter the realm of state coercive action. Because of her prior penal charges, she spent a month in jail and was then released with an ankle monitor. As a result, her asylum case suffered, and the ankle monitor made it difficult for her to work. It also made it a problem to rent a place because, as a device of surveillance, it endangered other undocumented immigrants living around her. Led to desperation, she cut the monitor off and got rid of it. Later, she had another problem involving the police and was detained again. She was then brought to the county jail, where she spent three days and was informed of an arrest warrant against her by immigration. While this was happening, she missed the date to go to court in relation to her asylum case. Then, an immigration official asked her to sign a document and informed her that her case had been dismissed. She asked the officer about her options: she could either sign and be deported, or else she would spend more time in prison. Rosario signed.

After twenty more days in detention, Rosario was deported on January 20, 2014. The initial joy with which her family received her quickly waned. With the help of a friend in the United States, she bought the strictly necessary luggage to head north, managing to cross Mexico and the Río Grande some days later. She was caught again, locked up in the Federal Detention Center in Houston, sentenced to forty days in prison for reentry, kept in custody by im-migration one more month, and finally deported in September 2014.

Though Rosario was willing to stay in Guatemala this time, her family started to demand that she reverse her gender transition. Her siblings told her that even if they accepted her for who she was, they did not know how to ex-plain the ambiguity of her gender to their children and larger family. Unwilling to conform to her sex assigned at birth, Rosario left once again. Since then, the cycle of migration and deportation that began for her in 2005 repeated in a more accelerated fashion, including two more trips, ninety additional days in detention in 2014, and one more deportation from Mexico.

Rosario's case illustrates the pervasiveness of confinement through perma-nent displacement. Set into motion by her nonbinary gender, Rosario's gen-der transition furthered her precarity and exposed her to state violence in the United States. Yet while she faced an overwhelming restriction in terms of her geographical movement, the cycle of migration and deportation persisted. Like many other migrants, increased border policing did not effectively deter successive crossings, and a seemingly temporary process of transit became a permanent state of confinement in motion.

Sheltering Transit

Even though Rosario was put in several carceral facilities, her journey was also filled with less obvious forms of confinement in which punitive and surveilling techniques were present in unexpected spaces. In her second-to-last attempt to cross the Guatemala-Mexico border in February 2016, Rosario was detained in the border city of Tapachula, Chiapas, and deported to Guatemala. It was the first time that Rosario could not reach the US border. As soon as she arrived in Tecún Umán, she again started the journey north. However, in 2014 the Mexican government had launched *"Programa Frontera Sur"* (Southern Border Program), rhetorically a humanitarian initiative to halt the mutilations, deaths, rapes, and kidnappings throughout migration routes, and aimed at "saving" migrants from human trafficking by coyotes and *polleros* (smugglers). Yet the program has become the most aggressive border control strategy of the Mexican state to date, an instrument to "stop migrants from reaching the [US] border to claim asylum" (Nazario 2015).

Rosario's last attempt to cross Mexico was completely different from her prior journeys. Because of increased border policing, she had to go around numerous immigration and military checkpoints. The areas surrounding these checkpoints worked as virtual enclosures through which migrants could circulate out of the direct sight of the state, but there they were more vulnerable to the abuses of anyone they happened to encounter. As Gilberto Rosas has shown in his analysis of *"cholos"* and *"chúntaros"* in the Nogales border zone, neoliberal sovereignty takes the form of "low-intensity warfare" undertaken by both the US and the Mexican states (2012, 11). This kind of sovereignty is necessarily "incomplete" because the state does not stop border crossers directly but in its very incompleteness "licenses" different forms of criminal violence to do the work of policing the border and instilling fear in transient migrants (2012, 11). For Rosas, sovereignty in the "new frontier" relies on historically racialized processes that have constituted poor male youth as criminal others (*cholos*) now preying on migrants in transit (*chúntaros*); it is about the "politicization of death and violence—even criminal violence—as new tactics of neoliberal governance and rule" (2012, 17). In the south of Mexico, precarious criminalized citizens also prey on migrants, halting their passage, a process often sanctioned by the state. For example, identical descriptions of aggressors and places of assault are told and retold by victimized migrants, without judicial authorities ever delivering justice, as migrant shelters and activists have persistently denounced. A historical analysis of how these criminal subjects have come into being, however, demands further research and theorization.

At the same time, as can be seen in Rosario's story, the decentralization of sovereign border policing in Mexico has been amplified beyond criminal violence. During her last journey, Rosario had to rely on the network of more than fifty shelters and soup kitchens that offer protection to undocumented migrants, as she was attacked by passersby from whom she tried to obtain directions. However, as a *chica trans*, she had difficulty finding shelter. In Tapachula, one of the most migrant-populated cities in Mexico—and the first urban area with shelters for those who cross the border through Paso del Coyote—one of the main shelters currently bans *chicas trans* on grounds of their "questionable" sexual behavior. In an interview, staff member Manuel explained that "transgenders" endanger the women because "they *really are* men," while also "provoking" the male population. For him, hosting "transgenders" would make it impossible for the shelter to guarantee the safety of (cis) guests or to enforce the rule that bans sexual encounters and expressions of affection.[11] During the interview, Manuel elaborated on other rules:

MANUEL: [Transgenders] are a source of trouble. We do not repudiate them. We respect. But they conduct business. . . . They do oral sex, anal sex. They do as they please, they dress as they please. Here, we have rules. [Women] should dress appropriately. They cannot be in small shorts, lycras, showing too much leg, too much skin. [Women] want to dress as if they were at home. . . . Even though it is understandable, we cannot allow that.

ME: Why?

MANUEL: Because I have a large male population, and they may riot.

ME: Has a riot happened?

MANUEL: No, but I will not wait for that to happen. I need to take precautions.

ME: Are there rules for men too?

MANUEL: No, just to wear a shirt always. They can use shorts.

Manuel's explanation about the origin of shelter rules illustrates the heavy policing of sexuality that is common in these spaces. Although other shelters do admit nonbinary genders, prevalent anxieties about *chicas trans*'s sexuality bring about a host of rules and an arbitrary regulation of space that often leads to their isolation. As with the establishment of a dress code, rules sometimes stem from a preventative, if arbitrary, approach. Other rules, however, implement the lessons learned in exceptional situations that challenge the management of shelter "safety." These rules tend to endure, increasingly controlling or rendering abject the bodies of *chicas trans*. Like state institutions, shelters do not just keep records of migrants' self-selected gender identity; they construct gender categories through registration processes and the classification of bodies that these entail.[12]

During Rosario's journey, in the absence of prompt aid, she continued her travel northward. Then, relying on locals and other migrants, she healed her open injuries, avoiding an infection. She also found people willing to feed her, provide her with some money, and give her short rides. For, as Nayan Shah has argued, "migrants' practices of social navigation, community building, and participation in interethnic social worlds . . . undermine the containment efforts of nation-states and empires" (2011, 2). And while these experiences are not necessarily free from violence, in my larger research I trace the extensive everyday practices of hospitality, solidarity, and care in the context of transit migration across Mexico, as ordinary people, often women and impoverished citizens, develop alternative forms of being and existing politically in the world in their encounters with noncitizens (see Balaguera 2017).

After fourteen days, Rosario arrived at a shelter in the southern state of Oaxaca, where I met her. Once at the shelter, Rosario was torn about what protection meant. The extreme lack of safety outside the shelter made her seek legal protection. Since she had been assaulted in Mexican territory, she had the right to file a report and request a humanitarian visa until her case was resolved. Yet life at the shelter was fraught with contradictions. As places where migrants can spend the night, eat, take showers, wash clothes, keep belongings safe, make calls, receive money from abroad, seek legal advice, be seen by physicians and psychologists—and, more important, be safe—shelters may also be confining. Enclosed by high-perimeter fences, barbed wire, and locked gates, and protected by twenty-four-hour guards, the rhythms of a shelter, with fixed eating times and mandatory curfews, have uneasy resemblances with carceral institutions. In them, migrants often feel as though they are locked up in prison, inasmuch as punitive, disciplinary, and biopolitical techniques permeate all aspects of everyday life (Foucault 1995, 2007, 2015).

Since July 2015, I have visited twenty migrant shelters in Mexico. In all of them, there are different administrative routines to deal with nonbinary genders and people of "diverse" sexualities. Like other institutions intended to discipline behavior, shelters are segregated by gender, so decisions ought to be made regarding how to allocate trans bodies in space. During Rosario's stay at the shelter, nonbinary individuals were lumped together and accommodated in a tent outside the female sleeping area.[13] Rosario never complained about the special treatment given to her, or the fact that she was called by her legal name and misgendered by shelter staff, but her permanent distrustful demeanor conveyed what her words did not. She would avoid interacting with other people as much as possible, as she understood that she could be bullied or harassed. In this sense, her isolation amplified the experience of confinement at the shelter, as she could not build community in that shared space.[14] A few days after I met her, she found out that she was HIV positive during the routine voluntary tests performed at the shelter. Her greatest fear was that other migrants would figure this out and vilify her. Shortly after I left the shelter, the volunteer coordinator told me that Rosario had decided to leave, giving up on her hopes of obtaining a humanitarian visa. She had left alone on top of the train. Without her mentioning it, the sense I got from this conversation was that it was unlikely that Rosario was still alive. Even though the train came twice a day, Mexican enforcement agencies had increasingly discouraged migrants from using this means of transportation, especially in the southern states of the country, where several migrants had died trying to escape from police operations aimed at keeping the train clear.[15]

The shelter system in Mexico is not completely or even primarily about confinement. It is run by Catholic priests and nuns devoted to social justice work, human rights defenders, informal grassroots associations of impoverished women who live next to the migration routes, and civil society organizations of different kinds. As benign havens for migrants, shelters also provide relatively safe research sites for journalists and academics, allowing them to access some of the darkest realities of the refugee crisis through the testimonies of survivors. It is common to find positive representations of these spaces both in the media and in scholarly works. For example, anthropologist Wendy Vogt has characterized the shelters as places of "hope," "justice," and "empathy" (2012, 80; 2013, 776). Others praise the political activism of their leaders (Frank-Vitale 2013, 8–9). In my larger research (Balaguera 2017), I highlight the radical transformations that shelters entail in terms of our democratic ethos, producing forms of "transnational citizenship from below" through the encounter between citizens and noncitizens they make possible.

However, lived experiences of transit migration reveal configurations of power that push us to think beyond the militarized strategies of state agencies. For Rosario, confinement in motion and confinement at the shelter through the disciplining of gender performance, the administration of shelter space, and the management of life and health were as real as the fear of police violence, limiting her capacity to act and sustain her life. Likewise, when shelters intervene so that migrants may access otherwise elusive rights and protections, they partake in a larger regime of sovereignty not reduced to the state. For example, an extended stay in shelters can be instrumental for migrants to obtain papers, which may make their circulation through Mexico less endangered.

Thus, confinement is often a precondition for freer circulation and access to elusive protections. In this sense, confinement as a characteristic technique of punishment and regulation is transferred from prisons and detention centers to the shelter system operating at the margins of the state.[16] Approximating rules and procedures characteristic of prisons, shelters come to reproduce, unintendedly, migrants' unfreedom and precarity.

As political theorist Ayten Gündoğdu argues, the condition of confinement exacerbates migrants' precarity due to their dependence on the "compassion" and "benevolence" of their captors, who may justify detention for the sake of expediency in processing asylum cases, while undermining refugees' political and human standing (Gündoğdu 2015, 120). Gündoğdu underscores the fundamental unfreedom that is attached to confinement, since migrants are reduced to the most basic survival functions (Arendt 1968, 297). Even if confinement in the shelter is not enforced by the state, and shelter administrators are not captors, the condition of captivity is upheld by the fact that they are de facto expelled from spaces of state protection, and their dependence on compassion becomes manifest. Yet the shelters are also spaces that facilitate new forms of collective action, new coalitions of citizens and noncitizens, and the politization of lives in transit without the requirement of a permanent political community.

Alejandra: Liminal Agency and Confinement

Shelter life is one possible embodied experience of confinement for transit migrants, but it may take multiple forms.[17] Even when there is outright coercion, it may be disconcerting for a captive person to make sense of her situation, as the first migration journey of Alejandra—a thirty-four-year-old *chica trans* from Guatemala—taught me. In 2007, Alejandra had left her home town in Guatemala with her friend Marina in a gesture of solidarity: "Marina was lesbian, and they killed her partner. . . . To this day, I haven't understood much. But you know, when someone dies, people invent thousands of lies. They said that she sold drugs. That's something I never saw and cannot judge. But because of that death, my friend was threatened. That's when I decided to travel with her."

Although Alejandra did not seem to believe that Marina's partner was involved in the drug business, her narrative indicated that death was a natural destiny for people who were part of it. By bringing up the question of sexual identity, Alejandra also suggested that being a lesbian was an additional danger that could explain her death. As Melissa Wright (2011) argues, blame-the-victim discourses often justify the murder of both women and "narcos," signaling the normalization of gender violence and the dehumanization of "criminals" in the context of the war on drugs. Following Wright's analysis, I do not claim that Alejandra and Marina's migration was forced by gender violence. Rather, I want to underscore the discursive normalization of violence and death that Alejandra's words conveyed.

As the rest of her story unfolded, it became apparent how those normalizing discourses may produce distinct subjects whose agency is unintelligible from the perspective of the liberal framework that informs our understanding of coercion and self-determination. The day they left, Alejandra and Marina met two men who offered them much-needed work in Veracruz, Mexico: "They said they were going to pay us 5,000 pesos a week.... We didn't even know how much that was, but we thought: 'that's good money.' So we left with them. They brought us by train, and a few days later we arrived in Reynosa."[18]

This is how Alejandra and Marina were *enganchadas* in Guatemala. *Enganchamiento* consists in recruiting a migrant to be smuggled by a coyote across the US border in return for monetary payment. For some migrants, coyotes perform vital protective functions that the state fails to fulfill in the context of militarized borders. In an informal conversation, a former coyote referred to himself as a "guide," someone who "helped" others in their transit journeys. Coyotes may or may not take advantage of migrants' fear and need of guidance and may be victims of violence themselves. Thus, migrants run the risk of being abandoned in the middle of their journey by coyotes, whether or not they are acting in bad faith. In the most unfortunate cases, coyotes can deceive migrants and then sell their victims to criminal groups that extort, torture, and profit from ransoms demanded from migrants' families located outside Mexico. All these possible scenarios may happen at once, as in the example of Alejandra and Marina.

For them, the trip from northern Guatemala to Reynosa, Tamaulipas (on the US border), hardly felt coercive for most of the time. They traveled willingly. Even after the *enganchadores* sold them to the Zetas cartel—a criminal organization that profits from kidnapping and claiming ransom for undocumented migrants, and is known for its brutal tactics to force compliance—they voluntarily entered a "security house" where they were kept captive for over a month. In several occasions, Alejandra was the agent of her own unfreedom:

> We entered that empty house. They told us to sit, and one of them asked, "Okay, who's going to the United States . . . ?" We were not going to the United States. But my stepfather was there, so I said: "Can I make a call . . . ?" I didn't know what I was getting into. That was my own stab. . . . I swear I didn't know I was kidnapped. At some point, they asked my family for money. They told me: "If you want to go to the United States, it's 5,000 dollars; if you want to go back to Guatemala, it's 2,500." My family [only had] 2,500 . . . . I thought, "Yes, sure; what I want is to

leave this place . . . where you do not even see if it's day or night." But . . .
I was very confused, constantly hearing the stories of people around me.

Alejandra had seen the tortures and forced labor of those who didn't have
someone to pay for them. That was the destiny of Marina, whom one of the Zeta
chiefs took as a "wife." The hardships Alejandra went through, shared by about
twenty people in the room and three hundred in the security house, also indicated to her that something was wrong. Yet, regardless of whether Alejandra had
been deceived or not, her interpretation of the conditions she faced while she
was kidnapped was striking, as she seemed to normalize them as an expected cost
for crossing the border without papers. In the end, Alejandra was released after
her family paid what turned out to be ransom: "When I had almost completed a
month there, . . . one of them . . . said to us: 'Welcome to Houston. . . .' We were
baffled. 'Yes, you have arrived,' he told us. . . . 'You are going to call your families
and tell them that you didn't suffer, that we gave you food and that you only had
to walk eighteen hours. If you don't do that, you can guess what's coming.' [After
I did what they asked], they dropped me at the migrant shelter in Reynosa."

Alejandra's testimony accounts not only for a blurry distinction between
kidnapping and *coyoterismo* but also for a contradictory liminal subjectivity.[19]
In the face of degrading treatment, Alejandra did not see her predicament as
one of unfreedom. At most, it was the expected price for crossing to the United
States. Migrating to the United States was not something she had wished to
do to begin with; it was a path driven by the inertia of her poverty, her gender, and normalized violence. Once she was in this situation, her agency was
both about and beyond surviving, as new life possibilities opened up. Although
there was a great silence in Alejandra's story regarding her identity, her transit
in gender was closely tied to her transit in space. If Alejandra seemed at times
to become the agent of her own unfreedom, her migration was itself a practice
that was both bounded by the borders and limits of her identity and past those
very limits (Butler 2000, 32–33).

The lingering lessons of Alejandra's confinement, nonetheless, exposed the
effectiveness of power techniques shaping lives in transit. As she insisted during the interview, her kidnapping had helped her become a "different person":
"When you are in that place, . . . you really learn the value of everything . . .
life is worth more than anything material or economic." Although the human
dimension of Alejandra's learning should not be dismissed, her transit was an
example of imposed docility, where the "disciplinary functions" of overlapping
transitions marked by confinement in motion unveiled the deeper disciplining
effects of what is otherwise seen as irrational violence (Hiemstra 2016, 437; see
also Golash-Boza 2015).

The Transit of Carceral Sovereignty

In the stories of *chicas trans*, the distinctions between shelter and homelessness, motion and boundedness, and freedom and unfreedom become blurred in embodied experiences of transit. Drawing on them, I have identified a proliferation of sites and forms of confinement that push contemporary gender-informed critiques on detention and incarceration, and our understanding of state sovereignty in the age of "global mobility" (Mbembe 2003, 31). Looking at extreme examples of intersecting transitions can expose with more force the ways in which "contemporary historical experience" is situated at the limits of sovereignty, while also redefining those limits (Berlant 2011, 96). These extreme experiences are not an exception but an allegory for a thriving carceral transnational system marked by decentralized practices of government, punishment, and discipline in assemblage, generative of lasting large-scale power effects.

As an enduring equation of state and sovereignty haunts our understanding of borders and the prison, elaborations on border policing, refugee camps, and mass incarceration have tended to be informed by a classical model that ascribes three major elements to the sovereign state: violence, territory, and decisionism (Weber [1919] 2007, 78; Schmitt 1985, 5). Yet, feminist critiques of the notion of sovereignty both at the level of the subject and of state power call into question this understanding.[20] As Lauren Berlant argues, "the sovereign concept" tied to "state privilege" "masks the wide variety of processes and procedures involved historically in the administration of law and bodies" (2011, 96).

As the cases presented in this essay illustrate, the proliferation of confinement that lives in transit endure is not reducible to the state's sovereign agency "to put people to death or to grant them life" (Berlant 2011, 97). Instead, it exposes an array of decentralized practices of government that discipline, regulate, punish, and shape life through carceral techniques of power. Rather than equating state and sovereignty, this study shows how transit migration becomes an occasion for both the expansion of the coercive functions of the state and the multiplication of agents and sites of government within a distinguishable, if hybrid, carceral regime of sovereignty.

As this study suggests, we can better understand the transformations unveiled by dynamics of transit not only by looking at the state's "waning sovereignty," whose symptom may well be an expansion of its walling, coercive, punitive, and confining capabilities (Brown 2010; Gündoğdu 2015). In addition, to be in transit, at the limits of sovereignty, warrants considering intersecting liminal configurations of power, whose transformations impact our world at large. As Foucault argues, the same punitive techniques perform different functions in different regimes (2015, 33). In this new regime, while neoliberal sovereignty extends state and nonstate violence to all realms of life—often pitting subaltern communities against each other (Reddy 2011; Rosas 2012)—the prison and the militarized policing of borders become increasingly "denatured" in scholarly and activist discourses.[21] The rapidly growing field of detention studies also attests to this critical shift. Under these conditions, the "carceral archipelago" of modern society that Foucault theorized in the 1970s—that is, "[a] subtle, graduated carceral net with compact institutions, but also separate and diffused methods"—explodes, even as we witness mass incarceration and mass deportations (1995, 297). Confinement is not only decentralized and multiplied; it is also part of a new regime that undoes modernity's familiar dichotomies. Blurring distinctions of shelter and homelessness, motion and boundedness, and freedom and unfreedom in the lives of *chicas trans* reveals the workings of "graduated" forms of sovereignty that do not only depend on state strategies "to remain globally competitive" (Ong 1999, 217; see also 2006). Instead, an assemblage of actors, sites, relations, and strategies produce this carceral regime, oftentimes as an unintended result of benign practices. This system, however, also produces conditions for the political encounter of otherwise heterogeneous subjects, as can be seen both in everyday practices of care and hospitality and in the collective struggles based on transborder solidarity and shared precarity. Confined subjects are not merely docile subjects.

NOTES

Reprinted with the permission of the University of Chicago Press. This essay originally appeared in *Signs: Journal of Women in Culture and Society* 43, no. 3 (Spring 2018): 641–64. My appreciation to the brave Central American *chicas trans* I have met in Mexico for allowing me entry into their world, and to the shelter network throughout the country for providing a space to develop my research. I am grateful to Alfonso Gonzales, Pasha Bueno-Hansen, and Nicole Guidotti-Hernández for their encouragement and their work as discussants of different versions of this essay at professional conferences between May and November 2016; to Elva Orozco, Alix Olson, Sonny Nordmarkden, Neelofer Qadir, and Alex Ponomareff for reading and commenting on early drafts; to Carolina Robledo Silvestre and the participants in the Seminario de Derecho Crítico at the Centro de Investigaciones y Estudios Superiores en Antropología Social (CIESAS) in Mexico City for discussing my essay at length during their November 2016 monthly meeting; and to the two anonymous reviewers for their insightful comments and suggestions for improvement. My research fieldwork in Mexico was possible thanks to generous funding from the Inter-American Foundation and the Graduate School at the University of Massachusetts Amherst.

1   In this essay, I use the Spanish term *chicas trans* (roughly translatable as trans girls) in lieu of the English "trans women" to account for how research participants identified themselves. By using this term, trans subjects distance themselves from the category "woman," possibly emphasizing a refusal to have their identity map onto the gender binary. In fact, my interviewees often referred to themselves as gay and trans, thus underscoring the importance of sexuality, ambiguity, and the irreducibility of the term *"chicas trans"* to gender.

2   See Castillo, Rangel Gómez, and Delgado (1999), Luibhéid (2002), Luibhéid and Cantú (2005), Schmidt Camacho (2005), and Rosas (2012).

3   This section is based on my interview with Natalia. Personal interview by the author, Mexico City, July 10, 2016. Throughout the essay, the names used for *chicas trans* are pseudonyms.

4   Interview with Julia, Vanessa, and Mónica. Personal interview by the author, Tapachula, June 16, 2017.

5   Interview with Marisa and Elena. Personal interview by the author, Tijuana, May 7, 2017.

6   Critiques of the narrative of "saving" have been broadly discussed in feminist scholarship. See, for example, Abu-Lughod (2002).

7   Notwithstanding the legacy of queer and trans activism against the carceral state, scholars in the field have been increasingly concerned about "queer investments in punitiveness," as when LGBTQ+ groups support legislation that criminalizes hate crimes, call for increased policing in gentrifying areas, or participate in the expansion of the security apparatus of the state (Lamble 2014, 151). For related critiques see Puar (2007), Stryker (2008), Bassichis, Lee, and Spade (2011), and Reddy (2011).

8   For a perspective on confinement more in line with my research, see Slack (2016).

9   The term "transmigration" is used by migration scholars to account for the transborder lives of those who cross international borders (Furman, Eps, and Lamphear 2016, 4). In the context of transit migration across Mexico, scholars use the term "transmigration" to mean "the movement of individuals from their place of origin through another without intention to settle and on their way to a final destination" (Cruz 2012, 1019). More broadly, trans studies have paid attention to different intersecting transitions, with contributors to the edited volume *Transgender Migrations* acknowledging the "movements and morphings of various kinds involving bodies and spaces in transit(ion) across multiple borders, temporalities, social, and sexual configurations" (Cotten 2012, 2).

10 This section is based on my interview with Rosario. Personal interview by the author, Ixtepec, August 7, 2016.

11 Personal interview with Manuel (pseudonym), staff member at a migrant shelter in Tapachula, December 1, 2016.

12 See Luibhéid's historical analysis of how the US immigration service has "produced and naturalized" sexual identities (2002, xxii).

13 At other moments, the same shelter allowed *chicas trans* to sleep in the female bedroom—as was the case of Natalia before she was transferred to the shelter for unaccompanied minors in Mexico City—or placed them in an old bathroom in disuse. Personal interview with ex-volunteer Valeria, Mexico City, March 28, 2017.

14 As Ayten Gündoğdu argues, spaces of confinement prevent asylum seekers and refugees from "participating in the ongoing constitution of a political and human community through their labor, work and action" (2015, 125).

15 Medios con M, *Plan Frontera Sur, cacería de Migrantes* (Southern border program: Migrant hunt), YouTube video, 28:01, July 30, 2015, https://www.youtube.com /watch?v=;rod_2F7eTUE&feature=;youtu.be.

16 Tellingly, the UNHCR has sought to provide shelter for asylum seekers initially confined at the Siglo XXI migratory station in Tapachula, as an alternative to widespread migrant detention (UNHCR 2014a). Personal interview with UNHCR regional office chief Javier Orejarena, Tapachula, June 12, 2017.

17 This section is based on my interview with Alejandra. Personal interview by the author, Saltillo, July 1–4, 2016.

18 In 2007, 5,000 Mexican pesos were approximately 400 US dollars.

19 On liminal and lateral agency, see Butler (2000) and Berlant (2011).

20 See Butler (2000), Ong (2006, chap. 3), Berlant (2011, chap. 3), and Rosas (2012).

21 See Foucault (1995, 304), Davis (2003), Gilmore (2007), Escobar (2016), and Golash-Boza (2016).

REFERENCES

Abu-Lughod, Lila. 2002. "Do Muslim Women Really Need Saving? Anthropological Reflections on Cultural Relativism and Its Others." *American Anthropologist* 104(3): 783–90.

Arendt, Hannah. 1968. *The Origins of Totalitarianism*. New York: Harcourt, Brace & World.

Balaguera, Martha. 2017. "Citizenship in Transit." Paper presented at the Annual Meeting of the American Political Science Association, San Francisco, September 1.

Bassichis, Morgan, Alexander Lee, and Dean Spade. 2011. "Building an Abolitionist Trans and Queer Movement with Everything We've Got." In Stanley and Smith 2011, 15–40.

Berlant, Lauren Gail. 2011. *Cruel Optimism*. Durham, NC: Duke University Press.

Bosworth, Mary. 2014. *Inside Immigration Detention*. Oxford: Oxford University Press.

Briggs, Laura. 2012. *Somebody's Children: The Politics of Transracial and Transnational Adoption*. Durham, NC: Duke University Press.

Brown, Wendy. 2010. *Walled States, Waning Sovereignty*. New York: Zone.

Butler, Judith. 2000. "Agencies of Style for a Liminal Subject." In *Without Guarantees: In Honour of Stuart Hall*, edited by Paul Gilroy, Lawrence Grossberg, and Angela McRobbie, 30–37. London: Verso.

Castillo, Debra A., María Gudelia Rangel Gómez, and Bonnie Delgado. 1999. "Border Lives: Prostitute Women in Tijuana." *Signs: Journal of Women in Culture and Society* 24(2): 387–422.

Cheng, Sealing. 2010. *On the Move for Love: Migrant Entertainers and the U.S. Military in South Korea*. Philadelphia: University of Pennsylvania Press.

Cheng, Sealing. 2012/2013. "Embodying the Sexual Limits of Neoliberalism." *The Scholar and Feminist Online* 11(1–2). http://sfonline.barnard.edu/gender-justice-and-neoliberal -transformations/embodying-the-sexual-limits-of-neoliberalism/.

Cidón Kiernan, María, Priscila Hernández Flores, and Prometeo Lucero. 2017. *"Sin refugio para las trans"* [Without refuge for trans women]. *Connectas News*, May. http://www.connectasnews.org/especiales/2017/transmigrantes.

Conlon, Deirdre, and Nancy Hiemstra, eds. 2016. *Intimate Economies of Immigration Detention: Critical Perspectives*. Florence, KY: Taylor & Francis.

Cotten, Trystan T., ed. 2012. *Transgender Migrations: The Bodies, Borders, and Politics of Transition*. New York: Routledge.

Cruz, Evelyn H. 2012. "Through Mexican Eyes: Mexican Perspectives on Transmigration." *Valparaiso University Law Review* 46(4): 1019–52.

Davis, Angela Y. 2003. *Are Prisons Obsolete?* New York: Seven Stories.

Escobar, Martha D. 2016. *Captivity beyond Prisons: Criminalization Experiences of Latina (Im)migrants*. Austin: University of Texas Press.

Foucault, Michel. 1995. *Discipline and Punish: The Birth of the Prison*. Translated by Alan Sheridan. New York: Vintage.

Foucault, Michel. 2007. *Security, Territory, Population: Lectures at the Collège de France, 1977–1978*. Basingstoke: Palgrave Macmillan.

Foucault, Michel. 2015. *The Punitive Society: Lectures at the Collège de France, 1972–1973*. Edited by Bernard E. Harcourt, translated by Graham Burchell. New York: Palgrave Macmillan.

Frank-Vitale, Amelia. 2013. "Central American Migrants in Mexico: Implications for U.S. Security and Immigration Policy." Center for Latin American and Latino Studies (CLALS) Working Paper Series No. 2: Religion and Violence in Latin America. https://papers.ssrn.com/sol3/Delivery.cfm/SSRN_ID2476525_code2213457.pdf?abstractid=;2412769&mirid=;1.

Furman, Rich, Douglas Epps, and Greg Lamphear, eds. 2016. *Detaining the Immigrant Other: Global and Transnational Issues*. New York: Oxford University Press.

García, María Cristina. 2006. *Seeking Refuge: Central American Migration to Mexico, the United States, and Canada*. Berkeley: University of California Press.

Gill, Nick. 2016. *Nothing Personal? Geographies of Governing and Activism in the British Asylum System*. Chichester: Wiley.

Gilmore, Ruth Wilson. 2007. *Golden Gulag: Prisons, Surplus, Crisis, and Opposition in Globalizing California*. Berkeley: University of California Press.

Golash-Boza, Tanya Maria. 2015. *Deported: Immigrant Policing, Disposable Labor, and Global Capitalism*. New York: New York University Press.

Golash-Boza, Tanya Maria. 2016. "The Parallels between Mass Incarceration and Mass Deportation: An Intersectional Analysis of State Repression." *Journal of World-Systems Research* 22(2): 484–509.

Gündoğdu, Ayten. 2015. *Rightlessness in an Age of Rights: Hannah Arendt and the Contemporary Struggles of Migrants*. New York: Oxford University Press.

Hernández, David. 2016. "Surrogates and Subcontractors: Flexibility and Obscurity in U.S. Immigrant Detention." In *Critical Ethnic Studies: A Reader*, edited by Nada Elia, David Hernández, Jodi Kim, Shana L. Redmond, Dylan Rodríguez, and Sarita Echavez See, 303–25. Durham, NC: Duke University Press.

Hiemstra, Nancy. 2016. "Deportation and Detention: Interdisciplinary Perspectives, Multi-scalar Approaches, and New Methodological Tools." *Migration Studies* 4(3): 433–46.

Lamble, Sarah. 2014. "Queer Investments in Punitiveness: Sexual Citizenship, Social Movements, and the Expanding Carceral State." In *Queer Necropolitics*, edited by Jin Haritaworn, Adi Kuntsman, and Silvia Posocco, 151–71. Abingdon: Routledge.

Lewis, Vek. 2012. "Forging 'Moral Geographies': Law, Sexual Minorities, and Internal Tensions in Northern Mexico Border Towns." In Cotten 2012, 32–56.

Luibhéid, Eithne. 2002. *Entry Denied: Controlling Sexuality at the Border*. Minneapolis: University of Minnesota Press.

Luibhéid, Eithne. 2013. *Pregnant on Arrival: Making the Illegal Immigrant*. Minneapolis: University of Minnesota Press.

Luibhéid, Eithne, and Lionel Cantú. 2005. *Queer Migrations: Sexuality, U.S. Citizenship, and Border Crossings*. Minneapolis: University of Minnesota Press.

Mbembe, Achille. 2003. "Necropolitics." Translated by Libby Meintjes. *Public Culture* 15(1): 11–40.

Mohanty, Chandra Talpade. 1986. "Under Western Eyes: Feminist Scholarship and Colonial Discourses." *Boundary 2* 12(3): 333–58.

Nazario, Sonia. 2015. "The Refugees at Our Door." *New York Times*, October 10. http://www.nytimes.com/2015/10/11/opinion/sunday/the-refugees-at-our-door.html?_r=;o.

O'Neil, Shannon K. 2016. "The Hidden Refugee Crisis in the Western Hemisphere." *Council on Foreign Relations*, November 1. https://www.cfr.org/blog/hidden-refugee -crisis-western-hemisphere.

Ong, Aihwa. 1999. *Flexible Citizenship: The Cultural Logics of Transnationality*. Durham, NC: Duke University Press.

Ong, Aihwa. 2006. *Neoliberalism as Exception: Mutations in Citizenship and Sovereignty*. Durham, NC: Duke University Press.

Puar, Jasbir K. 2007. *Terrorist Assemblages: Homonationalism in Queer Times*. Durham, NC: Duke University Press.

Reddy, Chandan. 2011. *Freedom with Violence: Race, Sexuality, and the U.S. State*. Durham, NC: Duke University Press.

Rosas, Gilberto. 2012. *Barrio Libre: Criminalizing States and Delinquent Refusals of the New Frontier*. Durham, NC: Duke University Press.

Schmidt Camacho, Alicia R. 2005. "*Ciudadana* X: Gender Violence and the Denationalization of Women's Rights in Ciudad Juarez, Mexico." *CR: The New Centennial Review* 5(1): 255–92.

Schmitt, Carl. 1985. *Political Theology: Four Chapters on the Concept of Sovereignty*. Cambridge, MA: MIT Press.

Shah, Nayan. 2011. *Stranger Intimacy: Contesting Race, Sexuality, and the Law in the North American West*. Berkeley: University of California Press.

Shah, Svati Pragna. 2014. *Street Corner Secrets: Sex, Work, and Migration in the City of Mumbai*. Durham, NC: Duke University Press.

Slack, Jeremy. 2016. "Captive Bodies: Migrant Kidnapping and Deportation in Mexico." *Area* 48(3): 271–77.

Spade, Dean. 2009. "Trans Law and Politics on a Neoliberal Landscape." *Temple Political and Civil Rights Law Review*, no. 18: 353–73.

Stanley, Eric A., and Nat Smith, eds. 2011. *Captive Genders: Trans Embodiment and the Prison Industrial Complex*. Edinburgh: AK Press.

Stryker, Susan. 2008. "Transgender History, Homonormativity, and Disciplinarity." *Radical History Review* 100: 145–57.

Suárez, Ximena, José Knippen, and Maureen Meyer. 2016. "A Trail of Impunity: Thousands of Migrants in Transit Face Abuses amid Mexico's Crackdown." Report of the Washington Office on Latin America. September. https://www.wola.org/wp-content/uploads/2016/10/A-Trail-of-Impunity-2016.pdf.

UNHCR (United Nations High Commissioner for Refugees). 2014a. "Beyond Detention: A Global Strategy to Support Governments to End the Detention of Asylum-Seekers and Refugees, 2014–2019)." Report, United Nations High Commissioner for Refugees, Washington, DC. http://www.unhcr.org/53aa929f6.

UNHCR (United Nations High Commissioner for Refugees). 2014b. "Children on the Run: Unaccompanied Children Leaving Central America and Mexico and the Need for International Protection." Report, United Nations High Commissioner for Refugees, Washington, DC. http://www.refworld.org/docid/532180c24.html.

UNHCR (United Nations High Commissioner for Refugees). 2015. "Women on the Run: First-Hand Accounts of Refugees Fleeing El Salvador, Guatemala, Honduras, and Mexico." Report, United Nations High Commissioner for Refugees, Washington, DC. http://www.unhcr.org/en-us/publications/operations/5630f24c6/women-run.html.

Vogt, Wendy A. 2012. "Ethnography at the Depot: Conducting Fieldwork with Migrants in Transit." In *Where Is the Field? The Experience of Migration Viewed through the Prism of Ethnographic Fieldwork*, edited by Laura Hirvi and Hanna Snellman, 66–86. Helsinki: Finnish Literature Society.

Vogt, Wendy A. 2013. "Crossing Mexico: Structural Violence and the Commodification of Undocumented Central American Migrants." *American Ethnologist* 40(4): 764–80.

Weber, Max. (1919) 2007. "Politics as a Vocation." In *From Max Weber: Essays in Sociology*, edited by Hans Heinrich Gerth and C. Wright Mills, 77–128. New York: Routledge.

Wolf, Sonja. 2014. "Central American Street Gangs: Their Role in Communities and Prisons." *European Review of Latin American and Caribbean Studies*, no. 96: 127–40.

Wright, Melissa W. 2011. "Necropolitics, Narcopolitics, and Femicide: Gendered Violence on the Mexico-U.S. Border." *Signs* 36(3): 707–31.

Yeates, Nicola. 2009. *Globalizing Care Economies and Migrant Workers: Explorations in Global Care Chains*. New York: Palgrave Macmillan.

Carne, Carnales, and the Carnivalesque

JOSÉ E. LIMÓN

At two in the afternoon a periodically unemployed working-class man in Mexican-American south Texas puts hot chunks of juicy barbecued meat with his fingers on an equally hot tortilla. The meat or *carne* has marinated overnight in beer and lemon juice. Antoñio or Toñio passes the meat-laden tortilla to one of the other eight mostly working-class men surrounding a rusty barbecue grill, but as he does so, the hand holding the food brushes against his own genital area, and he loudly tells the other, "¡Apaña este taco carnal, 'ta a toda madre mi carne!" (Grab this taco, brother, my meat is a mother!). With raucous laughter all around, I accept the full, dripping taco, add some hot sauce and reach for an iced down beer from an also rusty washtub.[1]

Some sixty years ago the Mexican thinker Samuel Ramos published his well-known and still culturally authoritative *Profile of Man and Culture in Mexico* (1934, 1962), an interpretive general narrative history of its subject since its indigenous beginnings. A kind of secondary precursor to my work, Ramos was trying to explain what he saw as the reduced sense of Mexican cultural life and its contradictions in his time. As part of his contemporary account, a kind of climax to his narrative, Ramos turns into an anthropological, if distanced, observer of everyday Mexican life, particularly male life. For example, the Mexican *pelado* or lower-class man

> belongs to a most vile category of social fauna; . . . a form of human rubbish . . . Life from every quarter has been hostile to him and his reaction has been black resentment. He is an explosive being with whom relationship is dangerous, for the slightest friction causes him to blow up.

According to Ramos, the Mexican lower-class man's

> explosions are verbal and reiterate his theme of self affirmation in crude and suggestive language. He has created a dialect of his own, a diction which abounds in ordinary words, but he gives these words a new meaning. He is an animal whose ferocious pantomimes are designed to terrify others, making them believe that he is stronger than they and more determined. Such reactions are illusory retaliations against his real position in life which is a nullity.

For Ramos, these verbal pantomimes, these explosive linguistic reactions are of a particular kind. This lower-class man's "terminology abounds in sexual allusions which reveal his phallic obsession; the sexual organ becomes symbolic of masculine force." The reproductive organs are a symbolic source of "not only one kind of potency, the sexual, but every kind of human power," as this man "tries to fill his void with the only suggestive force accessible to him: that of the male animal," and, continues Ramos, "so it is that his perception becomes abnormal; he imagines that the next man he encounters will be his enemy; he mistrusts all who approach him" (1962:59–61).

In this essay—this first instance of my own ethnographic work in contemporary south Texas—I want to discuss what Foucault calls discourses of power as these concern Mexican-American south Texas. You have already heard two examples of such discourses: one, the expressive, all-male humor of a group of *batos* (guys, dudes) articulated in and through the ritualistic consumption of barbecued meat in southern Texas, an event called a *carne asada*; and, two, Samuel Ramos' narratively imbedded commentary on the language and culture of the Mexican male lower class, a discourse tradition continued by Octavio Paz in the 1950s and applied directly to the Mexican-Americans of south Texas in the 1960s by anthropologist Joseph Spielberg (1974).

Somewhat mindful of Marcus' recent call upon Marxist ethnographers to provide analyses of the culture of the dominant as well as the dominated (1986), I have elsewhere tried to show how this second set of discourses, this interpretive tradition begun by Samuel Ramos, functions as a discourse of power with a larger international scope (Limón 1987). At critical moments in Mexican and

Mexican-American history, this interpretive tradition, perhaps unintentionally, helps to ratify dominance through its negative psychologistic interpretation of the Mexican male lower class and their language. As Ramos' commentary clearly illustrates, this discourse casts these classes in the idiom of human rubbish, animality, aggressiveness, and abnormality—in the Christian realm of the devil, if you will. This is a view, I might add, considerably shared by those—both Anglo and Mexican-Americans—who hold class power in southern Texas.

My chief purpose here, however, is to begin to develop an alternative but critical understanding of this lower-class male culture; to develop a third narrative discourse, if you will, one which I would like to think Foucault might have called an archeology of subjugated knowledges and practices, this in an effort to demonstrate *their* power as a discourse of the dominated even as I draw out its gender contradictions. My analysis will draw from recent Marxist perspectives on language, on the anthropology of natural symbols, but centrally on Bakhtin's sense of the carnivalesque, for these men are, I will argue, Bakhtinian *batos*.

Yet, as I contest Ramos in this analysis, I also wish to remain in dialogue with my primary precursors. Renato Rosaldo notes that "culturally distinctive jokes and banter play a significant role in constituting Chicano culture, both as a form of resistance and as a source of positive identity" (1989:150). Did Bourke and Dobie somehow semiconsciously recognize the cutting edge of such humor, and is this why they largely ignored it? Or did the linguistic complexity of such humor mark the limits of inquiry for these barely if at all fluent speakers of Spanish? Or, even more cutting edge, is the in-group character of humor such that they, as outsiders, were excluded? Jovita Gonzalez certainly recognized it in her jocular rendition of the devil in south Texas, although it is highly unlikely that as a bourgeois woman she could have entered the male *cantina* culture of her time, precursor to these scenes. Finally, some substantial portion of Américo Paredes' career has focused on male humor. More on this.

My rendering of this sociocultural process of "resistance" and "positive identity," as Rosaldo says, departs directly from Paredes' work. Though in this essay I return to the "same" Lower Rio Grande Valley where he studied humor, it is no longer the "same" semirural society of the 1960s but rather, by 1981–82, an emerging postmodern urbanizing political economy. Here we visit not Brownsville but Hidalgo County also noted earlier by Paredes, still a center of a multinational agribusiness-based economy but one now diversified by cheap labor industrial assembly plants (*maquiladoras*) across the river in Mexico and by drugs. Here we treat not the narrated bilingual-bicultural joke of the ascending middle class but rather the speech body play of a lower-class *fuereño* existence. Here humor becomes not existential angst and cultural ambivalence but carnivalesque critical difference, though never without its own internal contradiction, for the fact that here, in the tradition of my precursors save Captain Bourke, I deal with a world of men from which women are excluded qualifies the "positive" and "resistance" character of this humor.

Later that hot August Saturday afternoon in 1982, another man, a part-time auto parts salesman, in a ten-year-old pickup drives up to our barbecue session on the outskirts of McBurg, a designated "All American" city. He brings with him a couple of pounds of tripe intestines which will eventually be added to other offal and to the *fajita*, or skirt steak, now turning dark golden brown and sizzling in its fat on the barbecue grill. His *tripitas*—for all the meat parts are expressed in the diminutive—are turned over to Poncho, house painter, and the latest cook at the grill; Jaime, this new arrival (otherwise known as "el Midnight" because he is quite dark), begins to shake everyone's hand in greeting, saying, "¿Como estas?" (How are you doing?), etc. Expecting my turn, I put down my beer and dry my hand on my jeans, but Jaime never makes it past the second man he greets.

This is Simón, otherwise known as "el Mickey Mouse" because of his large ears. He has been a construction laborer most of his adult life except for three years spent at the state prison after he got caught on the highway to Austin transporting marijuana intended for the students at the university. ("¡Que pendejada!" "¡Tiré un beer can y me paró el jurado!"—What stupidity! I threw out a beer can and the cop stopped me!)

Simón takes Jaime's hand as if to shake it but instead yanks it down and firmly holds it over his own genital area even as he responds to Jaime's "¿Como estas?" with a loud "¡Pos, chinga ahora me siento a toda madre, gracias!" (Well, fuck, now I feel just great, thank you!). There is more laughter, which only intensifies when "Midnight" in turn actually grabs and begins to squeeze "el Mickey's" genitals. With his own free hand, for the other is holding a taco, "el Mickey" tries to pull away from Jaime, unsuccessfully. Finally in an effort to slip out of Jaime's grip, he collapses to the ground cursing and trying to laugh at the same time and loses his taco in the process. Jaime, however, has gone down on his knees and manages to maintain his grip even as he keeps saying over and over, "¡Dime que me quieres, cabrón, dime que me quieres!" (Tell me you love me, goddammit, tell me you love me!). "El Mickey" finally says "¡Te quiero dar en la madre!" (I want to beat the hell out of you), playing on the double meaning of *quiero* as "want" and "love." He takes a few semimock punches at Jaime's body and receives a few in return both carefully avoiding the face. Everyone is still laughing as el Mickey and Midnight, still on their knees, hug each other to a stop. As they help each other up, Jaime tells "Mickey," "Dejando de chingaderas, anda a traer otro taco y traile uno a tu papa" (All screwing around aside, go get another taco and bring one for your father), referring, of course, to himself. Doing or saying *chingaderas* (fuck ups), that is how these men label and gloss this activity, also sometimes *pendejadas* and *vaciladas* (stupidities, play routines) (see Spielberg 1974).

In the 1950s another distinguished Mexican intellectual, yet another second-ary precursor, had this story to tell about the Mexican lower-class male per-sonality and his language. "It is significant," says Octavio Paz, "that masculine homosexuality is regarded with a certain indulgence insofar as the active agent is concerned." The passive agent is an abject, degraded being. "This ambiguous conception," he continues, "is made very clear in the word games or battles—full of obscene allusions and double meanings—that are so popular in Mexico City."

> Each of the speakers tries to humiliate his adversary with verbal traps and ingenious linguistic combinations, and the loser is the person who cannot think of a comeback, who has to swallow his opponent's jibes. These jibes are full of aggressive sexual allusions; the loser is possessed, is violated, by the winner, and the spectators laugh and sneer at him. (1961:39-40)

Octavio Paz continues this commentary translated into English in 1961. "The Mexican macho," he says

> is a humorist who commits *chingaderas*, that is, unforeseen acts that produce confusion, horror, and destruction. He opens the world; in doing so, he rips and tears it, and this violence provokes a great sinister laugh . . . the humor of the *macho* is an act of revenge. (1961:81)

"Whatever may be the origins of these attitudes," Paz tells us, "the fact is that the essential attribute of the *macho*—power—almost always reveals itself as a capacity for wounding, humiliating, annihilating" (1961:82).

It is almost six o'clock on this evening outside of McBurg, at what our host Chema likes to call his *rancho* which amounts to less than one-quarter acre of dry, wholly undeveloped land with only a few mesquites to provide some shade from the hot south Texas sun. Chema bought the land, called a "ranchette" by local real estate agents, when he came into a little money from a workmen's in-jury compensation settlement. He fell from a truck while doing farm labor for extra money. Massaging his lower back for the still lingering pain, he says, "El pínche abogado Chicano se quedó con la mitad" ("The damn *Chicano* lawyer kept half"). Chema's only real notion for improving the property is to build an inevitable brick barbecue pit, but until he can afford it, he will have to haul the portable rusty one on the back of his pickup out to the *rancho*.

A few more men have come with more meat and beer, and a few have left playfully taunted by the others, "Tiene que ir a reportar a la vieja" (He has to go report to his old lady), knowing that eventually they'll have to go report to their "old ladies." The eating and drinking and the talk are still thick, and *conjunto* polka music is playing from a portable radio, although later this will be replaced by guitar playing and singing of, on the one hand, *corridos* with accompanying *gritos* (cries) and, on the other, American tunes from the fifties and early sixties such as "In the Still of the Night" by the Five Satins to which everyone will sing a cacophony of appropriate *sho do be do be doos*.

One of the men keeps insisting that he has to go; with equal insistence he is told to have another beer and to make a taco out of the very last of the cherished delicacy, *mollejitas* (glandular organs), but he is particularly insistent because his kids need to be picked up at the movies where, we discover, they have been watching Steven Spielberg's *E.T.—The Extra-Terrestrial*. Octavio is almost ready to leave when Chema, our host and ranch owner asks him: "Aye, 'Tavo. Sabes como de dice *E.T.* en espanol?" (Hey 'Tavo, do you know how to say *E.T.* in Spanish?). Before Octavio can even try to reply, a grinning Chema answers his own question correctly by saying *Eh Te*, but he is also holding his hand over his genitals and gesturing twice with it as he pronounces the two syllables. *Eh Te* does of course mean E.T. in Spanish, but is also the way a toddler might pronounce *este* or "this one," dropping a consonant *s*, as in *este papel*—this paper. In saying Eh Te and with his double gesture, Chema is calling attention, particularly Octavio's attention, to his penis—this one. But things get better . . . or worse . . . as the case may be. Chema continues his interrogation of Octavio. "¿Y, como se llaman los dos hermanitos de E.T.?" (And what are the names of E.T.'s two little brothers?). Chema demonstrates the answer with another genital double gesture, this time answering his own question with the Spanish *Eh Tos*, again exploiting the baby play language pronunciation of *estos* meaning *these*, referring, of course, to *these two* meaning his own testicles. Everyone, including Octavio, is laughing and all of us cannot help but look as Chema does his gestures and baby talk, and he isn't through yet. "And what," he asks, "is the name of E.T.'s mother?" This time, however, Octavio, who has obviously been conducting his own ethnography of this speech act, beats Chema to the answer with his hand at his crotch, loudly and triumphantly proclaims the answer, "¡Mama Eh Te!"; this time, Octavio has exploited the original *Este* (this one) and also the charged ambiguity of *mama* in Spanish, which depending on accent and syntax can mean "mother" or "suck." Laughing with the others, Octavio finally makes his way to the movie *E.T.* or *Eh Te* to pick up the kids; Chema is shaking his head and laughing and complaining about all of the meat juice he has managed to rub all over his crotch.

By seven or eight, more people start dispersing, a few latecomers arrive, a fire has been started, and one of the guitarists sings the *corrido* of Jacinto Trevino about a brave south Texas Mexican who shot it out with the Texas Rangers in

1906 in the town of Brownsville just down the river from McBurg (Paredes 1976). Finally, thinks your ethnographer, I get some real folklore of resistance and not all of the these *chingaderas*.

For at that moment, I am troubled, at least intellectually, by what I have reexperienced, having gone through such events several times in my life in south Texas but also in a few cantinas in Monterrey, in Los Angeles, in Mexico City. Are Ramos and Paz right when they speak of sexual anxiety, of wounding and humiliation? Are the *chingaderas* "unforeseen acts that produce confusion, horror, and destruction" amidst a "great sinister laugh"? And it does not help to have reread a recent anthropological study of such south Texas male humor specifically in this area near McBurg, in which Joseph Spielberg, also a native south Texan, concludes that this humor "can be characterized as verbal aggression aimed at another when he is most vulnerable" by his "own lack of discretion in bodily functions, social circumstances or by revealing his sentiments." In the tradition of Ramos and Paz, Spielberg also believes that "the principal theme of this humor" is "humiliation" (1974:46).

These discourses, as I say, troubled me then for they did not speak well of these, my people, and perhaps they do not speak well of me, for frankly, although with some ambivalent distance, I had a good time that Saturday afternoon and have had a good time since.

I had indeed gone to dominated southern Texas in 1982 looking for a folklore of resistance, carrying in my head the examples furnished by Genovese, by Gutman, by E. P. Thompson and George Rude, by Gramsci, and, of course, by Paredes, and I found instead a powerful yet contradictory sexual and scatological discourse—part of a greater Mexican working-class folk tradition left largely unexamined by my primary precursors. Yet, it is a tradition, as I say, delegitimized by the powerful authoritative intellectual discourses of Ramos and Paz and, in a more circumscribed but still effective way, by Spielberg. And I found difficult, and perhaps still do, its relegitimization, because this is at least the implicit burden carried by those who approach such materials from a Marxist cultural perspective. Certainly one alternative is simply to deny the burden and accept Ramos and Paz or perhaps some species of functionalist argument where these behaviors are seen as adaptive steam valves or as "communitas," so that as everyone leaves Chema's ranch they feel prepared to confront the labors they will face on Monday.

How can one rethink these materials as a Marxist narrative of "resistance," especially when they do not nicely lend themselves to such a reading as do peasant rituals of inversion, black spirituals, and English artisans? And when one has to contend with an extant authoritative interpretive discourse, especially one developed by members of the same general cultural group, for these—Ramos, Paz, and Spielberg—are *Mexican* observers; and, finally and most importantly, when one is faced with its manifest gender contradictions?

Writing with a Difference

We may begin this alternative reformulation by examining the central sexual symbolization that lies at the heart of the speech play and gesture that I have noted. Tonio's, Jaime's, Samuel's, Octavio's, and Chema's obvious and clear expressive manipulations of body and speech would certainly seem consistent with Samuel Ramos' observation that the Mexican lower-class man's

> terminology abounds in sexual allusions which reveal his phallic obsession; the sexual organ becomes symbolic of masculine force. In verbal combat he attributes to his adversary an imaginary femininity, reserving for himself the masculine role. By this stratagem he pretends to assert his superiority over his opponents. (1962:59–60)

For these commentators, aggression and its generative conditions, inadequacy and inferiority, are directly expressed through anal references and the theme of male sexual violation in this humor. I would not deny the existence of these values and meanings, given my earlier argument for the historical production of aggression. I would, however, argue that such references might be multivocal symbols possessing *several* meanings and not reducible to a single one that fits a preconceived psychoanalytical scheme.

It is too easy to rely on a simple and wild psychoanalysis when dealing with such physical references. Mary Douglas has warned us of the dangers and shortcomings of such simple psychologistic readings when they concern rituals dealing with the human body (1978). Some psychologists are fond of treating such rituals not as social acts but as the expression of private and personal infantile concerns. "There is," she believes, "no possible justification for this shift of interpretation just because the rituals work upon human flesh. . . ." Those who make this interpretive reduction

> proceed from unchallenged assumptions which arise from the strong similarity between certain ritual forms and the behavior of psychopathic individuals. The assumption is that in some sense primitive cultures correspond to infantile stages in the development of the human psyche. Consequently such rites are interpreted as if they express the same preoccupations which fill the mind of psychopaths or infants. (1978:115)

She argues for an alternative analytical model for the understanding of the human body in relation to society—one that is "prepared to see in the body a

symbol of society, and to see the powers and dangers credited to social structure reproduced in small on the human body" (1978:115). A society's definition
and treatment of the body and bodily pollution is, in her estimation, a critical
symbolic key for grasping its perceptions of its own structure and of its external
relationships. Such pollution—all forms of matter issuing from the body's orifices
as well as entering through them—may acquire symbolic proportions, as do necessarily the orifices themselves. The Coorgs of India, for example, are an isolated
mountain community sharing with other castes a fear of what is "outside and
below" their group. In their ritual behavior they "treat the body as if it were a be-
leaguered town, every ingress and exit guarded for spies and traitors" (1978:123).

I would submit that the *mexicano* on both sides of the border also has something to fear. This fear may not be simply an infantile concern with one's male
group and their simple sexual dominance. Rather, the themes of anality, pollution, and bodily penetration may also be symbolic expressions of an essentially
political and economic concern with social domination, not from below, as with
the Coorg, but from above—from the upper levels of the structure of power in
both countries. The marginalized working and unemployed classes where these
expressions abound constitute a body politic symbolically conscious of its socially
penetrable status. What Douglas claims for the Coorgs may be at least partially
applicable for Octavio, Samuel, Chema, and my other companions of those years:

> For them the model of the exits and entrances of the human body is a
> doubly apt symbolic focus of fears for their minority standing in the larger
> society. Here I am suggesting that when rituals express anxiety about the
> body's orifices the sociological counterpart of this anxiety is a care to pro-
> tect the political and cultural unity of a minority group. (1978:124)

There is certainly some evidence for this view in the often noted tendency
of the Mexican male but particularly the lower-class male to turn to the expression *chingar*—meaning sexual violation—to also express social violation, as
my companions often did when speaking particularly of their political/eco-
nomic relationships. "Me chigaron en el jale" (I got screwed at work), or during
one of the regular political discussions at the *carne asada*, "Pos gano Reagan, y
ahora si nos van a chingar" (Well, Reagan won, now we're all really going to get
screwed), and, finally "la vida es una chinga" (life is being constantly screwed),
which represents a quite reasonable perception of social conditions for these
men in this part of the world.

Others, the dominant Mexican-American and Anglo upper classes—*los chingones* (the big screwers), as these men commonly refer to them—always have
the ability to *chingar*, and it is entirely to the point that these are also men. It
is here, I suspect, that we can find a possible reason for the conversion of this

potential male social violation into the symbolic idiom of homosexuality. The routines, I will remind you, are called "*chingaderas.*" When Antonio seemingly threatens me with the meat that has passed by his genitals; when Octavio triumphantly says "¡Mama Eh Te!" they may indeed, as all Western men do, be expressing their latent anxiety about homosexuality. However, I am suggesting, partially following Mary Douglas' lead, that we need not just stop here. This homosexuality-in-play may also be reversing the sociosexual idiom of *chingar* as practiced by *los chingones* that continually violates the well-being and dignity of these working-class men.

But as I speak of play and games, I want to introduce yet another critical alternative perspective that speaks to a central flaw in Ramos, Paz, and Spielberg's understanding—or lack of it—of this speech play. It is important to recognize that even as my friends introduce the seeming aggressive idiom of sexual and social violation, they do so in a way that reframes that aggressive speech and gesture as play. Ramos, Paz, and Spielberg extract the sexual symbols in this play and give them their shallow reductive interpretations. They are not appreciative of these scenes as dynamic forums that interactionally produce meaning, mastering anxiety by inverting passive destiny through active play.

To begin with, *mexicanos* frame such scenes as ludic moments through native markers such as *relajando* and *llevandosale* (carrying on, bantering, playing), as in "nomas estabamos relajando" (we were just playing). We have a clear recognition of a play world in which open aggression can appear *only by mistake.* Such a mistake can occur when a novice or an unacculturated person fails to "recognize" the scene, or when he is less than competent in the requisite artistic skills. This latter consideration is crucial, for whatever latent aggression exists is not only rendered socially harmless to themselves but is turned into a basis for solidarity. The participants do this by interactionally creating an artistically textured discourse through skillful manipulations of allusion, metaphor, narration, and prosody.

Through interactionally produced play, through artistic creativity which does not deny the existence of aggression but inverts its negativity, the aggression of the world is transformed into mock aggression, mock fighting. What Bateson notes for nonhuman animals is also fundamentally true for these human artistic performers. These men mean something other than what is denoted by their aggressive language. Such language becomes like the "playful nips" which "denote the bite but [do] not denote what would be denoted by the bite" (1972:180). Art and play ultimately create paradox and fiction.

> Paradox is doubly present in the signals which are exchanged within the context of the play, fantasy, threat, etc. Not only does the playful nip not denote what would be denoted by the bite for which it stands but the

bite itself is fictional. Not only do the playing animals not quite mean what they are saying but, also, they are communicating about something which does not exist. (1972:182)

Aggression is what would be denoted by an actual bite—it is that something which is the hidden textual model for the playful nip, but is itself not denoted and therefore is negated at the moment of interaction. The playful nips of skillful artistic language produce a paradoxical effect, namely, the interactional production of solidarity, or as Latin Americans everywhere would say, *confianza*. Anthony Lauria notes that in Puerto Rico, "to indulge in *relajos* of any sort in the presence of anyone is to engage in a relation of *confianza*—or trust and familiarity with that person" (1964:62). As Lauria also notes, the ultimate paradoxical social result of the expressive scene is not aggression, humiliation, and alienation, but rather *respeto*. This—*respeto*—is the significance of ending a verbal exchange in mock punches, a hug, and a laugh. In one of Bateson's metalogues, his persona and that of his daughter engage in conversation:

DAUGHTER: Why do animals fight?

FATHER: Oh, for many reasons, territory, sex, food . . .

DAUGHTER: Daddy, you're talking like instinct theory. I thought we agreed not to do that.

FATHER: All right. But what sort of an answer do you want to the question, why animals fight?

DAUGHTER: Well, do they deal in opposites?

FATHER: Oh. Yes. A lot of fighting ends up in some sort of peace making. And certainly playful fighting is partly a way of affirming friendship. Or discovering or re-discovering friendship.

DAUGHTER: I thought so . . . (1972:18)

The artistic disclosure of friendship and respect in the *palomilla*'s interaction is not, in and of itself, ideological. That is, in a social vacuum, one could only construe it as play, friendship, and solidarity pure and simple. But, of course, these expressive scenes do not emerge in such a vacuum; they appear and are embedded in a postmodern political economy and a hegemonic culture that produce the marginalization and alienation that prevail among this class of *batos* in south Texas.

In these particular socioeconomic circumstances, play and its concomitant friendship become eminently ideological. As an emergent cultural performance, they represent an oppositional break—or critical difference—in the alienating hegemony of the dominant culture and society.

In a provocative article, Hearn notes that both mainstream and orthodox Marxist social science construe play as an activity ontologically secondary to the instrumental "real" world of politics and economics (1976–77). There is in such a construal a reproduction of capitalist categories of experience, a particularly unfortunate situation for Marxists. Hearn offers a corrective formulation of play which draws upon two nonorthodox Marxist theoreticians, Habermas and Marcuse. He notes the former's idea of language as symbolic interaction that "has a transcendental self-reflexive capacity which permits it to give expression to contradictions between appearance and reality, potentiality and actuality." Because it is not totally and automatically bound to reproduce the social order, "language has the potential for emancipating people from a dependence on reified cultural controls . . ." Thus, people have in their language "the capacity for reflexivity and transcendence which enables the creation of evaluative standards, allows the expression of contradictions, and supplies a conception of potentiality, of 'what can be'" (1976–77:147). These critical possibilities are greater for the least commodified and instrumentalized language—the emergent verbal art of marginalized peoples.

Hearn finds similar properties in Marcuse's concept of play. For Marcuse human play is the autonomous production of a dramatized, albeit temporal, vision of an alternative social order. In authentic, that is, non-commodified play, there is an emergent promise of "freedom from compulsion, hierarchy, inequality, and injustice" (1976–77:150). In its very ontology, play is neither secondary to instrumentalism nor its total denial. Rather it emerges as a critique, a constraint, and a transcendence of all instrumental activity. Ultimately, play— the free-flowing artistic exchanges of the men at Chema's *rancho*—has a subversive quality.

> In play while the limitations of the existing reality are exposed, a more satisfying—more equitable and just—order is celebrated . . . To the extent that play affirms the possibility of a "better world" it retains the potential for highlighting the negativity of and contributing to the subversion of the prevailing arrangements. (1976–77:150-51)

Mexicans and their verbal art draw upon the domains of language and play explored by Habermas and Marcuse, to produce a single phenomenon—human speech play. Through such speech play the participants continually produce a world of human value—of *confianza* and *respeto*. Such momentary productions, created in collective equality, negate the alienating constraints of the historically given social order that exists for *mexicanos* and affirms the possibilities, at least, of a different social order. The participants momentarily overturn the alienating effects even while reminding themselves of the real aggressivism in the world, that of *los chingones*, such as the upper middle classes of Brownsville who tell parody jokes about *curanderos* and *fuereños*.

Because the dominant discourse of power—that of Ramos, Paz, and Spielberg—has focused exclusively on the language of such scenes, I too have felt obligated to pay special attention to language even while recognizing that language is only part of a cultural contextual scene. Indeed, as I have suggested, it is the failure to recognize this total context of play that flaws this dominant discourse. In the world of Chema's *rancho*, it is necessary to recognize other symbolic elements that also constitute this play world as a temporary forum of nonalienation.

For example, this play scene is itself framed in another form of play—a kind of visible joke—namely, the very existence of Chema's *rancho*, that undeveloped little piece of land surrounded on all sides by huge ranches with oil drills or agribusiness factory farms; just a few miles away, for example, lie the beginnings of the King Ranch, parts of which, according to Mexican legend, were bought and paid for in blood. Chema's *rancho* is itself a source of constant humor, especially when, after a few beers, Chema begins to tell the other guys of his big plans for this little place. Inevitably someone will ask him, where are you going to put the cow? And, how is the bull going to screw her when you can't get them both on the place at the same time? The ultimate joke, of course, is the existence of this ranch dedicated not to capitalist mass agriculture but to friendship and play. While not a necessary condition, the very existence of this visible joke—this humorous incongruity—is productive of more jokes and play. As Mary Douglas says, "if there is no joke in the social structure, no other joke can appear" (1968:366).

Finally, there is my title—*carne, carnales*, and the carnivalesque. As the name of this event—*carne asada*—clearly indicates, and as I have suggested throughout, *carne*, meat, and its preparation and consumption are of central concern here. If, as Mary Douglas says, food is a code, then where in society lies the precoded message, and how does this message speak of hierarchy, inclusions, and exclusion (1971:61)? Or, as Appadurai reminds us, more specifically,

> When human beings convert some part of their environment into food, they create a peculiarly powerful semiotic device. In its tangible and material forms, food presupposes and reifies technological arrangements, relations of production and exchange, conditions of field and market, and realities of plenty and want. (1981:494)

What kind of meat is this socially, and what, if anything, is its message, its gastropolitics? These men are preparing and consuming those parts of a steer—the internal organs and the *faja*, or skirt steak—that are (were in 1982) clearly undervalued, low-prestige meats in the larger social economy, and, given their economic resources, that is not unexpected. (As an old Anglo rancher in the area told me, "We used to call that stuff 'Mexican leavings.'") What interests me is the way in which such meat parts—the discards of capitalist cattle ranching—are culturally mediated to convert them from low-prestige, rather tough and stringy protein into tasty, valued, social food. The use of the affectionate diminutive to name and linguistically "soften" this food—*fajita, mollejita, tripita*—is a case in point here and parallels the physical softening of the protein in much-valued, secretive marinades. (Indeed, it is rumored with awe and disgust that the marinade for Chema's meat, which is considered the best, has a touch of urine in it, some say from his wife.) When I hesitantly asked Chema about this, he said it was absolutely not true; he would never ask his wife to do such a thing. After a few seconds, he added, with a grin, "only a man's piss will do!" In this cultural mediation we get food that is an ever-present reminder of class status but which in its preparation negates that status.

The preparation and consumption of this meat also speaks to class difference in another way. The food is simply prepared, with the only utensils present being a sharp knife to cut the meat, the chiles, tomatoes, and onions for the sauce, and a fork to turn the meat. The sauce is prepared in the bottom parts of beer cans cut in half, and spoons are fashioned from the metal of the upper half. All of this preparation becomes a way for these guys to distinguish themselves from the dominant others—*los chingones*—who use plates, knives, forks, cups, and napkins. They also eat awful things like potato salad and lettuce with their meat which is bought and barbecued for them by their Mexican servants from across the border who cross the bridge to work in their large fashionable homes.

Finally, I am most interested in the way the consumption of food is a kind of interactional parallel to the charged language which paradoxically generated friendship. Everyone brings his low-prestige meat—a symbol of societal aggression—and contributes it to a central collective pile; everyone at some point or another takes a turn at shooing flies away, broiling and cutting the meat, and making the sauce. The tacos are made by everyone in random fashion, and since there are no plates they are passed along by hand, indeed, sometimes going through two or three sets of hands. These men at Chema's *rancho* and many others throughout south Texas, and, I might add, in the Texan outposts of central California, prepare and consume their own once low-prestige food collectively and nonhierarchically, even as they playfully assault each other with the charged language of friendship. The felt result is another discourse of power, but a power that does not dominate; rather and if only for brief moments, it liberates them from the contexts of alienation beyond Chema's *ranchos* where race and class still prevail.[2]

In this world at Chema's *carne* is closely linked to *carnales*, a kinship term used among brothers or close male friends. In the 1960s Chicano college students spoke in too self-conscious and slightly forced ways of *carnalismo*. These men never use this term, although when they hear it they can sense what it means. Rather, they freely use the term *carnal*—this folk term for brother or buddy which seems to me to be an appropriate native gloss for their cultural practice. In one too conscious and too keenly ideological moment, Chinito ("little Chinese man"), a young man with Asian features and the most educated among them (one year of college), holds up a piece of raw *fajita* and says, "esta carne es pa' mis carnales, esto es el carnalismo" (this meat is for my brothers, this is brotherhood). Another man, pained slightly by this apparent intrusion of linear ideology, immediately replies, "Mira cabron," and going for his genitals, says, "esta es la carne que te voy a dar" (Look, goddammit, this is the meat I'm going to give you). And it is only at this moment, when the others laugh hesitantly, that we see the possibility and the tones of real aggression. The world of too conscious ideology has intruded and must be rejected. One does not speak ideologically of friendship and community, one practices it in the symbolic action of meat, body, and language.

To unify these various revisionary perspectives, I want to think of these scenes as a present-day example of what Bakhtin calls the unofficial culture of the Middle Ages, the folk culture of Grotesque Realism, of the carnivalesque, the near realm of the Christian devil. The playful, sexual, and scatological language, the concern with minimalist consumption of meat taken from the internal stomach-centered parts of the animal, the concern with the body—all of these involve what Bakhtin called degradation, a principal aspect of the carnivalesque. But this is not degradation as the imprisoning bourgeois discourse of Ramos and Paz would have it.

> Degradation here means coming down to earth, the contact with earth as an element that swallows up and gives birth at the same time. To degrade is to bury, to sow, and to kill simultaneously, in order to bring forth something more and better. To degrade also means to concern oneself with the lower stratum of the body, the life of the belly and the reproductive organs; it therefore relates to acts of defecation and copulation, conception, pregnancy, and birth; it has not only a destructive, negative aspect, but also a regenerating one. To degrade an object does not imply merely hurling it into absolute destruction, but to hurl it down the reproductive lower stratum, the zone in which conception and a new birth takes place. Grotesque realism knows no other lower level; it is the fruitful earth and the womb. It is always conceiving. (Bakhtin 1984:21)

However, in adopting this Bakhtinian perspective on unofficial culture, heteroglossia, and the carnivalesque, one also has to note its political limitations and its uneasy relationship to Marxism. In a recent critical review of this tissue, Young seriously and persuasively questions the Marxist status of Bakhtin's thought on the carnivalesque in culture (Young 1985–86). Taken without critical revision, Young argues, Bakhtinian "carnival offers a liberal rather than a Marxist politics" (1985–86:92). That is, Bakhtin has offered a semi-idealist version of an essentialist humanistic oppositional Other. His carnivalesque is a transcendence of an unspecified general Foucauldian-like domination. Only by specifying the historical moment and social location of some of the carnivalesque; only by accounting for its class (and race) antagonistic character in a specific context can the carnivalesque be read as an expression of class contestative discourse. This I have tried to do. For it is specifically against the ruling bourgeois official culture of contemporary south Texas, including both Anglos *and* Mexican-Americans, that one must understand my companions. Their discourses of sexuality, the body, low food exactly counterpoint the repression and affectation of these ruling sectors throughout the region, a dominating culture whose most visible expression is the high societal celebration of George Washington's Birthday in Laredo, not that far from Chema's *rancho*.

But even as it sets limits to a dominant Anglo and Mexican class, perhaps the most encompassing significance for us of the carnivalesque as a total set of expressive practices is its critical relationship to the urbanized metroplex of cities and shopping malls linked by busy highways that now constitutes the reality of the Lower Rio Grande Valley. This emergent urbanizing postmodern political economy is based increasingly on low-wage service industries, high-tech farming, and on the same rapidly shifting patterns of consumption as everywhere else. Low-wage employment and protracted unemployment, as cheaper Mexican labor across the border is manipulated, lead to the long-term marginalization of men such as these on Chema's *rancho*, and, in turn, to the further marginalization of their spouses and to marital strain and divorce.

Finally and perhaps most critically in our own time there is the question of drugs. In the Lower Rio Grande Valley political economy, drugs are a commodity for personal use and, more attractively, for smuggling and dealing. These men, like poor young African-American men in the urban postmodern North, must constantly dance with this devil as a way of getting money and bringing stability and order into their pressured and fragmented lives. But, of course, this temptation to tap into the large amounts of money generated by the postmodern drug industry, wracked as it is by local violence, can only bring further stress. It is a situation captured vividly by the fine south Texas writer Rolando Hinojosa in his novel *Partners in Crime* (1985) as he traces the efforts of his modernist city detective protagonist, Rafe Buenrostro, to find meaning and order in the postmodern drug-fed culture that has descended upon his beloved Lower Rio Grande Valley in the 1970s.

It is not only in critical relationship to Ramos and Paz or the Anglo/Mexican dominant classes of South Texas that we must view the carnivalesque. The planned use and valuation of a "rural" setting, the insistence on simple meats recalling Dobie's *vaquero* cattle culture, the practice of bodily play and speech play to bring men together, all of these processes may also be understood as a critique of the totality of this new postmodern culture that has come to the Valley and the rest of south Texas, a bedevilment more insidious than the earlier coming of *los diablos tejanos*, the Texas Rangers—a late capitalism with no human face.

Yet, as Laura Cummings (1991) notes in a reply to an earlier version of this essay, the ritual reproduction of this expressive male culture of critical difference comes with a contradiction and at a cost. As I noted earlier, women are pointedly excluded from these scenes. What is centrally problematic in the male carnivalesque is the concomitant reproduction of a ritually enhanced sense of dominant masculinity which, its resistive edge notwithstanding, may be carried over into other spheres of lived experience with repressive consequences for women.

For this is a scene that has some clear capacity for lurching beyond the carnivalesque into a resemblance of Juan Pedro and his beer-drinking friends in Sandra Císneros' Texas short story, "Woman Hollering Creek." As his oppressed wife and the central protagonist, Cleofilas, watches from the margins, the effort of these men to communicate "bubbles and rises . . . gurgles in the throat . . . rolls across the surface of the tongue and erupts from their lips—a belch. . . ." as they try "to find the truth lying at the bottom of the bottle like a gold doubloon on the sea floor" (Císneros 1991:48).

Where are they, the women, in this male-dominated, too close approximation of the world of Gregorio Cortez? The place of women in the expressive world of south Texas—what my precursors rarely noted, including Jovita Gonzalez—and their particular warfare now appear as a revisionary task before us as we move beyond the paradoxical freedom and repression of *carne* and *carnales* to a different sense of the carnivalesque in another part of southern Texas well known to the residents of the Lower Rio Grande Valley—San Antoñio, Texas.

NOTES

Reprinted with the permission of Wisconsin University Press. This essay originally appeared in *Dancing With the Devil: Society and Cultural Poetics in Mexican-American South Texas*, 123–40 (Madison: University of Wisconsin Press, 1994).

1   Based on field research carried out, at various moments, during 1981 and 1982 under the partial auspices of a grant from the National Research Council and the Ford

Foundation. All personal names, including nicknames, as well as place names (except for Hidalgo County), are fictitious.

2   For a masterful descriptive and analytical account of working-class Mexican-American food culture in south Texas, see Montano (1992).

REFERENCES

Appadurai, Arjun. 1981. "Gastro-politics in Hindu South Asia." *American Ethnologist* 18:494–511.

Bakhtin, Mikhail. 1984. *Rabelais and His World*. Bloomington: Indiana University Press.

Bateson, Gregory. 1972. "A Theory of Play and Fantasy." In *Steps to an Ecology of Mind*. New York: Random House. 177–93.

Cisneros, Sandra. 1991. *Woman Hollering Creek and Other Stories*. New York: Random House.

Cummings, Laura. 1991. "Carne con Limon: Reflections on the Construction of Social Harmlessness." *American Ethnologist* 18:370–72.

Douglas, Mary. 1968. "The Social Control of Cognition: Some Factors in Joke Perception." *Man: The Journal of the Royal Anthropological Institute* 3:361–76.

Douglas, Mary. 1971. "Deciphering a Meal." In *Myth, Symbol, and Culture*, ed. Clifford Geertz. New York: W.W. Norton. 61–81.

Douglas, Mary. 1978 (1966). *Purity and Danger: An Analysis of the Concepts of Pollution and Taboo*. London: Routledge & Kegan Paul.

Hearn, Francis. 1976–77. "Toward a Critical Theory of Play." *Telos* 30:145–60.

Lauria, Anthony, Jr. 1964. "Respeto, Relajo, and Interpersonal Relations in Puerto Rico." *Anthropological Quarterly* 3:53–67.

Limón, José E. 1987. "Mexican Speech Play: History and the Psychological Discourses of Power." *Texas Papers on Latin America*, no. 87–06. Austin: University of Texas Institute of Latin American Studies.

Marcus, George E. 1986." Contemporary Problems of Ethnography in the Modern World System." In *Writing Culture: The Poetics and Politics of Ethnography*, ed. James Clifford and George E. Marcus. Berkeley: University of California Press.

Montano, Mario. 1992. "The History of Mexican Food Folkways of South Texas: Street Vendors, Offal Foods and Barbacoa de Cabeza." PhD dissertation, University of Pennsylvania.

Paredes, Américo. 1976. *A Texas-Mexican Cancionero*. Urbana: University of Illinois Press.

Paz, Octavio. 1961 (1951). *The Labyrinth of Solitude: Life and Thought in Mexico*. New York: Grove Press.

Ramos, Samuel. 1962 (1934). *Profile of Man and Culture in Mexico*. Austin: University of Texas Press.

Rosaldo, Renato. 1989. *Culture and Truth: The Remaking of Social Analysis*. Boston: Beacon Press.

Spielberg, Joseph. 1974. "Humor in Mexican-American Palomilla: Some Historical, Social, and Psychological Implications." *Revista Chicano-Requena* 2:41–50.

Young, Robert. 1985. "Back to Bakhtin." *Cultural Critique* 1:71–92.

PART IV

OTHERING

SPACES,

OTHERING

BODIES

The Erotic Zone: Sexual Transgression
on the U.S.-Mexican Border

RAMÓN GUTIÉRREZ

The images middle-class San Diegans have of Mexicans in general are often shaped by the immediate impressions and images they form of Tijuana. Like the Tijuanenses, who have deep kinship, social, and economic ties to San Diego and to southern California, San Diegans have deep-rooted and longstanding ties to Tijuana. Indeed, since the end of the nineteenth century, Tijuana's growth as a city, in large part, has depended more on prominent capitalists in San Diego than on those farther south in central Mexico. Tijuana's businesses were created with American technology to meet consumption demands located in San Diego and Los Angeles. The Santa Fe Railroad link, which by 1890 connected Los Angeles, San Diego, and Tijuana, is but one early example of this. The telephone wires and electric lines, which by 1914 tied Tijuana to an American economic infrastructure based in San Diego, is another.[1]

The line that marks the boundary between Mexico and the United States is a border that both binds and separates two spaces, two national territories that once were one, and two peoples of numerous classes and multiple ethnicities that are now quite impossible to pull apart. Thousands of Tijuanenses cross into the United States every day to work, to study, and to pass their leisure time shopping in fancy shops in La Jolla, strolling through Balboa Park, or stashing away their millions in San Diego's banks. Commerce and capital move ever more frenetically in the opposite direction as well. Billions of U.S. dollars flow into the *maquiladoras* just across the border. Millions of American tourists visit Tijuana yearly in search of inexpensive leather goods and black velvet paintings of Jesus Christ, Michael Jackson, and Che Guevara. Many San Diego boys count the days until they reach manhood with dreams of Tijuana's bestial sex acts, its drinking and debaucheries, which good Protestant mothers constantly caution their sons will only lead to hell, furry palms, and dissipation.

Educated middle-class San Diegans who understand the social and economic dynamics of the cultural space they inhabit, or whose daily lives are profoundly touched by Mexicans, know that Mexico's human geography is a complex and multifaceted universe never easy to describe in one breath or image. But for the majority of San Diegans, the less educated and more ignorant ones, Mexico and Mexicans are more a concept than a tangible reality. Caricatures, stereotypes, and images, born of ignorance, fed by fantasy, shaped and distorted by the media, and explained by folk aphorisms, are the currency of popular discourse. Whatever the genesis of these perceptions, distorted as they are, they shape the way middle-class Americans refract reflections of themselves onto the "illegal aliens," those nonhuman creatures from another world called Mexico, who constantly threaten to invade sovereign United States space and destroy the essence of American life.

My task here is to explore the way middle-class San Diegans express their fears, the way they construct "illegal aliens," imaginary Mexican enemies at their borders. Let me proceed with my most complex point regarding how Americans shape and organize their symbols of national identification, and conversely, how they shape national others, citizens of other nation-states.

David Schneider, the respected cultural anthropologist, in his book, *American Kinship*, argues that the symbol of "conjugal sexual intercourse" was the key symbol that shaped how middle-class white Americans understood kinship, or that complex set of human relationships that structures how individuals are related to each other:

> Sexual intercourse as an act of procreation creates the blood relationship of parent and child and makes genitor and genetrix out of husband and wife. But it is an act which is exclusive to and distinctive of the husband-wife relationship: sexual intercourse is legitimate and proper only between husband and wife and each has the exclusive right to the sexual activity of the other. . . . Sexual intercourse between persons who are not married is fornication and improper; between persons who are married

but not to each other is adultery and wrong; between blood relatives is incest and prohibited; between persons of the same sex is homosexuality and wrong; with animals is sodomy and prohibited; with one's self is masturbation and wrong; and with parts of the body other than the genitalia themselves is wrong. All of these are defined as "unnatural sex acts" and are morally, and in some cases, legally, wrong in American culture.[2]

The products of sexual intercourse, children born of shared blood and substance, are related to their parents naturally, or by the natural order of things. Father, mother, brother, sister, uncle, aunt, grandfather, and grandmother are related by blood, through acts that originate in intercourse and by a process that is deemed to be natural. People are also related through marriage and marriage is an institution rooted in law and custom. A husband and wife are related and duty-bound to each other through human laws. They are husband and wife, and their parents are in-laws (father-in-law, sister-in-law, son-in-law, etc.).

Middle-class white Americans organize their kin relationships around two orders: the order of nature, which is human and biological, and the order of law, which is based on the rule of reason. These two basic elements—nature and law—on which American notions of relatedness rest, are the basic oppositions through which spatial, political, philosophical, and zoological categories are often constructed and understood. One only has to take for an example how the United States of America defines citizenship and nationality to see this point. Americans are either born into the nation (the order of nature) or they enter it through a legal process (the order of law) and become citizens through a process we call "naturalization." Three types of citizens are possible in the United States: (1) those who are born American but are naturalized citizens of another country, (2) those who are born elsewhere but "naturalized" as Americans (quite frequently by marrying an American citizen), and (3) those who are American by birth and law.[3] Nature and law thus create citizens.

The nature/law code that derives from the domain of kinship creates other basic dichotomies, which are anchored to the symbol of conjugal sexual intercourse and are used to differentiate us/them, insider/outsider, male/female, law-abiding/criminal, human/animal, clean/dirty.

To form a mental picture of how American middle-class stereotypes of Mexico and Mexicans are logically constructed, we can begin at the spatial level, examining how Tijuana first developed as an escape valve for the sexually repressed and regulated American Protestant social body of San Diego. In this case, the international boundary between Mexico and the United States has long been imagined as a border that separates a pure from an impure body, a virtuous body from a sinful one, a monogamous conjugal body regulated by the law of marriage from a criminal body given to fornication, adultery, prostitution, bestiality, and sodomy.

Indeed, Tijuana really came into its own as a city in the 1920s primarily as a haven for American illegal activities. When Prohibition, the outlawing of the production and consumption of alcoholic beverages, was instituted in the United States in 1920, San Diegans rushed across the border to Tijuana to construct their gin mills and their saloons. Soon there were brothels, gambling houses, and all those pleasures and pains prohibited in respectable California society. San Diego newspapers frequently lambasted these activities. "Tia Juana Is a Disgrace to Mexico, a Menace to America," the *Los Angeles Examiner* announced in its headline, continuing that "Tia Juana is a plague spot and ought to be eradicated."[4] Although cries of shock and revulsion similar to these filled the pages of local tabloids, historian Vincent Z. C. de Baca argues that until the early 1940s, much of Tijuana's vice activity was owned and operated by American citizens who lived in Los Angeles and San Diego.[5] Prohibition was eventually abolished in 1935, but by that date the caricature of Tijuana as a den of vice and decadence—as a place of unruly and transgressive bodies—had been firmly fixed in the American psyche.

Shaping the images Americans have of the "other," of the Mexican that inhabits the deepest recesses of fantasy, are a series of concrete events that constantly crystallize the fear that seems to characterize sociocultural relations between San Diegans and Tijuanenses. Whether it be in the 1920s, the 1950s, or the 1990s, the Mexican rapist figures prominently in those fears. One can begin as early as 1926, with the famous Peteet case, to see how the fear and fantasy of rape constantly repeat themselves. The events of this case started on Saturday, 31 January 1926, when Thomas and Carrie Peteet and their two daughters, Clyde and Audrey, checked into Tijuana's San Diego Hotel. The family had crossed into Mexico for five days of vacation. A little gambling and a little drinking was all they had in mind. And, according to local witnesses, they did plenty of that. On Wednesday evening, 3 February, Thomas Peteet and his daughters entered the Oakland Bar, and before long Peteet, apparently drugged, passed out. His daughters met a similar fate, and in that state were abducted and raped. Mr. Peteet came to later that night, discovered by his wife in the street outside the Oakland Bar. The ordeal the girls had suffered was known the next day. Deeply humiliated and shamed when they returned home, the family committed suicide together. The case became a cause célèbre in San Diego. What sorts of outrages were being perpetrated on Americans across the border? Civic, religious, and temperance groups demanded a closed border. "Remove the menace of Tijuana and keep San Diego County a clean, safe, law-abiding community," the San Diego Law Enforcement League constantly proclaimed.[6] Eventually the furor died down, but before it did, this celebrated rape case had created an image of Tijuana and the Mexicans living there as brutes governed by lust and given to crime.[7]

Since the famous Peteet case, the shape of reporting on Tijuana has not changed very much. What is noted in stories are the unregulated sexual activities of American youth. The crimes they commit in Tijuana are rarely noticed; what is done to them makes the evening news.[8] As a headline in a recent story in the *Orange County Register* noted: "Tijuana's wild nights of partying lure teens south, where beatings, robbery and death sometimes await."[9] The story chronicles how young American boys and girls escape the natural-law authority of parents over children with trips to Tijuana where minors are served alcohol, indulge their sexual desires and fantasies, and create a disorder that is never permitted at home. At home, they would be breaking the law. The law codes that order and regulate the body and kinship in American thought stem from the symbol of conjugal marital intercourse. In Tijuana, American boys and girls desecrate marriage by soliciting prostitutes or by becoming the victims of rape. In American middle-class minds, Tijuana is a marginal area that lies beyond the border of the American body politic governed by nature and law. Mexico is a place where vice thrives. There, gambling, liquor, drugs, prostitution, and unnatural sexual activities flourish. And these activities constantly threaten to spill across the border to corrupt the American body politic.

If we cross the border into San Diego County to explore how middle-class San Diegans speak about and imagine the Mexican workers who actually cross the border to cook their meals, to clean their streets, to nurse their babies, and to build their homes, we find again a related set of stereotypes best understood by looking at the ways in which nature and law create the moral community of kinship.

The dominant rhetoric concerning Mexican workers in the San Diego area has been marked by two major depictions. First, Mexican workers are "illegal aliens" and thus a menace to public safety. They break the law. They engage in illegal acts, such as seeking work. In times of economic difficulty, they take away jobs that are meant for Americans, and thus are the reason for economic hardship. This argument is well known, and so are its fallacious assumptions, but it nonetheless gets reinformed continually because the Immigration and Naturalization Service, seeking illegals, frequently stages raids at factories and fields. The second depiction of Mexican workers is that they are physically dangerous because they are rapists, the source of drugs and diseases such as AIDS, and a menace to public health because they live in squalor and unsanitary conditions.

Regarding Mexican illegality, consider the 1989 survey sent to voters in San Diego by the American Immigration Control Foundation. The Foundation asked recipients of the survey for their opinions on "America's illegal alien crisis," informed them of what it considered the facts on "illegal aliens," and solicited their dollars. Full of xenophobic rhetoric, the leaflet posed a variety of questions. Question 3 asked: "Which of the problems associated with illegal aliens are the most personally disturbing to you?" The options, to name but the most inflammatory, were: "bilingual public education, bring in diseases like AIDS, loss of jobs for American citizens, drug trafficking and crime." The opening statement of the cover letter that accompanied the poll stated:

My forefathers and yours entered America legally. They understood through hard work, obeying the law and contributing to the nation's good, they would EARN the right of citizenship in this great land of opportunity. But what we're dealing with today is quite different. Statistics show our borders have become a floodgate for millions . . . who think little of breaking our laws and living off taxpayers like you and me.[10]

The "illegal alien" as a physically dangerous rapist is a stereotype that has a long history in U.S.-Mexican relations that goes back to the 1926 Peteet case. But more recently, paranoid fantasies about Mexican rapists have reemerged in American public discourse. In September 1986, hysteria over school-aged children who attended the Kelly School in Carlsbad, California, in the northern part of San Diego County, exploded as a result of two incidents. The first involved several migrant workers and a fifteen-year-old girl near the Kelly School. Apparently the girl was walking near the school when three Mexican migrants started to approach her from the front, and three more from behind. An acquaintance of the girl saw the men approaching her and immediately called out to the girl, thus avoiding a "bad situation." Community concern had already been fanned by a newspaper story in the 19 September 1986 issue of the *San Diego Union.* "Aliens Said Preying on School Kids," the headline read. The story quoted Border Patrol Assistant Chief Gene Smithburg reporting that "A new type of crime is being perpetrated by undocumented aliens, extorting lunch money from schoolchildren . . . it's really too bad that something like this happens. The kids are really intimidated." A public outcry was quickly heard and it led to a "roundup" conducted on horseback, helicopter, and all-terrain vehicles. Some three thousand "illegal aliens" were apprehended and returned to Mexico. The idea of adult single men, dark-skinned men, who congregated near innocent children, was more than parents could take. As one resident said, "We hit a nerve that runs through San Diego County."[11]

One sees another permutation of the fear of the Mexican rapist in the "Light Up the Border" campaign that was started in San Diego in 1989 by Muriel Watson, a middle-class white widow of a former U.S. Border Patrol agent. The main activity of "Light Up the Border" was to get citizens to drive in their cars to Dairy Mart Road, just off Highway 5, about one mile north of the Tijuana-San Diego border, and, at sunset, to turn on the headlights of their cars toward the border. The campaign was a huge success, counting over five hundred cars and some 2,500 participants. These individuals came to "Light Up the Border," says Watson, because "they just share my concern, they all had [newspaper] clippings: 'Oh, look at this, this 16-year-old girl was raped and her throat was slit and they rescued her just in time.' . . . So this was what motivated me . . . pure and simple."[12] Using body metaphors to describe her goals, Watson explained, "The light . . . was just meant to light up this area. . . . This is a main artery, this is a very tender spot."[13]

Many sensationalistic things have been written and reported about "Light Up the Border." This probably is due to the fact that the movement is composed of many desperate elements, among them neo-Nazis and skinheads who are motivated by racist and xenophobic ideas. But, in the mind of Muriel Watson, the movement's founder, her actions are born of a concern for the "aliens." She wants to protect the "aliens" from border rapists. Her intentions are totally altruistic. She and her followers, Watson says, are "good Americans" motivated only by the desire to uphold law and order. Certain physical things had to take place, and one of them was the message to the alien: "Look, you're crossing the border and it is against the law.[14] "Light Up the Border," says Watson, was started to create

a certain modicum of control. It's just like your own yard in your own house. If you have a fence up, then you keep kids from running across your lawn. . . . If you see somebody coming on, you're more aware of it and you're able to better control the flow of whatever goes across your own property. . . . I still ask the question: "Why are they coming the way they are?" and that has to be resolved. And there's no reason that between two reasonably civilized nations, that the border can't be respected.[15]

The idea that the nation's front yard is being littered with the refuse of rapists, robbers, and petty criminals has been expressed in much of the literature describing the tensions in the northern townships of San Diego County. Here, one of the constant complaints of Americans is that the "aliens" congregate at shopping centers and local business establishments, waiting for work. Gloria Carranza, Transient Issues Coordinator for the City of Encinitas, summed up this fear well:

The businesses were complaining that the large number of migrants was actually a negative impact to them because they were walking through the establishments or "hanging out" in the morning, looking for employment. In the afternoon they were hanging out, they would be drinking . . . just the intimidation factor of large groups of Hispanic males was an intimidation . . . [it was] a public safety issue.[16]

The composition of the Mexican workforce in Encinitas was large, single, and male—men who did not duplicate the American ideal of compulsory heterosexuality. Nina LeShan, a social worker, described this population and the root of the problem well when she said: "Most of the time, men come up here, and without their family or without any women."[17]

The image of the disease-infested Mexican is often juxtaposed and incorporated in public-safety arguments. In San Diego County the stereotype of the disease-spreading Mexican has become particularly potent primarily because the large-scale development of middle- and upper-class housing has suddenly put the residents of these new tracts in face-to-face contact with the cardboard and plastic shantytowns Mexican workers have constructed as their own shelters. These workers' camps have long existed, but went unnoticed when the area was still predominately rural. There they lived in the most rudimentary and rustic of conditions, without toilets, without running water, without heat or electricity. Then housing starts began. And as the number of Mexican workers arriving to build these fancy houses increased, so too the friction, fueled by the belief that the area was being overrun and that the encampments were a health menace to Americans. The city of Encinitas took the most strident measures against these "illegals." Using force, it proceeded "to clean them [the camps] up," stationing guards to assure that such squatter communities did not develop again. It is significant that the city of Encinitas wanted "to clean up" the camps, for, as Nina LeShan, a social worker and midwife to the Mexican migrants in the area stated, the Mexican were seen "as filth."[18]

In the public and official discourse of the city of Encinitas and its residents, the distinction between "us" and "them," between Americans and Mexicans, between citizens and "aliens," between persons who obey the law and those who are criminals, has been cast as "cleanliness" versus "dirt," as a distinction between healthy bodies and those infested with disease. "Dirtiness" represents the physical threat to the ideal order, to the orderly functioning of society.

Mary Douglas, the cultural anthropologist, in her book *Purity and Danger*, writes that symbolic schemes preoccupied with disease, hygiene, and dirt are often implicit comments about the ideal order of society. Douglas notes:

> If we can abstract pathogenicity and hygiene from our notions of dirt, we are left with the old definition of dirt as matter out of place. . . . It implies two conditions: a set of ordered relations and a contravention of that order.

Dirt, then, is never a unique, isolated event. Where there is dirt, there is a system. Dirt is the by-product of a systematic ordering and classification of matter, in so far as ordering involves rejecting inappropriate elements.[19]

What I have been arguing is that in the dominant Anglo-American middle-class culture of the United States, the symbol of marital sexual intercourse is the fundamental foundation on which the moral community rooted in nature and law rests. This is a moral community that grants citizenship principally to those persons who mirror its body order, and resists penetration and excludes those who do not—"illegal aliens," rapists, dirt, and so on. Cultural historian Sander Gilman has noted that coitus creates in all of us a sense of abandonment, an abandonment of the highly ordered and controlled world. Such moments represent the potential loss of control, not only of self, but of our private and public worlds. "Such disorder cannot be contained within the self. It must be expelled into the world. The projection of such disorder, a disorder exemplified by the sexual, . . . [often] take[s] the form of the thought-collective's fantasies about the Other, whether the 'sexual' or the 'racial' Other."[20]

In Mexico, the process of nation building began when single Spanish males raped Indian women. The result was cultural, social, and biological *mestizaje*, the heritage of race mixture that remains the dominant conquest legacy for Mexicans. In the United States, the nation was founded atop Puritan and Calvinist foundations, based on a strict morality and beliefs about what was natural and unnatural, who were and who were not kin by blood and marriage. That legacy of nature and law, which is at the very core of American middle-class kinship ideas, explains how Americans project their hysterias and anxieties and thereby symbolically construct Mexicans.

NOTES

Reprinted with permission from the author. This essay originally appeared in *Mapping Multiculturalism*, edited by Avery Gordon and Chris Newfield, 253-63 (Minneapolis: University of Minnesota Press, 1996).

1   Vincent Z. C. de Baca, "Moral Renovation of the Californias: Tijuana's Political and Economic Role in American-Mexican Relations, 1920-1935" (PhD diss., University of California, San Diego, 1991), 1-4.

2   David Schneider, *American Kinship: A Cultural Account* (Chicago: University of Chicago Press, 1980), 38.

3   David M. Schneider, "Kinship, Nationality, and Religion in American Culture: Toward a Definition of Kinship," in *Symbolic Anthropology: A Reader in the Study of Symbols and Meanings*, ed. Janet L. Dolgin, David S. Kemnitzer, and David Schneider (New York: Columbia University Press, 1977), 67-68.

4   "Tia Juana Is a Disgrace to Mexico, a Menace to America," *Los Angeles Examiner*, 11 February 1926; quoted in de Baca, "Moral Renovation of the Californias," 12-13.

5   De Baca, "Moral Renovation of the Californias," 10.

6   Quoted in de Baca, "Moral Renovation of the Californias," 8.

7   De Baca, "Moral Renovation of the Californias," 13–16.

8   See, for example, "Mexican Accuses U.S. of Disinformation Campaign," *San Diego Union*, 21 November 1986; "Pressure, Payoffs Curb Mexican Press," *Los Angeles Times*, 4 March 1987; "Views Differ over Coverage by U.S. Press of Mexico," *San Diego Union*, 11 October 1986.

9   *Orange County Register*, 1 December 1991: K1.

10 Quoted in Isabelle Fauconnier, "Perceptions of and Reactions to Undocumented Workers in San Diego" (senior thesis, University of California, San Diego, 1991), 5.

11 Daniel Wolf, *Undocumented Aliens and Crime: The Case of San Diego* (La Jolla, Calif.: Center for U.S.-Mexican Studies, 1988), 21.

12 Muriel Watson interview, transcript in Fauconnier, "Perceptions," 92.

13 Watson interview, transcript in Fauconnier, "Perceptions," 91.

14 Watson interview, transcript in Fauconnier, "Perceptions," 42.

15 Watson interview, transcript in Fauconnier, "Perceptions," 48, 88.

16 Gloria Carranza interview, transcript in Fauconnier, "Perceptions," 53–54.

17 Nina LeShan interview, transcript in Fauconnier, "Perceptions," 70.

18 LeShan interview, transcript in Fauconnier, "Perceptions," 74.

19 Mary Douglas, *Purity and Danger: An Analysis of the Conceptions of Pollution and Taboo* (London: Praeger, 1966), 35.

20 Sander L. Gilman, *Sexuality: An Illustrated History, Representing the Sexual in Medicine and Culture from the Middle Ages to the Age of AIDS* (New York: John Wiley and Sons, 1989), 3.

Medicalizing the Mexican: Immigration, Race, and
Disability in the Early Twentieth-Century United States

NATALIA MOLINA

Every few years, the debate over whether race is a social construction or a biological reality is rekindled.[1] A recent example is a March 2005 *New York Times* op-ed
piece by Armand Marie Leroi. In an editorial titled "A Family Tree in Every
Gene," Dr. Leroi, an evolutionary developmental biologist at Imperial College in
London, contended that racial differences are biologically identifiable realities
and asked readers to reconsider the idea that individuals share nearly as much
genetic similarity across races as they do within them.[2] The lively response to the
piece, which included comments from those in both the natural and social sciences, demonstrates that the so-called race question remains unresolved.

Historically, meanings of race have been understood in both biological and
social terms. In the eighteenth and nineteenth centuries, much scientific effort
was devoted to determining—and ranking—human racial groups.[3] Contemporary
scholars, however, especially those in the social sciences, tend to concur with
Michael Omi and Howard Winant (authors of the leading U.S. text on race as
a social construction), who argue that "as a result of prior efforts and struggles,
we have now reached the point of fairly general agreement that race is not a
biological given but rather a socially constructed way of differentiating human

beings."[4] Many scholars in the social sciences who view race as a social construction explicitly decouple concepts of race from biology. Their work shows how racial meanings evolved and how these concepts shape social life, determining, for example, where people live and how they are perceived by others.[5] Alas, this close attention to social construction may have exacted a price, shifting our focus from the corporeality of race so that important ways in which race is written (and continuously rewritten) on the body are sometimes overlooked.

Cultural practices have written race on the body so indelibly that, as some scholars have shown, they are almost indistinguishable from biological inscription. In *Stories in the Time of Cholera: Racial Profiling during a Medical Nightmare*, Charles Briggs and Clara Mantini-Briggs argue that when a cholera epidemic broke out among indigenous persons in the delta region of the Orinoco River in eastern Venezuela in 1992 and 1993, cultural reasoning held the victims themselves accountable. Health and government officials blamed the cultural beliefs and practices of the region's inhabitants and in the process "transformed individual bodies into natural bearers of disease."[6] Similarly, in his examination of hypertension and heart-disease studies and research on human genetic diversity, Troy Duster has demonstrated how scientists continue to use "a set of assumptions about race" to interpret their data, thereby ascribing disparities between groups to racial differences. As Duster convincingly argues, a methodology that privileges race as the main interpretive framework can lead investigators to miss or ignore other underlying causes of disease.[7] Both studies underscore the observation that Evelyn Hammonds, a historian of race and science, recently made regarding the sizable amount of work that remains to be done in challenging "the power of biology as a naturalizing discourse."[8]

A potentially useful step in mounting such a challenge is to initiate and sustain a conversation between historians investigating race and immigration and those conducting scholarship on disability. Our joint recognition of the body as a narrative site provides us with a shared border to use as a starting point: the modal subject. In the United States, the modal subject is neither raced nor disabled. Historically, race has provided a shorthand way to refer to difference, be it physical, cultural, or political, and thus also has been central in defining the modal subject (e.g., enfranchised/disenfranchised; citizen/alien, slave owner/slave). Likewise, the modal subject historically has been assumed to be independent and, by extension, able-bodied as well. The provisions of the 1790 Naturalization Act, which allowed only those deemed legally white to become naturalized citizens, are a case in point. Members of groups denied citizenship could not vote, testify in court, initiate lawsuits, or own property. With the modal subject by definition independent and by default able-bodied, those with disabilities were legally incapable of representing themselves, regardless of their race.

The concept of the modal subject draws attention to similarities in the ways in which race and disability have been used to exclude certain groups from the body politic. In each case, physical difference is identified and mobilized to figure specific groups discursively as outside the bounds of social membership. Studies of race and immigration and of disability provide a unique opportunity to understand the fallacy of the modal subject. To make the most of that opportunity, though, we need to conduct a *joint* conversation, one that deliberately reaches across the separate, isolated spaces—academic, private, and public—that are and have been the typical sites of discourse. We would be wise to remember that it was just such isolated discourse that shaped the Civil Rights Act of 1964, which for all its historic achievement in redefining the legal meaning of race fails to even mention disability, though the act was amended nine years later in 1973 with the inclusion of section 504.

This essay contributes to multidisciplinary perspectives in the academic field of disability studies by examining some of the social and political determinants of the status and role assigned to Mexican immigrants in early twentieth-century America. Because immigrants were considered advantageous only to the extent they filled critical gaps in the labor market, physical fitness was central to gauging a group's desirability. One way immigration advocates positively constructed Mexicans was by emphasizing this group's special affinity for manual labor. Mexicans, they argued, were uniquely able-bodied. They were capable of doing work whites could not do, as well as work that whites simply would not do. In contrast, when anti-immigrationists turned their attention to Mexican immigration in the aftermath of the 1924 Immigration Act, they emphasized how unfit Mexicans were, even as laborers. Calculating the worthiness of a given group on the basis of its members' perceived physical characteristics provided a way of calibrating racial difference as well. As a result, long after immigration legislation was passed (or, in some instances, was defeated), the arguments used to construct Mexicans as desirable or undesirable continued to resonate. Attributes, including corporeal characteristics, ascribed to Mexicans during immigration debates became central to the construction of the racial category *Mexican*.

The practice of judging an immigrant group's desirability based on their perceived physical abilities emerged well before the 1920s, of course. The 1882 Immigration Act legalized the exclusion of any immigrant deemed to be a "convict, lunatic, idiot, or any person unable to take care of himself or herself without becoming a public charge."[9] Although Mexicans were not categorized as disabled, they were constructed as nonnormative, and discourses that emphasized the body constituted a main vehicle for achieving this construction. In American immigration policy, the specific grounds for exclusion were malleable; the crucial step was simply to establish difference. And in that regard, as Douglas Baynton points out, the *concept* of disability played a key role. He notes that "beyond the targeting of disabled people, the concept of disability was instrumental in crafting the image of the undesirable immigrant."[10] Conversely, even the arguments in favor of Mexican immigration that emphasized Mexicans' physical capability as laborers became yet another way to mark them as racially distinct.

Mexican Immigration in Historical Context

In the early twentieth century, large-scale employers, particularly those in the agricultural, railroad, and mining industries, supported immigration to facilitate development in many parts of the Southwest. Projects requiring an infusion of labor included the expansion of railroad lines, construction of federally funded irrigation, and support for the increase in agricultural exports made possible by refrigerated boxcars. During the 1910s, employers turned to Mexican immigrants as a source of low-skilled, low-wage labor.[11] The number of Mexican employees grew steadily throughout the next few decades, assisted by an immigration policy that permitted a steady supply of low-cost Mexican labor.[12]

Although Southwestern capitalists generally welcomed Mexican immigration, not everyone else did. Labor unions, for example, opposed Mexican immigrants on the grounds that they competed with white laborers.[13] Anti-immigrationists also cited various social and fiscal costs as reasons to restrict entry. One issue that immigration opponents did not raise in the 1910s and early 1920s, however, was the state of Mexicans' health. This is a significant omission, as health factors were an important component of the social costs attributed to the presence of other immigrant groups. The Immigration Act of 1882 set forth rules and regulations that required those coming into the United States to be in good physical health, to be of sound character, and to demonstrate they were unlikely to become public charges. The Immigration Act of 1917 added a head tax and literacy requirement to these existing regulations. Concern over the potential costs of immigrants who were not fit for immediate employment contributed to the development of standardized and rigorous physical inspections, including medical evaluations, of southern and eastern Europeans and Asians, particularly Chinese, at ports of entry. At Ellis Island, for example, immigration inspectors weeded out European immigrants based on what the inspectors considered telltale signs of physical unfitness, such as hunched shoulders.[14]

Chinese immigrants, who generally were processed at a facility located on Angel Island in the San Francisco Bay, underwent physical inspections much different from those conducted at Ellis Island. U.S. Public Health Service (USPHS) workers operated under the assumption that disease resided naturally in the Chinese. Health inspectors believed the Chinese were naturally prone to diseases such as leprosy and hookworm. In depicting Chinese bodies as more susceptible to disease, and specifically to diseases that differed from those that afflicted other immigrants, public health officials showed that they were not only screening to determine who would be good laborers but also to determine who were fit to be citizens.[15]

Meanwhile, until the mid-1920s, Mexican immigrants crossed the border with relative ease (the Border Patrol was not created until 1924), and their health status was an issue only sporadically.[16] In Los Angeles, for instance, Mexicans (who represented the area's largest immigrant group by 1920) were not characterized as tubercular, even though they died of tuberculosis (TB) at a rate two times higher than the rest of the population of Los Angeles County.[17] County officials chose to define the high rate of TB among Mexican residents as a condition that did not threaten the general public. Thus health department staff did not compile and compare TB rates by race, as they did for birth- and infant-mortality rates (IMRs). Nor did they set up TB clinics. The Los Angeles County Health Department (LACHD) concentrated its outreach efforts on Americanization programs, such as well-baby clinics, rather than on tuberculosis treatment and prevention.[18] The disproportionate emphasis on high IMRs and, more specifically, on Mexican women, shifted the focus away from TB, thus enabling health officials to sidestep responsibility for improving overall housing conditions to help eradicate TB. The gendered approach to racialized health problems also helped divert attention from a crucial fact: Southern California's economy depended on Mexican immigrant labor. By focusing on high IMRs, health officials marked Mexican women as the source of health problems and, in so doing, helped male Mexican laborers escape further stigma.[19] Downplaying the presence of TB in Mexican communities during the early twentieth century meant that the disease generally did not serve as an impetus for reform, but neither did it prompt warnings against open immigration for Mexicans. So, for instance, in 1916, when Dr. William Sawyer of the California State Board of Health testified before Congress on tuberculosis cases in the state, he made no reference to Mexicans.[20] At the time, health officials took the position that Mexicans contracted tuberculosis *after* they arrived in the United States.

During Congressional hearings on the admission of Mexican agricultural laborers in 1920, many who favored continued immigration from Mexico emphasized Mexican bodies, constructing an image of these immigrants as ideal laborers. Mexicans may not have been culturally suited for citizenship, but certainly they were physically fit for hard work. Mexicans were consistently described as better able to perform strenuous labor than other groups, based on their physical ability. Testifying before the Committee on Immigration and Naturalization, Texas congressman Carlos Bee argued, "The Mexican is adapted for that special character of labor; whether in the providence of God he has been so constituted I won't say."[21] Judge Walter Timon, also of Corpus Christi, wrote, "The gathering of cotton is peculiar to the Mexicans and to the negro."[22] Of course, all of those who testified in this manner had a vested interest in the continued importation of Mexican labor because they lived in a region that relied on affordable casual labor. Perhaps not surprisingly, they increasingly described Mexicans as particularly well suited for physically demanding labor. Previously, pro-immigrationists had asserted that Mexicans would make good laborers because of their subordinate and docile natures, or they had focused on the idea that Mexicans were an especially good match for the seasonal nature of agricultural work—they were "birds of passage" who could be counted on to return to Mexico once their jobs were done.[23]

The emphasis on Mexicans' physical ability that emerged during the 1920 congressional hearings was significant given the biological racialism of the time. During the opening decades of the century, eugenicists argued that immigrants, particularly southern and eastern Europeans, should be barred from the United States because they were of inferior genetic stock and could not assimilate.[24] The anthropologist Franz Boas, now referred to as the father of American anthropology because of his enduring influence, tried to disprove these claims. He argued that racial characteristics once thought fixed were, in fact, mutable. Boas published his findings in 1911, in a study titled *Changes in Bodily Form*. After studying eighteen thousand children of European immigrants, Boas concluded that physical forms changed across generations. The types of physical features that marked immigrants as different, such as long skulls or round heads, physically morphed, becoming more "American" in as little time as one generation. Boas's work was included in a forty-two-volume report by the Dillingham Commission, published in 1912. The nine-member commission, appointed by Congress as part of the Immigration Act of 1907, assessed numerous aspects of the so-called immigrant problem in the United States.

Prior to the passage of the 1924 Immigration Act, the times when links between Mexicans and disease did impact border-crossing policies coincided with outbreaks of serious illnesses that could spread to large (white) populations. In 1916, a typhus epidemic began in a Mexican laborers' railroad camp in Los Angeles, infecting twenty-six people (twenty-two of whom were Mexican railroad workers). There were five fatalities, all Mexican. In the aftermath of the outbreak, health officials' and municipal leaders' desire to assure the public that Mexicans were a safe source of labor prompted the drafting of local measures to prevent any future outbreaks.[25] In addition, officials encouraged the USPHS to establish inspection stations along the border in Texas.[26] The need for stronger public health safeguards in border-crossing policy was underscored by an outbreak of typhus fever, also in 1916, which claimed four lives in El Paso, including that of W. C. Kluttz, a prominent local physician. In the aftermath of these deaths, Claude C. Pierce of the USPHS implemented much more detailed medical inspections at border-crossing stations. The new procedures, which were intensive and invasive, amounted to what the historian Alexandra Stern has termed an "iron-clad quarantine."[27] Because Mexicans were suspected of being "vermin infested," they were required to strip naked for physical examinations and then bathed in a mixture of soap, kerosene, and water. In the meantime, their clothes were disinfected.[28]

Disease outbreaks legitimized the increased fortification of the border and stigmatized Mexicans as disease carriers. Still, the link between disease and race was not yet as all encompassing as it would become after the passage of the 1924 Immigration Act. In the aftermath of the typhus and typhoid fever incidents, the medicalized aspects of border-crossing procedures intensified for Mexicans, based on the notion that they could spread infectious diseases. They were not, however, marked as having or being prone to the kinds of exotic and/or disabling diseases associated with other immigrants, especially the Chinese. Nor, unlike southern and eastern Europeans processed on Ellis Island, were they routinely tested for mental deficiency, insanity, or feeblemindedness. Border agents might call Mexicans foolish or stupid, but these labels were not formalized in ways that might lead to exclusion.[29] In sum, although there was an increase in the medical racialization of Mexican immigrants, the general construction of Mexicans as a fit workforce remained in place until after the 1924 Immigration Act.

Mexicans, as I have argued, were not medically racialized in the same ways southern and eastern Europeans were. For them, however, there was no possibility of "becoming American," culturally or physically. Mexicans' physical form was not the subject of criticism, but the lack of criticism meant that they were biologically suited only for manual labor (and not much else), which did nothing for improving their position in the U.S. racial hierarchy.

Medicalized Racial Exclusion after 1924

After the passage of the 1924 Immigration Act, attitudes toward Mexicans began to shift. The 1924 legislation established a national origins quota for southern and eastern Europeans, but it placed no such restrictions on immigrants from countries in the western hemisphere.[30] Mexicans could continue immigrating with few limitations. Many supporters of the 1924 Immigration Act were outraged by this imbalance. Mexicans were seen as inferior to Europeans; permitting their continued immigration while excluding southern and eastern Europeans was an affront to the logic of racial ordering. That Mexicans should have been barred from immigrating seemed so patently obvious that the act's lack of such prohibitions caught many Americans by surprise. Restrictionists' feverish efforts to extend the quotas to include Mexicans resulted in legislation proposed by U.S. Representative John C. Box of Texas in 1926.[31] Box attempted to show that Mexican "birds of passage" created various social and health problems while in the United States. Citing reports from Los Angeles–based institutions, he depicted Mexicans as responsible for overburdening charity departments and hospital services. Not surprisingly, agricultural employers and others who relied on large numbers of Mexican workers fought the Box proposal. The debate grew so heated that the House Immigration and Naturalization Committee chose not to act on the Box Bill.[32]

With the cessation of the flow of southern and eastern European immigrants, brownness came to signify the most important new threat to the racial hegemony of white native-born Americans. To ensure that Mexicans would be included in quota-based immigration legislation, it was imperative to depict them as dangerous. Anti-immigrationists began promoting an image of the racially inferior and diseased Mexican. Medicalized nativism proved central to this effort. Biologically based negative representations intensified during the mid- to late twenties and served as a key justification for the deportation of Mexicans during the Depression. Health officials made unprecedented contributions to the new view of Mexicans as an undesirable immigrant group.

Edythe Tate-Thompson, the director of California's Bureau of Tuberculosis (a division of the State Board of Health), held views on Mexicans and TB that represented a sharp departure from the attitudes of public health officials in the first two decades of the century. She wrote a forceful response to the open immigration policy. In "A Statistical Study of Sickness among the Mexicans in the Los Angeles County Hospital," she presented results of a study of Mexican TB rates and argued that Mexicans were a drain on municipal governments' budgets.[33] An important aim of the report's attention on the social costs of Mexican immigration was to prove false arguments by agricultural and business leaders that Mexican labor was an asset to the country. Tate-Thompson's contention that Mexican immigration should be limited was based on both biological and cultural grounds. She argued that Mexicans were inherently less able-bodied and thus were more prone to be infected by and to become spreaders of tuberculosis. Mexicans' biological makeup, she asserted, rendered them less able to fight off the progression of TB once infected. Her culture-based reasoning completed the picture: Mexicans ate poorly, lived in deplorable conditions, and, due to language barriers, were less likely to follow health codes. Combining these scientific and cultural arguments, Tate-Thompson arrived at a representation of

Mexicans as irresponsible and diseased. This image also conveniently masked systemic inequalities (such as segregation and dual labor-market segmentation) that were the actual basis for the conditions she observed and criticized.

Tate-Thompson also used her tuberculosis report to advocate immigration policy reform. She called on the federal government to fortify national borders by placing physicians at United States–Mexico ports of entry.[34] Health officials in El Paso, the site of the busiest of these entry points, had made similar requests during other disease outbreaks,[35] but Tate-Thompson's position was different. She argued for these reforms as a California state health official, based in Sacramento, twelve hundred miles from the El Paso port of entry.

During the years following the publication of her study, Tate-Thompson continued to pursue her agenda of identifying Mexicans as health burdens. In 1929, she wrote to the Los Angeles Board of Supervisors, asking them to create more selective admissions policies for Olive View Sanitarium, the county's tuberculosis facility. Her letter asserted that during 1925 and 1926 alone, Olive View had housed 374 tubercular Mexicans, at a cost of $300,000.[36] The sanitarium's official policy was to admit Mexicans who had established residency in California after living in the state for a year. The facility's supervisor, W. H. Holland, reported that contrary to Tate-Thompson's estimates, only 139 (23 percent) of Olive View patients were Mexican.[37] The discrepancy between the two sets of figures (374 versus 139) may reflect an error in tabulation on Tate-Thompson's part. It was common for patients with TB to be interned for several months. Thus Olive View patients who were counted as in residence in 1925 may have been counted again in the 1926 tally. In addition, Holland noted that 67 of those the report counted as Mexican were in fact U.S. citizens.

In addition to these efforts to limit public health expenditures to non-immigrants, Tate-Thompson persisted in her explicit use of public health issues as a springboard to influence immigration policy. In the California Department of Public Health's biennial report, she called for "shutting off the tide of [Mexican] immigration" in order to reduce California's tuberculosis mortality rates and to lower the economic costs associated with the disease.[38] She based her policy recommendation on the assumption that diseased Mexicans immigrated when their TB was in a latent stage; the infection moved into its more active and severe stages only after the carriers had settled in the United States.[39] Tate-Thompson referred in passing to "activities" that had begun "toward the restriction of migration of tubercular Mexicans into the United States," but she did not describe any specific programs.[40] She also noted that health authorities attempted to deport sick Mexican immigrants. When these attempts were unsuccessful, health departments would "care for [the ill] until the immigration authorities could deport them."[41]

Tate-Thompson's writings are especially important because they were widely used by those who supported restrictions on immigration from Mexico. For example, the editors of the *Grizzly Bear* magazine quoted her argument that Los Angeles County had become a dumping ground for poverty-stricken Mexicans. This development, the editors maintained, was part of a "carefully laid scheme to make the taxpayers of the county pay for the support and care of indigent foreigners."[42] Similarly, politicians who supported the 1928 Box-Harris Bill's quotas for Mexico rallied behind images of Mexicans as disease carriers whose cheap labor was outweighed by the high cost to taxpayers in terms of public health and social services.[43] "Not only do these people cause the county to spend thousands of dollars for relief, but they are compelling the expenditure of a great deal more public money in treating them for contagious diseases, including tuberculosis," Congressman Box charged during hearings on the bill. He, like the *Grizzly Bear* editors, quoted Tate-Thompson's assessment of Los Angeles County as a "dumping ground."[44]

Other California public health officials also went on record as endorsing the claim that Mexicans imported TB and other diseases. In a weekly bulletin issued in February 1928, the state health department published an article that asserted just such a link. The article ran alongside another piece that described immigration legislation under consideration that would decrease or eliminate immigration from Mexico, including the Box-Harris Bill.[45] In the bulletin, state health officials implored border officials to ensure that physical examinations at the United States–Mexico border were comparable to those conducted at stations with longer histories, such as those at Ellis Island and Angel Island.[46] They also urged U.S. Public Health Service staff to equip border stations with all the necessary "machinery" (most likely a reference to x-ray machines to test for TB) to adequately examine Mexicans crossing the border. California state health officials were not convinced that long-standing federal restrictions prohibiting the entry of individuals deemed unable or unlikely to be able to care for themselves due to illness were sufficient.[47] They expressed concern that Mexicans might pass the border inspections, but would later manifest signs of a chronic disease that had been in an inactive stage at the time they immigrated. Thus the officials called for the deportation of Mexicans who showed any sign of chronic illness within a year after being admitted to the United States. This, they hoped, would eliminate the possibility that these immigrants would seek state-funded services.

Just as lawmakers relied on the racialized knowledge produced by health officials, well-known eugenicists also began to use medical and public health standards as a gauge with which to determine the deleterious effects of immigration. They still relied on the tried and true racial tropes they had used against southern and eastern Europeans, confidently declaring, in the words of one "very intelligent" female writer in California, "Mexican peons can never be assimilated with white Americans."[48] Others (also referring to Mexicans as "peons") charged that Mexicans' "Indian stock" would result in national decay.[49] But eugenicists also began to rely on data public health officials had been amassing for over a decade. Birth- and disease rates became fundamental building blocks in the ongoing effort to construct Mexicans as dangerous.

Opponents of open Mexican immigration, including self-described eugenicists like Madison Grant, wrote numerous articles in support of the passage of both the Box and Box-Harris Bills. Medicalized constructions of Mexicans emerged as a common theme across these publications. With titles such as "The Menace of Mexican Immigration," "The Influx of Mexican Amerinds," and "Mexicans or Ruin," authors showcased their beliefs regarding the inferiority of Mexicans.[50] Some articles were published in extremist journals such as *Eugenics: A Journal of Race Betterment*. Others made their way into more popular mainstream publications, including the *Saturday Evening Post*, which claimed a circulation of over 2 million, revealing the degree to which eugenics-based notions of a racial hierarchy were part of mainstream culture before and during the Depression. The use of public health information to advance eugenicist arguments also demonstrates how a growing arsenal of knowledge in the field of public health gave eugenicists new ways of articulating their fears regarding immigrant bodies.

The image of the racially inferior, tubercular Mexican often was used to rally support for the restriction of immigration. For example, the University of California at Berkeley zoology professor and eugenicist Samuel Holmes, although perhaps best known for his preoccupation with birthrates as evidence of race suicide, also publicly advocated immigration limits. Holmes used tuberculosis statistics from the LACHD to support his position. He also quoted John Pomeroy, the county's chief health officer, as stating that the LACHD had "found four thousand [Mexicans] to have been infected before they crossed the border."[51] (There is no indication of any such finding in LACHD records.)

In the aftermath of the 1924 Immigration Act, attitudes toward Mexicans changed. Scientific racialism came to influence how people generally understood the category *Mexican*. Fears about southern and eastern European groups had often been expressed similarly—appearing, for example, in studies of craniotomy and treatises on race suicide. The post-1924 treatment of Mexicans, however, represents a significant break with the past. Mexicans go from typically receiving fairly casual medical scrutiny—relative to southern and eastern Europeans on the East Coast and Chinese immigrants on the West Coast—to being the objects of intense, negative assessment and then exclusion. This dramatic redefinition was brought about by means of a focus on their bodies, demonstrating the general principles of anti-immigrant bias within political and medical discourses.

Nonnormative physical attributes, including disease and disability, have served historically as grounds for writing groups out of the notion of the modal subject. Visual and rhetorical representations of the modal subject have routinely and compulsively depicted an actor who is white, male, and able-bodied. The categories of exclusion applied to Mexicans, who were deemed less than able-bodied because of diseases like tuberculosis, continued to overlap and inform one another for years to come. For example, when institutionalized in juvenile detention centers, mental hospitals, or prisons, Mexicans (immigrants and citizens alike) were routinely given the same kinds of biased IQ tests immigration inspectors had administered to southern and eastern European immigrants before permitting their entry into the United States.[52] Like the Europeans, Mexicans often scored poorly and were labeled feebleminded. That such a label could result in forcible sterilization provides another indication of how the discourses of race and disability reinforce one another.[53] In fact, the history of sterilization in the United States cannot be understood apart from the category of disability. One need only consider the U.S. Supreme Court's landmark ruling in *Buck v. Bell* (1927), in which the court supported a Virginia statute authorizing the compulsory sterilization of the mentally retarded for the purpose of eugenics. Defending the high court's ruling, Justice Oliver Wendell Holmes argued that "three generations of imbeciles [were] enough."[54]

The question of "who may give birth to citizens" remains salient, as legislation such as California's Proposition 187, passed in 1994 by an overwhelming majority and seeking to deny public services to undocumented immigrants, makes clear.[55] Ostensibly, Proposition 187 was directed at all undocumented immigrants, but within California's political and cultural climate, it was understood that the proposition's primary target was Mexicans. The two public services most discussed were education and nonemergency medical care, specifically infant and maternal care. Thus Mexican women and children would have been disproportionately affected (state court rulings eventually voided the proposition). Voters' endorsement of Proposition 187 starkly demonstrates the role race, like disability in *Buck v. Bell*, plays in marking groups against the modal subject.[56] These examples indicate not only that race, immigration, and disability studies are intimately connected but also that often it is difficult to discern where one ends and the other begins. Inquiry in these fields is relational. Thus, if we are to understand larger processes of exclusion and inclusion, we should take historical practice as our guide and deliberately blur the boundaries between the categories of race and disability in our methodologies, studies, and categories of analysis.

NOTES

This essay originally appeared in *Radical History Review* 94 (2006): 22–37. I would like to thank David Serlin and Charles Briggs for helping me think through some of the conceptual links between race and disability. I would also like to thank Ian Fusselman for his editorial help and support and Kathy Mooney for her editorial help. Parts of this essay are taken from my book *Fit to Be Citizens? Public Health and Race in Los Angeles, 1879–1939* (University of California Press, 2006).

1   Two notable examples of this ongoing cycle are Richard J. Herrnstein and Charles Murray, *The Bell Curve: Intelligence and Class Structure in American Life* (New York: Free Press, 1994); and Vincent Sarich and Frank Miele, *Race: The Reality of Human Differences* (Boulder, CO: Westview, 2004).

2   Leroi cited a well-known 1972 article by Harvard geneticist Richard Lewontin that argued, "If one looked at genes rather than faces . . . the difference between an African and a European would be scarcely greater than the difference between any two Europeans." Leroi goes on to counter Lewontin's findings, arguing that "gentic variants that aren't written on our faces, but that can be detected only in the genome, show similar correlations. It is these correlations that Dr. Lewontin seems to have ignored. In essence, he looked at one gene at a time and failed to see races. But if many—a few hundred—variable genes are considered simultaneously, then it is very easy to do so." Richard C. Lewontin, "The Apportionment of Human Diversity," *Evolutionary Biology* 6 (1972): 381–98; Armand Marie Leroi, "A Family Tree in Every Gene," *New York Times*, March 14, 2005.

3   See, for example, Matthew Frye Jacobson, *Whiteness of a Different Color: European Immigrants and the Alchemy of Race* (Cambridge, MA: Harvard University Press, 1998).

4   Michael Omi and Howard Winant, *Racial Formation in the United States from the 1960s to the 1980s* (New York: Routledge, 1986), 65.

5   Some notable examples of this scholarship include Keith Wailoo, *Dying in the City of the Blues: Sickle Cell Anemia and the Politics of Race and Health* (Chapel Hill: University of North Carolina Press, 2001); Nayan Shah, *Contagious Divides: Epidemics and Race in San Francisco's Chinatown* (Berkeley: University of California Press, 2001); Dorothy Roberts, *Killing the Black Body: Race, Reproduction, and the Meaning of Liberty* (New York: Vintage, 1997); Julyan Peard, *Race, Place, and Medicine: The Idea of the Tropics in Nineteenth-Century Brazilian Medicine* (Durham, NC: Duke University Press, 1999); John McKiernan-Gonzalez, "Fevered Measures: Race, Contagious Disease, and Community Formation on the Texas-Mexico Border, 1880–1923" (PhD diss., University of Michigan, 2002); Judith Walzer Leavitt, *Typhoid Mary: Captive to the Public's Health* (Boston: Beacon, 1996); Alan Kraut, *Silent Travelers: Germs, Genes, and the "Immigrant Menace"* (New York: Basic Books, 1994); Laura Briggs, *Reproducing Empire: Race, Sex, Science, and U.S. Imperialism in Puerto Rico* (Berkeley: University of California Press, 2002); Alexandra Stern, *Eugenic Nation* (Berkeley: University of California Press, 2005); and Charles L. Briggs and Clara Mantini-Briggs, *Stories in the Time of Cholera: Racial Profiling during a Medical Nightmare* (Berkeley: University of California Press, 2003).

6   Briggs and Mantini-Briggs, *Stories in the Time of Cholera*, 9.

7   Troy Duster, "Enhanced: Race and Reification in Science," *Science* 307 (2005): 1050–51.

8   See the Web site "Is Race Real?" organized by the Social Science Research Council, raceandgenomics.ssrc.org (accessed May 31, 2005).

9   Kraut, *Silent Travelers*, 70.

10 Douglas Baynton, "Disability and the Justification of Inequality in American History," in *The New Disability History: American Perspectives*, ed. Paul Longmore and Lauri Umansky (New York: New York University Press, 2001), 33.

11 U.S. employers had first recruited Chinese and then Japanese to work as low-skilled laborers. Chinese laborers were forced out through the 1882 Chinese Exclusion Act (and repeated ten-year extensions of its provisions); later, Japanese workers faced a similar form of exclusion, through the 1907-8 Gentlemen's Agreement and state laws passed in 1913 and 1920 restricting land ownership by "aliens."

12 According to the U.S. Bureau of the Census, the number of Mexican-born residents was 103,393 in 1900, 221,915 in 1910, and 486,418 in 1920. See Mark Reisler, *By the Sweat of Their Brow: Mexican Immigrant Labor in the United States, 1900-1940* (Westport, CT: Greenwood, 1976); David Gutiérrez, *Walls and Mirrors: Mexican Americans, Mexican Immigrants, and the Politics of Identity* (Berkeley: University of California Press, 1995); Camille Guerin-Gonzales, *Mexican Workers and American Dreams: Immigration, Repatriation, and California Farm Labor, 1900-1939* (New Brunswick, NJ: Rutgers University Press, 1994).

13 See Reisler, *By the Sweat of Their Brow*, esp. chap. 2.

14 Kraut, *Silent Travelers*; see also Amy Fairchild, *Science at the Borders: Immigrant Medical Inspection and the Shaping of the Modern Industrial Labor Force* (Baltimore, MD: Johns Hopkins University Press, 2003).

15 Shah, *Contagious Divides*; Erika Lee, *At America's Gates: Chinese Immigration during the Exclusion Era, 1882-1943* (Chapel Hill: University of North Carolina Press, 2003).

16 Mae M. Ngai, "The Strange Career of the Illegal Alien: Immigration Restriction and Deportation Policy in the United States, 1921-1965," *Law and History Review* 21 (2003): 69-108; Kathleen Anne Lytle Hernandez, "Entangling Bodies and Borders: Racial Profiling and the U.S. Border Patrol, 1924-1955" (PhD diss., University of California at Los Angeles, 2002); George Sánchez, *Becoming Mexican American: Ethnicity, Culture, and Identity in Chicano Los Angeles, 1900-1945* (New York: Oxford University Press, 1993).

17 "Mexicans in Los Angeles," *Survey* 44 (1920): 715-16. The first Los Angeles County Health Department annual health report to mention Mexicans with TB was the one in 1920. The reports were usually brief and mainly qualitative. Annual Health Report 1920, Department of Health Services Library, Los Angeles, CA.

18 Well Baby Clinics (WBCs) provided prenatal care to pregnant women and offered preventive medical care to babies and children under six. The clinics formed part of a national movement to improve children's health and thus significantly lower infant mortality rates. Initially, public health departments had tried to combat early deaths through the establishment of pure milk stations. See Richard Meckel, *Save the Babies: American Public Health Reform and the Prevention of Infant Mortality* (Baltimore, MD: Johns Hopkins University Press, 1990).

19 For a helpful discussion of gendered racism within the context of welfare, see Kenneth Neubeck and Noel Cazenave, *Welfare Racism: Playing the Race Card against America's Poor* (New York: Routledge, 2001), 29-35.

20   U.S. Congress and Senate Committee on Public Health and National Quarantine, Standardization of Treatment of Tuberculosis: *Hearings before the United States Senate Committee on Public Health and National Quarantine*, 64th Cong., 1st sess., January 17, 1916 (Washington, DC: Government Printing Office, 1917).

21   U.S. Congress and Senate Committee on Immigration and Naturalization, *Hearings on Admission of Mexican Agricultural Laborers*, 66th Cong., 2nd sess. (Washington, DC: Government Printing Office, 1920), 19.

22   *Hearings on Admission of Mexican Agricultural Laborers*, 27.

23   Camille Guerin-Gonzales, *Mexican Workers and American Dreams: Immigration, Repatriation, and California Farm Labor, 1900–1939* (New Brunswick, NJ: Rutgers University Press, 1994), ch. 2.

24   See Thomas A. Guglielmo, *White on Arrival: Italians, Race, Color, and Power in Chicago, 1890–1945* (New York: Oxford University Press, 2003); Jacobson, *Whiteness of a Different Color.*

25   See Molina, *Fit to Be Citizens?*

26   El Paso was the largest point of entry from Mexico into the United States during this period. See Sánchez, *Becoming Mexican American*, 39.

27   For an insightful analysis of this event, see Alexandra Stern, "Buildings, Boundaries, and Blood: Medicalization and Nation-Building on the U.S.-Mexican Border, 1910–1930," *Hispanic American Historical Review* 79 (1999): 41–81, esp. 45.

28   Stern, "Buildings, Boundaries, and Blood." For more on disease and medicalization along the Texas-Mexico border, see McKiernan-Gonzalez, "Fevered Measures."

29   The historian George Sánchez gives a good example of miscommunication arising from language barriers between a border agent and a Mexican crossing into the United States. The border agent interprets the miscommunication as a sign of stupidity on the part of the Mexican. See Sánchez, *Becoming Mexican American*, 54–55.

30   The 1921 Immigration Act had initiated a quota system that became known as the national origins principle. Immigration from eastern and southern Europe was limited to 3 percent of the population of each designated European country's citizens already in the United States at the time of the 1890 census. That amount was reduced to 2 percent under the 1924 Immigration Act.

31   The Box Bill, HR 6741, proposed extending the quota restrictions to countries in the western hemisphere. See Reisler, *By the Sweat of Their Brow*, 202 n. 19.

32   Reisler, *By the Sweat of Their Brow*, 202–4.

33   Edythe Tate-Thompson, "A Statistical Study of Sickness among the Mexicans in the Los Angeles County Hospital, from July 1, 1922 to June 30, 1924" (Sacramento: Bureau of Tuberculosis, California State Board of Health, California State Printing Office, 1925).

34   Tate-Thompson, "A Statistical Study of Sickness among the Mexicans in the Los Angeles County Hospital."

35   El Paso health officials had called for more stringent standards of public health to fortify the border during the 1917 typhus epidemic. See Stern, "Buildings, Boundaries, and Blood."

36   Letter from Tate-Thompson to Board of Supervisors, April 24, 1929, Los Angeles County Board of Supervisors, Los Angeles, CA, hereafter cited as "B of S." She also stated that she was concerned that migrants were coming to Los Angeles to seek

free medical care at the facility, even though they had not resided in California for very long and thus had not yet paid taxes to the state. Among the patients Tate-Thompson used as an example of this reprehensible behavior were migrants from Iowa and Kansas.

37   Letter to Board of Supervisors from Supervisor W. H. Holland of Olive View, 2/4/1927, B of S.

38   Edythe Tate-Thompson, "Migration of Indigent Tuberculosis Is Serious Problem," *Weekly Bulletin of the California State Department of Public Health*, June 15, 1929, 73–74.

39   Tate-Thompson, "Migration of Indigent Tuberculosis Is Serious Problem."

40   *July 1, 1928, to June 30, 1930* (Sacramento: California State Printing Office, 1931).

41   *July 1, 1928, to June 30, 1930.*

42   *Grizzly Bear*, December 1927, 3.

43   Like the 1926 Box Bill, the 1928 Box-Harris Bill would have extended the quota to all western hemisphere nations. Also like the Box Bill, Southwestern lobbyists helped defeat the bill in order to maintain a steady source of laborers from Mexico.

44   House Committee on Immigration and Naturalization, United States Congress, *Hearings before the Committee on Immigration and Naturalization, House of Representatives*, 70th Cong., 1st. sess., February 21 to April 5, 1928 (Washington, DC: Government Printing Office, 1928).

45   "For Control of Mexicans' Health," Weekly Bulletin of the California State Department of Public Health, February 11, 1928, 2–3.

46   For a history of immigration to these ports of entry, see Howard Markel and Alexandra Stern, "Which Face? Whose Nation? Immigration, Public Health, and the Construction of Disease at America's Ports and Borders, 1891–1928," *American Behavioral Scientist* 42 (1999): 1314–31. See also Kraut, *Silent Travelers*; Shah, *Contagious Divides*; and Fairchild, *Science at the Borders.*

47   Baynton, "Disability and the Justification of Inequality in American History," 33–57.

48   Quoted in Remsen Crawford, "The Menace of Mexican Immigration," *Current History* 31 (1930): 902–7, esp. 907.

49   Madison Grant, "Editorial: Immigration," *Eugenics: A Journal of Race Betterment* 3, no. 2 (1930): 74.

50   Kenneth Roberts, "Wet and Other Mexicans," *Saturday Evening Post*, February 4, 1928, 10–11, 137–38, 141–42, 146; Kenneth Roberts, "The Docile Mexican," *Saturday Evening Post*, March 10, 1928, 40–41, 165–66; Kenneth Roberts, "Mexicans or Ruin," *Saturday Evening Post*, February 18, 1928, 14–15, 142, 145–46, 149–50, 154; Crawford, "The Menace of Mexican Immigration"; C. M. Goethe, "The Influx of Mexican Amerinds," *Eugenics: A Journal of Race Betterment* 2 (1929): 6–9.

51   Samuel J. Holmes, "Perils of the Mexican Invasion," *North American Review* 227 (1929): 615–23. There are no reports by the LACHD on how many Mexicans may have had tuberculosis *before* they entered the United States.

52   See Kraut, *Silent Travelers.*

53   See Molina, *Fit to Be Citizens?* See also Natalia Molina and Anne-Emanuelle Birn, "In the Name of Public Health," *American Journal of Public Health* 95 (2005): 1095–97; Alexandra Minna Stern, "Sterilized in the Name of Public Health: Race, Immigration, and Reproductive Control in Modern California," *American Journal of Public Health* 95 (2005): 1128–38; and Stern, *Eugenic Nation.*

54 *Buck v. Bell*, 274 U.S. 200 (1927).

55 The court, however, immediately barred implementation of the law, pending settlement of the legal challenges lodged against it. Dorothy Roberts, "Who May Give Birth to Citizens?: Reproduction, Eugenics, and the Nation," in *Immigrants Out: The New Nativism and the Anti-immigrant Impulse in the United States*, ed. Juan Perea (New York: New York University Press, 1997).

56 Roberts, "Who May Give Birth to Citizens?"; and Pierrette Hondagneu-Sotelo, "Women and Children First: New Directions in Anti-immigrant Politics," *Socialist Review* 25 (1995): 169–90.

"Looking Like a Lesbian": The Organization of Sexual Monitoring at the United States–Mexican Border

EITHNE LUIBHÉID

I

While returning by taxicab from Juarez, Mexico, to El Paso, Texas, on January 6, 1960, Sara Harb Quiroz was stopped for questioning by an immigration service agent. Quiroz was not a newcomer to the United States. She had acquired permanent U.S. residency in July 1954, at the age of twenty, and lived in El Paso where she worked as a domestic. We do not know why she traveled to Juarez on that particular occasion, but her parents and her nine-year-old daughter lived there. Other familial, economic, and social ties also drew the residents of El Paso to Juarez. Documentation that explains why Quiroz was stopped no longer exists. But Albert Armendariz, the attorney who handled her case, believes she was stopped because of her appearance. "Based on looks. Based on the way she dressed. The way she acted. The way she talked."[1] In the eyes of the immigration inspector who stopped her, Quiroz seemed like a lesbian. Until as recently as 1990, lesbian immigrants were excludable and deportable from the United States.

II

The case of Quiroz provides us with a window into immigration service efforts to identify and exclude foreign-born women who were believed to be lesbians. Some scholars date lesbian and gay exclusion from 1917, when "constitutional psychopathic inferiors," including those with "abnormal sexual instincts," became excludable.[2] However, the most extensive records about immigration service efforts to police the border against lesbians and gay men date from after the passage of the 1952 McCarren-Walter Act. In anticipation of the act, the Senate Committee of the Judiciary recommended in 1950 that "classes of mental defectives [who are excludable] should be enlarged to include homosexuals and other sex perverts."[3] However, the final wording of the McCarren-Walter Act did not explicitly mention homosexuals. Instead, homosexual exclusion became rolled into the provision that barred entry by psychopathic personalities. A Senate report explained, "The Public Health Service has advised that the provision for the exclusion of aliens afflicted with psychopathic personality or a mental defect . . . is sufficiently broad to provide for the exclusion of homosexuals and sex perverts. This change in nomenclature is not to be constructed in any way as modifying the intent to exclude all aliens who are sexual deviants."[4] In 1965, lesbian and gay exclusion was recodified, this time under a provision barring entry by "sexual deviates."

To date, only cases involving men who were alleged by the Immigration and Naturalization Service (INS) to be gay have received substantive scholarly analysis. Little is known about the experiences of women.[5] By providing information about Quiroz's case, which is the only documented case involving a woman that has been uncovered to date, I renarrate the history of lesbian and gay immigration exclusion in a way that centers, rather than subsumes, specifically female experiences.[6] In addition, Quiroz's case raises questions about the complexities of mapping histories of immigrant, refugee, and transnational women while using sexual categories that substantially derive their meanings from metropolitan centers.[7]

This article's methodological and theoretical frameworks are drawn from Michel Foucault's *The History of Sexuality* (vol. 1). Though Foucault never explicitly addressed immigration, his work usefully points out that sex became something for the state to administer and manage. The nineteenth-century multiplication of discourses about sex unquestionably affected the U.S. immigration system, which took up these discourses and developed procedures for administering sex in relation to multiform objectives (that concerned not only sex but also gender, race, class, and constructions of nation). Foucault's discussion of how homosexual acts became reconstructed, as evidence of the existence of homosexual types, illustrates the general process whereby the administration of sex enabled relations of power to become organized and extended.[8] The example also draws attention to the specific ways that sexual categorizations became "freight[ed] . . . with epistemological and power relations," through which immigration monitoring became organized.[9] The incorporation of sexual categorizations into exclusion laws, as well as the development of procedures to detect and deter entry by those who fit the categorizations, is a key piece of how the immigration system came to exclude individuals on the basis of sexuality.[10]

That Quiroz encountered difficulties when entering at El Paso, because an agent suspected that she was a lesbian, clearly demonstrates that sexuality functioned as a "dense transfer point for relations of power" at the border.[11] But in analyzing her case, I resist making efforts to determine whether she was a lesbian, since such efforts participate in power relations that recirculate and naturalize dominant cultural notions of sexual "types."[12] Instead, my approach to Quiroz's case focuses on problematizing how mainstream institutions, including the INS, remain invested in constructing fixed boundaries around what homosexuality is. Such boundary marking involves operations by which mainstream institutions empower and legitimize themselves while producing diverse minoritized populations.

III

INS monitoring techniques contributed to the construction of the very sexualities against which they guarded the nation.[13] This fact becomes clear when we examine how immigrants came to be designated as excludable on the basis of homosexuality. Since there is no easy way to differentiate lesbians and gay men from heterosexuals, what led certain people to be singled out? On looking through case histories, it appears that immigrants came to INS attention as possible lesbians or gay men on the basis of checkpoints that were set up within the immigration process. These checkpoints served as particularly dense points where dominant institutions constructed (and individuals contested) the possible meanings of lesbian or gay identity, and of who should be included within these categories.

In thinking through the operation of these checkpoints, we must avoid two common and related mistakes. First, we should not imagine that coherent, predefined lesbian or gay identities always existed among immigrant applicants, and that the checkpoints simply captured these preformed "queer" subjects. To frame the issue in this way is to miss the myriad ways that these checkpoints often regulated the terms by which formation of identity occurs.[14]

Second, and conversely, we have to conceptualize lesbian and gay identities as being never reducible to these checkpoints. Though the checkpoints were dense power points in the dominant culture's production and policing of homosexuality, not all (potential) lesbian/gay subjects were equally affected. This is because lesbian and gay identities are also inflected by race, class, gender, cultural, and religious features that defy the possibility that there can be any uniform queer identity; equally, the checkpoints themselves reflected some degree of bias, such that they captured males more than females, and Latin Americans and Europeans more than Asians. Consequently, in looking at who was liable to become ensnared by these checkpoints, we should never imagine that this was the totality of the kinds of lesbian, gay, or "queer" identities that were passing into the United States.[15]

One of the richest sources of information about these immigration checkpoints comes from court records. Perhaps not surprisingly, almost all of the court cases that have been reconstructed concern men. Very striking are the numbers of men who ended up being targeted by the INS because of criminal convictions related to sexual activity. Writing about German-born Horst Nemetz, who had no criminal record connected to his sexual activities with men, Shannon Minter describes the extent to which male-male sexual practices remain heavily criminalized:

> His denial of public activity [for which he could have been convicted] means that he never made love on a beach, in a car, in a park, or in any of the other quasi-public places in which heterosexual couples occasionally engage in sexual relations. His denial of "recruiting" means that he never sexually propositioned a man in a bar, at a party, on the street, or anywhere outside his home. His denial of ever being arrested or questioned by the police means either that he was fortunate, or that he avoided gay bars, gay bathhouses, gay cruising areas in parks and bathrooms, and other places that gay men informally gather and socialize. It also means he never had the misfortune of expressing sexual interest to an undercover police officer posing as a gay man.[16]

Court cases confirm that significant numbers of immigrant men came to INS attention on the basis of sexual criminalization.

But given that lesbian sexual activity is not usually as heavily policed, how can we map lesbians onto this history of immigration exclusion? Less policing does not mean that lesbian sexuality is more socially acceptable than gay male sexuality. However, disbelief that women can have sex without the presence of a male penis—and the ways that gender, in conjunction with race and class, has differentially shaped the acquisition and formation of spaces where women could come together to have sex—means that lesbian sexuality has not been scrutinized and policed in the same ways as gay male sexuality. The result was that INS criminal record checks were more likely to affect men, rather than women, who engaged in same-sex activities. Were lesbians therefore relatively unaffected by the historic practices of homosexual exclusion? That is one possibility. A second possibility is that indicators other than criminal record checks were used to identify women who might be lesbians. Given the dearth of known lesbian exclusion cases, it is difficult to know what these indicators were.[17] The Quiroz case provides one (possibly unrepresentative) example.[18]

As mentioned earlier, the lawyer who handled Quiroz's case believes she was stopped because she looked, spoke, and acted "like a lesbian." Quiroz was also unlucky enough to encounter an immigration inspector who had undertaken a personal campaign to identify and expel women who he believed were sexual deviates: "There was this fellow who was at the International Bridge. . . . He had a thing for people, especially women . . . who were lesbian, or in his mind were deviates, and met the requirements of the statute [for exclusion]. . . . They would go to Mexico on a visit, and on the way back he would send them to secondary [inspection] where he would determine they were ineligible to enter. This officer was very, very good at making people admit that they were sexual deviates."[19] The importance of appearance is confirmed by testimony that was given to the INS by Quiroz's employer, to the effect that "the respondent usually wore trousers and a shirt when she came to work and that her hair was cut shorter than some women's."[20]

The use of visual appearance to monitor the border against possible entry by lesbians connects to a complex history. A 1952 Public Health Service (PHS) report to Congress mentioned visual appearance as one possible index of homosexuality. "In some instances considerable difficulty may be encountered in substantiating a diagnosis of homosexuality or sexual perversion. In other instances, where the action or behavior of the person *is more obvious, as might be noted in the manner of dress* (so called transvestism [*sic*] or fetishism) the condition may be more easily substantiated [emphasis added]."[21] This passage suggests that monitoring based on visual appearance operated around the notion of gender inversion—that is, homosexuals could be visually identified by the fact that gay men looked effeminate or lesbians looked masculine.[22] The PHS formulation connects to a broader cultural history of conceptualizing homosexuality as a problem of one gender being trapped in the other gender's body. Linked to that conceptualization were a range of endeavors to scientifically delineate, in a measurable and absolute way, the difference between homosexual and heterosexual bodies. Jennifer Terry has documented the activities of the

Committee for the Study of Sex Variants, active in New York City in the 1930s and 1940s. Members of the committee included "psychiatrists, gynecologists, obstetricians, surgeons, radiologists, neurologists, as well as clinical psychologists, an urban sociologist, a criminal anthropologist, and a former Commissioner of the New York City Department of Corrections."[23] This truly impressive array of professionals, scientists, and academics, connected together through their efforts to delineate how the homosexual was distinct from the heterosexual, conducted its research under the assumption that "the female sex variant would exhibit traits of the opposite sex. In other words, she would invert her proper gender role."[24] Under this guiding assumption,

> pathologists looked at skin complexion, fat distribution, coarseness of hair, the condition of the teeth, and commented on the overall facial and bodily structure of each subject. Radiologists took x-rays to determine cranial densities of the skull and "carrying angles" of the pelvis in order to identify anomalous gender characteristics. A dense skull was presumed to be masculine. "Graceful" and "delicate" pelvic bones were feminine.
>
> Endocrinologists measured hormonal levels. . . . Sketches of genitals and breasts were drawn in order to document particular characteristics of sex variance. . . . In analyzing the thirty pages of graphic sketches of breasts and genitals, Dr. Dickinson reported on the general genital differences recognizable in the female sex variant population. He identified ten characteristics which he argued set the sex variant apart from "normal women."[25]

These and other studies were formed around, and helped to keep alive, the notion that lesbians were visibly different from heterosexuals (and that lesbianism and heterosexuality were opposites). Thus, it was not surprising that immigration officers tried to identify immigrants who might be lesbians by using the index of gender-inverted appearance. Gay men were similarly sought.

The notion that lesbian and gay immigrants could be identified on the basis of appearance marks out an area where homophobia, racism, and sexism share some commonalities but also significant differences, in terms of an individual's ability to mediate costs associated with looking different. bell hooks, for example, frames the issue by writing, "While we can acknowledge that gay people of all colors are harassed and suffer exploitation and domination, we also recognize there is a significant difference that arises because of the visibility of dark skin."[26]

Nice Rodriguez has described altering her sexuality and gender appearance, so as to pass official scrutiny, during her migration from the Philippines to Canada:

On the day of her interview [for a visa at the embassy] she wore a tailored suit but she looked like a man and knew she did not stand a chance.

They did not want masculine women in that underpopulated land. They needed babymakers.... Her wife got mascara and lipstick and made her look like a babymaker. During her interview with the consular officer she looked ovulating and fertile so she passed it.

Canada had strict immigration laws, but even bugs could sift through a fine mosquito net.[27]

This account captures the process of "straightening up" that many lesbians undertake when they expect to deal with immigration officials. Straightening up includes practices like growing one's hair and nails, buying a dress, accessorizing, and donning makeup. Clearly there is privilege involved in the fact that the visual markers of lesbianism—unlike visual markers of race or gender—can usually be altered or toned down, so as to pass homophobic border guards.[28] But at the same time, the fact that one has to straighten up so as to avoid a penalty serves as a reminder that lesbianism is a difference. Consequently, Rodriguez suggests that her self-presentation as an ovulating and fertile woman wearing lipstick and mascara did not erase her lesbian difference, but instead confirmed the "bug"-like status of lesbians within the immigration system. Monitoring the border on the basis of visual appearance does lend itself to lesbian and gay male subversion, yet at the same time it marks out an area where the identity the INS is trying to contain and expel is also reestablished and reinforced.

The experiences of women of color like Quiroz further complicate analysis of visually based border monitoring. The visual, or that which gets seen, is driven by and redeploys particular cultural knowledges and blindnesses. Though the inspector who stopped Quiroz for questioning saw something different about her, there are many questions we need to ask about this. Was there really anything different about Quiroz to see? Was the difference he claimed to see really a lesbian difference, or was it another kind of difference that simply became named as lesbian through a combination of procedures and expediency? What cultural knowledges and blindnesses organized this inspector's regime of seeing, such that he picked out Quiroz for investigation? What are the connections between the inspector's suspicion that Quiroz was a sexual deviate and the long U.S. history of viewing and treating the bodies of women of color as sexually other? The use of visual judgment to monitor the border involves levels of complexity that have yet to be unraveled, when immigrant women of color with diverse sexualities are involved.

In the context of the El Paso–Juarez border where Quiroz was stopped, the regimes through which Mexican immigrants get visually evaluated are further complicated by the historical processes through which that border was imposed. Timothy Dunn explains that "for many decades, the [U.S.-Mexico] border was a tenuous social construct, established and maintained by force."[29] The border, which derived from the Texas Revolution of 1836 and the Mexican War of 1846–48, was "in large part either ignored or actively contested by *Mexicanos* in the region . . . because it was imposed on them and it disrupted their lives. . . . The full pacification of the region required some 70 years, and involved the prominent use of a variety of coercive measures both by the state and by Anglo groups."[30] The Border Patrol, created by the Immigration Act of 1924, became a key state institution through which the border was maintained. Border enforcement efforts have continually legitimated the subordination of Mexican-origin peoples in the region, regardless of whether they were citizens, residents, or immigrants. The scrutiny Quiroz received from immigration service officials derived from and further extended this history.[31] Immigration service techniques, which involved atomizing and evaluating her appearance, documents, and speech, also echoed and extended the historical processes whereby Latina bodies became racialized and sexualized in the context of imposing the U.S.-Mexico border. As Yvonne Yarbro-Bejarano reminds us, it is not only "our attitudes about our bodies, but our very bodies themselves" that are constructed within social relations, including the relations that Mexican immigrant women negotiate at U.S. southern borders.[32]

IV

Ways that lesbians (and gay men) might come to INS attention were not restricted to the visible, nor to the existence of police records. Individuals also became suspected of homosexuality during required premigration medical inspections; through the timing and location of their arrival (e.g., people coming into San Francisco just before the lesbian, gay, bisexual, transgender parade); because of information given to the INS by third parties; based on the contents of their suitcases; and as a result of information contained in the forms that all immigrants must complete. Immigration forms included questions about whether or not one was of good moral character or a sexual deviate or a psychopathic personality, and they also asked the applicant to list all affiliations. Anyone who participated in a lesbian or gay organization potentially had to list that fact. One could, of course, lie or omit information when completing the forms, but only at the risk of a substantial penalty if the INS found out.[33] No doubt there were other ways that lesbians and gay men came to INS attention, but these ways have yet to be uncovered. The impact of these methods for identifying women who might be lesbians was undoubtedly differentiated by race, nationality, class, and other features.[34]

V

Once immigrants came to INS attention as possible lesbians, the means used to officially exclude them was to issue them a Class A Medical Exclusion Certificate.[35] This practice no doubt inspired Richard Green's observation that "American immigration policy regarding homosexuals has been a marriage of one government bureaucracy with another: the Immigration and Naturalization Service (INS) and the Public Health Service (PHS)."[36] It is tempting to assume that use of a medical exclusion certification process signals that medical fears motivated the exclusionary treatment of lesbians and gays. But such a reading does not take into account the full complexity of how exclusion operated. Exclusion never involved only a simple "failure" of medical knowledge. And although medicine is one key discourse through which the homosexual has been constructed as a threatening type, it is not the only such discourse. Robert Podnanski's analysis notes that fears about "morality, subversion, or destitution may have motivated Congress" to enact lesbian and gay exclusion.[37] A plurality of discourses and institutional practices, not just one, underpinned exclusion. Furthermore, these discourses and practices were neither necessarily rational, nor commensurate with one another.

The workings of exclusion must therefore be grasped not at the level of lack or plenitude of knowledge but, rather, at the level of how homophobia is strategically organized and deployed within institutional circuits of power. As David Halperin writes, "Homophobic discourses are not reducible to a set of statements with a specifiable truth-content that can be rationally tested. Rather, homophobic discourses function as part of more general and systemic strategies of delegitimation."[38] Consequently, the practice of issuing Class A Medical Exclusion Certificates to immigrants who were judged lesbian or gay reflected not just that medicine was a key discourse through which lesbians and gay men were constructed as threatening "others" but also that medical practices provided a means through which a larger discourse of homophobia could be mobilized, channeled, and legitimated.[39] The medical exclusion certification process connected to the drive for rationalized efficiency. Its use required few additional resources, since the PHS already inspected the physical and mental health of aspiring immigrants, and had a system whereby "unfit" people could be certified for exclusion.[40] It was easy to add one more group to the list of those already weeded out.[41] The medical exclusion certification process further fit into the rationality that stressed scientific management, since it enabled deployment of disparate homophobic practices under the sign of medical intervention.

Issuance of medical exclusion certificates to suspected lesbian and gay immigrants was also congruent with the operations of other government apparatuses. During the massive World War II troop mobilizations, the handling of homosexuality in the ranks underwent a shift from criminalization to psychiatrization. Dishonorably discharging homosexuals for mental illness, rather than charging them with a crime, was deemed preferable on various grounds. Mental illness discharges eliminated time-consuming trials and costly imprisonment; they "made it easier for the military to extend its antihomosexual apparatus to women"; and the process could be conducted in a discretionary manner, without strict evidentiary requirements.[42]

After World War II, these military policies toward homosexuality "served as a model for senators who, in 1950, launched the most aggressive attack on homosexual employees that had ever taken place in the federal government."[43] Under Eisenhower, the attack widened further:

> The government's anti-homosexual policies and procedures, which had originated in the wartime military, expanded to include every agency and department of the federal government, and every private company or corporation with a government contract, such as railroad companies and aircraft plants. This affected the job security of more than six million government workers and armed forces personnel. By the mid-1950s, similar policies had also gone into effect in state and local governments, extending the prohibition on employment of homosexuals to over twelve million workers. . . . Similar policies were adopted independently by some private companies, and even by such private organizations as the American Red Cross.[44]

At the same time, the American Psychiatric Association (APA), "building on the standardized nomenclature developed by the Army in 1945," issued its first *Diagnostic and Statistical Manual of Mental Disorders* (*DSM-I*) in 1952. The manual "firmly established homosexuality as a sociopathic personality disorder."[45] This APA classification legitimated the PHS practice of issuing Class A Medical Exclusion Certificates to immigrants who were thought to be lesbian or gay.[46] Certification thus shared significant connections with military and employment apparatuses.

Foucault's *History of Sexuality* provides further specification of how the PHS certification system organized a circuit of homophobic discourses and practices. Within immigration monitoring, procedures were needed to ensure that "the will to knowledge regarding sex . . . caused the rituals of confession to function within the norms of scientific regularity."[47] Thus, although foreign-born peoples' sexuality could be inquired into at various points within the process, there had to be a way to make the process seem legitimately scientific, and to regularize what happened if information such as "I am a lesbian" was revealed. Five procedures, through which these aims could be accomplished, are described by Foucault: "[First] a clinical codification of the inducement to speak. . . . [Second] the postulate of a general and diffuse causality . . . that endowed sex with an inexhaustible and polymorphous causal power. The most discrete event in one's sexual behavior . . . was deemed capable of entailing the most varied consequences throughout one's existence. . . . [Third] the principle of a latency intrinsic to sexuality . . . [that] made it possible to link the forcing of a difficult confession to scientific practice. . . . [Fourth] through the method of interpretation. . . . [And lastly] through the medicalization of the effects of confession."[48] The case of Quiroz offers us an opportunity to examine how these procedures operated together, around the Class A Medical Exclusion Certification system, to create an integrated circuit of power, knowledge, and homophobic practices.

VI

The first feature of this discursive circuit involves the "clinical codification of the inducement to speak." Inducement to speak conjoins neatly with the third feature, the assumption of a "principle of latency intrinsic to sexuality . . . [that] ma[kes] it possible to link the forcing of a difficult confession to scientific practice." A very basic "inducement to speak" is built into the immigration system, in that one's ability to gain U.S. entry depends on willingness to respond to any and all questions of immigration officials. One risks a substantial penalty for lying or omitting information that the immigration service might consider pertinent to one's application.[49] This substantial inducement to speak is compounded during the experience of being held for secondary inspection, as happened to Quiroz when she attempted to reenter at El Paso. There are variations on how secondary inspection is conducted, but Armendariz offered one description of how intimidating the process can be: "When you go down to the bridge, these people [immigration officials] are kings. And they act like kings. They put them [i.e., people detained for secondary inspection] in a little room. And they keep them there for hours and don't feed them. And one comes in and asks a few questions and then leaves them alone. Then another comes in: 'We're going to put you in the penitentiary for five years, and we're waiting for them to pick you up and take you to jail. Unless you tell us the truth.' And then they end up transcribing what they [the detained] said. . . . In my 45 years, I have come across at least 1,000 people who insisted they did not say [what the INS statement says they said]. Under oath."[50] We do not know if this description reflects Quiroz's experience, but at a hearing before a special inquiry officer, she attempted to refute the statements that the INS obtained from her during questioning. The special inquiry officer's decision related that "the respondent testified in an attempt to impeach her statements (Exhibits 3 and 4). She said that the statements were not read to her and that she cannot read or speak English. She denied that she had ever been a lesbian and stated that she has a nine-year-old daughter. She testified that she signed the statements because she was told that everything would be all right."[51] Quiroz thus tried to contest the speech that was attributed to her. This is important, because it was primarily on the basis of her speech that she was constructed as a lesbian. If the speech could be impeached, the "evidence" of homosexuality became severely undermined.[52]

How the INS overturned Quiroz's impeachment efforts is interesting, because of the connections it reveals between inducement to speak, the forcing of a sexual confession, and the use of scientific practice to legitimate the whole proceeding. The INS testimony read:

> To rebut the respondent's testimony impeaching the statements, the Government had the two immigration officers who took the statements testify as witnesses. Their testimony was that the statement was read to the respondent at the conclusion, that it was made voluntarily, that she was cooperative, and that her answers were responsive to the questions. Their testimony was also to the effect that there was comprehension between them and the respondent in their speaking with her in the Spanish language during the taking of the statement. In passing it is to be noted that Dr. Coleman [the PHS surgeon who signed the Class A Medical Exclusion Certificate issued to Quiroz] during his testimony, stated that he was present during the taking of the statement (Exhibit 3) and that the respondent replied readily, was relaxed, cooperative, not under duress and did not show hesitancy or embarrassment.
>
> The respondent's attempt to impeach her sworn statements (Exhibits 3 and 4) must fail. Each statement recites at the end thereof that it was read to her. The first statement shows a material correction was made . . . and this was initialed by the respondent. . . . I shall therefore consider these two statements [signed by Quiroz] as true and correct.[53]

In essence, the INS argued that they followed proper procedures in the Quiroz case. These included correct administration of the immigration system, requisite adherence to legal doctrines concerning how evidence may be obtained, and validation by a medical authority.

But procedural propriety is not necessarily the key issue here. More significant, in light of Foucault's description of how an economy of discourses becomes organized to generate confession about sexual practices and feelings, is that there are procedures, and they did work together to ensure that Quiroz provided explicit statements about her sexuality. It was INS adherence to proper procedures that led Quiroz to confess "that she has had homosexual desires for at least a year, that she had homosexual relations on numerous occasions over this period of time with two women whom she named, that she had these relations both in El Paso, Texas, and Juarez, Mexico, and that the relations were had with weekly frequency. She described in detail the manner in which these homosexual relations were performed . . . the respondent stated that she enjoyed the sexual relations more with women than with men, and that she had entered into such relations voluntarily."[54] The very scientific and correct nature of the INS procedures operated as relations of force that induced a certain kind of speaking, or confessing, by this woman. It is difficult to believe that Quiroz would have freely volunteered this information to the INS, without being compelled to do so by the procedures. That INS procedures were scientific and proper, however, ensured their legitimation, and meant that their operation as relations of force had become invisible. Consequently, Quiroz's confession, but not the existence of procedures that compelled the confession, became the subject of adjudication in her case. Unfortunately for Quiroz, the alleged perversity of lesbians and gay men is often backed up by the claim that they willingly talk about their deviant sexual practices so as to recruit others into lives of depravity. The erasure of the induced nature of Quiroz's speech subjected her to this derogatory construction, which reconfirmed the original contention of the government about her undesirability. But the fact that her speech about sex was induced surely ranks as a significant perversity, too.[55]

A third feature of the economy of discourses, referred to by Foucault and evident in the medical exclusion process, was "the postulate of a general and diffuse causality . . . that endowed sex with an inexhaustible and polymorphous causal power. The most discrete event in one's sexual behavior . . . was deemed capable of entailing the most varied consequences throughout one's existence."[56] In Quiroz's case, this feature is perhaps clearest in the Board of Immigration Appeals judgment that "her relations with several women on many occasions demonstrated a pattern of behavior which was antisocial, irresponsible, lacking in social judgment and 'without any true judgment of what the results may be' (Doctor Schlenker's testimony, p. 33). To use the Public Health Service parlance, she has manifested a disorder of the personality which has brought her into conflict with 'the prevailing culture.'"[57] The mere fact that Quiroz testified to having sexual relations with two women was deemed evidence that she was irresponsible, antisocial, and personality disordered. The principle of "diffuse causality" is an ever-present resource on which the dominant culture can draw to justify penalizing lesbian and gay existence.

The fourth and fifth features of the economy, which visibly worked through the Class A Medical Exclusion Certificate system, were "methods of interpretation . . . [and] medicalization of the effects of confession."[58] In immigration exclusion cases, issues of interpretation play out at every stage of the process. For example, two key interpretive issues (along with many lesser ones) that emerged in the course of Quiroz's extended court battle to overturn the deportation order against her were: was she a lesbian, and, if so, did that mean she was necessarily a psychopathic personality? (After all, exclusion was based on a certificate issued to her for being a psychopathic personality, not for lesbianism.) The law became the key site within which these interpretive battles were fought—yet, medical and psychiatric interpretation also had a role within this process.

As we have seen, Quiroz's first line of defense in the preliminary case was to challenge the manner in which her statements were obtained and used as proof of homosexuality. She also bluntly denied that she was a homosexual and invoked the fact that she had a daughter as clear evidence of her sexual relations with men. Invoking her daughter played into hegemonic constructions of female heterosexuality. Quiroz's second line of defense drew on medical and psychiatric testimony to suggest that being a homosexual was not necessarily equivalent to being a psychopathic personality.

However, the government found that Quiroz's statements to the INS were unimpeachable. They thus found her to be a homosexual, even if she had a daughter. Regarding the second issue, the government acknowledged that there was a possible gap between homosexuality and a psychopathic personality. They even included the testimony of one of the PHS surgeons, who had signed Quiroz's exclusion certificate, that "there are persons who are sexual deviates who are not afflicted with psychopathic personality . . . but [the PHS doctor] is required to certify all homosexuals as psychopathic personalities regardless as to how he privately might feel."[59] Nonetheless, the INS ruled:

> The history of the enactment of Section 212(a)(4) of the Immigration and Nationality Act shows that Congress intended that homosexuals and other sex perverts were to be excluded from admission to the United States and that rather than make a separate class of homosexuals and sex perverts within the excluding provisions, these individuals are to be included within the category of individuals afflicted with psychopathic personality. . . . Notwithstanding the medical opinion of both physician witnesses that a person who is homosexual is not per se afflicted

with psychopathic personality and that other character traits must also be considered, Congress has intended that persons who are homosexuals are to be considered as being afflicted with psychopathic personality. It is on the basis of this clear intent of Congress that the United States Public Health Service, in its manual for the examination of aliens, classifies homosexuals and sexual deviates as being afflicted with psychopathic personality.[60]

Thus, within a legal framework, congressional intent to exclude lesbians and gay men—grounded in Congress's plenary power over immigration, which is not bound by common legal and procedural standards—was affirmed.[61] The order deporting Quiroz stood.

When the case was appealed to the Board of Immigration Appeals (BIA), Quiroz essentially employed the same two lines of defense. But the BIA responded even more harshly than had the special inquiry officer. Regarding the question of whether the evidence established that she was a homosexual, members of the BIA affirmed that Quiroz's original statements were unimpeachable. The BIA also addressed the fact that Quiroz had a daughter. The ruling related the circumstances behind the birth of the daughter: "When she was around sixteen years of age, respondent lived for about two months with a man who then deserted her, apparently when she became pregnant."[62] The board opinioned that "that affair of ten years ago does not establish that she is not now a homosexual" and furthermore, reconstructed that affair as a possible reason for her (to them, confirmed) present homosexuality. "There may be a causal connection between this earlier incident and her present problems." Quiroz's efforts to reconstruct herself within a heterosexual framework, through reference to the birth of her daughter, thus backfired, since the BIA used these same facts to advance the common homophobic proposition that unfortunate experiences with a man are the reason why a woman turns to lesbianism.[63] This only strengthened their case.

Regarding the possible gap between homosexuality and psychopathic personality, the BIA tartly ruled that "each psychiatrist or psychoanalyst may construe the term 'homosexual' and 'psychopathic personality' according to his own perspective, but within the Public Health Service and the Immigration Service, in order to achieve a degree of uniformity and fairness in the interpretation and administration of this law, we are bound to a more rigid system of classification." Therefore, within this interpretive struggle, the exigencies of uniform administration took precedence over psychiatric opinion. Not only did administrative need require that homosexuality be treated as equivalent to psychopathic personality, but furthermore, the BIA ruled, the two categories actually came together in the person of Quiroz herself. Because Quiroz had engaged in sexual relations with women, "it is our opinion that the respondent falls within the class of (psychopathic) persons defined by the two doctors who testified in this case." Not surprisingly, the BIA concluded that "since Congress unquestionably intended to include homosexuals within the class of aliens afflicted with psychopathic personality, no finding is possible in this case except that she is subject to deportation."[64] At the district court level, to which Quiroz next appealed, her counsel no longer tried to refute the finding that she was a homosexual. Instead, he concentrated on trying to undo the contention that a homosexual is necessarily a psychopathic personality. But the district court merely affirmed the legal overlap between the two, ruling that "since the record shows the plaintiff is a homosexual she is therefore a person of psychopathic personality."[65]

The Fifth Circuit brief for Quiroz again hinged on the argument that "the court erred in concluding as a matter of law that since the record shows that plaintiff is a homosexual, she is, therefore, a person of psychopathic personality."[66] Various arguments were marshaled to support this contention. The government's counterbrief acknowledged that Congress had not defined the term "psychopathic personality" and that there were no cases on which to rely for precedent. Nonetheless, Congress had (and has) the right to decide who shall be excluded from immigrating, and government documents suggested that Congress intended to exclude lesbians and gay men. Quiroz was sent yet another letter that ordered her deportation. Ultimately, Quiroz's lawyer was unable to drive a wedge between the notion of equivalence between homosexuality and psychopathic personality, despite engaging in a prolonged interpretive battle within the courts. He was also unable to challenge the evidence that was used to construct her as homosexual.

Quiroz had one last card to play, though. On June 23, 1961, the Fifth Circuit Court ruled against her and ordered her deportation by August 15, 1961. On August 2, 1961, she married Edward Escudero, and filed a motion to reopen her case. We will probably never know the circumstances surrounding this marriage. Was Quiroz a lesbian engaging in a sham marriage, with Escudero as either a willing participant or a dupe? Or did she enter into the marriage in good faith, perhaps trying to "go straight," or even from honest feelings of love, attraction, and affection? Whatever the circumstances, the motion filed on her behalf requested the right to reopen her case so as to "present evidence of her marriage and full rehabilitation, being new facts which touch upon the issue of deportability. . . . That since the order of deportation was entered herein, your applicant has married Edward Escudero, who joins this application, and that she is prepared to prove that she is, at this time, a normal individual and no longer a psychopathic personality."[67] Given the timing of the marriage, it certainly seems to constitute an effort to take the charges brought against her and use them to craft a response that satisfied dominant cultural terms regarding women and sexuality. The argument that her marriage offered evidence of "rehabilitation" and of becoming "a normal individual" fits neatly into mainstream assumptions that homosexuality can be "cured" (and even better, that lesbianism can be cured by finding the right man).

It was a brave effort. But marriage, too, failed to prevent Quiroz's deportation. This is because, as the INS noted in their "brief in opposition," "According to counsel's motion the new facts to be proven at the proposed reopening will show that the respondent has married since the order of deportation was entered, is now a normal individual and no longer a psychopathic personality. Even if all this should be proven, no application is apparent to the matter of the respondent's deportability, *which is based on her condition at entry* on January 6, 1960 and not on circumstances which may have arisen since that time" (emphasis added).[68]

Both sides thus tried to play on the temporal ambiguity of when one might be said to have "become" homosexual. Quiroz initially tried to deny her homosexuality; then she presented the birth of her daughter as evidence that she had had sexual relations with a man sometime in the past (which might cast doubt on present allegations of homosexuality); then, through marriage, she tried to construct homosexuality as a prior condition that was now "cured." The INS, for its part, refuted her initial denials. The BIA hearing then suggested that the circumstances surrounding the birth of her daughter may have "caused" her lesbianism. Finally, they invoked their legal power by which lesbianism was defined as significant at time of entry, regardless of any changes later. In the interpretive battle over the construction and penalizing of lesbianism, the INS eventually won.

We will never know with absolute certainty whether Quiroz was a lesbian. After all, lesbianism has no clear, predefined content that allows us to draw a marker between it and other forms of sexuality. But her case shows how the immigration service, in conjunction with larger circuits of power and knowledge, established the boundaries of who and what counted as a lesbian, and then confined Quiroz within that definition. The effects of Quiroz's battle and its resolution were indeed "medicalized" (the fifth feature mentioned by Foucault): Quiroz's Class A Medical Exclusion Certificate stood, and she was deported.

Quiroz's refusal of the lesbian label was certainly intended to avoid deportation. But other reasons may also have motivated her. Perhaps she did not consider herself a lesbian, despite reporting sexual relations with women. Anthropologists such as Joseph Carrier have documented how the construction of male homosexuality in Mexico differs from dominant U.S. constructions, such that men who have sexual relations with other men are not necessarily stigmatized as homosexual.[69] Carrier's work raises questions about how lesbian identity was constructed in the late 1950s and early 1960s in Mexican and U.S. communities that were familiar to Quiroz. It also raises questions about how Quiroz, who was situated at the intersection of several cultures, communities, and traditions, negotiated her sexual identity, which may have changed over time.[70] Though she reported sexual relations with women, did this make her a lesbian? If so, according to whose definition?

Even if Quiroz considered herself a lesbian, claiming the label was undoubtedly complicated by being a Mexican immigrant woman living in a U.S. border city. Oliva Espín notes that immigrant lesbians often remain situated within the contradictory space "between the racism of the dominant society and the sexist and heterosexist expectations of [their] own community."[71] Under those circumstances, female sexuality becomes a site through which cultural contestations are played out. Thus, Cherríe Moraga, among others, eloquently documents how declaring oneself a lesbian leaves Latinas vulnerable to the charge of *vendida*, or race traitor.[72] Yolanda Leyva further explains that silence, rather than public admission, enables many Latina lesbians to remain connected to family and community. "Latina lesbians have survived because of that silence, and the protection it has provided, despite the many limits and compromises it has imposed."[73] The INS charge that Quiroz was a lesbian, whether true or not, shattered the protective silence and jeopardized her access to family and community resources. The lesbian label may also have followed her to Mexico, through the gossip of other returnees, or when she was asked to explain her deportation to family and friends. Resettlement becomes very difficult under those circumstances. Quiroz's efforts to refuse the label of lesbian must be framed, therefore, within the context of multiple jeopardies and competing pressures that she faced as an immigrant woman living in a U.S. border city with an anti-Mexican history, as well as the incommensurabilities between different cultural practices of constructing and naming sexual identities.

For these reasons, and in the absence of documents other than official ones, I have resisted offering a judgment about whether or not Quiroz was a lesbian. My resistance is intended to foreground the dangers of reading immigrant women's sexualities within dominant U.S. frameworks—even when the reading is intended to assist in the formation of a counterhistory—because unqualified use of the term "lesbian" may arrogate immigrant women's experiences to U.S.-based paradigms that do not allow for theorization of the ways that immigrant status, allied with experiences of racism, cultural difference, and class exploitation, complicate sexual identities. As Quiroz's case shows, this arrogation may occur in conjunction with systemic violence that is imposed by the state (in the form of deportation). But it is important to emphasize that lesbians do cross borders. Immigrant lesbian lives remain little documented or understood, however.[74]

VII

In 1990, Congress repealed immigration provisions that excluded lesbians and gay men. A congressional report stated that "in order to make it clear that the U.S. does not view personal decisions about sexual orientation as a danger to other people in our society, the bill repeals the 'sexual deviation' exclusion ground [in immigration]." The end of exclusion based on sexual orientation has received little attention in studies of immigration. However, a congressional report demonstrates one way that this policy change has been framed and explained: "The law also needs to be updated in its treatment of sexual orientation. The term 'sexual deviation' (INA 212[a][4]) was included with the other mental health exclusion grounds expressly for the purpose of excluding homosexuals. Not only is this provision out of step with current notions of privacy and personal dignity, it is also inconsistent with contemporary psychiatric theories. . . . To put an end to this unfairness, Congress must repeal the 'sexual deviation' ground [for immigration exclusion]."[75]

Tempting as it is to attribute the repeal of exclusion as an outgrowth of current notions of privacy and personal dignity and contemporary psychiatric theories, this explanation is partial at best. As discussed above, exclusion never hinged solely on medical or psychiatric knowledge; rather, that knowledge was deployed as part of a larger strategic formation of homophobic discourses and practices. Alterations in the composition of that knowledge were not sufficient to generate repeal, unless alterations also occurred in the discursive economy as a whole.

One of the most significant alterations to the discursive economy that organized exclusion occurred more than a decade before the 1990 change. In 1979, the surgeon general directed the PHS to stop automatically issuing Class A Medical Exclusion Certificates solely on the basis of homosexuality. One factor bearing on the Surgeon General's decision was the fact that in 1973, trustees of the American Psychiatric Association (APA) "voted to remove homosexuality *per se* from the categories of mental disorder. In the next year, a referendum upholding the decision was passed by the full APA membership."[76] Until this APA action, homosexuality was listed as an illness; and even if its exact nature was disputed, the fact it was officially an illness meant that lesbians and gay men came under PHS purview. After 1974, however, in the absence of an official illness categorization, the PHS was arguably no longer responsible for lesbians or gay men (unless they had other medical or mental conditions).[77] Other factors, too, undoubtedly had a bearing on the surgeon general's decision.

When the surgeon general declared that the PHS would no longer automatically issue Class A Medical Exclusion Certificates to lesbians and gay men, he evoked a sharp response from John M. Harmon, Assistant Attorney General for the Department of Justice. In a memorandum to David M. Crosland, Acting Commissioner of the INS, Harmon excoriated the surgeon general for his decision and suggested he had overstepped the bounds of his authority. "Congress clearly intended that homosexuality be included in the statutory phrase 'mental defect or disease' and the surgeon general has no authority to determine that homosexuality is not a 'mental defect or disease' for the purpose of applying the [Immigration] Act," stated the memo.[78] Harmon ruled that the INS remained bound to exclude lesbians and gay men, even without PHS assistance. In 1980, the INS announced how exclusion would operate: "If an alien made an 'unsolicited, unambiguous admission of homosexuality' to an INS inspector or was identified as homosexual by a 'third party who arrived at the same time,' the alleged homosexual would be subject to a secondary inspection. At that inspection, the person would be asked whether he or she was a homosexual. If the person answered 'no,' entry would be permitted. If the person answered 'yes,' a formal exclusionary hearing would follow."[79]

In some respects, this approach to exclusion was not very different from before. Well before 1980, the INS relied on self-disclosure and identification by a third party (though not necessarily a party who arrived at the same time) to pick out immigrants who might be lesbians or gay men. Other identificatory practices, such as criminal record checks and inclusion of key questions on immigration application forms, operated both pre- and post-1980. Perhaps the main difference was simply the elimination of one step in the exclusion process: whereas pre-1980, a suspected lesbian or gay immigrant was sent to the PHS for certification before exclusion, after 1980, the INS skipped the certification process and excluded directly.

The growing questions and criticisms directed toward lesbian and gay exclusion in the 1980s therefore reflect not the implementation of new, egregious forms of border control, but the loss of the certification process. An array of practices was suddenly unbound from the legitimation offered by a medical exclusion certificate, in a way that made them available for further questioning and contestation. In addition, new political and social formations, including lesbian/gay legal defense and political advocacy groups, had also emerged, and they directly contested practices like exclusion. During the 1980s, "the question of how to identify lesbians and gay men had become an increasingly vexed one. . . . The INS's stated policy of relying on voluntary admission drew an openly arbitrary line between lesbians and gay men who, perhaps unaware of the consequences, announced their homosexuality to INS inspectors and those who did not. The enforcement of the procedure was, as even the State Department and some INS officials admitted, uneven and arbitrary . . . the legal uncertainties [arising from contradictory court rulings in the 1980s] and administrative inconsistencies surrounding the exclusion had made an already controversial provision increasingly difficult to justify."[80] Concern about discrimination against lesbians and gay men was voiced. Some public officials suggested that "a person's sexual orientation should be a private matter that had no relevance to immigration."[81]

The expression of these problematizations continued unchecked, since neither the medical certification system remained, nor did an equally effective new organization of homophobic discourses emerge. The diversity of problematizations meant that a wide spectrum of groups could find something to support in proposals to repeal the exclusion. "Those who supported [the exclusion's] elimination spanned a broad ideological range, including the Carter, Reagan, and Bush administrations, the Select Commission on Immigration and Refugee Policy, the American Psychiatric Association, and numerous civil rights organizations."[82] In 1990, Congress repealed immigration exclusion based on sexual deviation.

VIII

Since 1990, lesbians and gay men are no longer automatically debarred from emigrating to the United States. The change is significant. But the meanings of this change must be carefully evaluated. After all, although lesbians and gay men are no longer excluded, judicial interpretations of aspects of immigration law remain "heavily influenced by the categoric exclusion of lesbians and gay men under the 1952 Act" and by a heterosexual norm.[83] Lesbians and gay men are still likely to be excluded for lacking good moral character. They also remain unable to use long-term relationships with U.S. citizens or residents as a basis for gaining their own U.S. residency (a right that is available to male/ female couples). Once within the United States, lesbians and gay men must continually contend with homophobia.[84]

These are some of the effects of homosexuality that continue to make immigration difficult, even after 1990. To assess how homosexuality is likely to remain salient in immigration in the foreseeable future, we would need to examine the operation of major discourses and practices that are critical to the current production of homosexuality. We would also need to analyze how lesbian and gay identities may be reproduced within new collectivities that are no longer delineated within clear lesbian or gay parameters. For example, HIV has become a significant issue in the administration of the immigration system. And HIV, as Katie King observes, is both altering the terrain of what counts as the gay/lesbian community, and producing new collectivities that cannot be captured within a gay/straight model.[85] In addition to the reconfiguration of identities caused by HIV/AIDS, the 1990 Act also established "a new general category of exclusion based on mental or physical disorders. Although general in nature, this ground is linked carefully to behavior and potentially harmful activities . . . two requirements must be met if an alien is to be excluded because of a mental or physical disorder. The alien must be determined to have a mental or physical disorder and a history of behavior (or current behaviors associated with the disorder) that may pose a threat to the property or the safety of the alien or others . . . the standard is based on the behavior of the alien."[86] The standard of "harmful activities" and behaviors has the potential to be unfairly applied to lesbians and gay men in particular, as well as to produce new minoritized collectivities that include but are not limited to lesbians and gay men.

Clearly, then, despite the 1990 changes, lesbian and gay identities continue to have various kinds of salience in immigration. Nonetheless, the act is a key piece of legislation that makes new social justice strategies possible. Because the act protects foreign-born lesbians, gay men, and "queers" from automatic exclusion, a national movement to secure spousal immigration privileges for same-sex couples, as well as novel ways of publicly linking struggles around homophobia, racism, and anti-immigrant sentiment, have emerged.[87] Pre-1990, these political projects were greatly handicapped (if not virtually impossible), since foreign-born people who identified as lesbian, gay, or queer risked exclusion by announcing their presence, publicizing their struggles, or participating in organizing.

Repeal of exclusion based on sexual deviation is intelligible within a framework that is sensitive to the operations of power. Foucault writes:

Power must be understood in the first instance as the multiplicity of force relations immanent in the sphere in which they operate and which constitute their own organization; as the processes which, through ceaseless struggles and confrontations, transforms, strengthens, or reverses them; as the support which these force relations find in one another, thus forming a chain or system, or on the contrary, the disjunctions and contradictions which isolate them from one another; and lastly, as the strategies in which they take effect, whose general design or institutional crystallization is embodied in the state apparatus, in the formulation of the law, in the various social hegemonies.[88]

Lesbian and gay exclusion functioned until 1990 not because of its grounding in rational thought, but because of its ability to weave together a range of disparate, sometimes contradictory, and often clearly unreasonable homophobic discourses and practices, into a chain or system. This weaving together found institutional crystallization in the Class A Medical Exclusion System, which was supported by "the state apparatus, in the formulation of the law, [and] in the various social hegemonies." At the same time, this formation generated its own "disjunctions and contradictions." Contradictions included the ways that the formation contributed to production of the very sexuality against which it claimed to guard the nation. Quiroz's case offers a valuable window into the ways that border monitoring enabled the production of official immigration service definitions of lesbianism, around which exclusions—that potentially affected not just self-identified lesbians but any woman who did not clearly conform to current heterosexual standards—were organized. Quiroz's case, and her strategies of resistance, also provide information about the ways that sexual monitoring of the border was gender differentiated, even though suspected lesbians and gay men were barred from entry under a shared provision. As the case makes clear, racial and class histories integrally structure how gender and sexual identities are produced, negotiated, oppositionally deployed, and sanctioned at the border. Quiroz's case also raises critical questions about how migrant women negotiate sexual identities and communities when the threat of state-sanctioned exclusion or deportation structures their options. Though an end to exclusion in the broadest sense has not occurred, the transformation of conditions of struggle, and of relations between affected individuals and groups, is beyond question.

NOTES

Reprinted with permission from the University of Texas Press. This essay originally appeared in the *Journal of the History of Sexuality* 8, no. 3 (1998): 477–506. This essay is dedicated to Hiroko Taira. I also gratefully acknowledge the many forms of support that made this article possible. Support included funding from the Vice Chancellor for Research at the University of California, Berkeley; generous assistance from Albert Armendariz, Sr., Esq., and his staff; Shannon Minter's suggestion that I locate and interview Mr. Armendariz; legal information from Professor Carolyn (Patty) Blum and Susan Lee; theoretical assistance from David Lloyd; helpful suggestions from Jill Esbenshade, JeeYeun Lee, José Palafox at the National Network for Immigrant and Refugee Rights, Jasbir K. Puar, Carla Trujillo, and audience members at the American Studies Association Conference in 1996; encouragement from Jean Molesky Poz; interviews with four anonymous lesbian immigrants; critical feedback from Arlene Keizer and Alberto Peréz; and the continued support of my dissertation committee. The mistakes are mine.

1   Albert Armendariz, Sr., interview by author, El Paso, Texas, March 18, 1996.

2   Cited in *Matter of LaRochelle*, 11 I&N December 436 (Board of Immigration Appeals, 1965).

3   Senate Committee of the Judiciary, The Immigration & Naturalization Systems of the United States, 81st Cong., 2d Sess., 1950, S. Rep. 1515.

4   "Revision of Immigration & Nationality Laws," Senate, 82d Cong., 2d sess., 1952, Rep. 1137, 9.

5   A significant amount of information about the history of gay and lesbian exclusion has been reconstructed from the records of court cases. To date, *Quiroz v. Neely*, 291 F. 2d 906 (1961), is the only female court case that has been identified.

6   This article focuses on the exclusion of lesbians and gay men, specifically, in U.S. immigration. Though the contemporary notion of "queer" also includes people who are bisexual and transgendered, as well as various heterosexualities, these were not identities around which the policing of immigration was organized. Rather, the historical record suggests that Congress and the immigration service were specifically concerned with a homosexual threat. Court cases indicate that individuals who were sexually involved with both men and women were considered homosexual, rather than bi- or heterosexual. Indeed, they were considered to be particularly pernicious homosexuals, who deceitfully tried to hide their "condition" by becoming involved with people of the opposite sex.

7   Kieran Rose, "The Tenderness of the Peoples," in *Lesbian and Gay Visions of Ireland: Towards the Twenty-First Century*, ed. Íde O'Carroll and Eoin Collins (London, 1995), 74.

8   Foucault argues that, though particular sexual acts had a long history of being forbidden and subject to punishment, it was only in the nineteenth century that these acts became reconstructed as the signs of distinct types of personages, each endowed with a discrete sexual identity that the state needed to monitor and manage. For example, homosexual *acts* became reconstructed as the sign of a homosexual *type*. As a result, "the homosexual became a personage, a past, a case history, and a childhood, in addition to being a type of life, a life form, and a morphology, with an indiscreet anatomy and a possibly mysterious physiology . . . the homosexual was now a species." See Michel Foucault, *The History of Sexuality: An Introduction*, vol. 1 of *The History of Sexuality*, trans. Robert Hurley (New York, 1990), 43.

9   Eve Kosofsky Sedgwick, *Epistemology of the Closet* (Berkeley, 1990), 9.

10 The immigration service also excluded those who had committed sexual acts that were forbidden by immigration law, whether or not the person fit within a sexual identity category. As Janet Halley usefully reminds us, sexual types and sexual acts "are not mutually exclusive descriptors" (184), but rather, they interrelate in the production of categories of people who are marked out for exclusion. See Janet Halley, "The Status/Conduct Distinction in the 1993 Revisions to Military Anti-Gay Policy: A Legal Archaeology," in *GLQ* 3 (1996): 179–251.

11 Foucault, *The History of Sexuality*, 1:103. For Quiroz, the density of the relations of power also have to do with the fact that she was a Mexican woman, and as such, was connected to a larger history of strict immigration monitoring directed at people of Mexican origin attempting to enter the United States. See Leo Chavez,

Shadowed Lives: Undocumented Immigrants in American Society (Fort Worth, TX, 1992); Kitty Calavita, *Inside the State: The Bracero Program, Immigration, and the INS* (New York, 1992); Roger Rouse, "Making Sense of Settlement: Class Transformation, Cultural Struggle, and Transnationalism among Mexican Migrants in the United States," in *Towards a Transnational Perspective on Migration*, ed. Nina Glick Schiller, Linda Basch, and Cristina Blanc-Szanton, Annals of the New York Academy of Sciences no. 645 (New York, 1992); and other writings on Mexican migration.

12 There is a double problem here. Efforts to determine whether Quiroz was a lesbian sustain sexual categorizations, even if the efforts are motivated by affirmation of resistant and minority sexual subjects. Furthermore, these sexual categorizations substantially derive their meanings from metropolitan centers, which are materially and ideologically implicated in the production of immigrant women as racial or ethnic minorities. Thus, uncritical application of the term "lesbian" to a woman such as Quiroz can easily erase her different historical formation and complex positionality, without revealing anything about her sexuality.

13 For a discussion of how the U.S. is constituted as heterosexual, see Lauren Berlant and Elizabeth Freeman, "Queer Nationality," in *boundary 2* (1992): 149–80.

14 Thanks to Judith Butler for this succinct formulation. Two examples may help to illustrate how immigration checkpoints can regulate the terms by which identity is formed. I interviewed a woman who had had a sexual relationship with a woman in her country of origin and thought nothing of it—until she was asked by a State Department official, while applying to immigrate, if she was a homosexual. The fact of being asked, and the manner in which she was asked, made her rethink the significance of that sexual experience. A second, rather different, example concerns a woman who came to the United States, lived here for several years, and began to think of herself as a lesbian. But she knew that in order to adjust from immigrant to citizen status, she would one day be asked to account for her activities before immigration officials. Therefore, the woman did not feel free to join lesbian groups or activities until she held citizen status.

15 The fact that certain forms of queer identities were unlikely to be captured by these checkpoints does not make the fact of policing any less salient for all queer people, however.

16 Shannon Minter, "Sodomy and Public Morality Offenses under U.S. Immigration Law: Penalizing Lesbian and Gay Identity," *Cornell International Law Journal* 26 (1993): 799.

17 But we should not treat this dearth of court cases as further evidence that lesbians were unaffected by immigration policing; instead, we need to remain attuned to the ways that women are historically excluded/unrepresented within official documents, but were present historically and had an impact. See Yolanda Chavez Leyva, "Breaking the Silence: Putting Latina Lesbian History at the Center," in *The New Lesbian Studies: Toward the Twenty-First Century*, ed. Bonnie Zimmerman and Toni McNaron (New York, 1996), 145–52.

18 Aside from *Quiroz*, the only other lesbian immigration case I have ever seen cited is *In re Schmidt*, 56 Misc. 2d 456, 459–60 NY Sup. Ct. (1961). This case is cited by Minter, who describes the issue as follows: "A New York court applied Judge Hand's standard to a lesbian seeking naturalization after living and working in

the United States for fourteen years. The woman testified to having had a series of relationships with women, both before her entry to the country and after. Citing a New Jersey court that found 'few behavioral deviations . . . more offensive to American mores than . . . homosexuality,' the New York court dismissed the woman's petition for citizenship despite the fact that her behavior was private and violated no law." See Minter, 794.

19 Armendariz interview (n. 1 above). Armendariz estimates that this officer was single-handedly responsible for the exclusion or deportation of several hundred women for "sexual deviation."

20 Decision of the Special Inquiry Officer, case A8 707 653, U.S. Department of Justice, Immigration and Naturalization Service, El Paso, TX, March 25, 1960, 3.

21 House, 82d Cong., 2d sess., 1952, Rep. 1365, 47.

22 Of course, masculinity and femininity are culturally coded in very specific ways, so when one deals with culturally different and diverse populations of immigrants, this standard would provide only a shaky basis for identifying "deviants."

23 Jennifer Terry, "Lesbians under the Medical Gaze: Scientists Search for Remarkable Differences," *Journal of Sex Research* 27 (1990): 319.

24 Terry, "Lesbians under the Medical Gaze," 321.

25 Terry, 323, 332.

26 bell hooks, "Homophobia in Black Communities," in her *Talking Back: Thinking Feminist, Thinking Black* (Boston, 1989), 125.

27 Nice Rodriguez, "Big Nipple of the North," in *Piece of My Heart: A Lesbian of Colour Anthology*, ed. Makeda Silvera (Toronto, 1992), 35–36.

28 Of course, race and gender are not reducible to visible marks, either, and the visible certainly need not provide an accurate index of an individual's gender or race. In terms of race, this point is most thoroughly developed in writings about people with multiracial heritages. See, e.g., the essays in Maria P. P. Root, ed., *Racially Mixed People in America* (Newbury Park, CA, 1992).

29 Timothy J. Dunn, *The Militarization of the U.S.-Mexico Border, 1978-1992* (Austin, TX, 1996), 6.

30 Dunn.

31 Since Quiroz crossed the border, U.S.-Mexican border relations have undergone many changes. In the 1980s and 1990s, as part of a renewed war against both drugs and undocumented immigration, the U.S.-Mexico border region has become increasingly militarized. Dunn, among others, has documented the increased deployment of military technology, expansion of Border Patrol powers, involvement of the National Guard, and the growth of detention centers in the region, since the early 1980s. Civil and human rights abuses against residents of the region, especially against Latino-origin peoples, have become a significant issue. In addition to Dunn, see María Jiminéz, "War in the Borderlands," *Report on the Americas* 26 (1992): 29–33; American Friends Service Committee, *Sealing Our Borders: The Human Toll* (Philadelphia, 1992); Americas Watch, *Brutality Unchecked: Human Rights Abuses along the U.S. Border with Mexico* (New York, 1992).

32 Yvonne Yarbro-Bejarano, "De-constructing the Lesbian Body: Cherrie Moraga's *Loving in the War Years*," in *Chicana Lesbians: The Girls Our Mothers Warned Us About*, ed. Carla Trujillo (Berkeley, 1991), 146.

33 See National Lawyers Guild, "Crime Related Deportation Grounds and Criminal Offenses under the INA," *Immigration Law and Crimes* (Deerfield, IL, 1995). This essay notes that immigrants who willfully and materially misrepresent their cases are excludable.

34 For example, Attorney Ignatius Bau related that in Russia, men accused of homosexuality tend to be jailed, whereas women accused of lesbianism tend to be hospitalized. Consequently, the mark (or at least, the accusation) of homosexuality is visible in gender-differentiated ways in documents that Russian immigrants submit to the INS. (Telephone conversation with author, San Francisco, April 1995.)

35 When someone seemed potentially lesbian or gay, the INS did not always thoroughly investigate them. Instead, it could dispose of them without generating any record at all. Donald C. Knutson, counsel to the National Gay Rights Advocates, explained how this occurred: "If the border guard suspects because of that person's appearance or some other reason [that he or she is gay or lesbian], the normal practice has been to inform that person that he or she is not entitled to enter the country, that he or she has two options. One, get on the plane or boat or train or whatever and go back where you came from and you won't have any more trouble. If you persist, however, you must go before an immigration judge. You must go before a psychiatrist for a psychiatric examination, and then you will be excluded from this country, deported, and never permitted to come back again. Well, it is no wonder that statistics do not indicate that many people have taken that [second] course." (See House, *Exclusion and Deportation Amendments of 1983*, Hearing before the Subcommittee on Immigration, Refugees, and International Law of the Committee of the Judiciary, 98th Cong., 2d sess., H.R. 4509, 5227, Serial no. 98–72, June 28, 1984, 193.) Consequently, although medical certification provided the means to exclude suspected lesbians and gay men, exclusion could always be implemented more informally, simply by invoking the threat of the medical certification process.

36 Richard Green, "'Give Me Your Tired, Your Poor, Your Huddled Masses' (of Heterosexuals): An Analysis of American and Canadian Immigration Policy," *Anglo American Law Review* 16 (1987): 140.

37 Robert Podnanski, "The Propriety of Denying Entry to Homosexual Aliens: Examining the Public Health Service's Authority over Medical Exclusions," *University of Michigan Journal of Law Reform* 17 (1983–84): 347.

38 David M. Halperin, *Saint Foucault: Towards a Gay Hagiography* (New York, 1995), 32–33.

39 Foucault refers to such organization and deployment as a discursive economy: "The *economy* of discourses—their intrinsic technology, the necessities of their operation, the tactics they employ, the effects of power which underlie them and which they transmit—this, and not the system of representations is what determines the essential features of what they have to say [emphasis added]." Foucault, *History of Sexuality* (n. 8 above), 1:68–69.

40 The PHS remains involved in inspecting the physical and mental health of aspiring immigrants to this day. For more information, see Committee of the Judiciary, Subcommittee no. 1, House of Representatives, "Inquiry into the Alien Medical Examination Program of the U.S. Public Health Service," Special Series no. 12, *Study of Immigration and Population Problems* (Washington, DC, 1963).

41 As Foucault phrased it, "The exercise of power is not added on from outside, like a rigid, heavy constraint . . . but is so subtly present in them as to increase their efficiency." See Michel Foucault, *Discipline and Punish: The Birth of the Prison* (New York, 1979), 206.

42 Allan Bérubé, *Coming Out under Fire: The History of Gay Men and Women in World War II* (New York, 1990), 142.

43 Bérubé, 266.

44 Bérubé, 269–70.

45 Bérubé, 259.

46 Jill Esbenshade pointed out to me that there were connections between immigration and military policies during this time period. Thank you, Jill.

47 Foucault, *History of Sexuality*, 1:65.

48 Foucault, 1:65–67.

49 National Lawyers Guild (n. 33 above).

50 Armendariz interview (n. 1 above).

51 Decision of the Special Inquiry Officer (n. 20 above), 3.

52 Once her testimony had been taken, corroborating testimony had also been obtained from one Celia Rosales, named by Quiroz as one of her lovers during the past fifteen months—so it was not her speech alone that constructed her as lesbian. However, in many cases, speech about oneself, without such corroboration, was sufficient proof of homosexuality—making speech, and the relation of speech to the self, a very contested location. For more on the vexed relationship between self-disclosure and homosexual identity, see Sedgwick (n. 9 above), esp. 69–75.

53 Decision of the Special Inquiry Officer, 3–4.

54 Decision of the Special Inquiry Officer, 1.

55 The question of using "scientific practice" to "induce" immigrants to speak and to "force a difficult confession" has played out in many ways in immigration monitoring of lesbians and gay men. The PHS suggested, in a 1952 report to Congress, that some people might suffer from a "homosexuality of which the individual himself is unaware." In those cases, "some psychological tests may be helpful in uncovering homosexuality" (House Rep. 1365 [n. 21 above], 47). Green speculates that the tests in question were Rorschach inkblot tests (see Green [n. 36 above], 142, n. 7). Public Health Service psychological tests were not the only means used to force a confession about sexuality—a more dramatic example concerns Mexican Jaime Chavez, who was "held incommunicado under armed guard for over twenty-four hours [and] subjected to abusive questioning and an abusive search" (Exclusion and Deportation Amendments of 1983 [n. 21 above], 185). Chavez was treated in this way because he was suspected of homosexuality, based on the contents of his luggage.

56 Foucault, *History of Sexuality* (n. 8 above), 1:66.

57 Decision of the Board of Immigration Appeals, case A-8707653, U.S. Department of Justice, Washington, DC, June 2, 1960, 7.

58 Foucault, *History of Sexuality*, 1:66–67.

59 Decision of the Special Inquiry Officer, 2.

60 Decision of the Special Inquiry Officer, 5.

61 Historically, Congress has enjoyed plenary power over immigration matters, such that: "Congress has unbounded power to exclude aliens from admission to

the United States; Congress can bar aliens from entering the United States for discriminatory and arbitrary reasons, even those which might be condemned as a denial of equal protection if used for purposes other than immigration." See *Matter of Longstaff,* 716 F. 2d 1439 (5th Cir., 1983). Plenary powers are intended to ensure national sovereignty.

62 Decision of the Board of Immigration Appeals, 4.

63 This argument makes heterosexuality the norm from which all other sexualities are both derivative and deviant; it makes all women's sexual agency derivative of male actions; thus, it implies lesbianism is the result of heterosexuality gone wrong, become spoiled; in this way, it renders impossible the affirmation of women loving women, while constructing lesbians as degraded, sick, and inferior.

64 Decision of the Board of Immigration Appeals, 7.

65 Findings of Fact and Conclusions of Law, U.S. District Court for the Western District of Texas, El Paso Division, in Civil Action no. 2175, *Sara Harb Quiroz v. Marcus T. Neelly,* August 22, 1960, 2.

66 *Sara Harb Quiroz v. Richard C. Haberstroh,* U.S. Court of Appeals for the Fifth Circuit, case no. 18724, Brief of the Appellant, (March 1961), 2. (A more precise date is not given.)

67 Motion to Reopen, in the Matter of Sara Harb Quiroz, Now Sara Harb Escudero, case no. A8 707 653, To the District Director of Immigration and Naturalization Service of El Paso, Texas, August 7, 1961, 1.

68 U.S. Department of Justice, Immigration and Naturalization Service, Brief in Opposition, in the matter of Sara Harb Quiroz, case. no. A8 707 653, August 23, 1961.

69 See Joseph Carrier, *De los otros: Intimacy and Homosexuality among Mexican Men* (New York, 1995).

70 Thomás Almaguer has documented that Chicano men negotiate sexual identity in the intersections of Mexican/Chicano and dominant U.S. sexuality constructions. (See Thomás Almaguer, "Chicano Men: A Cartography of Homosexual Identity and Behavior," in *The Lesbian and Gay Studies Reader,* ed. Henry Abelove et al. [New York, 1993], 255–73.) How that process of negotiation might have occurred for immigrant Mexican women in the late 1950s is something about which we can only speculate. But we know that immigrant lesbians do not easily fit into what Leyva calls "the Anglo lesbian paradigm of the modern lesbian identity" (see Leyva [n. 17 above], 149), and other identity formations and traditions must be grasped if we are to theorize the richness of immigrant lesbian history.

71 Oliva M. Espín, "The Immigrant Experience in Lesbian Studies," in Zimmerman and McNaron, eds. (n. 17 above), 82.

72 Cherríe Moraga, *Loving in the War Years: lo que nunca pasó por sus labios* (Boston, 1983), 90–142.

73 Leyva, 145.

74 Espín, 79. See also Lourdes Arguelles and B. Ruby Rich, "Homosexuality, Homophobia, and Revolution: Notes toward an Understanding of the Cuban Lesbian and Gay Male Experience," pt. 1, *Signs: Journal of Women in Culture and Society* 9 (1984): 683–99, and "Homosexuality, Homophobia, and Revolution: Notes toward an Understanding of the Cuban Lesbian and Gay Male Experience," pt. 2, *Signs: Journal of Women in Culture and Society* 11 (1985): 120–35.

75 House, "Family Unity and Employment Opportunity Immigration Act of 1990," 101st Cong., 2d sess., September 19, 1990, Rep. 101–723, parts 1 and 2, 56.

76 Green (n. 36 above), 143. For a more detailed discussion of the APA's decision, see Ronald Bayer, *Homosexuality and American Psychiatry: The Politics of Diagnosis*, 2d ed. (Princeton, NJ, 1987). Neil Miller mentions that in an effort to contest the automatic labeling of homosexuality as a mental illness, gay activists "zapped" APA conventions and meetings, and at one panel discussion of the issue, "a psychiatrist . . . created a sensation by announcing that he was gay. It marked the first time that any psychiatrist in the United States had come out publicly; the drama of his revelation was heightened by the fact he found it necessary to wear a mask and speak through a voice altering device." See Neil Miller, *Out of the Past: Gay and Lesbian History from 1869 to the Present* (New York, 1995), 256.

77 Thanks to Carolyn (Patty) Blum for her comments on this matter.

78 John M. Harmon, assistant attorney general, to David L. Crosland, acting commissioner, INS memorandum, December 10, 1979, 2.

79 Green, 143.

80 Minter (n. 16 above), 780–81.

81 House, 100th Cong., 2d sess., Rep. 882, 23–24.

82 Minter, 781.

83 Minter, 787.

84 There are also difficulties with accessing political asylum, especially for lesbians.

85 Katie King, "Local and Global: AIDS Activism and Feminism," in *Camera Obscura* 28 (1992): 80. Note that in the late 1980s, HIV became a grounds for immigration exclusion, "although the law did not specifically list it as such. In 1993, Congress added HIV to the list of grounds for exclusion in the Immigration and Nationality Act." See "HIV as a Grounds of Inadmissibility: How It Works," in *Asylum Based on Sexual Orientation: A Resource Guide*, ed. Sydney Levy (San Francisco, 1996), I: E, 25.

86 House Report 101–723 (n. 75 above), 52–53.

87 This is a project that intersects with the more domestically oriented campaign for same-sex marriage.

88 Foucault, *History of Sexuality* (n. 8 above), 1:92–93.

Migrant Melancholia: Emergent Discourses of Mexican Migrant Traffic in Transnational Space

ALICIA SCHMIDT CAMACHO

It is not, then, just a question of mapping social relations (economic, sociological, or whatever) *on to* space. The fact that those relations *occur over* space matters. It is not just that "space is socially constructed"—a fact with which geographers have for a while been coming to terms—but that social processes are constructed over space.
—DOREEN MASSEY, *Spatial Divisions of Labor: Social Structures and the Geography of Production*

It was a Holiday Inn
downtown El Paso
where she crossed the line daily
paso por paso
mal paso que das
al cruzar la frontera
There was the work permit
sealed in plastic
like the smile
she flashed every morning
to the same uniformed eyes
—MARISELA NORTE, "Act of the Faithless"

Reports of migrant deaths and disappearances in the transnational circuit linking the United States and Mexico should disturb the fiction of the regulated border. The fate of the undocumented reveals the violence with which both states have acted over time to rationalize the boundaries of their territory and citizenship.[1] In recent years, sharp increases in the numbers of undocumented migrants and the concurrent escalation of border militarization have made the journey to the United States more hazardous and the possibilities of return to Mexico more uncertain. Furthermore, as migration increasingly extends outward from the Southwest, it challenges the dominant frameworks for depicting or explaining the Mexican presence in the United States. As the costs of Mexican labor migrations have become more visible, state institutions and communications media in both countries have had to address the hazards, both physical and psychological, of unauthorized entry and settlement in the United States. Disappearances of various sorts are revealed in the growing rosters of missing persons kept by the Mexican Office of Foreign Relations (Secretaría de Relaciones Exteriores) and immigrant organizations; these numbers reveal the instability of those narratives of kinship, class, and nationality that have historically functioned to delimit accounts of migration as loss or rupture for sending communities.

Given the recent developments, the melancholic aspect of the journey north has surfaced with a new urgency, putting the tale of the enterprising migrant "seeking a better life" in crisis. Stories of disappearance and lonely deaths put the flesh back on the bare-bones figure of the "guest worker" at a moment when the Mexican state confers neither a living nor rights to poor citizens and when U.S. officials and civilians alike routinely detain, abuse, and exploit migrants with little regard for international human rights conventions. The two nations collude in producing a class of stateless subjects whose personhood is discursively consigned to mere economic being as disposable labor, or legally reduced to the mere status of criminal trespassers.

In what follows, I examine the discourses that produce what I am calling "migrant melancholia" in order to consider the effects of the decade of Operation Gatekeeper, free trade, and neoliberalism for Mexican migrants and what these changes may signify for current understandings of human mobility and transnational community. Alongside established accounts of transnational labor and remittances, other narratives of loss and wounding have always coexisted in tension with the legitimating discourses of international cooperation, development, and economic opportunity that depict the sojourn in the United States as a matter of elective choice.[2] These narratives can be found across a number of media, including television documentaries on migration, *telenovelas* on Telemundo, Internet photos of missing migrants, and cultural productions by border artists. The narration of migrant sorrows constitutes a political act, cast against the prerogatives of neoliberal development and the global division of labor—in particular, the erosion of substantive citizenship and communal belonging but also the collusion with resurgent forms of racial governance in both countries.

I am especially interested in how women's border literature and testimonials provide a counternarrative to official depictions of migration as temporary economic necessity, just as they disrupt conventional narratives of male migration. In contrast to historic masculinist claims to cross-border unity between Mexico and *México de afuera*, women's testimonies reveal a distinct female imaginary operating in the border space, one that moves with ambivalence and caution through competing claims of family, class, and nation in the transnational arena. Women and children are increasingly protagonists of the border crossing, rather than simply dependents left behind by male breadwinners. Their accounts reveal how social relations structuring kinship and community are not simply reconstructed over transnational space but may also provide insufficient refuge from the perils of the cross-border passage.

Lost Citizens

In the days following the destruction of the World Trade Center, members of El Asociación Tepeyac de New York, an advocacy center for Latino immigrants, found themselves inundated with calls from households across Latin America, asking for news of missing relatives believed to be working in the United States. Eventually, El Asociación Tepeyac identified 113 cases of missing people and 857 displaced workers connected to the 9/11 disaster.[3] The organization has been instrumental in documenting these cases and helping survivors obtain relief funds. Just as impressive, however, are the hundreds of petitions for assistance in locating missing family members that may have no direct relationship to the events in New York and that remain unresolved. Esperanza Chacón, Director of Urgent Affairs for Tepeyac, argues that the enforced invisibility of undocumented workers in the United States makes it impossible to clarify the status of these reports of missing persons.[4] Despite the ready availability of cellular phones and electronic communications media for sustaining communal and familial ties among migrants, it was all too clear in 2001 that migration can still threaten sending households with dissolution and loss.

The events of 9/11 foreclosed on the plans of Presidents Bush and Fox for a binational agreement that would facilitate guest worker programs and provide amnesty to thousands of undocumented Mexicans residing in the United States. For Mexico, the losses at the World Trade Center provoked renewed debate about the implications of mass migrations and economic dependency for the exercise of state sovereignty and the coherence of its national community. In 2003, public pressure forced Gerónimo Gutiérrez Fernández, then Subsecretary for North America to the Office of Foreign Relations (SRE), to admit openly that his office received an annual average of five thousand requests for assistance in locating persons presumed missing in the course of emigration to the United States.[5] Mexican officials consider the actual number to be far higher, since the SRE figure only reflects the fraction of incidents where the state becomes involved. Gutiérrez Fernández reported that his office resolves 20 percent of the cases, but he did not elaborate on the specific outcomes of these investigations. The SRE has since outlined a proposal for creating an electronic database for biogenetic data that would assist the state in tracking and identifying the missing, a proposal made urgent by the rising costs of repatriating the remains of Mexicans who die abroad.

Ghosts of Development

As the United States and Mexico pursued policies of accelerated economic integration in the late twentieth century that exacerbated the demand for Mexican labor in the United States, on the one hand, and decimated communal Mexican agriculture, on the other, the U.S.-Mexican border has lost its peripheral status within national processes for either country. The unstoppable movement of people to the border cities and across the international boundary that began before World War I has exerted considerable pressure on the structures of governance, commerce, income generation, and justice for both nations as they have responded to rising levels of undocumented migration since the 1990s (and had to cope with the new exigencies of national security linked to the U.S. war on drugs and the war on terror). Mexican policies for stimulating economic growth and development have effectively redrawn the compact between the state and its poor, its working class, and its rural citizens. The neoliberal programs that culminated in the 1994 North American Free Trade Agreement were heralded by some as "Mexico's second revolution," not so much for their promise of social advancement as for their stark contrast to the revolution of 1910.[6] While nation-building reforms of the "institutionalized" revolution promoted economic restructuring in the name of redistributive reforms, the market-led restructuring of the Mexican economy following the 1980s subordinated social reform to economic growth at enormous cost to the urban and rural poor.

Although Mexican officials and financiers may argue that the first decade of NAFTA brought Mexico new foreign investment and jobs with the unexpected dividend of the democratic transition from PRI dominance, the actual economic and political benefits accruing from neoliberal reforms have largely bypassed the poorer sectors of society. The rapid restructuring of Mexican agriculture has only exacerbated the historical process of outmigration from the countryside and small towns. In this period, changes to the Mexican state have failed to extend democratic inclusion to marginalized populations, just as they have weakened those institutions that provide the substance of citizenship: access to goods and services, justice, security, and political representation. The forms of exchange and consumption that have underwritten neoliberal development depend on the social relations institutionalized in the border region: in particular, an economic caste system that demands workers well versed in both service and low-skilled labor, whose weak social integration assures that they make relatively few demands on either state.

Increased rates of interdiction at the Mexico-U.S. border, along with unprecedented levels of undocumented migration from Mexico and farther south, have added to the perils of the border crossing and settlement in the United States in the last decade.[7] Migrants confront the travails of the desert and anti-immigrant hostilities along the frontier as a passage through a space of death, or what Luis Alberto Urrea calls "the devil's highway."[8] Migrant fatalities have risen 500 percent over the last decade due to stricter U.S. border policing and the expansion of organized crime in the border region.[9] Mexican consuls apportion ever-greater percentages of their budgets to the forensic identification and repatriation of bodies, both of migrants who perish in transit and of those who die in the United States; they also face increased demands for assistance from families searching for missing relatives, now numbering in the thousands.[10] The space of death is not confined to the border, however, but incorporates the limited spheres of agency afforded undocumented people in the United States: Migrants occupy the legal minefield between labor and human rights protections, on the one hand, and U.S. immigration policy, on the other.

As a result, established patterns of seasonal migration for work have given way to higher rates of permanent settlement following the inception of Operation Gatekeeper in 1994.[11] Greater numbers of women and children are migrating from Mexico to the United States, both to obtain work and to unify families, despite conditions of increased risk.[12] Contracting with "coyotes," once simply optional, has become vital for successful crossings; traffickers are likely responsible for many of the recent disappearances of migrants now that the movement of people has become so lucrative for criminal entities in the region.[13]

The border crossing has always threatened migrants with disappearance or death, and certainly with dislocation from kin and community. The 2001 catastrophe in New York brought the fragility of transnational ties into focus once more during the same period that migrant remittances reached their peak share of Mexican GDP.[14] Mexican settlements in New York followed patterns established by earlier labor migrations; new arrivals to Manhattan and Long Island in the 1990s were just as successful in forming mutual aid societies and exerting economic and political force in their Puebla hometowns as their conationals in Los Angeles or Houston.[15] Many perils of recent migration are in fact not *new*, but the diffusion of migrant circuits beyond the southwestern United States does reflect significant changes in traditional forms of transnational settlement, even from older sending regions. Emigration has shifted from being a rural phenomenon to encompassing industrialized towns and cities, and every Mexican state now confronts the vast scale of out-migration to the United States. These demographic shifts correspond to stalled economic and political reforms in Mexico as state failure continues to promote mass emigration. Jorge Durand and Douglas Massey comment that in Mexico, "migrant networks are much stronger in rural than in urban areas because rural social networks are stronger and more dense."[16] If so, it remains to be seen whether newer migrants can mobilize the same forms of social capital as their predecessors.

Such transformations in Mexican political economy and state policy have profound implications for how displaced Mexicans, both internal and transnational migrants, may experience and express their nationality in the migratory circuit. Mexicans living abroad form hometown associations in order to provide resources for sending communities, a process the government seeks to co-opt through a program of matching funds for migrant remittances. Federal, state, and local authorities promise to match migrant donations on a three-to-one ratio, with the hopes of diverting private remittances to state expenditures. In Chicago, for example, a group of migrants from Indaparapeo, Michoacán, have pooled resources to establish a scholarship program for the town's youth, resisting the state government's suggestion that monies be set aside for new roads and drainage.[17] Grupo Indaparapeo chose to develop the town's human capital over state-run projects as a direct rebuke to officials for their failure to meet its most basic obligations to the townspeople. While the private contributions for the scholarship are always on time, Grupo Indaparapeo reports that matching funds are always in short supply. Members of the hometown association may be exercising the forms of *postnational* agency described in current studies of migration, but they do so in a concerted effort to recover and reconstitute *national* citizenship.[18] The Michoacán migrants designed the scholarship program so that townspeople will not have to leave home to seek their livelihood. After a century of out-migration, their initiative represents a purchase against loss and estrangement in the next generation.

Mourning and Migration

U.S. immigration policies and border policing have effectively cancelled the option for circular migration, making Mexicans much more likely to pursue permanent settlement in the United States. The coercive aspect of these developments warrants further inquiry. In fact, studies overwhelmingly show that most migrants do not wish to stay: "Left to their own devices, the vast majority would return to participate in Mexico's growth as an economy and a society."[19] The prevailing metric of immigration studies, centered as it is on the economic and social productivity of the migrant, cannot measure the melancholic aspect of the shift from circular migrations to a "national population of settled dependents scattered throughout the country" (12). A focus on the relative economic integration between migrants and sender communities, measured in remittances, may obscure the social upheaval and deformations of kinship that extended migrations impose on sender households. The unacknowledged costs of Mexican mobility find expression in the rumors of human traffic and bondage that circulate within migrant communities. The spectacular horror of these stories may correspond to actual incidents, but in their elaboration, rumors also project the phantasmagoric aspect of migrant imaginaries.[20] Lists of missing persons obtain symbolic significance as an inchoate form of contestation to the way government policies continue to displace the burden of maintaining transnational labor circuits from the state onto private individuals and households.

In his 1917 essay "Mourning and Melancholia," Sigmund Freud addressed the ways individuals contend with the death or absence of a beloved person, object, or idea. He noted that distress leads the mourner to deny the loss but that the healthy person will eventually relinquish the attachment and recover a capacity for everyday life. The melancholic person, he argued, refuses to "relinquish the lost object" and cannot therefore overcome the psychic burden of loss. For Freud, melancholia arises from a pathological or thwarted process of mourning, in which the absent object becomes constitutive of the melancholic self. Recent scholarship has applied Freudian models of mourning and melancholia to forms of subjection or abjection enacted in the political sphere.[21] Here I want to consider how the border crossing implies a psychic wounding for migrants and invests their nostalgic desires for return with political significance.

If current conditions make the option of circular migration unavailable to many migrants, then the notion of "home" may take on the qualities of the beloved object whose loss threatens the integrity of the border crosser's personhood. In the same way, the migrant's departure may constitute a catastrophic separation for the sending family and community. In a recent television documentary about a family in rural Michoacán that sent three sons to Kentucky for work, the mother of the young men describes a sense of desperation at her economic dependence on her children's remittances: "Yo sé que me va a ayudar, pero para mí cada partida es una muerte" (I know that it will help me, but for me every departure is a death).[22] Marcelo, the last son to leave, describes his trip to the United States through the Sonoran Desert as an indelible trauma:

> Yo no sabía si podía aguantar. Pasé tres días sin alimentos, tomando sólo tragitos de agua. El sol era tan caliente. Tenía tanta sed. Mi mamá estaba llorando. Eso me afectó mucho. Créo que me afectó psicológicamente.
>
> [I was not sure if I would make it. I went three days without food, taking only small sips of water. The sun was so hot. I was so thirsty. My mother was crying. This affected me. I think it affected me psychologically.][23]

This exchange, captured in an episode of *Assignment Discovery*, offers a rare pedagogy for U.S. viewers on migrant subjectivity. Marcelo's reflection on his border passage captures exactly the process of melancholic incorporation that Freud describes: As he recalls the hardships of his desert passage, the son makes no distinction between his mother's grieving and his own. Although his mother remained behind, the son narrates his experience as if his mother traveled alongside him in the desert—as a source not of comfort or protection but of the profound guilt and distress that Freud ascribed to the melancholic person.

By extension, we may consider how undocumented status itself might constitute a melancholic condition for migrants in the United States. In 2004, I participated in a local effort to uncover a confidence scheme to defraud undocumented migrants of thousands of dollars through the sale of false papers. That summer, a friend who migrated to New Haven from Veracruz, Rita (a pseudonym), told me that a woman she worked for had offered to assist her in obtaining legal status for herself and her family. While cleaning the home, Rita had observed her employer operating a business in immigration documents out of her home. This woman, a Latina resident of Hamden, Connecticut, said she was a New York immigration official, offering to process paperwork "under the table" and expedite clients' legalization. Dozens of Latin Americans came from New York, Connecticut, and New Jersey to pay fees of as much as $25,000 for the "green cards" that they thought would permit them to work legally, sponsor family members, and move freely between the United States and their home countries.[24]

Rita paid her employer approximately $2,500 to process paperwork for her husband, herself, and her four-year-old son, who had all entered the United States without authorization a few years earlier. She grew alarmed when I communicated my doubts about the veracity of the woman's promises and my concerns that Rita and her family could get into trouble because of the scam. At the time, Rita was a client of Junta for Progressive Action, an advocacy center that serves the predominantly Latino neighborhood of Fair Haven. Having seen the numbers of migrants falling for her employer's false promises, Rita made the courageous decision to report the criminal operation to the police. Junta's director, the attorney Kica Matos, and I mediated between the migrants and the police so as to secure promises that the police would not pursue the immigration cases of the people caught up in the scam. In January 2006, the alleged perpetrator of the crime, María Agosto, a fifty-five-year-old resident of New York, was arraigned in the Superior Court of Connecticut on charges of first-degree larceny and criminal impersonation. Rita was the chief witness in the proceeding.

As I translated for Rita and other victims during their exchanges with Hamden police, I came to understand how easy it was for the imposter to persuade her clients that she could help them circumvent the most elaborate and impenetrable apparatus of U.S. law enforcement, that of immigration. The people she stole from were hardly naive—they had experienced theft at the hands of coyotes, employers, immigration lawyers, and other migrants—but they were unwilling to relinquish the fantasy of reunion with the lost objects that haunted their residence in the United States—family and citizenship. As a Puerto Rican migrant herself, Agosto must have had intimate knowledge of her clients' melancholic disposition and just how far it would lead her clients into her trap. Even after she was exposed, having abandoned her Hamden residence without delivering the papers, many of her clients remained unwilling to accept the reality of their situation. Rita continued to confide to me after her testimony that she was certain that the police proceeding was a mistake and that perhaps Señora Agosto would return with her documents if she withheld her charges.

Proponents of anti-immigration measures commonly represent the undocumented as people with no respect for the rule of law. This assumption reflects a total misunderstanding of what "law" means for the unauthorized migrant. One could say that the undocumented come from countries where bribes are routinely paid to expedite state services; however, this explanation is, in my opinion, an inadequate answer to the question of how so many migrants came to pay unimaginable sums for the dream of legalization. It is precisely because of their investment in legality, both in practical and moral terms, that the victims of the Hamden scam could invest so heavily in false papers. The migrants did not deliberately seek to circumvent state authority when they paid the imposter to act on their behalf; rather, they sought incorporation into the state through the only means available. Beyond their desire for the goods of citizenship, freedom of movement, better wages, working conditions, and health care, the migrants were gullible because of their profound desire to be recognized as legitimate subjects, to inhabit the status of citizen. Even in simple economic terms, the theft of migrant earnings represents a terrible crime: Consider for a moment how many people were willing to work an inordinate number of hours under difficult conditions to amass $25,000 in the vain hope of bringing children north from Ecuador or Guatemala and making them into U.S. nationals.

The horror of the Hamden incident, then, comes from the reminder that it is so easy to exploit migrant desire. For many, the costs of entering the United States for work preclude the seasonal visits to Mexico that might placate the sense of loss and isolation. In New Haven, far from the ethnic centers of the Southwest, nationality is easily reduced to a consular card and the vague promises of protection it confers. For Mexicans here, U.S. citizenship or legal residence represents the single best option for securing a livelihood and retaining viable connections to family and hometown over time. And yet, the vast majority of the undocumented are unlikely to obtain such a prize.

The material and psychic hungers that propel migrants to abandon, in their quest for wages, the most basic elements of sociality—residence, kinship, language, culture, and landscape: in short, home—exert a violence that immigration scholarship and political discourse have yet to fully address. The condition of being "undocumented" does not simply imply a lack of legal protection or status but rather entails the active conversion of the migrant into a distinct category of stateless personhood. This peculiar status emerges with the contradiction between market demands for mobile labor and consumable goods and the immobility of rights beyond the bounds of the nation-state. Mexican migrants, like other displaced peoples, continually invent forms of agency within that space of opposition. It is a melancholy task. Stories of border mortality and disappearance are a means to narrate the other kinds of death that Marcelo's mother describes, the leave-taking that extinguishes one form of connection to make way for another. In this ritual of departure, the family enacts, in intimate form, the migrant's detachment from the state, a severing of citizenship that is also a death, a death that produces.

Disappearing Migrants

Current anxieties about border hazards also appear in popular media, in texts that narrate significant shifts in how migration is managed both at the level of lived experience and at the level of consumer culture. In December 2003, Telemundo aired the Mexican *telenovela El Alma Herida (The Wounded Soul)*, a serial melodrama devoted to a migrant family shattered at the border crossing.[25] The show earned strong ratings and became known as "una de las novelas más queridas por el público hispano."[26] The storyline followed familiar motifs for reinforcing national identity by depicting the dangers of pursuing material aspirations in the United States:

Una familia llena de esperanzas toma la difícil decision de cruzar la frontera en busca del sueño Americano, déjandolo todo atrás sin sospechar
que el destino les jugará una mala pasada separándolos trágicamente.

[Full of hope, a family makes the difficult decision to cross the border
in search of the American Dream. They leave everything behind, not
knowing that destiny is about to play them a bad hand, separating them
tragically from one another.][27]

The family does not make it across the border intact: The father and two
children meet up with abusive police, while the *pollero* forces Catalina, the
mother, across to the United States. The sixty-five episodes follow the daughter
and mother's efforts at family reunification, allegorizing the broader process of
Mexican migration since 1965. The border imposes total familial separation and
threatens its annihilation: The plot turns on the family's question of whether
the mother has died or abandoned them. The story ultimately ends in a blood-
bath, with the daughter electing between two male partners in two countries, a
choice which implies that her honor can be safeguarded only in Mexico. However contrived, *El Alma Herida* nevertheless departs from standard nationalist
discourse by anchoring its story in a female, rather than a male, migrant. The
status of the family depends on the recovery of the missing mother, not its
wage-earning father, while her recuperation comes through the agency of the
enterprising daughter Eugenia, who first crosses the border at age eleven. *El
Alma Herida* thus fulfills the function of melodrama to nourish a female spec-
tatorship; it does so through a migrant imaginary now thoroughly feminized.

For Mexicans living a precarious permanence in the United States, the
border operates as a critical juncture for imagining community and exerting
claims on either nation. In this context, the crossing *itself*—in its various legal,
economic, cultural, and social aspects—shapes the political disposition of the
larger transnational community of unauthorized migrants and noncitizens in
the United States and their hometowns in Mexico. Here I refer not only to the
political apparatus of the border, as it regulates the mobility of peoples or their
access to rights and citizenship, but also to the broader binational space that
contains the institutions devoted to national security, immigration, and trade
at the boundary checkpoints. The transborder corridor is not only the largest
urbanized region in Mexico; it is also one of the fastest-growing settlement
sites in the Western Hemisphere.[28] The complex communal ecologies of this
space do not simply give the border an internal sense of distinction and shared
identity; they also influence the form broader transnational linkages and communities may take. So, too, border cities socialize migrants in their passage
from citizenship to noncitizenship, authorized status to unauthorized status.

As greater numbers of people find themselves stranded in the border space because of failed crossings or deportation, or the availability of jobs in service work and export manufacturing created by neoliberal development, the normative force of this movement to the transnational corridor increases.[29]

This passage may exact different political costs for the federal government from those facing sender communities: Despite new legislation permitting migrants to cast absentee ballots in the upcoming presidential elections, the expatriate vote is likely to disappoint.[30] The stagnation of democratic reform in Mexico means that migrants may opt to retain hometown connections while resisting their interpellation as national subjects. According to Rodolfo Rubio, a researcher at El Colegio de la Frontera Norte, fewer than 10 percent are likely to register out of an estimated 4 million eligible voters, making it less possible for the migrant vote to sway the presidential election.[31] The cost of absentee voter registration effectively functions as a poll tax, repeating a long-standing process whereby the state discourages poor voters. Daniel Solis, director of the Alliance for Community Development in El Paso, argues that eligible voters, even those residing in the border, are "losing hope of better prospects at home and putting stock in their future as new immigrants."[32] The intense nationalism of migrants, in this context, may not extend to a sense of political obligation to the nation-state.

The new hazards and congestion of the border crossing may thus ultimately alter the social networks observed in studies of migrant communities.[33] The proliferating reports of migrant disappearances reflect the uncertainties of this period for sending communities in Mexico. It is impossible to examine the ephemeral Web sites devoted to the missing without considering the weight of the disappearances on the fragile linkages of kin and conationals in transnational space. Family photographs, passport pictures, and identification cards posted to sites operated by the Mexican consulate adopt both the form of official immigration documents and more personal narrative to describe the disappeared. "Odilon Vera Mendez, 32," listed by height, weight, hair and eye color, complexion, and facial features, appears online in a photograph depicting the young man at a track meet. The race tag on his chest, "L959," stands in for the official imprint of the state identification number, the mug shot, passport, or perhaps the Bracero registration number of past migrations. The photo caption reads: "Lugar de Origen: Huauchinango, Puebla. Últimos datos conocidos: Salió de Tetela de Ocampo, Puebla el pasado 13 de noviembre de 2001, con destino a Estados Unidos para trabajar, pero hasta la fecha su familia no tiene noticias de él."[34] Between the precision of Tetela de Ocampo, Puebla (population 25,859, 304.89 square kilometers in area, and 3,000 meters above sea level), and the uncharted route to work in the United States, the vast terrain of transnational space presents its threat to identity, to kinship, to territoriality itself.

The interrupted biographies of the disappeared represent a rupture in time and space for sending families and towns. For the bereft, not knowing whether the missing are alive or dead disrupts the narrative of transnational community, both in its symbolic unity and in the material sense of economic survival and the futurity of family lines. One image in particular, from the Consul General Web site, invites analysis: Azucena Quezada Olea, of Morelos, last seen in 2002.[35] The young woman in the photograph stands in a parking lot that could be anywhere in the north/south circuit of migrant travels. Her shirt bears the tourist logo for Kentucky, perhaps a sign of her connection to this new outpost of Mexican labor, or perhaps a souvenir of her tourist travel. The nondescript background is nonetheless an occasion for a portrait, for memorialization of the moment, of her being there. Azucena Quezada Olea smiles as she gazes out at the camera, one hand shyly at her face, another hand holding a young child. She occupies the whole of the image: The child next to her is only partly in the picture. The child looks so much like Azucena that the image can only imply their relatedness, yet the border of the photograph splits the child in half. What Roland Barthes would call the *punctum* of the image lies in this bisection of the child's figure.[36]

The photograph of the missing woman captures what seems ineffable in narratives of border crossing: the sense that the migrant occupies a place and no place at once. Disappearance does not only imply the loss of the woman herself, but the destruction her death or departure means for the child. Familial dislocation, occurring across national boundaries, puts children's identities and protection in crisis. Children lose their minimal political status once separated from their parents in the migrant circuit. In a larger sense, the photograph illuminates the profoundly unsettling ways in which transnational migration remakes kinship and reveals how kinship cannot mitigate against loss. In this instance, the vanishing of Azucena makes a ghost of her child.

The formal institutions that enshrine Mexican citizenship seem equally strained by the uncertainties of the border passage: the Office of Foreign Relations (SRE), which oversees Mexican consulates, vacillates between a discourse that interpellates migrants as full nationals and something approaching an official language of mourning. "Tu calidad de indocumentado no te convierte en delincuente," reads a Web site for the Consul General of New York, which goes on to explain the human rights protections that cover migrants in the United States.[37] Within this assertion is a latent recognition of the threat of loss—of personal sovereignty for the migrant, of national sovereignty for the Mexican state—inherent in the unauthorized border crossing. The transit from citizenship to unauthorized status in the United States is, in fact, a process of conversion, effected *through* violence—the sanctioned interdiction of the state, which may seize and remove migrants by its use of force or by the extralegal, informal aggressions of nonstate actors like the Arizona Minutemen.

The Instituto Nacional de Migración (INM/National Institute of Migration) generated controversy in recent years by issuing pamphlets to potential migrants that delineate the hazards of the border crossing. The guides contain emergency telephone numbers, the details of consular services and immigration documents, and information about migrants' protections under international law. With their graphic depictions of migrant deaths, the books become an inventory of *passing* as well as passage in pages devoted to the many ways the border can kill. In a section devoted to the Sonoran Desert, the *Guía del Migrante Yucateco* lists the symptoms of dehydration, only to conclude: "Si tienes estos síntomas, estás en peligro de morir lentamente."[38] The irony is, of course, that the Mexican government cannot do more than forecast this death. Mexican sovereignty does not extend to providing gainful employment to nationals at home, nor does it provide safe passage for those leaving the country.

This point came home to me in an interview with officers from the Grupos Beta de Protección a Migrantes (Beta Group for the Protection of Migrants), the Mexican border patrol in Ciudad Juárez, in 2003. C. Roberto Gaytan Saucedo, the interim director for the INM in Juárez, reported that the scale of migration makes the task of policing the desert region impossible. Officially a humanitarian operation of the INM, Grupos Beta claimed just seven officers for the vast Juárez metropolitan region in 2003. Like generations of border officers before him, Gaytan Saucedo admitted that every seizure of a migrant merely delays the eventual crossing.[39] Grupos Beta has resorted to posting signs in the desert about the perils of migration, advising women to purchase pepper spray as a defense against male aggressors. The empty gesture makes it clear that women alone are responsible for their personal safety. The state functions of security do not extend into this denationalized border zone, nor do they cover the bodies of women moving through this space. Mexican sovereignty and state power are so compromised in the border region that the Grupos Beta does not dare to venture into the path of armed criminal groups operating in the desert; the absurdity of pepper spray here makes a cruel joke of the state's disinterest in women's suffering. In March 2005, Claudia Smith, president of the Coalition in Defense of the Migrant, presented the statistic that one in ten women report being raped in the attempt to cross the border.[40]

In this context, the INM warning "Hay caminos sin regreso" doubles as an admonition and an admission of state complicity in migrant suffering.[41] Neoliberal governance has only exacerbated the government's role as a broker for cheap labor. The failure of market-led development has forced individual states to compete with one another for migrant remittances. Various states now issue their own localized migrant guidebooks, which combine the national discourse on the border crossing with promotions of regional identity and loyalty. The *Guía del Migrante Yucateco* offers information on Yucatecan clubs and mutual aid societies in California, stressing the interest of the state government in helping migrants organize abroad. "Yendo o viniendo Yucateco sigue siendo," it reads, displaying an official regard for how local Mayan ethnicity offers a vital resource for group survival in the United States.[42] Of course, those Yucatecos who perish or vanish do not remain Yucateco. On average, five migrants from southern Mexican states die every month trying to reach the northern border, and many more disappear. The state's invocation of human rights or cultural unity as a supplement to citizenship collapses under the pressure to obtain migrant remittances at any cost. The final assertion, "Cuida tu vida," underlines how life, in this instance, gets reduced to a vehicle for income generation.[43] In their ambivalent discourse of nationalism and mourning, migrant guides articulate contradictions in Mexican development: The links between nation building and migration mark the state's intimacy with death.

Women's Border Imaginaries

On May 10, 1948, "Concepción Zapata" presented her retablo to the Santísima Virgen de San Juan de los Lagos as a testament to the saint's protection during her sojourn in the United States.[44] The retablo, or votive painting, is a popular form of devotion that renders compensation for the miraculous intercession of the patron saint. The votive practice records a private act of supplication and gives witness to the person's deliverance from illness or danger. For Mexican migrants, the retablo combines a holy image with a visual rendition of perils faced in the border crossing, forming a closed narrative of departure and return once the painting is deposited in its shrine. As the patroness of Los Altos de Jalisco, La Virgen de San Juan de los Lagos has heard many stories of emigration and has made many border crossings of her own.[45] Alongside accounts of averted deaths and wondrous cures, this guardian of migrants knows the particular gender terror of the passage northward.

In her account of divine protection, Concepción Zapata relates:

> Dedico el presente RETABLO a la Sma. V. de San Juan de los Lagos por aberme salbado de un TEXANO que me llebara, me escodi [*sic*] debajo de un arbol con mi hermanito ala orilla de la carretera.
>
> [I dedicate the present retablo to the Holiest Virgen of San Juan de los Lagos for having saved me from a Texan who tried to carry me off. I hid under a tree by the side of the road with my little brother.][46]

Unlike conventional votive paintings, this retablo does not depict the traumatic encounter itself, but Concepción's act of devotion after the fact. The image places the kneeling figure of Concepción just beyond a drawn curtain, as if the viewer is looking in on a confessional. Staged this way, this public disclosure of the young woman's experience reinscribes the private, unspeakable nature of sexual aggression. The anonymous artist painted the nationality of the aggressor in capital letters, "TEXANO," as if to locate the threat of gender violence *en el otro lado*, on the other side. The story describes the peril of a young woman traveling alone, her younger brother too small to act as her guardian or chaperone. Concepción's narrative leaves open the question of what might have happened: She describes the male threat in the verb *llevar* (carry off) ("un TEXANO me llebara"), a taking that is both rape and capture. The verb shows how the sexual violation is discursively linked to disappearance, a taking from which there is no return. The story ascribes the agency behind the young woman's evasion of harm to the saint rather than to her own resourcefulness. Concepción's escape under the tree anticipates her enclosure back at home. The narrative figures the border as the open road, "la carretera," in opposition to the protective closeness of the interior space rendered in the painting.

In its reticence toward depicting Concepción as a fully autonomous agent in her border crossing, the retablo presciently anticipates current concerns about Mexican women's mobility through transnational space. Women's perceived sexual availability and vulnerability incite social anxieties about the nation's exposure at the northern frontier. The question of women's autonomy of movement takes on greater urgency at the international boundary, where disappearance can also be a matter of a change in political status altogether. The story of Concepción Zapata's miraculous deliverance speaks to us from midcentury San Luis Potosí as a testament to the ways sex has historically been constructed as a woman's price for a successful border crossing.[47]

Zapata traveled north to Texas at the height of the Bracero Program, a period of mass emigration in which women's mobility remained invisible in public discourse, rendering women migrants doubly undocumented. Some fifty years later, we might inquire into the strategies of rendering visible these journeys— artistic strategies for elucidating the complex relationships linking women's bodies, processes of deterritorialization, and the fabric of social bonds.

I'm Just Passing Through Here

By way of conclusion, I want to draw out the possibilities for locating alternate imaginaries of the border space in recent literary productions by women emerging from the transnational migrant circuit. For this, I turn to Los Angeles author Marisela Norte, whose spoken-word composition "Act of the Faithless" narrates the relationship between a young Chicana girl and her uncle's girl-friend, a Juárez woman who crosses the border for daily work in a luxury hotel in El Paso.[48]

> The story would have to begin with her.
> She worked as a maid
> in the El Paso Holiday Inn.
> El Paso
> Mal paso que te das
> al cruzar la frontera
> I mean
> I'm just passing through here.

Chicana poet and performer Marisela Norte is an "Eastside Girl," a voice for urban Los Angeles. Born in 1955 to Mexican parents who immigrated to Southern California in the 1930s and 1940s, Norte grew up in a community with strong kinship and cultural ties to Ciudad Juárez.[49] "Act of the Faithless" first appeared in recorded form in 1991, on the poet's album *Norte/Word*. Rather than publish her compositions in book form, Norte chose to circulate her work in a format that would make it available to a broader audience and would also retain the tex-ture of her voice. Norte's work exploits shifts in narrative time and perspective in order to convey the multiplicity of female subjectivity in the border space; her poem appropriates a working-class, migrant vernacular to delineate the complex alteration of female agency and perspective taking place in the border crossing.

In Norte's poem, the urban environs of Ciudad Juárez and El Paso appear as sites of economic and personal transactions that convert Mexican women into commodified beings. Norte's story of a young Chicana girl's relationship to her uncle's girlfriend, whom she calls her "aunt," embeds the relationship in a longer narrative on family, danger, and desire at the U.S.-Mexican border. But Norte tells us that if she were to tell her story straight, it would begin with the aunt cleaning rooms in the luxury hotel, "twenty stories high" above the squalor of the urban frontier. Their crossing into El Paso, narrated as a momentary depar-ture from the confines of class, is described as "a bad step" or a "wrong move." For the protagonist, the border crossing doubles as a change in cultural identity and a passage from girlhood to maturity. The story links the formation of the girl's critical consciousness to her separation from the maternal figure of her aunt.

Border crossing is doubly hazardous, both because *mexicanas* are pressed into the service of a foreign and punishing racial system in the United States and also, for the young narrator, because it signifies loss:

El paso con la frontera
Por vida
con safos
mas vale
as it is written
up and down that border
that runs up and down our backs
like a bad tattoo

The severing of national ties symbolized in the border forces an understanding of migrant identity as a violation, "the bad tattoo" marking emigrants to the United States in difference. The racial inscription of the migrant's body is analogous to the division of social space by the national boundary. "Por vida / con safos," the tags of graffiti that adorn the crossing, are ironic articulations of presence and ownership written into the interstices of nation and property that exclude migrant subjects. "The acceptance of difference," writes Ramón Saldívar, "does not diminish the pain of separation that difference implies," a loss that resides at the heart of identity.[50] Norte's poem turns on jagged inflections of loss within the gestures of intimacy between family and workers, on the particular forms of nonidentity produced in the border crossing.

"She was an aunt / I would know too briefly," Norte warns us from the beginning. Norte's poem enacts the dialectic of identification and disidentification that Saldívar prescribes, as she continually delivers an affirmative statement, "she cleaned up / decorated their home" only to more effectively communicate its negation, "with objects of rejection." As Norte's narrator visits the Holiday Inn with her aunt, her trip features an ascent "in the hotel elevator / from the basement / to the honeymoon suite," a crossing of class boundaries that far exceeds the physical distance of her journey from home. The young girl quickly perceives that this visit has significance beyond her entertainment, as her aunt shows her the workings of leisure and bourgeois values:

A slow curtain is pulled
by the delicate hand
holding the heavy gold cord.
Slowly and deliberately
she will expose,
letting out a little sigh.
She cannot believe it herself.
This is what it could all look like,
this view from twenty stories high.

Like a magician, the aunt ceremoniously presents her niece with a glimpse of a world of privilege wholly distinct from life as it is lived on the ground floor. The view signifies not only the romantic temporal disengagement from worldly cares promised by the tourist industry, however; here it is described in spatial terms as the deliberate construction of an insular social landscape. As the "delicate hand" that services this fantasy, the maid experiences the crossing of class boundaries as a kind of cognitive dissonance—even as she reveals it to her niece, "she cannot believe it herself."

The view alternately figures a space of possibility beyond the social restrictions of the border and reinscribes the aunt and niece's outsider status within this cosmopolitan realm. The statement "This is what it could all look like" reminds us that the landscape can only reflect the gazers' own social position. Looking out, the narrator situates herself in relation to the luxury that encloses her by reading the storefronts:

> There was a dance hall
> called El Peor es Nada,
> Better than Nothing,
> and then there was
> that narrow stretch of nothing,
> the remains of a dried-out sewer.
> She told me it was El Río,
> El Grande grande.
> Surely these were the things
> bad dreams were made of.

The place-names signify the absolute negation of the social mobility manifested in the gilded ornaments of the luxury suite. Even the river, made heroic in border legend, betrays its name by serving as the washed-out basin for pollution and waste generated in the tourist trade and the maquiladora industry. The repetition of "nothing" inscribes the landscape with a fatalism sharply divergent from Chicana feminist constructions of the border as a crossroads.[51] This nothingness exerts a material force on its subjects, expressed as the substance of nightmares. Norte's border insistently spatializes the racial and gender formations that make up the neocolonial tourist economy.

At first, the narrator wishes to experience her ascent to the luxury suite as an escape, to close her eyes:

> I only wanted to lay down
> and shut my eyes
> to the annoying Texas sun

in the sky
and make these feet
leave the ground
for one moment
and imagine the afterlife,
eternity at twenty stories high

Abandonment of her place under the "annoying Texas sun" connotes not only relief but also a kind of death. The ability to evacuate her subject position for that of the tourist is figured as immobility and stasis, not mobility or freedom of choice. The girl's lesson continues in a trip to the rooftop swimming pool. "If there's no one up there," the maid tells her, "you can take your shoes off / and put your feet in the water." This episode speaks to the innumerable hidden acts by which migrant women contest the dehumanizing control of their labor in forms of resistance that feminize class struggle. The act of putting her feet in the pool alleviates tiredness from long hours spent standing; it also signifies a transgression of the boundaries between the domestic worker and the customer. For the niece, getting her feet wet is an experience of what it means to be a tourist.

The inscription of race within a class hierarchy serves as the occasion for a struggle over the meanings of the girl's transnational identity:

You are not from here,
nor are you from over there,
you understand m'hija?
Entiendes?

The aunt understands her niece's identity as a condition of homelessness, of estrangement from both Mexican and U.S. national unities. She ascribes a particular cognitive advantage to the girl's ambivalent national status, but also an utter lack of a coherent identity. The narrator counters with a recitation that reclaims the border as the "sitio y lengua" which both authorize and give form to her utterance.[52]

Los dos idiomas?
Claro que sí.
Que no soy de aquí
Que no soy de allá
But I can speak
the language, I insisted,
both of them.
Entiendes?

One important detail of this exchange is the way the aunt distinguishes between her own border identity and her niece's. The niece belongs to both worlds on either side of the border; "she speaks both languages," though her aunt does not. The maid merely travels to render her services at the hotel. The whole of the girl's adventure in the pool is staged as a foreshadowing of her future travels beyond the confines of her border existence. This transient destiny is shaded with both pleasure and danger: "mal paso que das / al cruzar la frontera," she warns, "I mean, I'm just passing through here."

Norte's narrator takes pleasure in transgressing the boundaries of privilege. But as she imagines her immersion in the luxury pool, she is pulled back to the present by the sight of her aunt performing her duties as a maid, wiping down the patio furniture: "I watched her body move inside the uniform / ... / the sound of her nylon stockings." Immediately she senses her separation from her aunt's status as a worker and wishes to repudiate her fantasy. Her aunt, observing the girl in her dark glasses, laughs at her pantomime of the role of U.S. tourist: "Ahora sí pareces turista americana." Her niece, threatened with the gulf of difference opening between them, hands the sunglasses back:

> She began to laugh, but I shook my head.
> I don't belong here and neither do you.
> I'm just passing through here, remember?
> I'm not from here and neither are you.

The niece recognizes that her play creates a separation between her aunt as a worker and her own mobility of identifications. She refuses to identify as a tourist, seeking instead to make her aunt share in her own position of "passing through." But the aunt knows better.

Rather than assume that kinship unites the girl and her aunt within a shared class position, Norte allows us to see precisely how the labor of the maid figures in the production of her niece's cognitive desire as a writer. In a moment of great poignancy, the maid reveals how the lesson she gives her niece plays a part of her own gendered class struggle:

> She gave me a pair of sunglasses to wear
> "Toma, cuidate los ojos
> take care of your eyes.
> There's so much you should see."

The sunglasses signify both the trappings of class privilege and a shield against the potential harm of exposure that the girl faces in her formation as a writer. The aunt prepares her niece to bear witness and also, in a moment of great generosity, to protect herself. Here the poem contrasts the relative social mobility of the Chicana niece and the Mexican maid.

The poem articulates the divides of class and citizenship instantiated in the border, revealing how the girl's transient status at the border ("passing through") is simultaneously a matter of wounding and of agency. In the final scene of the poem, the narrator relates the conclusion to her poolside fantasy. As the maid pushes her cart toward the door back to the elevator, the voice of a U.S. tourist calls her back:

Excuse me. Señorita, can you come here, por favor?
. . . .
He waves an empty glass at her.
The wife looks up at him smiling
The "He's all mine" smile.

The drama of the formation of the girl's critical consciousness thus takes place within an ongoing conflict over the terms of sale for migrant women's labor. Opposed to the maid and her niece are a white tourist and his wife, who play out their heterosexual travel adventure against the neocolonial backdrop of the luxury hotel.

This final scene instructs us in the way the struggle over signification shares space with the class struggle over production:

I tug at her arm.
I point at the man now silent.
"There is too much to see," she said.
"Too much to remember."

By leaving open the problematic of seeing and narrating, Norte "problematizes women's discursive practices" in the border space: "There is too much to see / too much to remember."[53] The girl's formation as a border subject separates the cognitive agency of "knowing" and "seeing" from the security of kinship and rootedness. Her "passing through" is a process both of personal transformation and of leave-taking, dislocating her from the resourceful aunt she "would know all too briefly."

"Act of the Faithless" narrates the border traffic in Mexican women in terms that banish any fantasy of the border's dissolution or permeability. Through her protagonist's fond recollection of the aunt she has lost, Norte gives voice to the "longing for unity and cohesion" that critic Rolando Romero ascribes to Chicana/Chicano narrative, even as her story of fractured kinship refutes any notion of an organic class or kinship unity among Mexicans, migrants, and Mexican Americans across the boundary.[54] In this piece, Norte details the intimate and often conflicted relationships among women in this clandestine labor economy, relationships complicated by the constant presence of sexual danger, transgressive erotic relations, and personal violence accompanying the binational sale of women's labor.

Norte's work exists alongside the consular lists of the disappeared that preserve accounts of the missing as parents, children, partners, friends—they are a form of desperate contestation to the binational state apparatus that converts the undocumented into people without status, without a place. Yet the disappeared are nonetheless *present*; their stories of loss remake the narratives of kinship, community, and belonging that sustain the transnational circuit.

In closing, I want to consider the significance of other vanishings. Ciudad Juárez is not only the place of arrival and departure for thousands in the migrant circuit; throughout this period of increased migration, the city has been a final terminus of utter brutality for the victims of *feminicidio*.[55] The northern boomtown, whose principal function is to support the mobility of capital, goods, and labor, has been the site of unprecedented killings of girls and women, residents of the Juárez colonias.[56] Many more young women are missing. For more than a decade, state and federal officials have permitted the murders to continue with impunity. The nation that sends thousands of its people into the migrant labor circuit has little to offer as protection for the female citizens whose vitality and labors sustain the fragile social ecology of the border space. Images of the missing girls travel the same networks as the pictures advertising the names of disappeared migrants. Currently, El Paso and Ciudad Juárez are the sites of ardent campaigns against both the *feminicidio* and the death of migrants in the border crossing. The success of these local mobilizations will depend on effective witness to migrants' stories of bereavement and absence. There is much to admire in the melancholic will to deny loss, to refuse to surrender the lost object, to refuse to go quietly. The political forms we devise in this moment of global transformation must partner the melancholic work against the violence that bring the circuits of human mobility into traffic with death, an immovable death, a departure with no return.

NOTES

This essay originally appeared in the *South Atlantic Quarterly* 105, no. 4 (2006): 831–61. The author thanks the editor of this volume, Jane Juffer, along with SAQ managing editor Christi Stanforth for their contributions to this essay. Special acknowledgments are also offered to the staff at Junta, to "Rita," and to Elizabeth Alexander, Jorge Durand, Jonathan Fox, Kellie Jones, Alondra Nelson, Stephen Pitti, Arthur Schmidt, and María Aurora Camacho de Schmidt.

1   I use the term *undocumented* to refer to migrants who either enter the United States without proper documents or overstay their visas. Jeffrey S. Passel offers a useful discussion of the term. See Jeffrey S. Passel, "Estimates of the Size and Characteristics of the Undocumented Population" (Washington, DC: Pew Hispanic Center Project Report, March 21, 2005), www.pewhispanic.org (accessed November 18, 2005).

2   See, for instance, the works of Jorge Durand and Patricia Arias, *Experiencia migrante: iconografía de la migración México-Estados Unidos* (Mexico DF: Altexto, 2000), and María Herrera Sobek, *Northward Bound: The Mexican Immigrant Experience in Ballad and Song* (Bloomington: University of Indiana Press, 1993).

3   Asociación Tepeyac, "Missing But Not Counted," November 2002, compiled in 9/11 digital archive, *911digitalarchive.org/collections/asntepeyac* (accessed November 15, 2002).

4   Asociación Tepeyac, "Missing But Not Counted."

5   See press communications of the Secretaría de Relaciones Exteriores—México, sre.gob.mx (accessed January 5, 2006).

6   See Manuel Pastor and Carol Wise, "State Policy, Distribution, and Neoliberal Reform in Mexico," *Journal of Latin American Studies* 29 (1997): 419–56.

7   Passel, "Estimates of the Size and Characteristics of the Undocumented Population."

8   Luis Alberto Urrea, *The Devil's Highway: A True Story* (New York: Little, Brown, 2004).

9   This figure comes from Amnesty International, "United States of America: Human Rights Concerns in the Border Region with Mexico," May 20, 1998. Further details are available in statistics compiled by the Mexican Foreign Relations Office for the past decade. The figure is corroborated by various nongovernmental agencies, including the California Rural Legal Assistance Foundation of El Centro, California (www.crla.org). At the time of this writing, the U.S. Border Patrol has acknowledged the December 30, 2005, shooting of Guillermo Martínez Rodríguez, an eighteen-year-old Mexican national, who met his death just north of the San Ysidro crossing point in San Diego County. President Vicente Fox is under political pressure in Mexico for his weak response to the incident. The killing occurred just days after the U.S. House of Representatives had approved the installation of 700 miles of new walls along the border as part of the punitive immigration reform bill H.R. 4437, which would make undocumented entry into the United States a felony.

10 Miguel Escobar Valdez, consul for Mexico at Douglas, Arizona, interview by the author, Tempe, Arizona, April 9, 2004. For an illustration of consular functions related to the disappearance of Mexican migrants, see the Web site for the Mexican Consulate of New York, www.consulmexny.org/esp/proteccion_tabla _desaparecidos.htm (accessed November 20, 2005).

11 Durand and Massey, *Crossing the Border*.

12 Jeffrey S. Passel, "Unauthorized Migrants: Numbers and Characteristics" (Washington, DC: Pew Hispanic Center Project Report, June 14, 2005), www. pewhispanic.org (accessed November 2, 2005).

13 For data on the migrants' use of coyotes or *polleros*, see Jorge Durand and Douglas S. Massey, "What We Learned from the Mexican Migration Project," in Durand and Massey, *Crossing the Border*, 1–14. On human traffic, see Peter Andreas, "The

Transformation of Migrant Smuggling across the U.S.-Mexican Border," in *Global Human Smuggling: Comparative Perspectives*, ed. David Kyle and Rey Koslowski (Baltimore: Johns Hopkins University Press, 2001), 107–28. See also John Bailey and Jorge Chabat, eds., *Transnational Crime and Public Security: Challenges to Mexico and the United States* (La Jolla: Center for U.S.-Mexican Studies, University of California at San Diego, 2002).

14 See Roberto Suro, "Remittance Senders and Receivers: Tracking the Transnational Channels," Pew Hispanic Center Report written in partnership with the Multilateral Investment Fund (Washington, DC: Pew Hispanic Center, November 24, 2003), available at www.pewhispanic.org/page.jsp?page=reports (accessed November 15, 2005).

15 Robert C. Smith, "'Los ausentes siempre presentes': The Imagining, Making, and Politics of a Transnational Community between Ticuani, Puebla, and New York City" (PhD diss., Columbia University, 1994).

16 Durand and Massey, "What We Learned," 10.

17 Carrie Kahn and Lourdes García Navarro for National Public Radio, "Immigrants Run Scholarship Program for Mexicans," aired January 6, 2006, on *Morning Edition*. See npr.org.

18 The term *postnational* describes the exercise of political agency outside the migrant's country of origin. The term also references a range of loyalties, social networks, or political claims that extend beyond the boundaries of national citizenship. See Linda Basch, Nina Glick Schiller, and Cristina Szanton Blanc, *Nations Unbound: Transnational Projects, Postcolonial Predicaments, and Deterritorialized Nation-States* (Langhorne, PA: Gordon and Breach, 1994); Linda Bosniak, "The State of Citizenship: Citizenship Denationalized," *Indiana Journal of Legal Studies* 7.2 (2000): 447–510; Saskia Sassen, "The Repositioning of Citizenship: Emergent Subjects and Spaces for Politics," *CR: The New Centennial Review* 3.2 (Summer 2003): 41–66; and Yasemin Nuhoólu Soysal, *Limits of Citizenship: Migrants and Postnational Membership in Europe* (Chicago: University of Chicago Press, 1994).

19 Durand and Massey, "What We Learned," 13.

20 Accounts of human traffic, organ trafficking, and slavery are not only limited to the border cities, where narcotrafficking and the *feminicidio* in Ciudad Juárez have raised the specter of other forms of predatory violence. Spanish-language media catering to new immigrants commonly carries stories of superexploitation and crimes against migrants. Both Univisión and Telemundo maintain Web sites devoted to immigration. In addition, Telemundo carries the syndicated program *Sin Fronteras*, which is devoted to immigrant concerns.

21 See Judith Butler, *The Psychic Life of Power: Theories in Subjection* (Palo Alto, CA: Stanford University Press, 1997); David Eng and David Kazanjian, eds., *Loss: The Politics of Mourning* (Berkeley: University of California Press, 2002); and Ann Anlin Cheng, *The Melancholy of Race: Psychoanalysis, Assimilation, and Hidden Grief* (New York: Oxford University Press, 2001).

22 "Battling Beyond U.S. Borders," *Assignment Discovery*, 2005.

23 My translations and transcription.

24 Details of the case appear in Mary E. O'Leary, "Scam Cost Illegal Aliens $150G," *New Haven Register*, January 6, 2006.

25   *El Alma Herida* (The Wounded Soul) was a coproduction of Telemundo and Argos in Mexico. The program completed shooting in 2003 and aired in the United States throughout 2004.

26   "One of the most beloved novelas of the Hispanic public": Organic Broadcast Project, http://broadcast.organicframework.com (accessed November 18, 2005).

27   My translation. Story synopsis and cast information are available at http://tdmnovelas.tripod.com/elalmaherida/ (accessed November 18, 2005).

28   See Daniel D. Arreola and James R. Curtis, "Cultural Landscapes of the Mexican Border Cities," *Aztlán* 21.1–2 (1992–96): 1–48.

29   In fact, many of those stranded or deported are children. María Eugenia Hernández Sánchez, "Deported Children in Ciudad Juárez," paper presented at the Center for Latin American and Iberian Studies, Yale University, New Haven, CT, October 12, 2005.

30   "Mexican Expatriate Voter Registration Falling Flat," *Frontera NorteSur* (online news-group circulated by Center for Latin American and Border Studies, New Mexico State University at Las Cruces), November 21, 2005.

31   "Mexican Expatriate Voter Registration Falling Flat."

32   "Mexican Expatriate Voter Registration Falling Flat."

33   See especially Smith, "'Los ausentes siempre presentes'"; Roger Rouse, "Mexican Migration to the U.S.: Family Relations in a Transnational Migrant Circuit" (PhD diss., Stanford University, 1989); and Luin Goldring, "Diversity and Community in Transnational Migration: A Comparative Study of Two Mexican U.S. Migrant Communities" (PhD diss., Cornell University, 1992).

34   "Place of birth: Huauchinango, Puebla. Last known: He departed from Tetela de Ocampo, Puebla, on 13 November, 2001, en route to work in the United States, but to this date, his family has received no news of his whereabouts." Protección a Mexicanos, Consulado General de México, www.consulmexny.org/esp/proteccion_tabla_desaparecidos.htm (accessed November 12, 2005).

35   Protección a Mexicanos, Consulado General de México.

36   Roland Barthes, *Camera Lucida*, trans. Richard Howard (New York: Hill and Wang, 1981). "The punctum *punctuates* the meaning of the photograph (the studium) and as a result punctures or pierces its viewer" (27).

37   "Your undocumented status does not make you a criminal." Protección a Mexicanos, Consulado General de México.

38   "If you have these symptoms, you are in danger of dying slowly." Gobierno del Estado de Yucatán, *Guia del Migrante Yucateco* (Yucatán, 2004), 32.

39   The United States instituted an official border patrol unit in 1924. C. Roberto Gaytan Saucedo, interview by author, Ciudad Juárez, November 13, 2003.

40   Claudia Smith, quoted in "Rapes on the U.S.-Mexico Border Up," United Press International, March 18, 2005, www.feeds.bignewsnetwork.com/?sid=2768526633891249 (accessed March 18, 2005). Smith argues that given the low rates of reporting crime, the actual number of rapes may be much higher.

41   "There are paths of no return."

42   "Going or coming, you remain Yucatecan." *Guía del Migrante Yucateco*, 79.

43   "Protect your life."

44 Retablo of Concepción Zapata, in Jorge Durand and Douglas S. Massey, *Miracles on the Border: Retablos of Mexican Migrants to the United States* (Tucson: University of Arizona Press, 1995), 138–39.

45 Durand and Massey, *Miracles on the Border*.

46 Durand and Massey, *Miracles on the Border*, 138.

47 See Sylvanna M. Falcón, "Rape as a Weapon of War: Advancing Human Rights for Women at the U.S.-Mexico Border," *Social Justice* 28.2 (2001): 31–50.

48 Marisela Norte, "Act of the Faithless," in *Norte/Word* 062/Cr02 (Lawndale, CA: New Alliance Records, 1991).

49 My discussion of Marisela Norte is informed by Michelle Habell-Pallán's definitive work on the poet, "No Cultural Icon: Marisela Norte and Spoken Word—East L.A. Noir and the U.S./Mexico Border," in *Loca Motion: The Travels of Chicana and Latina Popular Culture* (New York: New York University Press, 2005), 43–80.

50 Ramón Saldívar, *Chicano Narrative: The Dialectics of Difference* (Madison: University of Wisconsin Press, 1990), 190.

51 This concept of the border appears in Gloria Anzaldúa, *Borderlands/La Frontera: The New Mestiza* (San Francisco: Aunt Lute, 1987), and Sonia Saldívar-Hull, *Feminism on the Border: Chicana Gender Politics and Literature* (Berkeley: University of California Press, 2000). See also Norma Alarcón, "The Theoretical Subject(s) of *This Bridge Called My Back* and Anglo-American Feminism," in *Criticism in the Borderlands: Studies in Chicano Literature*, ed. Hector Calderón and José David Saldívar (Durham, NC: Duke University Press, 1991), 28–39.

52 Emma Pérez, "Sexuality and Discourse: Notes from a Chicana Survivor," in *Chicana Lesbians: The Girls Our Mothers Warned Us About*, ed. Carla Trujillo (Berkeley: Third Woman Press, 1991), 159–84. Pérez's phrase "sitio y lengua" means "place and language/tongue."

53 The phrase comes from María Socorro Tabuenca Córdova and Debra A. Castillo, *Border Women: Writing from La Frontera* (Minneapolis: University of Minnesota Press, 2002), 64.

54 Rolando Romero, "Postdeconstructive Spaces," *Siglo XX/Twentieth Century II* (1993): 225–33, cited in Córdova and Castillo, *Border Women*, 15.

55 Since 1993, some 370 women have been murdered in Chihuahua City and Ciudad Juárez; approximately 137 were sexually assaulted before their death. Of these, 100 fit a pattern of serial killings. Some 75 of the bodies have not been identified or claimed. The mothers' organization Nuestras Hijas de Regreso a Casa (Bring Our Daughters Home) estimates that in addition to these documented killings, 600 women have disappeared from the Juárez/Chihuahua metropolitan areas. Amnesty International, "Mexico: Intolerable Killings: Ten Years of Abductions and Murders in Ciudad Juárez and Chihuahua," August 11, 2003, AI index: AMR 41/027/2003.

56 See my discussion of the *feminicidio* in Alicia Schmidt Camacho, "Body Counts on the Mexico-U.S. Border: *Feminicidio*, Reification, and the Theft of Mexicana Subjectivity," *Chicana/Latina Studies* 4.1 (2004): 22–60.

PART V

BORDER

CROSSINGS

"Awakening to a Nightmare": Abjectivity and Illegality in the Lives of Undocumented 1.5-Generation Latino Immigrants in the United States

ROBERTO G. GONZALES AND LEO R. CHAVEZ

The "abject" designates that which has been expelled from the body, discharged as excrement, literally rendered "Other." This appears as an expulsion of alien elements, but the alien is effectively established through this expulsion.—JUDITH BUTLER 1999:5

From 2003 to 2008, we listened to the stories of undocumented Latino young adults who have lived in the United States since childhood. We came to know many of these young people personally and interacted with them in community meetings, on school campuses, and at their homes. They spoke of their frustrations and struggles to make better lives for themselves and their families. Esperanza, a particularly bright 27-year-old woman who migrated to the United States from Jalisco, Mexico, with her parents and younger sisters at age 8 and aspires to be a journalist, told us that even though she has a BA from the University of California, her dreams are on hold. Articulating the frustrations of her present circumstances, she told us,

> I [don't] want to break the law, but everything you do is illegal because you are illegal. Everything you do will be illegal. Otherwise you can't live.

But I am still afraid. I don't want to jeopardize anything. I mean, I guess I am just ashamed. I looked [for work] and in most restaurants they would be like, "Why do you want to work for us if you have a BA?"

Esperanza, like many others we met during the course of fieldwork, told her story with an outpouring of emotion, as much of her young life had been spent trying to understand the confusing and contradictory experience of growing up in the United States but not being able to take part in important and defining aspects of being American. Over the course of our 3+ years in the field, we came across more than 200 young people with similar stories of frustration and shattered dreams. We spoke to the Orange County Immigrant Student Group, an organization made up of mainly undocumented college-age students working to pressure the US Congress to pass legislation to provide undocumented students a path to citizenship (Development, Relief, and Education for Alien Minors [DREAM] Act). We also interacted with less fortunate undocumented youth who, because of run-ins with the police, trouble in school, and economic circumstances, have not been able to move on to college. These young men and women struggle to make ends meet and find their place in society. We heard undocumented Latino youth speak of themselves as unwanted by the larger society even though the United States is the only country they really know.

Out of these experiences came our general research question: Does the undocumented status of young Latino men and women who came to the United States at a young age (whom immigration scholars call the 1.5 generation) affect their political, civic, and public selves? Our approach to this question is framed by what Sarah S. Willen has called "abjectivity," a term that combines abject with subjectivity (Willen 2007). Our contribution to thinking about abjectivity is to further elaborate how Foucault's notions of biopolitics and biopower, and Agamben's "states of exception," frame abjectivity's usefulness for understanding (im)migrant and racialized populations. We also argue that undocumented 1.5-generation Latinos, despite the structural constraints they face, are often active agents working to make the best of their situation and to change the laws that constrain their lives.

At the core of the concept of abjectivity is the word "abject," which means "to cast away" or "to throw away." Abject has been used to describe those in the lowest, most contemptible, and most wretched social status.[1] Julia Kristeva first pointed to the implications of a condition of abjection as an exclusionary practice that produced discrete subjects, a point that has influenced subsequent scholars (Kristeva 1982; Willen 2007).[2] As Judith Butler (1999:169) notes in the epigraph above, "The 'abject' designates that which has been expelled from the body, discharged as excrement, literally rendered 'Other.' This appears as an expulsion of alien elements, but the alien is effectively established through this expulsion." Various intersections of race, gender, sexuality, nationality, migrancy, and any number of other categories can demarcate the abject in society. For example, Nicholas De Genova (2008) examined what he called "American abjection," a form of racialized identity Mexican migrants projected onto US-born people of color. And Leo R. Chavez (2008) examined how the often vitriolic discourse about the children of undocumented immigrants in the United States, including the US-born ("anchor babies"), characterized them as abject, as unwanted and discardable.

For our purposes, it is the body of the nation from which undocumented children of immigrants' are expelled and the source of their abject status. Theirs are castaway (abject) lives, which, as James Ferguson noted, are lives disconnected from the life they had imagined for themselves (Ferguson 2002: 140–41). These rejected and abject subjects inhabit a liminal space where the boundary between their everyday lives *in* the nation and their lives as *part of* the nation is maintained as a way of ensuring their control and social regulation (Chavez 2008:115–16). But what about the subjective understanding of living an abject life?

Willen's research among undocumented migrants in Israel emphasized the importance of lived experiences, that is, subjectivity, within abject spaces. It is in this sense that abjectivity raises a question such as that posed by Paul Farmer (2003:30): "By what mechanisms, precisely, do social forces ranging from poverty to racism become embodied as individual experience?" Such a question leads to a methodological approach that examines experiences and practices that shape understandings of the world. As Marjorie O'Loughlin observed in relation to Merleau-Ponty's (1962, 1968) theoretical insights, it is crucial to ask, "How embodied subjectivities are produced through material relations with other embodied subjects" (O'Loughlin 1998:275).[3] Human beings, as O'Loughlin (1998:280) further observes, "are simultaneously *inside* their bodies and *embodied* as actors in the world. It is this dual sense of bodiliness—the lived experience of embodiment—which enables social agency, that is, the ongoing creation of collective life." It is in this sense that Sarah Willen (2007:8) called for a "critical phenomonology of 'illegality,'" one that examines illegality as a juridical status, as a sociopolitical condition, and, finally, as a mode of being-in-the-world.

We are interested in the experiences of living in abjection. Abjectivity speaks to how the "casting away" of individuals and populations shapes (or perhaps delimits) their social, economic, and biological life. We believe that abjectivity draws attention to the forces creating the condition of abjectivity. Abjectivity is the effect of social forces, but we must also ask about the causes of that condition. We argue that the practices of the biopolitics of citizenship and governmentality— surveillance, immigration documents, employment forms, birth certificates, tax forms, drivers' licenses, credit card applications, bank accounts, medical insurance, and mandatory car insurance—may frustrate anyone, citizen and noncitizen alike, because they enclose, penetrate, define, and limit one's life and actions. But for undocumented 1.5-generation Latino immigrants (and others in a similar status), these practices of governmental contact and surveillance can create enormous distress, detention, and even deportation (Inda 2006). These "rites of institution," as Pierre Bourdieu (1992) called them, are central to the power of nation-states to construct identities and produce, in a perverse way, the "sweet sorrow" of a sense of belonging (to borrow from Shakespeare). Thus, abjectivity underscores the link between the mechanics of biopower and the lived experiences of those most vulnerable to the exercise of power.

Our construction of abjectivity clearly draws on Michel Foucault's biopolitics, the development of techniques that work on the body to produce docile bodies (Foucault 1977, 1990 [1976], 1997; Gordon 1991).[4] This led Foucault, as Giorgio Agamben (1998) points out, to two research directives. The first focuses on the way power "penetrates subjects' very bodies and forms of life." The state, with its "political techniques (such as the science of the police) . . . assumes and integrates the care of the natural life of individuals into its very center" (Agamben 1998:5). Second, Foucault examines "the *technologies of the self* by which processes of subjectivization bring the individual to bind himself to his own identity and consciousness and, at the same time, to an external power" (Agamben 1998:5). Judith Butler (1997*b*) also argued that power and subject are interlocked in a paradox of subjectivization, or the formation of a self-conscious identity and thus agency.

We are also interested in the intersection of Foucault's two research directives, that is, how the practices targeting undocumented or unauthorized immigrants shape the lived experience of undocumented 1.5-generation Latinos and how they respond to such constraints. Agamben speaks of "bare life," the natural life that is distinct from the "good life," the political life in classic Western thought. In modern politics, bare life, once kept at the margins, is now increasingly included in the political order (Agamben 1998:9). But what happens to those objects of state regulation whose bare life is kept at the margins of the political order? They become states of exception, their lives bracketed as in the nation but not part of the nation, which allows them to become the object of laws and other techniques of regulation (Agamben 2005). These can include everyday experiences of ill treatment by the larger society, discrimination, and targeted police actions. When taken to its extreme, the state can target such exceptions, physically separate them from society, isolate them into "zones of social abandonment," and even engage in practices of genocide, extermination, or ethnic cleansing (Biehl 2005).[5]

But before such endpoints are reached, if ever, a set of practices can emerge that mark off or bracket a group as different, less than, unworthy, illegitimate, undeserving (Sargent and Larchanché-Kim 2006; Tormey 2007; Willen 2007; Zhang 2001). What marks the group as "Other" derives from particular histories and can coalesce around any number of traits: race, religion, sex, physical or mental disability, stigmatized disease, migration history, or citizenship status, among others. Importantly, it is not something inherent to the particular bracketed group that is important here, but the practices that make their lives miserable, constrained, limited, invisible or differently visible, stigmatized, feared, and even dangerous. And yet, despite these practices of exclusion, it is sometimes possible that a sense of inclusion emerges through everyday lived experiences such as working, forming families, making friends, paying taxes, playing sports, engaging in community affairs, and interacting with social institutions, particularly schools (Agamben 1998; Chavez 1998; Yuval-Davis 2006). These "zones of indistinction," as Agamben called them, are paradoxes in which the law and social practices legitimize that which law has prohibited (Agamben 1998; Coutin 2007).

Importantly, as Nicholas De Genova (2010:37) has noted, zones of indistinction, and bare life, are produced by sovereign (state) power. But we must note that, as we will show, undocumented 1.5 generation can, and do, resist total exclusion. The ultimate exclusionary act here is deportation, which De Genova (2010:34–35) has observed, is where "the whole totalizing regime of citizenship and alienage, belonging and deportability, entitlement and rightlessness, is deployed against particular persons in a manner that is, in the immediate practical application, irreducibly if not irreversibly individualizing."

Abjectivity leads us to examine the quotidian experiences of those who are the object of disciplinary practices and the subjects of exclusionary discourses of citizenship and belonging (Coutin 2000a; Reed-Danahay and Brettell 2008; Yuval-Davis 2006). How do the abject in a society internalize their subject status? What types of self-disciplinary practices do they engage in? How does everyday reality inform a sense of identity, belonging, and citizenship? At the same time, by including biopolitics as central to our formulation of abjectivity, we are also underscoring that power not only works to create docile bodies but that, as Foucault (1990 [1976]:95) so famously put it, "Where there is power, there is resistance." Thus, as we explore these questions, we are mindful of how, as Liliana Suárez-Navaz (2004:13) observed, "people situated at the margins of the hegemonic 'either-or' notion of belonging resisted their displacement." Focusing on the lives of undocumented Latino youth and the ways in which they understand, respond to, and critique their circumstances demonstrates the salience of this observation.[6]

Locating 1.5-Generation Latinos in a Condition of Illegality

The literature refers to the 1.5 generation as those who migrated at a young age,[7] in recognition of the fact that most or all of their schooling and much of their cultural and social development occur in the host country (Portes and Rumbaut 2001; Rumbaut 2004).[8] In contrast, older migrants (the 1.0 generation) who experience their formative years in their country of origin develop their worldview from experiences growing up there. In many respects, the 1.5 generation is more similar to the second generation, those born in the new country, than to those of the first generation who migrated at 15 years of age or older. Also, because the 1.5 generation come to the United States as young children, it is typically their parents who made the decision to migrate.[9]

The biopolitics associated with governmentality produce illegality.[10] "Illegal" refers to unauthorized residents who entered the county without permission from government authorities, or they may have entered with permission—tourist or student visas—but then overstayed visa end dates. Illegality, as Susan B. Coutin (2007:9) observed, has meant that "individuals can be physically present but legally absent, existing in a space outside of society, a space of 'nonexistence,' a space that is not actually 'elsewhere' or beyond borders but that is rather a hidden dimension of social reality." We would offer as a slight variation on Coutin's representation: to be illegally present is not to be "outside of society" but to be allowed to participate in some aspects of society (e.g., schooling) but not others (e.g., work) (Gonzales 2011). All children, regardless of immigration status, have access to primary and secondary education as a result of the US Supreme Court's decision in *Plyer v. Doe*. Access to higher education has focused on immigration status and in-state versus nonresident tuition. In California, Assembly Bill 540, signed into law in 2001, allowed undocumented students to attend publicly funded colleges and universities and pay in-state tuition, but they were ineligible for financial aid, which the California DREAM Act of 2011 now allows.[11]

As a condition, being "illegal" contributes to subjective understandings of the world and to identity (Coutin 2000a, 2000b; De Genova 2002; Menjívar 2006; Suárez-Navaz 2004; Willen 2007). As Sarah Willen (2007:11) has put it, "migrant 'illegality' [is] the catalyst for particular forms of 'abjectivity.'" Abjectivity, by drawing us back to biopolitics, suggests that adding to the despair of abjectivity is not just the condition of illegality but the state's holding out of the possibility of an end to that condition.

Moving from an illegal status to a legal one—to legal permanent residence—has become much more difficult as a result of changes in US immigration law, most notably the 1996 Illegal Immigration Reform and Immigration Responsibility Act (IIRIRA; Bunis and Garcia 1997).[12] IIRIRA's provisions included that apprehended undocumented immigrants can no longer demand a hearing and stay in the country until their case is adjudicated; they can now be sent home immediately, but they can appeal a deportation order because of a later legal decision (Stout 1978). Undocumented immigrants must now be in the United States for 10 years, rather than 7 years, before they can appeal a deportation decision, and they must prove good moral character and show that that deportation would cause extreme hardship to a family member who is a US citizen. Waivers of deportation for aggravated felonies are no longer possible, and this class of felonies has been greatly expanded. An individual sponsor for an immigrant must sign an affidavit and prove that his or her income (not her household's income) is at least 125% above the nation's poverty level (Chavez 2001).

Because of such obstacles to moving to legal status, public debates over comprehensive immigration reform include the possibility of a "path to citizenship" for the large (11–12 million) number of unauthorized residents (Passel and Cohn 2009). Although such proposals have gained little traction in recent years, the US Congress has considered a more focused reform for the undocumented 1.5 generation, known as the DREAM Act. Under the DREAM Act, most students of good moral character who came to the United States before they were 16 years old and had at least 5 years of US residence before the date of the bill's enactment would qualify for conditional permanent resident status if they met one of three criteria: (a) graduated from a 2-year college or a vocational college, or studied for at least 2 years toward a bachelor's or higher degree; (b) served in the US armed forces for at least 2 years; or (c) performed at least 910 hours of volunteer community service. Undocumented youth would not qualify for this relief if they had committed crimes, were a security risk, or were inadmissible or removable on certain other grounds. However, the DREAM Act has been in Congress, in some form, for nearly 10 years without passage.[13] The constant vacillation between hope and despair engendered by the possibility of immigration reform and the DREAM Act is a major disciplinary practice that informs the subject status of the undocumented young people whose lives are examined below (Gonzales 2008a, 2008b; Negron-Gonzales 2009; Olivas 1995; Ramirez 2008).

Abjectivity as experienced by those in a condition of illegality, therefore, is situational and not immutable, with the state having the power to maintain or mitigate that status (Bosniak 1998, 2000). An illegal or undocumented immigrant can sometimes, though with great difficulty, find a way to move to a legal immigration status, which often means greater economic, physical, and psychological stability. The liminal and unstable nature of abjectivity is both a source of life stress and a condition that allows for the possibility of change, which opens up a space for human action and resistance. Though lacking power, undocumented immigrants are not powerless. They have, as Saskia Sassen (2003:62) put it, a political *presence*. This becomes evident when we examine the political activism, what Isin and Nielsen (2008) call "acts of citizenship," of the young people examined here (Getrich 2008). Rather than falling into completely immobilizing despair and hopelessness, they often engage in personal acts of resistance (Butler 1997a), which range from making small steps to improve their lives through education and training to political activism aimed at immigration reforms to provide a path to citizenship for undocumented immigrants.

Exploring the Lives of 1.5-Generation Latinos

We examine the lives of young Latino immigrants who came to the United States at a young age and were living in Orange County, California. Our approach combines survey data and in-depth ethnographic interviews that grew out of extensive participant observation. Survey data provide general patterns in the lives of 1.5-generation Latinos in Orange County and indicate the constraints of illegality on their lives. In-depth ethnographic interviews and participant observation provide insights into the subjective understandings and practices of living in a condition of illegality for young Latino immigrants. Questions in both the survey and in-depth interviews focused on residence, family, education, work, discrimination, unauthorized status, political engagement, and daily, lived experiences, with extensive follow-up and probing in the in-depth interviews.

Orange County covers an area of 789 square miles, is largely urban, and contains 34 cities and numerous unincorporated communities (US Census Bureau 2006). It is the third most populous county in California, with an estimated 3,002,048 inhabitants in 2006, of whom 30.5% were foreign-born. With an understanding that it is difficult to estimate the undocumented immigrant population, they may account for about 10.2% of the county's overall population in 2006 (Fortuny et al. 2007; Paral 2006; US Census Bureau 2006). Latinos accounted for 32.5% of the county's population in 2005. Most Latinos are of Mexican heritage, but Latino immigrants are also from other nations in Latin America, particularly Central America.

Orange County is an excellent site for this study not just because of the large proportion and diversity of Latinos, but for other reasons as well. Even though it had a median household income in 2008 of $74,862 (almost $24,000 above the California average), it is an economically diverse county, ranging from modest working-class communities to wealthy communities (US Census

Bureau 2010). The southern half of the county has been an area of rapid growth in new middle class, upper-middle class, and exclusive (i.e., mostly white) residential communities. Latino immigrants often work in south county communities but find less expensive housing in the many working-class communities in the northern part of the county (Chavez et al. 1997).

Finally, Orange County has also been one of the areas where anti-immigration movements have found substantial support. In the early 1990s, Ronald Prince, one of the cofounders of the Save Our State (SOS) initiative, was based in Orange County. The SOS initiative was the basis for the 1994 California state initiative known as Proposition 187, the so-called anti–illegal alien initiative and a forerunner of Arizona's 2009 anti-immigration law (McDonnell 1994). Jim Gilchrist lives in Orange County and started the Minutemen Project to express concern with what he perceived as a lack of enforcement of the nation's borders (Delson 2005; Kelly 2005). In sum, the demographics of the county and the local concern for public policy issues surrounding immigration reform make Orange County a particularly apt place to examine issues related to 1.5-generation Latinos.

Survey data were collected between January 4 and January 30, 2006, from 805 Latinos and 396 non-Latino whites (hereafter simply "whites") in Orange County. Latinos were over-sampled to account for diversity in generation and immigration status. The Orange County Survey was conducted under the auspices of the Center for Research on Latinos in a Global Society (CRLGS), University of California, Irvine. The research protocol was successfully reviewed by the University of California, Irvine Office of Research Administration Institutional Review Board.[14] Interviewing Service of America conducted the telephone survey, using trained interviewers in both English and Spanish. Interviews were in the interviewee's language of choice. The survey used random-digit dialing on a sample from a database that includes all US directory-published household numbers, both listed and unlisted, combined with a sample that had identified Hispanic markers, such as unique first and last names.[15] Eligible participants were English- or Spanish-speaking men and women, 18 years of age or older, who were not institutionalized and who identified themselves as white (Anglo, Caucasian, non-Hispanic white) or Latino (Hispanic or more specific ethnic identifiers such as Mexican, Mexican American, and Salvadoran). If there was more than one 18 year old in the household, we asked for the one with the closest birthday. The response rate was 70%.

Although "Latino" and "Hispanic" are often used interchangeably, the term "Latino" is used here as a panethnic identifier of people of Latin American descent living in the United States. For the purposes of this analysis, respondents who were born in a Latin American country and/or self-identified as Latino,

Hispanic, or a specific Latin American nationality (e.g., Mexican, Salvadoran) were classified as Latino.

Survey questions focused on residence, family, education, work, income, discrimination, immigration status, political engagement, various social and economic experiences, use of medical services, and health. Questions of life stressors were drawn from research on an array of health outcomes and stress (Campos et al. 2007; Dressler 1996; Farley et al. 2005; Wallace and Wallace 2004). Not all questions in the survey are examined here.

Immigration status was assessed through two questions. First, we asked if the respondent was a legal permanent resident of the United States, a naturalized US citizen, or something else (the default category). We then asked if any of the following applied to their immigration status: awarded asylum, awarded Temporary Protected Status, applied for a work permit, applied for permanent residence, applied for political asylum. The default category consisted of those without authorization to be in the United States. As the findings below indicate, unauthorized immigrants differed significantly along a range of socioeconomic variables from legal permanent residents, naturalized citizens, and US-born citizens.

We also conducted 80 in-depth interviews, the majority (72) of which were with individuals of Mexican origin. Most of the in-depth interviews (76) were conducted by the lead author, the rest by the second author. Gonzales's research took place in several sites during three periods of field research in Orange County. The first included volunteering at two community-based organizations in Santa Ana during the 2002–2003 academic year, where he once or twice a week helped out and observed young adults in their natural environments. The fieldwork and the relationships made with key community interviewees helped him to identify initial respondents and use snowball sampling to identify subsequent interviewees (Chavez 1998; Cornelius 1982). The second phase of fieldwork took place from 2004 to 2007, during which he observed respondents in their workplaces, schools, homes, and in community settings. In 2009, he collected additional data and followed up with past respondents. All in-depth interviews were conducted in English.

Interviewees included 1.5-generation young adults who entered the United States without authorization and remain unauthorized, 1.5-generation young adults who entered the United States with visas and became unauthorized due to overstays, and 1.5-generation young adults who were once unauthorized and have since regularized their status (are either lawful permanent residents or naturalized citizens). Interviewees ranged from 20 to 34 years of age and were evenly divided by gender. Interviews ranged in time from 1 hour and 40 minutes to 3 hours and 20 minutes. Interviews were transcribed and coded.

Describing Abject Lives

We examine survey data first as a way of providing general patterns that distinguish 1.5-generation Latino immigrants from their first-generation counterparts and to suggest the contours of their abject status. Of the 805 Latinos surveyed, most (84.7%) were Mexican immigrants or of Mexican origin. There were, however, Salvadoran and other Central American immigrants, some South Americans, and a few immigrants from the Caribbean. Of the Latinos surveyed, 573 (71.2%) were first generation, meaning that they were born in a foreign country and migrated to the United States.[16] Of these, 130 respondents, or 22.7% of the first-generation Latino respondents, were in the 1.5 generation. Most (105, 82%) of the 1.5 interviewees were born in Mexico, with the rest coming in smaller numbers from the same countries mentioned above.

Surveyed 1.5-generation respondents were generally younger (median age 29) than first-generation adult migrants (median age 39), but they had more years of US residence (23 years and 16 years, respectively). The 1.5 generation also tended to have more years of schooling (median 12 years) than their older migrating counterparts (median 9 years), but less than second-generation Latinos (median 13 years) or whites (median 16 years). Income also varied by generation, with only 26% of those who migrated at age 15 or older (1.0 generation) having family income (interviewee's income plus spouse/partner's income, if applicable) of $35,000 or more, compared to 54% of 1.5-generation Latinos ($P < .01$), both of which were less than second-generation Latinos (71%) and whites (79%) in that upper income category. Young Latinos who migrated under age 15 were, compared to older migrants, more likely to speak all or mostly English at home (17.8% and 2.5%, respectively; $P \leq .001$), with friends (31% and 5.2%, respectively, $P \leq .001$), and at work (43.4% and 19%, respectively; $P \leq .001$).

Examining all 1.5-generation Latinos together masks the material conditions of illegality. About a third (32%) of the Latino 1.5-generation interviewees were unauthorized immigrants in the United States compared to 46% of the first generation who migrated at age 15 or older, a statistically significant difference ($P < .01$). Illegality had significant ramifications for all Latino immigrants, and for the 1.5-generation Latinos in particular. For example, undocumented 1.5-generation Latinos were able legally to attend a college or university in California, but they were not eligible for government-sponsored financial aid and thus often found meeting the costs of higher education difficult (Rincón 2008). Not surprisingly, given the financial obstacles, only 30.3% of the undocumented 1.5 generation had 13 or more years of schooling, compared to 50% of their legal resident counterparts.

Being undocumented also meant that those educated in the United States could not work legally. Consequently, among Latinos who migrated at a young age but were still unauthorized residents at the time of the interview, only 23.5% had a family income of $35,000 or higher, compared to two-thirds (67.6%) of legally resident 1.5-generation Latinos, a statistically significant difference ($P < .001$).

Living in a condition of illegality also results in beliefs and experiences among Latinos who differ significantly from Latino legal immigrants. Undocumented 1.5-generation Latinos were less likely than legal 1.5-generation Latinos to own their home (13% compared to 70%; $P < .001$), as well as second-generation Latinos (70%) and whites (86%). Compared to legal 1.5-generation Latinos, undocumented 1.5-generation Latinos held less positive beliefs about their quality of life in Orange County (13% compared to 35%; $P < .05$), were less satisfied with their neighborhoods (36% compared to 64%; $P < .05$), more likely to have lost sleep or worried excessively because of neighborhood problems (18% compared to 7%), were more often forced to move because of money problems (15% compared to 2%; $P < .01$), and more often did not have enough food to eat (18% compared to 8%). They were less likely to view police protection as excellent (13% compared to 26%; $P < .05$) and more likely to believe they had been treated unfairly by the police (18% compared to 6%; $P < .05$). These views and experiences indicate the social, material, and psychic costs of illegality and abjectivity.

Illegality places limits on what is possible, especially spatial mobility and engagement in transnational practices (Basch et al. 1994). Although both legal and undocumented Latino immigrants (60% and 67%, respectively) remitted money to a relative or friend in another country, legal 1.5 Latino immigrants were twice as likely as the undocumented 1.5 interviewees (84% compared to 42%; $P < .001$) to have visited their parent's home country in the year before the interview. They were also much more likely (13% compared to 3%) to participate in hometown or state-of-origin organizations associated with their country of origin. Communicating with relatives or friends transnationally was hampered by few undocumented 1.5-generation Latinos (39%) compared to legal 1.5 Latinos (73%, $P < .001$) owning a computer. Among those undocumented 1.5 generation who did have a computer, few (7%) compared to about half (49%, $P < .01$) of legal "1.5ers" used the computer to communicate with a relative or friend in another country.

Illegality also has physical or bodily costs as well. Few of the undocumented 1.5 Latinos had private or government medical insurance compared to their legal counterparts (42% and 71%, respectively; $P < .01$), the sine qua non for access to medical care in the United States. As a consequence, undocumented 1.5-generation interviewees were less likely (51% compared to 78%; $P < .01$) than legal 1.5 Latinos to have sought medical care in the 12 months prior to the interview. Moreover, they were less likely to exercise regularly outside of work or in addition to daily activities (49% compared to 69%; $P < .01$), a pattern ill-suited to maintaining good health.

Abjectivity does not result in complete surrender, or silencing, at least in terms of civic and political engagement. Indeed, perceived threats can, and did, lead to political activity among Latinos surveyed, even those without legal status. This can be shown most clearly in the relation between civic engagement and perceived discrimination.[17]

The survey asked about membership in community, sports, ethnic, and political organizations, and about political activities in the previous 12 months, such as contacting a governmental office to complain about a problem or get help; attending political rallies, meetings, or dinners for a political candidate; taking part in protests; contributing money to political candidates or campaigns; or volunteering time for an organization. About the same proportion of 1.0 (28.2%) and 1.5 (33.6%) generation Latinos surveyed answered yes to one or more of these examples of civic engagement and political participation. However, 31.8% of the 1.5-generation Latinos who were civically and politically engaged also perceive discrimination, compared to 19.2% of the 1.0-generation Latinos. The 1.5-generation Latinos were similar to their US-born counterparts, among whom 30.5% of the civic and politically engaged also perceived discrimination.

When facing perceived discrimination and threats, the 1.5 generation will respond, or resist. The survey was undertaken before the large marches and demonstrations by immigrants and their supporters in the spring of 2006. However, the in-depth interviews below were done during and after the marches, and as we will note, the fact that most of the interviewees participated in the marches reflects the survey's findings of civic and political engagement when faced with threats.

As these survey findings suggest, illegality significantly influences the daily experiences of those living in that condition, raising a number of questions. In what ways do 1.5-generation Latinos internalize their experiences? How do they make sense of the biopolitics that constitute their subjective understandings of the world? What practices have emerged to confront and resist a condition of abjectivity? The ethnographic aspects of our study help us to answer these questions.

"Awakening to a Nightmare"

In-depth interviews indicate that as undocumented adolescents move into adulthood, the technologies of biopolitics and the practices of governmentality become achingly apparent in their lives. They come face-to-face with illegality, a condition that they had been partially protected from by their age and by their parents. But as they began to anticipate the rites of passage common to adolescents and young adults in the United States, reality quickly entangled them. Like other youth, they desired to drive a car, work, vote, and join friends in social activities where a state-issued identification was required. However, each of these activities requires some form of state-issued identification, typically a driver's license or Social Security card, which are easy to get if one is a legal permanent resident or citizen of the United States. For those living in a condition of illegality, however, attempting to acquire such identification exposes them to government practices of control, surveillance, and punishment.

Thus, adolescence is a period of great stress and anxiety for undocumented youth (Coutin 2007, 2008). As children, most of them were not required to produce identification. It is only when they attempted to assert their position in the American mainstream that the importance of identification became essential. This was a defining moment, a challenge to their taken-for-granted identity and sense of belonging. This often came as a surprise to many who were unaware of their unauthorized immigration status or its significance.[18] As Julian, who has been in the United States since age 4, described it, "It was like awakening to a nightmare." Respondents grew into adolescence and adulthood steeped in US culture, and, because their unauthorized status did not pose too many restrictions as they grew up, many gave little thought to their legal status. In fact, many believed themselves to be just like their US-born peers.

Sergio was 16 years old when he discovered his unauthorized status. He had saved up money for over 2 years from various side jobs—a paper route and weekend job helping his father at a construction site—in order to buy his first car. But, as he said, "I was told at the DMV that I needed a Social [Security number]. So I went home and my mom told me I didn't have one. I couldn't believe it. What was I going to tell my friends? I had been all 'I'm gonna get my car before all of you.' But I couldn't. How could I tell them now I can't drive? I can't get my license. It really messed me up."

As a child, Sergio was not required to produce his Social Security number and, as a result, his early life was not defined by his legal status. However, the attempt to get a driver's license forced him to confront the implications of not having legal status.

The sudden awareness of their abject social status was often jarring and traumatic. Cesar's case exemplifies. He migrated to the United States from Mexico City as a child with his mother and brother, and his father followed a few months later. His father had completed 2 years of college in Mexico, and his mother up to the sixth grade, but both emphasized education for Cesar. Cesar excelled academically, taking honors and advanced placement classes, and was involved in student government, clubs, and sports. He wanted to pursue a career in pharmaceutical sciences. Upon graduation, he was accepted to seven universities. But problems suddenly arose:

> Once you get the acceptance letter, then you get sent a letter asking for residency. You know, proof of residency. And so, that's when reality struck, and that was around the second semester [senior year] of high school. All my friends were accepted [to college], making plans. That's when I was, I got a little bit depressed. I got a little bit frustrated. And even more so because I learned that I couldn't go to any of the schools I had gotten accepted to. I had to go the junior college route.

At that time, before Assembly Bill 540, Cesar would have had to pay non-resident tuition, at 3–5 times the cost of instate tuition, to attend a public college or university in California. Without the possibility of student loans, his family could not afford it. Cesar's depression lasted quite awhile. He could not understand how the value of hard work and his accomplishments could suddenly be so meaningless. He felt as though he was being punished: "I worked so hard, junior college was way below my standards."

Problems of Everyday Living

After growing up in the United States, undocumented young adults are forced to confront the consequences of illegality and must learn to live as an "illegal."[19] Whether the respondents were trying to move on to college, find jobs, travel, or open bank accounts, awareness of their status meant their plans had to be adjusted or even abandoned.

The sudden and dramatic changes that accompanied the awareness of the condition of illegality altered the lives of undocumented young adults in profound ways as they began to recognize the constraints on their lives. Becoming aware of the condition of illegality during adolescence and confronting its challenges was not a singular or uniform experience. Some respondents mitigated the constraints of their lack of citizenship status by continuing their education with private scholarships to attend college, a few with family financial support. Others, however, became despondent as their lives became narrowly circumscribed.[20] Rather than going to college, they had to try their luck in the low-skilled labor market, alongside adult migrants, many of whom were also without immigration documents. Some experienced trouble with the law, others early childbearing.

Many experienced a sense of hopelessness as they looked ahead to an uncertain future. Miguel was 4 years old when he was brought to the United States from Jalisco, Mexico. He believed during most of high school that he had his whole future laid out, but when his mother alerted him to the reality of his nonlegal status, everything was "turned upside down." As a result, his school attendance faltered and his grades fell. Others also recounted how their grades declined and their optimism about the future fell during their last year or two of high school.

Those who managed to attend college were able to ameliorate the daily stresses of illegality. It also allowed them to continue their education and the hope that they would find a way to become legal residents. As students, they would also reduce the risk of run-ins with police or immigration officials. As a result, many respondents felt less stress while on college campuses. However, driving to and from college increased that risk. Irene, a 22-year-old who came from Guerrero at age 6, was returning from classes at a California state university when she was pulled over by a police officer less than six blocks from her house and had to call her father to pick her up. This was an awakening for her because she felt a false sense of safety while in school, but away from college she was, in her words, "just another Mexican."

For 1.5-generation undocumented Latinos, like Irene, working and going to college meant they had to find a way to get there, and in Southern California, public transportation is often difficult and slow. Many who chose to take the bus described excruciatingly long commutes from Orange County to Los Angeles. Those who drove to work ran the risk of being stopped by the police for some minor infraction. Luis, a 26-year-old from Jalisco who is now enrolled in graduate studies, noted that driving meant that he had to "try his luck in the gauntlet every day." The dangers associated with driving caused many to pay close attention to traffic laws. They made sure to always drive under the speed limit and to avoid certain areas, such as those where immigration officials were known to have set up checkpoints to stop drivers and check for immigration documents. Interviewees spoke of avoiding certain cities in Los Angeles, Orange, and San Bernardino counties where local police have been deputized as immigration agents.

Even a minor traffic violation or accident can throw their lives into peril. Luz came to the United States from El Salvador when she was 2 years old. When the police stopped her for a minor violation, Luz and her children were left on the street after her car was towed away.

> I was coming from an appointment, and my son took off his seatbelt in the tantrum that he was throwing. And the cop passed by us and saw him without a seatbelt. And I couldn't pull aside to put his seatbelt back on because it was traffic time, and we were like in the middle of the road, so it was like "ahhh." The cop stopped me, and he gave me a ticket for not having a license and they took the car.

For most people, driving without a license would have resulted in a traffic ticket, but Luz also did not have automobile insurance. She and her four children were left on the sidewalk near a busy intersection, without their car and miles away from home. This incident triggered a fear in Luz for not only her own safety, but also that of her children. It also left a huge impression on her, as she became acutely aware that at any moment her life could change. As a result, Luz is fearful of everyday situations that could result in contact with the authorities.

Taking buses presented other risks. Interviewees said they stopped taking the bus in Santa Ana after reports that immigration agents were seen at the downtown bus station. Sonny, who was 8 when he came from Michoacan, Mexico, and left high school in tenth grade, told us about his cousin being stopped at a bus stop near Huntington Beach. The cousin was waiting with his girlfriend at a bus stop when local police stopped him and asked for his papers. When he was unable to produce them, they drove him all the way to Tijuana and dropped him off. At the time of the interview with Sonny, his cousin had been in Mexico for over a year. His family had been unable to come up with sufficient funds to bring him back to the United States. With no money on him, and no familiarity with Tijuana, he had a difficult time.

As the reality of the respondents' authorized immigration status became oppressively apparent, stories, news reports, and firsthand experiences served to set a climate of fear. Many interviewees told of changing their behavior patterns. A common experience among most was the continual looking over their shoulders. Especially when driving, many feared being pulled over by police. They made sure to always drive under the speed limit and obey traffic laws, in an almost exaggerated manner. They also learned to avoid certain areas with high levels of police activity. After an immigration raid in their apartment complex, Ramon and his girlfriend Maria, who were both undocumented and without high school diplomas, began spending most of their nonworking time locked up in their apartment. Maria, age 26, was not working at the time of our interview, so as to take care of their two children at home. She said that while she was bored at home, "at least I don't have to worry about what's going to happen to me or the kids." Maria and Ramon, who was 27, worry about what would happen if one of them were deported, as Maria said: "My biggest fear is our kids. I mean, what's going to happen if both of us get picked up and deported? What's going to happen to the kids? We worry a lot about that. About what's going to happen. I can't imagine what I'd do if something happened. It's scary. It's really scary."

Ramon related that Maria had been sick because of stress. Neither of them has medical insurance, and, with only Ramon working and not making enough some months to cover all of their expenses, they have avoided going to the doctor to check on Maria's condition. Others in our study developed similar physical manifestations of stress. Misto, a 22-year-old who came to the United States from Guerrero when he was 5, was forced to bypass college for work. He developed an ulcer as a result of his constant worry. Andrea, a college graduate who had been in the United States since she was 8, had to miss several days of work and school after experiencing chronic fatigue and recurrent headaches that sent her on regular trips to the doctor. Similarly, Grace, who was enrolled at the University of California at the time of her interview, has had to miss school and work because, "sometimes I can't even get out of bed."

Living on Hold

Undocumented 1.5-generation Latinos that have succeeded academically may desire greater levels of inclusion for themselves but are hampered by their illegality. Esperanza, whose story began this essay, excelled academically in her Anaheim high school and was heavily involved in extracurricular activities, including the school's band. As she said, "The whole band experience and community service . . . makes you so proud of your school and you represent it no matter what. It makes you feel so proud of them." She completed a BA from a University of California campus and would someday like to pursue a PhD or law degree. At the time of the interview, however, she was working and trying to survive as an undocumented immigrant. Esperanza spoke of how her life is constrained because of her unauthorized status:

> I know I can do so much more, but I can't because I can't live wherever. I can't choose where I live. I can't choose where I work. And the worst thing is that I can't choose my friends. In high school I was able to do that. I can't anymore. I can't even hang out with my high school friends anymore and that hurts a lot. Yeah, they want to do grown up stuff. I can't do anything that is 18 and over. I can't do anything. I can only hang out where little kids hang out. I can't hang out with them. I can't travel with them. I can't go out to dinner with them. I can't go to Vegas with them. If I want to go to a bar, I don't even have a drink. If they want to go to San Diego, if they want to go visits museums down there, if they want to go to Sea World, I can't go with them. I can't go to Los Angeles. I can't go to any clubs in L.A. I can't go to any clubs in L.A. because after the marches [in the Spring of 2006] they don't accept *matrículas* [identification provided by the Mexican government] anywhere.[21]

Esperanza's high school friends are doing well. Some have their own band programs, one is a city planner, others are moving ahead in business-related jobs or are teachers. As Esperanza notes: "They have their degrees and they are working at jobs they saw themselves working at. . . . They are following their dreams." Esperanza, on the other hand, moves from one low-paying job to another. She typically either finds work where employers do not ask for identification or stays until identification becomes an issue. She has held various jobs—minor office work as a receptionist and secretary, factory work stuffing envelopes, and in fast food restaurants—but she runs the risk of not getting paid when the issue of identification surfaces, which has previously happened. Sometimes she works for cash. Esperanza laments the humiliations she has had to endure as a person who is educated, speaks English, and, from the perspective of the recent immigrants she works with, appears to "have it easy" because she grew up in US culture. Alas, as a strategy for survival, on job applications she omits her university degree, even though she views the degree as her greatest accomplishment.

> So I tell them that I just dropped out of high school. But eventually they are going, it is going to come out, I know it. The people [working] at those places, like the cooks and the cashiers, they are either really young people, and I feel really old, like what am I doing there if they are all like 16, 17 years old, those who start working when they are very young. The others are like *señoras* who are 35 and have little kids and they know they dropped out of school, but because they have little kids they are still working at the restaurant. Thinking about that, it makes me feel so fucking stupid. And like the factories, too, because they ask me, "*Que estas haciendo aquí?* [What are you doing here?] You can speak English. You graduated from high school. You can work anywhere." They don't stop bugging me. (Quoted in Gonzales 2011:615)

In high school, before the reality of her abject status set in, Esperanza looked down on the types of jobs she now takes. Then she reconciled the work as temporary, not career work, until she could find a way to become a legal resident. She told herself there were some jobs she would not do—cleaning toilets, mopping floors—but her views are slowly changing. "I just need a job. It's become about survival. If it used to be a choice, it is not a choice anymore. I am to the point where yes, I will clean somebody's home. I will take care of them. I will clean up somebody's saliva. More and more it is getting to the point where I don't care."[22]

Although Esperanza finds it difficult to make plans for the future, she still yearns for legal residency and to hold a job where she can put her education to use. Although she recognizes the desperate conditions under which she is living, she has not given up all hope. She volunteers for an organization promoting passage of the DREAM Act, which would provide 1.5-generation undocumented immigrants like her a path to citizenship.

Cesar, who was introduced earlier, had similar feelings. After his initial despair, he became involved in student government and once again excelled academically. He transferred to UCLA, which was made possible by his parents, especially his mother, working extra hours and saving specifically for Cesar's tuition. Cesar also worked to pay tuition. Cesar graduated from the University of California, Los Angeles, and now dreams of applying to medical school and opening a nonprofit clinic. As Cesar said, "I decided about a year ago that I wasn't going to let my situation [being undocumented] handle me anymore. When I used to think about my situation, it was kind of like a block. I was like "Oh, no. I can't apply to med school. I can't do this. I can't do that."

Because he is not a legal resident and cannot work legally, Cesar works as a tutor, helping young people in the sciences. His students have included two high school valedictorians. Cesar reflected on his illegal status, which he said "defined who we are." Rather than give up, Cesar said he "pushed back" and continued his education and hoped for the day he can become a legal resident and put his education to use. For Cesar, being undocumented forced him to fight back, to develop self-confidence, and motivated him to achieve educationally. Cesar is aware of the self-disciplining caused by his abject status: "You put a positive spin onto this negative reality that you live in. It's kind of like, you know, when you're a little kid and you get scolded and they tell you to go to your room. It's like, okay, I've learned my lesson now. I've learned that I have to be humble. I learned that you have to work hard for what you need to work hard for. So, now, it's time for it to go away."

As these last examples suggest, for some adolescents and young adult undocumented immigrants, the condition of illegality can be paralyzing, resulting in a lack of mobility along multiple dimensions: educational, economic, and physical. Indeed, such feelings of paralysis, and the dangers associated with undocumented status, kept many respondents in a state of limbo.

For example, Dora, a 26-year-old from Zacatecas who has lived in Santa Ana since she migrated with her family at age 8, has held only one full-time job and one part-time job in her entire life. At the time of her interview, she was not working because of a fear of getting caught. However, she was living at home with her parents and other siblings who work. While she wants to contribute to household expenses, she is not required to do so. Such minimal expectations allow her to avoid situations that could put her face-to-face with the law. However, they also place many aspects of her life on hold.

For many of our respondents, waiting for the possibility of acquiring legal permanent residency status is full of uncertainty, and thus many refrain from making investments in their futures. Luz has experienced unsuccessful attempts at sponsorship by her mother and husband. Her hopes for a change in immigration status have turned into disappointment, as she is stuck in limbo, trying to make the most of her abject situation. At 22 when we first met, Luz was raising three children by herself. Her husband of 8 years was incarcerated and was not expected to be released anytime soon. Because he was convicted of a crime as a noncitizen, his legal permanent residency was revoked, and he faced deportation charges upon the completion of his served jail time. As Luz said, "If you get deported or something, everything that you worked for is going to be gone."

Wasted Lives

Many young undocumented immigrants who did not move on to college had to work in order to contribute to their families or meet their own needs. After high school, life became saturated by legal limitations and barriers caused by a lack of legal residency. Biopolitics penetrated our interviewees' behavior such that they constantly thought about ways to avoid immigration officials, police, and other authorities. They found themselves constantly looking over their shoulders, avoiding potentially dangerous situations and spending much of their time worrying. The stress of abjectivity was pronounced in their lives. The longer the time interviewees were out of school, the greater effect the condition of illegality had on their aspirations and expectations, the more biopolitics worked on their very being.

Take Pedro, for example. He came to the United States from Guatemala when he was 6 years old. Already, at 26, Pedro's aspirations have been derailed by his unauthorized status and a police record. After completing a day-labor job, the employer gave Pedro a check for his work. When Pedro tried to cash the check, the teller at the local currency exchange called Pedro's employer to verify the check's legitimacy. The employer denied writing the check, and the police were called. The police found different sets of identification on Pedro and took him to jail. He served over a month in prison and was serving a 3-year probation sentence when interviewed. Pedro currently lives with his childhood friends in a mobile home and does odd jobs to pay rent for his room.

Pedro has few aspirations other than living in a mobile home and does not see his life changing for more than 10 years. Pedro's outlook, however, is not unique. Other interviewees were similarly hesitant when it came to thinking about their futures. The opaqueness with which they viewed the future stemmed from the cumulative effects of illegality and the seemingly insurmountable number of barriers framing their lives.

Fear of detection and deportation sometimes render undocumented young adults immobile and afraid to invest time, money, or hopes in their future. Living their lives in a narrowly circumscribed present, several of these young men and women let go of aspirations to have anything more. When Sergio and his brother were in a car accident with another driver, the already unfortunate situation took on a magnified level of stress. Although they were not in the wrong, neither of them had a driver's license or insurance. Because of their illegality, they were left vulnerable and having to pay for the damages out of their own pockets. After the accident, Sergio bought a beat-up 1987 Chevy Cavalier for which he paid $900 because, he said, he could not buy a good car on his own. He figures that if he gets caught and has the car towed, he will lose only $900.

Sergio was 21 years old when interviewed. He occasionally worked on the weekends, taking jobs that hired for the day or weekend, but stayed away from anything resembling ongoing or permanent employment and did not drive.

> I've been offered jobs, but the thing is that it messes me up. There's ways around it but let's say, okay, there's a job I've been offered, if I get it, I have to buy fake papers. If I get caught with fake papers, that's a federal offense so I'll be screwed, and, I mean, I'm closer than I've ever been to getting my papers. I don't want to mess it up with something like that so I can't get it later on.

Sergio chose to take the safe route in hopes of someday being able to work freely without worry. He did not want to jeopardize his chances by getting caught with illicit citizenship papers. Nevertheless, his frustration grew with the years he has had to wait. At the time, Sergio indicated that he was frustrated and felt stuck in one place. "When you don't have papers you're not really motivated . . . you can't go anywhere." Three years later his girlfriend was pregnant with his child, and he felt as though he needed to provide financial support to his new family. He took a full-time job at a factory and carpooled with a coworker, a Caucasian male and former skinhead.

One evening after work, local police pulled them over and searched his co-worker's vehicle. In addition to finding a small amount of drugs in the car, they also found a homemade explosive device. Sergio was charged as an accomplice to a federal crime and ordered to serve 3 years in prison. In addition to serving prison time, Sergio was to be deported.

Like Pedro and Sergio, Luz dropped out of school at an early age. Now, with few options, she works as a cashier at a Greek-owned hamburger restaurant where she makes minimum wage and is subjected to ongoing verbal harassment by her racist employer. She sees her status as the most salient barrier to success.

> If I had the papers I wouldn't be in the situation that I am, because I would fight for what I want. . . . Sometimes there's people that just want the papers, you know, and they don't do anything, and they're just like at home, whatever. But I want my papers to get ahead, and I think a lot of people do, too, so I could work here, so I could get something.

Identity

The condition of illegality not only constrains daily life, but can leave an indelible imprint on identity. Catarina, 21 years old, came to the United States when she was 8 years old. Her father had come to the United States before Catarina and acquired legal permanent residency through the legalization program of the 1986 Immigration Reform and Control Act. Catarina's mother joined her husband, who was working as a gardener, in Santa Ana, California, where much of his family had preceded him and from whom they were able to get a great deal of help and support. Catarina's mother, although undocumented, worked as a housekeeper. When she became pregnant, she returned to Mexico to deliver Catarina because delivery was cheaper there, and she was not yet used to life in Santa Ana. Because of her family's fateful decision, Catarina was not born in the United States and was not a citizen when she came back to the United States at age 8. Catarina's undocumented status has plagued her pursuits at education and has influenced her sense of identity.

Catarina finished high school with a 4.0 GPA but knew she could not attend the University of California because, at that time, undocumented students would have to pay nonresident tuition, thousands of dollars more than regular tuition. Consequently, she went to community college and later transferred to a University of California campus. By this time, California law had changed as a result of Assembly Bill (AB) 540 so that students like Catarina could attend the university and pay instate tuition, with the proviso that they could not receive financial aid. When she heard AB 540 passed, Catarina said, "I cried, I cried. I was with my dad in my living room. My sister follows a lot of the legal stuff, and we had helped sign stuff to send to Governor Davis. We were involved, I was involved in student government in my community college, and it was like finally something, justice."

At the time of the interview, Catarina was finishing her senior year at the university, had a 3.9 GPA, and intended to apply to graduate school. Her father had acquired US citizenship and had sponsored his wife and children for legal residence, which Catarina was now in the process of obtaining.

Catarina identifies herself as Mexican. She does so because she is an immigrant and not a Chicana or Mexican American, which she associates with being US-born. But she also recognizes that society has pushed her toward emphasizing Mexican as an identity. For Catarina, her experiences as an undocumented immigrant have influenced her identity. Because she has not had the rights and privileges that come with being US-born and being a citizen, Catarina says she does not "think like a Mexican-American." As she said,

Having the barriers that I had, or not having all the opportunities that I see that a lot of the students have, and they might not be taking advantage of them for different reasons. I know I'm no one to criticize their decisions, but I think that's what really makes me consider myself a Mexican. I am an immigrant, immigrant Mexican. . . . You know you are not [American] because society keeps telling you that you're not. You don't have the opportunities that a Mexican American has, because you don't have the social security. So you have to make the decision. I don't fit in here. They don't want me in here. Then I fit there, with Mexicans. . . . I think if you have obstacles to integrating, one, they don't want you to integrate. Obviously, they have the obstacles for you not to integrate, so you get to the point where you know what, I don't want to integrate, whether you will eventually want me to integrate for any reason, I am no longer willing to integrate.

Despite her frustration with the obstacles she has faced, Catarina desires US citizenship because of the opportunities and rights it imparts. As she put it, "You need it [citizenship] in order to move on. If I am going to work hard, why not get the benefits?" Catarina also realizes that even though she identifies as Mexican, she is also American in many ways and that living in the United States for most of her life has shaped her sense of self and made her life different from if she had stayed in Mexico. Concerning what it means to be American, she said,

It can mean different things. It can mean being acculturated into American culture. It can mean having loyalty for America, for example, after September 11, I felt American. And it's amazing because regardless of political inequalities, I think of my life and what would it have been if I had not been here. And here I am. There are obstacles, but it's better. It's better here even with the inequalities. I guess it's human nature. We just want something better.

Abjectivity as a Way of Life

As the comments of the 1.5-generation undocumented Latinos testify, they are not living the lives they imagined for themselves. They grew up in US society and culture. The significant part of their education was in the United States, and, like other youth, they were for the most part inculcated in the values, desires, drives, ethics, and cultural practices of US youth. This is not to say that they abandoned, or did not carry around with them, cultural beliefs and practices of their countries of birth. They did, after all, live within families where they and their parents were immigrants. But that does not diminish the fact of lives lived in the United States, where they also learned about educational expectations, career goals, and the rites of passage so eagerly awaited by adolescents and young adults. However, even with the internalization of much of the culture of the larger society, their lack of immigration status places them closer to the structural position of undocumented immigrants who came as adults. It was also in this context that illegality and abject status came to frame their lives at a critical stage in their lives, the moment when they are making plans for their future and their move from the security of home to increasing engagement with the larger society.

The subjective experience of an abject status as related to illegality intersects harshly with issues of the economy, national policy, and power. During the early years of their lives, they became incorporated into the nation through their social relationships and public school experiences. Then, as they became aware of their lack of legal residency, they felt cast out, forced to live in the world as illegal subjects. They experienced a trauma of sorts, one that destabilized their sense of self. They were forced to come to terms with what the condition of illegality meant for their lives and their futures. Their bodies are the targets of disciplinary practices—biopolitics—which are designed to constrict their mobility and to construct subjective understanding of their lives as undocumented immigrants. But because their practices and subjective experiences were also often similar to those which constitute belonging among those born in the United States, our interviewees desired inclusion, to be considered as having qualified lives, as subjects in and of the nation.

The voices heard here indicate bitter lessons learned. With the awakening reality of their abject status as socially constituted noncitizens, these young people came to realize they were not like their peers. Even though they may have come to believe the civic lessons so essential to citizenship and to hold dear the values driving the American Dream, the illegality that defined their abject status left them with a clear sense of their difference. As noncitizens, they were full of discardable potential. No matter how hard they worked or how they self-disciplined, applied themselves, and self-engineered their very beings, they were to remain on the sidelines, waiting, leading abject lives on the margins of society, desiring government documentation of their presence. Knowing they have more to offer society and themselves, they wait for the possibility that future changes to immigration laws would someday ameliorate their condition. Some wilted under such pressure, while others resisted, pursued education and training, struggled to survive economically, contributed to organizations working to change the nation's immigration laws, and maintained hope in a future where they would be allowed full participation in society. For example, of the 76 in-depth interviews conducted during or after the immigrant marches of 2006, 65 had participated in at least one march.[23] This includes all but one of the interviewees quoted in this paper. Another 42 of the in-depth interviewees, including Catarina, Cesar, Misto, Grace, Esperanza, and Miguel, have contributed their time to organizations working to promote passage of the DREAM Act.

We interpret these acts of resistance as acts of cultural citizenship, which Flores and Benmayor (1997:15) define as a broad range of activities that disadvantaged groups use to claim space and rights in society. However, their lives are narrowly circumscribed by a multitude of regulations that protect citizens and ensure the persistence of an abject population against which citizens are defined, such as policies regarding immigration, detention, deportation, access to social services, medical care, driver's licenses, Social Security cards, bank accounts, work authorization, and many other micropractices of control. Despite, or even because of, these constraints on their lives, many of the young people examined here assert their cultural citizenship through their political activities and by continuing their education.[24] These acts blur the boundaries between objects and subjects of political power and are important forms of resistance to the condition of abjectivity that informs and frames their lives.

Finally, although 1.5-generation undocumented Latinos engage in both self-disciplining and resistance, their full integration into society is on hold. Their fates—whether they will continue living in a state of illegality, be allowed to become legal permanent residents, or be deported—are unknown to them. In the meantime, there is the suffering that goes along with the contradictions of being raised in a society that finds you discardable. Focusing on abjectivity among the undocumented 1.5 generation draws our attention to the practices of power that help construct the abject, such as laws targeting immigrants. But by no means is abjectivity limited in its applicability. There is much to be learned about the subjective understanding of living in an abject status among various individuals and groups who find themselves relegated to such a status.

By way of a postscript, young undocumented Latinos continue to have their fates and hopes raised and dampened by public policies and polarized political discourse. Under President Obama, the threat of deportation for undocumented immigrants actually increased. In 2009, for example, 387,790 people were deported, a 5% increase over 2008, the last year under George W. Bush's administration (Medrano 2010). In addition, the federal Secure Communities program, which works in cooperation with local police to locate undocumented immigrants, received criticism for deporting immigrants with minor offenses and for splitting apart families (Preston 2011a). Then, on July 26, 2011, Representative Luis Gutierrez (Illinois) was arrested for protesting, outside the White House, the one millionth deportation by the Obama administration, about half the number deported over 8 years under George W. Bush (DHS

2011:95). However, in a dramatic change in policy, the Obama administration, in August 2011, began reviewing all deportation cases in order to separate criminals from noncriminals. Those who have not been convicted of a crime would possibly receive a suspension of deportation and be allowed stay, and would also possibly be able to apply for work permits (Preston 2011b). This policy has raised the hopes of many. As one 21-year-old undocumented student who was brought to the United States as a boy and whose mother is facing deportation put it: "It makes me happy and hopeful. I hope they go through my mother's case, stop her deportation and, if possible, get her a work permit" (Goffard et al. 2011). While possibly reducing the risk of deportation for some of the undocumented 1.5 generation, it does not solve the problem of their lack of citizenship—rather, it creates another subclass of individuals living in limbo. The new deportation policy does not provide undocumented immigrants with a path to citizenship, which is something only Congress can do. Until Congress acts, the young people examined here will continue to live with uncertain futures.

NOTES

Reprinted with permission from the University of Chicago Press. This essay originally appeared in *Current Anthropology* 53, no. 3 (June 2012): 255–81.

1   See American Heritage Dictionary of the English Language, 4th ed. (Boston: Houghton Mifflin, 2006), s.v. "abject."

2   For examples of Kristeva's influence on scholars examining abjectivity, see Butler (1999); Chavez (2008); Ferguson (2002); Inda (2002, 2006); Willen (2007).

3   See Uli Linke's (2006) argument that the state also has a corporeal grounding.

4   Paul Rabinow and Nikolas Rose (2006:197) provide a sharper definition to Foucault's rather vague concept of biopolitics: "We can use the term 'biopolitics' to embrace all the specific strategies and contestations over problematizations of collective human vitality, morbidity and mortality; over the forms of knowledge, regimes of authority and practices of intervention that are desirable, legitimate and efficacious."

5   Agamben (1998) notes that Foucault did not apply his insights to twentieth-century totalitarian states and their concentration camps.

6   Although our focus is on the United States, we recognize that the lives of the children of immigrants vary across nation-states according to laws of citizenship and national philosophies and practices of inclusion. For information on a large multicountry project on this topic currently underway, see the Integration of the European Second Generation, available at http://www.tiesproject.eu/component /option,com_frontpage/Itemid,1/lang,en/. See also Maurice Crul and Liesbeth Heering's (2008) work among second-generation Turks and Moroccans in Amsterdam, and the research of the Organization for Economic Cooperation and Development (OECD 2007) for Europe. See also Kamal Sadiq's (2005, 2008) research on India, Malaysia, Indonesia, and Bangladesh.

7   There is no consensus on the cutoff age for the 1.5 generation. We use under 15 years of age in our analysis.

8   Problems also arise when children raised in the United States return, either voluntarily or involuntarily, back to their country of origin; see Boehm (2008); Hamann, Zúñiga, and Sánchez García (2006).

9   We understand that minors also migrate unaccompanied by parents or other family members. For our discussion here, we focus on undocumented youth who migrate and live with parents or other familial guardians.

10 For a discussion of the legal construction of the "illegal" and the "Mexican illegal alien," see Mae Ngai's (2004) book *Impossible Subjects*.

11 For research on California Assembly Bill 540 and its impact on undocumented students' lives, see Abrego (2006, 2008); Gonzales (2007, 2008a, 2008b); Olivas (1995).

12 Details of IIRIRA are available at http://www.ows.doleta.gov/dmstree/pl/pl_104–208.pdf.

13 According to the National Immigration Law Center (http://www.nilc.org/immlawpolicy/DREAM/Dream001.htm), the Development, Relief, and Education for Alien Minors (DREAM) Act (S. 1545), introduced on July 31, 2003, was reintroduced in the Senate on November 18, 2005. It passed the Senate Judiciary Committee on March 27, 2006. However, Congress failed to pass immigration reform, and with it the DREAM Act, in either 2006 or 2007.

14 Confirmation from the UC Irvine Office of Research Administration Institutional Review Board was received December 9, 2005 (HS# 2005-4671).

15 Both listed and unlisted numbers were included, avoiding potential bias due to exclusion of households with unlisted numbers (SSI 1990). In addition, telephone survey findings may not be generalizable to families without telephones. In Orange County, however, approximately 94% of Latinos and 99% of whites have telephones (CSCDC 1995). Despite these high proportions, there is still a limitation based on some members of the population without phones, e.g., recent immigrants and the unemployed.

16 The percentages cited in the discussion are based on the total of 799 Latinos who answered the question.

17 When asked if they felt as if someone was showing prejudice toward them or was discriminating against them because of their race or ethnicity in the past year, 13.1% of older migrating Latinos (the 1.0 generation) said yes, compared to 21.7% of the 1.5-generation Latinos and 24.8% of US-born Latinos. For the 1.0- and 1.5-generation Latinos, there was not a significant difference by immigration status, although the 1.5ers (and the second generation) were more likely to perceive discrimination in school, whereas the 1.0 generation were more likely to believe they faced discrimination in the workplace and when trying to find an apartment or house.

18 For a more extensive examination of the tension between acculturation, transitioning to late adolescence and early adulthood, and illegality, or the transition to illegality, see Gonzales (2008a, 2011).

19 See also Chavez (1998, chap. 9).

20 For a more in-depth discussion of the ways in which familial, institutional, and community mediators differently shaped respondents' trajectories, see Gonzales (2010, 2011).

21 For more on *matrículas*, see Varsanyi (2007).

22 This disdain for jobs held by their immigrant parents is common among US-born and raised children, as Kasinitz et al. (2008:173–204) found among the second generation in their extensive New York study.

23 For an example of second-generation Mexican American youth in San Diego, California, and their participation in the marches of 2006, see Getrich (2008).

24 For more on cultural and social citizenship, see Dwyer (2004); Ong (1996); Rosaldo (1997); Sassen (2003); Schiller and Caglar (2008); Stephen (2003).

REFERENCES

Abrego, Leisy Janet. 2006. "I can't go to college because I don't have papers": Incorporation Patterns of Latino Undocumented Youth. *Latino Studies* 4: 212–231.

Abrego, Leisy Janet. 2008. Legitimacy, Social Identity, and the Mobilization of Law: The Effects of Assembly Bill 540 on Undocumented Students in California. *Law and Social Inquiry* 33(3):709–734.

Agamben, Giorgio. 1998. *Homo Sacer: Sovereign Power and Bare Life*. Stanford, CA: Stanford University Press.

Agamben, Giorgio. 2005. *State of Exception*. Chicago: University of Chicago Press.

Auyero, Javier, and Debora Swistun. 2007. Confused Because Exposed: Towards an Ethnography of Environmental Suffering. *Ethnography* 8(2):123–144.

Basch, Linda, Nina Glick Schiller, and Cristina Szanton Blanc. 1994. *Nations Unbound: Transnational Projects, Postcolonial Predicaments, and Deterritorialized Nation-States*. Amsterdam: Gordon & Breach.

Bhabha, Homi K. 1994. *The Location of Culture*. London: Routledge.

Biehl, João Guilherme. 2005. *Vita: Life in a Zone of Social Abandonment*. Berkeley: University of California Press.

Bloch, A., and M. Chimienti. 2011. Irregular Migration in a Globalizing World. *Ethnic and Racial Studies* 34(8): 1271–1285.

Bloch, A., N. Sigona, and R. Zetter. 2009. *"No right to dream": The Social and Economic Lives of Young Undocumented Migrants in Britain*. London: Paul Hamlyn Foundation. [NS]

Bloch, A., N. Sigona, and R. Zetter. 2011. Migration Routes and Strategies of Young Undocumented Migrants in England: A Qualitative Perspective. *Ethnic and Racial Studies* 34(8): 1286–1302.

Boehm, Deborah A. 2008. "For my children": Constructing Family and Navigating the State in the U.S.-Mexico Transnation. *Anthropological Quarterly* 81(4): 777–802.

Boehm, Deborah A. 2011. "Here/not here": Contingent Citizenship and Transnational Mexican Children. In *Everyday ruptures: children, youth, and migration in global perspective*. Cati Coe, Rachel Reynolds, Deborah A. Boehm, Julia Meredith Hess, and Heather Rae-Espinoza, eds., 161–173. Nashville, TN: Vanderbilt University Press.

Bosniak, Linda S. 1998. The Citizenship of Aliens. *Social Text* 56:29–35.

Bosniak, Linda S. 2000. Universal Citizenship and the Problem of Alienage. *Northwestern University Law Review* 94(3):963–984.

Bourdieu, Pierre. 1992. Rites As Acts of Institution. In *Honor and grace in anthropology*. J. G. Peristiany and J. Pitt-Rivers, eds., 79–89. Cambridge: Cambridge University Press.

Bourdieu, Pierre, and Loïc Wacquant. 2000. The Organic Ethnologist of Algerian Migration. *Ethnography* 1(2): 173–182.

Bunis, Dena, and Guillermo X. Garcia. 1997. New Illegal-Immigration Law Casts Too Wide a Net, Critics Say. *Orange County Register*, March 31, news sec.

Butler, Judith. 1997a. *Excitable Speech: A Politics of the Performative*. New York: Routledge.

Butler, Judith. 1997b. *The Psychic Life of Power: Theories in Subjection*. Stanford, CA: Stanford University Press.

Butler, Judith. 1999. *Gender Trouble: Feminism and the Subversion of Identity*. New York: Routledge.

Butler, Judith. 2004. *Precarious Life: The Powers of Mourning and Violence*. London: Verso.

Campos, Belinda, Christine Dunkel Schetter, Julia A. Walsh, and Marc Schenker. 2007. Sharpening the Focus on Acculturative Change: ARSMA-II, Stress, Pregnancy Anxiety, and Infant Birthweight in Recently Immigrated Latinas. *Hispanic Journal of Behavioral Science* 29(2):209–224.

Chavez, Leo R. 1998. *Shadowed Lives: Undocumented Immigrants in American Society*. 2d ed. Ft. Worth, TX: Harcourt & Jovanovich.

Chavez, Leo R. 2001. *Covering Immigration: Popular Images and the Politics of the Nation*. Berkeley: University of California Press.

Chavez, Leo R. 2008. *The Latino Threat: Constructing Immigrants, Citizens, and the Nation*. Stanford, CA: Stanford University Press.

Chavez, Leo R., F. Allan Hubbell, Shiraz I. Mishra, and R. Burciaga Valdez. 1997. Undocumented Immigrants in Orange County, California: A Comparative Analysis. *International Migration Review* 31(2): 88–107.

Comfort, Megan M. 2008. *Doing Time Together: Love and Family in the Shadow of Prison*. Chicago: University of Chicago Press.

Cornelius, Wayne A. 1982. Interviewing Undocumented Immigrants: Methodological Reflections Based on Fieldwork in Mexico and the United States. *International Migration Review* 16:378–411.

Coutin, Susan Bibler. 2000a. Denationalization, Inclusion, and Exclusion: Negotiating the Boundaries of Belonging. *Journal of Global Legal Studies* 7:585–594.

Coutin, Susan Bibler. 2000b. *Legalizing Moves: Salvadoran Immigrants Struggle for U.S. Residency*. Ann Arbor: University of Michigan Press.

Coutin, Susan Bibler. 2007. *Nations of Emigrants: Shifting Boundaries of Citizenship in El Salvador and the United States*. Ithaca, NY: Cornell University Press.

Coutin, Susan Bibler. 2008. Deportation of Salvadorans Who Immigrated to the U.S. as Children: Preliminary Report. CARECEN, San Salvador.

Coutin, Susan Bibler, and Connie McGuire. 2011. Transnational Alienage and Foreignness: Deportees and Foreign Service Officers in Central America. Paper presented at the Humanitarianism and Migration conference, University of Colorado, Boulder, March 4.

Crul, Maurice, and Liesbeth Heering, eds. 2008. *The Position of the Turkish and Moroccan Second Generation in Amsterdam and Rotterdam: The TIES Study in the Netherlands*. Amsterdam: Amsterdam University Press.

CSCDC (California State Census Data Center). 1995. 1990 Census of the Population and Housing. Summary Tape File 4. Sacramento: California Census Data Center.

De Genova, Nicholas P. 2002. Migrant "Illegality" and Deportability in Everyday Life. *Annual Review of Anthropology* 31:419–447.

De Genova, Nicholas P. 2005. *Working the Boundaries: Race, Space, and "Illegality" in Mexican Chicago*. Durham, NC: Duke University Press.

De Genova, Nicholas P. 2008. "American" Abjection: "Chicanos," Gangs, and Mexican/Migrant Transnationality in Chicago. *Aztlan: A Journal of Chicano Studies* 33(2): 141-174.

De Genova, Nicholas P. 2010. the Deportation Regime: Sovereignty, Space, and the Freedom of Movement. in *the Deportation Regime: Sovereignty, Space, and the Freedom of Movement*. N. D. Genova and N. Peutz, eds., 33-65. Durham, NC: Duke University Press.

Delson, Jennifer. 2005. Profile of James Gilchrist. *Los Angeles Times*, April 11, B2.

Derrida, Jacques. 1993. Circumfession. In *Jacques Derrida*. George Bennington and Jacques Derrida, eds. George Bennington, trans. Chicago: University of Chicago Press.

DHS (Department of Homeland Security). 2011. *Yearbook of Immigration Statistics: 2010*. Washington, DC: US Department of Homeland Security, Office of Immigration Statistics.

Dingeman, Katie, and Susan Bibler Coutin. 2012. The Ruptures of Return: Deportation's Confounding Effects. In *Punishing Immigrants: Policy, Politics, and Injustice*. Charis M. Kubrin, Marjorie S. Zatz, and Ramiro Martinez Jr., eds. New York: New York University Press.

Dressler, William W. 1996. Culture, Stress, and Disease. In *Medical Anthropology: Contemporary Theory and Method*. C. F. Sargent and T. M. Johnson, eds., 252-271. Westport, CT: Praeger.

Dwyer, Peter. 2004. *Understanding Social Citizenship*. Bristol: Policy Press.

Farley, Tillman, Al Galves, L. Miriam Dickinson, and Maria de Jesus Diaz Perez. 2005. Stress, Coping, and Health: A Comparison of Mexican Immigrants, Mexican-Americans, and Non-Hispanic Whites. *Journal of Immigrant Health* 7(3): 213-220.

Farmer, Paul. 2003. *Pathologies of Power: Health, Human Rights, and the New War on the Poor*. Berkeley: University of California Press.

Ferguson, James. 2002. Global Disconnect: Abjection and the Aftermath of Modernism. In *The Anthropology of Globalization: A Reader*. J. X. Inda and R. Rosaldo, eds., 136-153. Malden, MA: Blackwell.

Flores, William V., and Rina Benmayor. 1997. Constructing Cultural Citizenship. In *Latino Cultural Citizenship: Claiming Identity, Space, and Rights*. W. V. Flores and R. Benmayor, eds. 1-23. Boston: Beacon.

Fortuny, Karina, Randy Capps, and Jeffrey S. Passel. 2007. *The Characteristics of Unauthorized Immigrants in California, Los Angeles, and the United States*. Washington, DC: Urban Institute.

Foucault, Michel. 1977. *Discipline and Punish*. London: Tavistock.

Foucault, Michel. 1990 (1976). *The History of Sexuality: An Introduction*, vol. 1. New York: Vintage.

Foucault, Michel. 1997. The birth of biopolitics. In *Ethics, Subjectivity and Truth*. P. Rabinow, ed., 73-80. New York: New Press.

Gerstle, Gary. 2001. *American Crucible: Race and Nation in the Twentieth Century*. Princeton, NJ: Princeton University Press.

Getrich, Christina M. 2008. Negotiating Boundaries of Social Belonging: Second-Generation Mexican Youth and the Immigrant Rights Protests of 2006. *American Behavioral Scientist* 52(4): 533-556.

Goffard, Christopher, Paloma Esquivel, and Teresa Watanabe. 2011. U.S. Will Review Cases of 300,000 Illegal Immigrants in Deportation Proceedings. *Los Angeles Times*, August 19, A1.

Goldring, L., C. Berinstein, and J. K. Bernhard. 2009. Institutionalizing Precarious Migratory Status in Canada. *Citizenship Studies* 13(3): 239–265.

Gonzales, Roberto G. 2007. Wasted Talent and Broken Dreams: The Lost Potential of Undocumented Students. *Immigration Policy In-Focus* 15(13): 1–12.

Gonzales, Roberto G. 2008a. Born in the Shadows: The Uncertain Futures of the Children of Unauthorized Mexican Migrants. PhD dissertation, University of California, Irvine.

Gonzales, Roberto G. 2008b. Left out but Not Shut Down: Political Activism and the Undocumented Student Movement. *Northwestern Journal of Law and Social Policy* 3(2): 219–239.

Gonzales, Roberto G. 2010. On the Wrong Side of the Tracks: The Consequences of School Stratification Systems for Unauthorized Mexican Students. *Peabody Journal of Education* 85(4):469.

Gonzales, Roberto G. 2011. Learning to Be Illegal: Undocumented Youth and Shifting Legal Contexts in the Transition to Adulthood. *American Sociological Review* 74(4): 602–619.

Gordon, Colin. 1991. Governmental Rationality: An Introduction. in *the Foucault Effect: Studies in Governmentality*. G. Burchell, C. Gordon, and P. Miller, eds., 1–51. Chicago: University of Chicago Press.

Hamann, Edmund T., Víctor Zúñiga, and Juan Sánchez García. 2006. *Pensando en Cynthia y su hermana*: Educational Implications of United States–Mexico Transnationalism for Children. *Journal of Latinos and Education* 5(4): 253–274.

Inda, Jonathan X. 2002. Biopower, Reproduction, and the Migrant Woman's Body. In *Decolonial Voices: Chicana and Chicano Cultural Studies in the 21st century*. A. J. Aldama and N. H. Quinones, eds., 98–112. Bloomington: Indiana University Press.

Inda, Jonathan X. 2006. *Targeting Immigrants: Government, Technology, and Ethics*. Malden, MA: Blackwell.

Isin, Engin, and Greg M. Nielson, eds. 2008. *Acts of Citizenship*. London: Zed.

Kanstroom, Daniel. 2007. *Deportation Nation: Outsiders in American History*. Cambridge, MA: Harvard University Press.

Kasinitz, Philip, John H. Mollenkopf, Mary C. Waters, and Jennifer Holdaway. 2008. *Inheriting the City: The Children of Immigrants Come of Age*. Cambridge, MA: Harvard University Press/Russell Sage.

Kelly, David. 2005. Minutemen Prepare to Lay Down the Law. *Los Angeles Times*, April 2, A-15.

Kristeva, Julia. 1982. *Powers of Horror: An Essay on Abjection*. New York: Columbia University Press.

Linke, Uli. 2006. Contact Zones: Rethinking the Sensual Life of the State. *Anthropological Theory* 6(2): 205–225.

McDonnell, Patrick J. 1994. Prop. 187 Win Spotlights Voting Disparity. *Los Angeles Times*, November 10, A3.

McGreevy, Patrick, and Anthony York. 2011. Gov. Jerry Brown Signs DREAM Act for State's Illegal Immigrants. *Los Angeles Times*, October 8. http://latimesblogs.latimes

.com/california-politics/2011/10/gov-jerry-brown-announces-he-has-signed-bill-allowing-illegal-immigrants-access-to-college-aid.html.

Medrano, Lourdes. 2010. Obama as Border Cop: He's Deported Record Number of Illegal Immigrants. *Christian Science Monitor*, August 12.

Menjívar, Cecilia. 2006. Liminal Legality: Salvadoran and Guatemalan Immigrants' Lives in the United States. *American Journal of Sociology* 111:999–1037.

Merleau-Ponty, Maurice. 1962. *Phenomenology of perception.* C. Smith, trans. London: Routledge & Kegan Paul.

Merleau-Ponty, Maurice. 1968. *The Visible and the Invisible.* A. Lingus, trans. Evanston, IL: Northwestern University Press.

Negron-Gonzales, Genevieve. 2009. Hegemony, Ideology and Oppositional Consciousness: Undocumented Youth and the Personal-Political Struggle for Educational Justice. In *Institute for the Study of Social Change.* Working paper no. 36. University of California, Berkeley.

Ngai, Mae M. 2004. *Impossible Subjects: Illegal Aliens and the Making of Modern America.* Princeton, NJ: Princeton University Press.

Nyers, Peter. 2003. Abject Cosmopolitanism: The Politics of Protection in the Anti-Deportation Movement. *Third World Quarterly* 24(6): 1069–1093.

OECD (Organization of Economic Cooperation and Development). 2007. *Jobs for Immigrants,* Vol. 1 of *Labor Market Integration in Australia, Denmark, Germany and Sweden.* Paris: OECD.

Olivas, Michael A. 1995. Storytelling out of School: Undocumented College Residency, Race, and Reaction. *Hastings Constitutional Law Quarterly* 22: 1019–1086.

O'Loughlin, Marjorie. 1998. Paying Attention to Bodies in Education: Theoretical Resources and Practical Suggestions. *Educational Philosophy and Theory* 30(3): 275–297.

Ong, Aihwa. 1996. Cultural Citizenship As Subject-Making: Immigrants Negotiate Racial and Cultural Boundaries in the United States. *Current Anthropology* 37(5): 737–762.

Paral, Rob. 2006. Undocumented Immigration by Congressional District. Immigration Policy Brief, October. http://www.robparal.com/downloads/undocumented_in_CDs.htm.

Passel, Jeffrey S., and D'Vera Cohn. 2009. A Portrait of Unauthorized Immigrants in the United States. Washington, DC: Pew Hispanic Center.

Peutz, Nathalie. 2006. Embarking on an Anthropology of Removal. *Current Anthropology* 47(2): 217–241.

Portes, Alejandro, and Rubén G. Rumbaut. 2001. *Legacies: The Story of the Immigrant Second Generation.* Berkeley: University of California Press.

Preston, Julia. 2011a. Federal Policy Resulting in Wave of Deportations Draws Protests. *New York Times*, August 17, A12.

Preston, Julia. 2011b. U.S. Issues New Deportation Policy's First Reprieves. *New York Times*, August 23, A15.

Rabinow, Paul, and Nikolas Rose. 2006. Biopower Today. *Biosocieties* 1:195–217.

Ramirez, Eddy. 2008. Should Colleges Enroll Illegal Immigrants? http://www.usnews.com/articles/education/2008/08/07/should-colleges-enroll-illegal-immigrants.html.

Reed-Danahay, Deborah, and Caroline B. Brettell. 2008. *Citizenship, Political Engagement, and Belonging: Immigrants in Europe and the United States*. New Brunswick, NJ: Rutgers University Press.

Rincón, Alejandra. 2008. *Undocumented Immigrants and Higher Education: sí se puede*. New York: LFB.

Rosaldo, Renato. 1997. Cultural citizenship, inequality, and multiculturalism. In *Latino Cultural Citizenship*. W. V. Flores and R. Benmayor, eds., 27–38. Boston: Beacon.

Rumbaut, Rubén G. 2004. Ages, Life Stages, and Generational Cohorts: Decomposing the Immigrant First and Second Generations in the United States. *International Migration Review* 38:1160–1205.

Sadiq, Kamal. 2005. When States Prefer Non-Citizens over Citizens: Conflict over Illegal Immigration into Malaysia. *International Studies Quarterly* 49: 101–122.

Sadiq, Kamal. 2008. *Paper Citizens: How Illegal Immigrants Acquire Citizenship in Developing Countries*. Oxford: Oxford University Press.

Sargent, Caroline F., and Stépanie Larchanché-Kim. 2006. Liminal Lives: Immigration Status, Gender, and the Construction of Identities Among Malian Migrants in Paris. *American Behavioral Scientist* 50(1):9–26.

Sassen, S. 2002. The Repositioning of Citizenship: Emergent Subjects and Spaces for Politics. *Berkeley Journal of Sociology* 46:4–24.

Sassen, S. 2003. The Repositioning of Citizenship: Emergent Subjects and Spaces for Politics. *New Centennial Review* 3(2): 41–66.

Sayad, A. 1999. *La Double absence: des illusions de l'émigré aux souffrances de l'immigré*. Paris: Editions du Seuil.

Schiller, Nina Glick, and Ayse Caglar. 2008. "And ye shall possess it, and dwell therein": Social Citizenship, Global Christianity, and Non-Ethnic Immigrant Incorporation. in *Citizenship, Political Engagement and Belonging: Immigrants in Europe and the United States*. D. Reed-Danahay and C. B. Brettell, eds., 203–225. New Brunswick, NJ: Rutgers University Press.

Sigona, N. 2012. "I've too much baggage": The Impact of Legal Status on the Social Worlds of Irregular Migrants. *Social Anthropology/Anthropologie Sociale* 20(1): 50–65.

SSI (Survey Sampling, Inc.). 1990. *Statistical Analysis of Sample*. Fairfield, CT: SSI.

Stephen, Lynn. 2003. Cultural Citizenship and Labor Rights for Oregon Farmworkers: The Case of Pineros y Campesinos Unidos del Nordoeste (PCUN). *Human Organization* 62(1): 27–38.

Stephen, Lynn. 2007. *Transborder Lives: Indigenous Oaxacans in Mexico, California, and Oregon*. Durham, NC: Duke University Press.

Stephen, Lynn. 2008. Negotiating Racial Hierarchies and Promoting Indigenous Culture: Oaxacan Immigrant Youth in California and Oregon. Paper presented at the Annual Meeting of the American Society for Ethnohistory, Eugene, Oregon, November.

Stout, David. 1978. Ruling Deals Blow to Deportation Policy. *New York Times*, May 19.

Suárez Navaz, Liliana. 2004. *Rebordering the Mediterranean: Boundaries and Citizenship in Southern Europe*. New York: Berghahn.

Suárez Navaz, Liliana, and Colectivo Al-Jaima, eds. 2007. *Las luchas de los "Sin Papeles" y la extensión de la ciudadanía: perspectivas críticas desde Europa y Estados Unidos* (The struggles of the "Sans Papiers" and the extension of citizenship: critical perspectives from EU and USA). Madrid: Traficantes de Sueños.

Suárez Navaz, Liliana, and Mercedes Jiménez. 2011. Menores en el campo migratorio transnacional: los niños del centro "Drari d'sentro" (Minors in the transnational migratory field "Drari d'sentro"). *Papers* 96(1): 1–33.

Suárez-Orozco, Carola, Hirokazu Yoshikawa, Robert R. Ternashi, and Marcelo M. Suárez-Orozco. 2011. Growing Up in the Shadows: The Developmental Implications of Unauthorized Status. *Harvard Educational Review* 81(3): 438–471.

Tormey, Anwen. 2007. "Everyone with eyes can see the problem": Moral Citizens and the Space of Irish Nationhood. *International Migration* 45(3): 69–100.

Tsing, Anna Lowenhaupt. 2005. *Friction: An Ethnography of Global Connection*. Princeton, NJ: Princeton University Press.

US Census Bureau. 2006. Orange County, California: Selected Social Characteristics in the United States; 2006, American Community Survey. http://factfinder.census.gov/servlet /ADPTable?_bm=y&-geo_id=05000US06059&-context=adp&-ds_name=ACS_2006 _EST_G00_&-tree_id=306&-_lang=en&-_caller=geoselect&-format=.

US Census Bureau. 2010. State and County Quickfacts: Orange County, California 2010. http://quickfacts.census.gov/qfd/states/06/06059.html.

US ICE. 2011. ICE Arrests More Than 2,900 Convicted Criminal Aliens, Fugitives in Enforcement Operation Throughout All 50 States, 18 Weapons Seized During Operation. News release. http://www.ice.gov/news/releases/1109/110928washingto ndc.htm.

Varsanyi, Monica. 2007. Documenting Undocumented Migrants: *Matriculas Consulares* As Neoliberal Local Membership. *Geopolitics* 12(2): 299–319.

Wallace, Rodrick, and Robert G. Wallace. 2004. Adaptive Chronic Infection, Structured Stress, and Medical Magic Bullets: Do Reductionist Cures Select for Holistic Diseases? *BioSystems* 77(1–3): 93–108.

Willen, Sarah S. 2007. Toward a Critical Phenomenology of "Illegality": State Power, Criminality and Abjectivity Among Undocumented Migrant Workers in Tel Aviv, Israel. *International Migration* 45(3): 8–38.

Wimmer, A., and N. Glick Schiller. 2002. Methodological Nationalism and Beyond: Nation-State Building, Migration and the Social Sciences. *Global Networks* 2(4): 301–334.

Yuval-Davis, Nira. 2006. Belonging and the Politics of Belonging. *Patterns of Prejudice* 40(3): 197–214.

Zhang, Li. 2001. *Strangers in the City: Reconfigurations of Space, Power, and Social Networks Within China's Floating Population*. Stanford, CA: Stanford University Press.

Zilberg, Elana. 2004. Fools Banished from the Kingdom: Remapping Geographies of Gang Violence Between the Americas (Los Angeles and San Salvador). *American Quarterly* 56:759–779.

Regions of Refuge in the United States: Issues, Problems, and Concerns for the Future of Mexican-Origin Populations in the United States

CARLOS G. VÉLEZ-IBÁÑEZ

Exactly 30 years ago, Gonzalo Aguirre Beltrán, one of the founding figures of Mexican anthropology, gave the first Bronislaw Malinowski Award address in my hometown of Tucson, Arizona. Without delving into any proposition of cosmic convergence, I find it remarkable that I should be honored for work closely identified with the Mexican population on the northern side of what may be termed the Greater Mexican Southwest (Bauman 1993). In that address, Beltrán laid out the various influences in the emergence of a Mexican applied anthropology and how the new Mexican state played a key role in the national integration of a people. He articulated the concept of *"regiones de refugio"* (regions of refuge) to describe isolated and frozen semicolonial ecological shelters that are regionally stratified and made up of indigenous populations in the countryside dominated by Latinos in cities (Beltrán 1979). All are intertwined within a series of caste relations that exercise control over the land, energy, and movement of subordinated Indian populations (Beltrán 1979:31).[1] For Beltrán such stratification could be resolved in part through the critical education of all groups, but more importantly through structural national reintegration in which the social relations of production, distribution, and consumption were altered in favor of more equitable economic and social treatments. The nation-building mission depended upon such changes, since resistance to democratization and equity would be normative at the regional level.

The nation-building project was promulgated not only by Beltrán, but earlier by Manuel Gamio, who is considered the father of Mexican anthropology and especially applied anthropology. His pathbreaking research on Mexican immigration to the United States in 1926 and 1927 was the first Mexican-led research on this population in the United States. Gamio, like Beltrán, also saw the state as the focal integrating force for a newly emergent Mexican revolutionary national identity and its heterogeneous populations. For Gamio, the northern border states were crucial, and he sought to take advantage of the repatriation process of the 1930s to tap into the knowledge base returning Mexican immigrants acquired in the United States.[2] His research, funded by the Social Science Research Council, was designed in part to test out some of his national theories (Gamio 1930; Paredes 1931). In fact, President Lázaro Cárdenas (1934–1940), in conjunction with American agricultural combines like Anderson and Clayton, developed specific agricultural and irrigation projects to attract this population back to northern Mexico. This program was developed by Gamio to balance the extreme structural and technical inequalities between nations (Walsh 2000).

Thus, Beltrán provided an important theoretical and methodological heuristic for understanding Mexican and Latin American populations and the applied approaches to be used for Mexican nation building. Gamio provided the first indication of the importance of northern Mexican populations, specifically those influenced by and born in the United States. Now, it seems to me that we must embark on an applied anthropological mission almost as important as the ones these two giants in Mexican anthropology undertook so long ago. We will face new "regions of refuge" in the United States that require thoughtful solutions comparable to nation building because of the demographic growth of the Mexican-origin population over the next 25 years—a population that will be as large as the population of Mexico was in 1962 (over 37 million) and one that in 50 years will be as large as the population of Mexico was in 1975 (over 60 million) (Lahmeyer 2002).

In the 30 years since Beltrán's first Malinowski Address, the Mexican-origin population in the southwestern United States emerged dramatically, and it continues to be fueled by the ever-present structural inequalities of the political economies of the United States and Mexico. These inequalities have reproduced new regions of refuge for large segments of the Mexican-origin population, not unlike those Aguirre Beltrán described for minority groups in Latin America and especially Mexico. For Beltrán (1979:18), minority groups, like colonized peoples, "experience the effects of the process of domination." But minority groups, while entitled to the benefits of citizenship by the national society, are denied them by what we now term regional or local levels of articulation.

For Beltrán, what marked minority group status was basically cultural differences that were accentuated regionally or locally and that did not allow the minority group to participate fully in the national society. In a sense, it is the cultural characteristics of the minority group that are used as rationales by dominant populations to justify continued supremacy at local and regional levels. Eventually minority groups come to believe they are so different culturally that their separation becomes normative.

Acute stratification, caste-like relations between populations, ecological isolation, institutional avoidance, political domination, economic subordination, unequal treatment, social distance, and lack of legal protection are consequences of real or imagined differences in culture. Citizenship, which differentiates the colonized from national minorities, allows minorities to change culturally and assimilate individually into the dominant culture. Nevertheless, depending on the severity of the cultural differences between groups, regions of refuge are created in relation to minorities regardless of the demographic differences between groups.

Several factors differentiate the regions of refuge Beltrán described for Mexico and Latin America from those in the United States. The U.S. versions have been created as: 1) an aftermath of the enormous loan repayments to the World Bank and the United States; 2) the structural relations between the U.S. and Mexico and, most recently, the North American Free Trade Agreement's (NAFTA) penetration throughout Mexico; 3) the neoliberal policies of the Mexican regime, including the elimination of credit to rural farmers, ejidos, and cooperatives, and the privatization of ejido lands; 4) the creation of border industries; and 5) the service and agricultural labor markets in the United States. These factors have served to stimulate migration as part of the commodity-exchange relations developed over the past 150 years between the U.S. and Mexico. As a result, Mexico's foreign debt alone:

[in 2000] stands at more than $161 billion, 181% higher than in the early 1980s, when the country declared a moratorium on payments. The current debt is equivalent to 40.3% of the gross domestic product of 1998, according to a report released by the Finance Secretariat in 2000. In this same year, each of Mexico's 96 million inhabitants owes $1,608, 96.3% higher than the 1980 figure. (Cevallos 2000)

These transnational capitalist extractions are creating a country almost prostrate economically, politically, socially, and ecologically. Mexico and its population are in fact a scrapped satellite periphery of the United States and international banking and monetary agencies.

The already developed structures of economic and political limitations in the United States incorporate Mexican Latinos, as well as indigenous Zapotecs, Mixtecs, and Mixes, fleeing economic and social adversity. All become "minority groups" in the new refuge, with indigenous populations even more disadvantaged economically, linguistically, and institutionally.

In the United States, such regions include an ideology that identifies Mexicans as "cheap" commodities, incorporated into poor or near-poor economic sectors and housed in restricted and equally poor urban or rural ecologies. These are part of a complex of marginal physical localities and regions, isolated from institutions, integrated into exploitive economies, unprotected in health, poorly represented politically, undereducated, and suffering from multiple social maladies. When coupled with cultural rationalizations of difference and a dominant ideology that values "whiteness," they intertwine to produce new regions of refuge.

Such regions have emerged at different periods of American history: first after the Mexican War, then again following the Mexican Revolution, and for the last 35 years in different ecological niches of the southwestern United States. The development of such regions may be formed for domestic and migrating populations. In rural areas, Mexicans inhabit colonias, townships, and villages where infrastructural investment is minimal, political representation nonexistent, educational and social services poor, and basic amenities absent. Subregions also emerge in cities like Los Angeles, Dallas, and Phoenix, where neighborhoods are in decay and Mexicans are incorporated into restricted barrios. For the most part, home ownership is denied them, or it is in the midst of econiches characterized by urban infrastructures like freeways, off-ramps, industrial parks, warehouses, junkyards, and graffiti-covered public housing that sits next to macadam-covered school grounds surrounded by cyclone fences topped by barbed wire.

Beltrán would recognize the stratification, the poverty, the miseducation, and the contending ethnic and class conflicts he described for Mexico in these new regions of refuge, especially those along the U.S.-Mexican border. He would not recognize how such regions could be developed for human habitation by the sheer determination and will of a vibrant population situated at the most disadvantageous positions within such regions. These modern refuges are likely to remain for at least the next 25 to 50 years because of the continuing economic and regional asymmetry between Mexico and the United States. The U.S. relies on poorly paid persons to fill the service, agricultural, and domestic roles necessary to provide low-cost vegetables, cheap milk and chickens, affordable nannies and domestic cooks, maids, gardeners, construction workers, and hundreds of sundry occupations few desire.

Not since the Mexican Revolution, which pushed almost a million Mexicans into the United States, and whose children became the "Mexican American Generation," has such a shift occurred in North America (Hall and Coerver 1988: 126). The size and scope of this Mexican movement rivals westward migration in the United States during the 19th century (Gonzalez 2000).

Part I. The Future in the Present: The Demography of Mexican-Origin Peoples

Education, income, labor, politics, health, social and community development, and culture are deeply interrelated. In conjunction with their physical environments, these issues emerge to form regions of refuge that present serious challenges at local, regional, national, and transnational levels. They must be examined and extrapolations to the future suggested if applied social sciences are to play strong programmatic and policy roles now or in the future.

Even a modest demographic expansion of the Mexican-origin population over the next 25 to 50 years has enormous consequences for what I have termed "the distribution of sadness" (Vélez-Ibáñez 1996). By this I mean the overrepresentation of Mexican-origin populations in the bilges of poverty, and among the undereducated, underemployed, and underrepresented who suffer from poor mental and physical health and lack in protection. They are also overrepresented in penal institutions and as war casualties. These most recent versions of regions of refuge have been forming for 25 years or more as the great restructuring of world economies emerged. Applied anthropology on both sides of the U.S.-Mexican border has enormous responsibilities in research and application, responsibilities comparable to those faced by Aguirre Beltrán's nation-creating period. We will have to deal with the many aspects of these new regions of refuge for many years to come.

On the other hand, for the Mexican-origin population there are also indicators of strong educational advancement between generations, a decline in poverty among the U.S. born, an increased percentage of upper-income households, and the creation of many small- and medium-sized businesses and enterprises. There has been a creative explosion in the performance arts and literature, as well as solid academic advancement in the social sciences, the biological and material sciences, and in medicine and engineering. These academic achievements could not have been possible without affirmative action and programs developed to increase the educational pipelines for the disadvantaged. But we have barely put a dent in the structure of these new regions of refuge.

The 2000 Census identified 35.2 million Latinos in the United States, of which almost 20.6 million were of Mexican origin (60%). Remarkable growth

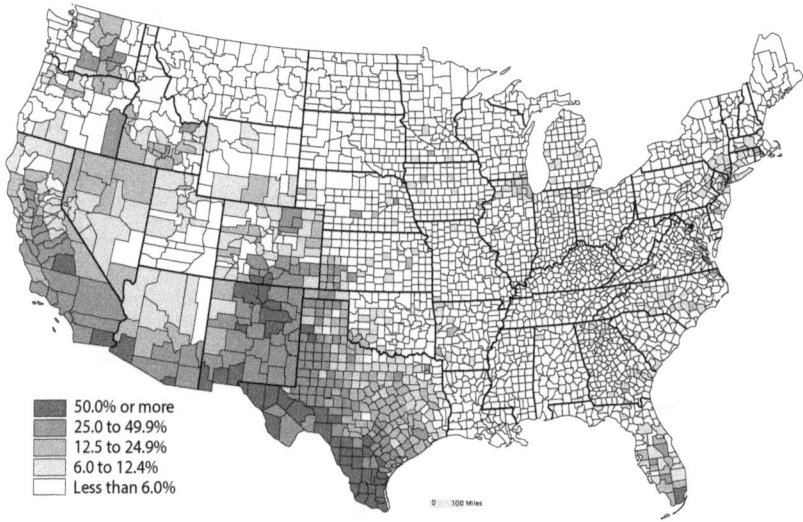

FIGURE 19.1. Hispanic Population as a Percent of the Total Population, by County, 2000. Source: U.S. Census Bureau, Census 2000 Redistricting.

characterized this population during the 20th century: 1.3 million Mexicans were reported in the 1930 census; 2.3 million persons of Spanish surname were reported in 1950; and 9.1 million persons of Spanish origin were reported in 1970.[3]

Mexican-origin populations continue to concentrate in the states bordering Mexico, but they are rapidly expanding to the Midwest and South (see figure 19.1). Recent Mexican immigrants have joined populations established since the eighteenth century to increasingly occupy urban landscapes in cities like Los Angeles, Santa Fe, San Antonio, San Diego, Tucson, San Francisco, and Albuquerque.[4] Cities like Phoenix, Dallas, Houston, and Long Beach have also witnessed dramatic population growth, especially between 1970 and 1980 when the total Latino population virtually doubled. In urban border areas like Brownsville-Harlingen, El Paso, and Laredo, Texas, Mexicans comprise over 60 percent of the population. The Los Angeles–Long Beach, California, area has the highest number of Latino households, of which the great majority is of Mexican origin (U.S. Census Bureau 1995). Over 70 percent of the Mexican-origin population in the United States lives in California and Texas and another 15 percent in Arizona, Illinois, Colorado, and New Mexico (Groggier and Trejo 2002:10). In each, regions of refuge constitute political ecologies of stratification and inequality, marked by cultural diversity and ethnic boundaries that are the analogs of economic constrictions and limitations of social structure.

Of the 10 places of 100,000 or more with the highest percentage of Hispanics, except for Miami, all are in largely Mexican-dominant cites of the South-

TABLE 19.1. Ten Places of 100,000 or More Population With the Highest Percent Hispanic, 2000

Place	Total Population	Hispanic Population	Hispanic Percent of Total Population
East Los Angeles, Calif.*	124,283	120,307	96.8
Laredo, Tex.	176,576	166,216	94.1
Brownsville, Tex.	139,722	127,535	91.3
Hialeah, Fla.	226,419	204,543	90.3
McAllen, Tex.	106,414	85,427	80.3
El Paso, Tex.	563,662	431,875	76.6
Santa Ana, Calif.	337,977	257,097	76.1
El Monte, Calif.	115,965	83,945	72.4
Oxnard, Calif.	170,358	112,807	66.2
Miami, Fla.	362,470	238,351	65.8

* East Los Angeles, California, is a census-designated place and is not legally incorporated.
Source: U.S. Census Bureau, Census 2000 Summary File 1.

west (see tables 19.1 and 19.2). With the exception of New York and Miami, cities in which Mexicans are dominant also constitute the largest Hispanic markets. The Strategy Research Corporation estimated the buying power of all Hispanics in the United States for 2002 at almost $430 billion—greater than the buying power of either Mexico ($404 billion) or Brazil ($398 billion). In fact, there are more Hispanics in the United States than in Peru and Venezuela (Whitefield 2001). There is also an increasingly visible presence not only in the rural Southwest, but also in the Great Plains, Midwest, and Southwest.

There are over 2,000 impoverished, rural colonias totaling approximately 1 million persons, in Arizona, California, New Mexico, and Texas. Colonias vary between "settlements" and communities.[5] Made up largely of clandestine makeshift housing, they are characterized by inadequate or nonexistent water supplies, sewage, or electrification, and surface drainage systems. The populations themselves are largely poor, with sizeable families, and sustained by a combination of local and migrant agricultural work. Figure 19.2 shows their distribution.

Colonias are part of the continuing "Mexicanization" of rural areas throughout the southwestern United States. After much of the non-Mexican population migrated out, Mexicans revitalized dormant or dying townships and villages (Allen and Rochin 1996:1, 3, 8, 18). Population projections for the foreseeable future provide a highly charged series of projections of increased Mexican-origin growth, both by birth and migration, and the continued development of highly complex regions of refuge.

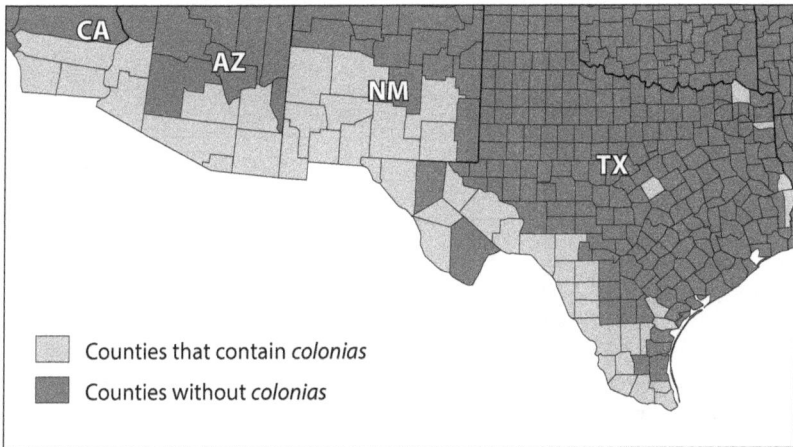

FIGURE 19.2. Location of *Colonias* Along the U.S.-Mexico Border. Source: Galán 2000.

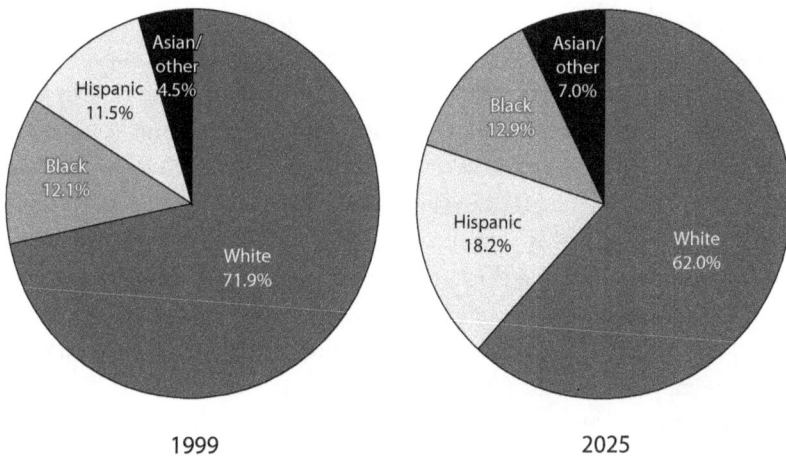

1999

2025

FIGURE 19.3. Racial and Ethnic Composition of the United States, 1999 and 2025.
Note: White, Black, and Asian/other categories exclude Hispanics, who may be of any
race. The Asian/other category includes American Indians, Eskimos, Aleuts, and Pacific
Islanders. Totals may not add to 100% due to rounding. Source: Population Reference
Bureau 2002.

Figure 19.3 provides the latest projections for the racial and ethnic composition in the twenty-first century.[6] This remarkable growth does not comprehensively tell the tale. For that we must look at the projected percent of native and
foreign-born population in 2100. We do not have a disaggregated projection
yet, but based on the 2000 census figures we can assume the same 60 percent
will be persons of Mexican origin.

TABLE 19.2. Ten Largest Places in Total Population and in Hispanic Population, 2000

	Total Population		Hispanic Population		Hispanic Percent of Total Population
	Number	Rank	Number	Rank	
New York	8,008,278	1	2,160,554	1	27.0
Los Angeles	3,694,820	2	1,719,073	2	46.5
Chicago	2,896,016	3	753,644	3	26.0
Houston	1,953,631	4	730,865	4	37.4
Philadelphia	1,517,550	5	128,928	24	8.5
Phoenix	1,321,045	6	449,972	6	34.1
San Diego	1,223,400	7	310,752	9	25.4
Dallas	1,188,580	8	422,587	8	35.6
San Antonio	1,144,646	9	671,394	5	58.7
Detroit	951,270	10	47,167	72	5.0
El Paso	563,662	23	431,875	7	76.6
San Jose	894,943	11	269,989	10	30.2

Source: U.S. Census Bureau, Census 2000 Summary File 1.

By using this approximate percentage we can surmise that by 2025, the Mexican-origin population will comprise approximately 37 million and by 2050 slightly less than 60 million. Mexico's total population will number over 160 million in 2050 (U.S. Census Bureau 2000a). With a growth rate of less than 0.5 percent by 2050, the Mexican population will grow at approximately 1 million persons per year. By 2100 it will total almost 214 million (World Bank 2002). By 2100, almost 115 million persons of Mexican origin will live in the United States. The Mexican-origin population in the United States is very young—it averages 24.5 years in comparison to 38 for the rest of the U.S. population—and age is an important consideration in all projections.

What then are the portents of this impressive growth for education, income, labor, politics, health, social and community organization, and culture? And what are the most salient issues that will emerge for the United States and Mexico?

Educational Attainment

Table 19.3 illustrates educational attainment of Mexican-origin men and women by generation and in comparison to other groups. Educational attainment for the immigrant generation is extremely low—almost half have less than 8 years of schooling. Only about 20 percent have completed secondary school, and less than 5 percent have completed high school. In the second generation, however, there is a dramatic increase for both men and women, but educational attainment slows down between the second and third generation (Groggier and Trejo 2002:11–13).

Educational attainment for this generation should be much greater than the preceding one, but Anglos are still three times more likely to graduate from college (Groggier and Trejo 2002:13). The third generation is almost four times less likely than Anglos to earn a postgraduate degree and half as likely as African Americans (Groggier and Trejo 2002). It should be remembered, however, that the great majority of Mexican-origin persons come from families that have been in this country less than two generations; at least half were born in Mexico and another fifth have at least one immigrant parent (Groggier and Trejo 2002:10).

Immigrant status does influence the undereducation of Mexican-origin persons in the United States, but the weak second to third generation educational influence is very worrisome. Gender is also an important factor, since Mexican women between the second and third generations have a lower completion rate at the bachelor's and postgraduate levels than men.

The intellectual loss for those who do not complete college cannot be overemphasized, especially for women who bear children and who are the primary socializing agents for subsequent generations. Such loss is felt in fragile communities where education is sorely needed. The lack of income for most Mexican communities is directly tied to the lack of education—both in the presence of those with less than an eighth-grade education and in an educational and opportunity system that does not seem to provide the intellectual or social scaffolding necessary for the third generation of Mexican-origin men and women.

And there is a fly in the ointment. Mean earnings of Anglos with a bachelor's degree are over $55,000, while Hispanics (read Mexican) average a little over $42,000; at the master's level, Anglos earn over $65,000 compared to $57,662 for Hispanics (U.S. Census Bureau 2000b). The difference between Anglo and Hispanic mean earnings for the same educational attainment must be related to noneconomic causes and factors. Such disparity could be part of the remaining structural bias within a political economy that reflects broader structural inequalities of an American region of refuge.

Income, Poverty, and Labor

In 2000, 24 percent of the Mexican population lived in poverty, compared to 9 percent of Anglos and 22 percent of blacks (Population Resource Center 2001). In fact, most Mexican households are below the median income of $38,000 and 71 percent of the population earns less than $30,000 a year. Figure 19.4 illustrates the unequal distribution of resources between foreign born and native born: 65.6 percent of Mexican immigrants and their U.S.-born

TABLE 19.3. Educational Attainment in the United States (Excluding California and Texas), by Race/Ethnicity and Generation, Ages 25-59

Education Level	Mexican Americans	
	Recent Immigrant	Earlier Immigrant
Men		
Avg. years of education	8.8	8.4
Percentage with 8 years ot less	44.9	48.7
Some high school	20.2	18.6
High school graduate	21.5	20.2
Some college	7.7	8.4
Bachelor's degree	3.9	3.4
Postgraduate degree	1.9	0.8
Total	100.0	100.0

Education Level	Mexican Americans	
	Recent Immigrant	Earlier Immigrant
Women		
Avg. years of education	8.5	9.0
Percentage with 8 years or less	48.3	43.6
Some high school	18.7	18.7
High school graduate	19.5	20.6
Some college	8.0	12.8
Bachelor's degree	4.5	3.1
Postgraduate degree	1.1	1.2
Total	100.0	100.0

Note: Recent immigrants are defined as those who arrived in the United States within approximately 10 years of the survey date.

Source: 1996–1999 CPS ORG data.

	2nd Generation	3rd+ Generation	3rd+ Generation Whites	3rd+ Generation Blacks
	12.1	12.4	13.5	12.5
	10.9	6.0	2.1	3.4
	14.3	16.1	7.0	14.3
	36.5	35.6	34.6	41.7
	24.4	27.2	26.2	26.7
	8.6	11.1	20.0	10.2
	5.4	4.0	10.1	3.6
	100.0	100.0	100.0	100.0

	2nd Generation	3rd+ Generation	3rd+ Generation Whites	3rd+ Generation Blacks
	12.1	12.2	13.5	12.8
	9.8	7.5	1.5	2.6
	14.7	14.0	6.1	13.9
	33.7	37.6	35.8	37.5
	29.2	29.7	28.7	29.9
	8.9	8.3	19.5	11.6
	3.7	2.9	8.5	4.6
	100.0	100.0	100.0	100.0

Percent

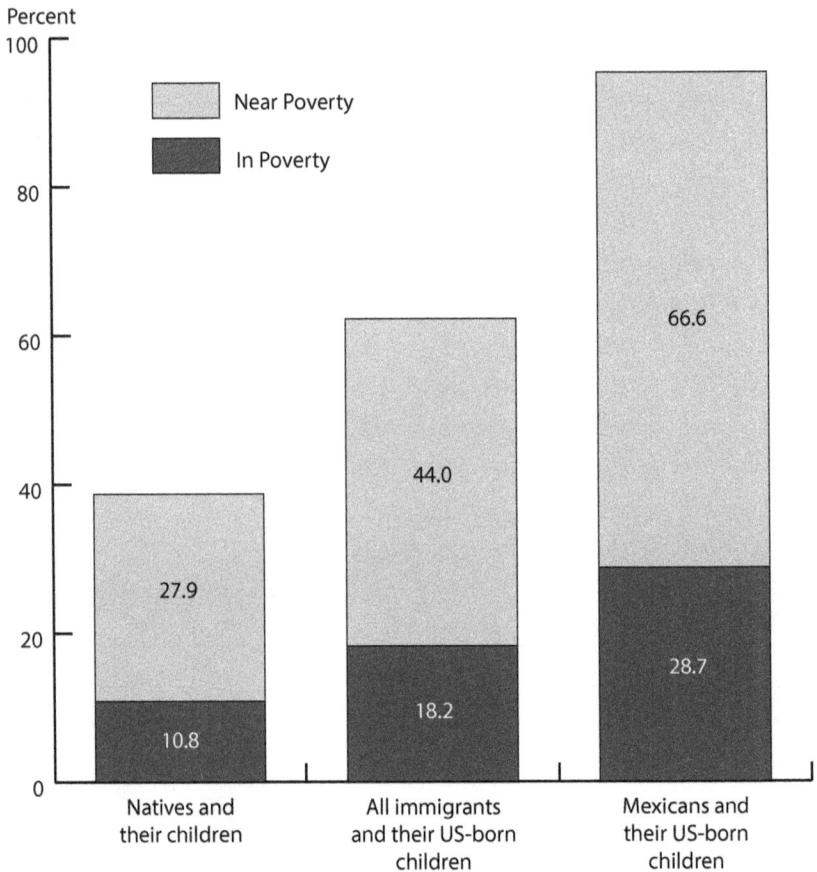

FIGURE 19.4. Poverty and Near Poverty in the U.S.
Note: U.S.-born children (under age 18) of immigrant mothers are included in the figures for all immigrants and Mexican immigrants are excluded from the figures for natives. Near poverty is defined as less than 200% of the poverty threshold. Source: Camarota 2001.

children live in or near poverty while only 27.9 percent of their native counterparts and their children live in or near poverty. Mexican immigrants and their U.S.-born children are 20 percent poorer than their counterparts from other cultural systems (Camarota 2001).

Figure 19.5 shows the stark income differences between natives and legal and illegal Mexican immigrants. The annual income of undocumented workers is less than half that of natives and three-quarters that of documented workers.

Between 1975 and 1990 the number of Latinos earning over $75,000 a year tripled, and the number of persons earning $50,000–$75,000 rose to 20 percent of the entire Latino population (U.S. Census Bureau 1997). Yet in comparison to other populations, Latinos did not fare well. For example, in California,

Dollars

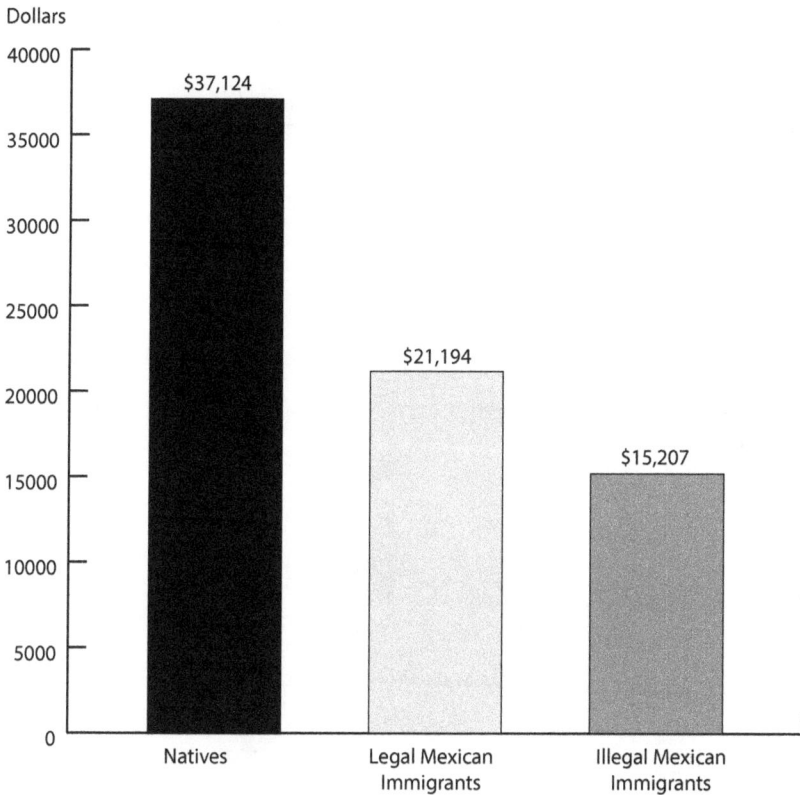

FIGURE 19.5. Estimated Average Annual Income by Legal Status for Mexican
Immigrants, 1999
Note: Figures for income from all sources for persons 21 and over who worked at least
part time in 1999. Source: Camarota 2001.

where more than 40 percent of the Mexican-origin population lives, the median income for Anglos was $27,000 a year in 1999. Asians were close behind
at $24,000 and African Americans were at $23,000. But Latinos, the largest
minority group in California, had a median income of only $14,500 (Lopez,
Ramirez, and Rochin 1999:9).

In 2001, only about 20 percent of Mexican-origin workers were employed in
managerial or professional capacities. For the most part, the structure of the
labor force reflects income distribution and educational levels (U.S. Census
Bureau 2001). Table 19.4 presents the occupational structure for U.S. workers
of Hispanic and Mexican origin.

Yet, labor, income, and educational statistics say little of the massive contributions the Mexican labor force makes to the American economy. Documented or undocumented, first generation to third, Mexican-origin populations

TABLE 19.4. Employed Mexican, Puerto Rican, and Cuban-Origin Workers by Sex, Occupation, Class of Worker, and Full- or Part-Time Status (in thousands)

Category	Total Hispanic Origin		Mexican Origin	
	2000	2001	2000	2001
Sex				
Total (all civilian workers)	14,492	14,714	9,364	9,577
Men	8,478	8,556	5,718	5,805
Women	6,014	6,159	3,646	3,771
Occupation				
Managerial and professional speciality	2,036	2,150	1,107	1,190
Executive, administrative, and managerial	1,072	1,148	602	667
Professional speciality	964	1,002	504	523
Technical, sales, and administrative support	3,504	3,556	2,060	2,143
Technicians and related support	303	338	171	198
Sales occupations	1,385	1,402	816	843
Administrative support, including clerical	1,816	1,816	1,073	1,102
Service occupations	2,867	3,000	1,818	1,884
Private household	251	234	133	124
Protective service	208	244	112	144
Service, except private household and protective	2,408	2,521	1,573	1,616
Precision production, craft, and repair	2,075	2,176	1,456	1,527
Mechanics and repairers	522	547	323	354
Construction trades	1,004	1,088	739	801
Other precision production, craft, and repair	550	541	394	373
Operators, fabricators, and laborers	3,202	3,134	2,202	2,225
Machine operators, assemblers, and inspectors	1,416	1,320	976	941
Transportation and material moving occupations	662	697	423	473
Handlers, equipment cleaners, helpers, and laborers	1,125	1,118	804	811
Construction laborers	281	300	220	230
Other handlers, equipment cleaners, helpers, and laborers	844	818	583	582
Farming, forestry, and fishing	807	698	721	607

Source: 2001 Household Data Annual Averages: Table 13, Employed Mexican, Puerto Rican, and Cuban-Origin by Sex, Occupation, Class of Worker, and Full- or Part-Time Status, U.S. Census Bureau, 2001.

support many parts of the economy and participate in myriad labor activities that few others dare to approach. More importantly, they are creating regions of refuge from little or nothing, revitalizing many urban and rural communities, and inventing ways to survive in very difficult circumstances. This population is creating and developing the foundations of and structure for civil society under debilitating circumstances. This has profound implications for what constitutes citizenship.

Part II. A Miniethnography of a Region of Refuge[7]

Creative, stubbornly persistent, and many times suffering from overwork and underpayment, Mexican-origin populations create social platforms from whence future generations will emerge. In the megacities of Los Angeles and Chicago, and in the growing urban hubs of Dallas, Phoenix, and Albuquerque, large networks of communities emerge amidst weak urban infrastructures, poor educational systems, oppressive physical ecologies, and, in some cases, the presence of dangerous gangs and urban violence. In rural areas, Mexican-origin populations, at great sacrifice and human cost, give life to barren landscapes or revive dead towns and villages. I am amazed at the many ways these people continue to thrive and suffer simultaneously. I would like to provide a simple example from my current work in New Mexico.

EL RECUERDO: A COLONIA OF NEW MEXICO

New Mexican colonias are largely situated along the serpentine Rio Grande, which begins in the Rocky Mountains of Colorado and flows 3,200 kilometers to the Gulf of Mexico. The 37 odd colonias in Doña Ana County, where the majority of the colonias have developed, all straddle either the Rio Grande or Interstate 25 and State Highway 32. The rest of the 148 colonias in New Mexico either border the Rio Grande or the international border.

Most colonias border agricultural fields and adjoining roads and are largely situated to provide labor to the surrounding farms. Four main venues offer colonia residents employment in the formal and informal economies: more than 70 percent of men and women work in agriculture; another 10 percent are labor contractors, foremen, and truck haulers; and a small percentage own very small businesses, such as informal garages, junkyards, hidden grocery stores, and home child care. A small but significant percentage (20%) engage in the underground economy, transporting undocumented relatives from Mexico to the United States and other less benign activities. This creates the basis for class mobility as well as transregional mobility and the establishment of colonia-like settlements in Alabama, Oklahoma, Mississippi, and other agricultural states thousands of miles away.

"El Recuerdo" is a perfect model for those colonias. It encompasses 80 acres and was first inhabited in 1987 after the original owner—a local rancher—sold four 10-acre parcels of undeveloped land to different families for $1,000 per acre. These families subdivided their parcels into ¾- to 1-acre plots and sold them for $3,000 each. By 1994, approximately 10 families had moved to Recuerdo, and by 2001, 31 households had been established in a combination of trailers, mobile homes, and finished concrete block homes. Most residents borrowed money from relatives, banks, moneylenders, or the landowner, who charged 10 percent interest per month. The owner could—and did—easily foreclose on the land and acquire any structures built on the property for failure to make a monthly payment. This credit relationship hung like Damocles's sword over the colonos and forced many to seek out moneylenders or become involved in underground activities to ensure they could make their land payment.

Lots generally are no less than three-fourths of an acre, and construction usually follows a sequence of settlement: a trailer first, then hybrids with permanent structures attached, then houses built entirely of block or adobe construction. Of the 40 dwellings in El Recuerdo, 30 are connected trailers, some of which have been ensconced within family-built brick homes. Many have no access to sewage or gas lines, and all, at one time or another, suffered from the lack of electricity and running water.

Eventually residents create "miracle" communities out of nothing. *Colonos* (colonists) literally fight for basic water services and electricity. For the most part, colonos rely on septic tanks that often overflow or incomplete sewage lines that allow overflow in pools of partially filtered but untreated sewage. Needless to say, children suffer from high rates of gastric and pulmonary diseases, while over 80 percent of persons 25 and over suffer from traces of hepatitis A.

Of the 27 households sampled (3 were elsewhere during the research), 11 live in trigenerational arrangements, 6 in clusters of two or more households on the same lot, and 5 share a single hearth. Sixteen nuclear families occupy the rest of the colonia. Total population is 177 persons, with a mean of 6.7 persons per household. Annual income is less than $25,000. Table 19.5 illustrates the range of income sources and labor activities in the community.

Every three to four months, *brigadas de limpia* (clean-up brigades) scour the colonia for broken bottles, plastic bags, assorted paper, discarded wrappers, and other trash strewn about by the strong winds that come from out of the hot desert in the summer. In the winter—the rainy season—these same brigades try to cover the perennial potholes created by trucks and cars that run

TABLE 19.5. Income and Labor Activities in El Recuerdo

Formal Economy		Informal Economy		Underground Economy	
Activity	Frequency	Activity	Frequency	Activity	Frequency
Agricultural contractor	2	In-house store	2	Confidential	10
Agricultural wage laborer	16	Babysitting	2		
Agricultural skilled laborer	3	Animal husbandry	2		
Agricultural packing warehouses	2	Cockfighting	1		
Dairy	2	Junkyard	1		
Bus driver	1	Tandas	6		
Trucker/Entrepreneur	1				
Mechanic	2				
Disabled	2				
Retired	3				

Source: Vélez-Ibáñez n.d.

over roadways weakened from the heavy rains which pour through the colonia. Located in a flood plain, Recuerdo is often threatened by rain from the surrounding low hills, and flooding is common. Before its present development, part of El Recuerdo was used as a dump and another part was a pasture for cattle belonging to a noncolonia owner. People from Hatch and other colonias continue to dump unwanted materials there. Ten or so cattle continue to use the pasture; in the evening they graze through the community, plowing up flowerbeds and urinating and defecating on the colonia itself. Children often run about barefoot with the obvious consequences.

Most residents work on nearby dairy farms for minimum wages; a lucky few have service or construction jobs in a nearby city. About a third travel the migrant stream for three or four months when the crop cycle of the area's chili and onions slows to a trickle of production. Pecans and cotton are largely machine-picked, and labor is limited to gathering what the machines cannot collect.

During January and February, and again in May, colonos migrate to Alabama, Oklahoma, Kansas, and Mississippi. Almost every household owns two trucks and automobiles that are called *muebles* (furniture). The term is symbolic of the nomadic nature of migratory existence in which their households are carried literally with them to points far from the colonias themselves. The term also attempts to soften the utilitarian function of vehicles with a more familial sense because the travel is strenuous, tiring, and saps family resources.

Such travel is part of an elaborate and complex mechanism developed to fill agricultural labor needs in the southeastern United States. The process often is initiated by telephone from labor contractors who communicate with *cuadrilla* (labor group) leaders, who then recruit kin and friends. This aspect of the migrant process also provides an avenue for class formation. Some individuals begin the process by purchasing a second-hand truck and driving to the onion, pecan, and chili fields, where they bag, box, or shovel product onto the pick-up truck's bed for transfer to a warehouse or processing plant. In time they invest in a larger truck and eventually haul products to markets. Simultaneously, the same individuals become involved in labor contracting and lead the cuadrillas to Alabama, Mississippi, or another state needing labor. Once established, however, the same individual purchases a garage, grocery store, and restaurant/bar in the new town, since the cuadrillas sometimes establish "colonias" in these distant locales. The individual will then recruit relatives to work in these establishments. They, in turn, serve as the basis for community life and function as central nodes for further recruitment for a trustworthy mechanic, familiar food and articles, and a meeting place for isolated Mexican families in an alien Anglo world.

Formative class aspects emerge. Those who work in these new businesses avoid the fields and the migrant stream and establish a lower-middle-class existence without having to rely on the vagaries of agricultural labor. Thus, some relatives jump from manual labor in Mexico to petty businesses in the United States. It is in this process that an emergent middle class forms "off the backs of others."

When insufficient kin are available, telephone calls are made to Mexico (usually Guanajuato, Chihuahua, and Zacatecas), and a relative who is a smuggler will charge $700 per person to arrange for transportation from the point of origin to a safe house or hotel. In some cases, relatives will be transferred to a ranch in Mexico close to the border and then moved into New Mexico through well-elaborated routes and communication links, the latter usually involving cell phones that are difficult to tap and to trace. Once safely housed in the region, immigrants then may be moved to other regions and states. But such safety is often illusory since border checkpoints are well manned, surveillance apparatuses technologically sophisticated, and roaming Immigration and Naturalization Service (INS) agents very familiar with the routes traveled by the smuggler and his kin.

Danger, anxiety, and indeterminacy often fill colonia residents with dread. Too often relatives are arrested and vehicles impounded, the latter representing very hard-earned capital. It must also be said, however, that those engaged in this underground economy represent only a small percentage of all residents of this and other colonias.

Money is always scarce and seldom sufficient to accomplish many of the basic life-cycle functions. The question then arises, if income is mostly negative, how are lots and homes purchased, improvements made, gardens grown, children clothed, food purchased, automobiles and trucks afforded, and the basic costs of daily living met? How are emergencies like illness, immigration raids and deportation of household members to Mexico, visits to relatives, travel to Alabama, and the other sundry costs dealt with?

The simple answer is a constant balancing of debt, credit, income, and expenditure. Such balancing involves: 1) shuttling between informal and underground economies; 2) pooling available resources and participating in rotating credit associations; 3) borrowing from local banks and loan sharks or using credit cards; 4) creating margins of favorable return on goods purchased in pesos and sold in dollars; and, finally, 5) reneging on loans from formal or informal credit sources. I discuss each in turn.

These approaches are not exclusive one to the other. Households are large, and extended households serve as a kind of "corporate" group in sharing of resources. Different individuals within households and within the larger network may engage in one or more of these activities at the same time. Which of the activities is most important depends on the life cycle of the household(s) and the number of household members present.

But there is a constant struggle to keep the negative income ratio to less than 20 percent. Transportation, gasoline, and food take up 55 percent of expenditures. Of this 55 percent, 70 percent is paid in auto or truck payments to banks, finance companies, or individuals, with interest in the 13 to 16 percent range per month. Vehicle insurance adds another 15 percent to the monthly cost. Gasoline costs an average of $200 a month, which adds another 10–15 percent of gross costs. Thus, fluctuations in gasoline prices, costs of periodic mechanical dysfunctions, tire replacements, and upkeep adds another 10–15 percent to the 55 percent already spent on transportation and food. Any fluctuation will automatically move households toward a greater negative income percentage, making informal and underground activities mandatory. At times, this will mean total reliance on underground activities. Such activities yield very large returns, but they also accrue very large risks.

Pooling resources and participating in rotating credit associations is a second important balancing strategy. The former usually involves pooling income, wages, and future earnings to make an initial down payment on land, trailers, or automobiles. Land in the colonias costs between $5,000 and $10,000 per acre, and three-quarters of an acre is needed to build or place a trailer. Based on payments of $150 per month on a 10-year mortgage, the actual price may double by the end of the payment cycle. A second-hand trailer costs between $3,000 and $10,000. A down payment of 20 percent is usually followed with installments between $100 and $300 per month, with interest around 15 percent. Therefore, the level of credit indebtedness for lots, housing, and necessary infrastructure, when added to the 55 percent, rises to about 75 percent.

Once married, individuals call upon their parents and siblings for assistance. Where two or more generations share the same land, a cycle of debt continues as new housing creates new debts. Meanwhile, the original generation assumes the costs of the land.

Rotating credit associations (RCAs) have two major functions: debt reduction and purchase of gifts for rituals or to defray the costs of everyday needs. For the most part, the amount is no more than $200 a month, with a rotation of five to six months. At one time an individual may receive between $1,000 to $1,200 and considerable relief is noted, especially during slack periods of employment. Many seek to have their fund collection fall in May or June and for the most part RCAs do not operate during these periods. RCAs are mostly in the hands of women and play a less important role than familial pooling.

Borrowing from banks is the prerogative of households that have been in the colonia area for one year or more and have established credit with stores or have a record of steady employment. Banks use a combination of safeguards with less regard for collateral and with a greater dependence on the local networks of farmers who vouch for the reputation of their employees and provide income information to banks when loans are solicited. But banks never provide more than 75 percent of the estimated maximum of any given loan. According to them, no household should exhaust its credit because it will return for more during the Christmas holidays, when most households visit Mexico and in some cases collect rent from lands left in the hands of relatives. At least one bank officer is sincerely concerned that colonia residents are often on the brink of insolvency, and borrowing more will put them at risk for foreclosure. In addition, one bank officer wanted the colonia borrower to have a cushion in case of emergencies for relatives in Mexico, not an infrequent occurrence. In some cases bank officers will not approve credit cards, not because colonia residents are poor risks, but because they think colonia residents are simply unacquainted with the mail as the means of repayment.

At times, colonia residents take advantage of the Mexican border 75 miles to the south to purchase Mexican foodstuffs and religious items for resale in the colonias. Carbonated drinks, candies, bakery goods, flour, sugar, beans, and spices are sold in tiny home-stores or simply stored and advertised through the dense information networks of the colonias. The return on investment is limited, given transportation costs, the limited quantities allowed by U.S. Customs, and the increasing costs of items. About 20 percent of households may be involved in these activities.

Reneging on debts is the last of the possible balancing measures, and the least desirable. Reneging on bank loans places the household in even greater risk, since banks may be the only source of cash for emergencies. If lots or homes are used as collateral, the household's most valuable asset may be eliminated. Farmer-bank relations are often close and personal relations between bank officers and farmers are also dense. As a result, employers may garnish wages.

Borrowing and reneging on informal borrowing may have both social and physical consequences, depending on the relationship with the creditor. Reneging on a relative, colonia resident, or friend has far-reaching consequences— failure to pay a debt breaks *confianza* (mutual trust), the central value in the many reciprocal and obligatory relations between colonia residents. Since reciprocal relations based on exchange endure even though the commodities they entail may not, reneging on debts places relations based on other obligations in danger. The rupture of relations is simply too dangerous socially for colonia residents, given their negative income, marginal economic stability, immigration status, and sundry other uncertainties and indeterminacies.

"Loan sharking" may also be present, especially among men. For the most part, women do not participate in this underground credit economy. Men usually contact other men, who then contract someone engaged in other underground activities and who may lend money at weekly interest rates. Reneging on such debts may result in physical violence. In one case, the borrower dared the lender to collect his debt and the lender together with his father, brothers, and cousins ambushed the borrower and broke his kneecaps.

The political ecology of the colonias reflects the asymmetry of the interaction between the labor needs of industrial agriculture and the labor regulatory role of the nation-state. It also reflects the meager provisioning of Mexican households, coupled with the lack of available housing stock. While these are in fact poor households, their inhabitants are also innovative and develop inventive practices using all available materials, wages, relationships, and opportunities to establish their homes in the midst of often unsettling physical conditions.

Colonias are the manifestation of one type of human subsidy that meets the needs of industrial agriculture. The colonias serve as available sources of labor, thereby freeing the state and industry from providing the basic provisioning necessary to develop healthy communities. It is only with great political struggle and local organizing that services are introduced, community formation made possible, relatively stable households formed, and some of the basic infrastructure for community living provided.

In fact, industrial agriculture demands an initially underpaid, underprovisioned, and largely uninsured and unprotected labor force. Colonias function as important platforms from which to gain profits in a risky and uncertain enterprise, one beset not only with declining local, regional, national, and international market prices but also with all the usual cost demands in farming, such as transportation, processing, marketing, chemicals, and equipment.

At one level, the entire edifice is dependent on the subsidies provided by the colonias, since their formation is a cost borne by the inhabitants themselves and only later by institutions. The reciprocal relationships of extended households used in the colonias, such as the exchange of money, information, and favors, provide a modicum of security and the basis of community life. This social capital makes up for the lack of monetary capital available to colonos and serves as a subsidy to the local and regional economy. The structure of credit and debts is associated with this subsidy function as well and undergrids the entire process. The underground economy provides an added invisible subsidy—the recruitment of relatives to fill the work needs of agricultural interests. Costs associated with such recruitment are entirely in the hands of those being recruited, and the risks to smuggler-relatives are also entirely debited to them. In no case is agriculture bearing any risk or cost associated with this process.

On the other hand, class mobility for some individuals is guaranteed by the same subsidy system, just as it guarantees social and economic inequality that is the central principle of social development in all capitalist systems. These subsidies of sacrifice, invention, reciprocity, indebtedness, and community formation are crucial links in the chains of debt and credit accrued by colonos. Yet this colonia and the 2,000 others in rural areas, as well as the urban networks created in the largest of our cities, form the basis of civil discourse, community relations, and political empowerment through self-development. The basis of participatory citizenship in all polities consists of exactly these webs of relationships, and, whether documented or not, migrant, immigrant, or native born are due political recognition as such.

There are many social and physical costs for those engaged in this chain of labor, debt, and community formation. In literally millions of instances, these chains tie households and individuals to a broader system of national and transnational production and economic ecology. These create the underlying structural conditions that guarantee statistical and actual overrepresentations in what I have termed "the distribution of sadness." Their implications for the future are profound and their solution mandatory, given the sheer weight of projected demographic growth.

The solutions lay in recognizing these colonias as regions of refuge and in extending and recognizing them as civil entities with all rights and duties of recognition by supraregional states. Equally imperative is forming an articulated transnational plan, rather than piecemeal approaches presently applied by state and national authorities. At the present rate of colonia increase—7 percent per year—by 2050 very large portions of unsuitable locations for human habitation will be occupied by desperate populations integrated within exploitive, largely debilitating, and oppressive political ecologies.

Part III. The Distribution of Sadnesses: The Prices of Subsidizing Regions of Refuge

There are special costs to be paid by significant parts of the Mexican-origin population for their roles in subsidizing the American economy and in the development of these regions. These roles are situated in their poor educational achievement, integration at the lowest rungs of the occupational ladder, low income, and in the struggle to develop stable communities in the midst of nothing in rural areas or networks of relations in dangerous urban areas. I refer to the actual costs paid as the "distribution of sadness," in that these appear as bulges in the statistical distribution of mental and physical health problems, of premature deaths for young people, in the early and too frequent incarceration of young men, and in the political disempowerment of sizeable parts of the population. Among the most terrifying sadnesses are those of an overrepresentation in war. Once more, young Mexican-origin servicemen and women will be overrepresented in another U.S. international adventure; one in which they will again become physical and mental casualties of the dogs of war, led by failing old men who themselves largely escaped the call of their own generation.

PHYSICAL AND MENTAL SADNESSES

To be in or near poverty almost guarantees associations with certain types of illnesses. These are in part the consequences of low-wage employment, but equally important is having little or no health access or insurance. More than 40 percent of working Latino adults have no insurance and only 20 percent of all poor Latinos have medical coverage. In compassionate Texas, 39 percent of Hispanics between the ages of 18 and 64 have no medical coverage (Sumaya 2002). While listed as "Hispanic," more than 90 percent of the Texas Spanish-speaking population is of Mexican origin, and 30 percent of all Mexicans in the U.S. reside in Texas. Even more remarkable is that in this most compassionate state, formerly led by a most compassionate governor, and now led by a most compassionate president, 80 percent of employed Mexicans are not covered by health insurance.

In general, there is little wonder the death rates among Mexican-origin populations are considerably higher than those of other populations. Taking Arizona

TABLE 19.6. Average Age at Death from all Causes by Gender and Ethnicity in Arizona, 1990–2000

Year/ Gender	All Ethnic Groups[1]	White Non-Hispanic	Hispanic	Black	American Indian	Asian
1990						
Total	68.4	70.6	58.5	58.1	51.4	NA
Male	65.4	67.9	54.6	55.5	48.7	NA
Female	72.2	73.9	64.1	61.6	56.1	NA
1991						
Total	68.5	70.8	57.6	58.8	52.3	NA
Male	65.6	68.1	54.7	54.4	50.4	NA
Female	71.9	73.7	61.5	64.4	54.8	NA
1992						
Total	68.7	71.1	58.3	57.8	52.8	NA
Male	65.8	68.5	54.8	54.7	49.0	NA
Female	72.4	74.2	63.7	62.3	58.7	NA
1993						
Total	68.6	71.1	57.9	56.2	51.9	NA
Male	65.6	68.3	54.7	54.1	49.3	NA
Female	72.2	74.3	62.7	59.2	55.8	NA
1994						
Total	68.4	71.0	56.6	56.8	52.0	NA
Male	65.2	68.2	52.5	54.5	48.7	NA
Female	72.2	74.2	62.3	60.6	57.2	NA
1995						
Total	68.5	71.0	57.4	57.4	52.2	NA
Male	65.2	68.2	53.1	53.7	48.2	NA
Female	72.4	74.2	63.6	62.9	57.8	NA
1996						
Total	69.6	72.4	56.5	57.8	52.9	62.1
Male	66.1	69.2	52.6	54.9	49.9	60.6
Female	73.6	75.9	62.4	61.3	57.2	63.9
1997						
Total	71.0	73.1	61.3	61.9	55.4	64.2
Male	67.5	70.1	57.2	57.6	51.2	61.4
Female	74.9	76.3	67.4	67.7	61.4	68.0
1998						
Total	71.2	73.4	61.8	62.5	56.5	62.7
Male	67.9	70.5	57.4	59.4	53.2	60.8
Female	74.9	76.5	68.0	66.3	61.2	62.7

Year/ Gender	All Ethnic Groups[1]	White Non-Hispanic	Hispanic	Black	American Indian	Asian
1999						
Total	71.7	74.1	59.2	60.5	55.7	63.9
Male	68.8	71.5	56.2	57.8	51.8	62.3
Female	74.9	77.0	63.3	63.9	60.6	65.5
2000						
Total	71.6	73.9	59.2	60.8	55.4	62.3
Male	68.7	70.9	55.8	56.8	51.6	61.6
Female	74.9	77.0	63.7	65.8	60.4	63.0

Source: ADHS 2001: Table 2D-1.

1. Include records with other/unknown ethnic groups.

as a case in point (Table 19.6), the average age at death from all causes in 1990 was 54.6 years for Mexican males and 65.4 for Anglo males. Ten years later, in 2000, the average age of death by all causes for Mexican males was 55.9 and 70.9 for Anglo males (ADHS 2001). This gain for Anglos and stasis for Mexican-origin males is an artifact of health practices, labor, and homicide. As Table 19.6 shows, similar dismal average ages for African Americans and American Indians remained relatively unchanged except for a four-year increase in longevity for American Indians. Women in all cases fared better than men, but Anglo women had an average age at death in 1990 of 73.9, while Mexican women lived an average of 9 years less. This advantage grew for Anglo women to almost 14 years by 2000. In 1990, Mexican women lived an average of 10 years more than men, but 10 years later it had decreased to 8 years. The reason for the decrease is unknown.

What then accounts for such disparities between groups? For Mexican-origin populations in general, chronic illnesses remain untreated because of lack of insurance. Mexican-origin women suffer twice the rates of cervical cancer of Anglo women and have the highest mortality rates due to breast cancer (Intercultural Cancer Council 2001). The latter condition is primarily because only 38 percent of Mexican-origin women age 40 and older have regular screenings, and high cervical cancer rates are also due to the lack of screening procedures (Intercultural Cancer Council 2001). Mexican-origin men get hurt and are killed more often on the job than women, and they are more often victims of homicide than are either women or Anglos.

Accidents, most work-related, are the third highest cause of death among Latinos in general and apply to Mexican-origin populations even more so than other populations given the structure of occupational participation (Table 19.7). Malignant neoplasms are strongly associated with exposure to

TABLE 19.7. Ten Leading Causes of Death among Hispanics in the U.S., 1999

Rank	Hispanics in the United States
1	Diseases of heart
2	Malignant neoplasms, including neoplasms of lymphatic and hematopoietic tissues
3	Accidents (unintentional injuries)
4	Cerebrovascular diseases
5	Diabetes mellitus
6	Chronic liver disease and cirrhosis
7	Assault (homicide)
8	Chronic lower respiratory diseases
9	Influenza and pneumonia
10	Certain conditions originating in the perinatal period

Note: Rates per 100,000 population in specified group. Race and Hispanic origin are reported separately on the death certificate. Cause of death (Based on the 10th Revision, International Classification of Diseases, 1992).
Source: Public Health Service Monthly Vital Statistics Report, 2001 Report.

chemical agents, and especially vulnerable are men who work in agriculture, construction, and mining. Noticeably, deaths by homicide are the seventh most common cause of death for Latinos (CDC 2001).

In California, which has 8 million Mexican-origin persons (or 40% of all Mexicans), homicide is the leading cause of death among males aged 15–24 and the second leading cause of death for males aged 25–34. Homicide is also the second leading cause of death among Latina females aged 15–24 in California. Many such deaths are alcohol related: 10 per 100,000 Latinos died in alcohol-related homicides compared with less than 3 per 100,000 Anglos (CDC 1998). In 1995, Latinos comprised almost 46 percent of all homicide victims, compared to 26.2 percent for African Americans and 20.6 percent for Anglos (CDJ 1995).

Such violence is also turned inward. Thirty-four percent of all Latinas surveyed had experienced domestic violence. In California, 40.6 percent of all Latino arrests were for domestic violence in 1998. The percentage for domestic violence arrests increased by 8 percent between 1988 and 1998 (California Department of Corrections 1999).

Such levels of violence cannot but develop a sizeable distribution of post-traumatic stress on entire families and singularly on women, who are the major targets for abuse. Mexican-origin populations have similar rates of psychiatric disorder to Anglos, but those born in the U.S. had higher rates of depression and phobias than those born in Mexico. In fact, the Mexican born had lower prevalence rates of all lifetime disorders than Mexicans born in the

U.S. All studies point to the fact that Mexican-born immigrants have better mental health than U.S.-born Mexicans (DHHS 2001). It would seem that while parents leave debilitating regions of refuge, U.S.-born Mexicans emerge in new ones.

Rates of substance abuse and dependence among U.S.-born Mexican males exceed those of Mexican-born males by a ratio of 2 to 1. U.S.-born males have higher rates of substance abuse than Mexican-born youth as well (DHHS 2001). When coupled with the fact that "Latinos (most of whom are of Mexican origin) are nearly four times as likely as Anglos to be in prison at some point during their lifetimes," then rates of mental disorders are likely to be higher among them because greater rates of mental disorders are found among incarcerated persons than the general population (DHHS 2001).

For many Mexicans, U.S. born or not, escape from such regions and from incarceration also meant joining the military service. The history of Mexican participation in the military is long and distinguished, but an inordinate number became casualties in almost every conflict since World War I. At present, 14 percent of Marines are Latinos, most of Mexican origin. The Army, Navy, and Air Force have focused their recruitment efforts on high schools with large concentrations of Mexican-origin youth, and services have established Reserve Officer Training Corps (ROTC) chapters in the same schools. The first U.S. casualties in the war in Iraq were a Guatemalan Marine shortly followed by a Mexican Marine—neither were citizens. Whether to be used as commodities, for war, or as candidates for prison, we simply must not allow this to occur.

Conclusions

If the future seems less than promising for so many Americans of Mexican origin, it behooves us to treat the symptoms and causes of the creation of the many versions of regions of refuge.

A partial solution lies in the recognition of colonias and urban networks as civil societies. These must be treated politically on a national and transnational level on their civil status, as reflected by their self-development and community formation, rather than on the basis of individual birth or legal status. Or to say it a bit differently, if communities are formed, then these should be the units of citizenship, and civitas becomes the glue for national and transnational protection, not individual birthright or passing an immigration test. Given their rate of growth, no draconian measures can stop their development.

However, the educational attainment of persons in Mexico has to be addressed if those communities are to become even stronger. Whether documented or undocumented, a Mexican labor force with an educational attainment similar to that of Asians in the United States—13 years or so—would be an intellectual and social force to be reckoned with. The information technology field holds great promise for Mexicans in Mexico, since it is a relatively low capital-intensive market that needs a well-educated labor force. Educational quality will determine the efficacy of such a sector. An educated Mexican labor force would help shorten the gap between first and second generations and reduce the need for special education programs. The first generation would receive all of the advantages of parents who can influence strongly the education of their children, defend themselves in the job market, and contribute even more to what could become a more vibrant economy.

On the other hand, the second- to third-generation gap needs to be addressed immediately. If the demographic expansion previously described is certain, then each gap between the second and third generation can only mean this gap will be maintained and many more generations will suffer. Therefore, programs designed to accentuate intellectual abilities and skills, as well as opportunities, need to be developed for exactly these generations. The emphasis would be on developing the social scaffolding that may have been weakened by class movement from one generation to another, with specific attention to the highest intellectual preparation for this generation through special preparatory programs. These would accentuate cognitive, compositional, computational, and scientific skills and could be developed as bridge programs between junior colleges and universities, since a very large percentage of Mexican-origin students attend junior colleges as part-time students. This combination of junior college attendance with part-time jobs weakens the preparatory base for advanced university-level instruction. As well, special attention to enrollments in Research I universities may also result in added generational benefits. The cost of such suggestions would be roughly two B-2 bombers over a ten-year period to fill the gap between generations and assist in the revamping of the educational opportunity structure of the Mexican system as well.

But whatever solutions emerge, we must deal with the overarching inability of poor and near-poor Mexican-origin populations to provision their households. Simply said, this is an issue of human rights too often dismissed by reference to a declared "cheap labor" rationalization that accompanies the word "Mexican." This treatment of the Mexican population as an often-devalued commodity, or at best a commodity to be bought and sold like any other feature of value, must be removed from the clutches of economistic definitions in which the humanity of a population is reduced to a market rationalization.

I argue that we are looking at a potentially new area for examining and reporting human rights violations. No existing instrument of the United Nations or other intergovernmental agency considers the inhumane conditions faced by people when they cross borders voluntarily for economic reasons to be human rights issues, nor do these address the impacts of local, regional, and national dislocations on human beings because of economic changes (see Nagengast, Stavenhagen, and Kearney 1992). International instruments, most notably the UN's International Covenant on Economic, Social, and Cultural Rights (ICESCR) (UN 1976) do, of course, call for basic economic, social, and cultural rights, including "the right of everyone to just and favourable conditions of work" (UN 1976: Article 7); an adequate standard of living, including adequate food, clothing, and housing (UN 1976: Article 11). While Article 2 states that rights specified in the ICESCR pertain to all, it also says that "Developing countries . . . may determine to what extent they would guarantee the economic rights recognized in the present Covenant to non-nationals" (UN 1976: Article 2(3); Vélez-Ibáñez 2004).

Yet there is no attention to a broader strategic mission that includes an operationalized method of integrating within the strategic decision-making process of corporate investments and outlays concomitant guarantees to the stable and predictive provisioning of households. I take the view that economic institutions—local, national, and transnational—must have integrated within their strategic "thought-range" the appropriate provisioning for human households and the deconstitution of regions of refuge. Economic processes initiated by capital institutions seldom recognize either political or economic borders of any sort, nor does this approach suggest any. Therefore, I do not distinguish the necessity of differentiating the provisioning households and the development of reconstituted regions of refuge between those created by migration, by natural birth rates, or by a combination of both. I argue that one of the most pressing human rights issues for the new century is the continued devalorized commodification of Mexican-origin populations.

It is only by enormous struggles and extraordinary human effort that many parts of the Mexican-origin population manage to emerge relatively whole within different versions of these regions of refuge. But they do so with real and tangible costs—cultural, social, and physical. Without decent wages, too often our populations have to dip into the grey interstitial corners of making a living to survive and to deal with bare versions of what allows human beings to emerge without immense psychic and physical damage.

The hard work to be done analytically includes how best to capture the most important variables linking the structures of each region of refuge to the broader political ecology and economy and to other regions. In rural areas, each will be marked by distinctive and similar physical ecologies like agricultural valleys, intensive and extensive organizations of production, available land for purchase or sale, and the invaluable relation to water. At the social and cultural level, how political influence is exercised and who has access to it would be crucial elements to research and to understand. In urban areas, different elements would have to be considered, like home ownership, control of local schools, funding patterns, stratification of legal and judicial access, and the economic investment and consistency of local businesses as they relate to the communities upon which they depend. Certainly religious and juridical authorities play crucial roles in how drugs, gangs, and violence are treated. In concert with the analysis of household dynamics and generational opportunities and change, as well as their limitations, urban subregions could be characterized and relations of obstruction, ideologies of subordination, practices of exclusion, and economic exploitation and misrepresentation could be addressed within an action-oriented application of the subregion.

Each region of refuge will have specific characteristics—some unique, some the same—but in their entirety they will constitute an integrated anthropological vision from which to gauge as well as to apply our knowledge for the benefit of the populations that are in need now and that in the future may be even more in need.

I have provided you with a glimpse of the present for many Mexican-origin populations and argued that we face many challenges to the thorny issues of immigration, health, education, community formation, social relations, and labor. These are all interrelated, and each may have applied to it specific approaches for possible alleviation, but without a broader synthetic framework, we are sure to fail. That framework must incorporate an anthropological vision akin in scope and application to Aguirre Beltrán's, for to borrow from him more specifically, much of the Mexican-origin population of the United States ends up in regions of refuge in which it is difficult to establish stable social platforms from whence future generations could arise as whole human beings.

NOTES

Reprinted with permission from *Human Organization*. This essay originally appeared in *Human Organization* 63.1 (Spring 2004): 1–20. This essay has been slightly adapted due to the unavailability of the original data used for Figures 6 and 7 included in the original text.

1   Beltrán also suggests that it is technological backwardness and cultural disadvantage that propagates and permits such dominance, which is not a position assumed by my use of the phrase for the United States.

2   Between 1929 and 1935, almost a half million Mexican-origin persons were "voluntarily" deported or forced to go to Mexico. One-third were American citizens (Vélez-Ibáñez 1996:288).

3   Unless otherwise stated, "of Mexican origin" refers to persons born in both Mexico and the United States. The most current population report, by Roberto R. Ramirez

and Patricia de la Cruz (2002), indicates that the Mexican-origin population now numbers over 25 million, or almost 67 percent of all Hispanics. Most continue to live in the Southwest.

4 Many of these cities were founded as the Spanish colonies expanded from Mexico beginning in the 16th century. Santa Fe, for example, was founded in 1610, three years after Jamestown, and Albuquerque 100 years later, San Antonio in 1731, San Diego in 1769, Tucson and San Francisco in 1776, and Los Angeles in 1781 (Vélez-Ibáñez 1996:37–62).

5 The former are characterized by isolated, nucleated households with little horizontal or vertical relations and the latter (fewer in number) are largely associated with the landlords who sold them the property in the first place.

6 In fact, even the middle-range series projections for 1990 have already proven to be too low by over 5 million Latinos, of which at least 60 percent are of Mexican origin (Population Reference Bureau 2002).

7 This mini-ethnography is being published as "The Political Ecology of Debt Among Mexican Colonias in the Southwestern United States" in the *Journal of Development Studies* (Vélez-Ibáñez n.d.).

REFERENCES

Allen, Elaine M., and Refugio I. Rochin. 1996. *White Exodus, Latino Repopulation, and Community Well-Being: Trends in California's Rural Communities*. Research Report No. 13. Julian Samora Research Institute, Michigan State University, East Lansing, Michigan.

Arizona Department of Health Services (ADHS). 2001. Average Age at Death from All Causes by Gender and Ethnicity: Arizona, 1990–2000. Table 2D-1, Arizona Health Status and Vital Statistics 2000. Office of Epidemiology and Statistics, Bureau of Public Health Statistics, Arizona Department of Health Services. http://www .hs.state.az.us/plan/report/ ahs/ahs2000/t2d.htm (November 21, 2003).

Bauman, Richard, ed. 1993. *Folklore and Culture on the Texas-Mexican Border: Américo Paredes*. Austin: University of Texas Press.

Beltrán, Gonzalo Aguirre. 1979. *Regions of Refuge*. Monograph Series No. 12. Washington, DC: Society for Applied Anthropology. (Originally published in 1973 as Regiones de refugio: Obra antropologica, Volumen noveno. Universidad Veracruzana e Instituto Nacional Indigenista. Mexico City: Fondo de Cultura Económica.)

California Department of Corrections. 1999. Report on Arrests for Domestic Violence in California (1998). Criminal Justice Statistics Center Report Series, Vol. 1, No. 3. Sacramento: California Department of Corrections.

California Department of Justice (CDJ). 1995. *Homicide in California, 1995*. Office of the Attorney General, California Department of Justice. http://caag.state.ca.us/cjsc /publications/homicide/homipub.htm (November 21, 2003).

Camarota, Steven A. 2001. Poverty and Income. In *Immigration From Mexico: Assessing the Impact on the United States*. Center for Immigration Studies. http://www.cis.org/ articles/2001/mexico/poverty.html (November 21, 2003).

Centers for Disease Control and Prevention (CDC). 1998. *WISQARS Leading Causes of Death Reports, 1981–1998*. Web-Based Injury Statistics Query and Reporting System

(WISQARS), National Center for Injury Prevention and Control. Washington, D.C.: Centers for Disease Control and Prevention. http://webapp.cdc.gov/sasweb/ncipc/ leadcaus9.html (December 16, 2003).

Centers for Disease Control and Prevention (CDC). 2001. *U.S. Department of Health and Human Services Public Health Service Monthly Vital Statistics Report.* Washington, D.C.: Centers for Disease Control and Prevention.

Cevallos, Diego. 2000. *Jubilee 2000 Musters Support Against Debt.* Third World Network. http://www.twnside.org.sg/title/musters-cn.htm (November 21, 2003).

Galán, Hector. 2000. *The Forgotten Americans: Focus La Colonias.* KLRU and PBS Online. http://ww.pbs.klru/forgottenamericans/focus.htm (November 21, 2003).

Gamio, Manuel. 1930. *Mexican Immigration to the United States: A Study of Human Migration and Adjustment.* Chicago: University of Chicago Press.

Gonzalez, Juan. 2000 *Harvest of Empire: A History of Latinos in America.* New York: Viking Press.

Groggier, Jeffrey, and Stephen J. Trejo. 2002. *Falling Behind or Moving Up?: The Intergenerational Progress of Mexican Americans.* Berkeley, Calif.: Public Policy Institute.

Hall, Linda B., and Don C. Coerver. 1988. *Revolution on the Border: The United States and Mexico, 1910-1920.* Albuquerque: University of New Mexico Press.

Intercultural Cancer Council. 2001. *Hispanics/Latinos and Cancer.* http://iccnetwork.org /cancerfacts/cfs4.htm (November 21, 2003).

Lahmeyer, Jan. 2002. *Mexico: Historical Demographical Data of the Whole Country. Population Statistics: Growth of the Population Per Country in a Historical Perspective, Including Their Administrative Divisions and Principal Towns.* http://www.library.uu.nl/wesp/populstat /Americas/mexicoc.htm (September 11, 2003).

Lopez, Elias, Enrique Ramirez, and Refugio I. Rochin. 1999. *Latinos and Economic Development in California.* Sacramento: California Research Bureau.

Nagengast, Carole, Rodolfo Stavenhagen, and Michael Kearney. 1992. *Human Rights and Indigenous Workers: The Mixtecs in Mexico and the United States.* San Diego: Center for U.S.-Mexican Studies, University of California.

Paredes, Américo. 1931. *The Mexican Immigrant: His Life Story.* Chicago: University of Chicago Press.

Population Reference Bureau. 2002. *The Changing American Pie, 1999 and 2025.* Population Reference Bureau, Ameristat, August 2000. http: //www.prb.org/AmeristatTemplate .cfm?Section=Estimates__Projections&Template=/Topics.cfm&InterestCategoryID =587 (November 21, 2003).

Population Resource Center. 2001. Executive Summary: A Demographic Profile of Hispanics in the U.S. Population Resource Center. http://www.prcdc.org/summaries/ hispanics/hispanics.html (November 21, 2003).

Ramirez, Roberto R., and Patricia de la Cruz. 2002. *The Hispanic Population in the United States: March 2002. Current Population Reports,* P20-545. 1-7. Washington, D.C.: U.S. Census Bureau.

Sumaya, Ciro. 2002. The Changing Population and Health Implications for Hispanics/ Latinos in Texas (2002). Powerpoint presentation, Texas Lulac Latino Health Summit, College Station, Texas: Texas A&M Health Science Center. www.srph.tamushsc .edu/presentations/lulac/pdf (November 21, 2003).

United Nations (UN). 1976. International Covenant on Economic, Social, and Cultural Rights (ICESCR). Articles 2(3), 7, 11. http://www.hrweb.org/legal/escr.html (November 24, 2003).

U.S. Census Bureau. 1995. Housing in Metropolitan Areas—Hispanic Origin Households (March 1995). Statistical Brief, SB95-4:1-4. Washington, D.C.: U.S. Census Bureau.

U.S. Census Bureau. 1997. Statistical Abstract of the United States, 1996. Tables No. 709 and 729. Department of Commerce. Washington, D.C.: U.S. Census Bureau.

U.S. Census Bureau. 2000a. Projections of the Resident Population by Race, Hispanic Origin, and Nativity: Middle Series, 2075 to 2100 (NP-T5-H). Population Projections Program, Population Division. Washington, D.C.: U.S. Census Bureau. http://www .census.gov/population/projections/nation/summary/np-t5-h.txt (November 21, 2003).

U.S. Census Bureau. 2000b. Table 9, Earnings in 1999 by Educational Attainment for People 18 Years Old and Over, by Age, Sex, Race, and Hispanic Origin: March 2000 (revised 2002). Washington, D.C.: U.S. Census Bureau.

U.S. Department of Health and Human Services (DHHS). 2001. Mental Health: Culture, Race, and Ethnicity—A Supplement to Mental Health: A Report of the Surgeon General. Rockville, Md.: Substance Abuse and Mental Health Services Administration, Center for Mental Health Services, U.S. Department of Health and Human Services. http://www.mentalhealth.samhsa.gov/cre/default.asp (November 25, 2003).

Vélez-Ibáñez, Carlos G. 1996. *Border Visions: Mexican Cultures of the Southwest United States*. Tucson: University of Arizona Press.

Vélez-Ibáñez, Carlos G. 2004. The Commoditization and Devalorization of Mexicans in the Southwest United States: Implications for Human Rights Theory. In *Human Rights, Power, and Difference: Expanding Contemporary Interpretations of Human Rights in Theory and Practice*. Carol Nagengaust and Carlos G. Vélez-Ibáñez, eds. Oklahoma City: Society of Applied Anthropology, Monograph.

Vélez-Ibáñez, Carlos G. n.d. The Political Ecology of Debt Among Mexican Colonias in the Southwestern United States. Journal of Development Studies. In press.

Whitefield, Mimi. 2001. Mining the Market: Hispanic Consumers Hold Promise, Purchasing Power. The Miami Herald (Miami, Florida), October 17. http://www .strategyresearch.com/subpages/inthenews/news2.html (November 26, 2003).

Walsh, Casey. 2000. Remembering the "Milagro Mexicano": Historical Memory, Regional Identity, and the Political Economy of Cotton in Matamoros, Tamalhuilpas—1935-Present. Paper presented at the Center for U.S.-Mexican Studies' Seminar on Mexico and U.S.-Mexico Relations, La Jolla, California, May 21.

World Bank. 2002. Mexico: Projection with Net Reproduction Rate = 1 by 2010. 2002 World Development Indicators, CD-ROM. Washington, D.C.: World Bank. https// www.bancomundial.org.mx/pdf/Poblacion.pdf (November 21, 2003).

The Battle for the Border: Notes on Autonomous Migration,
Transnational Communities, and the State

NÉSTOR RODRÍGUEZ

The global landscape in the late twentieth century presents a dramatic socio-
geographical picture: the movement across world regions of billions of capital investment dollars and of millions of people, and concerted attempts to facilitate
the former and restrict the latter. Capital, in its various forms, e.g., corporations
and financial funds, circulates among core countries and peripheral regions of the
world economy. In the former setting, international funds finance such enterprises
as real-estate development, service industries, and stock and money markets. In
the latter, it gravitates to a host of financial and production activities, including
banking, mining, manufacturing, and the exploitation of natural resources. Numerous international economic agreements (GATT, NAFTA, EC, etc.)[1] emerge to
facilitate the transnational movement of capital. Two agreements (the EC and
NAFTA) attempt to establish regional economic communities with few or no restrictions on the transnational movement of capital. Human movements across
nation-state borders are just as dynamic: 100 million people relocate across the
world regions of Eastern and Western Europe, Asia, Africa, Latin America and
the Caribbean, and North America (*Migration World*, 1994).

For some, this global scene represents a fundamental change threatening the established world system of nation-states. Among the most urgent issues listed by the vocal leaders of those concerned with these dynamics are the relocation of jobs to less-developed countries and the loss of control over national borders. In the United States, dramatic measures are being implemented to halt the immigration of people who enter the country without papers (the "illegal aliens"). In workplaces, these measures include the enactment of federal regulations to create a new worker status of "authorized worker," pilot projects to verify authorized-worker status through centralized computer data in Washington, D.C., and pilot projects to draw on the collaborative support of employers in replacing unauthorized workers with authorized workers. At the U.S.-Mexico border, the measures include a large increase in the number of U.S. border agents, a human fence of Border Patrol agents in El Paso, construction projects to erect fences, ditches, walls, and other physical barriers, and calls by visiting political candidates for the deployment of U.S. troops. In California, voters approved a referendum to exclude undocumented residents from public-supported services, and in other regions of the country, county and city officials acted to rid undocumented immigrants from public social welfare programs. Across the country the anti-immigrant mood raises the issues of the need for a national identification card and the denial of citizenship to U.S.-born children of undocumented parents.[2]

These attempts to halt undocumented immigration and to curtail legal immigration I refer to as "the battle for the border." On the U.S. government side, the principal actors include the large bureaucracies of the Immigration and Naturalization Service, the Border Patrol, the National Security Council Working Group on Illegal Immigration, units of the National Guard and Army Reserves, well-financed special-interest groups and think tanks, and university scientists developing new border surveillance technology. On the migrants' side, the principal actors include men, women, and children from mainly working-class backgrounds with little education and income, as well as persons fleeing political persecution. The migrants' side also includes smugglers, who often share a social background with the immigrants they bring, and sometimes employers. Before it became illegal in 1986 to hire undocumented workers, big and small employers played a major role in attracting these migrants.

The battle for the border is more than just a struggle to "stem the tide" of an undocumented migrant wave; the battle for the border is fundamentally about social-historical development. It is about the changing significance of nation-states in the global order, and thus of the changing relevance of nation-state boundaries. It is a struggle to maintain nation-state borders in a global context made increasingly fluid by the heightened transnational migration of capital and labor. Although the nation-state system expedited the political-administrative consolidation of the world economy in an earlier era (Cohen, 1987), by the late twentieth century the presence of multinational capital and international labor has increasingly countered this function.

Globalization has usually been conceptualized in terms of capital's ability to mobilize and integrate economic resources and activities among different world regions (e.g., see Dicken, 1992). However, the autonomous social action of working-class and peasant communities in developing countries also has significantly increased transnational development. Autonomous international migration organized by workers, their families, and communities has significantly challenged the status of the U.S.-Mexico border by making it increasingly irrelevant. By the late twentieth century, large numbers of migrants had constructed transnational communities between U.S. settlement areas and places of origin back home (e.g., see Hagan, 1994). In many ways, these transnational structures functioned as if the border did not exist. The battle for the border, which will eventually be lost, is thus a reaction to this worker-led transnational sociospatial reconfiguration. The battle for the border is more than just a move to control illegal immigration; it is a struggle to resist attempts by working-class communities in peripheral countries to spatially reorganize their base of social reproduction in the global landscape. This attempted change by foreign working-class communities seriously challenges the established stratified sociospatial global order.

In the sections below I discuss the battle for the border in the southern United States from three perspectives. The first involves what I term "autonomous migration," that is, the movement of peoples into the U.S. independent of state authorization and regulation. The second concerns the growth of transnational communities, which circulate resources between migrant points of destination and origin for social reproduction. The third is the reaction of the state to reinsert the border as a meaningful divide in community lives. I end the essay with critical remarks concerning social-scientific research on undocumented migration and with comments regarding the prospects of the battle for the border.

Autonomous International Migration

By "autonomous international migration" I mean international migration organized by workers, their families, and communities independent of intergovernmental agreements. It is the movement of people across nation-state borders outside state regulations. Autonomous migration means that working-class communities in peripheral countries have developed their own policies of international employment independent of interstate planning. As such, autonomous international migration can be considered to be state-free migration, i.e., a process that decenters the state as the regulator of human movements across international boundaries. Through autonomous migration undocumented workers themselves have created a guestworker program, which many U.S. employers have supported.

It is important to understand that autonomous migration means more than unauthorized ("illegal") border crossings: it means a community strategy implemented, developed, and sustained with the support of institutions, including formal ones, at the migrants' points of origin and U.S. points of destination. Precisely because core institutions (legal, religious, local governmental, etc.) support this migratory strategy, undocumented migrants do not perceive its moral significance as deviant. Migrants may see their autonomous migration as extralegal, but not necessarily as criminal. (Thus, while some migrants may use the Spanish term *ilegal* to refer to an undocumented worker, they never use the term "criminal.") It is also important to understand that migrant communities do not formally acknowledge autonomous migration as policy; this policy is neither written in any legal document nor declared by any official. It emerges as popular policy as families and other community institutions adopt autonomous migration as an approved course of action for social reproduction.[3]

AUTONOMY AS SELF-ACTIVITY

While the concept of autonomy as self-activity can be traced back to Marx's writing in *Capital*, several unorthodox Marxist groups have used the concept since the 1930s to analyze the former Soviet bureaucracy and workers' autonomous struggles against unions and the Communist Party (Cleaver, 1979). From the 1930s to the 1950s, C. L. R. James and Raya Dunayevskaya in the Johnson-Forest Tendency movement used the concept to analyze autonomous labor struggles in the United States, including independent black struggles, and in the Soviet Union. From 1949 to 1967, Cornelius Castoriadis and Claude Lefort, founders of a French revolutionary group and journal called *Socialisme ou Barbarie*, also used the concept to critique the Soviet bureaucracy and reified concepts of orthodox Marxism. Since the early 1970s, several Italian Marxist theorists (e.g., Mario Tronti, Toni Negri, Sergio Bologna, Franco Piperno, and Oreste Scalzone), working together in the group and magazine *Potere Operaio* (*Workers' Power*) have used the concept to analyze independent and spontaneous worker struggles in Italian northern factories (Cleaver, 1979). According to these theorists, these worker struggles, which involve many migrants from southern Italy, are waged not only against capital, but also against their "official" organizations, i.e., the Communist Party and unions. In the late

1970s and 1980s, Harry Cleaver and several co-analysts in the United States used the concept of autonomy to analyze workplace struggles of Latino immigrant workers, and, more recently, the Zapatista revolt in the southern Mexican region of Chiapas.[4]

In an essay entitled "The Return of Politics," Lotringer describes the growth of autonomous struggle among Italian working-class groups as a characteristic of postindustrial social conflict in which the division between the factory and society is increasingly disappearing. Lotringer's comments on the Italian Autonomy movement characterize some of the basic features of autonomous struggles: "Autonomy is a "body without organs of politics, anti-hierarchic, anti-dialectic, anti-representative. It is not only a political project [sic], it is a project for existence" (Lotringer and Marazzi, 1980: 8).

To paraphrase at the level of workers' struggles, the workers' self-activity is not channeled through political parties; it challenges the hierarchies of organizational labor, refuses to follow capital's plans for (dialectical) development, and seeks to express its own voice. The purpose of the workers' self-activity is survival.

Some comparisons between Lotringer's characterization and autonomous migration are obvious: undocumented migrants are not organized into political groups,[5] they contradict capital's global stratification, they articulate their own international policy, and their purpose is survival. Autonomy, according to Lotringer (1980), refuses to separate economics from politics, and politics from existence. From the perspective of the many large and culturally dynamic Latino migrant settlements in the United States (e.g., see Pedraza and Rumbaut, 1996: Chapters 25–28), one can observe that undocumented migrants refuse to separate economics from community, and community from ethnicity.

Though autonomy as self-activity has been analyzed mainly in the form of industrial worker struggles, it is also present in other arenas of social life. In Latin American rural areas, for example, landless peasants have a history of autonomously taking over plots of land for farming (e.g., see Foley 1991), and in Latin American cities, poor working-class people have created shantytowns of *callampas, favelas, pueblos jovenes,* and *villas miserias* through autonomous invasions of land for self-built housing (Green, 1991). Lúcio Kowarick describes the conditions that lead to autonomous, sudden eruptions for improved neighborhood services among shantytown residents in Sao Paulo: "These movements [are] nurtured by a series of social bonds forged in neighborhood interactions, in the common experience of living in neglected districts, in the delays in public transportation, in accidents, illness, and floods" (Kowarick, 1994: 37). For Kowarick (1994), "micromovements" among shantytown residents occur when, under certain circumstances, subjective accumulated experiences link conflicts and demands.

It is one thing to argue that marginalized populations participate collectively in independent and spontaneous demands for change, but it is quite another to posit that these activities constitute social forces that are altering or even restructuring global structural arrangements. Yet, the latter is precisely the basis for my thesis of the battle for the border, that is, that autonomous migration has recomposed the settlement space of communities in peripheral countries in a manner that pays little heed to the nation-state divide. This has occurred not only through the migration of millions of undocumented migrants, but also through these migrants' development or fortification of community structures that transcend the border and at various levels (social, cultural, economic, etc.) unite U.S. settlement areas with communities of origin back home. From this perspective, the state's battle for the border concerns more than controlling the border—*it is about maintaining a border.*

Studies of social change that remain wedded to the structural level of impersonal forces have often failed to recognize the transformative power of human agency by ordinary men and women, including undocumented immigrants. At the structural level, according to Michael Peter Smith (1989), the social actions and struggles of ordinary men and women remain invisible as mediums as well as outcomes of social structures. Smith comments on the human dimension of structural change as follows: "Although impersonal conditions constitute the historical context within which people act, people are not merely passive recipients of these structural economic and political conditions. They are creators of meaning, which is also a wellspring of human action and historic change" (Smith, 1989: 355).

Commenting on the unrecognized condition of this human role, Smith states: "[S]cant attention has been paid to the varieties of agency exercised by popular classes and to the dynamics of their resistance to dominant structural tendencies in the larger political economy" (Smith, 1989). Smith's words are a late twentieth-century restatement of what unorthodox Marxists had earlier termed autonomous struggles. This is illustrated by Cleaver's comments on studies of worker autonomy by Italian New Left theorists:

> From the study of the reality of autonomy among rank-and-file workers . . . they were able to articulate with new sharpness and depth the position that the working-class is not a passive, reactive victim . . . and that its ultimate power to overthrow capital is grounded in its existing power to initiate struggle and to force capital to reorganize and develop itself. (Cleaver, 1979: 52)

Cleaver points out, however, that studies that remain confined to the "economic" sphere are sure to miss the major social conflicts that affect societal change through other arenas. When social scientists and political groups do recognize social struggles in other arenas (e.g., shantytown housing), there is often a tendency to devalue these conflicts as mere appendages to workplace movements (Kowarick, 1994).

From the perspective of autonomous migration, human agency means more than the formation of undocumented work forces. As undocumented migrants participate in activities of the larger immigrant community, it also means the development of community forces that, while marginally situated, eventually affect core institutional sectors in mainstream society. This includes various examples, such as political activism to counter proposed restrictions against immigrant populations and the organizing of soccer leagues that socially appropriate and culturally recompose public spaces in many U.S. cities. In some cases, the migrants' impact of human agency is mediated by mainstream institutions. For example, constituting a large consumer market, undocumented migrants also have attracted considerable attention from mainstream businesses. In some cases, the Spanish-language and Latin themes used in the advertising by these businesses have substantially restructured the symbolic aspect of social environments previously regulated by the dominant culture.

Viewing autonomous migration as a source of human agency contradicts the perception of undocumented migrants as a docile, job-happy, helpless population. Instead, from the perspective of human agency, undocumented migrants take on the role of historical actors restructuring sociospatial contours across global regions. Several conditions are at the base of this social action. One condition, undocumented status itself, seemingly affects this social action in opposite ways. On the one hand, the restrictions of undocumented status motivate undocumented migrants to implement survival strategies that through social networks recompose work forces and settlement spaces (Hagan, 1994). On the other hand, undocumented status keeps many migrants unattached from bureaucratic systems, allowing them short-term benefits to maneuver and survive with greater ease. The benefits of this include entering the country without state approval, locating jobs without applying for worker certification, and in some cases circumventing income-tax systems to keep a greater share of their usually low incomes.

The human agency associated with the autonomous migration of undocumented migrants is reminiscent of the experiences of earlier U.S. immigrants, who arrived and adjusted with little state intervention. Describing the rise of mass immigration from Europe in the 1815 to 1860 period, Maldwyn Allen Jones (1992) concludes,

The mass immigration of the nineteenth century originated as a self-directed, unassisted movement. . . . Here lies a key to the patterns both of distribution and of adjustment. That immigrants moved entirely as individuals or in family groups, that they received virtually no aid or direction, and that they were subject to control neither by European nor by American agencies or governments would largely determine their destination in the New World and the nature of their reaction to it. (Jones, 1992: 98–99)

As Jones describes (1992: Chapter 6), nativistic movements soon emerged to counter the large-scale immigration patterns of the mid-1800s. The tactics used by these movements to discredit new European immigrants were fairly similar to today's methods.

A variety of immigrant characteristics, e.g., racial, linguistic, and religious, have been associated with the rise of anti-immigrant movements, but it is also the rise of immigrant settlement space that draws heated controversy as it forms the basis for the growth of immigrant communities. In attacks against new Irish immigrants in the 1830s and 1840s, for example, nativist Protestants entered Irish districts to burn down Catholic religious centers (Jones, 1992).

TRANSNATIONAL COMMUNITIES

In the late twentieth century, many new immigrant settlement spaces in the United States, as well as in other countries, have developed into transnational communities. These communities span between the migrants' settlement spaces in the U.S. and their communities of origin. Transnational communities maintain constant interaction across nation-state boundaries. Containing a host of formal and informal sectors, transnational communities are products of human agency. Many transnational communities were developed mainly by autonomous migration before the enactment of the Immigration Reform and Control Act (IRCA) of 1986. These communities play a major role in facilitating the migration, settlement, and survival of many undocumented persons who enter the U.S. In many ways, transnational communities carry out functions of social reproduction across international boundaries as if these boundaries did not exist (see Goldring, 1995; Smith, 1994; and Kearney, 1991).

Transnational communities challenge the relevancy of the border because they constitute an alternative to a state-supported global order of nation-state divisions that attempts to correlate national space with race and ethnicity. For Michael Kearney (1991: 54, 55), today's transnational communities, and the transnational age in general, represent a passing beyond the "modern age" in which forms of "organization and identity . . . are not constrained by national boundaries." Kearney also refers to this phase as a post-national age.

What also should be recognized about the transnational age from the perspective of transnational communities is the role of self-activity by mainly low-income migrants. While broad economic and political forces pressured populations to migrate, the social and individual actions of migrants, however, played a central role in building transnational communities. This involved developing neighborhoods, creating formal and informal organizations, opening ethnic businesses, and establishing linkages with institutions in the larger society, e.g., labor markets and school systems. It was a phenomenal task, considering that before the enactment of IRCA these processes were accomplished mostly by migrants who not only lacked legal immigrant status, but often also faced heated opposition from established residents (e.g., see Rodríguez and Hagan, 1992). The intensification of opposition, such as through Proposition 187, in the 1990s further turned some transnational community settings in the United States into contested terrains.

To be sure, through their promotion of technological development in transportation and communication, two economic sets of mainstream actors in the U.S. also played a major role in the emergence of transnational communities. One set consisted of highway construction firms that lobbied aggressively to promote government expenditures on highway development. A result, initially promoted as a national defense weapon, was the interstate highway system of over 45,000 miles built at a cost of over $129 billion (Koch and Ostrowidzki, 1995). Interstates and other superhighway systems developed over the last 40 years greatly facilitated travel not only for U.S. citizens, but also for newcomers. The ability to journey on a single highway for hundreds of miles through unknown areas greatly facilitates travel for many new immigrants seeking to reach distant destinations. Texas' well-developed highway system, the largest in the country, no doubt played a major role in attracting the many Mexican bus lines that now transport thousands of migrants yearly between Texas cities and Mexican localities.

While superhighways improved the ability to travel, high-tech electronic systems revolutionized the ability to communicate, greatly enhancing transborder telecommunication in transnational communities. Along with jet travel, high-tech communication enabled transnational community members to substantially transcend the spatial separation between communities of origin back home and immigrant settlement areas in the United States. Many migrants in transnational communities now enjoy same-day, if not instant, communication with family members back home, even in some of the most remote areas of Latin America (Rodríguez, 1995b). Indeed, in some cases migrants stay continually in touch with friends and relatives as they make their way to the United States through Central America and Mexico. Also, after entering the country, new Latino migrants are able to continue viewing their favorite television programs through international Spanish-language television systems and thus maintain a cultural continuity with communities back home. For Mexican migrants, two mega-wattage radio stations, one in Monterrey and one in San Luis Potosí, provide continuous evening and early morning musical and news programs reaching from southern Mexico to the U.S. interior.

The actions of several members of a Maya immigrant group in Houston demonstrated how migrants can appropriate high-tech telecommunication technology to strengthen transnational community ties and maintain traditional practices. Using two fax machines, one in a migrant's home in Houston and the other in the group's Guatemalan home *municipio* of San Cristóbal Totonicapán, members of the Maya group organized an elaborate *quinceañera* celebration for a family member back home. Through faxes sent between Houston and the *municipio*, families in both settings were recruited to participate in the event's religious ceremony and to assist in preparing a feast for several hundred invited guests. The migrant organizers of the event used faxes not only to recruit families, but also to select traditional background motifs and to schedule payments for ceremonial materials and food supplies.

The use of high-tech communication in transnational communities will continue to increase substantially in the 1990s, since telecommunication companies are investing billions of dollars to expand their operations in the United States and abroad (see CWA *News*, 1993). In some Latin American countries, telecommunication companies are among the fastest growing industries and have greatly enhanced the capacity of the local communities' residents to communicate with relatives abroad. In Mexico, for example, the ratio of telephones per 100 population increased from 5.4 in 1976 to 9.6 in 1986, a 78% increase (U.S. Bureau of the Census, 1992; 1978).

In addition to providing a host of functions for social reproduction among migrant households in the United States and in communities of origin, transnational communities also constitute a social political space (Smith, 1994), enabling the transnational circulation of migrant struggles in various relational spheres. Nagengast and Kearney (1990), for example, report the formation of a pan-Mixtec transnational association developed by Mixtec migrants to defend themselves in California and Oregon on issues regarding discrimination, exploitation, health, and human rights. The Mixtecs, who migrate from Oaxaca, also meet with Mexican officials on the U.S. side of the border to discuss abuses Mixtecs face as indigenous communities in Mexico. Conflict between Sprint Long Distance and Latino telemarketers in the San Francisco area showed another political dimension of transnational communities. When Sprint fired 235 Latino telemarketers in its San Francisco facility in July 1994 for demanding a union election, a Mexican telecom union offered to care for telemarketers' families that lived in Mexico until the case was reviewed by U.S. authorities (CWA News, 1994). The Mexican union also obtained the Mexican government's commitment to investigate the firings of the Latino telemarketers under the NAFTA labor agreement (CWA News, 1996).

At another level, transnational communities represent political space for gender relations. To the extent that female migrants use transnational communities to leave traditional gender roles back home and seek self-defined opportunities through their migrant roles, it is possible to conceptualize transnational communities as a means of empowerment for some women (e.g., see Hondagneu-Sotelo, 1994). Of course, this opportunity may vary among migrant women according to factors such as age and marital status. Undoubtedly, however, for many women, whether migrant or abandoned wives back home, the transnational community remains one more social structure exploited by men.[6]

Finally, transnational communities, as outcomes of human agency, represent the lengthy struggles by migrant workers to reunite with their families and communities, against the designs of an international capitalist system that values foreign migrant labor but provides no assistance for its maintenance and reproduction (see de Brunhoff, 1978; Burawoy, 1976). The Bracero Program, which imported five million Mexican farm workers from 1942 to 1964, epitomized this labor system (see Garcia, 1980; Olivas, 1990). Organized through the state, the program yearly imported thousands of Mexican workers for seasonal work in the fields of U.S. agribusiness. When the *braceros* completed the harvest, they were sent back to Mexico until the next season. *Braceros*, all men, were not allowed to bring their families to the United States. The poor communities from which the *braceros* originated bore all the costs of developing and reproducing this migrant labor force (Burawoy, 1976). Undocumented Latino immigration since the late 1960s, in which whole families migrate and community structures are extended north of the U.S.-Mexican border, represents a different system of migrant labor. It is a system of autonomous migration where working-class migrants themselves determine which resources for the social reproduction of their families and communities are brought to the United States and which resources are maintained back home.

State Strategies Against Autonomous Migration

The state in capitalist society is not a monolithic institution mindlessly following the plans of capital. On many social issues, various agencies of the state may offer different goals and agendas. In some cases, it is even possible to think of state policies as negotiated outcomes among different state offices (Skocpol,

1985). The operation of the Bracero Program, for example, involved disagreements between the Department of Agriculture, which generally favored it, and the Department of Labor, which at the end worked to curtail the program (see Craig, 1971; see also Calavita, 1992). Yet it is possible, I believe, to conceive of a capitalist state in terms of the tendency of state agencies in capitalist society to work within policy contours that historically have favored the reproduction of the capitalist system. Of particular significance has been the state's role in regulating or attempting to regulate immigrant labor, formally and informally.

I contend that the goal of current state activities to control undocumented immigration goes beyond an attempt to regain control of the border. It is more an attempt to end autonomous migration, which for many years has been a creative power of transnational communities. Stopping the self-directed migration of communities across the border will end the transnational survival strategy for many migrant families who have yet to achieve legal immigrant status. It will also limit the social resources of the many legal immigrant families who have undocumented family members.

Recent state strategies to control autonomous migration have included several approaches. The implementation of IRCA in 1986 had a three-pronged approach: bring undocumented immigrants into the legal system through amnesty and legalization, close the labor market for undocumented labor by prohibiting the hiring of undocumented workers, and increase the number of border enforcement agents (Hagan and Baker, 1993). Although undocumented immigration apparently slowed down for a few years after the passage of IRCA, by 1990 the INS was apprehending as many illegal Latino entrants as it had in pre-IRCA days.[7] IRCA actually strengthened autonomous migration by enlarging, through legalization, the support base consisting of immigrants with legal residence in the United States. The 2.7 million migrants (mainly Mexicans) who legalized under IRCA made the transnational community stronger for undocumented members by becoming more stable sources of social support (Hagan, 1994).

In the 1990s, the state moved with greater interest to control undocumented immigration by restricting the access of undocumented migrants to the social wage, i.e., the "indirect wage" of public human service programs used mainly by working-class persons (Withorn, 1981; de Brunhoff, 1978). While the federal government moved to restrict undocumented residents from public housing subsidized by the Department of Housing and Urban Development, local governments acted formally or informally to restrict undocumented persons from indigent health and medical care in public institutions (e.g., see Asin, 1995). Many public-supported colleges and universities also acted to exclude undocumented students (Rodríguez, 1994). Although undocumented migrants felt the restrictions, for many it did not represent a dramatic change since they depended on internal survival strategies more than on social wage programs. Indeed, through social networks, transnational communities provided assistance to those in need (Hagan, 1994), though this is not always a given (see Menjívar, 1996).

A third state strategy to emerge in the 1990s was to forcefully confront autonomous migration at the border, for example, to impose physical barriers at the U.S.-Mexico borderline to stop illegal entry. The barriers varied by region, but included barbed wire and steel fences and a human wall of Border Patrol agents in El Paso. More than stopping undocumented entry, the strategy attempted to reimpose the border as a major divide in the lives of transnational Latino working-class people. As such, the strategy became a space war, as the state struggled to politically reinforce international boundary space to restrict the autonomy of foreign migrant labor. Additionally, the U.S. state attempted to deter undocumented Central American immigration by mobilizing the Mexican state to apprehend U.S.-bound Central Americans in Mexico.

Similar to the interdictions of Haitian migrants at sea, the campaign to stop Central American migrants in Mexico reflected, in my view, the U.S. state's desire to avoid legal and political struggles in the United States with activist organizations that work in defense of migrants and political refugees inside and outside transnational communities. Throughout all the major border points and immigrant settlement areas, numerous community-based organizations have developed to take on the state in legal and political struggles on behalf of migrants (Rodríguez and Urrutia-Rojas, 1990). Many of these organizations involve immigrant residents of transnational communities, but some are composed mainly of U.S.-born activists. When community organizations working to protect undocumented Central Americans came together to form the Sanctuary Movement in the 1980s, the state attempted to suppress the movement through its Operation Sojourner, which gathered information to prosecute movement members (Crittenden, 1988). By the mid-1990s, transnational communities contained numerous broad-based organizational networks working to mobilize community sectors on behalf of migrant and refugee rights and against proposed state policies to restrict immigrant populations. One network has called for and organized toward a massive immigrant march on Washington on October 12, 1996, the Latin American *Día de la Raza* (Columbus Day). The plan is to recompose immigrant political struggles from the local level to the level of the country.

Even state actors do not think that border enforcement alone is sufficient to control undocumented immigration. In their promotion of NAFTA, Mexican and U.S. state representatives viewed sustained economic growth in Mexico as essential for halting this immigration (Teitelbaum and Weiner, 1995). From the perspective of NAFTA, the state strategy for control of undocumented migration is thus inter-regional development. Yet, the strategy faces very uncertain prospects, even without considering the vacillating conditions of the Mexican economy. NAFTA's long-term success, for example, will require an agricultural restructuring that will undoubtedly release a massive army of rural migrants (Barry, 1995). This scenario, cited by *zapatista* rebels in Chiapas as one reason for their revolt (Ross, 1995), is reminiscent of the rural enclosure movements that accompanied Europe's Industrial Revolution. Displaced from their peasant livelihoods, many of Europe's unemployed rural people made their way to the United States (Jones, 1992). This option remains a viable one for the Mexican case.

Conclusion

The late twentieth century has inaugurated a new age of global capitalist development. Just as capital has expanded globally to seek new resources for its existence, many working-class communities in peripheral regions of the world economy have extended their base for survival across nation-state boundaries. They have done so autonomously through undocumented migration. This has created a new transnational person, a person who out of necessity has become very adaptable to new settlement environments (Kearney, 1995). Undocumented migrants have developed transnational communities that recompose the global spatial contours of class structures and class relations. They have accomplished this through self-activity and through capital's developments of new communication and transportation technology. This transnational development seriously challenges the continuing existence of rigid nation-state boundaries.

If the depictions of working-class transnational man and transnational woman sound farfetched, it is because social science has failed to capture the self-activity and human agency of undocumented migrant communities. This failure has resulted from at least two methodological factors. One factor has been the constant use of the individual as the unit of analysis in research of undocumented immigration. At this level, the reconstructive power of undocumented migration is limited to the individual; when the higher aggregate level of the household is used, it is usually examined as a unit struggling for existence and not as a source of structural social change. The resulting picture is one of a victimized population of docile, job-happy migrants in settings where only capital has power and workers passively suffer the consequences. A second factor has been the almost permanent use of the nation-state as the moral unit of analysis (Sjoberg and Vaughan, 1971). What benefits the nation-state is taken as a fixed value, and thus the effects of undocumented migration are measured against the "national interest," not from the standpoint of what benefits migrant communities or humankind in general. As Kearney (1991) maintains, this is an official social science that is dependent on conceptual categories provided by the dominant system and that works in the service of the nation-state. It is also a social science theoretically unprepared to capture important transnational changes in a post-national era.

What does the future of the battle for the border hold? It will continue and more than likely become a war for the border as even more potential institutional actors (e.g., international banks and health-care systems) also wear down nation-state boundaries in search of greater markets. Certainly, migrants, legal and undocumented, will continue to play a major role in this development, as U.S. employers will continue their historical role of attracting migrant labor. This was evidenced by California Governor Pete Wilson's trip to the U.S. Congress, soon after Proposition 187 was passed, to recommend the reintroduction of a *bracero* migrant program. Wilson's recommendation clearly indicated that the purpose of the battle for the border is not to end labor immigration, but to terminate its autonomous origin.

NOTES

Reprinted with permission *from Social Justice: A Journal of Crime, Conflict, and World Order*. This essay originally appeared in *Social Justice* 23.3 (Fall 1996): 21–37.

1   See Cornelius, Martin, and Hollifield (1994) for a description of the policy context of international migration in different world regions. This context includes the General Agreement on Tariffs and Trade (GATT), the North American Free Trade Agreement (NAFTA), and the European Community (EC).

2   The calls and proposed measures to limit undocumented immigration are listed regularly in major U.S. newspapers. Also, see examples in *Migration World*, a magazine of the Center for Migration Studies in Staten Island, New York.

3   I base these comments on my observations, since 1988, in the Guatemalan highland *municipio* of San Cristóbal Totonicapán (see Rodríguez, 1995a; 1995b). The *municipio* and other surrounding ones in the Guatemalan highlands have sent a large number of undocumented migrants to the United States since the early 1980s.

4   Many papers and publications using an autonomous perspective are listed in Cleaver et al. (1991). Also, see Cleaver (1994).

5   I do not mean to imply that undocumented migrants do not participate in political groupings, which they certainly do. What I mean is that the undocumented have not organized into a formal political group, such as a political party.

6   For example, see "Irma's Story: The Life of an Illegal Alien" in Nathan (1991). For comparative materials from Britain, see Mama's (1993) "Women Abuse in London's Black Communities."

7   See INS apprehension figures in U.S. Bureau of the Census (1994: Table 323). INS apprehension figures are poor indicators for estimating how many migrants enter the country because nonmigrant factors, e.g., the number of border enforcement agents, affect the number of apprehended entrants. Yet, the trends shown by apprehension statistics may represent changes in actual undocumented migration.

REFERENCES

Asin, Stefanie. 1995. "A New Look at Gold Card Safeguards: Closer Checks Ahead for Hospital District." *Houston Chronicle* (February 23): A-21.

Barry, Tom. 1995. *Zapata's Revenge: Free Trade and the Farm Crisis in Mexico*. Boston: South End Press.

Burawoy, Michael. 1976. "The Functions and Reproduction of Migrant Labor: Comparative Material from Southern Africa and the United States." *American Journal of Sociology* 81,5: 1050–1087.

Calavita, Kitty. 1992. *Inside the State: The Bracero Program, Immigration, and the I.N.S.* New York: Routledge.

Cleaver, Harry. 1994. "Introduction." In *¡Zapatista!: Documents of the New Mexican Revolution*. Brooklyn, New York: Autonomedia: 11–24.

Cleaver, Harry. 1979. *Reading* Capital *Politically*. Austin, Texas: University of Texas Press.

Cleaver, Harry, Jim Fleming, and Conrad Harold (eds.). 1991. "Bibliography." Jim Fleming (ed.), Harry Cleaver, Michael Ryan, and Maurizio Viano (trans.), Antonio Negri, *Marx Beyond Marx: Lessons on the* Grundrisse. Brooklyn, New York: Autonomedia: 222–242.

Cohen, Robin. 1987. "Policing the Frontiers: The State and the Migrant in the International Division of Labor." Jeffrey Henderson and Manuel Castells (eds.), *Global Restructuring and Territorial Development*. Beverly Hills: Sage: 88–111.

Cornelius, Wayne A., L. Philip Martin, and James F. Hollifield (eds.). 1994. *Controlling Immigration: A Global Perspective*. Stanford, Cal.: Stanford University Press.

Craig, Richard B. 1971. *The* Bracero *Program*. Austin, Texas: University of Texas Press.

Crittenden, Ann. 1988. *Sanctuary: A Story of American Conscience and the Law in Collision*. New York: Weidenfeld and Nicolson.

CWA News. 1996. "Sprint/*La Conexión Familiar* Workers Tell of Rights Abuses at International Forum." Vol. 56,3 (March): 12.

CWA News. 1994. "Sprint Long Distance Shuts Latino Telemarketing Office to Avoid Union Election, Spread Fear." Vol. 54,7 (September): 3.

CWA News. 1993. Vol. 53,9 (November): 7.

de Brunhoff, Suzanne. 1978. *The State, Capital, and Economic Policy*. London: Pluto Press.

Dicken, Peter. 1992. *Global Shift: The Internationalization of Economic Activity*. New York: Guilford Press, 2nd edition.

Foley, Michael W. 1991. "Agenda for Mobilization: The Agrarian Question and Popular Mobilization in Contemporary Mexico." *Latin American Review* 26,2: 39–74.

Garcia, J. R. 1980. *Operation Wetback: The Mass Deportation of Mexican Undocumented Workers in 1954*. Westport, Conn.: Greenwood Press.

Goldring, Luin. 1995. "Blurring Borders: Transnational Community, Status, and Social Change in Mexico-U.S. Migration." Paper presented at the 1995 meetings of the American Sociological Association, Washington, D.C.

Green, Duncan. 1991. *Faces of Latin America*. London: Latin American Bureau.

Hagan, Jacqueline, Maria. 1994. *Deciding to Be Legal: A Maya Community in Houston*. Philadelphia: Temple University Press.

Hagan, Jacqueline, and Susan Gonzalez Baker. 1993. "Implementing the U.S. Legalization Program: The Influence of Immigrant Communities and Local Agencies on Immigration Policy Reform." *International Migration Review* 27,3 (Fall): 513–537.

Hondagneu-Sotelo, Pierrette. 1994. *Gendered Transitions: Mexican Experiences of Immigration*. Berkeley: University of California Press.

Jones, Maldwyn Allen. 1992. *American Immigration*. Chicago: University of Chicago Press, 2nd edition.

Kearney, Michael. 1995. "Theorizing Transnational Personhood and Community in the Age of Limits." Unpublished paper.

Kearney, Michael. 1991. "Borders and Boundaries of State and Self at the End of Empire." *Journal of Historical Sociology* 4,1 (March): 52–74.

Koch, Wendy, and Vic Ostrowidzki. 1995. "Paving a Way of Life: Interstate Highway Revolutionized America, But at What Cost?" *Houston Chronicle* (November 19): A-6.

Kowarick, Lúcio. 1994. "Introduction." Lúcio Kowarick (ed.), *Social Struggles and the City: The Case of São Paulo*. New York: Monthly Review Press: 31–40.

Lotringer, Sylvere, and Christian Marazzi. 1980. "The Return of Politics." *Semiotext(e) Italy: Autonomia*, Post-Political Politics 3,3: 8–23.

Mama, Amina. 1993. "Woman Abuse in London's Black Communities." Winston James and Clive Harris (eds.), *Inside Babylon: The Caribbean Diaspora in Britain*. London: Verso: 97–134.

Menjívar, Cecilia. 1996. "Immigrant Kinship Networks: Vietnamese, Salvadorans, and Mexicans in Comparative Perspective." *Journal of Comparative Family Studies* 28,1: 1–24.

Migration World. 1994. "International Migration Growing in Size and Importance." Vol. 22,4: 3.

Nagengast, Carole, and Michael Kearney. 1990. "Mixtec Ethnicity: Social Identity, Political Consciousness, and Political Activism." *Latin American Research Review* 25,2, 61–91.

Nathan, Debbie. 1991. *Women and Other Aliens: Essays from the U.S.-Mexico Border*. El Paso, Texas: Cinco Punto Press.

Olivas, Michael A. 1990. "The Chronicles, My Grandfather's Stories, and Immigration Law: The Slave Traders Chronicle as Racial History." *St. Louis University Law Journal* 34: 425–441.

Pedraza, Silvia, and Rubén Rumbaut (eds.). 1996. *Origins and Destinies: Immigration, Race, and Ethnicity in America*. New York: Wadsworth.

Rodríguez, Néstor. 1995a. "The Real 'New World Order': The Globalization of Racial and Ethnic Relations in the Late Twentieth Century." Michael Peter Smith and Joe R. Feagin (eds.), *The Bubbling Cauldron: Race, Ethnicity, and the Urban Crisis*. Minneapolis: University of Minnesota Press: 211–225.

Rodríguez, Néstor. 1995b. "Lessons on Survival from Latin America." *Forum for Applied Research and Public Policy* (Fall): 90–93.

Rodríguez, Néstor, and Jacqueline Hagan. 1992. "Apartment Restructuring and Latino Immigrant Tenant Struggles." *Comparative Urban and Community Research* 4: 164–180.

Rodríguez, Néstor, and Ximena Urrutia-Rojas. 1990. "Impact of Recent Refugee Migration to Texas: A Comparison of Southeast Asian and Central American Newcomers." Wayne H. Holtzman and Thomas H. Bornemann (eds.), *Mental Health of Immigrants and Refugees*. Austin, Texas: Hogg Foundation for Mental Health: 263–278.

Rodríguez, Roberto. 1994. "Central American Students Organize to Be Seen and Heard." *Black Issues in Higher Education* (April 21): 26–30.

Ross, John. 1995. *Rebellion from the Roots: Indian Uprising in Chiapas*. Monroe, Maine: Common Courage Press.

Sjoberg, Gideon, and Ted R. Vaughan. 1971. "The Sociology of Ethics and the Ethics of Sociology." Edward Tirayakian (ed.), *The Phenomenon of Sociology*. New York: Appleton-Century-Crafts: 259–276.

Skocpol, Theda. 1985. "Bringing the State Back In: Strategies of Analysis in Current Research." Peter R. Evans, Dietrich Rueschemeyer, and Theda Skocpol (eds.), *Bringing the State Back In*. Cambridge: Cambridge University Press: 3–43.

Smith, Michael Peter. 1994. "Can You Imagine?: Transnational Migration and the Globalization of Grassroots Politics." *Social Text* 39 (Summer): 15–33.

Smith, Michael Peter. 1989. "Urbanism: Medium or Outcome of Human Agency?" *Urban Affairs Quarterly* 24,3 (March): 353–357.

Teitelbaum, Michael S., and Myron Weiner. 1995. *Threatened Peoples, Threatened Borders: World Migration and U.S. Policy*. New York: W. W. Norton.

U.S. Bureau of the Census. 1994. *Statistical Abstract of the United States: 1994*. Washington, D.C.

U.S. Bureau of the Census. 1992. *Statistical Abstract of the United States: 1992*. Washington, D.C.

U.S. Bureau of the Census. 1978. *Statistical Abstract of the United States: 1978*. Washington, D.C.

Withorn, Ann. 1981. "Retreat from the Social Wage: Human Services in the 1980s." *Radical America* 15,1–2 (Spring): 23–32.

Yo Era Indígena: Race, Modernity, and the Transformational Politics of Transnational Labor

MIREYA LOZA

Their sombreros and serapes undoubtedly hung in those dreary bunkhouses, for they were bareheaded, and their rough black hair look[ed] as if [it was] never combed.

These *mestizos* and Indians varied in skin color.—TED LE BERTHON

Indians from Tlaxcala, small wiry men who spoke only the tribal tongue, showed up in Yuba City.—ERNESTO GALARZA

Published seven years after the initiation of the Bracero Program in 1949, *Aventuras de un Bracero: Relatos de Seis Meses en Estados Unidos*, remains one of the few bracero memoirs depicting the conditions Mexican workers experienced in the United States.[1] Bracero-turned-author Jesús Topete has his protagonist recount his six-month experience in the United States as a guest worker. His narrative not only reveals details about the bracero experience but also highlights popularly held notions of race in Mexico. In one anecdote, he writes about the excitement that the protagonist and his fellow workers felt when they heard that women would be coming in to work alongside braceros harvesting potatoes in California. The men were looking forward to working alongside tall, beautiful *"gringas,"* because they spent so much time laboring only in the company of men. The protagonist was then extremely disappointed when *"chichimecas* speaking English" arrived. Here he used a term that technically refers to the Nahua people of Mexico, but it is also used as a derogatory way to indicate indigeneity. Thus, he both insulted the women and emphasized racist concepts of idealized Mexican beauty in which indigenous women are unattractive. He even claimed that some of the men in the camp were better looking than these groups of women.

Topete says he developed a tense relationship with these Mexican American women because they made fun of the braceros, viewed them as unmodern, and often asked them if cars and telephones existed in Mexico. When one of the women asked him why he did not speak to them, he told her that he did not like to be mocked. Furthermore, the women spoke English boastfully in front of the braceros as if they were gringas and Spanish in front of the gringos, claiming they were Mexican. But the Spanish she spoke, according to him, was not even that good because it was clear that she used terms from the most remote mountains in Mexico. He went on to say, *"La cara de totonacas se les ve a tres kilómetros* [You could see their *totonaca* (indigenous people of Totonacapan) faces from three kilometers away]."[2] Here he references another indigenous population as a way to insult these women, while he also maps indigeneity onto Mexico's rural and remote areas.

The protagonist saw himself as belonging to a group that stood above rural indigeneity; as he explained, he was a cosmopolitan man from Guadalajara who had experienced modern Mexican cities with skyscrapers, movie houses, theaters, and parks. The memoir thus reveals the racialized perception that indigenous communities conflicted with or only existed outside of cosmopolitan modernity, in both Mexico and the United States. In Topete's schema, one could not be both "Indian" and modern. Although these women also strived for a cosmopolitan identity, the protagonist felt he could decipher their true identity as "Indian." His indictment also illustrates racialized relationships of power, where his modern cosmopolitan identity trumps what he perceived as these women's "true" racial identity. The protagonist intended the words *"totonaca"* and *"chichimeca"* to be insulting and belittling. Although these women inhabited new lands in which these notions of racialized appearance were understood differently, they continued to be racially inferior in his eyes, and many braceros shared this sentiment. Mexican racial systems were at once flexible and rigid. Indians could become mestizos, but a hierarchy still existed, with whiteness at its pinnacle. That is to say, although mestizaje functioned as a spectrum of mixture, whiteness had more value, and Topete felt more entitled to it.

Topete's description of this scene reveals popular perceptions about the place of indigenous communities in Mexican racial hierarchies, while it also

demonstrates how race is an important construct that defined social boundaries in the transnational communities of Mexico and the United States during
the Bracero Program. Although many braceros were in the process of inhabiting new geographic areas, they rooted their racial frameworks in Mexican
social hierarchies and discourses of Mexican modernity. In the United States,
migrant workers challenged and reconfigured Mexican meanings of beauty,
belonging, and labor, thus reframing racial categories. Braceros negotiated
American and Mexican racial constructs, as well as their implications, when
being managed by American growers. While Topete's novel demonstrates how
braceros grounded racial meanings in perceptions of Mexican indigeneity, his
writing simultaneously renders indigenous braceros invisible. By 1940, the
Mexican census estimated that "Indians" composed about 20 to 25 percent of
the population.[3] However, the population of Mexican indígenas was perhaps
much higher, given that census takers, politicians, and anthropologists held
the power to determine whether an individual was "Indian." Furthermore, the
state was invested in decreasing the population identified as Indian in order to
reinforce the national racial identity of mestizo.[4] The state pressure to transform indigenous communities into mestizos makes it very difficult to determine the numbers of indigenous braceros that participated in the program.

Scholars have explored the racism embedded in the discourses of Mexican
president Manuel Ávila Camacho and other government officials as they envisioned guest workers to be the racially undesirable members of the Mexican
nation and most in need of modernization. Historian Ana Rosas argues that the
Mexican government viewed braceros as an "intellectually, culturally, and socially
inferior race."[5] They constructed the indigenous subject as socially and racially
deviant and an impediment to Mexican modernity. This racism was based on
the Mexican history of colonization, the oppression of indigenous communities,
and nation-building strategies that focused on the mestizo as the ideal citizen. If
the mestizo rural peasantry was marginalized because of its indigenous heritage,
where did that leave populations that identified only as indigenous and did not
claim whiteness or mestizaje? Historian Robert Buffington keenly observes, "In
Modern Mexico . . . Indians would be productive citizens or be damned!"[6] That
is to say, there was no place for a modern indigenous future. The Bracero Program thus became a way for indigenous communities to become "productive"
citizens by learning to labor in the United States. Their bodies would be disciplined abroad and ready for integration upon their return to Mexico.

This essay focuses on the experiences of indigenous braceros and their crucial role in shaping narratives of Mexican modernization through the Bracero
Program. Mexican elites viewed indigenous people as deviant subjects who
needed to be remade into Mexican mestizos for incorporation into the nation.[7]

Their stories reveal how some indigenous bracero communities strived for this inclusion in the project of Mexican modernity by marking their transformation from indigenous peasant to Mexican laborer, while others rejected this premise. In learning the framework of modernity, bracero communities increasingly used the discourses of civilization, class, and race to explain the changes happening in their families, towns, and rural villages. Indigenous women evoked these discourses and argued that their husbands became more "civilized and modern" because of the program.[8] Indigenous braceros often highlighted the impact of language and attire as manifestations of the modernizing power of migration. In indigenous communities, such as the Zapotecs of Teotitlán del Valle, braceros recalled buying their "first pair of shoes and coming home with tailored pants."[9] In this context, they viewed the Mexican rural past as uncivilized, and dress standards signaled a world of difference.[10] Changes in attire became emblematic of the transformative power of bracero modernity. Men experienced the modernizing powers of the program through the Mexican and U.S. states' management of their bodies, through their new purchasing power and consumption, and finally through language and literacy, all of which shaped racial and ethnic identity and changed how these men understood and represented themselves.

The racial and ethnic identities of distinct bracero populations also shaped how individuals understood their place in the racialized landscape of the United States and their relationships with other braceros. Examining the experiences of indigenous braceros can help us question assumptions that these guest workers were racially and ethnically homogeneous. Furthermore, placing indigenous workers at the center highlights how American labor management created and perpetuated a distinct racialized system when hiring Mexican migrants. Some indigenous communities yearned to secure bracero contracts, but American officials informally barred them from the program simply because of their inability to speak Spanish proficiently. As a result, indigenous migrants were more likely to enter the United States as undocumented workers. In Mexico, official documents and processing stations utilized the dominant language of Spanish, making it more difficult for non–Spanish speakers. Conversely, other employers targeted populations to work in specific crops deemed suitable for indigenous bodies, such as picking dates. Discriminatory practices often placed these groups in dangerous jobs. This forced many indigenous braceros to rely on assistance more from hometown social networks than from other immigrant communities. For example, while many mestizo braceros from northern states like Jalisco had prior experience working in the United States and could rely on their social networks for support, many of the indigenous braceros from the central and southern states of Mexico did not share this advantage.[11] Some men from these geographic areas were the first of their communities to enter U.S. territory.[12]

The communities I focus on include the Purépecha residing in Michoacán; Mayans residing in the Yucatán; and Mixtecs, Nahuas, and Zapotecs from central Mexican states who relocated to Southern California. These communities created strong ties with the Bracero Justice Movement and were willing to be interviewed for the Bracero History Project. I trace indigenous populations through archival documents that label individuals as "Indian" and through oral histories with indigenous populations and nonindigenous populations. Many within the bracero community claimed indigenous identities because of language, while others did so through narratives emphasizing family history and culture. The lines of racial and ethnic identity were not always clear-cut; accordingly, interviewees spoke about their complicated dances across these lines and along spectrums of mestizaje. While few historians have focused on these intersections of Mexican indigeneity and migration, several anthropologists, such as Seth Holmes, Lynn Stephens, Liliana Rivera-Sánchez, and Adriana Cruz-Manjarrez, have produced pioneering works that document the contemporary migration of these communities.[13] In addition, organizers in the Bracero Justice Movement have identified indigenous communities affected by the Bracero Program in almost every geographic region of Mexico, from the northern border to southern states like the Yucatán. While my research does not encompass all the indigenous communities that participated in the Bracero Program, it does include some of those who settled permanently in the United States.

Like mestizos, indígenas wrote to the Mexican presidents pleading for work contracts. These letters reveal not only the conditions that caused them to seek out contracts, but also the additional burdens they faced. In March 1944, a group of Purépecha wrote to President Manuel Ávila Camacho requesting entry into the program because of the disaster caused by the eruption of the Paracutín volcano in Michoacán. They asked the president for the immediate "immigration of the Purépecha race," because the eruption had ruined their crops.[14] Once in Mexico City, the group of indígenas spent more than sixty days trying to enter the program. Their situation grew "precarious" because they had been lied to and deceived by false promises of contracts.[15] The next month, they wrote to the president yet again, explaining that they could not return because many had sold everything they owned to get this far and that their poverty in Mexico City had driven the men to sleep in public parks. Returning home would mean that they had "failed."[16] Over 200 indígenas signed the letter. Some wrote their names confidently in cursive, while others had shakier signatures or wrote in block print, and still others simply left their thumbprint in lieu of a signature.

Situations like these had become such a problem that a group of women in Mexico City wrote to the president to complain that their streets and sidewalks had become "dorms" and "public urinals." They saw these men as a "danger to families" and children.[17] Three years later, Josefina González Flores, a fifteen-year-old young woman from the predominantly Purépecha area of Pátzcuaro, Michoacán, wrote to the president. "For the sake of God, can you give my father, Zacarias González Flores, a card so he can go work?" In the past, her father had held a six-month contract that had enabled him to buy a small lot, and with much sacrifice they had managed to cover their small home with a roof. Josefina added that if they had to sell it, "Where will we go?"[18] While indigenous men from Michoacán traveled a long way in the hopes of enrollment, those from southern states with large indigenous communities traveled much further, adding to their costs. Félix Aguilar gave up after he found it nearly impossible to enter the program in Mexico City in March 1944. He wrote to the president simply requesting fare to return to his home state of Yucatán.[19] Aspiring braceros continued to write the president in hopes of securing contracts, citing the need to work. By the late 1950s, Abel Matamoros, a Mixtec, pleaded for contracts for his group that had traveled from Oaxaca to Empalme Sonora.[20]

The class position of these workers shaped their decisions to settle in the United States or to return to Mexico. Families who owned their own homes and arable land in Mexico, as well as those who had other viable means to make a living, were more likely to return home. While some men had more economic and social reasons to return to Mexico, others found ways to ease their transition into life in the United States. Spanish-speaking indigenous braceros found avenues of social incorporation within the program, and some built friendships with mestizo braceros and people in Mexican American communities. Some men believed that their experiences laboring in the United States altered their sense of self, as Julio Valentín May-May's statement, "*Yo era indígena,*" indicates. Other men, like Pedro Domínguez, openly embraced their indigenous identity on American soil despite the marginalization and the stigma, defying the Mexican state project that characterized their indigeneity as deviant and in urgent need of change.[21] Ultimately, the statements of both of these men reveal racialized logics of modernity.

Solving the "Indian Problem"

Modernizing Mexican indigenous communities through an emerging mode of labor management was a central concern of the dictatorship of Mexican president Porfirio Díaz (1883–1911). Scholar Jason Ruiz explains that the Mexican elite invested in the notion that "Mexico had much to gain if Americans saw the potential in Indian labor, and it appeared that the regime actively strove to spread the message that Indians could become better and more modern workers." At the turn of the century, a bureaucrat in Mexico's Ministry of Development, Otto Peust, claimed that Indians were "inert and only cultivate what is indispensable for their own consumption. Higher salaries do not make them more active; to the contrary, they make Indians work less, because they acquire what they need a little faster."[22] Here Peust creates a logic that justifies indigenous labor exploitation. Despite their resistance, "Indians" urgently needed to be transformed into modern workers so that they could become valuable citizens. Moreover, this discourse posited that "Indians" required rigid systems of management so that they could be "remade into something better."[23] The Bracero Program drew on these Mexican discourses of race and labor to create a sense that U.S. systems of labor management offered an opportunity for Mexican indígenas from the most rural areas of Mexico to recast and remake themselves into modern Mexican subjects and thus better citizens.

After the Mexican Revolution, policy makers, anthropologists, and intellectuals identified the Mexican Indian as the "problem" that Mexico faced in its efforts to create a cohesive national project that would unify and modernize the state. The perception of the "Indian problem" was based on three assumptions: first, contemporary indigenous populations were "the tired, tattered remnants of once-great races"; second, Indians represented an "obstacle to national progress"; and third, "only racial and cultural *mestizaje* could unify the nation."[24] In the 1920s, intellectuals, such as José Vasconcelos, argued that Spanish and indigenous miscegenation in Mexico created the racially ideal national subject: the mestizo. However, these discourses of mestizaje obfuscated the realities of marginalization and racism that Mexican indigenous communities faced.[25] Vasconcelos's ideas of miscegenation amounted to whitening projects whereby indigenous populations would move away from their indigeneity in order to become incorporated into the nation. Through racial mixing, "the inferior traits of non-whites would be replaced by those of the whites."[26] In an effort to build a national identity, mestizaje was coupled with *indigenismo*. Historian George Sánchez explains that, as a construct, indigenismo was "a product of non-Indians, which sought to exalt the native Indian of Mexico while destroying his culture and land base," and its goals were "to construct a sense of unifying nationalism among a diverse and unwieldy population."[27]

By the 1920s, Manuel Gamio, a prominent Mexican intellectual and the father of Mexican anthropology, pushed for the temporary migration of rural peasantry to the United States as a means of modernizing Mexican populations and to *"forjar patria* [forge a sense of nationhood]."[28] Many of Gamio's ideas were shaped by his doctoral work in American anthropology with Franz Boas, who specialized in the study of Native American communities.[29] Gamio's U.S. training and vision for Mexico demonstrates what historian Natalia Molina describes as racial scripts, or the "ways in which the lives of racialized groups are linked across time and space, and thereby affect one another, even when they do not cross paths."[30] His work was premised on a cultural relativist approach in which "cultural manifestations of different peoples" could not "be placed in a single and unique hierarchy of values, as unilineal evolution had required."[31] Gamio borrowed from the ideas of anthropologists working with Native American populations and adapted these ideas to challenge Mexican ideas about the racial inferiority of indigenous Mexicans. He wanted to fold indigenous populations into the Mexican national project, explaining, "Our end should be to make the national race homogeneous, unify the language, and make the different cultures that exist in our country converge into one."[32] Leading intellectuals thus "redefined the term Indian, making culture rather than race a determining factor."[33] As a result, they reduced the number of Mexicans who were considered Indians, making mestizaje easier to achieve, as there was no longer a need for racial mixing, because culture, "not biology, distinguished the Indian from the non-Indian."[34]

While Vasconcelos and Gamio ideologically incorporated indigenous populations into state-building projects through mestizaje and indigenismo, Mexican president Lázaro Cárdenas (1934–40) created an economic vision of incorporation through agricultural reform. Cárdenas redistributed lands through *ejidos*, a communal land system in which many indigenous populations could hold lands that could not be bought or sold as private property.[35] This was one element of the *cardenista* program, which could be used to assimilate indigenous communities into the national polity.[36] His plans of progress rested on the idea of Mexicanizing the Indians, not indigenizing the Mexicans.[37] These ejidos were not seen as the end point or the fruits of the Mexican Revolution but instead as a tenuous opening from which to incorporate these populations into a modern industrial future.[38] If they could learn to labor on their own communal lands under the strict state regulations of the ejido system, they could perhaps cultivate "modern" work habits that would allow them entry into industrial systems. This ejido system "would serve as an indispensable tool for managing change and introducing peasants to new habits of work, consumption, and clock time."[39]

Mexican politician José Gómez Esparza illustrated these concerns by explaining that the Indian problem was fundamentally economic and that they could be "first taught to work" in order to make them "productive subjects" with the subsequent desire to "eat, dress, and live better."[40] While President Manuel Ávila Camacho worked to undermine the agrarian reform put in place by Cárdenas, he also looked for new ways to incorporate the rural peasantry and indigenous communities into the national economy that were not predi-cated on land redistribution.[41] The Bracero Program represented one method for "modernizing" the Mexican Indian, even as artists, poets, and archaeolo-gists deployed discourses of indigenismo to carry out the cultural work of cast-ing indigenous populations as foundational to Mexico's past but in need of change to find a place in Mexico's future.[42]

In a current propelled by indigenismo, by 1945 mestizo intellectuals and art-ists were attempting to recover Mexican indigenous histories in a celebratory and romanticized fashion; however, this did not change the fact that these communities faced racism and inequality as part of their everyday lives.[43] Earlier efforts to emphasize "culture" rather than race in the formation of indigenous identities resonated, as signifiers of racial identity became more tied to class, patterns of consumption, language, and labor than to strict as-sessments of phenotypical racial features. In this period, indigenous popula-tions could take on a mestizo cultural identity if they consumed items that represented the modern Mexican subject and learned to labor in ways that disciplined their bodies. This is not to say that phenotype was irrelevant, but that racial identity could shift on the spectrum of mestizaje.

To be sure, this was not the first time Mexican government officials placed hopes of modernization on migration. In fact, during the first iteration of a Mexican guest-worker program, begun during World War I, officials empha-sized the skills that workers could gain.[44] In the 1920s and the 1930s, the Mexi-can government used land-reform policies to "lure U.S.-resident Mexicans and the U.S.-acquired skills back home."[45] During this period, the Mexican consul-ates encouraged the return of immigrants to their homeland with headlines like "*México llama a sus hijos* [Mexico calls to her children]."[46] They represented powerful pleas rooted in ideas of family and belonging that aimed at moving Mexicans across the border once more.

By 1942, the Bracero Program held the potential to introduce the Mexican peasantry and indigenous populations to modernization in the American fields, without needing to redistribute wealth through Mexican land reform. Mexican officials cloaked the program in the racialized terms of Mexican modernity and as serving as a social and technological project for rural peasants of Mexico. Learning to be managed by Americans would also make this population more malleable for reincorporation into the Mexican economy. In this state-to-state project, braceros were essentially socialized into modernity in an effort to push Mexico forward technologically in the areas of agriculture and industry.[47]

Being a modern Mexican meant one would wear commercial shoes and pants instead of village-made sandals and clothes. Similarly, one would speak the national language of Spanish instead of an indigenous language. According to scholar Stephen R. Niblo, leading Mexican intellectuals, such as Manuel Gamio, argued for models in which indigenous transformation could take place through consumption. They believed that these groups needed to "live better" and that their needs should be satisfied with "goods and services," thus "overcoming the old customs that oppose every change."[48] For indigenous Mexicans, the border-crossing journey and the experience of working in the United States could bring about these changes and thus take these communities one step closer to the racial project of mestizaje.

Gamio's investment in studying both indigenous populations in Mexico and the migration of Mexicans to the United States shows how racial scripts could cross national boundaries. Ideas of race were not tightly attached to one nation but bled across borders. Mexican and U.S. racial scripts about indigeneity intertwined in this historical moment when Native Americans were also being relocated from reservations to urban centers. Federal policy shifted so that Native Americans would be encouraged "to live like other Americans without federal restrictions."[49] Proponents believed that "moving to urban areas to work and live would improve their standard of living."[50] As it was for Mexican indigenous communities, the promise of integration into the nation was premised on migration, work opportunities, and consumption. These indigenous communities across borders had similar problems framed within discourses of poverty, and the proposed solution was migration to sites of labor that could teach these populations capitalist agendas of labor rooted in measures of work and time. Unlike the Mexican nation-state, however, the United States did not provide a national racial identity that Native Americans could strive for. In Mexico, mestizaje was presented as the solution to integrating indígenas, and there were a myriad of avenues to transform indígenas to mestizo. The Bracero Program represented one such avenue in which the Mexican state invested little but reaped great rewards.

Indigenous Mexicans in the Popular Imaginary

Not everyone believed in the modernizing potential of the Bracero Program or its ability to recast the racial identity of indigenous communities. Some middle-class Mexican critics problematized the consequences of the program; they infantilized indigenous Mexicans and represented these individuals as children in need of state protection. Shortly after the implementation of Public Law 78 in 1951, which extended the Bracero Program, the Mexican magazine *Hoy* depicted the plight of the bracero through a caricature on its cover (figure 21.1).[51] Standing on either side of a small indigenous boy are two larger male figures. The boy wears a *serape*, with the word *campesino* (peasant) written

FIGURE 21.1 *Hoy* 747 (June 16, 1951).

across it. On the left side is the American grower with a gun in his holster, and the words *humillaciones* and *discriminaciones* (humiliation and discrimination) written along the bottom of his Western shirt. On the right side stands a Mexican mestizo with the words *malos tratos* and *humillaciones* (poor treatment and humiliation) inscribed across his large belly. Both figures peer down with wide, menacing grins as if they are waiting to eat the child. The barefoot child is dressed in *pantalones de manta* (white linen pants) and a *serape*, symbols of his indigeneity. While his wide-open arms signal that he is waiting to be picked up by one of these patriarchal figures, the look on his face does not communicate excitement. Instead, it is as if he recognizes his poor and limited options, as Mexico is depicted as just as menacing as the United States. In fact, the Mexican character is fatter and fuller than the American figure, whose mouth is closer to devouring the child. The image articulates the indigenous bracero's dilemma anchored in racial discourses.

Mexican visions of indigeneity resonated with racial scripts in the American Southwest, in which Mexicans were already considered more "Indian" than Spanish, and this status held strong implications in the area of agricultural labor.[52] Their perceived indigenous ancestry made them exploitable labor because they were viewed as an inferior race with little potential for self-governance. American representations of the labor of Mexican indigenous populations "implied that the Mexican Indian was racially suited to primitive forms of labor—and that the subordination of Mexicans in general was justifiable on racial grounds."[53] Historian Natalia Molina explains that in the United States, "Mexicans were considered nonwhite because of their indigenous heritage, but access to resources, land, and money moved them up the social hierarchy."[54] This was also true in Mexico, as "Indians" could climb the social ladder similarly via resources, land, and money, which laboring as a bracero could provide.

Braceros were commonly depicted as indigenous in the popular culture of Mexico. Another image, titled "*Salto Mortal*," or deadly leap or somersault, was provided by cartoonist Arias Bernal and printed in *Siempre*, a Mexican political magazine (figure 21.2).[55] In the image, a bracero under the circus big top leaps toward Uncle Sam, positioned on a trapeze. With his legs tightly hooked around the trapeze, Uncle Sam appears made up to look like a clown performer. His arms are firmly extended in an effort to catch the worker, and money flows out of his pockets. The bracero is wearing white cotton pants, a shirt, and a sombrero, and he is the only figure without shoes. It is unclear whether the indigenous bracero is looking toward Uncle Sam or toward the money fluttering around him. It is also unclear whether the worker will be successful as he attempts to grasp Uncle Sam's hands. The Mexican mestizo looking on from the background is dressed, like the figure in the previous cartoon, in a *charro* outfit.

SALTO MORTAL   Por ARIAS BERNAL

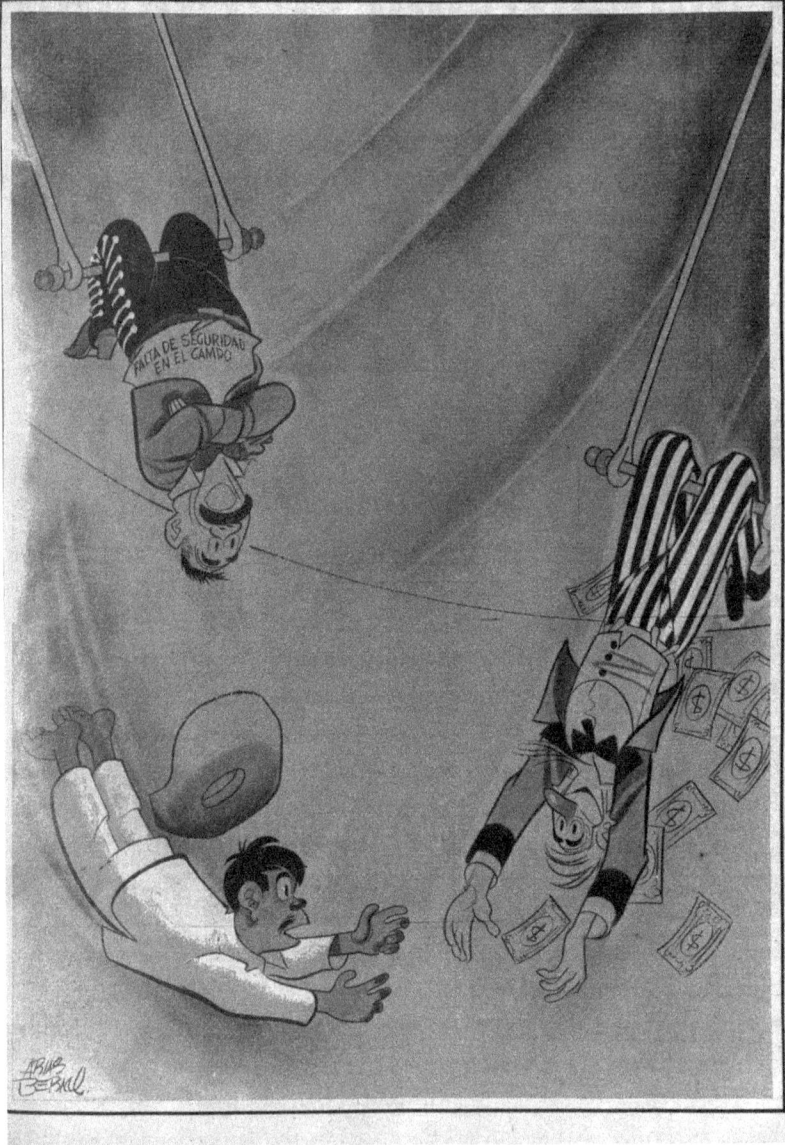

FIGURE 21.2 *Salto Mortal,* by Arias Bernal, *Siempre! Presencia de Mexico* 4, no. 31 (January 23, 1954).

How much do you know
about your nation's agriculture

Agricultural Life FARM QUIZ

United States Agriculture	California Agriculture	Agricultural Life
Its troubles, values, growth.	Its oddities, importance, economy.	Its contents— facts from this issue.

"Boots and Sandals"

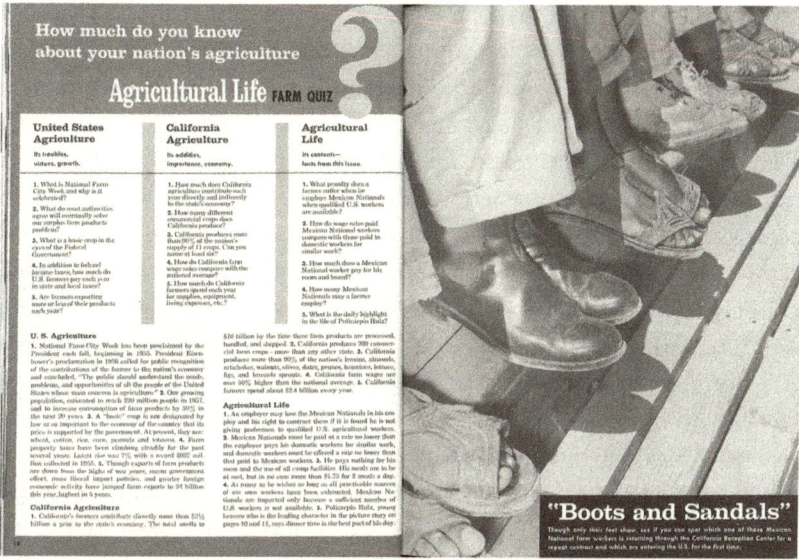

FIGURE 21.3 "Boots and Sandals," featured in *Agricultural Life*.

The figure of the *charro*, a traditional Mexican horseman with much more social status than a ranch or field hand, gained popularity in the Mexican golden age of cinema and was elevated to a national symbol that embodied mestizo ideals of masculinity. His outfit, shoes, fair complexion, and full mustache connote not only that he is of a higher class than the indigenous worker, but he is also racially distinct. On the mestizo's shirt appears the message, *"Falta de Seguridad en el Campo* [lack of security or safety in the field]," meaning that he does not care that the bracero is in danger, suggesting that the indigenous worker is expendable. The mestizo looks toward the spectacle from the safety of his trapeze, recognizing that the only person in danger is the worker. He and Uncle Sam are secure, while the bracero is in mid-flight with no trapeze or safety net in sight.

To the vast majority of Americans, the men who came through the Bracero Program were indistinguishable from one another, thus solidifying a national and racialized identity that was imposed on them. In addition to marveling at their physical appearance, Americans gawked at these men's clothes, sandals, and hats because these objects represented racial difference and aided in the depiction of these figures as "primitive" and "unmodern."[56] Photographers like Leonard Nadel captured the brownest bodies on the way to work camps and in the fields. Writers such as Lawrence and Sylvia Martin became captivated by these laborers' brown flesh and clothing, describing the braceros as including "every Indian type in the republic and every mixture of Indian with Spanish"; their regional identities could be deciphered through their attire.[57]

As men entered the United States in sandals and returned to Mexico with shoes and boots, they embodied modernization.[58] The sandals were not only a functional piece of attire but, like sombreros, also connoted regional identity, as many areas of Mexico created distinct styles. While on a guest-worker contract, Gabriel Martínez Angel compared the sombreros and sandals of his compatriots from different regions and explained that these articles suggested not only where workers were from in Mexico but also their class background, as laborers with more money would have more complicated woven leather straps on their sandals.[59] In the processes of becoming modern, some braceros did away with symbols of indigeneity and regional identity in order to adopt a broader Mexican national identity that incorporated American consumer goods. In order to assess these changes, American academics looked to Mexican intellectuals to make sense of the racial world of Mexicans. Vocal critic and scholar of the Bracero Program Henry P. Anderson noted in his studies the impact of the Bracero Program on indigenous communities. He utilized racially charged categories presented in the demographic studies of Gilberto Loyo and Lucio Mendieta y Nuñez to illuminate the place of indigenous populations in Mexico on their journey toward a teleological transition into the "modern world."[60] Language and footwear became one of the key indicators of moving away from an "Indian world" and into modernity. Anderson described those who belonged in the core segment of the "Indian world" as barefoot and as "native"-language speakers. He viewed the attire of Mexican braceros as a key sign of indigeneity and noted the malleability of this racial and ethnic category, as Mexican laborers transitioned from bare feet, to *huaraches*, and finally to shoes.[61] For these intellectuals, language closely follows these transitions. Class distinctions are implicit in the scholarship on which Anderson drew for his understanding of the movement of braceros from the "Indian world" to the "modern world."[62]

Since attire signaled modernity, many indigenous braceros were eager to consume the proper symbols of entry into the Mexican nation. Indigenous braceros argued that the program fundamentally changed the dress styles of some indigenous communities, because braceros who left for the United States with *pantalones de manta* (typically simple white cloth pants) returned wearing the newest American apparel. These *pantalones de manta* were similar to those popularly worn by many mestizo communities but were considered part of their enduring indigenous heritage. American anthropologist Oscar Lewis described these pants as "ancient white *calzones* [underwear]" that villagers pair with "huaraches."[63] For Lewis, this supposedly primitive underwear signaled not only poverty but also indigeneity. Poverty had become so interwoven with indigeneity that embracing mestizo modernity also became a route to escape poverty. The Bracero Program gave Mexicans the economic opportunity to do away with these symbols of poverty and adopt the consumer symbols of modernity, progress, and uplift, such as boots and Levi's. Although the change from "sandals to shoes" affected all poor braceros, the meanings ascribed to this change became particularly complex for indigenous communities as narratives of modernization collided with shifting meanings of race.

While the Bracero Program could transform the male indigenous rural peasant into a productive mestizo citizen, it did not hold the same potential for indigenous women. Social workers turned their eyes toward indigenous women who could not participate in the program and who needed the attention of the state in order to "adapt" to their newly modern husbands, fathers, brothers, and children.[64] *Christian Science Monitor* author Lucile Rood explained in a 1944 article, "Many of the Indian women and children from the hinterland made their first journey to the big city capital of their country when they accompanied their men to the point of debarkation last spring." Fascinated by "primitive" ways of life and fixated on tattered yet colorful attire, Rood cast this group as the greatest beneficiaries of the Bracero Program. These women dealt with intense repercussions from the departure of their loved ones: "[The] primitive unity of the Indian family dependence has made the grief of separation doubly hard for some of these women, but they have accepted it stoically."[65] The families of indigenous braceros in this article faced deplorable living conditions in Mexico City, which, coupled with their lack of knowledge of how to cash checks, write letters to their bracero family members, and adapt to a modern environment, created situations that in Rood's mind could only be addressed by a social worker. Mexican social workers focused on women living in camps along roadsides and in the "slums of the great city," to offer "free instruction in child hygiene, home and personal sanitation, knitting, sewing and cooking." These social workers also tailored programs for the families of braceros that taught the "rudiments of reading and writing so they might communicate with their husbands and sons."[66] Snapshots of indigenous women sitting and standing with striped *rebozos* (shawls) wrapped around their shoulders or placed over their heads accompanied the article. Rood described them as the "typical" group of wives affected by this migration.

Ultimately, what these and other popular perceptions of the time made clear was that "Indians" needed to be prepared for the modernization that the Bracero Program would bring. Rood argued that the income from bracero remittances could be used to buy "better clothing" and "better housing" that more closely resembled model homes that would reorganize their "primitive" way of life. It was essential for these indigenous women to learn new ways of living so that they could be "given" a "broader point of view" that would improve their condition. They would have to shed their "Indian" ways in order to accept modern comforts, moving them from the "hinterland" to incorporate them into broader Mexican society. Because indigenous women would not learn to be modern by traveling and laboring in the United States, Mexican social workers would prepare these women to adapt to the changes brought home by their bracero husbands and fathers. They could not gain entry into modernity through their own experiences in Mexico; instead, that would require mediation by their male bracero family members.

These post–Mexican Revolution depictions of indigenous Mexican communities emerged as central to Mexican national identity. And although intellectuals of the day superficially celebrated indigenous history and culture, they continued to perpetuate the popular notion that indigenous people were historic relics, not subjects of a modern Mexico. During the Bracero Program, receiving communities relied on both Mexican popular culture and American scholars of Mexican "Indians" in order to address the social needs of indigenous braceros and develop systems of racialized labor management.

Racial Imaginaries, Indigenous Imaginaries

Depictions of Mexican indigenous populations circulated throughout areas where braceros were heavily employed, such as Southern California. In the early period of the program, growers in San Bernardino County attempted to address the compounded social isolation indigenous braceros felt by urging them to attend public events specifically organized for them. In the first years of the program, growers and receiving communities attempted to address concerns of braceros by creating social spaces that were at times anchored by racially essentialized perceptions of who the men were. On July 26, 1944, the Claremont Colleges created an event for braceros featuring Mexican American performers called the Padua Players, from the Padua Hills theater troupe.[67] The Padua Hills Theater was managed under the Padua Institute by Bess and Herman Garner, who thought that the theater could expose the general public to Mexican culture and teach Mexican Americans the dance, music, and history of Mexico and California.[68] A group of indigenous braceros with six-month contracts attended the event, held in the Balch Auditorium of Scripps College.[69]

During this period, many of the Padua Players' productions featured young Mexican American women, as many young men were off at war. Furthermore, the scripts featured "Mexican women soldiers during the Mexican Revolution (*soldaderas*) and Mexican matriarchs (*Tehuanas*) in southern Mexico."[70] Productions, such as *Como Siempre*, featured young women dressed in colorful *huipils*, embroidered blouses, and headdresses in an attempt to depict indigenous populations of Oaxaca. Historian Matthew Garcia argues that although the play provided young women the opportunity to portray strong female roles, it also catered to the prejudiced sensibilities of American audiences by portraying "Mexican men as effeminate, lazy alcoholics" and indigenous women as "wedlock tyrants."[71] These ideas further reified the notions in the world of growers and labor management that these men required not only close guidance, but also labor structures that could make them productive workers and patriarchs. Although indigenous braceros were encouraged to attend this play, the image that they encountered of Mexican indigeneity seemingly supported American visions that positioned these workers and men in need of American cultural guidance.

Like this early group of braceros, Pedro Domínguez, a Purépecha from Janitzio, Michoacán, confronted an unexpected depiction of his own community while attending a film with his *patrón* (boss or landowner). At one point, the patrón invited Domínguez to take the day off and accompany him to the local theater to watch the Mexican movie *Maclovia*, which was set in Janitzio. Perhaps the patrón felt drawn to cinematic depictions of Mexicans so he could further his knowledge of his workers. Released in 1948 in Mexico, this movie became a popular frame of reference for Domínguez's patrón and his fellow braceros for understanding Purépecha communities. The film depicts a legendary love story between a Purépecha couple in Janitzio: Maclovia, played by Maria Félix, and José Maria, played by Pedro Armendáriz. The movie explores relations between the indigenous people and outsiders as they fight over the military occupation of Janitzio and the abuse of power by a self-identified "white, with blue eyes," sergeant who is in love with Maclovia.

During the golden age of Mexican cinema, indigenous images flourished as directors placed brown bodies among scenic vistas. Mestizos were cast as the indigenous protagonists, while indigenous communities were relegated to the backdrop. These images commonly circulated across the border.[72] Sharing a movie experience with his patrón was an extraordinary experience for Domínguez, as guest workers rarely shared spaces of leisure with management. The patrón expressed surprise when he found out that the beautiful site of the movie was, in fact, where Domínguez was from. "That *patrón* did not believe I was from there." The patrón replied, "You're not from there, only rich people should live there because it is so beautiful in the movie." To which Domínguez responded, "I am from there. . . . I felt really proud."[73] For the patrón, beauty was reserved for the rich, and it seemed like a contradiction that indigenous people could live in such a picturesque landscape.

Pedro Domínguez recognized that his patrón and others did not know he was Purépecha because language was one of the key markers of racial and ethnic identity. "No one knew I was indigenous," he explained, until they heard him speak Tarascan.[74] He pointed out that many men from indigenous communities felt embarrassed and hid their indigenous identity by not speaking languages that would irrevocably racialize them as indígena. Popular depictions of Purépechas caused many in his camp to express fascination with them. He and his friend from Janitzio spoke in Tarascan, and other braceros listened with curiosity to what they were saying. Domínguez said, "They [monolingual Spanish speakers] were very interested in learning Tarasco,"[75] because being bilingual in Spanish and an indigenous language could make them indispensable employees in the context of managing indigenous communities. Speaking an indigenous language also came at a risk because it would racialize a Mexican bracero as indigenous and hence make him vulnerable to shaming, additional exploitation, and marginalization. But Domínguez did not hide his indigeneity, emphasizing, "Why should I be embarrassed? Why would I say that I am Spanish if I am indigenous?"[76] His statement provided a challenge to the hegemonic discourses that positioned transitioning away from indigeneity as a vital function of the program. Implied in these racial scripts is the assumed desire of indigenous populations to embrace racial and ethnic change as the only entry into the national project of mestizaje. Domínguez acknowledged that the core of this project privileges whiteness coded as "Spanish," and he rejected that notion and challenged the assumption that indigeneity should cause embarrassment. Through his rejection of mestizaje, he defiantly stood against the racial project of Mexican modernity and embraced indigeneity. He posed a critique of the narrative of racial transformation that both Mexico and the United States promoted within the program.

Although many could not tell the specific ethnicity of Mexican guest workers, some contractors, farmers, foremen, managers, and community members noted these differences in order to more effectively develop systems of labor management. As Elizabeth Esch and David Roediger explain, "Racial managerial knowledge was often tantalizingly close to being systematized but remained more effective if informally wielded by lower managers who hurried and pushed workers, and often hired and fired them."[77] In the case of contractors and farmer-owners, some specifically targeted or avoided indigenous braceros based on their racialized perceptions that specific groups were better suited for certain types of agricultural labor. Although indigenous labor was incorporated into the railroad component of the program, there is more evidence in both oral histories and the archives of their use in agriculture.

Reading and managing brown bodies informed behaviors at several points in the contracting process: first at the contracting station; then in medical examinations; and finally in being selected or assigned to a particular growers' association or grower. Elvon De Vaney, a former contractor for the cotton industry in Texas, described his preferences for laborers using biologically racist terminology. "There was only one type of individual or group of individuals we kinda shied away from and this was the little bitty short Indian fellas from way down on the southern end of Mexico." His knowledge of Mexican geography intersected with his understanding of racial difference, as he went on to explain:

> They was so short ... they couldn't get the tube up ... it's about a forty-foot pipe. ... So we had to shy away from them little guys especially in the [irrigation]. ... They were kinda dwarf, midget type. ... The closer to the border, usually the better educated in our ways of farming they'd be. ... We tried to get boys ... if they were from the states of Durango or Zacatecas, San Luis Potosi ... what we'd call the mountain states ... those boys were generally bigger and stronger. They were meat eaters, ranch country-type folk. ... They were bigger and stronger and more stable. A lot of time, Chihuahua and border state boys were kinda rascals, just a little bit a lot of times, so if we had a choice we'd get your mountain type fellars.[78]

For De Vaney, indigenous braceros were not as sought after as the taller mestizos from the mountainous areas of Mexico because the "dwarfs" or "midget" types were seen as unviable for working in cotton production. De Vaney went on to explain that when choosing braceros he also avoided men from the border, as the ideal bracero came from the country and not cities. He perceived mestizos from the border as more assertive and indigenous populations as more docile. Perhaps because of the proximity to the United States, braceros from borders areas were more likely to have experience working in the United States and therefore more knowledge of how to maneuver through and resist exploitative practices in the fields. Defiant braceros could use the program to enter the United States and skip out on their contracts if better opportunities presented themselves. It was the job of contractors like De Vaney to find a workforce that could stick out the contracts and would not complain when growers violated the terms of the contract.

Braceros understood what the various visual markers meant and manipulated them to perform particular identities to their advantage. De Vaney stated, "Our selectors learned this first, you see an ol' kid coming and if he had on pointed shoes, kinda high top boots and zoot suit britches ... you'd kind of just thumb him over the side ... and get the ol' boy with the hat behind him. That had on him a big ol' straw hat and the rubber tire shoes cause you'd know more or less that he was a farmer. ... This other might be a ukulele player over on Juárez." Migrant workers became aware of this, and, as De Vaney explained, "it wasn't too long before till they wised up, to what was taking place, they'd pack their zoot suit britches and their sharp pointed shoes in a suit case and get the ol' tire casing sandels and that's the way they'd come through the selection line. . . . And then as soon as you'd select them they'd put on their sharp pointed boots."[79] Cosmopolitan men, border dwellers, and urban zoot suiters learned to perform indigeneity, poverty, or general naïveté about the program in order to garner favor. These new performances of race and class upended the visual knowledge of growers. Laborers utilized managements' symbols of identification in order to recast themselves as "ideal" braceros. They understood how to navigate American racial ideologies and used that knowledge to their own advantage.

Some Mexican workers along the border also had English-language skills that could make them more difficult to exploit. Bracero Rosendo Alarcón Carrera explained that on one contract near the final years of the program, he worked in Pecos, Texas, with a grower who, in his eyes, broke the rules of the contract by having the braceros work for other growers. The group of workers found out because, as Alarcón Carrera described, one bracero in his group "knew a lot of English and spoke to us." This English-speaking bracero, from Juárez, Mexico, understood what other braceros could not because of the language barrier and organized the braceros into reporting the grower to the growers' association.[80] Situations such as these led growers and contractors to view men whom they caught "passing" as country folk as more troublesome and less effective field workers.

Growers, like foremen and contractors, believed that their ideal laborer was a man from an agricultural community with little to no education and few literacy skills. These values were embedded throughout the contracting process as officials in Mexican processing stations inspected the hands of braceros in search of calluses that were indicative of agricultural work.[81] This set of characteristics sought by employers placed indigenous laborers in a double bind: going from the most desirable because of their exploitability to the least employable because of their perceived low level of intelligence and presumably weaker physique. The simultaneous attractiveness and unattractiveness of utilizing indigenous labor demonstrated how labor management's narratives of race impacted workers. Esch and Roediger argue that this is a larger trope in American histories of labor management, as being "able to preside over such contradictions require[d] that managers pretend to possess a knowledge of race and of human behavior that they could never have had."[82] As I will describe later, indigenous men with some Spanish-language skills could, like the zoot suiter playing the role of campesino, manipulate these understandings to their advantage.

Other industries that participated in the Bracero Program, such as date-palm cultivators, specifically targeted indigenous men because of the perception that they were physically and psychologically suitable for this kind of work. The medical community validated these ideas by deploying "scientific" and "statistical" language deemed objective. In one such report that appeared in *Today's Health*, a publication of the American Medical Association, Thomas Gorman explained, "An interesting recent development in the examination of workers is the testing of their physical aptitude for different crops. The accident rate in working on date palms has been cut noticeably by using young men who work well at heights."[83] The medical community backed the date-palm growers' racialized ideas of labor by deploying discourses that tied the men's physical bodies to aptitudes for working with particular crops.

Mestizo and indigenous braceros understood the racialized discourses of labor management and the scientific racism at the core of these logics. When I first met Nahua bracero Nemecio Meza in Los Angeles in 2006, he broadened my perceptions of the bracero experience by confiding in me that speaking little Spanish was his biggest challenge in the program, as he was raised in the state of Puebla-speaking Nahuatl. I was also interested in the way he sensed growers' perceptions of indigenous communities. He explained that the date-palm industry targeted Zapotecs and Mixtecs from Oaxaca, because "they were not a tall people, they were short. They could withstand [high] temperatures because their land was very hot."[84] Nemecio drew a parallel between Oaxaca's climate and Southern California's hot and arid date-growing area. This assessment also rested on racist scientific discourse of human adaptation, and although Nemecio claimed an indigenous identity, he saw himself as very distinct from Zapotecs and Mixtecs. This belief also pointed to a hierarchy and tensions within Mexican indigenous populations that deemed certain indigenous people ideal for particular work.

As many employers targeted rural peasants who supposedly had little education, it became counterintuitive to provide formal education programs in the United States. In some geographic areas, English and literacy courses fell out of favor quickly. Ernesto Galarza recorded the perceptions of E. C. Rosenberger, a manager for the Upland Heights Orange Association, stating, "His idea was that the more the Mexican worker was educated, the harder he became to handle. As far as he was concerned, he preferred to have them left alone."[85] Education could have serious implications for the management of guest workers. According to Galarza, growers "felt that [the workers] were already getting far more out of life than they had ever before enjoyed; they were learning habits of spending totally out of proportion to their needs or condition in life; and the more they earned, the more they wanted. Educating them was just another way of looking for trouble."[86] Literacy meant that these men could also read their contracts and come to a better understanding of their rights as guest workers in the United States. Many managers and foremen chose men they felt they could easily handle and oversee. Some went so far as to take advantage of these men based on illiteracy in both the English and the Spanish languages.

The Language of Modernity

Non-Spanish-speaking braceros often experienced exploitation that was compounded by their inability to express themselves in the dominant languages of Spanish and English. Employers and fellow braceros could take advantage of these workers, knowing that it was more difficult for them to protest. Employers created discourses that pathologized indigenous workers in order to reinforce power relations and limit their recourse. Zapotec men, like Antonio Feliciano Ramirez and his friend Juan F. Torres, experienced this firsthand when they found themselves working in Plainsboro, New Jersey, for the Pennsylvania Railroad Company in 1945.[87] It is likely that this was not Torres's first guest-worker contract in the United States, as he had some rudimentary English skills but spoke little to no Spanish.

In the summer of 1945, Feliciano Ramirez injured himself at his work site. Although other workers witnessed the accident, he did not report it immediately. The nature of the incident is not exactly known, but he suffered severe back pain and lesions to his left eye. When he decided to inform his supervisor, J. P. Zealy, about his injury, he asked his friend Torres to act as his interpreter. Zealy did not believe that the accident had indeed occurred at the workplace, and he also downplayed the severity of the injuries. In the formal report, Zealy wrote, "My observation reveals that he [Ramirez] is either slightly demented or greatly faking." Moreover, Zealy found it difficult to believe Ramirez because he could not establish the precise date of his injury. Zealy could have answered this question by asking Ramirez's co-workers, but he did not show any interest in interviewing witnesses to the accident.

Ultimately, Ramirez signed off on an injury report that did not recognize his rights to proper settlement for his injuries. His case was reviewed, and a formal hearing took place. Ramirez also visited a doctor who verified his injuries, but he was still unable to establish that he had been, in fact, wounded on the job. Management asked Ramirez to return to work, but when his injuries prevented him from carrying out his job, the company terminated his contract, thus forcing him to return to Mexico. Before his departure, Ramirez signed documents that authorized his friend Torres to represent his interests and collect compensation for his injury. During a review of the hearing, many questions about translation arose, as Torres acquired legal counsel that argued that Ramirez's language abilities could not accurately express his answers to the questions he was being asked during the hearing. His representative pointed out:

The last question in the record of the July 28 hearing is: "Has this investigation been conducted in a fair and impartial manner according to the rules and regulations?" The answer recorded is: "Yes, this investigation has been conducted in a fair and impartial manner. I have—the statement in its entirety and it is true and correct to the best of my knowledge." The irrelevance of this question and answer given is obvious. Ramirez is an illiterate. The rules and regulations covering the proceedings in which he was involved were totally beyond his knowledge and understanding. He could not possibly have read the statement in its entirety. Neither could it have been read to him, since the interpreter did not know how to read either in English or Spanish.[88]

The hearing revealed that the company did not provide Ramirez with a proper translator, as Torres was not literate in either English or Spanish, and the extent of his ability to speak Spanish was also not clear. The legal representation to the case argued that there were many additional errors in translation and that Ramirez had signed documents that were not made clear to him.

Additionally, Ramirez's legal counsel took offense that Zealy pathologized Ramirez as either demented or a liar. They wrote:

> A moment's thought will suggest that Mr. Zealy did not have to venture into psycho-logics and neurology to find probable reason for Ramirez' inability to remember dates and places. If the American, English speaking supervisor were to find himself in the midst of Zapoteca Indians; if he were to be interviewed by a Zapoteca Indian with the aid of a Mexican who could not read or write Spanish or English; and if the supervisor did not know a word of Zapoteca and only a few words in Spanish, it is likely that he would not be able to remember dates, places, and names to the satisfaction of his questioner.[89]

It is unclear whether Ramirez did in fact receive compensation in Mexico for his injury, but what is clear is that Zealy believed that he could manipulate the circumstance because of Ramirez's inability to express himself in the dominant languages of Spanish and English. Despite his vulnerability, Ramirez created avenues to attempt to address grievances. He authorized Torres to work on his behalf in hopes that his bilingual friend would be able to resolve the conflict. Though allowing his friend to represent his interests ultimately did not work in his favor, Ramirez's story is an example of how indigenous braceros relied on fellow community members for support. Similar linguistic networks of support arose in agricultural fields across the United States as monolingual indigenous men attempted to secure contracts and navigate their daily lives. These linguistic circles became an important resource for indigenous people to make their way through the program and deal with discrimination.

As early as 1944, racialized systems for managing indigenous braceros emerged and were heavily shaped by linguistic circles. In one of Ernesto Galarza's studies of Mexican guest workers in San Bernardino County, he noticed the growing presence of indigenous populations, specifically Purépechas: "In one camp there is a group of nine Indians from one village in Mexico. They speak only their own Tarascan dialect." Galarza further explained that, in addition to the field foreman, who only spoke English, the employers also hired a Mexican who understood Tarascan to work as a translator between the foreman and the workers. "Through him, orders and instructions are relayed to the Indian group."[90] Monolingual Tarascan speakers strategically stuck together during contracting to ensure that a functional linguistic circle could be developed once at the work site. Some growers took it upon themselves to reinforce these circles by purposely hiring groups from shared linguistic communities. This also streamlined communication with management. Another grower went so far as to employ an assistant camp manager who was described as "a local well-educated Mexican Indian." Perhaps the grower felt compelled to emphasize that this person was "well educated" in order to validate the valuable role the local would come to play in the camp. Even mestizo braceros noted that indigenous laborers were preferred for certain types of agricultural work and deployed racist logics that highlighted the indigenous body in order to understand growers' preferences.[91]

In these labor-management systems, bilingual indigenous braceros became prized employees and took on what we might call middle-management roles. Nemecio Meza described how, ten years after Galarza's study, these systems of labor management of indigenous groups persisted. He explained to me that "for every ten people, they looked for a Oaxacan who spoke Zapotec and Spanish to serve as a translator for his people. And then the boss would ask the translator of the group of ten Oaxacans . . . he would tell them what they needed to do or how to work. Everything their boss wanted he would tell the translator. That's how they did it at that time."[92] Unlike Spanish-speaking braceros, indigenous workers directed complaints and concerns toward indigenous middle management, and those individuals could choose whether to translate these concerns and raise them or to ignore them. Furthermore, they also held the power to shift translations as they saw fit. Language centralized power into the hands of a few and thus streamlined the use of indigenous braceros in American systems of labor. This also makes it highly likely that these prized laborers would be given preference for special contracts, ensuring their return to particular sites and giving some the opportunity for family reunification.[93]

FIGURE 21.4 Isaias Sánchez's identification as an experienced date worker. Bracero History Archive.

Contractors and management in the date industry believed that indigenous braceros were ideal for the type of labor needed in date harvesting and also relied on the social networks of indigenous braceros to recruit more temporary laborers. Isaias Sánchez was an indigenous bracero who spoke Spanish and actively sought out date-palm work. Although he had experience tending to several different crops, he acquired skills working in date-palm fields specifically because he valued how easy it was for him to obtain contracts working in that industry. Some braceros considered it undesirable work because falling from a tall palm tree could mean death or permanent disability. Sánchez, on the other hand, found it made it easier for him to obtain contracts. While many other men waited for days, weeks, or months at processing centers in Mexico, he recognized that he could capitalize on a specialized expertise in order to avoid long waits. On one of his trips, Sánchez arrived at the contracting center to find that there was a slight shortage of braceros to work the date palms. A center worker approached him and asked if he could bring him thirty laborers. Sánchez went back to his hometown and recruited friends. Eventually, after Sánchez gathered enough experience as a date worker, he was given an identification card that helped him obtain bracero contracts more quickly (figure 21.4). During one call for date workers, only five men had an identification card, making him the envy of other workers who awaited contracts. Because Isaias spoke Spanish as a first language and was connected to indigenous communities, he became a prized employee. Although language could easily have marked him as mestizo, he identified with indígenas and understood the power of language and identity.

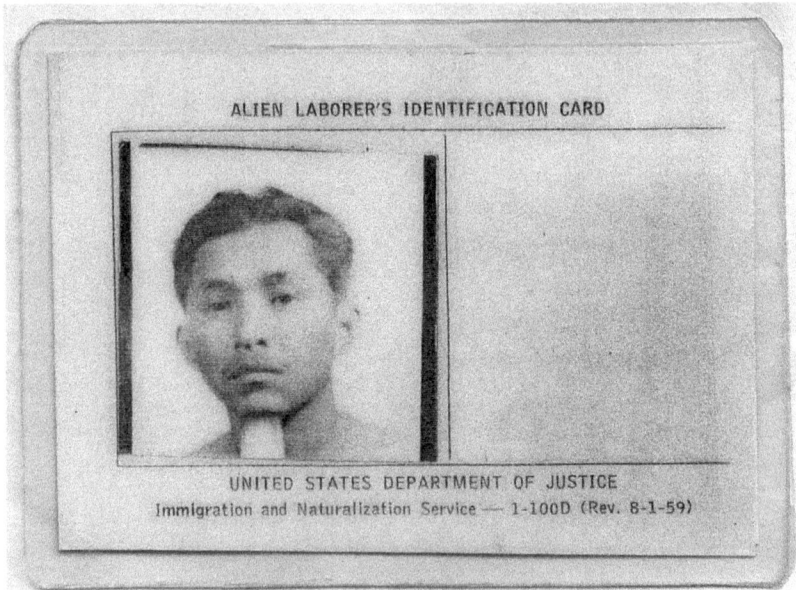

FIGURE 21.5 Julio Valentín May-May's bracero identification, front side, June 19, 1962. Bracero History Archive

As other indígenas learned to speak, read, and write Spanish, they could also take a step closer toward projects of mestizaje, whereby the nation could imagine and celebrate indigenous culture and history from the vantage point of the mestizo. Educational volunteers, fellow workers, foremen, and growers could all provide moments of linguistic learning in the accepted dominant languages. In Mexico, language was a powerful symbol of race, and monolingual speakers of indigenous languages were cast in more rigid racial terms, as anthropologists, census takers, and government officials were more likely to label a monolingual as indigenous. Spanish-speaking indígena braceros could more fluidly alter their own racial identity and assert a mestizo identity in Mexico. This racial claim could be augmented by Spanish literacy. While growers in the United States could see physical difference and could decipher contours of indigeneity, Mexico provided a setting where racial identity could work in a fluid spectrum, which, of course, had its limits. Indigenous populations could work toward a mestizo identity, but they could never solely assert the Spanish or European identity that composed a prized part of mestizo identity.

Indigenous communities understood the power of language in Mexico through a racializing lens long before they went to work in the United States. Some families who sought greater economic opportunities and incorporation, or simply wanted to bypass the labor discrimination tied to indigeneity, encouraged their children to learn Spanish. Mayan bracero Alonso Ayala explained, "My father didn't like us to speak Mayan, and my mom spoke Mayan."[94] Harking back to a colonial period of indigenous labor exploitation, he explained that he had gotten tired of working in a hacienda system. *Patrónes* in this system often viewed indigenous populations as an exploitable source of labor. Ayala explained, "It was like slavery."[95] He finally decided to leave in search of a guest-worker contract, because, "well, because things were difficult here. We worked hard and we earned very little."[96] According to Ayala, in order to increase economic opportunities, indigenous parents encouraged their children to speak Spanish. This proved to be a valuable skill, because during the program Ayala experienced less isolation than workers who could not speak Spanish or English.

Even multilingualism did not lead to complete integration with fellow braceros because many workers brought with them mestizo Mexican attitudes toward indigenous populations that affected whether some workers would express an indigenous identity. Like Julio Valentín May-May, Ayala recalled that other braceros made fun of Mayans and caused some Mayans so much discomfort that they would not speak their language. He remembered that "many . . . were embarrassed to speak Mayan."[97] Braceros who held a command of Spanish, like Ayala, could potentially distance themselves from indigenous racialization by refraining from speaking indigenous languages.

Some braceros took advantage of educational opportunities to learn Spanish, not only because it held the potential to circumvent discrimination but also because it provided an avenue for social incorporation into camp life and into a broader social world upon their return to Mexico. In the early years of the Bracero Program, growers and receiving communities often offered English classes and literacy courses, but some educators quickly determined that they would have to include basic education in Spanish as well. Patricia Sahera, a resident of an agricultural community in Salem, Oregon, joined a group of young women who taught such courses. Many of these women studied Spanish during high school, and their command of the language ranged from basic to advanced. During her time as an instructor, Sahera came in contact with indigenous braceros who challenged her notions of the racial and ethnic homogeneity of Mexican migrant workers. Twice per week, during the evenings, she taught an English-language course using a Sears catalog for illustrations. Sahera recalled, "I can remember using the Sears' catalog a lot to get pictures of things because some . . . of the Mexicans, well they were from Mexico but they were Indians who did not speak Spanish and they would relate to the picture well and you could give them the Spanish and the English or the ones that spoke Spanish, we tried to stress the English and we all laughed, some of those ladies were quite good with their Spanish."[98] Perhaps it was amusing that these young women held a better command of Spanish than these native-born Mexicans. Sahera also explained that many of the Spanish speakers assisted the non-Spanish speakers. Many of these young volunteers taught indigenous men basic Spanish so that they could then teach them a bit of English. Through the program, non-Spanish-speaking Mexicans gained language skills that would prove useful upon their return to Mexico. Sahera's incorporation of the Sears catalog also further exposed laborers to modes of popular consumption. As braceros turned the pages, they saw a cornucopia of American goods and imagined themselves in the newest Levi's jeans and dapper shoes.

Braceros, such as Nemecio Meza, explained that it was through their guest-worker contracts that they gained much greater exposure to the Spanish language than they had had in Mexico. He was raised speaking Nahuatl and learned Spanish at the age of fifteen. As a traveling musician, Meza's father became very fluent in Spanish, even though Meza's mother and grandmother never learned Spanish. In 1959, Meza found himself traveling with his father to Empalme, Sonora, to try to obtain a bracero contract. This was familiar terrain for Meza's father because he had gotten several contracts previously. They waited for a contract together in Empalme, but officials in the contracting center sent them to two different employers. Meza ended up working in a very large farm in Cucamonga, California, and later obtained two additional contracts in King City, California, and Lorenzo, Texas. Meza encountered many contracting and work difficulties but lamented that his greatest struggles were with language. He had been practicing Spanish for only five years by the time he arrived in the United States as a bracero. Meza explained that his experiences as a bracero in the American Southwest strengthened his command of Spanish, which later facilitated his migration from Puebla to the Mexican border after his bracero contracts ended, and eventually during his move to Los Angeles. While the acquisition of Spanish-language skills could lead to their reincorporation into the Mexican economy upon their return home, the ability to speak Spanish also became a key factor that affected a bracero's decision to stay, as he could find support and social integration into already existing Mexican communities in the United States.

Although indigenous bracero Isaias Sánchez did speak Spanish, his family attempted to dissuade him from pursuing a contract because of his illiteracy. "You don't know how to read, you don't know how to write," his father angrily noted.[99] So how could he venture out of the country? But Sánchez was convinced that he, like many other laborers with limited literacy, could figure it out. By the time Sánchez was eighteen years old, his father was already in the United States on what Sánchez called an "adventure." When his father came back, Sánchez told him he had obtained the paperwork he needed to seek out a bracero contract. After a previously unsuccessful attempt to secure a contract, Sánchez made his way to the border in April 1955. Since his efforts to obtain a contract in Irapuato failed, Sánchez believed he could find success at the contracting stations on the border. He did not know how to read and write well, but in 1959 a maternal great-uncle, Bruno, taught him how to write his name. Prior to learning, Sánchez used his fingerprint in place of his signature. Bruno approached him and said, "Look, Shorty, you have a chance to at least learn to sign your name. I am going to show you."[100] Sánchez accepted and said, "That man taught me. He went to the store and brought me back a chalkboard, the Coca-Cola kind. And on it he started writing letters and all of that."[101] Bruno told Sánchez, "Let's renew our contract and you will not use your fingerprint,"[102] meaning he would use his signature in lieu of his fingerprint. He learned enough to write his wife a letter. This was a great triumph for Sánchez, as he was able to work and learn in the United States in ways that he could not in Mexico. Through the Bracero Program, he continued to go back and forth from his hometown to the United States until 1964. Eventually, after the termination of the program, he settled in California.

Navigating Ethnic and Racial Hierarchies

While bilingual indigenous braceros like Sánchez could rise to the ranks of middle management, those who only spoke indigenous languages could feel intense alienation. In the chaotic contracting centers, separation from their linguistic circle could open indigenous men up to additional isolation, exploitation, and violence. For many mestizos, these experiences could be associated with Anglos and Mexican Americans, but indigenous workers often experienced these at the hands of their mestizo counterparts. Unlike mestizos and bilingual indigenous people, monolingual speakers of indigenous languages were also less likely to find the support they needed to break contracts and move to urban centers on their own. Their dependency on the few bilingual workers who played the role of interpreters also meant they could easily be taken advantage of by these same men.

As one of only two Tarascan speakers at his work site during his first contract, Pedro Domínguez felt intense isolation. He was a guest worker in the United States for three consecutive years, for approximately six months per year. Braceros from other indigenous communities in Oaxaca attempted to communicate in their native language with Domínguez and his friend, but they were unable to understand each other. He said, "There were the Oaxacans as well and they spoke to us, but we could not understand them because they speak in another way and we could not understand them, and the same goes for them. I think they could not understand us either."[103] They made efforts to build broader social networks. Domínguez described how he sought out relationships with other Tarascan speakers: "We looked for each other, because we were unhappy."[104] In an attempt to feel less isolated and help each other, they built networks of community and support based on their language group.

Managers in the fields noted the tensions between mestizos and indigenous braceros, and in some cases attempted to mediate it. Felix Flores, a Purépecha from Janitzio, Michoacán, explained the racial and ethnic tensions in the program. In order to deal with the discrimination that could potentially arise, one of the men who brought Felix Flores to a field in Texas gave a speech about equality as he dropped off the new braceros. Flores recounted, "In the barrack he would tell them . . . 'Look, guys, paisanos [fellow countrymen], here are the other paisanos. You're going to treat each other like people. You're going to treat each other like brothers. You're going to treat each other like nephews. You're not going to fight. And they speak another language, and you another language, and others speak other languages.'"[105] This particular camp employed braceros from various mestizo and indigenous communities, and the contractor knew that the indigenous braceros were susceptible to intra-ethnic tensions and racially discriminatory practices. The contractor attempted to circumvent these issues early on by addressing mestizo braceros directly. Some Tarascan braceros avoided speaking in front of other braceros because they did not want to call attention to themselves and be stigmatized. Many Mexicans recognized the relationship the Purépecha community had forged with ex-president of Mexico Lázaro Cárdenas and viewed the Purépecha as leftists and communists. Flores recalled that non-Tarascan speakers would at times tell them "that we were Bolsheviks," because they were speaking Tarascan.[106]

Flores recalled mestizo discrimination and social marginalization of indigenous braceros. He recounted how men working at his camp called a group of workers with large sombreros venados, or deer, because they used blankets with deer on them, while the indigenous braceros were referred to as enanitos, or dwarfs. These taller men intimidated the indigenous braceros. When the venados teased them, the men from Janitzio said, "Relax don't pay attention, if we pay attention they will throw us over there."[107] Flores thought they could be easily tossed aside and physically assaulted by the venados. He explained, "They are tall and we are short."[108] They felt their stature prohibited them from defending themselves physically, but they found the support and advice they needed to face the situation within their close-knit circle. They created networks of solidarity to deal with unfair treatment and the menacing presence of the venados.

Isaias Sánchez also illuminated these tensions, but he experienced them across the country in Southern California's date industry. He remembered that when he was fifteen, men from his largely Zapotec hometown of San Pedro Apostol, Oaxaca, returned from the program: "The first ones that came [back] in 1945, the first men that came here, they had gone over there and they said that the United States is, 'cool, there is a lot of work, and you make a lot of money.'"[109] After several failed attempts to obtain a contract in 1955, he finally succeeded in becoming a bracero, making him one of the 126,453 men who left the state of Oaxaca as a bracero in the years 1951–64.[110] Sánchez used to get angry with fellow braceros who would make fun of the indigenous braceros who spoke to each other in their native languages. "They humiliated them, they said things to them," he explained.[111] In response, Sánchez recalled, "I said to them, 'Don't say anything to them. What they are speaking, they speak it because they understand each other that way. And why do you get involved, you have no right to offend them.' 'And who are you?' 'I am part of them!' We got into it."[112] He explained, "Well they would insult them, they would say bad words to them, and that's not fair, that's not fair."[113] Sánchez pointed out to his friend, "They don't even understand you if you insult them, because they only know how to speak very little Spanish."[114] He took the treatment of other indigenous braceros personally and felt compelled to stand up to the injustices committed against them.

Julio Valentín May-May, a Mayan from the Yucatán, also experienced racism and discrimination directly. In May 1962, he left his hometown of Cansahcab to embark on the long and arduous journey of obtaining a contract. When he was finally issued one, May-May entered the United States through Calexico, California. Officials of the Bracero Program sent him to work in Blythe, California, which is located in the Sonoran desert near the Arizona state border. The grueling work and hot climate killed eight people, by May-May's count. It was common for the temperature to climb into the high 90s and over 100 degrees Fahrenheit in May and June. Many men from his town decided to return to Mexico rather than work in these harsh conditions. The high mortality rate May-May witnessed demonstrated that indigenous populations were targeted as expendable laborers who could work in dangerous conditions.

During his time in the United States, it was clear to May-May that some people did not like him because he was Mayan. In the fields, one worker stole May-May's boxes of produce in order to take credit, and payment, for May-May's work. "He hates me," May-May concluded and explained that just because braceros spoke Mayan, "[the mestizo bracero] disliked them."[115] This bracero was prejudiced against indigenous Mexicans and thought he had the right to exploit their labor by stealing their boxes of produce and receiving payment for them. Some mestizos worked toward implementing racial hierarchies in order to claim positions that placed them above indígenas.

In the face of this blatant racism, May-May could have chosen to stop speaking his language, but instead he explained that when he found another Mayan speaker he would speak Mayan, "so that others could not listen."[116] He found many advantages to speaking Mayan and creating linguistic social circles. Many of the large-scale farms in Blythe used barracks lined with bunk beds to house braceros. The housing was sparsely furnished and personal space was very limited; privacy was almost nonexistent. There was very little space for personal items, and many men struggled with the inability to find privacy. Under these dehumanizing conditions, Mayans found ways of creating private social spaces in public through the Mayan language. Non-Mayan speakers could not eavesdrop or join the conversation, and Mayans shared information and advice in this private sphere. They connected with each other through conversations in indigenous languages and fought to create confidential and intimate spaces in public settings.

One of several Nahua braceros working in the grape industry in Fresno, California, in the late 1950s, Florencio Martínez Hernández utilized indigenous language circles to organize a strike around pay. "We spoke in *mexicano* and they couldn't understand us, [and] in that way we could organize even though it was prohibited, and fight for a just salary. We created the strike in *mexicano*," Martínez Hernández said.[117] He used the word *mexicano* to refer to Nahuatl because it is popularly known in Mexico as the language of the Aztecs. For the duration of the strike, Nahuatl speakers decided to speak solely in that language. After a month on strike and several threats of deportation, the grower finally agreed to meet the demands of 160 braceros, the majority indígena. Martínez Hernández proclaimed, "We didn't understand English and they didn't understand *mexicano*, so we were even."[118] For Martínez Hernández, Nahuatl became a critical tool for challenging exploitation and unfair practices. Braceros used the private linguistic circle created by speaking Nahuatl to fight for their labor rights and in the process dispel the myth that indígenas were a docile workforce.

While some men remember how indigenous languages helped them form support networks, other bracero indígenas were wary of placing too much trust in each other. Felix Flores pointed out the threat of braceros being assaulted on their return trips, which, as he explained, were just as dangerous, if not more, than the departure because of the cash they were often carrying. Flores was deeply disturbed by the reality that many of the assaults were perpetrated by men from the same hometown, as they often knew how much their friends had saved. But the real root of the problem of theft was that illiterate and indigenous-language–speaking families had few avenues for communication. Domínguez points out that since his contracts only lasted forty-five days, he did not write his family. He also explained that even if he had written them, they did not know how to read. Their lack of Spanish literacy led Domínguez to believe that his effort to communicate with his family through letters was in vain. Although other illiterate mestizo braceros experienced the same hurdles in communication, Domínguez's problem was compounded by his family's lack of Spanish-language proficiency. This uncertainty with the process of communicating the instructions his wife needed to cash money orders led him, along with other braceros, to carry large sums of their earnings back to Janitzio.

Isaias Sánchez noted that indigenous families could overcome these hurdles through the help of their children or friends who were well educated and spoke Spanish. Starting from the moment of their departure, this support network helped them gather the paperwork necessary to obtain a guest-worker contract. They then continued through the contracting process with indigenous bracero support networks, which functioned through language groups. When Sánchez worked in Arkansas, he was approached by a group of indigenous men from Oaxaca, and someone in the group pleaded with him, "Paisano don't leave us, if you are going to leave, we will leave with you. You can tell us when we will change money, when we will leave to Oaxaca. You can help us."[119] Sánchez responded, "Of course."[120] There were about eighteen in the group that Sánchez led back to Oaxaca. Once in the state, they knew how to get back to their hometowns. During his many contracts, Sánchez filled various roles within indigenous communities, including guide, translator, and barber—all of which were facilitated by his learning to read and write in Spanish after he became a bracero.

Temporary Contracts, Shifting Identities

Indigenous braceros stood at the center of narratives about the modernizing potency of the program, and their experiences illuminate the contours of this racial project. These oral histories challenge mestizo-centered histories of the Bracero Program and narratives that solely focus on Anglo-Mexican racial tensions or intra-ethnic tensions between Mexican migrants and Mexican Americans. Both these schemas look past the racial and ethnic heterogeneity of Mexican communities. The experiences of indigenous communities disrupt long-standing ethno-normative constructs developed around the Bracero Program, chief among them the assumption that the United States was hiring (and that Mexico was providing) "fixed" national subjects. Indigenous bracero experiences draw our attention to new dimensions of this modernity project by pointing to their own self-representations, the program's bureaucratic dealings with them, and the limits and possibilities of their relationships to mestizo braceros. Moreover, issues of consumption, language, and migration brought on by the program changed the lives of indigenous bracero families and thus brought them closer to the racialized nation-building projects intricately tied to mestizaje. Although indigenous communities have much in common with mestizos in terms of the economic situations that drove families to participate in the program, the uncertainties of the contracting process, labor exploitation in the United States, and the difficulties of family separation, oral histories shed light on the ways indigenous bracero families dealt with these specific issues differently than their mestizo counterparts. They created systems of support centered on linguistics in order to participate in the program and to cope with marginalization, violence, and ethnic and racial tensions.

The experiences of Mexican indigenous communities affected by the program bring Mexican racial and ethnic relations into relief and offer up a distinct perspective of the guest-worker program. The racial discrimination, threats of violence, experiences of marginalization, and solidarity that indigenous communities felt draw out the conflicting place of indigenous communities within Mexico and in historical transnational circuits. Indigenous communities were incorporated into the Mexican national project through their labor as braceros, as some strengthened their command of Spanish, learned to write, and changed their attire. From pants to shoes to language, these shifts signaled an entry into modern Mexico. These shifting terrains also signaled that not only was it possible to enter the project of Mexican modernity by working abroad, but it also bolstered the assumption that these communities needed to be modernized. In addition, it perpetuated the false logic that mestizaje was the only avenue toward a Mexican modernity that created no space for the future of Mexican indigenous populations. Ultimately, indigenous populations deviated from the ideals of a Mexican modern future. While some remade themselves as mestizos abroad, others defied the racial national project by reasserting their identity as *indígenas*.

Mestizaje is such a powerful racial ideology that it naturalizes a person's transition from indígena to mestizo, obscuring the national, political, and economic forces behind this transition. This complicated shift demonstrates the charged racialized underbelly of discourses of modernization. The ideology of mestizaje splits communities, repeatedly placing studies of indigenous populations in the hands of anthropologists and archaeologists, leaving indígenas with a rich body of ethnography and ancient history but a slim history as modern subjects. It also naturalizes the role of mestizos as central subjects in modern Mexican history. This, in turn, renders the historical imprint of Mexican indigenous communities' migrations across the United States virtually invisible. Nationalist mestizo ideologies have not only obscured the social production of race but they have also propagated heteronormative romanticizations of the Mexican family. As a result, bracero practices that deviate from these norms have been hidden in the camp shadows. But, as I learned in speaking with braceros, the Bracero Program gave some men the opportunity to remake themselves and occupy a space in the predominantly homosocial world of braceros.

NOTES

Reprinted with permission from the University of North Carolina Press. This essay originally appeared in *Defiant Braceros: How Migrant Workers Fought for Racial, Sexual, and Political Freedom*, 21–62 (Chapel Hill: University of North Carolina Press, 2016).

1 Jesús Topete, *Aventuras de un Bracero*, 52.

2 Topete, *Aventuras de un Bracero*.

3 Horacio Labastida, "¿La economía indígena: Un límite de la Revolución?" *Novedades*, November 23, 1952.

4 Doremus, "Nationalism, Mestizaje, and National Identity," 381. As the national project, mestizo identity was utilized to marginalize indigenous communities and render peoples of African descent invisible.

5 Ana Elizabeth Rosas, *Abrazando El Espíritu*, 20.

6 Buffington, *Criminal and Citizen in Modern Mexico*, 144.

7 Buffington, *Criminal and Citizen in Modern Mexico*, 164.

8 Interview with Orfa Noemi Soberanis.

9 Stephen, *Transborder Lives*, 96.

10 Niblo, *Mexico in the 1940s*, 24.

11 Indigenous communities from Mexican border states experienced longer histories with border crossings. For more, see Meeks, *Border Citizens*.

12 The migration routes of these guest workers shaped contemporary immigration patterns, as several scholars have traced present-day Mixtec, Zapotec, and Mayan immigration to regions of the Pacific Northwest, Southern California, New York, and then south to the Bracero Program. In her ethnography, Rocio Gil Martínez de Escobar followed contemporary Mixtec families from Santa María Tindú, Oaxaca, to towns in Oregon and Southern California. She argued that these families stepped into the same transnational employment circuits that their parents and grandparents forged during the Bracero Program. In some cases, such as migration to New York, the children and grandchildren of braceros did not follow the same route of migration to a particular destination, but their descendants claim connections to the United States through their families' experience with the Bracero Program. Activists within the Bracero Justice Movement argue that children of braceros are following in the footsteps of their parents and are reclaiming this experience as an explanation for their own migration and claims of belonging. For more, see Gil Martínez de Escobar, *Fronteras de Pertenencia*; and Rivera-Sánchez, *Belongings and Identities*.

13 Cruz-Manjarrez, *Zapotecs on the Move*; Holms, *Fresh Fruit, Broken Bodies*; Rivera-Sánchez, *Belongings and Identities*; Stephen, *Transborder Lives*.

14 Letter to the President from Antonio Toledo Martínez et al., March 6, 1944, microfilm box 793_6_6, MAC, AGN.

15 Summary of Letter to the President from Antonio Toledo Martínez, February 29, 1944, microfilm box 793_6_6, MAC, AGN.

16 Letter to the President from Antonio Toledo Martínez et al., March 6, 1944, microfilm box 793_6_6, MAC, AGN.
17 Summary of Letter to the President from Estela Merino et al., April 26, 1944, microfilm box 793_6_6, MAC, AGN.
18 Letter to the President from Josefina González Flores, April 4, 1948, vol. 593, exp. 546.6/15, MAC, AGN.
19 Summary of Letter to the President from Félix Aguilar, February 29, 1944, microfilm box 793_6_6, MAC, AGN.
20 Letter to the President from Abel Matamoros, August 7, 1959, vol. 715, exp. 546.6/15, ALM, AGN.
21 Interview with Julio Valentín May-May; interview with Pedro Domínguez.
22 Ruiz, *Americans in the Treasure House*, 145; Weiner, *Race, Nation, and Market*, 39.
23 Ruiz, *Americans in the Treasure House*, 145.
24 Buffington, *Criminal and Citizen in Modern Mexico*, 163.
25 For more on mestizaje, see Vasconcelos, *The Cosmic Race/La Raza Cósmica*.
26 Doremus, "Nationalism, Mestizaje, and National Identity," 380.
27 Sánchez, *Becoming Mexican American*, 119.
28 Sánchez, *Becoming Mexican American*, 122.
29 Bonfil Batalla, *México Profundo*, 115.
30 Molina, *How Race Is Made in America*, 6.
31 Bonfil Batalla, *México Profundo*, 115.
32 Gamio, *Forjando Patria*, 28.
33 Doremus, "Nationalism, Mestizaje, and National Identity," 377.
34 Doremus, "Nationalism, Mestizaje, and National Identity."
35 Needler, *Mexican Politics*, 13.
36 Cullather, *Hungry World*, 50.
37 Niblo, *Mexico in the 1940s*, 313.
38 Cullather, *Hungry World*, 54.
39 Cullather, *Hungry World*.
40 Greaves, "La Política y el Proyecto de Educación Indígena del Avilacamachismo," 101.
41 Niblo, *Mexico in the 1940s*, 105.
42 For more on indigenismo, see Tarica, *The Inner Life of Mestizo Nationalism*.
43 Urías Horcasitas, *La Historia Secreta del Racismo en Mexico*.
44 Alanis Enciso, *El Primer Programa Bracero y el Gobierno de Mexico, 1917–1918*.
45 Deborah Cohen, *Braceros*, 4.
46 Sánchez, *Becoming Mexican American*, 116.
47 Garcia y Griego, *Importation of Mexican Contract Laborers to the United States*; Ana Elizabeth Rosas, *Abrazando El Espíritu*; Schmidt Camacho, *Migrant Imaginaries*.
48 Niblo, *Mexico in the 1940s*, 34.
49 Fixico, *Urban Indian Experience in America*, 10.
50 Fixico, *Urban Indian Experience in America*.
51 *Hoy* 747 (June 16, 1951).
52 For more on Mexican indigeneity in the United States, see Menchaca, *Recovering History, Reconstructing Race*; for more on "racial scripts," see Molina, *How Race Is Made in America*.
53 Ruiz, *Americans in the Treasure House*, 50.

54 Molina, *How Race Is Made in America*, 26.

55 Mraz, "Today, Tomorrow, and Always," 116–58.

56 Jesús Topete, *Aventuras de un Bracero.*

57 Lawrence and Sylvia Martin, "To Earn 'Miracle' Wages," *Post*, July 11, 1943, box 25, folder 6, EGP.

58 Lawrence and Sylvia Martin, "To Earn 'Miracle' Wages."

59 Interview with Gabriel Martínez Angel.

60 Report of Progress by Henry P. Anderson, January 1–December 31, box 17, folder 4, EGP.

61 *Huaraches* are Mexican handmade sandals.

62 Cline, *The United States and Mexico.*

63 Lewis, *Life in a Mexican Village*, 201.

64 For more on the role of Mexican social workers in bracero families, see Ana Elizabeth Rosas, *Abrazando El Espíritu.*

65 Lucile Rood, "Changes for Mexican Families as Men Return from U.S. Work," *Christian Science Monitor*, November 17, 1944, 12.

66 Rood, "Changes for Mexican Families as Men Return from U.S. Work."

67 "A Study of Mexican Nationals in the Nine Camps of the Cucamonga, Upland, Ontario, and Chino Districts of San Bernardino County, California," summer 1944, box 17, folder 8, EGP.

68 Garcia, *A World of Its Own*, 131.

69 "A Study of Mexican Nationals in the Nine Camps of the Cucamonga, Upland, Ontario, and Chino Districts of San Bernardino County, California," summer 1944, box 17, folder 8, EGP.

70 Garcia, *A World of Its Own*, 136.

71 "A Study of Mexican Nationals in the Nine Camps of the Cucamonga, Upland, Ontario, and Chino Districts of San Bernardino County, California," summer 1944, box 17, folder 8, EGP.

72 This was not the first Mexican feature film set in Janitzio, as there was also a 1934 film titled *Janitzio.*

73 Interview with Pedro Domínguez. Pedro Domínguez: *Ese patrón no creía que yo era de allí. 'No, tú no eres de allí, pues allí ha de vivir pura gente rica porque se ve pues muy bonito en la película. . . . Yo soy de allí. Yo me sentía muy orgulloso.*

74 Interview with Pedro Domínguez. *Nadie sabía que yo era indígena.*

75 Interview with Pedro Domínguez. *Tenían mucho interés ellos de que se enseñaran eso, Tarasco.*

76 Interview with Pedro Domínguez. *¿Yo, por qué me va dar pena? ¿Yo, pa' qué voy a decir que soy español, pues yo soy indígena?*

77 Roediger and Esch, *Production of Racial Difference*, 15.

78 Interview with Elvon De Vaney by Jeff Townsend on March 9, 1974, SWC.

79 Interview with Elvon De Vaney by Jeff Townsend.

80 Interview with Rosendo Alarcón Carrera. Rosendo Alarcón Carrera: *Sabía mucho inglés y él nos platicaba.*

81 Leonard Nadel, "An Official Examines a Bracero's Hands for Calluses during Processing at the Monterrey Processing Center, Mexico," Item #1592, http://bracero archive.org/items/show/1592 (January 8, 2015), BHA.

82   Roediger and Esch, *Production of Racial Difference*, 8.
83   "They Helped Feed America," *Today's Health*, October 1957.
84   Interview with Nemecio Meza. Nemecio Meza: *Los contrataban porque no eran gente muy alta, eran chaparritos. Aguantaban mucho la temperatura, como su tierra de ellos era bastante caliente.*
85   "Problems of the Mexican Nationals in the Nine Camps of Cucamonga, Upland, Ontario, and Chino Districts of San Bernardino County, California," summer 1944, box 17, folder 8, EGP.
86   "Problems of the Mexican Nationals."
87   Report on Antonio Feliciano Ramirez, undated, box 17, folder 9, EGP. For more on the Railroad component of the Bracero Program, see Driscoll de Alvarado, *The Tracks North.*
88   Report on Antonio Feliciano Ramirez, undated, box 17, folder 9, EGP.
89   Report on Antonio Feliciano Ramirez.
90   "A Study of Mexican Nationals in the Nine Camps of the Cucamonga, Upland, Ontario, and Chino Districts of San Bernardino County, California," summer 1944, box 17, folder 8, EGP.
91   Sarricolea Torres, "Cuerpos Masculinos en Tránsito," 247.
92   Interview with Nemecio Meza. Nemecio Meza: *Pero en diez personas buscaban a un oaxaqueño que hablara su idioma, el zapoteco, y español para que podría interpretar a sus gente. Y ya el mayordomo le preguntaba al intérprete del grupo de diez personas, oaxaqueños, les decía lo que tenía que hacer o cómo se trabajaba. Bueno todo lo que quería el mayordomo de aquel le decía al interprete de ellos. Así se entendían en ese tiempo.*
93   For more on special contracts, see Ana Elizabeth Rosas, *Abrazando El Espíritu*, 66.
94   Interview with Alonso Ayala. Alonso Ayala: *A mi papá no le gustaba que hablemos maya, y mi mamá hablaba maya. El nos hablaba así, en castellano y ella en maya.*
95   Interview with Alonso Ayala. Other indigenous bracero families shared similar experiences with the hacienda system. See Interview with Orfa Noemi Soberanis.
96   Interview with Alonso Ayala. Alonso Ayala: *Pos porque aquí estaba dura la cosa. Está duro el trabajo de aquí y se ganaba poco.*
97   Interview with Alonso Ayala. Alonso Ayala: *A muchos . . . les da pena hablar maya.*
98   Interview with Patricia Sahera.
99   Interview with Isaias Sánchez. Isaias Sánchez: *No sabes leer, no sabes escribir.*
100 Interview with Isaias Sánchez. Isaias Sánchez: *Mira chaparrito, tú tienes chanza de aprender aunque sea a firmar. Yo te voy a enseñar.*
101 Interview with Isaias Sánchez. Isaias Sánchez: *Ese hombre me enseñó. Fue a la tienda me trajo un pizarrón, de esos de la Coca-Cola. Y ahí empezó a poner las letras y todo eso.*
102 Interview with Isaias Sánchez. Isaias Sánchez: *Vamos a renovar contrato y no vas a poner el dedo.*
103 Interview with Pedro Domínguez. Pedro Domínguez: *Estaban los de Oaxaca también pero ellos nos platicaban, pero no les entendíamos porque ellos hablan de otra forma y uno no puede entenderles, pues a ellos también. Yo creo ni ellos también nos entendían a nosotros.*
104 Interview with Pedro Domínguez. Pedro Domínguez: *Sí, nos buscábamos, como que no estábamos contentos . . .*
105 Interview with Felix Flores. Felix Flores: *Él le decía en la barraca . . . 'Mira muchachos, paisanos, aquí están otros los paisanos, se van a tratar como gente, se van a tratar como her-*

manos, se van a tratar como sobrinos. No se van a pelear y ellos hablan otro idioma y ustedes otro idioma y otros otro idioma.

106 Interview with Felix Flores. Felix Flores: *Que nosotros éramos Bolcheviques.*

107 Interview with Felix Flores. Felix Flores: *Cálmense, no hagan caso, que si hacemos caso nos avientan hasta allá.*

108 Interview with Felix Flores. Felix Flores: *Ellos son altos y nosotros chaparros.*

109 Interview with Isaias Sánchez. Isaias Sánchez: *Los primeros que vinieron en 1945, los primeros hombres que vinieron aquí, fueron unos que llegaron allá y dijeron que Estados Unidos '[es]ta bien suave, [hay] mucho trabajo y gana mucho dinero.'*

110 Mize and Swords, *Consuming Mexican Labor*, 8.

111 Interview with Isaias Sánchez. Isaias Sánchez: *Los humillaban, les decían cosas.*

112 Interview with Isaias Sánchez. Isaias Sánchez: *Yo les decía, 'No les digan nada. Lo que están hablando ellos, ellos lo que hablan porque ellos así se entienden.' 'Y tú, ¿[por] qué te metes?' 'Tú no tienes ningún derecho de ofenderlos.' 'Y tú, ¿quién eres?' 'Porque yo soy parte de ellos.' Nos agarramos a fregazos.*

113 Interview with Isaias Sánchez. Isaias Sánchez: *Pues los insultaban, les decían malas palabras, y eso no se vale, no se vale.*

114 Interview with Isaias Sánchez. Isaias Sánchez: *'Si los insultas,' le digo ni te entienden. Porque ellos saben hablar poco castellano, pero poco.*

115 Interview with Julio Valentín May-May. Julio Valentín May-May: *Ya le caí mal.*

116 Interview with Julio Valentín May-May. Julio Valentín May-May: *Porque no oigan los otros.*

117 Ramirez Cuevas, "Cuando los Braceros se Fueron a Huelga en California."

118 Cuevas, "Cuando los Braceros se Fueron."

119 Interview with Isaias Sánchez. Isaias Sánchez: *Paisano, no nos dejes, si tú te vas a ir, nos vamos contigo. Tú nos vas a decir cuando vamos a cambiar el dinero, cuando nos vamos a ir a Oaxaca. Tú nos ayudas.*

120 Interview with Isaias Sánchez. Isaias Sánchez: *Seguro que sí.*

BIBLIOGRAPHY

Primary Sources

Manuscript Collections

Digital Archive
    Bracero History Archive
    Mexico City, Mexico
    Archivo General de la Nación Fondo Adolfo López Mateos
        Fondo Manuel Ávila Camacho
        Fondo Miguel Alemán Valdés
    Stanford, California
        Special Collections and University Archives, Stanford University Ernesto
        Galarza Papers

Oral Histories

Alarcón Carrera, Rosendo. Interview for Bracero History Archive by Laureano Martínez on May 28, 2003, in Durango, Durango.

Ayala, Alonso. Interview for Bracero History Archive by Mireya Loza on July 9, 2008, in Cansahcab, Yucatán.

De Vaney, Elvon. Interview for Southwest Collection at Texas Tech University by Jeff Townsend on March 9, 1974, in Lubbock, Texas.

Domínguez, Pedro. Interview for Bracero History Archive by Mireya Loza on June 27, 2008, in Patzcuaro, Michoacán.

Flores, Felix. Interview for Bracero History Archive by Mireya Loza on June 26, 2008, in Janitzio, Michoacán.

Martínez Ángel, Gabriel. Interview for Bracero History Archive by Edwin R. Ubeda on September 1, 2005, in Chicago, Illinois.

May-May, Julio Valentín. Interview for Bracero History Archive by Mireya Loza on July 9, 2008, in Cansahcab, Yucatán.

Meza, Nemecio. Interview for Bracero History Archive by Mireya Loza on May 12, 2006, in Los Angeles, California.

Sahera, Patricia. Interview for Bracero History Archive by Mireya Loza on July 29, 2008, in Salem, Oregon.

Sánchez, Isaias. Interview for Bracero History Archive by Alma Carrillo on May 20, 2006, in Coachella, California.

Soberanis, Orfa Noemi. Interview for Bracero History Archive by Mireya Loza on July 9, 2008, in Cansahcab, Yucatán.

Secondary Sources

Alanis Enciso, Fernando Saul. *El Primer Programa Bracero y el Gobierno de Mexico, 1917–1918.* San Luis Potosi: Colegio de San Luis, 1999.

Bonfil Batalla, Guillermo. *México Profundo: Reclaiming a Civilization.* Austin: University of Texas Press, 1996.

Buffington, Robert M. *Criminal and Citizen in Modern Mexico.* Lincoln: University of Nebraska Press, 2000.

Cline, Howard F. *The United States and Mexico.* Boston: Harvard University Press, 1953.

Cohen, Deborah. *Braceros: Migrant Citizens and Transnational Subjects in the Postwar United States and Mexico.* Chapel Hill: University of North Carolina Press, 2011.

Cruz-Manjarrez, Adriana. *Zapotecs on the Move: Cultural, Social, and Political Processes in a Transnational Perspective.* New Brunswick: Rutgers University Press, 2013.

Cullather, Nick. *The Hungry World: Americans' Cold War Battle against Poverty in Asia.* Boston: Harvard University Press, 2010.

Doremus, Anne. "Nationalism, Mestizaje, and National Identity in Mexico during the 1940s and the 1950s." *Mexican Studies/Estudios Mexicanos* 17, no. 2 (Summer 2001).

Driscoll de Alvarado, Barbara. *The Tracks North: The Railroad Bracero Program of World War II.* Austin: CMAS Books, Center for Mexican American Studies, University of Texas at Austin, 1999.

Fixico, Donald L. *The Urban Indian Experience in America.* Albuquerque: University of New Mexico Press, 2000.

Gamio, Manuel. *Forjando Patria: Pro Nacionalismo*. Boulder: University of Colorado Press, 2010.

Gamio, Manuel. *A World of Its Own: Race, Labor, and Citrus in the Making of Greater Los Angeles, 1900–1970*. Studies in Rural Culture. Chapel Hill: University of North Carolina Press, 2001.

García y Griego, Manuel. "The Importation of Mexican Contract Laborers to the United States, 1942–1964." In *Between Two Worlds: Mexican Immigrants in the United States*, edited by David G. Gutiérrez. Wilmington: Scholarly Resources Inc., 1996.

Gil Martínez de Escobar, R. *Fronteras de Pertenencia: Hacia la Construcción del Bienestar y el Desarollo Comunitario Transnacional de Santa María Tindú, Oaxaca*. Mexico City: Universidad Autonoma Metropolitana, 2006.

Greaves, Cecilia. "La Política y el Proyecto de Educación Indígena del Avilacamachismo." In *Historias, Saberes Indígenas y Nuevas Etnicidades en la la Escuela*, edited by María Bertley Busquets, 95–119. Mexico City: CIESAS, 2006.

Holms, Seth M. *Fresh Fruit, Broken Bodies: Migrant Farmworkers in the United States*. Berkeley: University of California Press, 2013.

Lewis, Oscar. *Life in a Mexican Village: Tepoztlan Restudied*. Urbana: University of Illinois Press, 1951.

Meeks, Eric V. *Border Citizens: The Making of Indians, Mexicans, and Anglos in Arizona*. Austin: University of Texas Press, 2007.

Menchaca, Martha. *Recovering History, Constructing Race: The Indian, Black, and White Roots of Mexican Americans*. Austin: University of Texas Press, 2001.

Mize, Ronald L., and Alicia C. S. Swords. *Consuming Mexican Labor: From the Bracero Program to NAFTA*. Toronto: University of Toronto Press, 2011.

Molina, Natalia. *How Race Is Made in America: Immigration, Citizenship, and the Historical Power of Racial Scripts*. Berkeley: University of California Press, 2014.

Mraz, John. "Today, Tomorrow, and Always: The Golden Age of Illustrated Magazines." In *Fragments of a Golden Age: The Politics of Culture in Mexico since 1940*, edited by Gilbert M. Joseph, Anne Rubenstein, and Eric Zolov, 116–58. Durham: Duke University Press, 2001.

Needler, Martin C. *Mexican Politics: The Containment of Conflict*. Westport: Praeger Publishers, 1995.

Niblo, Stephen. *Mexico in the 1940s: Modernity, Politics, and Corruption*. Wilmington: SR Books, 2000.

Ramirez Cuevas, Jesus. "Cuando los Braceros se Fueron a Huelga en California." La Jornada (October 19, 2003), http://www.jornada.unam.mx/2003/10/19/mas-jesus.html (November 23, 2015).

Rivera-Sánchez, Liliana. "Belongings and Identities: Migrants between the Mixteca and New York." PhD diss., New School University, 2001.

Roediger, David, and Elizabeth D. Esch. *The Production of Difference: Race and the Management of Labor in U.S. History*. New York: Oxford, 2012.

Rosas, Ana Elizabeth. *Abrazando El Espíritu: Bracero Families Confront the US-Mexico Border*. Berkeley: University of California Press, 2014.

Ruiz, Jason. *Americans in the Treasure House: Travel to Porfirian Mexico and the Cultural Politics of Empire*. Austin: University of Texas Press, 2014.

Sánchez, George J. *Becoming Mexican American: Ethnicity, Culture, and Identity in Chicano Los Angeles, 1900–1945.* New York: Oxford University Press, 1993.

Sarricolea Torres, Juan Miguel. "Cuerpos Masculinos en Tránsito: Una Etnografía con Hombres, Mujeres, y Familias Migrantes de Jerez, Zacatecas, 1940–1964." PhD diss., El Colegio de Michoacán, 2014.

Schmidt Camacho, Alicia. *Migrant Imaginaries: Latino Cultural Politics in the U.S.-Mexico Borderlands.* New York: New York University Press, 2008.

Stephen, Lynn. *Transborder Lives: Indigenous Oaxacans in Mexico, California, and Oregon.* Durham: Duke University Press, 2007.

Tarica, Estelle. *The Inner Life of Mestizo Nationalism.* Minneapolis: University of Minnesota Press, 2008.

Topete, Jesús. *Aventuras de un Bracero.* Monterrey, Mexico: Gráfica Moderna, 1961.

Urías Horcasitas, Beatriz. *La Historia Secreta del Racismo en Mexico (1920–1950).* Mexico City: Tusquets, 2007.

Vasconcelos, José. *The Cosmic Race/La Raza Cósmica.* Baltimore: Johns Hopkins University Press, 1997.

Weiner, Richard. *Race, Nation, and Market: Economic Culture in the Porflrian Mexico.* Tucson: University of Arizona Press, 2004.

PART VI

NEW BORDER

IMAGINARIES

Tijuana: Hybridity and Beyond:
A Conversation with Néstor García Canclini

FIAMMA MONTEZEMOLO

Translated by John Pluecker

FIAMMA MONTEZEMOLO: Néstor, when I asked you for an interview, you pointed out that you had undertaken your last research on Tijuana in 2000. "Since then," you said, "I have continued to follow its process of disintegration and transformation in newspapers, in academic articles and through friends' stories. I would say that for me, Tijuana is no longer, as I wrote in *Hybrid Cultures*,[1] a laboratory of postmodernity but rather perhaps a laboratory of the social and political disintegration of Mexico as a consequence of a calculated ungovernability."

There are several points that I would like to tease out with you. The first is this: Why were you interested in Tijuana in the eighties?

NÉSTOR GARCÍA CANCLINI: I first went to Tijuana in 1979. At that time the federal government under President López Portillo thought it was necessary to strengthen Mexican identity in the border region due to its proximity to the United States. I was doing fieldwork in Michoacán on indigenous craftwork and its transformation due to contact with the city and tourism. I was fascinated to find a very different

Mexico in the border region with a discourse distinct from the rest of the country. Border towns had more of a relationship with the United States than with the Mexican capital. Many people had never been south of Guadalajara.

Later, in 1984, I was invited to do a study of the public served by the Centro Cultural de Tijuana (CECUT). The Centro had been built in 1982 as part of a project to strengthen identity and develop local cultural facilities. CECUT existed primarily as a building and only later as a cultural programme. We agreed—I and two other anthropologists—to do a study not only of the CECUT's audience but also to try to understand Tijuana's cultural needs. I also suggested that focus groups of people in a variety of professions select the most representative parts of the city. We found interesting evidence that their perception of Tijuana was not strictly territorial: for example, someone answered "Balboa Park," which is in San Diego. There was a certain transterritoriality or urban transnationalism.

Through interviews and fieldwork with artists, intellectuals and academics from the Colegio de la Frontera Norte, journalists and photographers, we demonstrated that the city was an extraordinary cultural and economic force. Significantly that while Mexico underwent no economic growth during the eighties, Tijuana experienced a leap of approximately 10 percent.

FM: That's what they say: When Mexico does badly, Tijuana does well . . .

NGC: The image of Tijuana that emerged through fieldwork was very different from the stereotypes in the US or Mexican newspapers. In the eighties, Tijuana was for many synonymous with emigrants from all over Mexico who came to form a kind of synthesis of Mexicanness, and at the same time an incredibly dynamic place of business, tourism and sexual spectacle. All of this gave rise to complex interactions, a diversity of cultural demands and expectations in regard to what a cultural centre as large as the CECUT could offer, very different from audiences of museums and cultural centres in Mexico City.

In the nineties, I went back to Tijuana to participate with InSite, an important binational artistic event organised in Tijuana and San Diego. I worked with Manuel Valenzuela on a study of the repercussions of the "border art" and "public art" which every two or three years experimented with new aesthetic, urban and institutional configurations.[2] I was interested in the complexity of migratory processes and the existence of multiple borders. The cliché of the Mexican–US border was just coming undone and different perspectives were recognised, not only

FIGURE 22.1 Ingrid Hernández, *Neighborhood,* 2006, digital photograph, 90 × 75 cm, collection of the artist

FIGURE 22.2 Ingrid Hernández, *Shop at the outskirts*, 2007, digital photograph, 50 × 40 cm, collection of the artist

between Tijuana and San Diego, but also between San Diego and El Paso, or between Tijuana and Ciudad Juárez.

In part because Tijuana represented the synthesis of contemporary processes—restructuring relationships between metropolis and peripheries, interethnic creativity, the change from national cultures to globalised flows—Tijuana as a multicultural city was held up as an emblem of postmodernity. Many of us who shared those experiences or studied them saw the border, along with the drama of immigration and the violent asymmetries between the United States and Mexico, as a space in which the dying certainties of nationalism were being destabilised and an unforeseen creativity might emerge. This perspective was developed in the analyses of Latin American critics and curators, as well as in the articles about InSite by *Art in America* and *Art Forum*.[3] Sociologists like Larry Herzog asked themselves if Tijuana "could become the next Hong Kong."[4]

Nevertheless, in the following years, I began to notice the risks involved in sustaining the notion of Tijuana as a laboratory of postmodernity. I remember speaking to John Kraniauskas, an English cultural critic, about the border as a place where the territorialised stereotypes of Mexicanness were breaking down. He made a very pertinent point: that I was paying much

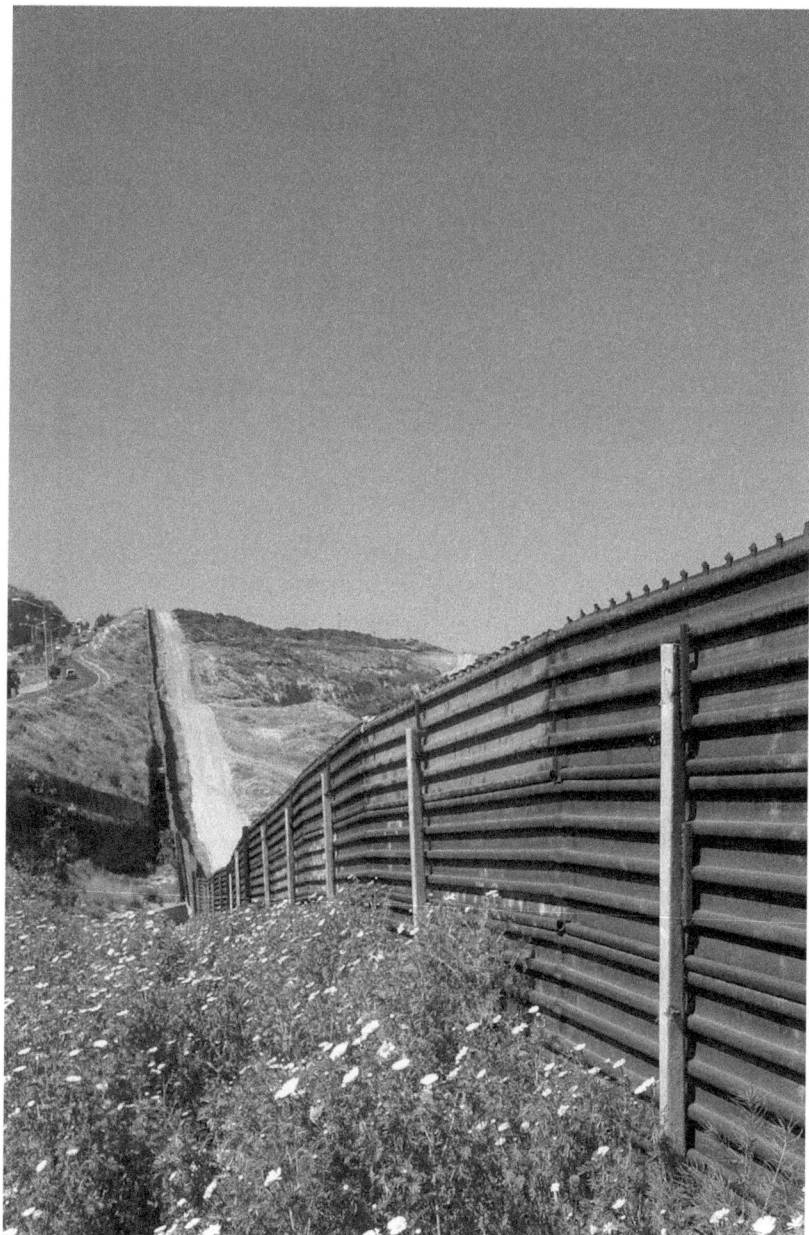

FIGURE 22.3 Ingrid Hernández, *Border fence Tijuana-San Diego*, 2005, digital photograph, 60 × 50 cm, collection of the artist

FIGURE 22.4 Ingrid Hernández, *Two residential areas,* 2004, digital photograph, 50 × 40 cm, collection of the artist

more attention to the phenomenon of de-territorialisation rather than to the re-territorialisation sought by the migrants, who were now converted into new residents of the border.

Changes in the Conceptualisation of Borders

FM: At one time, did Tijuana seem like a vanguard to you?

NGC: I saw Tijuana as a very advanced place but also with serious social and economic backwardness. If one considers the structures of work in the maquiladoras,[5] for example, or social disintegration, the brutal effects on families torn apart by migration, this process can't be simplified to fit into a single historical direction. I would not use the word vanguard, but without a doubt those contemporary contradictions were made more obviously visible, in a more intense way, than in other regions of Mexico.

As time passed, it became necessary to oppose hasty thinking that referenced cities like Tijuana, or borders like the one between Mexico and the United States, as a way to justify theories about the predominance of nomadism. A way of thinking had emerged which celebrated the fluidity and the permeability of the border. Some artistic movements, although still motivated by the exaltation of nomadism, attempted a new kind of analysis. The changes generated during the development of InSite represent this shift quite well. The time that artists and intellectuals from many countries spent living in this area, after being invited by the binational programme to carry out projects, gave them the opportunity to discover the variety of situations and actors. They didn't arrive with previously completed work, rather they went through a process of immersion in the area before beginning their production, even though they were not required explicitly to refer to the border. By following these processes and seeing their ambivalence, the artists took positions or avoided the question of the border, and thereby made the diversity and the ambivalence clear. One of the contrasts that I first noticed was that while foreign artists used the public space of Tijuana with much more freedom, contrasting their search for forms with the local culture and border conflicts, many Latin American artists who went to San Diego to make their artworks ended up hiding it in a basement: it was as if the urbanism of San Diego, and getting a grasp of that urban fabric, made their interventions that much more difficult. Some artists have used the open spaces, above all Chicano muralists, but there were in general few instances of public art within the city. The lack of urban structure in Tijuana seemed to be more propitious to the utilisation of space than the layout of isolated neighbourhoods in San Diego, linked together by highways.

FM: If we are all positioned subjects—in the sense of the term provided by Donna Haraway, Renato Rosaldo, Trinh Minh-ha and other cultural theorists—what was the influence of your own "positionality" in relationship to your reading of Tijuana in that historical period? Do you think you grasped that idea through your own de-territorialisation and hybridity?

NGC: In 1976, when I left Argentina after the military coup and moved to Mexico, I experienced several migration processes: one was the change in country, another was the disciplinary migration because I was schooled in philosophy and in Mexico I began to do fieldwork as an anthropologist. We worked on Michoacán with a group of researchers with the idea not only of studying Purépecha communities in isolation in their own territories, but also instances of migrating, travelling to distant festivals to sell their craft products. For me, it was vital to the anthropological project at that time to recognise the multiple outflows and exchanges that in the end redefined Purépecha culture.

FM: I imagine that you, being from Argentina, would have had a bit of a different relationship with Mexico, at least initially, from that of a Mexican. We're talking about a Mexican nationalism that can be quite strong.

NGC: Yes, and with a role played by the State that I had never known in Argentina. Many people have asked me about the cultural shock I experienced when I arrived in Mexico and I always say that there wasn't much confrontation, because the strong feeling of terror I brought with me from Argentina contrasted with a very welcoming Mexico. I quickly found work, good conditions for putting together research teams, funding for fieldwork and publishing. Two books of mine were published which did not appear in Argentina because of repression and censorship. Mexico had a steady rate of development, due to the single-party hegemony of the PRI (The Institutional Revolutionary Party [*Partido Revolucionario Institucional*]), and at the same time was opening up to dissident thought.

A few years later, I wrote a few pages about my own disaffection or difficulty in adapting to Mexican ways of being and acting. An appendix in *The Imagined Globalization*[6] explains my subject position in relation to this text about globalisation. I wasn't speaking from a neutral place, but rather out of the tension between a number of cultures, that of an Argentinian who studied in France, who went to Mexico as an exile and admired certain lifestyles in the United States and Europe and rejected others, discovering the relativity of each culture and the necessity of thinking interculturally.

Tijuana and the Debate about Hybridisation and Ethnicity

FM: Your theory of the hybrid has provoked a number of reactions both at a local level and internationally. Some have adopted it with enthusiasm and others have interpreted it as a theory out of touch with the "real condition" of the city. There is the problem of opposition to someone from another culture, an outsider with the power to speak and make decisions without local consent; there's also the problem laid out by *tijua-*

nense writers like Heriberto Yépez who feel that the theory of the hybrid is somehow a pacified Hegelian synthesis dressed up as something new, referring to a lack of resistance. The fact is, the theory of the hybrid has had more success outside the city than in the city itself.

NGC: Some of those critiques are understandable. They have helped make clear that, by interpreting social processes with the category of hybridity, we run the risk of covering up contradictions. I wrote a new introduction to *Hybrid Cultures* in 2001 to debate that question and return to the intense debate about hybridisation which took place in Spanish and in English during the nineties. Many works appeared, for example Homi Bhabha's book,[7] and an enormous number of international journals, with entire issues devoted to the topic. I began to see that hybridisation, as a central process of modernity and postmodernity, also had to be articulated along with concepts of contradiction and inequality. Hybridisation, as an initial process of fusion, had to be differentiated from the consequences which later emerged as it was unpacked. When there is migration, there is what anthropologists in another period called "cultural contact," and which is almost always hybridisation. But it is not enough to look at what can be fused together: we must also consider what is left out, other processes of contradiction and of conflict. Hybridisation is not a synonym for reconciling things that are different or unequal.

FM: I felt that the work on hybridity implied a political thought beyond those Western oppositions of traditional/modern, white/not-white, feminine/masculine. There's a certain categorisation of the same and the other in these dualisms that is now very much in question, as always inherently hierarchical.

NGC: Yes, the emphasis on hybridisation was an effort to oppose identitarian essentialisms, and nationalism in Mexico and in other countries.

FM: In the United States as well, I would say.

NGC: Yes, in opposition to the segregating multiculturalism which compartmentalised ethnic groups and immigrants. All of that was there, but as time passed I realised that from an epistemological and methodological point of view, the concept of hybridisation is a descriptive. It allows us to describe multiple processes of fusion which can be religious syncretism, ethnic *mestizaje*, musical and cultural fusion, et cetera, but in each case we have specifically to analyse how those fusions are always partial—that they leave a great deal out—how they operate in the midst of conflicts and social inequalities that persist and are sometimes made worse by the contact itself. So hybridisation is not the destination, it is not the only concept for describing a societal state, and much less a satisfactory state. It is the recognition that cultures cannot develop in an autonomous way, isolated from what is happening on the global stage.

FM: Do you think that hybridity and a less solid conception of identity, an overly plural conception of identity, could weaken a politics of resistance or of self-determination? There is a certain fear that the politics of differences is going to destroy the politics of opposition. Paul Gilroy suggested the possibility of moving beyond these two oppositions through the notion of anti-anti-essentialism, that is, an identity which is neither monolithic and essentialised, nor completely useless because it is too fragmented by difference.[8] We are talking about a third possibility: an identity which is sensitive to differences, while at the same time open to alliances based on situational affinities. For example, I am thinking of the anti-globalisation movement that in Genoa was able to bring together feminists, environmentalists, pacifists and immigrants.

But even with this Gilroyan vision, a more general problem remains of reconciling hybridity with hegemonies and subalternities that continue to exist in the relationships between nation-states and that do not seem ready to collapse. How to reconcile the amount of biopolitics present on the border with the theory of multiplication of identities? How do we reconcile the discourse of auto-representation with the discourse of the hybrid?

NGC: A certain evolution within the social sciences in the last ten to fifteen years has meant that certain key concepts have been altered. Today, we speak of processes of identification more than of identity, of interculturality more than of hybridisation. What significance do these conceptual changes have? *Identity* always carries with it the risk of over-valuing self-affirmation and of essentialising it, freezing it. Identities are temporary sedimentations of processes that have been changing and will continue to change. So it does not mean much to say "we do this in the name of Chicano identity" or "we act this way because of our Brazilian identity." These identities designate abstract fusions of certain particularities, which in a certain historical moment were able to organise themselves into a group or nation but which continue to change in different ways in different regions of the same country, depending on contact with the outside world.

We can localise this analysis, say, in regard to Tijuana in the eighties. I am referring to the conflict between those who promoted the regional culture of Tijuana with its complexity and its heterogeneous make-up, and the national unifying cultural policies emanating from Mexico City, which sought to establish the canons of Mexicanness for northern residents.

Processes of identification instead are more dynamic and require us to take as a reference point that with which we identify ourselves, not to think of identity as something that we possess, as if it were a self-contained substance that belongs to us as a group. I'm thinking of Arjun Appadurai's *Modernity at Large* and his criticism of essentialist conceptions of identity and culture.[9] I still insist on the importance of examining the processes of hybridisation, but interculturality allows us to understand that cultures act among themselves without predefining what is going to happen or what is happening. We have to analyse the many forms of interculturality that imply acceptance, rejection, dominations, hegemonies, a multiplicity of forms of interaction. We know that there are historical moments in which the affirmation of a community, of a group, is valuable and necessary for survival.

FM: It's necessary to essentialise at times, in order to move to the level of politics.

NGC: We can understand, at this moment, the importance and value of ethnic and national identity affirmation in Bolivia. Although, from a theoretical or more general point of view, we would prefer a more fluid interaction with what is outside the actual nation. But I understand that now—after five hundred years of *criollo* white domination, subordination and exclusion of indigenous people—there is not only an indigenous president but also a completely indigenous cabinet. This is a historic event. It would be beneficial, if they had time, to articulate this historical bloc we call Bolivia on new axes.

FM: You're making me think of my work on Zapatismo in the early nineties. I noticed their dynamic use of "ethnic" in their communiqués. The first communiqués put much less emphasis on a certain "indigeneity" or "Mayanness," while the later communiqués made greater use of that concept, because it was understood that the use of ethnicity would not necessarily isolate the group but rather would strengthen it in a globalised world under the threat of dominant homogenisation. A certain identity-based localism was very attractive for many lost souls (including myself), from a West looking for alternatives to itself. Zapatismo and its ethnic specificity came to be understood as a possibility for resistance.

NGC: We would also have to include in that analysis the marginalisation of the Zapatistas within Chiapas by the Mexican state and the army, which made it difficult for them to construct a national or international alternative. In the first communiqués, Zapatismo had three agendas: a local one for Chiapas and the indigenous communities; another agenda for the country; and—let's not forget that the insurgency began on 1 January 1994 when NAFTA [North American Free Trade Agreement] went into effect—it also proposed an international agenda for Mexican relations with the world. That last part later became diplomatic relations: looking for solidarity from foreign countries. Inside Mexico, they began to fail for many reasons not solely due to the Zapatistas but rather to the Mexican political system and to its social movements. Their calls for solidarity organised an alternative power base, and that also contributed to rooting themselves more deeply in the indigenous, the ethnic and in more local demands.

FM: Doesn't it seem interesting to you that a city renowned as "postmodern," "Bajalta," a megalopolis tied to LA, shows such obvious signs of an industrial reality (like that of the maquila) generally associated with the modern Fordist era? A city in which half the population still does not cross the border, while the other half crosses mainly to shop or to work or to share a kind of "Bajalta-ness," unless it has to do with family relationships or specific friends, possibly among the upper-middle classes. In five years of experience in Tijuana, I realised that certain theoretical concepts like hybridity and transculturation or transnationalism operate more effectively in relation to certain social classes or specific ethnic groups. For example, young people of the upper-middle classes who have access to the internet, who have passports and access their own surroundings. Or we see that the idea of a more open border is more in use from a Chicano point of view than from a specifically *fronterizo* (frontier-corridor) perspective. As we said previously, there are many people in Tijuana who never cross the border and for whom the border remains simply a wall which unfortunately is not at all porous.

NGC: Transculturality, or the trans-city or the trans-border, was over-exaggerated. It exists more as a circuit than as a space, more as a possibility of a constant and fluid exchange, sometimes with great obstacles, than as a shared culture. When one crosses from Tijuana to San Diego or from San Diego to Tijuana, one immediately notices the differences in the spatial layout, the care of the front yards, the traffic on the streets.

FM: Even in the attitude . . . My *tijuanense* friends, almost invariably, when they cross the border into San Diego drive differently, with a respect for the law and traffic signals.

NGC: Perhaps the notion of Bajalta, of transborder, isn't very productive. It is more helpful to talk about circuits. Looking for cheaper prices to produce goods and an ease of coming and going corresponds to global movements, not only between Mexico and the United States, but that also occur with Jakarta or African countries. This allows the mobility of capital and goods which circulate and accumulate in a way very different from Fordism.

FM: Yes, that's true. But I was referring more to the local working conditions in the maquila . . . without unions, without rights, with women in a majority because they are less educated, more vulnerable, and thus easier to manipulate. They are fixed in a historical moment that we thought was already over. I would differentiate the dynamics of the finished product from that of the production itself. Those two conditions would seem to belong to two different periods, which paradoxically continue to exist contemporaneously in Tijuana.

NGC: But this is a characteristic of capitalist development in most of the world. In the central countries, despite the current economic crisis, a higher level of well-being in labour terms persists, for instance better collective bargaining contracts. When the same companies appear in peripheral countries, they impose the most unjust conditions, not only on production but also on services. The great transnationals like Walmart, for example, exploit workers more in Latin American because the legal structure in these countries is weaker and it's easier to corrupt the authorities.

FM: It's well known that the maquiladoras are now moving from Mexico to China because there are even more advantages there for the companies.

Again, it seems to me that Tijuana is caught between two different kinds of violence: the violence of the border and of the Foucauldian polarity of biopolitics/biosecurity, and the violence of the drug-trafficking and kidnappings taking place across Mexico. How did this condition arise? Did the events of September 11 in the United States and others in Mexico itself create this explosive situation?

NGC: It began before September 11. The repression of immigrants, the organisation of Ku Klux Klan–like groups, laws restricting rights . . . all of this was already evidence of a social and cultural uneasiness in the US and of forms of racist discrimination previous to the extension of the border wall ordered during the Bush administration. It also has to do with the increase in emigration of labour from Mexico and other Latin American countries due to the reorganisation of agricultural production that stemmed from deindustrialisation and free trade agreements. Along with those processes of social and economic regression, during the last decades of the twentieth century there was a steady acceptance of the advance of informality and illegality in labour relations, the growing power of drug-traffickers who were even conceded political protection. The death of Colosio, the PRI presidential candidate in 1994, took place in Tijuana, but it was never cleared up in an acceptable investigation in which national forces were implicated. That's why it's possible to say that from that time on Tijuana was the laboratory of the sociopolitical disintegration of Mexico as a consequence of a calculated ungovern-ability. With that disintegration, the volume of migration increased, and also the possibility of sending remittances to relatives in Mexico: a very precarious equilibrium was maintained in this way between the population which was lost and the survival of those who stayed behind.

FM: Remittances make up the third highest source of income in the Mexican economy.

NGC: But they are decreasing. It seems that the annual level of remit-tances at twenty-five billion dollars a year will not be seen again and im-migration specialists offer several explanations: one is the recession and the loss of jobs in the US; another is that the second or third generation of immigrants in the US, with all their local commitments (paying for the car, the house, the kids' education), don't have enough money left to maintain their relationship with Mexico. Then, there are also the barri-ers of increased border controls for sending money.

These facts at least partially explain the repositioning of Tijuana and other Mexican border towns in relation to the worldwide restructuring of the markets. The impact of the recent economic crisis in the US is greater in Mexico, thanks to NAFTA and an increased and more consoli-dated dependency on the US. More than 90 percent of Mexican trade is with the US, unlike other Latin American countries, such as Argen-tina or Brazil, who divide their commercial relationships between Eu-rope, the United States and their regional neighbours. The way the Free

Trade Agreement was established, with free passage of goods but not of people, also has a large influence. The Mexican government was not able to include migration in the treaties. And there has also been a growth of so-called informality throughout the country, as demonstrated along the border by illegal trafficking in goods, people and drugs, in shady businesses of all kinds, immigrant exploitation, kidnappings and violence in the dispute for public space and commercial networks.

FM: Are we seeing a resurgence of the "Leyenda Negra"?[10]

NGC: It is no longer the same "Leyenda Negra" of the last century which stigmatised Tijuana in particular. What's happening in Tijuana is in some way what is happening throughout Mexico: incredibly violent killings, dismembered bodies, corruption at all levels of the police and the State. The conflicts between mafias, the decapitated cadavers, the police and political complicity are reproduced in regions far from the border: Acapulco, Michoacán, Mexico City.

FM: The main difference involved in the violence in Tijuana is that the city is caught between two violences: the one that it shares with the entire country, and the border one which is biopolitical, related to hyper-identification like fingerprinting, iris scans, the power to look inside my body for proof of my citizenship and of my intention to return to my country after my visit. This "secondary" inspection is very illustrative— an obsessive review of your identity, your "legality" and your intentions on crossing the border. Any attempt at intrusion by an undetermined identity is blocked. There is a logic in the feared secondary inspection that forcefully marks the divide between the "First" and "Third" Worlds, where not even the slightest ambiguity is permitted. If you are Mexican, you will be admitted, but only under certain conditions.

The statistics speak of illegal migration and commuters but also insist on the 42 percent of people who wait in line for hours under the glaring sun to "go shopping." Many Mexican consumers are infatuated with spending their savings in San Diego or *"en el otro lado."* This topology shines a light on the "most agreeable and inoffensive" category of visitors, those who are not ambiguous non-residents, who are possibly middle class, with a light skin tone, with understandable English, and who, after an afternoon of shopping, go "back home," to their own territory of juridico-political belonging.

Borders become mise-en-scène in two ways. The "white" upper-middle-class Mexican, schooled in certain educational environments, economically stable, a "consumer" who knows that it isn't difficult to play the role of the useful "alien," is the same character who is generally well accepted inside Mexico as well—a country which at times reproduces historical racial dynamics very similar to those of Western countries. It is this ambiguity which creates this sense of danger, the uncertain identities, the shady intentions both inside and outside the nations of belonging, the same motives for provoking the suspicions of the agents on any border that seeks to preserve the imaginary homogeneity of a nation-state. In this sense, the border continues to be a highly bio-politicised place, not only as an obvious judicial system of inclusion/exclusion, but also as a stage for the national projects of Mexico and the United States.

Lost Creativity and the Appropriation of the Different

FM: Tijuana lives between two myths that do not just characterise the perception of the city but also that of the "Third World" in general: the creativity and violence, Rousseau's "noble savage," and the other as a dangerous and sinister being. A certain West still perceives a certain "Other" in this double vision. An "exceptionalisation" of the Other, whether in a positive or a negative way, comes to the same end: a distorted perception. *Tijuanense* artists became relevant without any real sense of discrimination (often independently of their real value, indubitable or not), because the West still needs its noble savages. Their creativity becomes something "natural," innate, in opposition to a West considered functional and rational. The West keeps looking for its Josephine Baker, to exploit the Other through a creativity which is seemingly out of reach for it. A trend that has taken the postcolonial peripheries to the peak of fashion and which tomorrow—capricious and unpredictable—will consign these internal and external others once again to a new oblivion.

NGC: We find various processes in what you are saying. There are international movements which broaden the field of legitimacy of the artistic mainstream and have continually incorporated a selective sample of African, Asian and Latin American artists. The majority of the art produced on these three continents circulates on a local or national level, but an increasing number of artists are being invited to the celebrity Biennials and to the Biennials now being developed in the so-called Third World: Johannesburg, São Paulo, etc. We can also see the development of a cosmopolitan culture in Tijuana, partly thanks to InSite. That kind of artistic and cultural development didn't exist in Tijuana in the eighties and artists had more difficulty showing their work. Hardly anyone crossed the border to show their work on the other side; they went as spectators. That changed because now Tijuana, with a better educational system and sustained quality production, has local audiences and international resonance.

FM: Among other things, the new art school at the Universidad Autónoma de Baja California . . .

NGC: Yes, publications, shows, visits and residencies by mainstream artists. All of this has attracted the attention of international art magazines, of US curators, to find out what's happening in the city. A new type of author and artist has appeared who doesn't speak as a *tijuanense* or about Tijuana any more, but rather with a certain style that has international echoes. I'm thinking of Marcos Ramírez Erre, Luis Humberto Crosthwaite and others. It's not that they cease to represent a place, but that "they have to recognise me, not because I'm *tijuanense*, but because I'm an artist who produces work of a value." The phenomenon of the collectives also seems very interesting to me, like Bulbo, for example, a media collective with anthropological interests. The intervention of artists from outside the city is also important, like Judith Werthein's artwork Brinco, of the shoes to cross the border. It is a matter of positioning oneself as one would for somewhere else. I'm thinking of the work of Erre, the Trojan horse left for a time next to the immigration checkpoints between Tijuana and San Diego: a gigantic wooden horse with two heads, one looking towards the United States and the other towards Mexico, later reproduced in Valencia, Spain to examine borders between Europe and Latin America, and adopted as a symbol of the Biennial, "Encuentro entre dos mares" ("Encounter between Two Seas").

FM: My criticism is more directed at a certain way of curating. I remember an artist from Tijuana who told me: "curators just aren't interested in art that's not related to the border, that's why if one wants to enter a certain circuit, one has to produce works about the border."

NGC: That process of exoticisation remains widespread. No one demands that German, French or American artists should represent the place they're from. The most introspective artist from Mexico, Gabriel Orozco, seems forced—despite his best efforts to distance himself from Mexicanness—to provide signs of Mexicanness, no matter what.

FM: Is this obsession with a certain "Mexicanness," always associated with Mexican artists, related to a discourse of alternative modernity?

NGC: We see different situations. In some cases, exoticising is necessary to reaffirm a culture that is thought to be in decline: there are those who, to shake up the market, offer something which is somehow novel or provocative. In addition, there's a desire on the part of peripheral artists to be accepted by hegemonic circuits. Nor must we forget that the art market has become a place for the safe investment of huge sums of money and tax write-offs. But what has happened in the last few years—unlike the period of neo-Mexicanism—is that after 1989 and the fall of the Berlin Wall, Europe started looking more to the East than to Latin America. Since then Latin American artists have been steadily displaced by the emergence of Asian countries in the Western artworld, with new actors from China, India, Korea.

Artists as Anthropologists

FM: The possibility of an ethnographically related art in Biennials and artistic events geopolitically positioned in strategic areas, possibly Third World areas, seems highly problematic. I am thinking of Hal Foster's criticisms. Involving an "other" is supposed to be important because, as Foster says, the "other" is "dans le vrai," just because of being situated in those cultural, ethnic, economic, social or gender margins.[11]

NGC: An aspect of what Foster calls the "ethnographic turn" in contemporary art is of course very attractive to me as an anthropologist. This is more interesting right now than a sociology of art or a sociological art. In general, sociology tends to work with structured social situations, and anthropology with more intersubjective questions, paying more attention to the variations of behaviour, experience, and not only what is determinative. In this sense, art, as work focused on the evolution of the I and the alterity of the other, is a discipline also interested in experience.

Another coincidence that allows us to talk about an ethnographic art is that both art and anthropology have dedicated much work to unmasking the institutions that sediment or freeze objects. Anthropological criticism of the institutionalising codification of museums is analogous to the concern of a lot of artists.

In this ethnographic turn we find what Foster calls "a nostalgia for the real," the search to reinsert art into life, as the vanguards said in the first half of the twentieth century. It is a turning back to everyday experience, to spectators participating as actors, listening to society from the inside again. I find similarities between what happens with the ephemeral interventions of artists and what is happening with anthropological work. Even though ethnographic work tends to be more long term, there is a moment when the anthropologist leaves, writes or teaches on the basis of what he or she saw of the people who lived in that place. The capacity of the anthropologist is limited in what it can accomplish, but often he or she aspires to modify society or intercultural relationships between societies. The artist also wants to intervene, but more on a symbolic level. The anthropologist's question is: "What have I revealed? What did I discover in this aspect of social life? How can it change? Is my description useful or not?" In so far as art intervenes in symbolic relationships, what the artist can provide is rather a change in the way society is perceived and represented, providing the possibility of seeing in a new way.

Given that the symbolic is indeed part of society, there is a possibility of intervening in the real, while acting on the symbolic. But all of this is, of course, very uncertain. What we call ethnographic art has enhanced the role of art, avoids reducing it to elitist circles and suggests other ways of relating socially. In other cases, deconstruction of the institution—or of border codification, as in Tijuana—can be converted into a game for the well informed that reverts to the most inscrutable artistic practices once again.

With regard to your question of artistic and ethnographic practices in the peripheral countries, discrimination is prevalent because we live on the divide created by the hegemonic control that stems from a mainstream metropolitan art and the separate and alternative developments without access to that mainstream. But there are also other experiences that, although not called ethnographic art, occur within Europe and the central countries. I am thinking of the intervention of Santiago Sierra at the Venice Biennale in 2003. He closed the Spanish pavilion with a wall across the main entrance and a sign that read, "if you want to come in, you must enter through the back, where armed guards will request a document proving Spanish national identity." He shone a spotlight on the exclusion of foreigners from Spain, and also, in a way, spoke of the difficulty of representing a country, the pointlessness of an artist taking on the burden of national representation in a globalised event.

FM: It seems odd to me that one Spaniard would think him- or herself capable of representing the entirety of Spain. As Stuart Hall said, "Just being black doesn't mean I can represent any black person."

NGC: I don't know if it is right to ask art to occupy the space left empty by politics. Perhaps the real work of the artist is that of producing experiences, or making hidden experiences visible, interpreting them and suggesting forms of thinking and memory, projections into the future without having to produce measurable results. It's the most devious and elliptical design of the symbolic.

FM: At the same time, there are artists who are looking to change their point of intervention. Not so easy if you involve a "community"—with all the risks inherent in that—unsure if that will change its conditions, typically underprivileged, as a consequence of the artistic intervention. Who is this experience for? Only for the artist's audience? Difficult to say it's for the community in question, which—once the artist is gone—returns to its daily situation of uncertainty. The artist takes his or her success away, which often doesn't seem to get beyond a certain narcissism and notoriety. I have doubts about relational art in situ. I feel that the ethical remains outside of it—for example, that wonderful InSite video produced by Itzel Martínez about the street girls. What will it take to the girls when InSite ends? Specifically, what will it take them that could help them in their incredibly difficult daily lives?

NGC: There is still another aspect: the relationship between the artist and the media. A large part of the artistic circuit has become eloquent through its media relationship. Many artists aim to perturb, to surprise, so the media covers their work, providing it with a boost of far greater reach. But this requires subordinating oneself to the logic of the media which is ephemeral, which almost never generates community, but rather simply a show with a manipulated message. Even so, interaction between art and the media has at times produced interesting results. I am thinking of the work of Krzysztof Wodiczko in Tijuana. He projected the stories of maquila women onto the huge "ball" of the CECUT building, telling of their abuse at the hands of bosses, husbands and men in general. He worked with psychologists in Tijuana to do these interviews. The women gave their testimonies and their faces appeared in the projected video. The criticism levelled was that the artist would leave the women to face vengeful reprisals for their public denunciations. For the artist, this work was very successful, for the women we don't know . . . we would have to speak with them.

FM: A piece on the after-effects of an artwork seems called for. That is the ethical aspect I was talking about. It leaves me perplexed. Of course, this also happens with the anthropologist. Staying for more months or years does not spare the anthropologist from similar questions that arise in his or her "heart of darkness," as Conrad said.

NGC: It is analogous, even though the interventions have different purposes. Another recourse is that the artist, instead of creating work alone, involves local organisations of women or migrants, with the hope that these could capitalise on part of the work.

FM: But the problem remains: why choose women or indigenous people, that is, why maintain this idea of the subaltern subject of alterity—now in fashion, previously dismissed and perhaps tomorrow rejected once again—as the truth for all of us who do not belong to that specific alterity? Besides, it empowers certain groups or actors that the artist chooses dialogue with instead of others, thus creating more hierarchies locally between those who participated in the project and those who were left out.

NGC: I ask myself what would have happened if Wodiczko had dared to interview the men who were accused of doing these things, the bosses at the maquiladoras or the husbands.

FM: It would be interesting to include more contradictory voices in the work.

NGC: The emphasis that we now place on interculturality, on not speaking from one place only, removes us from the period of György Lukács and the later subalternists when it was thought that certain social positions generated truth: the proletariat in capitalism, women in the condition of gender, or indigenous people in possession of the truth about interethnic society. It seems to me that the truth, or the representations which most approximate it, must be in more places than one and in more interactions.

FM: The comparative turn can multiply points of view, providing more partial truths. I'd like to conclude with a question about specific geopolitical categories born in the post-Bandung era that we could judge as being less rigorous but still utilised. Is Tijuana, Mexico City, Mexico in general "First" or "Third" World or both?

NGC: These are categories that are less and less precise, even though they continue to be used. The category of Third World, which includes Asia, Africa and Latin America, spans continents different from each other and within themselves. It includes a reality so immense as to be meaningless. I would call it a category useful in order to unify those excluded from the perspective of the "metropolis": "people who are like us." But the "us" is not homogeneous either, not even inside Europe. We can see the problems the European Union has had trying to make its members identify themselves as European.

NOTES

Reprinted with the permission of RightsLink and Taylor & Francis. This essay originally appeared in *Third Text* 23, no. 6 (2009): 733–50. I am grateful to Surpik Angelini and the Transart Foundation for funding my travels to Mexico City and making possible this conversation.

1   Néstor García Canclini, *Hybrid Cultures: Strategies for Entering and Leaving Modernity*, trans Christopher L Chiàppari and Silvia L López, University of Minnesota Press, Minneapolis, 1995.

2   Néstor García Canclini and Jose Manuel Valenzuela Arce, *Intromisiones compartidas: Arte y sociedad en la frontera México/Estados Unidos*, FONCA—InSite San Diego/Tijuana, 2000.

3   See, for example, Jan Tumlir, InSite 05, *Artforum*, November 2005 and Nico Israel, Over the Border, *Artforum*, May 2005.

4   Lawrence A. Herzog, *From Aztec to High Tech: Architecture and Landscape Across the Mexico-United States Border*, Johns Hopkins University Press, Baltimore, MD, 1999.

5   A maquila is a factory that imports materials and equipment on a duty-free and tariff-free basis for assembly or manufacturing and then re-exports the assembled product, usually back to the originating country. A maquila is also referred to as a "twin plant," or "in-bond" industry. Nearly half a million Mexicans are employed in maquiladoras.

6   Néstor García Canclini, *Consumers and Citizens: Globalization and Multicultural Conflicts*, trans George Yúdice, University of Minnesota Press, Minneapolis, 2001.

7   Homi Bhabha, *The Location of Culture*, Routledge, London, 1994.

8   Paul Gilroy, *The Black Atlantic: Modernity and Double-Consciousness*, Harvard University Press, Cambridge, MA, 1993.

9   Arjun Appadurai, *Modernity at Large: Cultural Dimensions of Globalization*, University of Minnesota Press, Minneapolis, 1996.

10 *La Leyenda Negra* (The Black Legend) is a term coined by Julián Juderías in his 1914 book *La leyenda negra y la verdad histórica (The Black Legend and Historical Truth)* in reference to British Hispanophobia in the Early Modern period, resulting in the depiction of Spain and Spaniards as "cruel," "intolerant" and "fanatical."

11 Hal Foster, *The Return of the Real: The Avant-Garde at the End of the Century*, MIT Press, Cambridge, MA, 1996.

The Art of Witness

ROSA-LINDA FREGOSO

There are 268 nails encircling the *Ni una más* crucifix. Two-hundred-sixty-eight nails in memory of women and girls murdered in Ciudad Juárez. After cross-ing the Paso del Norte International Bridge, we spot it immediately, the large wooden memory-cross on the Mexican side of the border, facing traffic that passes into El Paso. It is attached to a twelve-foot metal panel and bears a plac-ard etched with the "¡Ni una más!" ("Not one more!") slogan, in remembrance of the women and girls.

I've stood before this memory-cross on many occasions. This time, my sister Angela accompanies me and we are both grief-stricken by its scale, the throng of six-inch spikes that once held tags with the names of the deceased women. It is a haunting sight to behold. Two-hundred-sixty-eight iron spikes. I try to count as I walk closer, wrap my fingers around one's surface, cold and raspy to the touch, close my eyes, and try to conjure up the lives the *Ni una más* crucifix mourns.

FIGURE 23.1 Memory-cross at Juárez toll booth as cars approach Paso del Norte bridge to El Paso, Texas, 2007. Photo by Angela Fregoso. Courtesy: Rosa-Linda Fregoso.

I

"Acompáñenos" is how Paula Flores phrases her plea, looking at us with dark, pensive eyes. In May of 2007, I am sitting next to my research collaborator, Cynthia, at a gender violence conference sponsored by Stanford University when Paula asks the audience to accompany the mothers of women and girls

who were murdered and disappeared in Ciudad Juárez, for monthly protests against the government.[1]

I could not refuse. As a mother, I connected deeply with Paula, who has survived a mother's most unfathomable fear: the brutal and unresolved murder of her teenage daughter, Sagrario González, in 1998.

Sagrario left home on the morning of April 16 and never returned. She was not accustomed to traveling alone to work at CAPCOM, a maquiladora or assembly plant located twelve miles away from her home on the outskirts of Juárez, but recently her shift changed from the one she shared with her father and sister, Guillermina. To get to work on time, Sagrario caught the bus at four in the morning.

The morning shift ended at three in the afternoon and by ten, she had not returned home. Her father and sister first sought help from the municipal police, who hinted she may have eloped with her boyfriend, Andres. Yet he was still working the late shift at the plant. The special prosecutor's office charged with investigating crimes against women proved equally dismissive, forcing the Gonzalezes to wait seventy-two hours before filing a missing person's report.

For days the family searched frantically, visiting area hospitals and clinics, interviewing friends, retracing Sagrario's habitual routes. Joined by friends and neighbors, the family organized *rastreos* or combings of the desert area, where other female bodies had been found.

Two weeks after Sagrario disappeared, police recovered a young woman's body in the desert area known as Loma Blanca. "I took my son, Chuy, with me to the police station and we identified the body," says Paula. "It was Sagrario. She was still wearing the company smock with her name embroidered on it." Sagrario had been stabbed five times and strangled. The body was too decomposed to determine evidence of sexual violence.

Despite the pain and anguish inscribed on her face, Paula remains a dauntless activist-mother, survivor of death threats and multiple assaults on her family, extortion attempts, menacing intimidations by incompetent and corrupt police authorities, all aimed at ending her unyielding campaign for justice on behalf of her daughter and hundreds of women who have suffered similar fates in the border city of Ciudad Juárez.

By 2007, over 450 women and girls had been murdered and hundreds disappeared in the border state of Chihuahua alone, and still the gender crimes remain unsolved and largely uninvestigated. The widespread disregard for the severity of violence against women is largely attributed to police corruption and the involvement of powerful groups in the murders and disappearances. To be sure, the murder rate for men is higher in Ciudad Juárez, but killing men does not involve sexual violence. Nor are men disappearing at the same rate as women. As writer Elena Poniatowska noted, "Mexico is the only country where four-hundred-and-fifty assassinations of women go unpunished. The problem is impunity and misogyny."[2]

The news about the monthly protests spread online and in June 2007, activists from the United States heeded Paula's request for "accompaniment" and convened in El Paso, Texas, for the trek across the border to march along with the mothers and witness the first of several monthly silent vigils. Inspired by the weekly protest marches undertaken by the "Mothers of the Plaza de Mayo" in Argentina, the mothers of Juárez pledged to march in front of the state government building that houses the Office of the Special Prosecutor for Homicides against Women until their claims for justice were validated.

For over a year, my sister and freelance photographer, Angela, my research collaborator, Cynthia, and I accompanied the mothers and family members during these monthly protest marches in front of government buildings. Along with their demands for justice, they created a community and reclaimed public space by employing vernacular and religious cultural practices like painting crosses, installing altars, designing posters and elaborately decorated dresses memorializing their daughters and sisters.

Starting with the brushing of crosses on pink backgrounds in 1999, mother-activists launched their initial campaign for justice for Juárez's women. Paula and her eldest daughter, Guillermina, designed the cross campaign when they founded *Voces sin eco*, the first alliance of mothers of the deceased and disappeared girls and women. "We named the group 'Voices without an Echo' because nobody would hear the cries of the women," Paula tells me.

As part of their campaign to raise public awareness, the mothers painted black crosses over pink backgrounds on utility poles throughout the city. "My daughter, Guillermina, came up with the idea of the cross campaign," says Paula. "The first cross was painted on the 20th of March of 1999, and every time an assassinated body of a girl was discovered," Paula adds, "we'd get together to paint a cross in her memory, so that she would not be forgotten."

For Paula, the cross's pink background represents women: "because we live in a machista society and pink is usually associated with girls." Her daughter Guillermina shared a more pragmatic reason for their choice of pink: "When I envisioned the cross campaign, we decided to use the leftover pink paint from the painting of our house in the colonia Lomas de Poleo."

The black crosses on pink backgrounds are ubiquitous in Juárez, visible on many streets throughout the city. "The cross is no longer found solely in Juárez," Paula declares. "It's present worldwide. We named our group 'Voices

FIGURE 23.2 Black cross on pink background painted on a utility pole in Ciudad Juárez, 2007. Photo by Angela Fregoso. Courtesy: Rosa-Linda Fregoso.

without an Echo' but we've had a great echo because throughout the world that cross represents the impunity on the part of government authorities. It stands for the memory of the girls, for the protests that continue permanently, and for our plea for respect," Paula adds. "And I have stated publicly, 'once the assassinations of girls and women end, I will personally remove each and every cross that we have painted on electrical poles.'"

II

When Angela, Cynthia, and I arrive at the meeting place on the US side of the Paso del Norte International Bridge, six members of the Christian Peacemakers Team are waiting with twelve other international observers, many holding large crosses painted in the iconic pink that has come to represent the campaign for justice for the women of Juárez.

At nine in the morning the hot streak is already drifting in. It takes us longer to reach the protest site than we had anticipated. A multiracial group of eighteen individuals parading down Juárez city-central, holding pink crosses—some bearing elaborately adorned dresses that symbolize a murder victim—we are a definitely noticeable presence. I wonder how the locals perceive us: As Christian do-gooders or foreign agitators? As instigators? As witnesses in solidarity with a cause? Or as defacers of the city's reputation, as the local authorities allege?

A few blocks into the city the local police stop us to ask about the purpose of our trip. Cynthia speaks for the group: "We are here to witness a protest march in front of the Special Prosecutor's office." To which the officer quips, "Estamos para proveérles vigilancia" ("we are here to provide you with vigilance"). Just in case, Angela snaps a few photographs.

On the hour-long walk, I talk briefly to B. of the Christian Peacemakers Team, a soft-spoken, mild-mannered white man from the Midwest. "I'm with a Borderlands delegation, on a fact-finding mission to the US-Mexico border," B. tells me. "We heard about the march from Sally so we decided to join the protest."

"I know Sally. She's a nurse who works with migrant support groups and one of the founders of Amigos de Juárez," I respond.

Along with Cynthia, Sally established the local support group to help the mothers and their families in their demands for justice. It's not surprising that the Christian Peacemakers Team would hook up with Sally. She is active in border issues and the CPT's "borderlands project" partners with local groups working to end violence against migrants. They provide medical assistance, food, and water to border crossers, and monitor the activities of the Border Patrol and vigilante groups like the Minutemen. In partnership with locally based organizations like No More Deaths Coalition and Healing Our Borders, the CPT oppose a militarized border, advocating for a comprehensive and humane immigration policy that reunites families and provides a pathway to citizenship.

When we arrive at our destination, the headquarters of the Special Magistrate for Homicides against Women, Paula is the first mother to greet us. "We are so grateful you came to support us. Without the international observers here, the news media would probably ignore our demonstration."

FIGURE 23.3 group from the United States preparing to cross the border into Ciudad Juárez, 2007. Photo by Angela Fregoso. Courtesy: Rosa-Linda Fregoso.

The mothers are already installing the altar as homage to their daughters. Each family member wears a memorial T-shirt bearing the image of their loved one, the date of her murder or disappearance, and the name of the newly formed organization, *Movimiento de Familias Fortalezidas para Exigir Justicia*.

It is the postcards of photographs that first captivate us. Dozens of stand-up postcards bearing images of nearly alike young women: long, dark hair, a smile, a name imprinted to the right of each photograph: Sylvia Arce, Paloma Angelica, Miriam Cristina, Diana Yazmin—all in boldface letters. "They are meant to be mailed to the Governor of Chihuahua," I tell my sister as I grab one. "See, his name and address is imprinted on the back, and there's a space for a personal message and a postage stamp. They were designed by the activist-mothers from the *Centro de Derechos Humanos* in Chihuahua City."

The postcards are casually arranged on the granite seating area that surrounds a bronze sculpture where the mothers and family members create vernacular resistance culture. They seem mindful as they collaborate to arrange the objects on their altar installation. One mother hangs her daughter's school uniform next to a white, organza-trimmed dress; another places a framed photograph above the handwritten sign with a message to the Governor,

FIGURE 23.4 Postcards of "disappeared" women, 2007. Photo by Angela Fregoso. Courtesy: Rosa-Linda Fregoso.

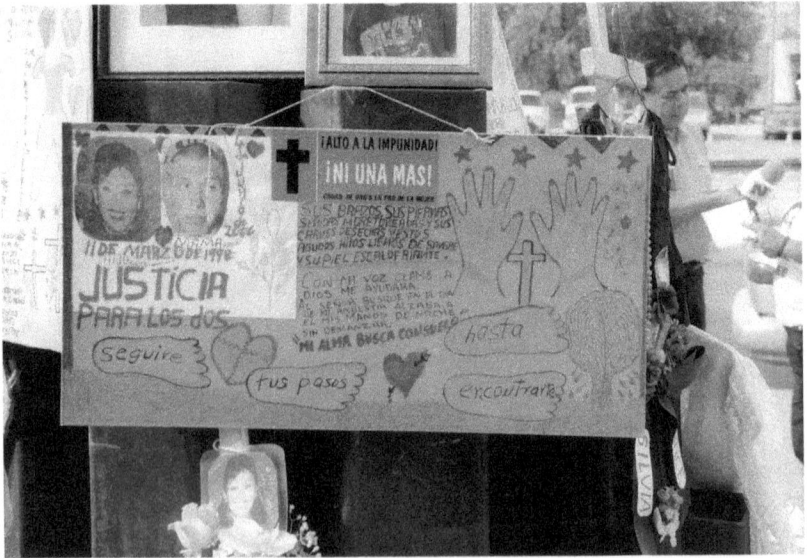

FIGURE 23.5 An altar installation memorializing the women and girls, 2007. Photo by Angela Fregoso. Courtesy: Rosa-Linda Fregoso.

demanding justice; others add their own *ofrendas* (offerings) to deceased loved ones: a favorite stuffed animal, posters conveying heartfelt messages, love notes on decorated hearts, a small photo of a disappeared sister in the center of a cutout butterfly, interspersed flowers and candles—each item arranged with utmost care.

Vernacular culture as expressed in altar-making practices enables the mother-activists to share their collective grief with witnesses in a public space and create consciousness about the value of female lives in Mexico.

III

"Altar making is a female-centered practice," Laura Pérez writes. This vernacular practice represents "a terrain of female agency for indigenous mestizas . . . a space of some religious and gender freedom, as well as creativity for the socially marginal and oppressed."[3] Crafted within the domestic sphere of the home, this culturally hybrid, vernacular cultural tradition conjures up the unseen but felt presences in our lives: deceased loved ones, ancestors, and deities. The home altar is an homage to the dead, a space for meditation and memory, and for invoking the spirits. It is also a private vernacular space for mourning and healing their suffering.

In taking the vernacular tradition into the streets, the mothers of Ciudad Juárez transformed the altar into an insurgent, radical act. "They transformed the private act of suffering of victimized families into a public discourse that makes evident the absence of public standing and civil rights for the economically poor on the borderlands."[4] In so doing, mother-activists remade an intimate cultural practice into a communally shared one, at once spiritual and political: an offering and a protest, a space for mourning/healing *and* for expressing demands for justice. This convergence of the secular and the sacred reminds me of what Chicana artist Amalia Mesa-Bains once called *politicizing spirituality*.[5]

Part of a broader tradition of social activism by Mexican American and Mexican communities on the border, *politicizing spirituality* involves the fusion of Mexican Catholic vernacular culture with public protests. Demonstrations against militarizing the border often incorporate religious practices: carrying of the sacred image of the Virgen of Guadalupe, installing crosses, or lighting *luminarias* in honor of migrants who perish crossing the border. In *politicizing spirituality* Latino protestors draw from a religious-based morality of "right" and "wrong" to condemn US immigration and border policies, and in this case, feminicides.

IV

It is almost ten in the morning and already there are nearly two hundred protestors gathered and more flocking in. A caravan of mothers with *Justicia para Nuestras Hijas* from Chihuahua City arrived early yesterday. Some bring signs with handwritten messages; others carry placards with the photo of a deceased or missing loved one. An elderly couple holds a pink cardboard female silhouette with a black cross painted on its head. There are a dozen colorful dresses hanging on pink crosses placed throughout the plaza. Yesterday, Irene Simmons with the ReDressing Injustice project held a workshop with mothers from Ciudad Juárez and Chihuahua City, where they decorated dresses in honor of their daughters.

The dresses on the pink crosses illustrate the transformative power of vernacular culture in activist politics. The cross symbolizes the crucifixion of Jesus Christ but in this instance, hanging a dress on a cross disrupts its masculine meaning, as Pineda-Madrid suggests: "These practices, by publicly linking female humanity to crucifixion, destabilize a male-centered Christian social imaginary."[6]

The dresses hang interspersed throughout the grounds. One dress is black, layered with tiny pink crosses, the slogan "Ni una más" centered prominently; a pale pink quinceañera dress bears the name "Ana María," next to the date of her disappearance. One mother carries a school girl's uniform hanging on a pink cross; another holds a black dress adorned with a bouquet of flowers. Sagrario's dress stands beside the entrance to the Special Prosecutor's office.

I notice Pilar and several women from Casa Amiga, the women's crisis center, lined up on both sides of the heavily trafficked boulevard, holding up photo placards at cars that inch by. Drivers honk and wave in support, but one furiously yells: *"se lo merecían por como se vestían"* ("they deserved it because of how they dressed"), to which we holler back, *"ignorante," "sexista," "machista."*

The man's attitude does not surprise me. Many residents are largely indifferent to crimes affecting the most vulnerable members of the community. "In Ciudad Juárez, it is socially acceptable to verbally abuse a woman in public, especially if she is poor," journalist Isabel Velásquez once confided. Nearly all of the women murdered and disappeared are poor.

Authorities have made it a point to vilify and blame the victims for their murders. "Your daughter led a double life: maquiladora work by day; prostitution by night." Or as police alleged to Paula: "Your daughter probably left town with another man."

Excitement builds as more protestors flock in. There are a dozen reporters from local and national media mingling around, taping interviews with the

FIGURE 23.6 Dress in honor of Sagrario González, gifted by Irene Simmons to her mother, Paula Flores, 2007. Photo by Angela Fregoso. Courtesy: Rosa-Linda Fregoso.

mother-activists. One radio journalist approaches Paula and asks, "What do you want to accomplish with these protests?"

"I want to arrive at justice. Simply. To where we see that no more girls disappear, that they don't appear dead. That's what I want to accomplish," Paula responds.

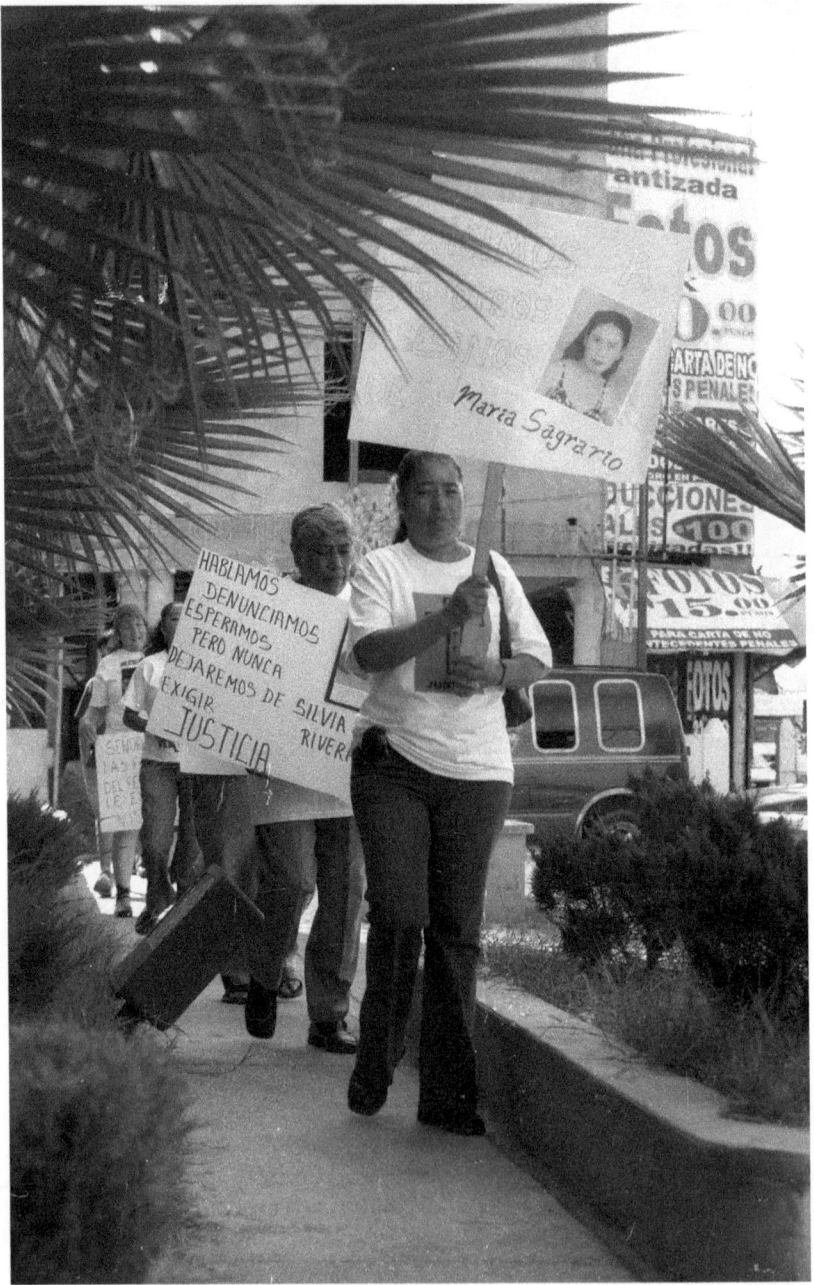

FIGURE 23.7 Led by Paula Flores, mothers silently march for one hour, 2007. Photo by Angela Fregoso. Courtesy: Rosa-Linda Fregoso.

At 10:15 the mothers and family members gather at the far side of the plaza and start their hour-long vigil. We stand as witnesses, observing as the families march silently, single file, around the perimeter of the plaza. Paula Flores leads the group, followed by thirty other relatives, each bearing a poster with an image of their deceased relative, a handwritten demand for justice, or a dress hanging from a pink cross.

I feel the weight of their anguish and breathe deeply as my eyes begin to dampen, my heart heavy with sorrow. Some onlookers talk among themselves, other witnesses stare intently; their gazes appear as stricken as my own. We are witnesses to something greater than this moment. The cross the mothers bear becomes our own. We are witnesses with a response-ability, an ability to respond to the fathomless cry of their suffering. We are witnesses to the suffering of others whose relationship to us is in the bonds that suture our humanity.

V

As part of my research on gender violence in Mexico, I visited Ciudad Juárez regularly, often pausing before the cross with 268 iron spikes to recite a silent prayer for the women and girls. The *Ni una más* cross is one of the most potent and visible symbols of vernacular resistance culture. It faces oncoming traffic to one of three bridges linking the cities of Juárez and El Paso, where over 100,000 people cross the border daily. Unemployed workers from Aceros de Chihuahua, wanting to contribute to the *Ni una más* cause, assembled the cross from scrap wood ties for railroad tracks and later, a coalition of women's rights activists in Chihuahua City named *Mujeres de negro* (Women Wearing Black) gifted the *Ni una más* cross to the mothers of Juárez because it embodied their collective struggles to end intolerable deaths, their sorrow and desire for justice and life.

On International Women's Day (March 8) 2002, *Mujeres de negro* embarked on a pilgrimage they called *Éxodo por la vida*, spanning 223 miles from Chihuahua City to Ciudad Juárez. Mothers, sisters, daughters, elderly and young women, housewives, students, and professionals braved the arctic winds lashing the Sonoran Desert. The women wore black capes to mark their outrage and grief, pink hats for life, and a determined refusal to forget the daughters murdered in the state of Chihuahua. "An exodus is always for life," writes journalist Victor Quintana.[7] "Its profound biblical content is just that: a departure from the land of death and slavery, the waters of the sea part and open way for the traverse of the desert and arrival to the promised land."

Accompanying the pilgrims on their ten-day traverse of the Sonoran Desert— their departure from "the situation of slavery, submission and death befalling the land of assembly plants"—the cross bears witness to *Mujeres de negro*'s courageous trek across the desert, to prayers, chants, and songs along the way, like the "Hymn Ni Una Más" composed by longtime human rights activist Lucha Castro:

> *Paso a paso llegarán*
> *Las mujeres caminarán*
> *Rumbo a Juárez llegarán*
> *La justicia llegará.*
>
> ***Ellas gritan "ni una más"***
> ***Ellas gritan "ni una más"***
> ***Ni una más. Ni una más,***
> ***ni una más, ni una más.***
>
> *Ellas buscan dignidad, paz*
> *Justicia y libertad*
> *También amor y equidad*
> *Ellas buscan solidaridad*
>
> ***Ellas gritan ni una más . . .***
>
> *Paso a paso sembrarán*
> *La conciencia expandirán*
> *Sembrarán, sembrarán*
> *La conciencia llegará*
>
> ***Ellas gritan ni una más . . .***
>
> *No se cansan de gritar*
> *Ni tampoco de luchar*
> *Van sembrando dignidad*
> *Y extendiendo ni una más*
>
> ***Not one more, they shout, not one more . . .***

Transported on a pick-up truck, the cross arrived with *Mujeres de negro* at the outskirts of Juárez where hundreds of supporters joined them, marching through the city streets, chanting "¡Ni una más, ni una más, ni una más!" When they reached their destination at the International Paso del Norte Bridge, several men lifted the cross off the truck and with power tools fastened it to a large metal panel where the wooden cross with 268 iron spikes remains to this day, facing hundreds of people who cross the border daily into the "promised land."

FIGURE 23.8 Mothers installing an altar, 2008. Photo by Angela Fregoso. Courtesy: Rosa-Linda Fregoso.

VI

The crowds dwindled in the subsequent monthly protests. Gone were the throngs of supporters, reporters, and the festive mood of the first march. In August, six international observers accompanied the mother-activists, whose numbers had diminished from thirty to nine.

"Division among the mothers is an open secret," we are told. Turf wars, battles over leadership, tactics and agendas—the schism endemic to social movements—plagued Juárez's mother-activists as well. For unknown reasons, a prominent local feminist warned one group of mothers against participating in the monthly protests.

The core group of mother-activists remained undeterred. Paula Flores, Eva Arce, and Malú Andrade greeted us on subsequent protests, even as they seem disappointed by the small numbers of protestors and observers. "Few but confident," Doña Eva quipped. Paula echoed the bravura, "We may not be many (*muchas*) but we are '*machas*'!" We laugh, feeling heartened by their spirited tenacity.

On one occasion, federal police with automatic weapons guard the entrance to the Public Ministry, casting an ominous shadow. "They weren't here the last time," I whispered to Cynthia. "They're trying to intimidate the mothers," she responded, "which makes the presence of the internationals even more important."

As news spread about the government's offensive against the drug cartels, international observers were reluctant to cross the border into Juárez. A South African journalist who writes on animal rights once joined Angela, Cynthia, Sally, and me; another time a reporter from Indy Media came along. When the government moved the Special Prosecutor's office miles away from the city center, only six mothers and their children participated in the silent vigil.

The vernacular practices of resistance remained unchanged: install the altar, fasten dresses on crosses to nearby trees, walk silently in a circle for sixty minutes, handhold the signs or photographs. Of all the monthly protests we attended, the one held in early November represented the boldest demonstration against the government's negligence. On the celebration of Days of the Dead, the mothers symbolically reclaimed public space, using vernacular cultural practices that enabled family members to be present but not consumed by their experiences of suffering.[8]

VII

After crossing the international bridge, four international observers, including my sister and me, meet Paula and drive to a designated spot on the outskirts of Ciudad Juárez where we park on the side of the road, next to a telephone pole branded with the iconic black cross on pink. In this mostly barren spot, a village dog appears, glancing at us as it strolls across the hill behind the telephone pole, before disappearing.

Half an hour later we caravan in the direction of the Pan-American Highway connecting Ciudad Juárez with Chihuahua City—three cars and a dark blue pickup truck transporting a metallic pink cross so large its horizontal beam, with the word *"Justicia"* painted in black, reclines over the truck's cabin. Three women with Albuquerque's Peace and Justice Center and Amnesty International ride in the car behind us. We stop once for Consuelo, who emerges from the *colonia* on a hillside. Her one-year-old daughter, Veronica, was murdered twelve years ago.

Forty minutes later, Paula announces, *"Ya llegamos,"* pointing to a gigantic modernist sculpture in the shape of an asymmetrical portal that stands above the hillside to our left, facing Ciudad Juárez's incoming traffic. Designed by Pedro Francisco, the *Umbral de Milenio* sculpture was installed at the turn of the twenty-first century to welcome visitors arriving into the City of Juárez. As we drive up the hill into the parking lot, I recognize several members of *Familias Fortalezidas*.

Amid the scrubby desert flora and fauna sits the *Umbral de Milenio*, anchored onto a granite base, light reflectors illuminating the sculpture from below.

FIGURE 23.9 Caravan on the Pan-American Highway, 2007. Photo by Angela Fregoso. Courtesy: Rosa-Linda Fregoso.

Behold the scenic panoramic view of Ciudad Juárez to the north, the Pan-American Highway to the west below us, and the Sierra Madre to the south. The splendor petrifies me when I think of countless female bodies dumped or buried on this torrid landscape.

On this chilly November day, the cool desert breeze tempers the sun's brightness. Close to fifty people are gathered at the Tierra Blanca park, including ten journalists, fifteen witnesses, and over twenty family members wearing memory T-shirts, their children's playful laughter filling the air. The mood feels somber and festive on this *Día de los muertos* when mourning the dead intersects so profusely with celebrating life.

As Paula approaches the media, she exclaims: "Today we are here to commemorate the women who were assassinated. This monument is meant as a 'welcome' to the city and beside it we are going to place *our* cross so that it is known that Ciudad Juárez is also the capital of feminicides," Paula continues. "The *Justicia* cross is our protest to the authorities. On this Day of the Dead, we want the world to know that the crimes against women continue."

One of the reporters questions Paula about the Governor's recent statement that "feminicides are a myth."

"My daughter was not a myth," Paula quips. "A myth is something invented. I named her Sagrario and I didn't invent that. In my case, there is an empty place for Sagrario, which the Governor wants to erase."

"Tierra Blanca is a public park," says another reporter. "Did you receive permission to install the cross?"

Paula responds indignant, "The government didn't ask me for permission to murder my daughter. So why should we ask for their permission?"

Paula's son-in-law, Felipe, drives the truck off the road onto an unpaved area north of the *Umbral*. After conferring for a few minutes, relatives work in tandem for nearly an hour. Some use shovels and pitchforks to dig a hole deep enough to bury the steel drum that holds the *Justicia* cross in place. Once they finish, six women and men haul the steel drum off the truck and, after almost dropping it twice, they manage to roll it into the dug-out, while others are mixing quick-drying cement with sand, gravel, and water in plastic tubs. A few minutes after pouring the cement mixture around the barrel, the newly affixed cross towers over its onlookers at least twenty feet from the ground, gigantic from our perspective, miniscule next to the *Umbral de Milenio*.

We stand next to the journalists, observing as events unfold. Before Felipe parks the truck beside the cross, a father fastens a floral wreath onto it. The father, Guillermina, and Malú then climb onto the truck's flatbed and with black markers start writing onto the cross the names of their female kin while Paula recites: "Sagrario González, Sylvia Arce, Veronica Castro, Lilia Alejandra . . ."

Paula's chant reverberates across the desert, drowning out the traffic's hum emanating from the Pan-American Highway below, the tone in her voice becoming more anguished with each additional name. We stand silently, our hearts heavy with sorrow, love, and compassion. When it becomes evident that Guillermina can no longer reach the cross's uppermost section, a six-foot photo-journalist with the Mexico City–based newspaper *Reforma* suddenly

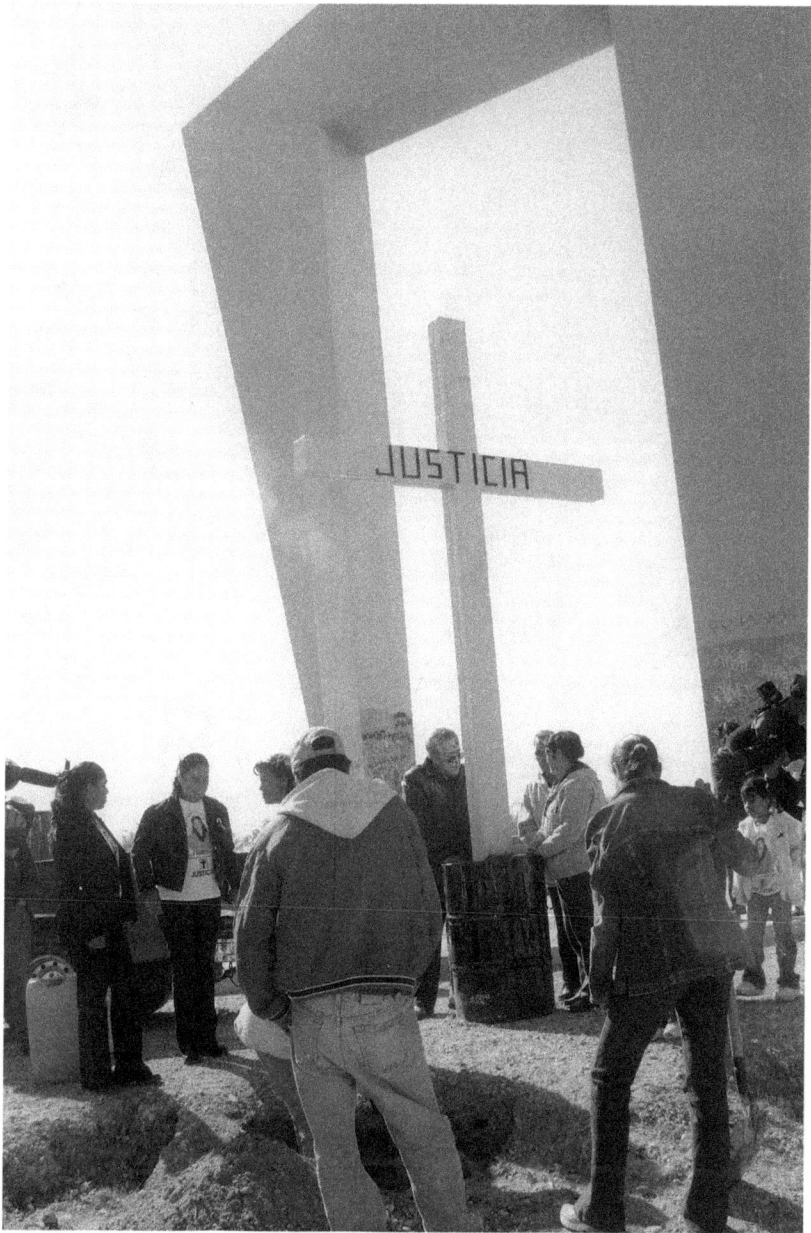

FIGURE 23.10 Families installing the *Justicia* cross beside the *Umbral de Milenio* monument, 2007. Photo by Angela Fregoso. Courtesy: Rosa-Linda Fregoso.

FIGURE 23.11 Photojournalist and family members write names on the *Justicia* cross, 2007. Photo by Angela Fregoso. Courtesy: Rosa-Linda Fregoso.

FIGURE 23.12 Families of the female victims of feminicide, 2007. Photo by Angela Fregoso. Courtesy: Rosa-Linda Fregoso.

climbs on the flatbed, and moving his camera aside, grabs a marker to pen the final names onto the cross.

We are tear-stricken by his act. Undoubtedly trained to remain detached and objective from events he witnesses, this photojournalist chooses not to remain indifferent, allowing himself to be stirred by compassion, to be impelled by Paula's recitation of the female victims' names echoing in the desert winds.

Our interdependence and response-ability to the suffering of others is profoundly captured in this spontaneous act of solidarity on the part of the photo-journalist. This singular, heartfelt act also evidences the transformative power of vernacular cultural practices of resistance. By installing the cross and inscribing onto it the names of the women and girls, mother-activists and their supporters reclaim public space and create an alternative social imaginary in which their sufferings are transformed into communal consciousness.

After the cross installation, family members assemble the Day of the Dead altar below the cross, placing photographs of their deceased loved ones, teddy bears, *papel picado*, candied skulls, bowls of fruit and nuts, votive candles, and dozens of *cempasuchitl* or marigold flowers. Two parallel lines are drawn with salt on the ground, "To help in the soul's transition," Guillermina confides, as a mother places her daughter's school uniform in the center, its sleeves

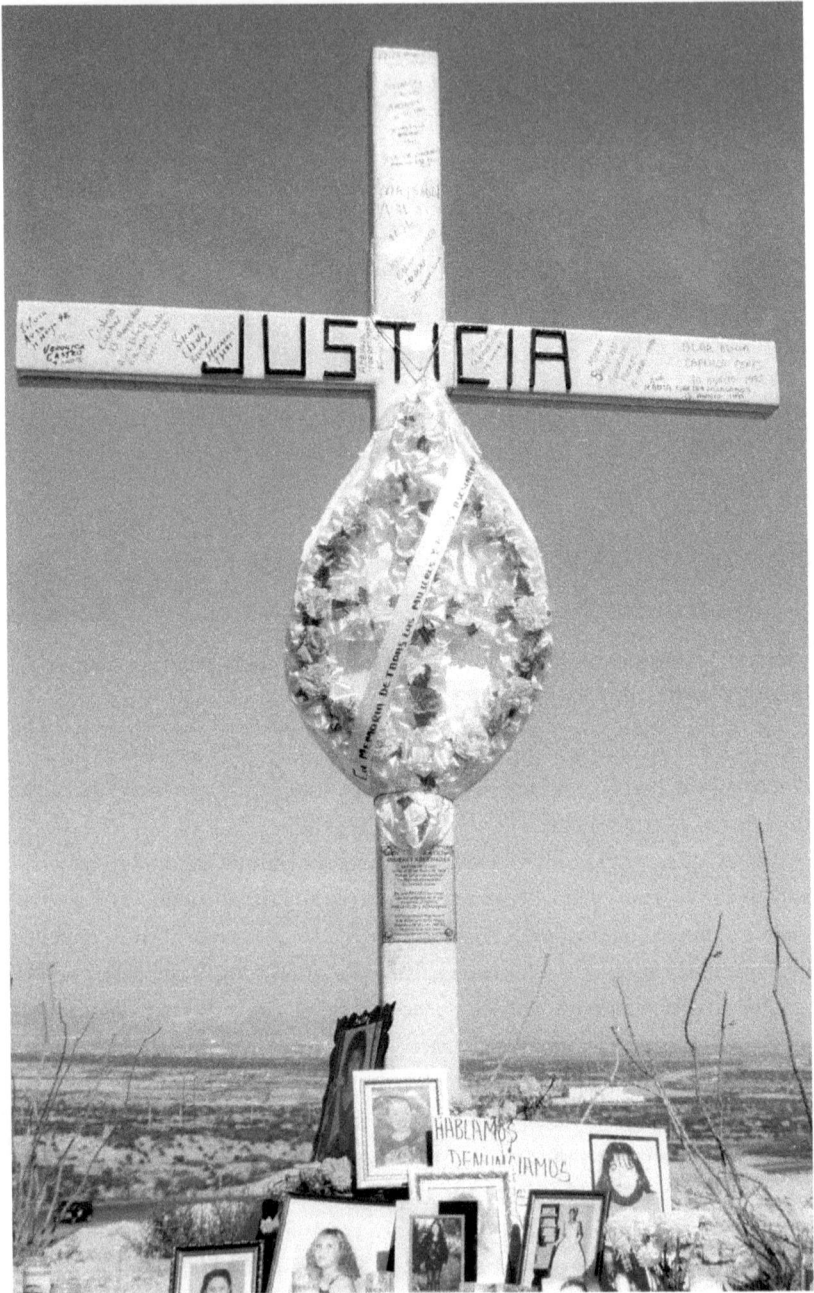

FIGURE 23.13 The *Justicia* cross, 2007. Photo by Angela Fregoso.
Courtesy: Rosa-Linda Fregoso.

extending Christ-like on the cross. Once the altar is complete, adults and children form a circle around the *Justicia* cross and *Día de los muertos* altar, and chant prayers for the souls of their deceased.

"Angela, take a picture of all of us, for our memories," Malú cries out.

Before departing, my sister and I walk over to the *Justicia* cross and read the words inscribed onto its metallic plaque: "IN MEMORY OF ALL THE WOMEN ASSASSINATED," followed by details about the cross campaign: "The painting of crosses began on March 20, 1999, by a group of families of the women who were assassinated in Ciudad Juárez. It is a protest against all the authorities, a demand for JUSTICE, PREVENTION AND CONSCIENCE. The pink background represents a woman and the black cross represents mourning for the women who have been assassinated in this city."[9]

As we stand there paying our final respects to the girls and women of Juárez memorialized by the *Justicia* cross, I recall the soulful words of Alice Walker: "The world cannot be healed in the abstract . . . healing begins where the wound was made."

NOTES

Reprinted with permission from Indiana University Press. This essay originally appeared in *Chiricú Journal: Latina/o Literatures, Arts, and Cultures* 2, no. 1 (2017): 118–36. This essay is based on my memories, notes, and reflections. It is deliberately written in the style of an impressionistic essay rather than in an academic style. For this reason I refrain from presenting an "argument" and a "methodology." I'm deeply grateful to Linda Watanabe McFerrin of Left Coast Writers, whose workshops have enabled my incursions into a different type of writing. I also thank fellow participants of these workshops for their invaluable feedback.

1   "Feminicide = Sanctioned Murder: Gender, Race, and Violence in a Global Context," conference held at Stanford University, May 16–19, 2007.

2   Keynote Address at the May 2007 Stanford conference.

3   Laura Pérez, *Chicana Art: The Politics of Spiritual and Aesthetic Altarities* (Duke University Press, 2007), p. 93.

4   Quoted in Nancy Pineda-Madrid, *Suffering + Salvation in Ciudad Juárez* (Fortress Press, 2011), 115.

5   Amalia Mesa-Bains, "The Interior Life: The Works of Patssi Valdez," in *The Painted World of Patssi Valdez* (exhibition catalog), May 5–July 4, 1993, Boathouse Gallery, Plaza de la Raza, 9.

6   Pineda-Madrid, 119.

7   Víctor M. Quintana S., "Mujeres en éxodo por la vida," *La Jornada*, 13 Nov. 2009, goo.gl/Oobk2V, consulted Mar. 2016.

8   Quoted in Pineda-Madrid, 93.

9   The cross remained in front of the *Umbral* for eight years and was removed sometime in 2015, according to Paula Flores.

Amnesty or Abolition? Felons, Illegals, and the Case for a New Abolition Movement

KELLY LYTLE HERNÁNDEZ

Nearly 10 percent of California's residents are prisoners, parolees, felons,[1] or undocumented immigrants.[2] Although differently constituted, these groups form a caste of persons living in the Golden State for whom neither democracy nor freedom is guaranteed. Prisoners, parolees, and undocumented immigrants cannot vote. Parolees, felons, and undocumented immigrants are variously denied access to public housing, food stamps, educational loans, and employment. Prisoners, deportees, and immigrant detainees are forcibly removed from their families and communities, while undocumented immigrants, parolees, and persons under warrant live with the constant fear of arrest.[3]

Disfranchised, denied core protections of the social welfare state, and imprisoned, detained, or under threat of warrant or deportation, the status of undocumented immigrants, prisoners, and ex-offenders in the United States pivots on shared exclusions from full political and social membership. This story of democracy denied and freedom unfound is one of clear racial significance across the country, with Blacks and Latinos comprising an extraordinary 60 percent of the total prison population in the United States. Home to a substantive slice of the nation's undocumented and incarcerated populations, California is a heartland of racial exclusion in the United States today.

In recent years, legal scholars have detailed the increasingly tangled world of exclusion rooted in felony conviction and unsanctioned migration.[4] The series of civil disabilities that have been heaped on citizens convicted of felony charges since the 1970s, namely drug offenders, have gutted the substance of their citizenship rights. Today, according to legal scholar Juliet Stumpf, the "status of an ex-felon strikingly resembles that of an alien" as "criminal offenders [have been]—literally—alienated" by limitations upon the right to vote, restricted employment opportunities, and exclusions from welfare benefits.[5] The criminal justice system, in other words, has created a legal framework by which the rights and benefits of citizenship are stripped away from US citizens until they mirror (and, at times, dip below) those of noncitizen immigrants within the United States. As US citizens have slipped toward what Stumpf describes as "alienation" through the criminal justice system, the status of immigrants in the United States has tipped toward criminalization through the implosion of criminal law and immigration law. In particular, Congress has greatly expanded the list of offenses that trigger deportation for *legal* immigrants while immigration law enforcement has become better coordinated among federal, state, and local officials. The result is that everyday criminal law enforcement activities are now harnessed to identify undocumented immigrants and enforce US immigration law. The rise of "crimmigration" law, as legal scholars like to say, has transformed the lives of immigrants in the United States. Minor criminal violations and everyday legal infractions, ranging from shoplifting to traffic violations, now routinely trigger one of the state's most consequential sanctions—deportation.

This essay explores the historical development of the alienation of citizen offenders and the criminalization of immigrants in the United States; in particular, it chronicles how immigration control and mass incarceration emerged as the systems of social control that frame alienated citizens and criminalized immigrants as a racialized caste of outsiders in the United States today. Pulling back the layers of citizen alienation in our modern democracy, and charting how our nation of immigrants came to deport so many for so little, reveals a story of race and unfreedom reaching back to the era of emancipation.

Immigration Control

Perhaps most Americans believe their ancestors arrived legally in the United States but few today are aware that Congress left immigration almost unregulated for almost a century after the Revolution. During that time, practically

FIGURE 24.1 Courtesy of the Huntington Library Collection.

any person who reached American shores of their own volition could enter the United States to work. Immigration control began nearly 150 years ago, during the US Civil War, long before our current struggles at the US-Mexico border.

About one year into that brutal war, Northern congressmen learned of a devious plot by slaveowners in Louisiana. Ever more anxious about the specter of emancipation, plantation owners had quietly begun to import Chinese contract workers. Popularly known and derided as "coolies," these workers were regarded as a racially inferior and unfree political caste that, in the case of emancipation, could be used to replace black slave labor across the South. Learning of the plan, Congress passed the Anti-Coolie Act of 1862, which prohibited US citizens from importing these workers into the United States. Passed to prevent the reinvention of slavery in the American South, the Anti-Coolie Act of 1862 functioned as the nation's "last slave-trade act and its first immigration law."[6]

Keeping Chinese workers out of the country, Congress reasoned, would prevent the creation of a new form of "unfree" labor in the United States. And yet, even as they considered additional "protective" measures, Frederick Douglass, the brilliant abolitionist orator and former slave, offered a stinging critique. Douglass firmly supported unrestricted immigration from the world over and challenged claims that Chinese immigrants would reintroduce "the slave prob-lem" to the United States.

"It was not the Ethiopian as a man, but the Ethiopian as a slave and a coveted article of merchandise, that gave us trouble," argued Douglass.[7] The problem of slavery, in other words, was not rooted in the bodies of enslaved persons but rather in the laws that organize inequitable social relations and protect the mar-ginalization of humans. This was the radical abolitionist critique that Douglass had cut during the movement, and then war, to end slavery. When he applied his wisdom to the congressional effort to halt Chinese immigration, he hinted that the quest for immigration control was at its core an anti-abolitionist proj-ect. It degraded human rights, fueled forms of racial thinking, and encompassed strategies of exclusion that African Americans were battling against in the years after the Civil War in their struggle to achieve full emancipation. In this, the black freedom struggle was directly tied to immigration politics and Douglass recognized the critical importance of opposing the rise of immigration control.

But Douglass's abolitionist critique went unheeded. Congress continued to pass legislation restricting immigration into the United States. In time, the rise of a US immigration control regime would write a new chapter in the story of unfreedom. In particular, increasingly restrictive immigration legislation created the "illegal alien" as a substantively marginalized political category in American life.

Creation of the Illegal Alien

The creation of the illegal alien unfolded in the decades following the Anti-Coolie Act, as Congress dramatically expanded the limitations placed on legal entry into the United States. In 1882, Congress banned Chinese workers and all "lunatics, idiots, convicts, those liable to become public charges, and those suffering from contagious diseases." In 1885, *all* contract workers were prohib-ited from entering the United States. In 1891, polygamists were added to the list of banned persons and, in 1903, anarchists, beggars, and epileptics joined the growing list. In 1907, Congress also excluded imbeciles, feeble-minded per-sons, unaccompanied minors, those with tuberculosis, and women of immoral purposes. That same year, the President signed a Gentlemen's Agreement with Japan that strictly regulated and limited Japanese immigration to the United States. By 1924, Congress had categorically prohibited all persons of Asian ori-gin from entering and introduced a national origins system, which limited how many immigrants could enter the United States each year; it favored Western European immigrants. In effect, Congress had prohibited much of the world from legally entering the United States.

The congressional project to restrict immigration thus took shape between the 1880s and 1920s as the United States, from northeastern manufacturing to southwestern agribusiness, was rapidly becoming one of the world's most robust industrial economies. Despite numerical and categorical limitations, immigrant workers still arrived by the hundreds of thousands. Not all were qualified to legally enter the country. To evade immigration restrictions, they crossed the borders without inspection, used fraudulent documents to enter at ports of entry, overstayed visas, and violated conditions of legal residency.[8] Immigration restrictions in an era of mass global migration, in other words, triggered the creation of "illegal immigration" as a new realm of social activity. As people from other countries stepped around US immigration restrictions, they stepped into the socio-political category of the illegal alien.

As immigrants entered in violation of US immigration laws, the Supreme Court faced tough new questions regarding the status of persons not formally authorized to be within the United States. In a series of decisions made during the late-nineteenth century, often referred to as the Chinese Exclusion cases, the court established a framework for shaping the rights and status of unauthorized persons living in the United States. In *Chae Chan Ping* vs *United States* (1889), the Supreme Court established that immigration control was, as a matter of foreign affairs, a realm of unmediated congressional and executive authority.[9] According to the decision, "The power of exclusion of foreigners being an incident of sovereignty belonging to the government of the United States . . . cannot be granted away or restrained on behalf of anyone. . . . The political department of our government . . . is alone competent to act upon the subject." Thus, the US Supreme Court limited the "reach of the Constitution and the scope of judicial review" over the development of immigration law by defining it as a matter of sovereignty and thereby a zone of unmediated federal power.[10]

In the 1893 *Fong Yue Ting* decision, the court held that the federal government's right to expel foreigners was "absolute" and "unqualified"; therefore, immigrants, even lawful permanent residents, could be deported from the country at any time for any reason. This decision also established that "deportation is not a punishment for crime" but rather an administrative process of returning immigrants to the place where they belonged. Defining deportation as "an administrative process" was highly significant because much of the Bill of Rights applies only to criminal punishment. Accordingly, the court held in *Fong Yue Ting*, "the provisions of the Constitution, securing the right of trial by jury, and prohibiting unreasonable search and seizures, and cruel and unusual punishment, have no application."[11] In these two decisions, each saturated with ideas of Chinese immigrants as "hordes of barbarians" and "alien races incapable of assimilation," the foundation for the rights and status of persons coming to be known as "illegal aliens" in the United States was established.[12] For the first time since slavery, an entire category of people in the United States could be imprisoned without a trial by jury. Their homes could be searched without warrants, they could be detained without being arrested, and punished by Americans in ways Americans could not be.

Over the next century, the Supreme Court would decide immigration cases when framed as constitutional issues regarding the rights of persons in the United States; but the federal project for immigration control, in general, developed with little oversight from the courts and limited application of the Constitution.[13] Therefore, the "illegal alien" developed as a uniquely marginal, political category of persons in post–Civil War America.

The Threat of Deportation

For unauthorized immigrants, their distance from the Constitution and the formal power of immigration control are compounded by the fear of deportation, which limits their ability to fully exercise their rights as persons and workers in the United States. In particular, as the regime of US immigration control expanded over the course of the twentieth century, the threat of deportation—once a fairly remote concern—now hangs over workplace disputes, limits mobility along roadways, and shapes the most intimate family decisions about marriage, divorce, housing, and child rearing. In effect, the US immigration regime has constructed the political category of the illegal alien as an expansive site of social inequalities that constitutes, as historian Mae Ngai argues, a "caste unambiguously situated outside the boundaries of formal membership and social legitimacy."[14]

No institution in US history has played a more significant role in defining the caste of "illegal aliens" than the US Border Patrol. With the mandate to detect and apprehend persons for unauthorized entry into the United States, Border Patrol officers spend their working hours literally bringing bodies to the consequential but relatively broad and abstract political category of illegal immigrant. Unauthorized immigration is a field of social activity constituted by everything from expired visas and border jumping to false statements and unemployment. The Border Patrol translates this broad field of social activity into an identifiable social reality of persons policed, apprehended, detained, and deported for violating US immigration law. Therefore, the making of the political category of the "illegal alien" an everyday reality in American life is rooted in the decisions and discretions made by the US Border Patrol in the pursuit of immigration law enforcement.[15]

The Border Patrol

Congress established the US Border Patrol in 1924 to enforce the enormous web of immigration restrictions that had developed since the passage of the Anti-Coolie Act of 1862. Their jurisdiction stretched along the Canadian border, spanned the US-Mexico border and, in time, extended to include the Florida Gulf Coast region and various coastlines. In addition to preventing persons from crossing into the United States without official sanction, the Border Patrol's job included policing borderland regions to detect and arrest persons defined as illegal immigrants. At first, Border Patrol officers in the US-Mexico border region were confused about how to translate their broad mandate and jurisdiction into a practical course of law enforcement. Thousands of excluded persons—Asians, unaccompanied minors, persons with trachoma—regularly violated US immigration law. Even US citizens routinely violated immigration restrictions by refusing to cross through official ports of entry. Working in far-flung offices in border communities, Border Patrol officers were given no guidance from national immigration officials regarding how to prioritize the enforcement of US immigration restrictions. The officers, for example, could have raided brothels or policed the primary racial targets of US immigration restrictions, namely Asians. But the early officers of the US Border Patrol took an unexpected approach.

Hired from local border communities, Border Patrol officers along the US-Mexico border focused almost exclusively on apprehending and deporting undocumented Mexican workers. Ironically, Mexico's migrant workers were not categorically prohibited from entering the United States, but they often evaded the administrative requirements for legal entry, such as paying entrance fees and passing a literacy test and health exam. For the working-class white men, hired from local border communities, who worked as Border Patrol officers during the 1920s and 1930s, directing US immigration law enforcement toward Mexican border crossers—the primary labor force for the region's dominant agribusiness industry—functioned as a means of wrestling respect from agribusinessmen, demanding deference from Mexicans in general, achieving upward social mobility for their families, and/or concealing racial violence within the framework of police work. Although they were satisfying more personal and local interests in immigration control, by targeting unsanctioned Mexican immigrants instead of the many other possible targets of immigration control, Border Patrol officers effectively Mexicanized the set of inherently and lawfully unequal social relations that emerged from the regime of US immigration control in the Mexican border region. Mexicanizing the caste of illegals remained a regional story until concerns regarding national

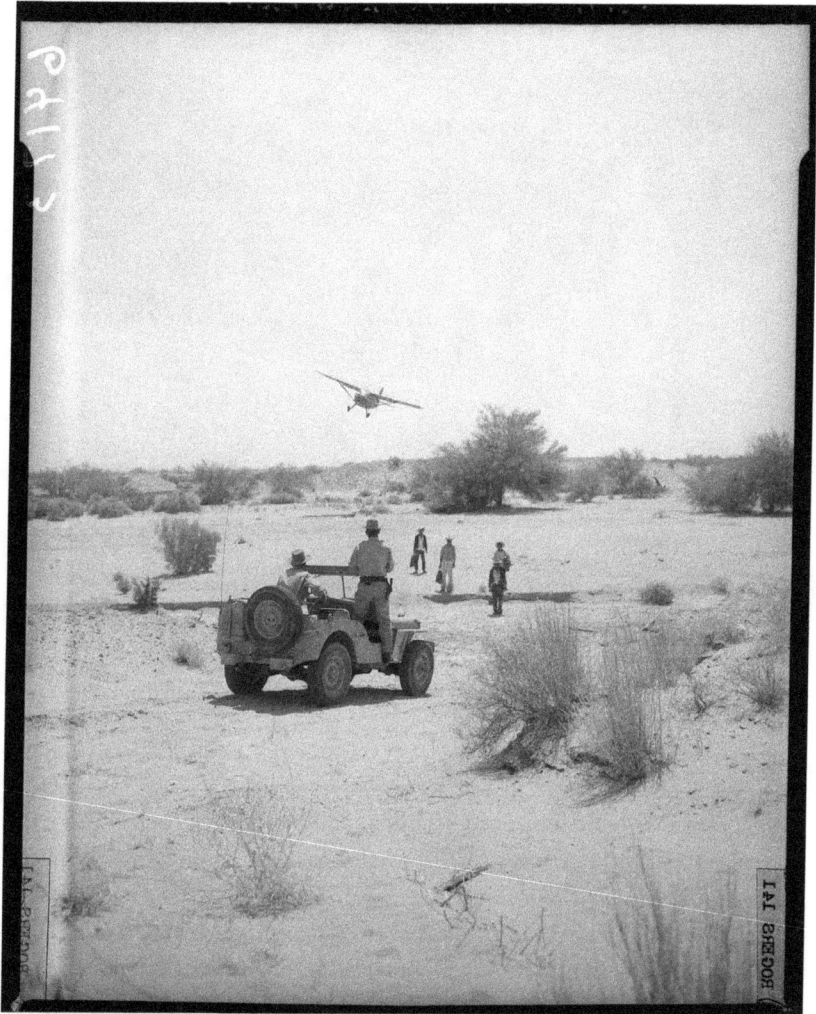

FIGURE 24.2 Courtesy of Los Angeles Times Photograph Archive, Charles E. Young Research Library, UCLA.

security during World War II forced the Border Patrol to become a more centrally operated institution.

During World War II, Congress transferred the Border Patrol's parent agency, the Immigration and Naturalization Service (INS), from the Department of Labor to the Department of Justice. Located within the Department of Justice, immigration control entered into the growing bureaucracy of federal law enforcement under the US Attorney General and alongside the FBI, US Marshals, and the Bureau of Prisons. With new resources, tighter supervision,

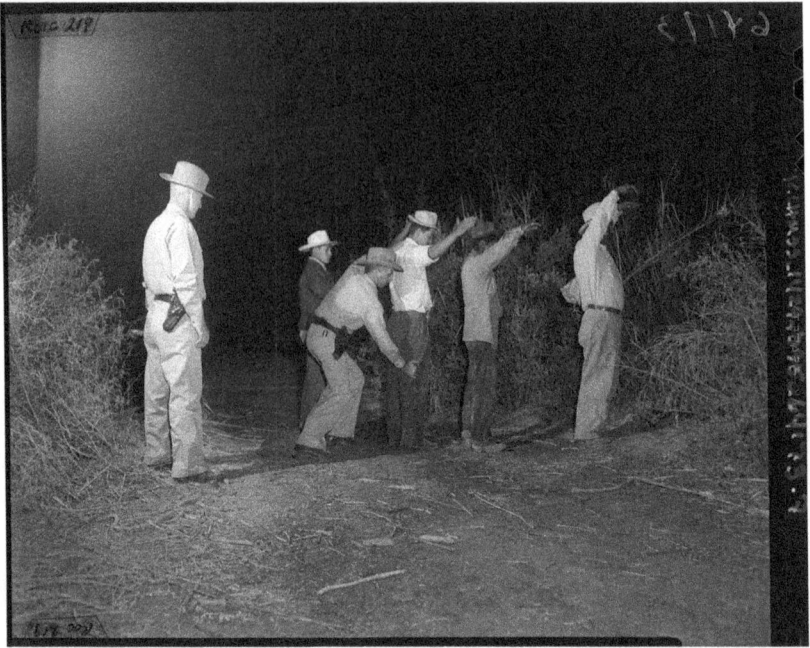

FIGURE 24.3 Courtesy of Los Angeles Times Photograph Archive, Charles E. Young Research Library, UCLA.

more personnel, and improved training, these were the years when the Border Patrol's national focus turned toward policing unsanctioned Mexican immigration.

This turn was primarily influenced by the establishment of the Bracero Program, a US/Mexico contract labor program launched in 1942. Between 1942 and 1964, over four million Mexicans legally worked in the United States through the Bracero Program. Still, a large number of Mexican nationals crossed the border without sanction in search of work. To protect a binational program designed to import legal Mexican workers in the United States, the US Border Patrol adopted an aggressive campaign to work with Mexican authorities to deport illegal Mexican workers. To increase the number of deportees, Special Mexican Deportation Parties were established. By 1944, this program had significantly increased the number of Mexicans apprehended each year. Concurrently, the number of Mexicans as a percentage of the total number of apprehensions nationwide shot up to over 90 percent.

By the early 1950s, the US Border Patrol's Special Mexican Deportation Parties were apprehending hundreds of thousands of Mexican immigrants each year. In May 1954, the Border Patrol announced that a crisis of unsanctioned

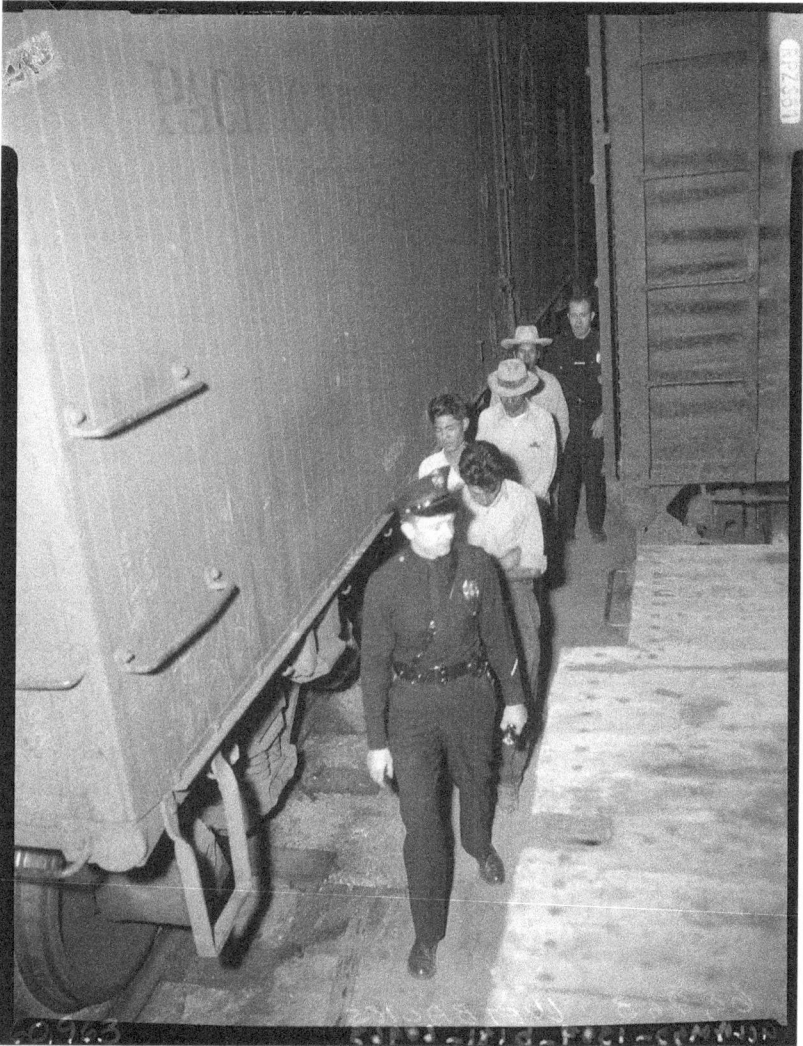

FIGURE 24.4 Courtesy of Los Angeles Daily News Negatives, Charles E. Young Research Library, UCLA.

Mexican immigration had developed along the US-Mexico border and that it would soon launch a major campaign to end that crisis. A few weeks later, in the now infamous Operation Wetback campaign of 1954, Border Patrol task forces swept across the Southwest and declared to have solved the so-called "wetback problem" by deporting over one million Mexican nationals.

After the campaign and into the mid-1960s, Border Patrol apprehensions along the US-Mexico border dropped dramatically.

Operation Wetback is often cited today as evidence that immigration law enforcement, if aggressively pursued, can successfully end unsanctioned migration. But aggressive enforcement is not how the Border Patrol scored its successes during the summer of 1954. The Border Patrol significantly overreported the number of persons apprehended during Operation Wetback and achieved a declining number of apprehensions after the campaign by demobilizing the task forces. Assigned to two-man horse patrols, officers simply could not apprehend the same number of persons as the days when they worked in deportation task forces. Reduced immigration enforcement, rather than aggressive immigration enforcement, was how the US Border Patrol achieved a declining number of apprehensions in the years after Operation Wetback. Still, the Border Patrol's proclamations of triumph along the US-Mexico border opened a series of questions regarding practices and priorities of US migration control in the future.

Rise of the Criminal Alien

In the years after Operation Wetback, Border Patrol officials carefully reinvented immigration control as a matter of crime control. As early as November 1956, officers were instructed that, "the word 'wetback' . . . should be deleted from the vocabulary of all Immigration officers" because "today's apprehensions consist in the main part of criminals, often vicious in type, and of hardened and defiant repeaters." To defeat the image of a poor worker crossing the border without sanction, a Border Patrol supervisor instructed officers that, "whenever a criminal record exists, we use the words, 'criminal alien,' and when no criminal record exists, the words, 'deportable alien.' I feel this change will have a psychological effect on the public and courts that will benefit the Service."[16] The linguistic turn toward approaching migration control as a matter of crime control, supported by the emerging War on Drugs throughout the country, reconfigured the everyday activities of immigration law enforcement.

Drug Wars

The War on Drugs is most often associated with Ronald Reagan and the 1980s but the 1940s and 1950s were critical years in the development of the campaign.[17] Between 1946 and 1951, the Uniform Narcotic Drug Acts created mandatory minimum prison sentences for drug convictions. In 1951, the Boggs Act established a mandatory minimum of two years even for first-time offenders. The ascent of drug control legislation reached a new level with the passage of the Narcotics Control Act of 1956, which imposed life imprisonment and even the death penalty for certain drug offenses, and made drug convictions a trigger for deportation for immigrants. Here were the state's ultimate sanctions: life in prison, death, and banishment.

The Border Patrol was deeply impacted by the rise of drug control as a federal law-enforcement initiative. In 1955, Congress designated all Border Patrol officers as customs inspectors and gave the organization primary authority over drug interdiction between official ports of entry. In addition, the Border Patrol began targeting immigrant prostitutes and drug runners. The INS detention centers along the US-Mexico border had been established to function as staging centers from where detainees were prepared for deportation or the more widely used form of forcible removal known as "voluntary return." With a new focus on arresting and deporting "criminal aliens," these centers adopted new policies and procedures to handle criminals rather than migrants. In particular, the INS began strip-searching all detainees upon entrance to the immigrant detention facilities and detained migrants for longer periods to run criminal background checks on all deportees.

By the late 1970s, immigration control was thoroughly enmeshed in crime control and drug interdiction in the US-Mexico border region.[18] During the 1980s, this implosion of law enforcement activities was reinforced with federal legislation that intimately bound immigration law to criminal law. The Anti-Drug Abuse Act of 1988 established a long list of retroactively applied "aggravated" felonies that triggered deportation for immigrants, including lawful permanent residents. Shoplifting, passing bad checks, and drug possession all constituted aggravated felonies subject to automatic deportation proceedings. The Anti-Drug Abuse Act, therefore, created new ways for immigrants to be marked as illegal and thereby deported.[19] By the mid-1990s, nonviolent offenses including document fraud, vehicle trafficking, and skipping bail were all added to the list of aggravated felonies that triggered deportation. In 1996, the Antiterrorism and Effective Death Penalty Act defined a single conviction of "moral turpitude" as a deportable offense while the Illegal Immigration Reform and Immigrant Responsibility Act, also passed in 1996, defined any conviction that carried a minimum sentence of one year as a deportable offense. By the turn of the twenty-first century, the new legislation had substantively expanded the deportability of legal immigrants while undocumented immigrants became more likely to be arrested for minor infractions via federal programs that coordinate with and reimburse localities for checking the immigration status of persons detained on ancillary charges.[20] The Criminal Alien Program (CAP) and Secure Communities program, for example, have allowed federal authorities to identify undocumented immigrants throughout the country among persons detained for misdemeanors and traffic violations.[21]

Today, over 60 percent of all deportations from the United States are triggered by criminal convictions, mostly traffic offenses, nonviolent drug crimes, and immigration-related violations.[22] After serving their criminal sentence, most immigrants who are identified for deportation will spend over one month in a detention facility, most likely a rented-out jail bed in one of several hundred jail facilities throughout the country that contract with Immigration and Customs Enforcement. In this era of mass incarceration, it is in jails and prisons across the United States where the paths of criminalized immigrants awaiting deportation have crossed with those of alienated citizens.

Mass Incarceration

Incarceration is an old story in the United States: jails reach back to the colonial era and prisons developed during the early nineteenth century. However, mass incarceration is a relatively recent phenomenon in American life.[23] Whereas the country's per-capita prison population remained relatively stable between the mid-nineteenth and mid-twentieth centuries, it began to tick up in the 1970s before exploding during the 1980s. Today, the United States holds over two million people behind bars. A total of seven million people—or 3.2 percent of the total adult population—are currently under some form of correctional supervision, and an estimated 50 million people have criminal records.[24]

The growth in the prison population has demanded an expansive set of institutions to hold, process, service, and monitor these millions of people. According to political scientist Marie Gottschalk, if one includes prisoners, probationers, parolees and their families, employees of correctional institutions, and residents in communities where prisons are built, mass incarceration directly impacts the daily lives of tens of millions of people throughout the country.[25]

California hosted one of the most dramatic prison booms in the late twentieth century. Fueled by new drug laws and sentencing practices, the state prisoner population increased by nearly 500 percent between 1982 and 2000. By 1992, California boasted the largest prison system in the Western world, with over 50 percent more prisoners than the US federal prison system and 40,000 more than the prison systems of Great Britain and Germany combined.[26] The state built twenty-three new prisons between 1982 and 2000, compared to twelve prisons built between 1852 and 1964.[27] Today, the Department of Corrections and Rehabilitation is California's largest state agency, with over 54,000 employees servicing nearly 161,704 inmates and 104,872 parolees.[28]

Like immigration control, mass incarceration is a zone of racial inequity. African Americans and Latinos, together, constitute 67 percent of the total state-prison population, but the rate of incarceration is significantly higher for the former. As of 2005, African American men were incarcerated at a rate of 5,125 per 100,000 in the general state population, compared to 1,142 for Latinos, 770 for whites, and 474 for men of other races. By the mid-1990s, five times as many black men in California were in prison than were enrolled in public higher education.[29] Among women, African Americans were incarcerated at a rate of 346 per 100,000 in the population, compared to 80 for whites, 62 for Latinas, and 27 for women of other races.[30] Today, black women are among the fastest growing prison populations.

Scholars and activists have been detailing since the mid-1980s how mass incarceration significantly shapes the life chances of African Americans, specifically as Congress and state legislatures restrict the social rights and benefits afforded to citizens convicted of a felony.[31] The right to vote, parental rights, and access to welfare benefits, including public housing, food stamps, and educational loans, for example, can be revoked for felony drug convictions. With higher rates of incarceration, African Americans are unevenly impacted by these "collateral consequences" of imprisonment. Yet to fully understand the meaning of mass incarceration at the turn of the twenty-first century, it is important to, once again, return to the nineteenth-century struggle for abolition.

In December 1865, upon Northern victory in the Civil War, Congress ratified the Thirteenth Amendment to the United States Constitution, which declared that "Neither slavery nor involuntary servitude, except as a punishment for crime whereof the party shall have been duly convicted, shall exist within the United States, or any place subject to their jurisdiction."[32] With its adoption, black emancipation from Southern slavery was accomplished, but the abolition struggle was incomplete, as convicts emerged as legitimate subjects of involuntary servitude. Into the twentieth century, in prisons and jails across the country, involuntary servitude flourished under the protection of the Thirteenth Amendment. Incarceration, in other words, functioned as a zone of exception in post-emancipation America.[33]

In 1868, Congress ratified the Fourteenth Amendment, which protected the citizenship status of freed slaves by firmly conferring citizenship upon all persons born or naturalized in the United States. In the decades ahead, municipalities and states would limit the substance of black citizenship with Jim Crow laws designed to marginalize African Americans under the rubric of "separate but equal." State legislatures also significantly altered the rights and privileges of citizenship according to convict status. According to California's 1872 Penal Code, for example, persons convicted for felonies and sentenced to life in state prison were defined as "civilly dead," and those convicted and sentenced to any term less than life in state prison lost *all* civil rights, other than those individually adjudicated or protected.[34]

Over the years, various rights and protections have been granted to California's inmates—by 1914, the right to receive correspondence: in the 1975 Inmate Bill of Rights, the right to marry, bring civil lawsuits, make wills, and create powers of attorney. Court decisions have also protected inmate access to health care and, most recently, the US Supreme Court upheld an order to protect inmates from the "cruel and unusual punishments" that accompany rampant overcrowding in the California prison system. Still, the many "collateral consequences" for felony conviction constitutes mass incarceration as a rights-stripping modality in the political landscape of the state and nation.

"Collateral consequences" is a term for the many social and political consequences attached to felony conviction. For example, in addition to disfranchisement for incarcerated felons and parolees in the State of California, federal law prohibits persons with drug convictions from being on or near the premises of public housing and maintains a lifetime ban on welfare benefits for persons with drug convictions. Such bans and exclusions are the material evidence that the criminal justice system operates as a broad-reaching system of social stratification that holds persons aloft from full citizenship and social belonging. Given the deeply racialized dimensions of mass incarceration in California and across the country, legal scholar Michelle Alexander refers to mass incarceration as the "new Jim Crow."[35]

But African Americans have not always constituted such a disproportionate number of inmates in California. In the 1920s, African Americans comprised 7 percent of the state and federal prison population in California.[36] During World War II, tens of thousands of African Americans migrated to the West Coast to take jobs in the region's growing industrial sector. Still, the black presence in the California prison system did not skyrocket until deindustrialization and the War on Drugs accelerated during the early 1980s.[37]

As the escalation of the War on Drugs swept increasing numbers of underemployed African Americans into the California prison system, it was also increasing funds for immigration control in the US-Mexico borderlands. During the 1970s, new investments in border enforcement for drug interdiction allowed the overall project of immigration control to expand. By the early 1980s, the Border Patrol routinely apprehended over one million persons per year and, by the close of the decade, increasing numbers of undocumented immigrants were being convicted of immigration violations and drug charges prior to deportation. The Urban Institute reports that the number of unauthorized immigrants sentenced in federal courts increased by 167 percent between 1991 and 1995, compared with 13 percent for citizens. In these years, immigration violations and drug crimes, most occurring in the Southwestern United States, constituted 85 percent of all offenses for which undocumented immigrants were convicted.[38]

The Illegal Immigration Reform and Immigration Responsibility Act (1996) further pushed undocumented immigrants into the prison system for nonviolent crime by increasing penalties for unsanctioned migration and requiring detention of immigrants undergoing deportation hearings. Today, Latinos, principally Mexicans, make up the largest group of inmates in federal prison; and undocumented immigrants, alongside Black women, represent one of the fastest growing incarcerated populations in California.[39]

In the jails and prisons of the Golden State, the crossed paths of felons and illegals clarify the meaning of mass incarceration and immigration control. For the Mexicanized caste of illegals, the arrival in US jails and prisons confirms that the US immigration control system is busy not only removing people from the United States but also in delivering them to peculiar institutions where far-reaching and racialized social, political, and economic inequities are now defined within the United States. For the African Americans who are unevenly represented among California's convict population, the arrival of undocumented immigrants in the prison system strengthens the prison's function as a special reserve for those without full citizenship rights in the United States. This tangle of alienated citizens and criminalized immigrants is a deeply historical construct that reaches up from the unfinished abolition struggle of the nineteenth century and across the twentieth-century experience with race and inequity to define today's caste of felons and illegal immigrants.

In the years ahead, as we grapple with the yet unfulfilled promises of immigration reform and prison reform, the success of our efforts will rest in remembering the history to which we respond. Since the era of emancipation, the rise of immigration control and mass incarceration has created a racialized caste of outsiders within the United States. Bigger jails with better food and improved health care—while immediately needed—will never address the larger and deeper problem of alienated citizens living in states of internal exile, both within and beyond the prison walls. Similarly, amnesty and paths to citizenship—while urgently needed—will never be enough. As the case of African Americans makes clear, citizenship can be gained and lost (time and again). Today it is the criminal justice system that renders the substance of citizenship, itself, unpredictable. In other words, a path to citizenship for undocumented immigrants in an era of mass incarceration may not be as valuable as it seems if pursued without a challenge to the inequities of mass incarceration; however, understanding the long history that brought us here carries within it alternatives to consider. At the beginning of it all, there was an abolitionist's critique. "It was not the Ethiopian as a man, but the Ethiopian as a slave and a coveted article of merchandise, that gave us trouble," explained Frederick Douglass in 1869. Like the slave, the caste of felons and illegal immigrants is a construct. We will need an abolitionist critique to imagine and build a world without it.[40]

NOTES

Reprinted with the permission of the University of California Press. This essay originally appeared in *Boom 1*, no. 4 (2011): 54–68.

1   In this essay, the terms "illegal alien," "convict," and "felon" are not used to refer-ence human beings but rather political categories created by immigration and criminal law. When referring to persons, either the terms unauthorized immigrant, unsanctioned immigrant, undocumented immigrant, or persons convicted of a felony are used.

2   California's total state population in 2010 was 37,253,956. Of this number, there are an estimated two million undocumented immigrants, an estimated 1.5 million ex-felons, and 170,000 currently in prison.

3   Voluntary Return was a process established during the 1920s to be used in lieu of formal deportation proceedings. Under Voluntary Return, immigrants waive their right to a deportation hearing and are not formally deported from the country but are required to leave the country. Most forced removals from the United States occur as Voluntary Returns rather than formal deportations. Immigrant detainees are persons held in detention facilities that are either administered or contracted with by Immigration and Customs Enforcement. Most detainees are held while disputing a deportation order or while awaiting deportation.

4   Examples of recent scholarship include Nora V. Demleitner, "Preventing Inter-nal Exile: The Need for Restrictions on Sentencing Collateral Consequences," 11 *Stanford Law and Policy Review* 153 (1999); Teresa Miller, "Citizenship and Severity: Recent Immigration Reforms and the New Penology," 17 *Georgetown Immigration Law Journal* 611 (2003); Juliet Stumpf, "The 'Crimmigration Crisis': Immigrants, Crime and Sovereign Power," 56 *American University Law Review* 367 (2006), 367–419; Yolanda Vazquez, "Perpetuating the Marginalization of Latinos: A Collateral Consequence of the Incorporation of Immigration Law into the Criminal Justice System," *Howard Law Journal* 54 (2011), 639–74. See also, "Policing, Detention, Deportation, and Resis-tance," a special volume of *Social Justice: A Journal of Crime, Conflict and World Order* 36, no. 2 (2009).

5   Stumpf, "The Crimmigration Crisis," 399.

6   Moon Ho-Jung, *Coolies and Cane: Race, Labor, and Sugar in the Age of Emancipation* (Baltimore: Johns Hopkins University Press, 2006), 38.

7   Frederick Douglass, "Our Composite Nationality" (1869).

8   Patrick Ettinger, *Imaginary Lines: Border Enforcement and the Origins of Undocumented Immigration, 1882–1930* (Austin: University of Texas Press, 2009).

9   The political branches of government include Congress and Executive Branch through the US Attorney General.

10 Quote from "Crimmigration Crisis," 392. For information on the cases discussed above, see Gabriel Chin, "Chae Chan Ping and Fong Yue Ting: The Origin of Plenary Power," *Immigration Law Stories*, David Martin and Peter Schuck, eds. (Foundation Press, 2005); Ian Haney Lopez, *White by Law: The Legal Construction of Race* (New York: New York University Press, 1996).

11 *Fong Yue Ting v. United States*, 149 US 698, 730 (1893).

12 Quoted in Chin, 20.

13 For a discussion of the rights granted to undocumented immigrants, see Miller, "Citizenship and Severity," 620–24.

14 Mae Ngai, *Impossible Subjects: Illegal Aliens and the Making of Modern America* (Princeton: Princeton University Press, 2004), 2.

15 The following discussion of the US Border Patrol is derived from my book, *Migra! A History of the U.S. Border Patrol* (Berkeley: University of California Press, 2010).

16 November 2, 1956 and November 15, 1956 untitled memos. National Archives and Records Administration 56364/43.3, 94, 59A2038.

17 David F. Musto, *The American Disease: Origins of Narcotics Control* (New York: Oxford University Press, 1999), 231. See also Peter Smith, ed., *Drug Policy in the Americas* (Boulder: Westview Press, 1992).

18 See Peter Andreas, *Border Games: Policing the U.S.-Mexico Divide* (Ithaca: Cornell University Press, 2000); Timothy Dunn, *The Militarization of the U.S.-Mexico Border, 1978–1992: Low-Intensity Conflict Doctrine Comes Home* (Austin: Center for Mexican American Studies, University of Texas at Austin, 1996).

19 David Hernandez, "Pursuant to Deportation: Latinas/os and Immigrant Detention," *Latino Studies* 6, nos. 1–2 (Spring/Summer 2008).

20 Vazquez, "Perpetuating the Marginalization of Latinos," 655–57.

21 Hernandez, "Pursuant to Detention," 45. See also Bill Ong Hing, "The Immigrant as Criminal: Punishing Dreamers," 9 *Hastings Women's Law Journal* 79 (1998).

22 Vazquez, "Perpetuating the Marginalization of Latinos," 665. This does not include the nearly one million removed from the United States each year under "voluntary return."

23 For an analysis of the rise of mass incarceration, see David Garland, *The Culture of Control: Crime and Social Order in Contemporary Society* (Chicago: University of Chicago Press, 2001). See also Garland, ed., *Mass Imprisonment: Social Causes and Consequences* (New York: Russell Sage Foundation, 2001). See also Heather Thompson, "Why Mass Incarceration Matters: Rethinking Crisis, Decline, and Transformation in Postwar American History," *Journal of American History* 97, no. 3 (December 2010), 703–34.

24 Demleitner, "Preventing Internal Exile," 12.

25 Marie Gottschalk, *The Prison and the Gallows: The Politics of Mass Incarceration in America* (Cambridge: Cambridge University Press, 2006), 1–3.

26 Franklin Zimring and Gordon Hawkins, *Prison Population and Criminal Justice Policy in California* (Berkeley: University of California at Berkeley, Institute of Governmental Studies Press, 1992), 1.

27 Ruth Wilson Gilmore, *Golden Gulag: Prisons, Surplus, Crisis, and Opposition in Globalizing California* (Berkeley: University of California Press, 2007), 7.

28   "Weekly Report of Population, As of Midnight June 8, 2011," Data Analysis Unit, California Department of Corrections and Rehabilitation (June 13, 2011), http://www.cdcr.ca.gov/Reports_Research/Offender_Information_Services_Branch/Population_Reports.html [accessed 15 June 2011].

29   "From Classrooms to Cell Blocks: How Prison Building Affects Higher Education and African American Enrollment in California," Center on Juvenile and Criminal Justice (October 1996).

30   "California's Changing Prison Population," Public Policy Institute of California, August 2006.

31   Some examples of more recent work include Katherine Beckett and Steve Herbert, *Banished: The Transformation of Urban Social Control* (New York: Oxford University Press, 2010); Jeff Manza and Christopher Uggen, *Locked Out: Felon Disenfranchisement and American Democracy* (New York: Oxford University Press, 2006); Sarah Wakefield and Christopher Uggen, "Incarceration and Stratification," *Annual Review of Sociology* 36 (2010), 387–406; and Bruce Western, *Punishment and Inequality in America* (Russell Sage Foundation, 2006).

32   Thirteenth Amendment to the United States Constitution.

33   Opposition from the labor and prison reform movements dramatically reduced the use of coerced prison labor during World War II. For information on convict labor between the 1860s and 1940s, see Alex Lichtenstein, *Twice the Work of Free Labor: The Political Economy of Convict Labor in the New South* (New York: Verso, 1996); Ward McAfee, "A History of Convict Labor in California," *Southern California Quarterly* 72 (Spring 1990), 235–54; Rebecca McLennan, *The Crisis of Imprisonment: Protest, Politics, and the Making of the American Penal State, 1776–1941* (Cambridge: Cambridge University Press, 2008); David Oshinsky, *"Worse Than Slavery": Parchmann Farm and the Ordeal of Jim Crow Justice* (New York: The Free Press, 1996); Robert Perkinson, *Texas Tough: The Rise of America's Prison Empire* (New York: Metropolotan Books, 2010).

34   For more information on the historical development of the rights of prisoners, see "Civil Death: Capacity of a Convict to Contract," *California Law Review* 2, no. 5 (July 1914), 401–2; "Civil Status of Convicts," *Columbia Law Review* 14, no. 7 (Nov. 1914), 592–94; Nathaniel Cantor, "The Prisoner and the Law," *Annals of the American Academy of Political and Social Science* 157 (Sept. 1931), 23–32; Alec Ewald, "Civil Death": The Ideological Paradox of Criminal Disenfranchisement Law in the United States," *Wisconsin Law Review* (2002), 1045–1138; Rebecca McLennan, "The Convict's Two Lives: Civil and Natural Death in the American Prison," in eds., David Garland, Randall McGowen, and Michael Meranze, *America's Death Penalty: Between Past and Present* (New York: New York University Press, 2011); M.W.S., "Constitutional Rights of Prisoners: The Developing Law," *University of Pennsylvania Law Review* 110, no. 7 (May 1962), 985–1008; Harry David Saunders, "Civil Death—A New Look at an Ancient Doctrine," *William and Mary Law Review* 11, no. 4 (1970), 988–1003.

35   Michelle Alexander, *The New Jim Crow: Mass Incarceration in the Age of Colorblindness* (New York: The New Press, 2010).

36   See Patrick A. Langan, "Race of Prisoners Admitted to State and Federal Institutions, 1926–1986," Publication #NCJ-125618, Bureau of Justice Statistics, US Department of Justice (May 1991); and Patrick Langan, John V. Fundis, Lawrence Greenfield, and Victoria Schneider, "Historical Statistics on Prisoners in State

and Federal Institutions, Yearend 1935–1986," publication # NCJ-111098, Bureau of Justice Statistics, US Department of Justice (May 1988).

37 Wilson Gilmore, *Golden Gulag*, 110–11.

38 Rebecca Clark and Scott Anderson, "Illegal Aliens in Federal, State, and Local Criminal Justice Systems," Urban Institute, 30 June 2000. See also, Jonathan Simon, "Refugees in a Carceral Era: The Rebirth of Immigration Prisons in the United States," *Public Culture* 10, no. 3 (1988), 577–606.

39 For additional information, see Michael Welch, "The Role of the Immigration and Naturalization Service in the Prison-Industrial Complex," *Social Justice* 27, no. 3 (2000), 73–88.

40 Prison abolitionism is already a robust political movement. See www .criticalresistance.org for more information.

How to Tame a Wild Tongue

GLORIA ANZALDÚA

"We're going to have to control your tongue," the dentist says, pulling out all the metal from my mouth. Silver bits plop and tinkle into the basin. My mouth is a motherlode.

The dentist is cleaning out my roots. I get a whiff of the stench when I gasp. "I can't cap that tooth yet, you're still draining," he says.

"We're going to have to do something about your tongue," I hear the anger rising in his voice. My tongue keeps pushing out the wads of cotton, pushing back the drills, the long thin needles. "I've never seen anything as strong or as stubborn," he says. And I think, how do you tame a wild tongue, train it to be quiet, how do you bridle and saddle it? How do you make it lie down?

"Who is to say that robbing a people of its language is less violent than war?"—RAY GWYN SMITH[1]

I remember being caught speaking Spanish at recess—that was good for three licks on the knuckles with a sharp ruler. I remember being sent to the corner of the classroom for "talking back" to the Anglo teacher when all I was trying to do was tell her how to pronounce my name. "If you want to be American, speak 'American.' If you don't like it, go back to Mexico where you belong."

"I want you to speak English. *Pa' hallar buen trabajo tienes que saber hablar el inglés bien. Qué vale toda tu educación si todavía hablas inglés con un 'accent,'*" my mother would say, mortified that I spoke English like a Mexican. At Pan American University, I, and all Chicano students were required to take two speech classes. Their purpose: to get rid of our accents.

Attacks on one's form of expression with the intent to censor are a violation of the First Amendment. *El Anglo con cara de inocente nos arrancó la lengua.* Wild tongues can't be tamed, they can only be cut out.

Overcoming the Tradition of Silence

Ahogadas, escupimos el oscuro.
Peleando con nuestra propia sombra
el silencio nos sepulta.

En boca cerrada no entran moscas. "Flies don't enter a closed mouth" is a saying I kept hearing when I was a child. *Ser habladora* was to be a gossip and a liar, to talk too much. *Muchachitas bien criadas*, well-bred girls don't answer back. *Es una falta de respeto* to talk back to one's mother or father. I remember one of the sins I'd recite to the priest in the confession box the few times I went to confession: talking back to my mother, *hablar pa' 'trás, repelar. Hocicona, repelona, chismosa,* having a big mouth, questioning, carrying tales are all signs of being *mal criada.* In my culture they are all words that are derogatory if applied to women—I've never heard them applied to men.

The first time I heard two women, a Puerto Rican and a Cuban, say the word *"nosotras,"* I was shocked. I had not known the word existed. Chicanas use *nosotros* whether we're male or female. We are robbed of our female being by the masculine plural. Language is a male discourse.

> And our tongues have become
> dry   the wilderness has
> dried out our tongues   and
> we have forgotten speech.

—Irena Klepfisz[2]

Even our own people, other Spanish speakers *nos quieren poner candados en la boca.* They would hold us back with their bag of *reglas de academia.*

Oyé como ladra: El lenguaje de la frontera

Quien tiene boca se equivoca.
—Mexican saying

"*Pocho*, cultural traitor, you're speaking the oppressor's language by speaking English, you're ruining the Spanish language," I have been accused by various Latinos and Latinas. Chicano Spanish is considered by the purist and by most Latinos deficient, a mutilation of Spanish.

But Chicano Spanish is a border tongue which developed naturally. Change, *evolución, enriquecimiento de palabras nuevas por invención o adopción* have created variants of Chicano Spanish, *un nuevo lenguaje. Un lenguaje que corresponde a un modo de vivir.* Chicano Spanish is not incorrect, it is a living language.

For a people who are neither Spanish nor live in a country in which Spanish is the first language; for a people who live in a country in which English is the reigning tongue but who are not Anglo; for a people who cannot entirely identify with either standard (formal, Castillian) Spanish nor standard English, what recourse is left to them but to create their own language? A language which they can connect their identity to, one capable of communicating the realities and values true to themselves—a language with terms that are neither *español ni inglés*, but both. We speak a patois, a forked tongue, a variation of two languages.

Chicano Spanish sprang out of the Chicanos' need to identify ourselves as a distinct people. We needed a language with which we could communicate with ourselves, a secret language. For some of us, language is a homeland closer than the Southwest—for many Chicanos today live in the Midwest and the East. And because we are a complex, heterogeneous people, we speak many languages. Some of the languages we speak are:

1. Standard English
2. Working class and slang English
3. Standard Spanish
4. Standard Mexican Spanish
5. North Mexican Spanish dialect
6. Chicano Spanish (Texas, New Mexico, Arizona and California have regional variations)
7. Tex-Mex
8. *Pachuco* (called *caló*)

My "home" tongues are the languages I speak with my sister and brothers, with my friends. They are the last five listed, with 6 and 7 being closest to my heart. From school, the media and job situations, I've picked up standard and working-class English. From Mamagrande Locha and from reading Spanish and Mexican literature, I've picked up Standard Spanish and Standard Mexican Spanish. From *los recién llegados*, Mexican immigrants, and *braceros*, I learned the North Mexican dialect. With Mexicans I'll try to speak either Standard Mexican Spanish or the North Mexican dialect. From my parents and Chicanos living in the Valley, I picked up Chicano Texas Spanish, and I speak it with my mom, younger brother (who married a Mexican and who rarely mixes Spanish with English), aunts and older relatives.

With Chicanas from *Nuevo México* or *Arizona* I will speak Chicano Spanish a little, but often they don't understand what I'm saying. With most California Chicanas I speak entirely in English (unless I forget). When I first moved to San Francisco, I'd rattle off something in Spanish, unintentionally embarrassing them. Often it is only with another Chicana *tejana* that I can talk freely.

Words distorted by English are known as anglicisms or *pochismos*. The *pocho* is an anglicized Mexican or American of Mexican origin who speaks Spanish with an accent characteristic of North Americans and who distorts and reconstructs the language according to the influence of English.[3] Tex-Mex, or Spanglish, comes most naturally to me. I may switch back and forth from English to Spanish in the same sentence or in the same word. With my sister and my brother Nune and with Chicano *tejano* contemporaries I speak in Tex-Mex.

From kids and people my own age I picked up *Pachuco*. *Pachuco* (the language of the zoot suiters) is a language of rebellion, both against Standard Spanish and Standard English. It is a secret language. Adults of the culture and outsiders cannot understand it. It is made up of slang words from both English and Spanish. *Ruca* means girl or woman, *vato* means guy or dude, *chale* means no, *simón* means yes, *churo* is sure, talk is *periquiar, pigionear* means petting, *que gacho* means how nerdy, *ponte águila* means watch out, death is called *la pelona*. Through lack of practice and not having others who can speak it, I've lost most of the *Pachuco* tongue.

Chicano Spanish

Chicanos, after 250 years of Spanish/Anglo colonization have developed significant differences in the Spanish we speak. We collapse two adjacent vowels into a single syllable and sometimes shift the stress in certain words such as *maíz/ maiz, cohete/ cuete*. We leave out certain consonants when they appear between vowels: *lado/lao, mojado/mojao*. Chicanos from South Texas pronounced *f* as *j* as in *jue (fue)*. Chicanos use "archaisms," words that are no longer in the Spanish language, words that have been evolved out. We say *semos, truje, haiga, ansina,* and *naiden*. We retain the "archaic" *j*, as in *jalar*, that derives from an earlier *h*, (the French *halar* or the Germanic *halon* which was lost to standard Spanish in the 16th century), but which is still found in several regional dialects such as the one spoken in South Texas. (Due to geography, Chicanos from the Valley of South Texas were cut off linguistically from other Spanish speakers. We tend to use words that the Spaniards brought over from Medieval Spain. The majority of the Spanish colonizers in Mexico and the Southwest came from Extremadura—Hernán Cortés was one of them—and Andalucía. Andalucians pronounce *ll* like a *y*, and their *d*'s tend to be absorbed by adjacent vowels: *tirado* becomes *tirao*. They brought *el lenguaje popular, dialectos y regionalismos*.[4])

Chicanos and other Spanish speakers also shift *ll* to *y* and *z* to *s*.[5] We leave out initial syllables, saying *tar* for *estar, toy* for *estoy, hora* for *ahora (cubanos* and *puertorriqueños* also leave out initial letters of some words.) We also leave out the final syllable such as *pa* for *para*. The intervocalic *y*, the *ll* as in *tortilla, ella, botella*, gets replaced by *tortia* or *tortiya, ea, botea*. We add an additional syllable at the beginning of certain words: *atocar* for *tocar, agastar* for *gastar*. Sometimes we'll say *lavaste las vacijas*, other times *lavates* (substituting the *ates* verb endings for the *aste*).

We use anglicisms, words borrowed from English: *bola* from ball, *carpeta* from carpet, *máchina de lavar* (instead of *lavadora*) from washing machine. Tex-Mex argot, created by adding a Spanish sound at the beginning or end of an English word such as *cookiar* for cook, *watchar* for watch, *parkiar* for park, and *rapiar* for rape, is the result of the pressures on Spanish speakers to adapt to English.

We don't use the word *vosotros/as* or its accompanying verb form. We don't say *claro* (to mean yes), *imagínate*, or *me emociona*, unless we picked up Spanish from Latinas, out of a book, or in a classroom. Other Spanish-speaking groups are going through the same, or similar, development in their Spanish.

Linguistic Terrorism

> *Deslenguadas. Somos los del español deficiente*. We are your linguistic nightmare, your linguistic aberration, your linguistic *mestizaje*, the subject of your *burla*. Because we speak with tongues of fire we are culturally crucified. Racially, culturally and linguistically *somos huérfanos*—we speak an orphan tongue.

Chicanas who grew up speaking Chicano Spanish have internalized the belief that we speak poor Spanish. It is illegitimate, a bastard language. And because we internalize how our language has been used against us by the dominant culture, we use our language differences against each other.

Chicana feminists often skirt around each other with suspicion and hesitation. For the longest time I couldn't figure it out. Then it dawned on me. To be close to another Chicana is like looking into the mirror. We are afraid of what we'll see there. *Pena*. Shame. Low estimation of self. In childhood we are told that our language is wrong. Repeated attacks on our native tongue diminish our sense of self. The attacks continue throughout our lives.

Chicanas feel uncomfortable talking in Spanish to Latinas, afraid of their censure. Their language was not outlawed in their countries. They had a whole lifetime of being immersed in their native tongue; generations, centuries in which Spanish was a first language, taught in school, heard on radio and TV, and read in the newspaper.

If a person, Chicana or Latina, has a low estimation of my native tongue, she also has a low estimation of me. Often with *mexicanas y latinas* we'll speak English as a neutral language. Even among Chicanas we tend to speak English at parties or conferences. Yet, at the same time, we're afraid the other will think we're *agringadas* because we don't speak Chicano Spanish. We oppress each other trying to out-Chicano each other, vying to be the "real" Chicanas, to speak like Chicanos. There is no one Chicano language just as there is no one Chicano experience. A monolingual Chicana whose first language is English or Spanish is just as much a Chicana as one who speaks several variants of Spanish. A Chicana from Michigan or Chicago or Detroit is just as much a Chicana as one from the Southwest. Chicano Spanish is as diverse linguistically as it is regionally.

By the end of this century, Spanish speakers will comprise the biggest minority group in the U.S., a country where students in high schools and colleges are encouraged to take French classes because French is considered more "cultured." But for a language to remain alive it must be used.[6] By the end of this century English, and not Spanish, will be the mother tongue of most Chicanos and Latinos.

So, if you want to really hurt me, talk badly about my language. Ethnic identity is twin skin to linguistic identity—I am my language. Until I can take pride in my language, I cannot take pride in myself. Until I can accept as legitimate Chicano Texas Spanish, Tex-Mex and all the other languages I speak, I cannot accept the legitimacy of myself. Until I am free to write bilingually and to switch codes without having always to translate, while I still have to speak English or Spanish when I would rather speak Spanglish, and as long as I have to accommodate the English speakers rather than having them accommodate me, my tongue will be illegitimate.

I will no longer be made to feel ashamed of existing. I will have my voice: Indian, Spanish, white. I will have my serpent's tongue—my woman's voice, my sexual voice, my poet's voice. I will overcome the tradition of silence.

My fingers
move sly against your palm
Like women everywhere, we speak in code. . . .

—Melanie Kaye/Kantrowitz[7]

"VISTAS," CORRIDOS, Y COMIDA: *MY NATIVE TONGUE*

In the 1960s, I read my first Chicano novel. It was *City of Night* by John Rechy, a gay Texan, son of a Scottish father and a Mexican mother. For days I walked around in stunned amazement that a Chicano could write and could get published. When I read *I Am Joaquín*[8] I was surprised to see a bilingual book by a Chicano in print. When I saw poetry written in Tex-Mex for the first time, a feeling of pure joy flashed through me. I felt like we really existed as a people. In 1971, when I started teaching High School English to Chicano students, I tried to supplement the required texts with works by Chicanos, only to be reprimanded and forbidden to do so by the principal. He claimed that I was supposed to teach "American" and English literature. At the risk of being fired, I swore my students to secrecy and slipped in Chicano short stories, poems, a play. In graduate school, while working toward a Ph.D., I had to "argue" with one advisor after the other, semester after semester, before I was allowed to make Chicano literature an area of focus.

Even before I read books by Chicanos or Mexicans, it was the Mexican movies I saw at the drive-in—the Thursday night special of $1.00 a carload—that gave me a sense of belonging. *"Vámonos a las vistas,"* my mother would call out and we'd all—grandmother, brothers, sister and cousins—squeeze into the car. We'd wolf down cheese and bologna white bread sandwiches while watching Pedro Infante in melodramatic tear-jerkers like *Nosotros los pobres,* the first "real" Mexican movie (that was not an imitation of European movies). I remember seeing *Cuando los hijos se van* and surmising that all Mexican movies played up the love a mother has for her children and what ungrateful sons and daughters suffer when they are not devoted to their mothers. I remember the singing-type "westerns" of Jorge Negrete and Miguel Aceves Mejía. When watching Mexican movies, I felt a sense of homecoming as well as alienation. People who were to amount to something didn't go to Mexican movies, or *bailes* or tune their radios to *bolero, rancherita,* and *corrido* music.

The whole time I was growing up, there was *norteño* music sometimes called North Mexican border music, or Tex-Mex music, or Chicano music, or *cantina* (bar) music. I grew up listening to *conjuntos,* three- or four-piece bands made up of folk musicians playing guitar, *bajo sexto,* drums and button accordion, which Chicanos had borrowed from the German immigrants who had come to Central Texas and Mexico to farm and build breweries. In the Rio Grande Valley, Steve Jordan and Little Joe Hernández were popular, and Flaco Jiménez was the accordion king. The rhythms of Tex-Mex music are those of the polka, also adapted from the Germans, who in turn had borrowed the polka from the Czechs and Bohemians.

I remember the hot, sultry evenings when *corridos*—songs of love and death on the Texas-Mexican borderlands—reverberated out of cheap amplifiers from the local *cantinas* and wafted in through my bedroom window.

Corridos first became widely used along the South Texas/Mexican border during the early conflict between Chicanos and Anglos. The *corridos* are usually about Mexican heroes who do valiant deeds against the Anglo oppressors. Pancho Villa's song, *"La cucaracha,"* is the most famous one. *Corridos* of John F. Kennedy and his death are still very popular in the Valley. Older Chicanos remember Lydia Mendoza, one of the great border *corrido* singers who was called *la Gloria de Tejas.* Her *"El tango negro,"* sung during the Great Depression, made her a singer of the people. The everpresent *corridos* narrated one hundred years of border history, bringing news of events as well as entertaining. These folk musicians and folk songs are our chief cultural mythmakers, and they made our hard lives seem bearable.

I grew up feeling ambivalent about our music. Country-western and rock-and-roll had more status. In the '50s and '60s, for the slightly educated and *agringado* Chicanos, there existed a sense of shame at being caught listening to our music. Yet I couldn't stop my feet from thumping to the music, could not stop humming the words, nor hide from myself the exhilaration I felt when I heard it.

There are more subtle ways that we internalize identification, especially in the forms of images and emotions. For me food and certain smells are tied to my identity, to my homeland. Woodsmoke curling up to an immense blue sky; woodsmoke perfuming my grandmother's clothes, her skin. The stench of cow manure and the yellow patches on the ground; the crack of a .22 rifle and the reek of cordite. Homemade white cheese sizzling in a pan, melting inside a folded *tortilla.* My sister Hilda's hot, spicy *menudo, chile colorado* making it deep red, pieces of *panza* and hominy floating on top. My brother Carito barbecuing *fajitas* in the backyard. Even now and 3,000 miles away, I can see my mother spicing the ground beef, pork and venison with *chile.* My mouth salivates at the thought of the hot steaming *tamales* I would be eating if I were home.

SI LE PREGUNTAS A MI MAMÁ, "¿QUÉ ERES?"

> Identity is the essential core of who
> we are as individuals, the conscious
> experience of the self inside.
> —Kaufman[9]

Nosotros los Chicanos straddle the borderlands. On one side of us, we are constantly exposed to the Spanish of the Mexicans, on the other side we hear the Anglos' incessant clamoring so that we forget our language. Among ourselves we don't say *nosotros los americanos, o nosotros los españoles, o nosotros los hispanos.* We say *nosotros los mexicanos* (by *mexicanos* we do not mean citizens of Mexico; we do not mean a national identity, but a racial one). We distinguish between *mexicanos del otro lado* and *mexicanos de este lado.* Deep in our hearts we believe that being Mexican has nothing to do with which country one lives in. Being Mexican is a state of soul—not one of mind, not one of citizenship. Neither eagle nor serpent, but both. And like the ocean, neither animal respects borders.

> *Dime con quien andas y te diré quien eres.*
> (Tell me who your friends are and I'll tell you who you are.)
> —Mexican saying

Si le preguntas a mi mamá, "¿Qué eres?" te dirá, "Soy mexicana." My brothers and sister say the same. I sometimes will answer *"soy mexicana"* and at others will say *"soy Chicana" o "soy tejana."* But I identified as *"Raza"* before I ever identified as *"mexicana"* or "Chicana."

As a culture, we call ourselves Spanish when referring to ourselves as a linguistic group and when copping out. It is then that we forget our predominant Indian genes. We are 70 to 80% Indian.[10] We call ourselves Hispanic[11] or Spanish-American or Latin American or Latin when linking ourselves to other Spanish-speaking peoples of the Western hemisphere and when copping out. We call ourselves Mexican-American[12] to signify we are neither Mexican nor American, but more the noun "American" than the adjective "Mexican" (and when copping out).

Chicanos and other people of color suffer economically for not acculturating. This voluntary (yet forced) alienation makes for psychological conflict, a kind of dual identity—we don't identify with the Anglo-American cultural values and we don't totally identify with the Mexican cultural values. We are a synergy of two cultures with various degrees of Mexicanness or Angloness. I have so internalized the borderland conflict that sometimes I feel like one cancels out the other and we are zero, nothing, no one. *A veces no soy nada ni nadie. Pero hasta cuando no lo soy, lo soy.*

When not copping out, when we know we are more than nothing, we call ourselves Mexican, referring to race and ancestry; *mestizo* when affirming both our Indian and Spanish (but we hardly ever own our Black ancestry); Chicano when referring to a politically aware people born and/or raised in the U.S.; *Raza* when referring to Chicanos; *tejanos* when we are Chicanos from Texas.

Chicanos did not know we were a people until 1965 when Cesar Chavez and the farmworkers united and *I Am Joaquín* was published and *la Raza Unida* party was formed in Texas. With that recognition, we became a distinct people. Something momentous happened to the Chicano soul—we became aware of our reality and acquired a name and a language (Chicano Spanish) that reflected that reality. Now that we had a name, some of the fragmented pieces began to fall together—who we were, what we were, how we had evolved. We began to get glimpses of what we might eventually become.

Yet the struggle of identities continues, the struggle of borders is our reality still. One day the inner struggle will cease and a true integration take place. In the meantime, *tenemos que hacerla lucha. ¿Quién está protegiendo los ranchos de mi gente? ¿Quién está tratando de cerrar la fisura entre la india y el blanco en nuestra sangre? El Chicano, sí, el Chicano que anda como un ladrón en su propia casa.*

Los Chicanos, how patient we seem, how very patient. There is the quiet of the Indian about us.[13] We know how to survive. When other races have given up their tongue, we've kept ours. We know what it is to live under the hammer blow of the dominant *norteamericano* culture. But more than we count the blows, we count the days the weeks the years the centuries the eons until the white laws and commerce and customs will rot in the deserts they've created, lie bleached. *Humildes* yet proud, *quietos* yet wild, *nosotros los mexicanos*-Chicanos will walk by the crumbling ashes as we go about our business. Stubborn, persevering, impenetrable as stone, yet possessing a malleability that renders us unbreakable, we, the *mestizas* and *mestizos*, will remain.

NOTES

Reprinted with permission Aunt Jude Books. This essay originally appeared in *Borderlands/La Frontera: The New Mestiza*, 2nd ed., 75–86 (San Francisco: Aunt Lute Books, 1999).

1   Ray Gwyn Smith. *Moorland Is Cold Country*, unpublished book.

2   Irena Klepfisz, "*Di rayze aheym*/The Journey Home," in *The Tribe of Dina: A Jewish Women's Anthology*, Melanie Kaye/Kantrowitz and Irena Klepfisz, eds. (Montpelier, VT: Sinister Wisdom Books, 1986), 49.

3   R.C. Ortega, *Dialectología Del Barrio*, trans. Hortencia S. Alwan (Los Angeles, CA: R.C. Ortega Publisher & Bookseller, 1977), 132.

4   Eduardo Hernandéz-Chávez, Andrew D. Cohen, and Anthony F. Beltramo, *El Lenguaje de los Chicanos: Regional and Social Characteristics of Language Used By Mexican Americans* (Arlington, VA: Center for Applied Linguistics, 1975), 39.

5   Hernandéz-Chávez, xvii.

6   Irena Klepfisz, "Secular Jewish Identity: Yidishkayt in America," in *The Tribe of Dina*, Kaye/Kantrowitz and Klepfisz, eds., 43.

7   Melanie Kaye/Kantrowitz, "Sign," in *We Speak In Code: Poems and Other Writings* (Pittsburgh, PA: Motheroot Publications, Inc., 1980), 85.

8   Rodolfo Gonzales, I Am Joaquín / *Yo Soy Joaquín* (New York, NY: Bantam Books, 1972). It was first published in 1967.

9   Kaufman, 68.

10 Chávez, 88–90.

11 "Hispanic" is derived from *Hispanis* (*España*, a name given to the Iberian Peninsula in ancient times when it was a part of the Roman Empire) and is a term designated by the U.S. government to make it easier to handle us on paper.

12 The Treaty of Guadalupe Hidalgo created the Mexican-American in 1848.

13 Anglos, in order to alleviate their guilt for dispossessing the Chicano, stressed the Spanish part of us and perpetrated the myth of the Spanish Southwest. We have accepted the fiction that we are Hispanic, that is Spanish, in order to accommodate ourselves to the dominant culture and its abhorrence of Indians. Chávez, 88–91.

"Wavering on the Horizon of Social Being"
The Treaty of Guadalupe-Hidalgo and the Legacy of Its Racial
Character in Américo Paredes's *George Washington Gómez*
MARÍA JOSEFINA SALDAÑA-PORTILLO

Which Century Is It Anyway?

In 1891, José Martí issued the following warning to his fellow *panamericanistas* (Pan-Americanists) about U.S. expansionist designs in his now famous essay "Nuestra América" ("Our America"):

> But there is yet another danger which does not come from within, but from the difference in origins, methods and interests between the two halves of the continent. The hour is fast approaching when our America will be confronted by an enterprising and energetic nation seeking close relations, but with indifference and scorn for us and our ways. And since strong countries, self-made by the rifle and the law, love, and only love, strong countries; since the hour of reckless ambition, of which North America may be freed if that which is purest in her blood predominates, or on which she may be launched by her vengefull [*sic*] and sordid masses, her tradition of expansion or the ambition of some powerful leaders, is not so near at hand, even to the most timorous eye, that there is not time to show the self-possessed and unwavering pride that would confront and dissuade her.[1]

The hour of U.S. "reckless ambition" seems once again on us, spurred, in part, by vengeful masses and rapacious leaders who refuse to mourn the victims of 9/11 or the passing of imperial power, and instead melancholically re-enact both. The cold war that embroiled Latin America in the U.S. bloody quest for ideological hegemony may well be over; U.S.–backed dictatorships and death squads appear to have receded temporarily behind the indifference of democracy. The world is now more polarized economically than at any point in the previous half century as the imposition of "free trade" policies and treaties spreads across the hemisphere, indeed across the entire Third World. And the United States is clearly the victor here, the center of economic power in the discrete, urbane neocolonialism of the post–Cold War world. Yet the current Bush administration is intent on returning us to a crass (by contrast) geopolitics of empire reminiscent of the eighteenth and nineteenth centuries. This nation, "self-made by the rifle and the law," revises or refuses international law as it simultaneously pursues military ventures in Afghanistan, Iraq, *and* Colombia under the cover of counterterrorist protective measures. George Bush Sr. promised us a new world order, and yet his son seems intent on returning us to an old world order of imperialist design—old, at least, for Latin America. History, indeed, seems intent on repeating itself.

Thus recent institutional calls for a transnational American and ethnic studies continue to be as timely as when Martí issued his call for a hemispheric knowledge production of the ties binding "our America" as a counterforce to the ambitions of one lone country from its northern hemisphere. In this essay, then, I answer such calls by returning us to the scene of the Mexico–United States war, perhaps the earliest expression of U.S. imperialism in *nuestra América*. The 1848 Treaty of Guadalupe-Hidalgo not only ended the conflict between Mexico and the United States; it initiated the racialization of "Mexican Americans" in relation to Anglo-Americans, but also in relation to indigenous populations who suddenly found themselves under the jurisdiction of a new imperial power. The racial logic enacted by the treaty served the purposes of future expansionist ambition in Latin America; however, it also established a tenuous border between Indian identity and Mexican American identity, one that continues to trouble Chicano nationalism.

While the larger aim of this essay is to contribute to an analysis of the evolving racial logic undergirding U.S. imperialism, its more discrete aim is to trace the lasting influence of the Treaty of Guadalupe-Hidalgo on the construction of contemporary Chicano identity. I am interested in how the treaty facilitated the racial subjection of formally enfranchised Mexican citizens into disenfranchised U.S. citizens, and how this racialized subjection finds echo in, as one example, contemporary Chicano literary production. How did such distinct representations of indigenous peoples emerge in the United States and Mexico? How, in other words, did the "Indian" come to occupy such different psychic spaces in the national imaginaries of the two countries, and more poignantly, in the national imaginary of Chicanos? The answers to these questions can be traced back, in part, to the racial logic set in motion by the Treaty of Guadalupe-Hidalgo. Postcolonial "Mexican," "U.S.," and subsequently "Chicano" subjectivities emerged from the treaty's legacy of representing and differentiating "Indian identity" in what today constitutes the Southwest.

The first half of my title—"wavering on the horizon of social being"—is taken directly from Judith Butler's *The Psychic Life of Power* because I find that the phrase perfectly captures the predicament of subaltern subjectivity as it wavers, flickers, at the margin of social recognition: "The temporal paradox of the subject is such that, of necessity, we must lose the perspective of a subject already formed in order to account for our own becoming. That becoming is no simple or continuous affair, but an uneasy practice of repetition and its risks, compelled yet incomplete, wavering on the horizon of social being."[2] Through a reading of the treaty, of the history immediately preceding and following its enactment, and of Américo Paredes's *George Washington Gómez* (1990), I attempt to enter the temporal paradox suggested by Butler in the hopes of gaining perspective on the process of "becoming" Chicano, of becoming subjected as (n)either white (n)or Indian at the margins of social being.

Faulty Analogies and the Fungible Indian

The historical scholarship on the Treaty of Guadalupe-Hidalgo divides into three camps, according to legal scholar Christopher David Ruiz Cameron. In his article "One Hundred Fifty Years of Solitude: Reflections on the End of the History Academy's Dominance of Scholarship on the Treaty of Guadalupe Hidalgo," Ruiz Cameron identifies the first camp as the "traditionalists," those historians who have interpreted the treaty as the "recorded deed of the biggest 'land grab' in American history." Since the traditionalists see the treaty as nothing more than the codification of the U.S. interests in Mexico that led to war, it stands to reason that U.S. courts would repeatedly interpret the treaty in favor of U.S. claimants and against the newly annexed Mexicans. Ruiz Cameron labels the second school of historians the "revisionists." The historians in this camp insist the treaty provided real protections for the civil and property rights of Mexicans. Unfortunately, they argue, the Mexican claimants, accustomed to a continental-style legal system, were culturally ill equipped for navigating the U.S. common-law legal system. Thus, from this perspective, if the Mexicans lost their rights and lands, it was the fault of neither the treaty nor the U.S. courts, but of culture. Finally, according to Ruiz Cameron, there are the "reclamationists." These historians interpret the treaty as a living document which not only guaranteed the civil and human rights of displaced Mexicans in 1848 but continues to do so today. Thus these rights remain and may still be claimed by Mexican Americans through the courts.[3]

Historians from all three camps have been primarily concerned with interpreting the legacy of just two of the treaty's twenty-three articles, Articles 8 and 9. These two articles are at the heart of scholarly research because together they presumably guaranteed the land and civil rights of the newly annexed population. It thus behooves us to cite the articles at length. Article 8 begins,

> Mexicans now established in territories previously belonging to Mexico, and which remain for the future within the limits of the United States, as defined by the present treaty, shall be free to continue where they now reside, or to remove at any time to the Mexican Republic, retaining the property which they possess in the said territories, or disposing thereof, and removing the proceeds wherever they please, without their being subjected, on this account, to any contribution, tax, or charge whatever. . . .
>
> In the said territories, property of every kind, now belonging to Mexicans not established there, shall be inviolably respected. The present owners, the heirs of these, and all Mexicans who may hereafter acquire said property by contract, shall enjoy with respect to it guarantees equally ample as if the same belonged to citizens of the United States.

It would appear there is little room for interpretation: annexed Mexicans are entitled to the preservation of their property, whether or not they elect to become U.S. citizens. Similarly, Article 9 seems straightforward as to this population's civil rights:

> The Mexicans who, in the territories aforesaid, *shall not preserve the character* of citizens of the Mexican Republic . . . shall be incorporated into the Union of the United States and be admitted, at the proper time (to be judged of by the Congress of the United States) *to the enjoyment of all the rights of the citizens of the United States* according to the principles of the Constitution; and in the meantime shall be maintained and protected in the free enjoyment of their liberty and property, and secured in the free exercise of their religion without restriction. (Emphasis added)

Traditionalists, revisionists, and reclamationists uniformly agree on the failure of the U.S. government to have delivered on this promise of the "enjoyment of all the rights of citizens of the United States" to the newly annexed Mexicans or to have protected the property rights of Mexicans. They differ only as to where they attribute responsibility for this failure. In other words, all three camps of historians described by Ruiz Cameron locate this failure in the execution of the treaty, rather than in the content of these articles. They read the meaning of the articles as self-evident.[4]

This widespread agreement among historians on the failure of the treaty to have delivered on its promise to annexed Mexicans has led early Americanist scholar David Kazanjian to identify a "broken promise" discourse within the preponderance of Chicano scholarship on the treaty. In *The Colonizing Trick: National Culture and Imperial Citizenship in Early America*, he writes,

> There is a long and varied tradition of representing Article IX's promise of "all the rights of the citizens of the United States" to annexed Mexicans as a "broken promise," given the extensive, post-war racial exploitation of Mexican-Americans in the U.S. In particular, complex articulations of this "broken promise" discourse emerged from post–WWII Chicano and Mexican-American activists who, variously in California, Texas, and the Southwest, sought to use the Treaty's promise as a lever for anti-racist, anti-colonial struggles.... However, as that quite supple activist work has more recently been translated into institutionalized civil rights discourse and, in turn, into the work of literary critics on the U.S.-Mexico War period, it has at times become a more static and unidimensional call for the fulfillment of the promise of equal rights. But what exactly does it mean to call for the fulfillment of Article IX?[5]

As early as the 1940s, according to noted historian Mario T. García, Chicano activists from both ends of the political spectrum based their pursuit of civil rights in the United States on the premise that the terms of the treaty remained unfulfilled. Thus both the conservative League of United Latin American Citizens (LULAC) and the radical *Asociación Nacional México-Americana* (ANMA; National Mexican American Association) regularly invoked the "broken promise" of the treaty when demanding the fulfillment of their guaranteed civil rights from a recalcitrant U.S. government.[6] However, as Kazanjian has suggested often occurs, the critical distance between historian and historical actors collapses in García's account when he adopts their position himself without comment: "These [cultural] differences had been recognized by the Treaty of Guadalupe Hidalgo, which . . . had promised to protect the Mexican's distinct culture and heritage. These guarantees, however, had not been fulfilled and arriving Anglos had abused the Mexican's culture, language, political rights, and economic holdings."[7] Like García, many other Chicano scholars in the humanities and social sciences proceed according to this commonsense assumption that a promise has been broken.[8] To begin challenging this seemingly commonsense discourse of a broken promise among Chicano activists and scholars alike, let us return to Kazanjian's compelling question: What exactly does it mean to call for the fulfillment of Article 9? What if its meaning is not self-evident but a matter of interpretation?

Kazanjian argues persuasively that the fulfillment of the promise of Article 9 formally requires of Mexican Americans that they give up, relinquish, the "character" of Mexicanness in order to enjoy "all the rights of the citizens of the United States" promised by the treaty. As the first sentence of Article 9 stipulates in the prohibition "shall not preserve the character," Kazanjian suggests, "the first step on the road to becoming a U.S. citizen is a negation, a becoming un-preserved, disposed of, lost, wasted" (207). Becoming a U.S. citizen requires the loss of a Mexican character that is both national and racial. The vernacular of the day, according to the *Oxford English Dictionary*, reinforces this interpretation, defining *character* as a distinctive, visible mark or set of features that represents "the sum of the moral and mental qualities which distinguish an individual or a race as a homogeneous whole; the individuality *impressed by nature* and habit on man or nation" (emphasis added). It is not just a question of semantics, or rather it is precisely semantics that facilitate a rereading of Article 9 and of the quality of its promise. The use of the term *character* in the treaty as interchangeable with citizenship suggests the intertwined nature of racial, moral, and national character in mid-nineteenth-century U.S. governmentality. However, this imbrication of racial, moral, and national character is not inexorable. To the contrary, the racialization of Mexicans encoded in Article 9 suggests that there exists the possibility for Mexicans, at least for some Mexicans, to shed this "sum of . . . moral and mental qualities . . . impressed by nature and habit on man or nation."

Chicano nationalism since the early seventies, however, steadfastly refuses this requirement of negation, of unbecoming, as a condition for the fulfillment of the promise of U.S. citizenship. Instead, through the mythology of Aztlán,[9] Chicanismo reinforces Mexican "character," insisting this character be interpreted as an indigenous heritage accessed through Mexico's unique history of *mestizaje*.[10] Indeed, the broken promise interpretation of the Treaty of Guadalupe-Hidalgo facilitates an analogy between the treatment of Chicanos in the Southwest and the treatment of indigenous peoples in Mexico. Both populations are minoritized and suffer a similar fate of discrimination, exploitation, and violence as a consequence of the failure of racist governments to fulfill their juridical obligations. As one example of the power of this analogy for Chicano nationalism, in late July 1996, Chicano leaders in solidarity with the Ejercito Zapatista de Liberación Nacional (EZLN, Zapatista Army of National Liberation) traveled to the liberated territories in Chiapas to communicate officially with the EZLN leadership. In this special meeting, they identified themselves to the EZLN leadership as *los indios del norte* (the Indians from the North).[11]

Participating in this meeting, I felt troubled by this analogy at the time, and here I would like to trouble the analogy itself by reading another article from the treaty that is almost entirely ignored by Chicano scholarship.[12] The U.S. Senate struck Article 10 from the treaty,[13] so Article 11 directly follows Article 9. It begins:

> Considering that a great part of the territories, which, by the present treaty, are to be comprehended for the future within the limits of the United States, *is now occupied by savage tribes*, who will hereafter be under the exclusive control of the Government of the United States, and whose incursions within the territory of Mexico *would be prejudicial in the extreme*, it is solemnly agreed that all such incursions shall be forcibly restrained by the Government of the United States whensoever this may be necessary; and that when they cannot be prevented, they shall be punished by the said Government, and satisfaction for the same shall be exacted all in the same way, and with equal diligence and energy, as if the same incursions were meditated or committed within its own territory, against its own citizens. (Emphasis added)

The article then lists the various ways in which the U.S. government must protect Mexican citizens and their property from the "savage tribes" that roam the newly annexed territories. Whether these Mexicans find themselves in Northern Mexico or in the southwestern United States, it is incumbent on the U.S. government to protect them from the savage Indians. The article ends by stipulating *"the sacredness of this obligation* shall never be lost sight of by the said Government" (emphasis added). The language of Article 11 varies from the narrowly legal language of negotiated settlement in the rest of the treaty. With its repeated pleas for protection from Indian raids and kidnapping, it is more detailed than the preceding two articles concerning the rights of annexed Mexicans. Clearly inserted at the behest of the Mexican government, Article 11 is vehement in its insistence that the U.S. government exert "equal diligence and energy" in defending both Mexicans and U.S. citizens from savage Indians. Article 11 is, in fact, the only place in the treaty invoking the "sacredness" of the U.S. "obligation" to Mexico.

Indeed, I would suggest that the tone of Article 11 betrays a certain hysteria on the part of the Mexican government with regard to the tribes it considered "prejudicial in the extreme." Here, the Mexican government is primarily alluding to the Apache and Comanche tribes, but also to the Navajo and Shoshone tribes as well. All these Indian tribes had, with considerable success, defended the territory from Hispanicization by Mexican settlers over the previous one hundred years.[14] Defense of the northernmost settlements in what is today Tamalhuipas, Sonora, Coahuila, Nuevo Leon, Arizona, New Mexico, and Texas had cost the recently independent Mexican government a fortune, hence the attempt to shift this economic burden onto the U.S. administration.[15]

The adamant tone of Article II, however, also masks a profound psychic anxiety—an anxiety over delineating the exact nature of the Mexican character alluded to in Article 9. The last sentence commits the U.S. government to act against the "savage tribes" imperiling Mexican safety "as if the same incursions were meditated or committed within its own territory, against its own citizens." The "as if" structure of the sentence requires a parity of treatment for Mexicans before the U.S. government, a parity between Mexican and U.S. citizens that, in fact, exceeds the newly established geographical border between the two nations. Article II, I would suggest, posits an equality between Mexican character and U.S. character. However, this equality—this sameness before the law—is established by policing the "savage tribes" as the actual border between civilized and uncivilized character. Article II anxiously differentiates Mexican character from the savageness of indigenous populations on the one hand, and compares it to the unproblematically civilized character of the victors in the U.S.-Mexican war on the other. At this historical and juridical conjuncture, indigenous subaltern subjectivity flickers at the margins of social recognition in the Southwest. Indigenous subalterns are the horizon, the threatening limit in the distance, against which, or rather within which, annexed Mexicans attain social visibility in the new geopolitical landscape of the Southwest.

Thus, while the broken promise of the Treaty of Guadalupe-Hidalgo is often the basis for analogies made between U.S. Chicanos and Mexican Indians in contemporary scholarship, popular culture, activism, and literature,[16] Article II of the treaty suggests that the Mexican government at the time was particularly anxious about the United States drawing just such analogies between newly annexed Mexicans and "savage tribes."[17] The analogy in contemporary Chicano nationalism and culture, then, occludes this anxious repudiation of the savage Indian character recorded in Article II. By representing Chicanos as *los indios del norte*, the analogy forgets the historical differences between southwestern Indians and Mexicans, differences enshrined by the treaty itself. Mexicans annexed by the United States gained rights through the treaty by being rigorously differentiated from Indians, those "savage tribes," who then became the target of joint Mexican and U.S. extermination efforts. The analogy between Chicanos and Indians thus depends on pushing the indigenous subaltern subject to the margins of social recognition.[18]

The romanticization of indigenous identity in Chicano culture, however, does not emerge whole cloth out of the fanciful imaginings of border subjects selectively reading the Articles 8 and 9 of the Treaty of Guadalupe-Hidalgo.

The annexed Mexicans were given two choices in these articles. They could either retain their Mexican character, eventually relocating to the southern side of the border, or they could relinquish their Mexican character and remain on the northern side of the divide. Article 9 suggests Mexicans relinquish their character in implicit exchange for U.S. character. And yet Article 11 reveals a prescient anxiety among Mexicans that their character might be mistaken as Indian savagery. And indeed, the U.S. government repeatedly read annexed Mexicans as rebellious, barbaric, and incapable of properly holding landed property. Neither black nor white, Spanish nor Indian, the majority of annexed Mexicans lingered in dangerous proximity to Indian difference. Thus annexed Mexicans were pulled into an ambivalent identification with a "savage" Indian difference, ambivalent because they were simultaneously asked to disavow this difference by the treaty's terms for inclusion as U.S. citizens. The treaty, then, constitutes the record of this ambivalent identification taking place as racial formations began transforming the Southwest.

Before proceeding to an analysis of the psychic consequences of this requirement for identification and disavowal through a literary reading of Américo Paredes's *George Washington Gómez*, let us flesh out the record by reconstructing the content of this bodily character. What constituted Mexican "character"— national, racial, moral—in the mid-nineteenth century? More specifically, what was the character of the Mexican colonists of the Southwest? How did Mexico define indigenous identity legally and biologically? What were the standards of civilization under the jurisprudence first of Spain and then Mexico? In other words, how did the nuanced and flexible racialization projects of Spain and subsequently Mexico get rigidly reinscribed by the United States?

¿Quien tiene razón? Racial Formations in the Southwest

Martha Menchaca, in her landmark book *Recovering History, Constructing Race*, provides a window of analysis into nineteenth-century racial formation among the Southwest colonists first under Spanish colonial rule and then during Mexican independence. Spanish colonial rule is notorious for its promotion of *mestizaje* as a form of conquest. Indeed, larger land grants and labor forces were awarded to those *peninsulares* (Spanish-born colonials), particularly military officers and soldiers, who married Indian women. In fact, Spanish men who refused to marry their concubines were penalized by having their *encomiendas* revoked.[19] In addition, the Catholic Church would not baptize children born of unwed couples.[20] Thus, for the first seventy-five years of colonial rule in Mexico, the Spanish administration promoted intermarriage and childbearing as a form of governmentality. It was not until 1575 that Spain changed its position on inter-marriage, prohibiting the upper echelons of the Spanish colonizers from mar-rying Indian women, though there was no such prohibition on midlevel criollo (Mexican-born colonists of presumably "pure" Spanish decent) administrators. Furthermore, the crown continued encouraging military men to intermarry through pecuniary incentives.[21]

Spanish colonial rule was similarly liberal with regard to the intermarry-ing of enslaved blacks. The slave trade to Mexico began in 1527 and continued through the mid-1600s. Though short-lived, it had a dramatic impact on the racial composition of Mexico. By the 1646 census, enslaved blacks exceeded the number of Spaniards in the territory: 130,000 slaves, 125,000 Spaniards (60–61). Unlike the Anglo-American colonizers, however, the Spanish empire did not question the fundamental humanity of the enslaved and thus accorded them more extensive legal rights, including the right of male slaves to choose their marital partners. As mestizos and the indigenous peoples of Mexico were juridically free, and the condition of the child followed that of the mother, an extraordinary incentive existed for exogamy. Indeed, the 1742 census rec-ords more than a quarter of a million free *afromestizos*—the term coined for the children of blacks and Indians or mestizos—in the Mexican territory.

Though the racial *casta* (caste) system under colonial rule was flexible, espe-cially regarding marriage, it was nevertheless hierarchical in the distribution of privileges and power. Thus while the crown made no legal distinction between them, only the *peninsulares* were allowed to hold high-level public office in the colonial and church administrations, while criollos held midlevel administra-tive positions in government, or high offices in the military and colleges (63). Though mestizos were permitted to enter craft guilds, their mobility in the guilds remained limited. Consequently, the majority, like *afromestizos*, were forced to enter the military or wagework (154–56).[22] Indigenous populations provided labor services for *conquistadores* (colonizers), but Spanish colonial rule primarily organized them into separate Indian townships and granted large tracts of communal lands under the auspices of the Catholic Church.[23] Given this hierarchical structure, the majority of colonists to the current U.S. South-west during the early eighteenth century were criollos, mestizos, and *afromes-tizos* from the middle echelons of the *casta* system who hoped to fare better on Mexico's northern frontier. According to Menchaca: "The irony of this seem-ingly liberating event was that the colonists of color were able to find a place where the quality of their lives indeed improved, at the cost of entrenching the same colonial order that oppressed them."[24] However, Menchaca's own re-search demonstrates that the colonial order on the frontier was not quite "the same" as in the interior.

The U.S. Southwest was not only racially diverse under Spanish colonialism; racial formations were also very much in flux, as census records of nonmission settlements in Texas from 1780 and 1796 confirm. Once again, from Menchaca's *Recovering History, Constructing Race*:

> The majority of settlers were classified as Spaniards and *afromestizos*, while Indians and *mestizos* constituted the smallest percentages. For example, in San Antonio (excluding mission communities) 61 percent of the residents in 1780 were registered as Spaniards (*N* [number] = 885), 25 percent as *afromestizos* (*mulattos, lobos*, or *coyotes*) (*N* = 361), 6 percent as Indians (*N* = 85), and 3.5 percent as *mestizos* (*N* = 51).[25] Furthermore, though the largest number of residents were registered as Spaniards, the majority of the heads of household were *afromestizos*. About eighty-six of the families reported that the male head of household was *afromestizo*. That same year in La Bahía the census reported a similar demographic composition. In the nonmission settlements 63 percent (*N* = 340) reported that they were Spaniards, 34 percent *afromestizos* . . . (*N* = 183), and 4 percent *mestizo* (*N* = 21). Furthermore, the census identified 52 percent of the heads of households as *afromestizos*. A similar pattern emerged in Laredo. The 1789 census reported that 45 percent were Spanish (*N* = 321), 22 percent *afromestizo* (*N* = 155), 17 percent *mestizo* (*N* = 121), and 16 percent Indian (*N* = 111). In 1793 in Nacogdoches 24 percent were Spaniards (*N* = 109), 28 percent *afromestizo* . . . (*N* = 130), 2 percent Black (*N* = 10), 26 percent *mestizo* (*N* = 117), and 6 percent Indian (*N* = 29).[26]

Menchaca does not speculate on the meaning of either the low percentages of *mestizos* or the preponderance of *afromestizos* as heads of households in San Antonio and La Bahía, where the majority of residents were registered as Spaniards. I would suggest that the census figures reflect the instability of racial categories in the Southwest over the hundred-year period of its initial colonization. Since the first wave of northern colonization began in the late 1600s, it is entirely possible that the small percentage of mestizo colonizers registered by the late 1700s indicates successful efforts by mestizos to have themselves reclassified as criollos, and therefore Spanish. Similarly, census-takers may also have classified the children of *afromestizo* men and criollo or mestiza women according to the racial condition of their lighter-skinned mothers. Historically, under Spanish legal codes, it was possible for nonwhites to have their status changed to criollo as a reward for brave deeds on behalf of the crown, and certainly influential *peninsulares* and criollos changed the classification of their mestizo offspring as they saw fit. Furthermore, in the northern colonies, *afromestizos* and mestizos could change their classification to criollo if they were skilled craftsman desperately needed on the frontier. Indeed, census records from all over the northern frontier, but especially Texas and Arizona, confirm that many mestizo and *afromestizo* colonists changed their status from one census to the next.[27]

My point here is not to suggest that Mexico's northern frontier was a multiracial paradise, on the verge of becoming a race-blind society, under Spanish colonial rule. Rather, I want to suggest that even as *peninsulares* and *indios* appeared to exist as steadfast categories on either end of a rigid *casta* hierarchy, racial boundaries were in fact relatively porous within the system, especially on the northern frontier. One boundary, however, was not porous, indeed it remained necessarily impenetrable. All of the subject categories within the *casta* system, from the highest peninsular priest to the most recently encountered, "pacified" Indian, were granted a certain humanity and were accordingly ascribed differential political, economic, and civil rights. Though differentially racialized, all were subject to the nuanced governmentality of a Spanish empire that recognized their civility. The absolute limit of this recognition, indeed establishing the very terms of identity among the different racial bodies within the *casta* system, were the "savage" Indian tribes that refused to recognize this governmentality. Hence there were literally hundreds of Indian tribes in the northern states of Sonora, Cahuila, Arizona, Texas, New Mexico, and California—living either within Spanish missions or outside of them—that recognized the governmentality of Spain and that were, in turn, recognized by the crown as possessing an assimilable moral and racial character; they were *of* the empire; they were considered *gente de razón* (people of reason).

By the time of Mexican independence in 1821, the census had, in fact, stopped using racial categories altogether and simply divided those under colonial rule into two groups, each increasingly deracinated. The dominant category was the *gente de razón*, which included *peninsulares*, criollos, *afromestizos*, mestizos, and all detribalized Indians who recognized solely the sovereignty of Spain. The subordinate category was that of *indio*, including all Christianized (or at least pacified) Indians who recognized Spanish sovereignty but maintained their own separate governing systems in their townships and tribes. The new categories for enumerating subjects suggest a deracination not because race suddenly did not matter but because racial character became subordinate to the characteristic of possessing reason. All racialized bodies, except those of the *indio*, possessed the character of reason "because they practiced Spanish-Mexican traditions, they were Catholics, and they recognized only the sovereignty of the government of Spain."[28] However, I would further suggest that the category of *indio* also became deracinated by the new terms of the census precisely because racial character was subordinated to the characteristic of possessing reason. At any point, pacified *indios* could become *gente de razón* by adopting the three characteristics enumerated above: by forgoing their aboriginal culture, language, and sovereignty in favor of Spanish-Mexican culture, language, and sovereignty. Thus racial character becomes less a question of biology than a question of culture. Put differently, what determines Spanish-Mexican character is a series of identifiable politico-cultural traits, rather than simply racial ones. Clearly, the privileged politico-cultural traits remain those of the white Europeans, but other racial bodies are capable of fully assimilating this politico-cultural character. And always, beyond the limits of this sign system stand the "savage" Indians, incapable of assimilating this politico-cultural character of reason.

The newly independent government of Mexico formalized and extended this assimilationist racial philosophy. Mexico's first constitution, promulgated in 1824, recognized whites, *afromestizos*, mestizos, and all pacified Indians as equal citizens with equal rights to land, public office, and education.[29] Furthermore, the Mexican government prohibited distinguishing between Indians and non-Indians in all government, church, and census documents.[30] The Mexican government was committed to the liberal tenets of equality and private property, and it regarded the crown's racial policy toward Indians as paternalistic and exploitative. Thus its new policies made the secularization and complete acculturation of all pacified Indians compulsory. As Menchaca points out, "the difference between the new republic's proclamation[s] and Spain's previous legislation was that the new racial policy was to be enforced with deliberate speed. This meant that Indians were to be assimilated and incorporated as practicing citizens, even if they refused."[31] The Mexican government's chief weapons in its assimilationist arsenal were the disentailment of all corporate property, including the church lands held communally by tribal Indians. Volumes have been written on the negative impact of nineteenth-century liberal reforms on the indigenous populations of Mexico.[32] My concern here is to flesh out the meaning of the Treaty of Guadalupe-Hidalgo's category of Mexican "character." From the historical perspective I have sketched, I suggest that the racial content of this character, particularly with regard to pacified Indians, was considered highly mutable. As with the Spanish colonial administration, races recognizing the sovereignty of the Mexican government and adopting its politico-cultural traits were designated as *gente de razón* and considered to be of Mexican national character. Again, it was the savage Indian who existed as the horizon of humanity, as the border to be policed.

Thus, in 1848, when Article II of the treaty was executed, Mexican national, and indeed moral, character encompassed Indian racial character. Simply put, racial character did not exclude an individual from national citizenship. Citizenship was instead based on the possession of reason, with reason defined as the acceptance of Mexican sovereignty and politico-cultural traits. Peaceful

Indians were full citizens precisely because they were seen as capable of reason, as capable of full acculturation into the *gente de razón* of Mexico—whether or not they wanted this acculturation. Thus whereas the Mexican government drew a discrete and definitive line between assimilated or pacified Indians within the nation and resistive Indians who threatened national character by refusing to subject themselves to Mexican sovereignty, the U.S. government drew no such fine distinctions.

To the U.S. Congress, it made little or no difference if Indians were Christianized or pacified; all Indians were deemed unassimilable to U.S. national character and so retroactively rendered noncitizens of Mexico. Within one year of the treaty's execution, "Congress racialized the Indians of the Southwest and determined they were distinct from Mexicans."[33] Agents of the Bureau of Indian Affairs, in consultation with ethnologists, visited Mexican communities to determine which were Indian. Any communities retaining forms of tribal council, permissible under Spanish and Mexican law, were immediately classified as such and subjected to the Northwest Ordinance of 1787—which determined that "Indians did not own the land they inhabited"—as well as to the Indian Intercourse Acts of 1802 and 1834—which established the reservation system (234). *Afromestizos* fared no better; the U.S. Congress refused to acknowledge that *afromestizos* had been full citizens of Mexico. In 1850, New Mexican legislators passed the Organic Act of 1850, which extended citizenship to all annexed Mexicans, regardless of race. The U.S. Congress superseded the New Mexican legislature, however, and its reasons for doing so bear examination. According to Menchaca,

> Under the Organic Act of 1850, citizenship was extended to all former citizens of Mexico. That year, however, U.S. Congress refused to recognize that Mexico had "ever" extended rights to Blacks. The U.S. Congress also ruled that Blacks could not become citizens anyway since Hispanos had to pledge allegiance to the new government to become citizens and under the new system of law Blacks did not have this privilege. Thus, since Blacks were not allowed to take the citizenship oath, the Organic Act could not apply to them. (225)

Once again the issue of character becomes central to this judicial logic of U.S. racial policy. Allegiance to the United States required giving up one's Mexican character in exchange for U.S. character. The Catch-22, however, was that U.S. character precluded the assimilation of a reified notion of blackness—blacks were incapable of allegiance to the nation—just as it precluded the assimilation of a reified notion Indianness. Thus lost in the loss of Mexican character under the terms of the treaty is its nuanced, multiracial nature, exchanged for the immutable categories of U.S. racism.

Furthermore, the U.S. Congress abrogated ultimate responsibility in determining the citizenship and rights of annexed Mexicans to the legislatures of the new states and territories. This worked to the great disadvantage of detribalized Indians, *afromestizos*, and mestizos. None of the legislatures of the other new states and territories were as progressive as New Mexico's legislature initially was. To the contrary, California, Texas, and Arizona extended full political rights, including the right to vote and own property, solely to white Mexican males. The pertinent question thus became, who was white enough to be declared a white Mexican? It was up to local and state government agents to determine if the degree of Indian or black racial "character" among annexed Mexicans was significant or not and thus to decide which annexed Mexicans should be enfranchised or disenfranchised accordingly. In the balance hung the right to retain property and civil rights, or in the case of *afromestizos* in the slave state of Texas, their very freedom. In all the annexed territories and states, but especially in California and Texas, descendants of the original Southwest colonizers repeatedly went to court to challenge their classification as nonwhites. Plaintiffs were forced to trace bloodlines back generations, arguing that the presence of black or Indian blood was so infinitesimal as to not merit their classification as nonwhite. Thus Mexicans of mixed racial heritage suddenly found themselves in a position of having to disassociate themselves from themselves, from their Indian and black racial heritage. The anxiety recorded in Article II over the possibility that annexed Mexicans would be identified with savagery proved well founded. Well into the twentieth century, mestizos, *afromestizos*, and detribalized Indians were simultaneously identified with the abject racial character of Indians and forced to disavow any such identification if they hoped to attain any rights. And indeed, in several cases throughout Texas, Arizona, and California, Mexican American plaintiffs filed suits against school districts, arguing that Mexican children should not be subject to school segregation because they were white, not Indian: *Independent School District v. Salvatierra* (1930, Texas); *Roberto Alvarez v. Lemon Grove School District* (1931, California); *Mendez v. Westminster* (1946, 1947, California); *Delgado v. Bastrop* (1948, Texas); and *Gonzales v. Sheely* (1954, Arizona).

What's in a Name?

In order to analyze further the psychic consequences of this structure of identification and disavowal, it is necessary to move between the historical register and the literary one. Américo Paredes wrote most of *George Washington Gómez* (*GWG*) between 1936 and 1940.[34] Paredes has emerged as a key figure in the development of Chicano studies. He was a renowned folklorist of southwest Texas, and he published a number of scholarly works in which he collected and translated ballads and stories from the Mexican American population living along the border. He is one of the earliest scholars of Mexican American culture and one of the first Chicano professors at the University of Texas at Austin to receive tenure in the Departments of English and Anthropology. His books are mainstays of Chicano studies courses. A native of Texas himself, Paredes wrote GWG while living in his hometown of Brownsville, in the heart of the segregated Rio Grande valley. Thus he would have been personally acquainted with this requirement for identification and disavowal that had become an integral part of racial formation among Mexican Americans in the Southwest. Indeed, the novel documents the life of a man fatefully named George Washington Gómez who comes from the Rio Grande valley and who is trapped in just such a psychic structure of identification with and disavowal of Indian difference. Or rather, the novel traces his psychic development within the constraints of this racial structure of subject formation from the moment of his birth to the moment of his return to the valley as a U.S. army spy during World War II.

Part I of the novel takes as its historical backdrop the 1915–17 revolt in which a coalition of Mexican and Mexican American insurgents attempted to overthrow the U.S. government and establish an independent republic.[35] The insurgents, led by Aniceto Pizaña and Luis de la Rosa, launched hundreds of attacks against Anglo farms and businesses. The motto on the seditionists' flag read "igualdad e independencia" (equality and independence), and their army was called the Liberating Army for Races and Peoples.[36] The novel begins with four Texas Rangers patrolling the *llano* (the plain) in search of a fictional character named Anacleto de la Peña, an amalgamation of the two insurrection leaders. De la Peña and his men, like Pizaña and de la Rosa, are waging war against Texas in an attempt to establish the "Republic of the Southwest."

As Ramón Saldívar explains in an essay entitled "The Borderlands of Culture: Américo Paredes's *George Washington Gómez*": "[The novel] takes especially as its moment the 1915 uprising in South Texas by Mexican Americans attempting to create a Spanish-speaking republic of the Southwest. Dismissed as 'Mexican Bandits' by Anglo historians, the *sediciosos* (seditionists) . . . were acting under a carefully considered revolutionary manifesto, the 'Plan de San Diego,' that called for the union of Texas Mexicans with the American Indians, African Americans and Asian Americans to create an independent border republic of the Southwest."[37] This fictionalized representation of the seditionist movement, however, provides not only a historical backdrop for the action of the novel but a psychological backdrop for the protagonist's subjective development. In its citation of this particular historical moment, the text posits as a political horizon a utopian structure of identification in which national, racial, and moral character remain unalienated from each other for the multiracial subjects of the Southwest. Indeed, the seditionists' call for "equality" and for the liberating of "races" indicate that central to their cause was a desire to reinterpret the meaning of racial character in the face of maligning Anglo misinterpretation and discrimination. However, as this revolt fails, the utopian ideal of unalienated identification, of unalienated character, remains just that, an ideal that recedes into nostalgia even before the protagonist is born.

The novel opens, then, with four rangers having just encountered a seditionist named Lupe García. They dismiss him as nothing more than a savage bandit incapable of expressing national allegiance to any republic, even the Republic of the Southwest. In addition, the third-person narrative voice informs us, the rangers let him pass because they feared the deadly aim of García's rifle. Thus the character of this dark-skinned Mexican emerges as at once abject and highly threatening, due to his association with Indian savagery. With the dismissal of García by the rangers, the policing of seditious acts is displaced within the text onto the adjudication of character. In the very next scene, the rangers find themselves called on to decipher the ambiguous character of the light-skinned Gumersindo Gómez, George Washington Gómez's expectant father. The rangers encounter Gumersindo with an Anglo doctor. The two are rushing to deliver the novel's protagonist, Gumersindo's son:

> The two sour-faced Rangers were staring at the red-haired man [Gumersindo], as though trying to place him. The man fidgeted in his seat and avoided their eyes. Finally one of the Rangers spoke, "What's your name, feller?"
>
> "He doesn't speak much English," Doc Berry said.
>
> "Mexican, eh?" said MacDougal. "For a minute there I thought he was a white man." He looked steadily at the man, who began to show signs of nervousness.
>
> "He's a good Mexican," Doc said. "I can vouch for him."
>
> "He's okay if you say so Doc," MacDougal answered. "But it's getting kinda hard these days to tell the good ones from the bad ones. Can't take any chances these days. But he's all right if you say so."[38]

Gumersindo's racial formation is indecipherable to the rangers because he is light-skinned; or rather, it is ambiguous, and thereby dangerously deceiving. It is clear to the rangers that he is not a black man, and yet it is not at all clear that he is a white man—a certainty that would immediately clarify any ambiguity over his character. Thus the Rangers must move to a register other than race, and they ask him his name. Once Doc Berry clarifies that the passenger, though redheaded, is in fact a Mexican, the question of Gumersindo's character comes sharply into focus. Doc Berry immediately vouches for him: "He's a good Mexican." The ambiguity of the annexed Mexican's racial formation is immediately shifted onto the ambiguity of his Mexican moral character. The ambiguity over the nature of Mexican character is never fully resolved, never fully assimilated into "good" character, however, as the rangers' response of "if you say so Doc" is hardly a resounding acceptance of Doc Berry's appraisal. Instead, it continues to be hard to "tell the good ones from the bad ones." And indeed, in response to the short-lived revolt of 1915–17, the Texas Rangers indiscriminately killed hundreds of Mexican Americans.[39] In addition, according to sociologist David Montejano, a historian of Texas, Anglo residents of south Texas "formed vigilante committees, which administered 'summary justice' to Mexican subjects."[40]

In the very next scene, the Gómez family decides on the name of the couple's first son. As Saldívar suggests, the naming scene is "an exemplary instance of Althusserian interpellation, the process whereby an 'individual' is 'appointed as a subject in and by the specific familial [and political] ideological configuration in which it is "expected" once it has been conceived.'"[41] However, let us examine more closely the familial and political configurations available to the boy as subject and then consider the psychic consequences of the newborn's "appointment" in the social. The boy's grandmother initiates the naming process by insisting that he needs to be baptized in the Catholic Church. Meanwhile, María, the baby's mother, has been feeding him:

> The baby . . . was feeding greedily at his mother's breast. Born a foreigner in his native land, he was fated to a life controlled by others. At that very moment his life was being shaped, people were already running his affairs, but he did not know it. Nobody considered whether he might like being baptized or not. Nobody had asked him whether he, a Mexican, had wanted to be born in Texas, or whether he had wanted to be born at all. The baby left the breast and María . . . [asked] "And what shall we name him?"[42]

The child is oblivious to the terms of his own subjection as a "foreigner in his native land," as a subject of indeterminate character. Indeed, the indeterminacy of his character is reflected in the various hailings that ensue. Gumersindo first responds to Maria's question by crying out "Crisósforo!" But Feliciano, Maria's brother and a member of the seditionist uprising, belittles his brother-in-law's aristocratic pretensions: "Sounds like *fósforo* to me. . . . Who wants to be named after a safety match?" The grandmother then attempts to hail the boy into Catholic subjection by suggesting the name José Ángel, but Feliciano again interrupts this narrative interpellation, commenting that the weight of the name "would ruin him for life!"[43]

Feliciano instead tries twice to hail the boy into the subjection of Mexican revolutionary nationalism. He first suggests the name "Venustiano," after Ve-

nustiano Carranza, the iconic, though corrupt, leader of the 1910 Mexican revolution. Feliciano's very interest in the Mexican revolution makes evident his
inability to relinquish the character of Mexican citizenship, as required by the
Treaty of Guadalupe-Hidalgo's Article 9. Instead, he cannot but be interested
in the politics of a revolution transpiring right across the border from his home.
Indeed, the porous nature of the Rio Grande border is precisely what preserves
this character, as many exiled revolutionary leaders, including Ricardo Flores
Magón, were headquartered in the Mexican American towns along the border.[44]
Feliciano then suggests "Cleto," after the fictionalized local seditionist hero Anacleto de la Peña. The difficulty in adjudicating the division between Mexican and
American is made evident in Feliciano's rapid choice of names for the boy. Feliciano clearly sees the southwestern seditionist leader and the Mexican revolutionary leader as on par. And yet the seditionist goal of establishing an independent,
multiracial Republic of the Southwest was not encompassed by the goals of the
Mexican revolution. Nevertheless, for Feliciano, Mexican character inheres in
the seditionist movement, hence his easy slide from one name to another. From
the racist perspective of the Anglos in south Texas, the Mexican character of the
seditionist movement was equally self-evident. As Montejano suggests,

> Most Texans saw these disturbances as pure and simple Mexican ban-
> ditry whose origins lay in revolutionary Mexico. The very discovery of
> [the "Plan de San Diego"] was seen as evidence of "foreign" influence.
> Some claimed that Mexican revolutionary leaders—either Victoriano
> Huerta or Venustiano Carranza—had authored the plan to pressure
> Woodrow Wilson into recognizing their claims to the Mexican presi-
> dency. . . . To a large extent, these explanations about outside influence
> were based on the common belief among Texans that "their Mexicans"
> would never organize such an uprising.[45]

It is precisely the fact that the character of "their Mexicans" always lingers
in dangerous proximity to Mexican character which makes possible the interpretation of "foreign influence" for Anglo-Texans. In other words, although
the treaty demands that annexed Mexicans "shall not preserve the character
of citizens of the Mexican Republic," it is nevertheless impossible for them to
shed this character, as it is biologically tied to their mixed racial character in
the eyes of Anglo governmentality.

In response to Feliciano's suggestions for names, "Gumersindo smiled absently and shook his head."[46] The phrasing of this response is particularly compelling. It suggests that by "smiling absently," Gumersindo absents himself from
the revolutionary nationalism so powerful in defining Mexican character during the period represented in the novel. Furthermore, with an almost reflexive

shaking of his head, Gumersindo rejects this interpellation for his child as well. When Feliciano insists the boy would "do fine if he's half as good as Anacleto," the text continues, "'It isn't that,' answered Gumersindo in a soft voice. 'It isn't that'" (15). The response suggests that Gumersindo may find the national character represented by the names Venustiano and Anacleto to be neither reprehensible nor ignoble. Rather, the "it isn't that" suggests that Gumersindo, unlike his seditionist brother-in-law, recognizes the deadly consequences of retaining Mexican character for his son, and the "soft voice" registers his quiet acceptance of its necessary loss. Indeed, Gumersindo is later killed by Texas Rangers for being the brother-in-law of the seditionist Lupe García. However, the psychic consequences of *not* identifying with a revolutionary character are equally deadly: in order to assume U.S. character, one is required to disavow, to kill, that which savagely resists one's own racial subjection as abjection. It is a double death, as killing the resistance simultaneously kills any possibility for an integral self for the racialized subject of the Southwest.

The grandmother continues the naming scene by insisting that the child should be named after his father because "that's the way you tell families apart. When he grows up people will say, 'Oh, you're Gumersindo Gómez, the son of Gumersindo Gómez and María García, and old Gumersindo Gómez, he was your grandfather.' That's the way to keep track of people and no need to put it down in writing" (15). The grandmother attempts to interpellate the boy-child into the primary site of subject formation in the Southwest, the patriarchal tradition that grants social recognition to Mexican males without any "need to put it down in writing." Importantly, this patriarchal semiotics recognizes the child's mother as well, even though María García is folded into the generations of Gumersindos. But again, Gumersindo rejects this primary interpellative scene, with its folkloric, oral nuances, in another attempt to differentiate his child from inherited Mexican character: "I said I didn't want him to have my name" (15).

Once the three cultural cornerstones of "Mexican character" have been rejected—Catholic tradition, revolutionary nationalism, and folkloric patriarchy—as appropriate ideological scenes for the child's appointment as a subject, María offers her opinion: "I would like him to have a great man's name. Because he is going to grow up to be a great man who will help his people." Just as quickly as María's last name gets folded into the generations of Gumersindos in patriarchal interpellation, Maria's words get folded into Gumersindo's narrative for his son's interpellation into U.S. character. Though she has made no mention of Anglos, Gumersindo responds, "My son. . . . He's going to be a great man among the Gringos. A Gringo name he shall have! Is he not as fair as any of them? Feliciano, what great men have the Gringos had?" (16). Gumersindo completely misinterprets María's words. He not only confuses the "a great man who will help his people" for "a great man among the Gringos" but further misinterprets her words by equating the moral characteristic of greatness with the physical characteristic of having fair skin, "Is he not as fair as any of them?" Having previously rejected the names of great Mexican men, Gumersindo's words establish greatness and fair skin as the purview of U.S. character with the questions he directs toward Feliciano.

Feliciano tries to disrupt this assimilative appointment to subjection for his nephew by disrupting the racialized equation between U.S. character and greatness. He answers Gumersindo, "They are all great. . . . Great thieves, great liars, great sons-of-bitches." Gumersindo ignores his brother-in-law, however, and continues, "I was thinking of the great North American, he who was a general and fought the soldiers of the king." Once again the grandmother tries to intervene and return the boy's destiny to a Mexican narrative of interpellation, "That was Hidalgo, but he was a Mexican." Gumersindo will not be deterred, however, in his quest for his son's assimilation of U.S. character. "'I remember,' said Gumersindo, 'Wachinton. Jorge Wachinton. . . . Once he crossed a river while it was freezing. He drove out the English and freed the slaves'" (16). Gumersindo insists on the boy's assimilation into a racialized U.S. character with his desire to interpellate his light-skinned son into a legacy of liberty (driving out the English) and of equality (emancipating the slaves). And yet Gumersindo exemplifies the difficulty, if not impossibility, of such an as-similative appointment as subject for Mexicans. Gumersindo himself disrupts the successful interpellation of the boy by confusing the slave owner with the emancipator of the slaves, and naming him after the former. And indeed, the failure of assimilation is underscored in the next chapter in which Gumersindo is killed by the four marauding *rinches*. Although the four Texas rangers had already met him—and Doc Berry had already vouched for his character—the rangers nevertheless "mistake" Gumersindo for a seditionist, reinforcing the ambiguous racial character of the Mexican in the Southwest.

The final result of the naming scene recognizes the structure of identification and disavowal that positions the boy's racial character in dangerous proximity to Indian difference. George Washington Gómez's grandmother defiantly mispronounces the phonetically hispanicized name "Wachinton" as "Guálinto," regardless of Feliciano's repeated attempts to correct her. The nickname Guálinto sticks with the protagonist through four-fifths of his narrative life. It thoroughly displaces his proper name. Although Gumersindo tries to disavow the identification with Indian difference by naming his boy after Anglo "greatness," it is the Indian identification that sticks. Thus when Feliciano enrolls the boy in primary school and the teacher asks his name, Feliciano reflexively answers "Guálinto Gómez." Miss Cornelia, the teacher, comments

"'Strange name isn't it? Is it an Indian name?' 'Yes,' said Feliciano, 'It's an Indian name.' He looked at Guálinto and then he looked away" (110). It is significant that Miss Cornelia misreads Guálinto's ambiguous racial character as Indian. After all, it is her job as a member of the educational state apparatus to properly interpellate the child into *U.S.* character. Instead, she misreads his racial character as Indian, as inassimilable. As another example of an annexed Mexican in the text who strives toward assimilation into U.S. character, Miss Cornelia sees herself in competition with Guálinto for enfranchisement. Understanding that many are called to U.S. character, but few may enter, Miss Cornelia takes it on herself to miseducate the annexed Mexican children in her charge, or rather to properly educate them on their distance from acceptable, civilized character. Neither of Mexican character nor of U.S. character, Guálinto is consigned to the margins of social recognition as an approximate Indian.

However, why does Feliciano agree with Miss Cornelia's reading of the name of his beloved nephew? It is certainly not because he wants to consign Guálinto to the margins of social recognition. Rather, I would argue that this is Feliciano's taciturn bid at prescribing a livable psychic life for his nephew, thus he looks at him and then looks away. Feliciano knows that the psychic life appointed to Guálinto by his proper name—U.S. first names, Mexican last name—is simply an unlivable subject position. Indeed, Guálinto is tormented from the beginning of the novel until its end by the consequences of his proper name. Feliciano hopes that the (mis)identification of Guálinto with Indian difference might offer his nephew a viable alternative, a psychic life lived in "savage" resistance to the interpellative call for the disavowal of Mexican character. For Guálinto to relinquish his Mexican character so that he may fully embrace his U.S. character is for him to become undone psychically. Thus Guálinto foreshadows his own psychic unraveling by literalizing the violent process of "unbecoming" Mexican. On a drunken evening at the end of his senior year in high school, Guálinto shoots and kills his uncle, the seditionist Lupe García. It is important that Guálinto does not know it was his uncle that he killed, or that Lupe García was a seditionist, for he is metaphorically killing a Mexican heritage he never fully comprehended. Indeed, the structure of identification and disavowal makes it impossible to comprehend his Mexican heritage. In order to enjoy "all the rights of the citizens of the United States," the boy must not only relinquish his rich Mexican heritage but denounce it at great psychic cost. This killing metonymically stands in as a rite of passage for Guálinto's own deadly assimilation into U.S. character. It is immediately after this event that Guálinto leaves the Texas valley for college, after which he enlists in the army.

When the novel continues in part 5, Guálinto has returned to the valley as a counterintelligence spy. He is posing as a Washington lawyer working for an unnamed real estate company interested in buying land in Texas, though he has actually been sent by the government to spy on his Mexican American cohort of former friends. The government believes that these friends may be involved in seditious activity and treason. Instead, they have organized a multiracial political party to challenge the racist and classist Democratic machine in the next election. His friends hope that Guálinto has returned to be their leader. However, Guálinto has no interest in joining the party they have formed. Indeed, Guálinto no longer exists, as the protagonist has changed his name to George G. Gómez in a literalization of his assimilative efforts.

Not only does our adult protagonist shed his childhood nickname in part 5, but by the time George returns to the Rio Grande valley as a lawyer/spy, he has legally dropped "Washington" from his name as well. Although one may be tempted to read this second name change as a clandestine disavowal of his apparent patriotic allegiance to the United States, such a reading would be mistaken. In a literary flashback, the reader is informed that George decides to change his name legally only after meeting his future father-in-law. While George greets Ellen's father with a polite "very pleased to meet you," his fiancé's father replies with racist alacrity, "George Washington Go-maize. . . . They sure screwed you up, didn't they, boy? . . . You look white but you're a goddam Meskin. And what does your mother do but give you a nigger name. George Washington Go-*maize*" (284, my emphasis). The narrator informs us, "It was then that he decided to legally change his name to George G. Gómez, the middle G for García, his mother's maiden name" (284). Ellen's father insists on doubly racializing this white-*looking* imposter. First, the father stresses George's dangerous proximity to Indian character by stressing his mispronunciation of the second syllable of George's last name as "maize." However, it is his name's association with blackness that appears to be the most damning for George. Ellen's father refuses to acknowledge the name's association with the first U.S. president, except by proxy, calling it a "nigger name" because of its historic use by blacks. This prompts George to drop "Washington" in a desperate bid to disassociate himself further from racial taint and its implications. In other words, although George *looks* white, his future father-in-law reminds George of the impossibility of his assimilating white character, insisting instead on George's denigrated, miscegenated, Mexican "character." Indeed, the phonetic pronunciation of the word "Meskin" implies that his skin is as "messed up" as his naming. Although the narrator indicates that George chooses the "G" as a tribute to his mother, I suggest that the G stands for Guálinto, as it is the resistant Indian character of his youth who haunts the adult George, not the patriot of the Potomac.

The expense of disavowing his Mexican character, however, is such that Guálinto's bid for assimilative subjection must be undone every evening.

George G. Gómez is haunted in his dream life by Guálinto, by the Indian differ-ence in Mexican character that he cannot fully relinquish without relinqushing subjection itself. Thus every night he re-enacts a childhood fantasy of Guálin-to's by dreaming he is a participant in the battle for Houston on the Mexican side of the Mexican–U.S. war, only this time the Mexican army, reinforced by Texas rancheros, wins the war and "Texas and the Southwest remain forever Mexican":

> He woke with a start, stared at the unfamiliar ceiling of the bedroom and cursed softly to himself. Again, the same mother-loving dream. The third time this past week. Goddam ridiculous, having daydreams of his boyhood come back to him in his sleep. . . .
>
> He would imagine he was living in his great-grandfather's time, when the Americans first began to encroach on the northern provinces of the New Republic of Mexico. Reacting against the central government's inef-ficiency and corruption, he would organize *rancheros* into a fighting militia and train them by using them to exterminate the Comanches. Then, with the aid of generals like Urrea, he would extend his influence to the Mexi-can army. He would discover the revolver before Samuel Colt, as well as the hand grenade and a modern style of portable mortar. In his daydreams he built a modern arms factory at Laredo, doing it all in great detail, until he had an enormous, well trained army that included Irishmen and es-caped American Negro slaves. Finally, he would defeat not only the army of the United States but its navy as well. He would reconquer all the terri-tory west of the Mississippi River and recover Florida as well.
>
> At that point he would end up with a feeling of emptiness, of futility. Somehow, he was not comfortable with the way things ended. There was something missing that made any kind of ending fail to satisfy. (281–82)

The protagonist's primary identification with Indian difference is initially foisted on him by the very terms of Article II of the Treaty of Guadalupe-Hidalgo. The Indian name "Guálinto," however, comes to stand in for an unconscious strategy of resistance to the racism encountered by a little boy growing up decades later in the segregated Southwest. Guálinto must necessarily be retained in this unconscious return to his boyhood dream life for his subjec-tivity to hold together, even if publicly Gómez must renounce the identifica-tion in the hopes of enjoying all the rights of U.S. citizenship. Importantly, his daydreams of reestablishing the Mexican character of the Southwest are his-torically accurate, for in them he practices winning the war against the United States by exterminating the Comanche. Thus Guálinto Gómez's utopic dream life still maintains the Spanish-Mexican distinction between a multiracial *gente de razón*, capable of including "Irishmen" and "American Negro slaves," and the savage Indians who hover on the other side of the border of Mexican national character. Indians like himself, however, are not only part of Mexican national character but redeem it from "the central government's inefficiency and corruption." There are no such fine distinctions made by the U.S. government, though, between "good" Indians and "bad." And so every day, George G. Gómez, assimilated and light-skinned, wakes from his dream identity to live a life of quiet desperation as a first lieutenant of counterintelligence who must disavow his seditious and savage "Indian" friends in order to save himself.

Concluding Remarks

The character of George G./Guálinto Gómez embodies, in literary form, the psychic split enacted by the Treaty of Guadalupe-Hidalgo in the racial construction of Chicanos. From the Mexican colonists' perspective in the Southwest, the treaty granted all *gente de razón* the right of full enfranchisement into U.S. national citizenship. Though excluding the "savage," the term encompassed *afromestizos* and Indians. However, from the perspective of a conquering U.S. imperial power, the treaty prescribed the whitening of the Mexican population. Enfranchisement required disavowal of a rich, racial logic of inclusion. It required the abandonment of the very terms of sovereign Mexican character, its mestizo and Indian heritage. The legacy of this interpretation of the treaty can be found not only on the Indian reservations that riddle the U.S. Southwest but in the insistence of use of the term *Hispanic* in describing people of Latin American descent, for the very etymology of the term—of Spain—whitens its subject. However, the terms of this enfranchisement are not only about loss but also about an accretion of power to those who accept these terms, for the treaty requires the enfranchisement of whitened annexed Mexicans into a logic of domination of racial others. Thus, in the loss of Mexican character, what is gained is the privilege of conquest. Hence, George G. Gómez returns to the Rio Grande valley as an agent of neocolonial power, to spy on his former friends.

Paredes's novel richly documents the psychic effect of this legacy for Chicano subjection. When Chicanos embrace an Indian past categorically denied them by the U.S. interpretation of the treaty, they embrace an Indian identity that remains at the margins of social recognition. But not only at the margins of normative, racist social recognition of imperial America but at the margins of Mexican American social recognition as well. For to recognize this savage Indian in oneself was, for generations of Mexican Americans, to willfully embrace one's own disenfranchisement, as George G. Gómez attests. Thus his family denies him knowledge of the violation of his family's civil and human rights.

Though they nickname the child "Guálinto," they refuse him knowledge of his father's violent death at the hands of Texas Rangers and of the family's seditious ties to a resistance movement in the hope that he may possibly grow up to be a "great man among the Gringos."

Furthermore, in the embrace of Indian identity by Chicano nationalism, the treaty's history of stark racial division between colonized mestizos and Indians becomes disavowed. To reclaim Indian heritage without a recognition of the differences 150 years of U.S. racialization has wrought among southwestern indigenous peoples confined to reservations, African Americans, and southwestern mestizos, is to reclaim an innocent history that is not so innocent after all. Hence the psychic split registered by George G. Gómez reflects the difficult and ambivalent place of Indian identity in Chicano subject formation. Chicanos continue to struggle with the place of an Indian identification foisted on a population by a racist state's interpretation of the treaty, and yet one also denied them, as knowledge of full import of the Indian contribution to mestizo history is methodically erased from the register of social recognition.

NOTES

This essay originally appeared *Radical History Review* 89 (2004): 135–64.

1   José Martí, "Our America," in *Tres documentos de nuestra América (Three Documents of Our America)*, ed. Roberto Romaní Velazco (Havana, Cuba: Casa de las Americas, 1979), 176–77.

2   Judith Butler, *The Psychic Life of Power: Theories in Subjection* (Stanford, CA: Stanford University Press, 1997), 30.

3   Christopher David Ruiz Cameron, "One Hundred Fifty Years of Solitude: Reflections on the End of the History Academy's Dominance of Scholarship on the Treaty of Guadalupe Hidalgo," in *The Legacy of the Mexican and Spanish-American Wars: Legal, Literary, and Historical Perspectives*, ed. Gary D. Keller and Cordelia Candelaria (Tempe, AZ: Bilingual Review Press, 2000), 1–2.

4   Indeed, this is precisely what Ruiz Cameron, as a Latino critical legal studies scholar, takes issue with in his rereading of the treaty. From his perspective, the very content of Articles 8 and 9, the letter of the law, is "indeterminate": "Neither the traditionalist, revisionist, nor the reclamationists fully appreciate the role that indeterminacy played in shaping the outcome of cases in which Treaty rights were litigated" (Ruiz Cameron, "One Hundred Fifty Years of Solitude," 3). Although Latino critical legal theorists like Ruiz Cameron have begun to question this commonsense interpretation of the treaty, suggesting instead a more volatile and open meaning, the consensus prevails among Chicano scholars, as it does among historians, that a promise has been broken in the implementation of the law.

5   David Kazanjian, *The Colonizing Trick: National Culture and Imperial Citizenship in Early America* (Minneapolis: University of Minnesota Press, 2003), 206–7.

6   Mario T. García, *Mexican Americans: Leadership, Ideology, and Identity, 1930–1960* (New Haven, CT: Yale University Press, 1989), chaps. 2 and 8.

7   García, *Mexican Americans*, 204.

8   See, for instance, Julian Samara and Patricia Vandel Simon, *A History of Mexican-American People* (Notre Dame, IN: University of Notre Dame Press, 1993); Zaragosa Vargas, ed., *Major Problems in Mexican American History* (Boston: Houghton Mifflin, 1999); Arnoldo Carlos Vento, *Mestizo: The History, Culture, and Politics of the Mexican and the Chicano* (Lanham, MD: University Press of America, 1998). In literary studies, see, for example, Luis Valdez and Stan Steiner, *Aztlan: An Anthology of Mexican American Literature* (New York: Vintage, 1972); or Leticia M. Garza-Falcón, *Gente Decente: A Borderlands Response to the Rhetoric of Dominance* (Austin: University of Texas Press, 1998). One notable exception to this commonsense approach to the treaty's interpretation is Richard Griswold del Castillo, *The Treaty of Guadalupe Hidalgo: A Legacy of Conflict* (Norman: University of Oklahoma Press, 1990), in which he systematically reviews the history of treaty negotiations through the history of its interpretation by the Chicano movement. Griswold del Castillo meticulously distances himself from the spectrum of interpretations of the treaty's legacy. Even while he clearly sympathizes with those most adversely affected by this legacy, he never assumes this commonsense himself. Rather, he traces the history of interpretation from its evolvement as anything but commonsensical in General Santa Ana's and President Polk's political negotiations through its mobilization by civil rights activists in the 1980s. Another exception is David Montejano, *Anglos and Mexicans in the Making of Texas, 1836–1986* (Austin: University of Texas Press, 1987), which I will discuss in greater detail later. Rather than assume that a promise has been broken in the implementation of the treaty, Montejano assumes that "the inferior political status of the Mexican was sanctioned by the Treaty of Guadalupe Hidalgo" (311).

9   Aztlán is the mythical, geographic origin of the Aztecs, presumably located to the northwest of Mexico City. In the 1960s and 1970s, Chicano nationalists recuperated Aztlán from Aztec lore, insisting it was located in the contemporary U.S. Southwest. Through this recuperation, Chicanos justified their nationalist claims on the Southwest as originary.

10 While *mestizaje* could be translated as "mixture" or "racial hybridity," these terms are reductive, as they fail to convey the complex history of *mestizaje* as a racial ideology in Latin America. "Mixture" and "racial hybridity" are, in turn, too neutral or too celebratory. Although frequently put to revolutionary use, *mestizaje* has an implicit hierarchical structure that shifted in balance according to historically specific circumstances. For an extended discussion of the history of *mestizaje* in Mexico, see María Josefina Saldaña-Portillo, *The Revolutionary Imagination in the Americas and the Age of Development* (Durham, NC: Duke University Press, 2003), chap. 6.

11 The meeting took place one day after the "International Meeting for Humanity and against Neoliberalism," which was also hosted by the Zapatistas in Oventic, Chiapas. The EZLN had invited all Chicanos to stay for one extra day to meet with the leadership and discuss ways of enlisting Mexican Americans and Mexican immigrants to help with the solidarity movement. I attended the meeting I am describing. Though I was not a member of the Chicano solidarity group making the statement that we were the *indios del norte*, I was a representative from another solidarity group and thereby nonetheless implicated by the statement.

12	Once again, the exception is Griswold del Castillo, who recognizes the article's implications for the Apache and Comanche. Griswold del Castillo, *Treaty*, 70–72.

13	Article 10 stipulates the validity of all Mexican land grants made to the annexed Mexicans. It specifies that all titles issued by any and all Mexican authorities must be respected, including those existing in Texas before its independence in 1836. The article would have further clarified the property rights of annexed Mexicans, though it is impossible to say whether its inclusion would have protected these rights. The full text of the deleted article reads: "All grants of land made by the Mexican Government or by the component authorities, in territories previously appertaining to Mexico, and remaining for the future within the limits of the United States, shall be respected as valid, to the same extent that the same grants would be valid, if the said territories had remained within the limits of Mexico. But the grantees of lands in Texas, put in possession thereof, who, by reason of the circumstances of the country since the beginning of the troubles between Texas and the Mexican Government, may have been prevented from fulfilling all the conditions of their grants, shall be under the obligation to fulfill the said conditions within the periods limited in the same respectively; such periods to be now counted from the date of exchange of ratifications of this treaty: in default of which the said grants shall not be obligatory upon the State of Texas, in virtue of the stipulations contained in this Article.

"The foregoing stipulation in regard to grantees of land in Texas, is extended to all grantees of land in the territories aforesaid, elsewhere than Texas, put in possession under such grants; and, in default of the fulfillment of the conditions of any such grant, within the new period, which, as is above stipulated, begins with the day of the exchange of ratifications of this treaty, the same shall be null and void."

14	According to anthropologist Martha Menchaca, the Apache occupying the Southwest were themselves, in fact, relatively recent arrivals to the territories of Texas, Arizona, and Sonora: "The Lipan Apache first appeared in West Texas during the late 1600s, and by the mid-1700s hundreds more had arrived"; "at that time [early to mid-1700s] hundreds of Apaches descended into Arizona and Sonora and began to occupy territory already claimed by other Indians. The Opata and Pima, to protect their land, resumed their alliances [with Spanish colonists] in return for military assistance." Martha Menchaca, *Recovering History, Constructing Race: The Indian, Black, and White Roots of Mexican Americans* (Austin: University of Texas Press, 2001), 108, 119. The Pueblo in Arizona and New Mexico also saw the Apache as enemies, according to Menchaca, and turned to the Spaniards for defense: "Most Pueblo villages were enemies of the Navajo, who resided in present northern Arizona, and the Apache, who were dispersed throughout Arizona and New Mexico. Warfare frequently broke out when Apaches and Navajos raided Pueblo villages in search of food. To keep them at a distance and to protect crops during harvest season, Pueblo villagers often sought the military aid of their colonial neighbors" (90).

15	Griswold del Castillo lists Article 11 as the principal reason for the negotiation of the Gadsden Treaty in 1853: "This task [of enforcing Article 11] turned out to be impossibly expensive. More than 160,000 Indians lived in the border region, and many of them, particularly the Apaches and Comanches, had a long history of raiding pueblos on the Mexican side. In an attempt to comply with its obligations, the United States stationed more than eight thousand troops along the border. The cost of keeping the peace turned out to be more than the cost of the original treaty. Between 1848 and 1853, military expenditures in New Mexico alone rose to 12 million dollars and the raids continued. In 1868 the Mexican government presented claims for damages that amounted to more than 31 million dollars." Griswold del Castillo, *Treaty*, 59. Needless to say, the U.S. government was anxious to be released from the provisions of Article 11.

16 See, for example, in history, Rodolfo Acuña, *Occupied America* (New York: Harper and Row, 1988); in literature, see Ana Castillo, *Mixquiahuala Letters* (Binghamton, NY: Bilingual Press/Editorial Bilingue, 1986); Gloria Anzaldúa, *Borderlands/La Frontera* (San Francisco: Aunt Lute Press, 1998); or Richard Rodriguez, *Days of Obligation* (New York: Viking, 1992). See Guillermo Gomez-Peña's performance piece *Border Brujo* (1993) in popular culture. It is not the intention of this article to question the productive power of this analogy; to the contrary, it has spurred some of the most extraordinary works of Chicano culture, particularly in the visual arts. Rather, my purpose is to explore more fully the structure of ambivalent identification at the center of the fecund psychic space provided for or generated by this analogy.

17 By troubling this popular analogy in contemporary Chicano nationalism, however, I do not mean to diminish the history of discrimination and violence Chicanos have suffered in the United States. In 2000, for instance, while George W. Bush was campaigning for president, it was widely reported that four out of the five poorest towns in the country were located along the border of Texas. My hometown of Laredo, of course, was among them. Thus the criminal violence of poverty inflicted on Chicano populations along the southwest border is not at issue. Rather, I trouble this analogy between Chicanos in the United States and Indians in Mexico because the analogy occludes as much as it reveals.

18 As Comandante Moises said to those earnest Chicano activists more than six years ago, "Ustedes sufren la discriminacion alla en el norte, pero nostros aqui nos estamos muriendo de hambre" (You may suffer from discrimination up north, but here we are dying of hunger). We should not read Comandante Moises's comment as suggesting a simplistic hierarchy of oppression, for down that road lies madness—the impossible impasse so often reached by the scarcity-based model of multiculturalism. Rather, his differentiation between discrimination and dying demonstrates how Chicano subject constitution depends on a romanticization of indigenous identity that, in effect, consigns the indigenous subaltern to the margins of the social. The demands of the pluralistic civil rights discourse of Chicano nationalism, encapsulated in the analogy between Chicanos and the Mexican Indians, operate through an occlusion of the international division of labor between rural subalterns in Mexico and the urban poor in the United States as well. This analogy also occludes the contemporary indigenous identity of northern Native Americans, as well as the specific history of Chicanos and Native Americans working in coalition toward related but differentiated aims in the 1980s. For a sophisticated discussion of this shared history of struggle that refuses to collapse the differences in the social formation of Native Americans and Chicanos, see Rodolfo O. de la Garza et al., *Chicanos and Native Americans: The Territorial Minorities* (Englewood Cliffs, NJ: Prentice-Hall, 1973).

19 *Encomienda* literally means "a thing held in trust." The Spanish crown awarded
    Indian laborers to Spanish conquistadors as *encomiendas*, presumably in exchange
    for the conquistador taking charge of the moral and physical needs of the Indians in
    their trust. The *encomienda* system was different from slavery in that the Indians were
    legally free, drew a wage, and were bound to the conquistador for only a set duration.

20 Menchaca, *Recovering History*, 54–55.

21 Menchaca suggests that the reasons for these changes were twofold. First, as
    the colonies were settled, Spanish nobility was encouraged to emigrate to the
    Americas to assume the administrative and executive positions. Thus the taboo
    of miscegenation was of greater concern once the elite of Spain became involved
    in the settlement of the Americas. Second, with most of the central valley of
    Mexico pacified, as it was by the late 1500s, intermarriage became less important
    as a military strategy. Furthermore, in 1592, the crown actually amended the law
    so that all employees of Spain, except for the military, were actually *required* to
    take European-born spouses. As Menchaca explains, "By this time, the crown was
    not solely interested in creating a White elite class; it had become necessary to
    form a loyal class with limited social commitment to the inhabitants of Mexico."
    Menchaca, *Recovering History*, 56.

22 Menchaca also reminds us that though mestizos enjoyed more social prestige than
    Indians, this did not translate into a better economic position: "They were also
    often ostracized by the Indians and Spaniards and did not enjoy certain legal privi-
    leges accorded to either group. For example, most *mestizos* were barred by royal
    decree from obtaining high- and mid-level positions in the royal and ecclesiastical
    governments. Moreover, the Spanish crown did not reserve land for the *mestizos*
    under the *corregimiento* system (a form of labor extraction from Indian villages) as
    it did for the Indians. The best economic recourse for most *mestizos* was to enter
    the labor market or migrate toward Mexico's northern and southern borders" (64).
    Afromestizos, though free, clearly fared no better economically than mestizos.

23 Hector Díaz Polanco, *Indigenous Peoples in Latin America: The Quest for Self-
    determination*, trans. Lucía Rayas (Boulder, CO: Westview, 1997), 29–34, 52–58.

24 Menchaca, *Recovering History*, 68.

25 The terms *mulattos, lobos* (wolves), and *coyotes* each indicate a varying degree of
    "black blood" in the parlance of the census takers and of popular culture at the time.

26 Alicia Tjarks, "Comparative Demographic Analysis of Texas, 1777–1793," *Southern
    Historical Quarterly* 77 (January): 291–338; Gilbert Hinojosa, "The Religious Indian
    Communities: The Goals of the Friar," in *Tejano Origins in Eighteenth-Century San
    Antonio*, ed. Gerald E. Poyo and Gilbert Hinojosa (Austin: University of Texas
    Press, 1991), 61–83, both cited in Menchaca, *Recovering History*, 116–17.

27 Menchaca, *Recovering History*, 111.

28 Menchaca, *Recovering History*, 167.

29 Though it became illegal to introduce new slaves to Mexico, the remaining ten
    thousand slaves were not immediately freed. Instead, a legal infrastructure was
    established for emancipating slaves over a period of ten to fourteen years. This
    delaying of emancipation was a response to political pressure from the southeast-
    ern states whose representatives pleaded for time for slave owners in their states

to switch labor sources. This infrastructure was rendered mute when in 1829, President Vicente Guerrero, of African decent, issued an emancipation proclamation with absolutely no exceptions for the territories. This was a major factor in the Texas war of independence, since by 1829, slave-owning Anglos made up the majority of the state's population and resented the central Mexican government's interference in their affairs.

30 Menchaca, *Recovering History*, 162, 168–69. The only exception to this prohibition was the northern frontier, where a large number of recently Christianized Indians were still under the tutelage of the Catholic Church. Consequently, although there was a wave of northern migration between 1821 and 1848, especially to California, the censuses from this period only distinguish citizens by trade, with the exception of the newly Christianized Indians, whom it counted separately (167–71).

31 Menchaca, *Recovering History*, 160.

32 Again, for a bibliography and analysis of nineteenth-century *mestizaje* in Mexico, see chapter 6 of my *Revolutionary Imagination in the Americas and the Age of Development*.

33 Menchaca, *Recovering History*, 218.

34 In the introduction to the first edition of GWG (1990), Rolando Hinojosa states that the entire novel was written over the course of these four years (5). However, this seems unlikely. In the last section of the book, "Leader of His People," the protagonist has returned to the Rio Grande valley during World War II, and he has joined the army as a counterintelligence spy. Thus this section appears to have been written later than the rest of the book. Américo Paredes, *George Washington Gómez: A Mexicotexan Novel* (Houston: Arte Publico, 1990).

35 Manuel G. Gonzales, *Mexicanos: A History of Mexicans in the United States* (Bloomington: Indiana University Press, 1999), 117.

36 Montejano, *Anglos and Mexicans*, 119, 117. For a complete account of the insurrection that turned the Rio Grande valley "into a virtual war zone," see 117–28.

37 Ramón Saldivar, "The Borderlands of Culture: Américo Paredes's *George Washington Gómez*," in *Mexican Americans in Texas History: Selected Essays*, ed. Emilio Zamora, Cynthia Orozco, and Rodolfo Rocha (Austin: Texas Historical Association, 2000), 177.

38 Paredes, GWG, 5–6.

39 According to Montejano, the rangers' retaliation was so indiscriminate that even Walter Prescott Webb, a historian of the Texas Rangers, acknowledged that "many innocent Mexicans were made to suffer" in "an orgy of bloodshed." Webb quoted in Montejano, *Anglos and Mexicans*, 127.

40 Montejano, *Anglos and Mexicans*, 119.

41 Saldivar, "Borderlands of Culture," 178.

42 Paredes, GWG, 14.

43 Paredes, GWG, 15–16.

44 Gonzales, *Mexicanos*, 117.

45 Montejano, *Anglos and Mexicans*, 117–18.

46 Paredes, GWG, 16.

Contributors

LEISY J. ABREGO

GLORIA ANZALDÚA

MARTHA BALAGUERA

LIONEL CANTÚ

LEO R. CHAVEZ

RAÚL FERNÁNDEZ

ROSA-LINDA FREGOSO

ROBERTO G. GONZALES

GILBERT G. GONZÁLEZ

RAMÓN GUTIÉRREZ

KELLY LYTLE HERNÁNDEZ

JOSÉ E. LIMÓN

EITHNE LUIBHÉID

MIREYA LOZA

ALEJANDRO LUGO

MARTHA MENCHACA

CECILIA MENJÍVAR

NATALIA MOLINA

FIAMMA MONTEZEMOLO

AMÉRICO PAREDES

NÉSTOR RODRÍGUEZ

RENATO ROSALDO

GILBERTO ROSAS

MARÍA JOSEFINA SALDAÑA-PORTILLO

SONIA SALDÍVAR-HULL

ALICIA SCHMIDT CAMACHO

SAYAK VALENCIA TRIANA

CARLOS G. VÉLEZ-IBÁÑEZ

PATRICIA ZAVELLA

Credits

Chapter 1. Gilbert G. González and Raúl A. Fernández, "Empire and the Origins of Twentieth Century Migration from Mexico to the United States," *Pacific Historical Review* 71, no. 1 (2002): 19–57. Reprinted with permission from the University of California Press.

Chapter 2. Cecilia Menjívar and Leisy J. Abrego, "Legal Violence: Immigration Law and the Lives of Central American Immigrants," *American Journal of Sociology* 117, no. 5 (2012): 1380–1421.

Chapter 3. Gilberto Rosas, "Necro-subjection: On Borders, Asylum, and Making Dead to Let Live," *Theory and Event* 22, no. 2 (2019): 303–24. Reprinted with permission from Johns Hopkins University Press.

Chapter 4. Lugo Aleandro, "Reimagining Culture and Power against Late Industrial Capitalism and Other Form of Conquest through Border Theory and Analysis," in *Fragmented Lives, Assembled Parts: Culture, Capitalism, and Conquest at the U.S.-Mexico Border*, 213–30 (Austin: University of Texas Press, 2008). Reprinted with permission from the University of Texas Press.

Chapter 5. Sayak Triana, "Tijuana cuir," *Queer Geographies* (Beirut, Tijuana, Copenhagen, Dinamarca: Museet for Samtidskunst, 2014), 90–95. Reprinted with permission from the author.

Chapter 6. Américo Paredes, "The United States, Mexico, and 'Machismo,'" *Journal of the Folklore Institute* 8, no. 1 (June 1971): 17–37, translated into English by Marcy Steen. Originally published as "Estados Unidos, Mexico y el Machismo," *Journal of Inter-American Studies* 9 (January 1967): 65–84. Reprinted with permission from Indiana University Press.

Chapter 7. Martha Menchaca, "The Spanish Settlement of Texas and Arizona," in *Recovering History, Constructing Race: The Indian, Black, and White Roots of Mexican Americans* (Austin: University of Texas Press, 2001), 97–126. Reprinted with permission from the University of Texas Press.

Chapter 8. Lionel Cantú, "A Place Called Home: A Queer Political Economy of Mexican Immigrant Men's Family Experiences," in *Perspectives on Las Américas* (New York: John Wiley, 2008), 259–73. Reprinted with permission from John Wiley and Sons.

Chapter 9. Patricia Zavella, "Migrations," in *I'm Neither Here nor There* (Durham, NC: Duke University Press, 2011). Reprinted with permission from Duke University Press.

Chapter 10. Renato Rosaldo, "Changing Chicano Narratives," in *Culture and Truth: The Remaking of Social Analysis*, 147–67 (Boston: Beacon Press, 1993). Reprinted with permission of the author.

Chapter 11. Sonia Saldívar-Hull, "Feminism on the Border: From Gender Politics to Geopolitics," in *Criticism in the Borderlands*, ed. José David Saldívar and Hector Calderon, 203–20 (Durham, NC: Duke University Press, 1991).

Chapter 12. Martha Balaguera, "Trans-migrations: Agency and Confinement at the Limits of Sovereignty," *Signs: Journal of Women in Culture and Society* 43, no. 3 (Spring 2018): 641–64. Reprinted with permission from the University of Chicago Press.

Chapter 13. José E. Limón, "Carne, Carnales, and the Carnivalesque," in *Dancing with the Devil: Society and Cultural Poetics in Mexican-American South Texas*, 123–40 (Madison: University of Wisconsin Press, 1994). Reprinted with permission from the University of Wisconsin Press.

Chapter 14. Ramón Gutiérrez, "The Erotic Zone: Sexual Transgression on the U.S.-Mexican Border," in *Mapping Multiculturalism*, ed. Avery Gordon and Chris Newfield, 253–63 (Minneapolis: University of Minnesota Press, 1996). Reprinted with permission from the author.

Chapter 15. Natalia Molina, "Medicalizing the Mexican: Immigration, Race, and Disability in the Early Twentieth Century United States," *Radical History Review* 94 (2006): 22–37.

Chapter 16. Eithne Luibhéid, "'Looking like a Lesbian': The Organization of Sexual Monitoring at the United States-Mexican Border," *Journal of the History of Sexuality* 8, no. 3 (1998): 477–506. Reprinted with permission from the University of Texas Press.

Chapter 17. Alicia Schmidt Camacho, "Migrant Melacholia: Emergent Discourses of Mexican Migrant Traffic in Transnational Space," *South Atlantic Quarterly* 105, no. 4 (2006): 831–61.

Chapter 18. Roberto G. Gonzalez, Leo R. Gonzales Chavez, "'Awakening to a Nightmare': Abjectivity and Illegality in the Lives of Undocumented 1.5-Generation Latino Immigrants in the United States," *Current Anthropology* 53, no. 3 (June 2012): 255–81. Reprinted with permission from the University of Chicago Press.

Chapter 19. Carlos G. Vélez-Ibáñez, "Regions of Refuge in the United States: Issues, Problems, and Concerns for the Future of Mexican-Origin Populations in the United States," *Human Organization* 63.1 (Spring 2004): 1–20. Reprinted with permission from Human Organization.

Chapter 20. Néstor Rodríguez, "The Battle for the Border: Notes on Autonomous Migration, Transnational Communities, and the State," *Social Justice* 23, no. 3 (Fall 1996): 21–37. Reprinted with permission from *Social Justice: A Journal of Crime, Conflict, and World Order*.

Chapter 21. Mireya Loza, "Yo Era Indígena: Race, Modernity and the Transformational Politics of Transnational Labor," in *Defiant Braceros: How Migrant Workers Fought for Racial, Sexual, and Political Freedom*, 21–62 (Chapel Hill: University of North Carolina Press, 2016). Reprinted with permission from the University of North Carolina Press.

Chapter 22. Fiamma Montezemolo, "Tijuana: Hybridity and Beyond: A Conversation with Néstor García Canclini," *Third Text* 23, no. 6 (2009): 733–50. Reprinted with permission from Taylor & Francis.

Chapter 23. Rosa-Linda Fregoso, "The Art of Witness," *Chiricú Journal: Latina/o Literatures, Arts, and Cultures* 2, no. 1 (2017): 118–36. Reprinted with permission from Indiana University Press.

Chapter 24. Kelly Lytle Hernández, "Amnesty or Abolition?" *Boom* 1, no. 4 (2011): 54–68. Reprinted with permission from the University of California Press.

Chapter 25. Gloria Anzaldúa, "How to Tame a Wild Tongue," in *Borderlands/La Frontera: The New Mestiza*. 2nd ed., 75–86 (San Francisco: Aunt Lute Books, 1999). Reprinted with permission from Aunt Lute Books.

Chapter 26. María Josefina Saldaña-Portillo, "Wavering on the Horizon of Social Being: The Treaty of Guadalupe-Hidalgo and the Legacy of Its Radical Character in Américo Paredes's *George Washington Gómez*," *Radical History Review* 89 (2004): 135–64.

Index

Arroyo, Antonio Vanegas, 151

Art Forum, 566

Art in America, 566

Asociación Nacional México-Americana (ANMA;
National Mexican American Association),
643

Asociación Tepeyac de New York, El, 404

Assignment Discovery, 409

assimilation, 47, 69, 74, 269, 271, 298, 365, 468,
525, 651–52, 661–62. *See also* migration

Associated Press, 37

asylum, 3, 90–93, 96, 102–3, 301, 308–10, 401n84,
440. *See also* refugees

autonomous migration, 502–4, 510–11

Aventuras de un Bracero (Topete), 518–19

Ayala, Alonso, 545

Aztec empire, 12, 665n9

Aztlán, 644, 665n9

Baker, Josephine, 578

Bakhtin, Mikhail, 326, 338–39

Bank of America, 30

Barbarous Mexico (Turner), 14

Barlow, Andrew D., 23

Barrio Boy (Galarza), 266, 271–75

Barrio Libre, 87–88

Barrios de Chungara, Domitila, 287–88

Barthes, Roland, 279

Bateson, Gregory, 333–34

Bau, Ignatius, 398n34

Baynton, Douglas, 357–58

Bee, Carlos, 358–59

Beltrán, Gonzalo Aguirre, 466–69, 470, 496n1

Benjamin, Walter, 77n9, 298

Berlant, Lauren, 317

Bernal, Arias, 529

Bernstein, Marvin, 24

Berthon, Ted Le, 518

bilingualism, 275–76, 326–27, 542. *See also*
English language; Spanish language

Billy the Kid, 167n28

biopolitics, 95–97, 431, 433–34, 436, 444, 451, 455,
457n4, 575. *See also* death; Foucault, Michel;
power

Boas, Franz, 350, 524–25

Boatright, Mody C., 163

bodies: and disability, 356–58; and disease, 356,
491; and illegality, 434; inspection of, 365,
378–79, 398n40, 406, 577; and purity, 347–49,
352–53, 356, 360; and race, 356, 359, 650; and

sexuality, 376–77; and society, 331–32. *See also*
disability

Bolivia, 289, 573

Border Industrial Program, 32, 40n13

Borderlands (Anzaldúa), 4, 288–90

Border Patrol, 88, 237, 240, 242, 590, 613–17, 619

borders: and class, 121–20; and disease, 360, 363,
365; formal definitions of, 106; imaginaries of,
351, 417–18, 507, 568–69, 577; and inspection
of bodies, 360–61, 398n40; media perceptions
of, 411–12; necessity of crossing, 97; physical
barriers, 57, 237, 242–43, 501, 512, 567, 575–76;
and purity, 347–48; social forms of, 119, 222;
and surveillance, 303, 310, 378–79. *See also*
migration; U.S.-Mexico border

border theory, 4, 109–11, 121, 124, 202–3, 288–90

Bosworth, Mary, 307

Bourdieu, Pierre, 50, 112–13, 434

Bourne, Jenny, 295

Bowie, James, 161

Bowra, C. M., 156

Box, John C., 362, 370n43

Box-Harris Bill, 364–65, 370n43

Bracero History Project, 522

Bracero Justice Movement, 522

Bracero Program, 417, 510–11, 514, 518–20, 522,
526–29, 531–35, 537, 543–49, 551, 553n12, 616

Brazil, 31, 576

Breaking Bad, 99

Brexit, 99–100

Briggs, Charles, 356

British empire, 14

Buck v. Bell, 366

Buffington, Robert, 520

Burke, Kenneth, 128n12

Bush, George H. W., 392, 640

Bush, George W., 404–5, 456, 575–76, 667n17

Butler, Judith, 141, 396n13, 431–34, 641

Caddo Indians, 169, 171, 179

Calabazas, 189

California DREAM Act of 2011, 437

California Inmate Bill of Rights, 622

California Proposition 187, 14, 366, 439, 508, 514

Camacho, Manuel Ávila, 153–54, 520, 522–23,
525–26

Campos, Rubén, 151

Canada, 377–78

Canary Islands, 178–80

Canclini, Néstor García, 7, 142, 563–83

de Tejada, Sebastián Lerdo, 23
detention studies, 306–7, 317–18. *See also* incarceration
deterritorialization, 109–10, 126n3
De Vaney, Elvon, 537–38
Devil's Highway, 226, 406
Diagnostic and Statistical Manual of Mental Disorders (DSM-I), 381
Díaz, Porfirio, 15, 17, 23, 151, 523–24. *See also* Porfiriato
Dillingham Commission, 360
disability, 356–57, 362–63, 366. *See also* bodies
disability studies, 357
disappeared people, 413–14, 424
discursive economy, 398n39
distribution of sadness, 489–90
Dobie, J. Frank, 270, 291, 326, 340
Dole, 32
Domínguez, Pedro, 523, 535–36, 547–48
Dos por Uno, 256n80. *See also* remittances
Douglas, Mary, 331, 333, 336, 352
Douglass, Frederick, 610–11, 624
DREAM Act, 437–38, 449, 456
drug trade, 92, 100–103, 143, 303–4, 308–9, 314–15, 327, 339–40, 397n31, 426n20, 453, 496, 600
Dryden, John, 156
Dulles, John Foster, 14–15, 31
Dunayevskaya, Raya, 503
Dunn, Timothy, 379
Durand, Jorge, 406
Durkheim, Emile, 113, 122–23
Duster, Troy, 356

education: access to, 52, 58, 64, 71–73, 246, 436–37; barriers to, 451, 539; benefits of, 203, 292, 437, 445, 448–49; costs of, 445, 450; and decision to migrate, 225, 230, 248; and language, 274, 544–46; and race, 474–76; rates of attainment, 493–94. *See also* literacy
Ejercito Zapatista de Liberación Nacional (EZLN), 644–45, 665n11
El Cañon, 177
Ellis Island, 358, 364
El Paso Valley, 183
El Salvador, 54, 56, 59, 63–64, 298, 447
endriago subjects, 138–40, 143–44
Engineering and Mining Journal-Press, 24
English language, 203, 272, 274, 276, 538–41, 545, 629, 631, 633. *See also* bilingualism

Erre, Marcos Ramírez, 579
Eschbach, Karl, 243
Escudero, Eward, 387
Esparza, José Gómez, 525
Espín, Olivia, 389
Estrada, Ezequiel Martínez, 149, 156, 161
Estrada, Mónica, 232
"Ethnicity, Ideology, and Academia" (Sánchez), 283
ethnography, 105n18, 265, 268, 580–81
eugenics, 365–66

Falcón, Sylvanna, 240
Familias Fortalezidas, 600–601
familism, 205, 208, 211, 218n4
family separation, 61, 64, 412
family stage migration, 233
family unity, 229, 244–45, 372, 389, 412, 418
Fanon, Frantz, 90
Farmer, Paul, 49, 433
fascism, 120
Feliciano Ramirez, Antonio, 540–41
felonies, 56, 437, 624n1
femicide, 98, 424, 426n20, 588, 602, 605. *See also* women
femininity, 92–93, 138, 206, 216, 232. *See also* gender
feminism, 109–10, 121, 128n14, 141, 158–59, 202, 268, 275, 282–90, 295–96, 299, 307. *See also* Chicana feminism; transfeminism
Ferguson, James, 433
Fernández, Gerónimo Gutiérrez, 405
Fernández-Kelly, Patricia, 295
Fierro, Martín, 162
First World/Third World dichotomy, 288, 577–78, 583
Flores, Paula, 586–90, 594–95, 599
folklore, 150–53, 156–57, 162, 165, 266, 270–71, 330, 658
Fong Yue Ting decision, 612
food, 324–40, 635
Fordism, 140, 575
Fore We Are Sold, I and My People (Fernández-Kelly), 295
Fort Saint-Louis, 169
Foster, Hal, 580
Foucault, Michel, 77n5, 95–96, 108–10, 126nn4–5, 127n7, 318, 325, 373, 381–82, 384, 393, 395n8, 398n39, 399n41, 434, 457n4, 575. *See also* biopolitics

www.ingramcontent.com/pod-product-compliance
Lightning Source LLC
Chambersburg PA
CBHW030854270326
41929CB00008B/413